Dear Reader,

Welcome to the Galileo Press *Discover SAP* series. This new series has been developed as part of our official SAP PRESS imprint to help you discover what SAP is all about and show you how you can use the wide array of applications and tools to make your organization more efficient and cost effective.

Each book in the series is written in a friendly, easy-to-follow style that guides you through the intricacies of the software and its core components. If you are completely new to SAP, you can begin with "Discover SAP," the first book in the series, where you'll find a detailed overview of the core components of SAP, what they are, how they can benefit your company, and the technology requirements and costs of implementation. Once you have a foundational knowledge of SAP, you can explore the other books in the series covering Financials, CRM, SCM, and more. In these books you'll delve into the fundamental business concepts and principles behind the tool, discover why it's important for your business, and evaluate the technology and implementation costs for each.

Whether you are a decision maker who needs to determine if SAP is the right enterprise solution for your company, you are just starting to work in a firm that uses SAP, or you're already familiar with SAP but need to learn about a specific component, you are sure to find what you need in the *Discover SAP* series. Then when you're ready to implement SAP, you'll find what you need in the SAP PRESS series at *www.sap-press.com*.

Thank you for your interest in the series. We look forward to hearing how the series helps you get started with SAP.

Jenifer Niles
Vice President

Galileo Press, Inc.
100 Grossman Drive
Suite 205
Braintree, MA 02184

 **PRESS**

SAP PRESS is a joint initiative of SAP and Galileo Press. The know-how offered by SAP specialists combined with the expertise of the Galileo Press publishing house offers the reader expert books in the field. SAP PRESS features first-hand information and expert advice, and provides useful skills for professional decision-making.

SAP PRESS offers a variety of books on technical and business related topics for the SAP user. For further information, please visit our website: *www.sap-press.com.*

Brian Schaer
Time Management with SAP ERP HCM
2008, ~500 pp.
978-1-59229-229-5

Manuel Gallardo
Configuring and Using CATS
2008, 162 pp.
978-1-59229-232-5

Hans Jürgen, Richard HaÐmann, Anja Junold
HR Reporting with SAP
2008, 435 pp.
978-1-59229-172-4

Martin Esch, Anja Junold
Authorizations in SAP ERP HCM
2008, 336 pp.
978-1-59229-165-6

Greg Newman

Discover SAP® ERP HCM

Galileo Press

Bonn • Boston

ISBN 978-1-59229-222-6

1st Edition 2009

Editor Jenifer Niles
Copyeditor Ruth Saavedra
Production Editor Kelly O'Callaghan
Cover Designer Jill Winitzer
Photo Credit Photos.com
Layout Design Vera Brauner
Typesetter Publishers' Design and Production Services, Inc.
Printed and bound in Canada

To Cath,
My love, my life, thank you.

Contents at a Glance

Contents

PART I   Workforce Process Management

PART II Talent Management

13 Employee Performance Management 315

14 Enterprise Compensation Management 335

PART III End-User Service Delivery

15 Employee Self-Service 371

16 Manager Self-Service 391

17 Employee Interaction Center 409

Acknowledgments

Writing a book on such a broad and complex subject would not have been possible without the encouragement, advice, wisdom, patience, and support of many friends around the world.

I would like to offer special thanks to; Andy, Brad, Chris, Dagmar, Doug, Evan, Ian, Isaac, Jason, Jeff, John, Manuel, Marco, Sally, Srinivas, Steen, Steve, Sven, Raf, Raghav, Raj, Rangachary, the GD team, Titia, Wilfred, and Venki for their input into this book.

Extra thanks need to go to Jenifer Niles at Galileo Press, for her patience and support coaching a first time author through this process.

I would also like to take this opportunity to thank my wife Cath, my parents, my brothers, my extended family and all my friends for their love, support and encouragement before, after and during this writing process.

I hope you find this book informative and easy to read, I hope it goes some way to helping you to discover the breadth and width of the SAP ERP HCM solution and that it helps you make good use of this excellent product.

Preface

The world of human resources related technology is one that continues to grow and evolve at a tremendous pace. The SAP ERP Human Capital Management (HCM) component continues to keep ahead of this growth, making it a constantly evolving and developing solution. Numerous great books are available from SAP PRESS on specific parts of the SAP ERP Human Capital Management solution, but there was no overall introduction explaining what all of the parts of the SAP ERP Human Capital Management solution can do — and how they can benefit your HR department, your employees, and your company.

The component is so broad that few customers implement all of its parts at one time; most choose just the parts that meet their specific and immediate needs and budget. A second group of customers already have parts of SAP ERP HCM up and running in their company, but they are unaware of the new offerings and parts of the solution that have been developed to make the most of advances in technology. And, a third group includes those who have not yet implemented the component, but are interested in learning what it has to offer.

This book has been written to meet the needs of all of these customers, by providing a single source overview of the entire SAP ERP HCM solution. The book explains the features and capabilities, avoids jargon wherever possible, and shows the benefits that real companies have achieved in implementing these solutions.

The following sections outline specifically who will benefit from this book, how the book has been structured, and what topics are covered.

Whom This Book Is For

If you're a business decision maker considering implementing SAP ERP HCM in your business, this book will help you become familiar with the terminology, concepts, components, and technology.

For decision makers considering SAP ERP HCM, this is the one resource you should read. It will provide you with an in-depth overview of the functions and tools available, and it will provide real-world insight through case studies of companies who have used it successfully to solve their HR issues.

If you're a manager dealing with a new SAP ERP HCM solution in your team or department, and you want to help your people succeed and become more productive, this book gives you the information you need to appreciate how all of the various features and tools in SAP components might make your people more efficient.

If you're an IT person who has never worked with SAP ERP HCM, you'll get a quick, solid grounding in those components, and you'll be able to understand how those components can solve your business problems.

And, if you're a consultant considering entering the world of implementing and/or supporting SAP ERP HCM, this book serves as a tutorial to help you better understand this part of the SAP universe, its features, benefits, and how it interfaces with other SAP solutions.

What You Will Discover

My intent in writing this book was to provide a simple and straightforward introduction to SAP ERP HCM and its many components; to introduce and explain the capabilities, concepts, terms, and solutions that make up the solution; and, most important for such an broad product, to look at how these many components are integrated, how they share data, and how we can use this strong integration to increase the overall capabilities of the solution. Each chapter covers a different component of SAP ERP Human Capital Management in considerable detail so that you can see the available functionality and relate it to how each component works in a real business.

Learning about SAP ERP HCM sometimes feels like learning another language, so to help beginners with this process, I tried to define business and SAP relevant terms in a way that anyone with a reasonable understanding of human resources can understand. I also made every attempt to give you examples and case studies to make SAP and its products relevant to you and your company. Not every chapter could be served well by a case study, so in those chapters I did not include one.

Navigational Tools for This Book

Throughout the book, you will find several elements that will help you access useful information:

- ➕ Tips call out useful information about related ideas, and provide practical suggestions for how to use a particular function.
- ▶ Notes provide other resources to explore, or special tools or services from SAP that will help you with the topic under discussion.
- ☒ Examples provide you with real-world illustrations of functions at work.

Marginal texts provide a useful way to scan the book to locate topics of interest to you. Each appears to the side of a paragraph or section with related information.

This is a marginal note

Case studies explain how real companies are using different parts of the SAP ERP HCM solution to benefit their business.

What's In This Book?

We begin the book with a short introduction to SAP ERP and the Human Capital Management component. Following that, the book is divided according to the three core parts of the SAP ERP HCM com-

Read the book in sequence, or go to specific chapters or sections as needed

ponent. Within each part, the chapters cover a separate part of the solution.

The following is an overview of what each part of the book covers:

Part 1

Workforce Process Management, really the core function of the SAP ERP HCM component, enables companies to manage employee and organizational data, and to manage complex employee relationships, such as globally mobile employees and those with multiple concurrent employment contracts. We will look at the solutions for managing your employee benefits programs, maintaining all aspects time entry, and maintenance. We will look at how the system meets global payroll and legal reporting requirements. And we will look at how processes and forms across all of these areas can be defined in the system to speed up processing and cut down on manual processing and errors.

Part 2

In this part of the book, we cover Talent Management. We look at solutions for recruiting, developing, training, managing, and compensating your employees. We explore the e-Recruiting online recruitment portal, explain the capabilities of the solution in the areas of career and succession management, and explore the powerful solutions that enable your company to manage every aspect of your employees' performance management and compensation programs in a way that benefits both your employees and your company.

Part 3

Part three covers End-user Service Delivery. This area embraces the Internet and new technology to empower your employees, managers, and administrators to take charge of their own data, tasks, and processes — and to process them via the Internet. Employee Self-Service gives each employee their own portal to access their own data, make changes, and complete many HR related tasks — such as creating leave requests, printing payslips, requesting training, and applying for internal vacancies. Manager Self-Service allows managers to monitor their team; view absence and attendance records; oversee time recording; approve leave, training, and transfer requests; and requisition new employees. Managers also have access to all of the reports they commonly need, freeing up HR departments' time by giving managers access to the information they need to do their jobs effectively. The Employee Interaction Center enables companies to deliver consistent, well informed, and well managed service to managers and employees, from anywhere in the world.

At the end of the book, there is a glossary of SAP and human resources systems terminology covering all of the key terms used in the book. In addition, the book also includes an index that you can use to go directly to certain points of interest.

I hope that this straightforward overview of SAP ERP HCM will help you discover the information you need to assess your own business needs; determine which components to explore further with your SAP support team, SAP implementation partner, or SAP account representative; and help you take advantage of the many benefits that SAP ERP HCM has to offer for effectively managing your employees, their data, and all of your human resource information needs.

PART I
Workforce Process Management

This part of SAP ERP HCM contains the key functionality that enables you to manage your company's core employee- or workforce-related processes, including storing and accessing employee data, mapping your organizational structure and keeping it up to date, and managing your benefits, time, attendance, and payroll functions globally. It also allows you to deliver functionality available in more recent areas of HR management, including managing global employees and employees with multiple employment contracts, and automating processes and forms for web delivery.

SAP ERP HCM is divided into eight sections, each managing a different part of the core processes of your employee administration.

> *Employee Administration*
> By using a centralized database that provides administrators, managers, and employees with up-to-the-minute data, this function of SAP ERP HCM enables companies to effectively manage all of the core processes and data related to employee administration. It enables companies to automate these processes to make them as efficient as possible and free your HR team members to concentrate on more strategic value-adding tasks.

> *Organizational Management*
> SAP ERP HCM provides companies with the ability to centrally create and maintain an up-to-the-minute and integrated graphical representation of their company structure. This organizational hierarchy then forms the backbone of many subsequent decisions, operations, and processes within your SAP ERP HCM solution.

> *Global Employee Management*
> As companies continually expand around the world, the ability to effectively manage globally mobile workforces becomes more and more important. This function provides your company with a set of processes and objects that allow you to manage every step of an employee's international assignment, from predeparture checks to repatriation.

> *Concurrent Employment*
> Another increasingly relevant part of human resource management is the concurrent employment function that allows companies to automatically maintain and process employees with multiple, simultaneous employment contracts within the company. Full integration with central data maintenance and time, payroll, and finance postings means that multiple employment scenarios are no longer a confused mess of paperwork and records.

> *Benefits Management*
> Benefits management is evolving as a business practice and becoming more complex. The benefits management function provides the means for companies to effectively manage all of their benefits offerings globally. It provides powerful tools allowing companies to quickly and efficiently maintain employee benefits data and maintain and report on their benefits offerings.

> *Time and Attendance*
> As one of the largest areas of SAP ERP HCM, the Time and Attendance function covers every aspect of employee time recording, from initial data entry through online time sheets, and working time evaluation and interpretation, to managing vacation entitlements and calculating piecework payments. As such, it provides time administrators with effective ways to manage large volumes of data.

> *Payroll and Legal Reporting*
Situated at the heart of any company, the SAP ERP HCM payroll and legal reporting function enables companies to run large complex payroll solutions for any type of organization in over 50 countries. A powerful calculation and processing framework enables large parts of payroll to be processed automatically and calculated quickly, which allows companies to minimize the time they spend checking and fixing errors.

> *HCM Processes and Forms*
Taking advantage of recent advances in form-related technology, this function uses the power of Adobe Forms to enable your company to create web-delivered, interactive forms. These forms can then be linked to automated processes to ensure that your HR team and employees can complete any forms and process them with the minimum of effort.

Each of these eight sections is explained in its own chapter within Part I.

Introduction

1

It is often said that employees are the most valuable resource a company has. It doesn't matter how good your product is, how nice your shops are, or how good your solution is; without happy, motivated, and effective employees, your company will fail. There are many aspects to maintaining an effective workforce in your company. One of the core enablers of an effective workforce is a human resources system. The SAP ERP Human Capital Management (SAP ERP HCM) solution provides companies with the broadest, most well-integrated total solution for managing their human capital.

SAP ERP HCM is part of the SAP Business Suite Enterprise Resource Planning (SAP ERP) solution. SAP ERP provides a set of powerful solutions that enable companies to align their strategies and operations to enhance productivity and profitability across all aspects of their operations. SAP ERP provides software solutions covering the following areas:

> **SAP ERP Financials**
> This solution enables companies to turn their finance operations into strategic business partners by providing a comprehensive financial management solution that covers every aspect of account-

ing, financial supply chain, treasury, compliance, and reporting for even the largest global company.

> **SAP ERP Operations**
> The SAP ERP Operations solution allows companies to maximize their operational efficiencies and productivity by providing operational management with tools to automate and streamline operation processes, streamline operations, increase collaboration through the provision of accurate and timely information, and apply operational performance by applying strategic insight into your operational processes.

> **SAP ERP Corporate Services**
> Corporate services helps companies effectively manage all of the essential support services that enable them to meet their strategic goals. The solution encompasses all aspects of corporate operations from project and portfolio management to real estate and asset management tools, environmental health and safety systems, and travel management. The solution optimizes these key processes to enable companies to operate in a streamlined, cost-efficient environment, managing risks and driving business value.

> **SAP ERP Human Capital Management**
> The topic of this book, the SAP ERP HCM solution transforms the role of your HR department from a passive transactional department to a proactive technology-enabled department delivering a wide range of services to employees and management across a variety of platforms.

The SAP ERP HCM component has evolved over several decades to enable HR departments to complete their transactional tasks in an efficient manner and to provide the tools required to deliver on strategic HR goals such as effective recruitment and talent management, accurate time recording, effective compensation management, and continual employee development.

SAP ERP HCM is divided into four key areas, although this book will only cover the three core areas: Workforce Process Management, Talent Management, and End User Service Delivery. The four areas and their related functions are illustrated in Figure 1.1.

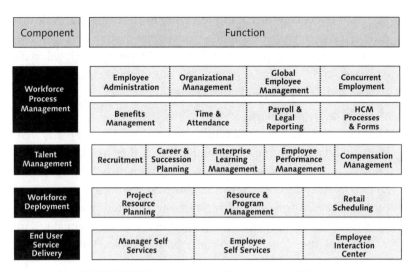

Component	Function			
Workforce Process Management	Employee Administration	Organizational Management	Global Employee Management	Concurrent Employment
	Benefits Management	Time & Attendance	Payroll & Legal Reporting	HCM Processes & Forms
Talent Management	Recruitment	Career & Succession Planning · Enterprise Learning Management · Employee Performance Management		Compensation Management
Workforce Deployment	Project Resource Planning	Resource & Program Management		Retail Scheduling
End User Service Delivery	Manager Self Services	Employee Self Services		Employee Interaction Center

Figure 1.1 The SAP ERP HCM Solution and Its Components and Functions

What does SAP ERP HCM Offer You?

Before we dive into more details of the HCM application modules, let's take some time to get a brief overview of the capabilities of each of the components:

> **Workforce Process Management**
> The core of your HR system, this component allows your company to perform its core transactions in an efficient, highly automated manner. Focused around the core tasks of administering employee data, managing your organizational structure, administering benefits, managing employee working time and payroll and legal reporting, the component also delivers solutions to enable companies to effectively manage global employees and employees on multiple employment contracts and automate and web-enable their core HR processes and forms.

> **Talent Management**
> Taking advantage of the seamless integration between the different parts of SAP ERP HCM, this component enables companies to effectively manage their employees, or "talent." The solution uses cutting edge technology to create structured process-oriented solu-

31

tions for effectively managing recruitment, learning and training, career management, performance, and compensation management. The tools enable companies to develop and implement global, standardized, and equitable solutions to ensure that their talent is motivated and delivering maximum benefit.

> **Workforce Deployment**
> There is no sense having speedily recruited, career-oriented, well-trained and well-compensated employees if they are not deployed effectively to meet your company's requirements. The Workforce Deployment component provides companies working in retail and professional services and delivering project-related work with a set of tools to ensure that the right employees with the right skills are available at the right time to meet both company and customer needs.

> **End User Service Delivery**
> The very nature of HR leads to high volumes of transactions and numerous HR, employee, and manager interactions. The End User Service Delivery component is designed to ensure that your company can deliver its HR services to its customers in an efficient, standardized, and cost-effective manner. It can do this by providing employees and managers with their own web-delivered self-service tools to manage their own data and the tasks related with managing their team, with little or no input from the HR team. Interactions between employees, managers, and the HR department that cannot be handled automatically by the self-service applications are handled by the Employee Interaction Center, a powerful relationship management tool that enables companies to deliver consistent, standardized, and cost-effective employee and manager services from anywhere in the world.

As you can already see, the SAP ERP HCM solution offers a wide range of services, many of which are worthy of a book of their own. To explore all these HCM areas in this book, we will look at each of the parts of this solution, their capabilities, their integration, and a selection of case studies illustrating their applications in the real world.

As with the other Discover books, there is no right or wrong way to read this book. Different readers have different requirements of the book, but we have tried to cater in some way to everybody's needs. Some readers may be looking at SAP ERP HCM for the first time and will probably benefit most from starting at the beginning of the book and working through chapter by chapter. The first part of the book, Workforce Process Management, covers what is traditionally known as the core components of SAP ERP HCM upon which all of the other components are effectively built, so starting with these chapters will help you better understand the later chapters. Other readers who have already had some exposure to SAP ERP HCM can pick and choose the chapters that they read depending on their immediate needs.

One of the key benefits of SAP ERP HCM is its extensive, robust integration. This means the solutions described in many of the chapters rely heavily on the solutions described in earlier or later chapters, so you may find yourself paging forward and back through the book.

In the next chapter we will begin our discovery of SAP ERP HCM by looking at Workforce Process Management, the core components of SAP ERP HCM that enable your company to effectively create, store, process, and manage the data of your company's most precious resource: its employees.

2

SAP ERP HCM Employee Administration

In today's rapidly globalizing marketplace, companies around the world grow, expand, acquire, and merge at a rapid pace. As a result, companies are faced with maintaining unprecedented volumes of employee data. The challenges and complications of storing and accessing sensitive employee data globally, while also making it accessible and tailoring it to local and regional demands, presents major issues for companies.

The SAP ERP HCM Employee Administration functionality is designed to face these demands and has three key purposes. First, it acts as a centralized database for all of your employee master data, enabling system users, management, and employees to access up-to-date, consistent and relevant information to support decision making. Second, it's the part of SAP ERP HCM where you define your company structure, and create a framework that meets your processing and reporting requirements while working well for your employees. Third, it's designed to enable your company to automate and streamline most of your day-to-day HR processes, saving you time and money and allowing your HR department to focus on strategic rather than administrative activities.

Because Employee Administration is the core function of SAP ERP HCM, it's the bedrock that all of your other SAP ERP HCM components are built upon. It is critical that you understand the Employee Administration functions and keep in mind their possible impact on other SAP ERP HCM components when designing and implementing the system.

This chapter will give you an understanding of how Employee Administration is used, how it's structured, and how it integrates with other SAP ERP HCM components, along with some of the key concepts behind Employee Administration in general.

How SAP Employee Administration Fits into an Enterprise

Because it is the central database for storing employee data, the Employee Administration function is the key component in SAP ERP HCM. When companies use SAP ERP HCM, this function is the most frequently accessed part of the solution.

All other employee-related HCM processes, such as recruiting, performance management, and payroll, reference and make decisions based on the data stored in this function, so employee administration sits at the heart of your company.

The Employee Administration function is built around the Personnel Administration (PA) component, which is where all of your employees' data is stored. A large amount of the information input into other SAP ERP HCM components ends up stored in PA and can be accessed from Employee Administration. This means that in addition to your core employee data, you can view data from many of the other SAP ERP HCM components from inside the Personnel Administration component.

To understand SAP ERP HCM Employee Administration, we need to answer the following questions:

1. What information can you store in Employee Administration?
2. How does SAP ERP HCM refer to this information?

3. How is employee data stored?

4. What can you do with it?

What Information Can You Store in Employee Administration?

As befitting an SAP ERP HCM system that is used by over 10,000 companies around the world, you can store almost any data in Employee Administration. The data is stored in various forms, beginning with employee data, which is stored in records called *infotypes*.

SAP ERP HCM is used by over 10,000 clients worldwide

 Example

> Each employee record has multiple infotypes: one that contains details of his current organizational assignment, one that details his basic pay, one for bank details, and one for his address.

Employee Administration's main purpose is to store infotypes that record the history of a person's employment with your company. Every employee has many infotypes stored for his employee number, so in Employee Administration, among other things, you can quickly view all of the positions that an employee has held in your company and all of the changes to salary over his employment history. Having your employee data stored in infotypes gives you a logical, controlled, and secure structure that ensures your administrators can access and maintain the data in a way that makes Employee Administration efficient and streamlined.

Infotypes are the key concept behind Employee Administration

SAP ERP HCM delivers over 650 standard infotypes catering to all of your employee data storage requirements, ranging from recording your employees' civil awards and decorations (Infotype 0861) to the finer details of their garnishment orders (Infotype 0195).

SAP ERP HCM delivers over 650 standard infotypes

We'll talk more about infotypes and the other objects used to store employee and organizational data in the following sections, but you'll also need to configure your company structure in Employee Administration so that you can map out where your employees physically and legally work. So first, let's look at the structures that SAP ERP HCM uses to define the legal and physical structure of your company.

How Is Your Company Defined in Employee Administration?

Before you can organize your employee data in SAP ERP HCM, you need to set up your company structure, which is largely determined by your legal and reporting requirements. Employee Administration uses three separate but related structures to map your company into Employee Administration:

Enterprise Structure

The enterprise structure represents your company's legal set up

The *enterprise structure* is the method used for defining how your organization is set up in SAP ERP HCM. Aligning your company correctly to this structure is one of the most important steps of an SAP implementation, because the enterprise structure defined here can have important ramifications on later decisions, not just in Employee Administration but in many other SAP ERP HCM components as well.

The SAP objects that combine to make up the enterprise structure are shown in Table 2.1.

Object	Description	Example
Client	SAP system clients have an independent status both in legal and organizational terms. The clients in a SAP system can be distinguished by a three-character alphanumeric code. Generally, you will have a client for production, one for testing, and one for development.	001 – Connells International Curtain Company Production System
Company code	These are set up as part of the Finance component, but they are subsequently used in SAP ERP HCM. Legal entities, currencies, and countries are set at a company code level.	CO01 – England Curtain Company CO02 – USA Curtain Company
Personnel area	These are sub-units of a company that are specific to Personnel Administration; they usually define such things as geographical locations and function areas. A personnel area can only belong to one company code.	P001 – England Operations P002 – Scotland Operations P0003 – West Coast Operations P004 – East Coast Operations

Table 2.1 SAP Enterprise Structure

Object	Description	Example
Personnel subarea	A further subset of personnel area, these are used to define grouping and defaults for payroll processing and time management decision making.	S001 – Factory Operations S002 – Head Office S003 – Deliveries

Table 2.1 SAP Enterprise Structure (Cont.)

Personnel Structure

As opposed to the enterprise structure, which defines the organization from a legal and physical point of view, the *personnel structure* defines the organization from the employees' point of view. Because the personnel structure is used to separate and group all of your different types of employees, it's frequently used as a decision point in payroll processing, time management, and shift planning, so it's vital that these groupings cater to all of the separate categories of employees within your company.

The personnel structure represents how your employees are grouped

The personnel structure in SAP ERP HCM is defined by the objects in Table 2.2.

Object	Description	Example
Employee group	Used to classify different types of employees at a high level, defining the different types of workforces and terms and conditions of employment	01 – Directors 02 – Management 03 – Salaried Staff 04 – Wage Staff 05 – Temporary Workers 06 – Pensioners
Employee subgroup	A subset of an employee group, the lowest level of granularity when it comes to defining your employees	04-01 – Apprentices 04-02 – Craftsmen 04-03 – Laborers
Payroll area	A grouping of employees with the same payroll rules, for example, pay period, pay date, calculation method	P1 – Monthly Payroll P2 – Weekly Payroll P3 – Bi Weekly Payroll

Table 2.2 SAP Personnel Structure

Organizational Structure

The organizational structure defines your company's hierachy

The third of the key structures used in Employee Administration is the *organizational structure*. This will be covered in more detail in Chapter 10, but in brief, the organizational structure represents the functional structure of employees in the organization. It defines the organizational hierarchy, the reporting and authority lines, and organizational groupings. The organizational structure is defined by the personnel development (PD) objects as shown in Table 2.3.

Object	Description	Example
Organizational unit	A logical, functional grouping of the organization. When arranged in a hierarchical order within an organization, they form an organizational structure.	Finance Department, Payroll Office, Mechanics Workshop, Special Response Team
Position	A position in an organization is an individual assignment held by a specific employee	Head Mechanic Diesel Mechanic Petrol Mechanic Small Engine Mechanic Apprentice Mechanic
Job	A general set of work duties, tasks and responsibilities; the same job may define many positions in an organization	Manager Mechanic Apprentice Mechanic
Organizational key	A customer-specific subset of the organization used for control of authorizations	CO01S001 England Head Office CO02S001 USA Head Office

Table 2.3 SAP Organizational Structure

Figure 2.1 shows an example organizational structure with organizational units, positions, and one employee.

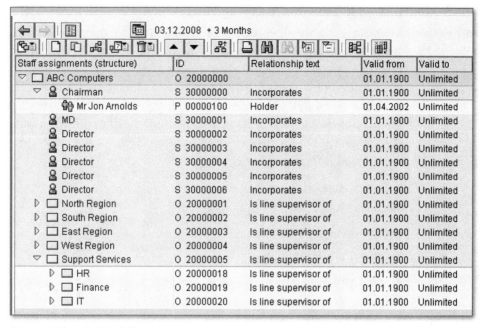

Figure 2.1 Organizational Structure

How Is Employee Data Stored?

Now that you have a general understanding of the SAP ERP HCM structure behind your company and how it is stored in Employee Administration, let's look at the different types of information we can store in Employee Administration and the structures that SAP ERP HCM uses to control this information. The main elements relating to storing employee data we need to understand are:

> Infotypes

> Wage types

> Pay structures

> Work schedules

These are ERP-specific terms for the different structures used to store employee data.

41

Infotypes

Recording, accessing, reporting, and maintaining your employee data is the primary aim of the SAP ERP HCM system. To do this, a structure called an *infotype* is used to store pieces of employee data together in logical groups. These infotypes provide a storage structure, facilitate data entry and maintenance, and let you store data for specific timeframes, or validity periods. As mentioned earlier, infotypes are the key concept in Employee Administration. Some of the most commonly used infotypes include:

> 0000 – Actions

> 0001 – Organization Assignment

> 0002 – Personal Details

> 0007 – Work Schedule

> 0008 – Basic Pay

> 0014 – Recurring Payments and Deductions

> 0015 – Additional Payments and Deductions

Infotype records are valid for a specific period of time, so, for example, as an employees' salary is changed during his employment, the employee will build up a chain of date-based infotype records showing a history of his salary changes.

Each infotype is defined by a four-digit key, and where subsets of the infotype data are required, the infotypes have *subtypes*. These subtypes are also defined by a four-digit key.

Infotypes fall into the following categories:

> Personnel Administration infotypes

> Personnel Development infotypes

Let's explore these in a little more depth.

Personnel Administration Infotypes

Personnel Administration infotypes can be maintained via the Maintain Master Data transaction. Figure 2.2 shows a transaction with an example employee and some of the infotypes maintained with it.

Personnel Administration infotypes are always created for a specific employee

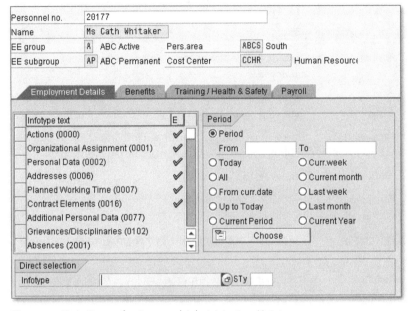

Figure 2.2 Main Screen for Personnel Administration Maintenance

Personnel Administration infotypes are used to record employee-based information. Within Personnel Administration there are two different types of infotypes:

> *International infotypes*

 – These are used by many countries, and it's worth noting that within this set, SAP allows *country-specific views of international infotypes* to provide more flexibility.

> *Country-specific infotypes*

 – Where required, SAP has also provided *country-specific infotypes* to meet country-specific requirements.

International Infotypes

These are the most widely used infotypes and are used for storing information that is required by most companies regardless of the employees' country. Some examples of the most commonly used international infotypes and infotype subtypes are listed in Table 2.4.

Infotype	Subtype	Name	Description
0000		Actions	Records details of personnel actions performed on employee
0001		Organizational Assignment	Stores details of employees' positions in the organization, their work locations and details of their employment
0002		Personal Data	Stores employees' key personal information: name, date of birth, gender, ID number, marital status, and so on
0006		Address	Employees' addresses
0006	0001	Permanent Address	Employees' home addresses
	0004	Emergency Address	The address of an employee's emergency contact person
	0005	Mailing Address	The preferred address for the employee to receive mail from the organization

Table 2.4 Examples of International Infotypes

Figure 2.3 shows Infotype 0006 Address subtype 0001 Permanent Address.

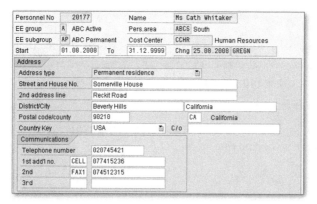

Figure 2.3 Address Infotype

Country-Specific Views of International Infotypes

SAP has succeeded in making infotypes very flexible in that an international infotype can have different fields available for input depending on the country of the employee whose data it holds. So, the fields contained in the infotype change depending on the country's statutory or organizational requirements.

Ex Example

In Infotype 0002 Personal Data, the country-based information is displayed depending on the employee's location.

You can see specific country fields in Table 2.5.

Country	Country-Specific Field
Great Britain	National ID Number
Ireland	PRSI Number
U.S.A.	Social Security Number
Canada	Social Insurance Number

Table 2.5 Examples of Country-Specific Data in International Infotypes

Figure 2.4 shows Infotype 0002 Personal Data for Great Britain.

Personnel No	20177				
EE group	A ABC Active	Pers.area	ABCS South		
EE subgroup	AP ABC Permanent	Cost Center	CCHR	Human Resources	
Start	28.12.1974 To	31.12.9999	Chng 25.08.2008 GREGN		

Name
FOA key	Ms			
Last name	Whitaker	Birth name		
First name	Cath	Initials	C.M.	
Middle name	Megan			
Name Format	Form-of-Address Key,First N	Name	Ms Cath Whitaker	

Additional data
Natl.ins.no.	AA516454B		
Birth date	28.12.1974	Birthplace	Wolverhampton
Gender	Female		
Nationality	British GB		
Language	English		

Marital status
Mar.stat.	Marr.	Since	24.01.2004
No. child.	11		

Figure 2.4 Infotype 0002 for Great Britain with Country-Specific Field National Insurance Highlighted

Country-Specific Infotypes

Many companies require information to be recorded that is only relevant to employees in one country. SAP ERP HCM accommodates this through the use of country-specific infotypes. These infotypes are only visible and available to the employees in that country and are designed to meet the specific needs of the country.

Some examples of country-specific infotypes are shown in Table 2.6.

Infotype	Name	Country
0013	Fiscal Data	Germany
0039	Additional Organizational Assignment	Austria
0048	Residence Status	Switzerland
0088	Maternity Data	Great Britain
0222	Superannuation	Australia

Table 2.6 Examples of Country-Specific Infotypes

Country-specific infotype subtypes are also delivered for international infotypes when a new infotype is not required, but country-specific data is required for the infotype (Table 2.7).

Infotype	Name	Subtype	Name	Country
0006	Address	US01	Paycheck Location	U.S.A.
0021	Family Members	J1	Guarantor	Japan
0045	Loans	B230	Mortgage	Belgium
0057	Membership Fees	AR03	Wood Workers Union	Argentina
0057	Membership Fees	MX01	Single Workers Union	Mexico

Table 2.7 Examples of Country-Specific Infotype Subtypes

Now you have an overview of the employee-focused Personnel Administration infotypes. Next, let's look at the more generic Personnel Development infotypes.

Personnel Development Infotypes

Personnel Development infotypes (PD infotypes) differ from Personnel Administration infotypes in that they are not specific to employee records but instead are defined for Organizational Management (OM) objects. Personnel Development infotypes are used in the Organizational Management and Personnel Development components to hold and link the followings types of information:

> Personnel Development:
>
> - Employee potential and qualifications
> - Career and succession planning
> - Employee appraisals and development plans

> Organizational Management:
>
> - Organizational units
> - Positions
> - Jobs
> - Relationships between objects

Personnel Development infotypes are very different from Personnel Administration infotypes and are used for very different tasks in Personnel Development and Organizational Management. Their use will be covered in more detail in the respective chapters on these topics.

Figure 2.5 shows the most common infotype in Personnel Development, Infotype 1000: Object.

Personnel Development infotypes are not always employee focused

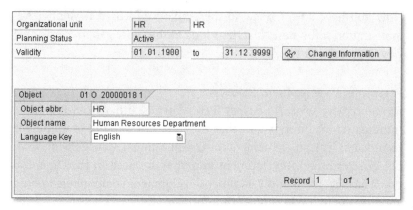

Figure 2.5 Example of a Personnel Development Infotype

Another key element in Employee Administration is the concept of a *wage type*.

Wage Types

Wage types are used to store payroll-related figures

Wage types are used in Personnel Administration and Payroll for storing the amounts, rates, and time units of payments and deductions that are subsequently used in payroll processing to calculate an employee's pay.

Wage types are primarily stored as components of an employees' pay in Infotype 0008 (Basic Pay), or as a one-time or recurring payment and deduction on either Infotype 0014 (Recurring Payments/Deductions) or Infotype 0015 (Additional Payments and Deductions).

The concepts behind wage types and their use in the payroll process are covered in more detail in Chapter 8, Payroll and Legal Reporting. In brief, wage types are defined by a four-digit customer-defined code. Wage types can be defined as payments or deductions and can store the following information for payroll processing:

> Wage type number/code

> Name

> Number

> Unit

> Rate

> Amount

> Costing information

Figure 2.6 shows a payment wage type assigned to an employee.

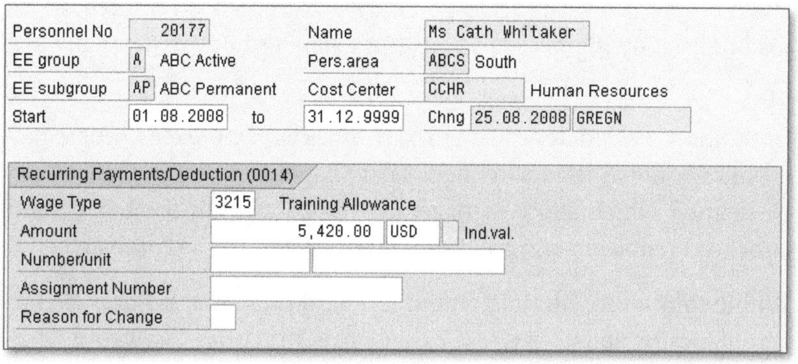

Personnel No	20177		Name		Ms Cath Whitaker	
EE group	A	ABC Active	Pers.area	ABCS	South	
EE subgroup	AP	ABC Permanent	Cost Center	CCHR		Human Resources
Start	01.08.2008	to	31.12.9999	Chng	25.08.2008	GREGN

Recurring Payments/Deduction (0014)

Wage Type	3215	Training Allowance
Amount	5,420.00 USD	Ind.val.
Number/unit		
Assignment Number		
Reason for Change		

Figure 2.6 Example Wage Type for a Training Allowance Assigned to an Employee

In addition to wage types, SAP ERP HCM also uses an element known as pay structures.

Pay Structures

Pay structures are used to define and group employees into their salary- and pay-related groups. They are especially useful for managing complex groupings of employees in highly structured work environments, where industrial-relations-related employee groupings and definitions are required, and also for employee populations where salary bands or grades are utilized. There are two basic types of pay structures that can be defined in SAP Employee Administration: Pay Scales and Pay Grades. Pay scale structures are typically defined for hourly or wage employees and those working under collective bargaining agreements. Pay grade structures are typically defined for salaried or non-wage employees.

Example

Pay structures are used to group employees into regional, legal, financial, or industry groups and are then used to manage the salary or pay rates within those groups.

Pay scales hold all of your rates of pay

Pay scales commonly define specific rates of pay, including steps or levels of pay. They can be set to be overwritten or, if required, to be read-only, allowing no deviations from standard or pre-defined wage rates.

In addition, pay grades can be used for salaried employees, where pay is typically not as rigidly defined. Salary bands, grades, and ranges can be defined which allow management ranges within the bands, and enhanced reporting and analysis of salaries within the company.

Within Employee Administration, standard programs are provided to automatically update pay scales and pay structures, as well as employee data, so that changes in employment agreements and company pay policies can be quickly reflected.

The pay scale hierarchy is shown in Table 2.8.

Object	Description	Example
Pay scale type	The highest level of pay structure; used to define a specific area of economic activity for which a collective agreement is valid	01 – Metal Workers Union 02 – Curtain Makers Union 03 – United Kingdom Collective Agreement
Pay scale area	Defines an additional structure grouping for pay, usually based on geographical or regaional variations in pay among wage or labor employees	A001 – South East England A002 – Scotland A003 – Wales A004 – The rest of England

Table 2.8 SAP ERP HCM Pay Scale Structure

Object	Description	Example
Pay scale group	A data element linked to a specific combination of pay scale type and pay scale areas, a pay scale group usually defines specific jobs or roles that have specific pay requirements or contracts	MASTCUR1 – Master Curtain Maker APPRCUR1 – Apprentice Curtain Maker
Pay scale level	A more detailed breakdown of a pay grade in which specific pay steps within a group exist	00 – Level 3 $52.00 01 – Level 2 $45.82 03 – Level 1 $22.45
Employee subgroup grouping for collective agreement provisions	Used to assign different pay scale types and areas to specific employee groups and subgroups	1 – Hourly wages 2 – Monthly wages 3- Salaried employee

Table 2.8 SAP ERP HCM Pay Scale Structure (Cont.)

The pay grade hierarchy is shown in Table 2.8.1.

Object	Description	Example
Pay grade type	The highest level of a pay grade structure; used to define a specific type of structure that is associated with a certain group of employees.	01 – Executive 02 – Technology Union 03 – General
Pay grade area	Defines an additional structure grouping for pay, usually based on regional or geographical differences within a pay grade structure.	A001 – San Francisco A002 – USA A003 – London A004 – England

Table 2.8.1 SAP ERP HCM Pay Grade Structure

Object	Description	Example
Pay grade	A data element linked to a specific combination of pay grade type and pay grade area, a grade typically defines a specific range or band of salaries within which an employee's salary will fall.	TECH1 TECH2 Exec1 Exec2 GRD27 GRD26 GRD25
Pay grade level	A more detailed breakdown of a pay grade which can also hold a specific range of salaries and a control or reference point against which salary evaluations can be performed.	00 – 21,000 USD – 28,500 USD 01 – 26,400 USD – 32,000 USD 03 – 29,300 USD – 34,500 USD

Table 2.8.1 SAP ERP HCM Pay Grade Structure (Cont.)

Work Schedules

Work schedules allow you to map and manage your employee working times

The accurate recording and management of employee working time is one of the key aims of any SAP ERP HCM system. SAP ERP HCM uses work schedules to record your employees' planned or contracted working times. A work schedule allows you to view an employee's planned working time for any day, including planned start time (or range of start times), breaks (morning, lunch, afternoon, or as required), and planned finishing time.

You can quickly see an employee's planned working hours for a specific week, month, or year. Defining and mapping employees to the correct work schedule is immensely important to companies that operate in complex factory, manufacturing, or other labor environments. Knowing when employees should be at work, on a break, or not at work gives shift managers, roster supervisors, and time sheet administrators valuable information to manage employee working times effectively. Companies that have mainly salaried staff working normal office hours are generally not as concerned about recording and tracking their employees working time. However, work schedules are still important to these types of companies so they can effectively manage vacations, sick leave, and other absence- and attendance-related activities. Work schedules are made up of the following components (Table 2.9).

Object	Description	Example
Daily work schedule	Define the authorized working times and break times for a single day; can record fixed working times, flextime, and days off	DWS Start End Total 00A 8:00am 5:00pm 7.5hrs 00B 9:00am 6:30pm 8.0hrs OFF 0.0hrs
Break schedule	Used within a daily work schedule to define employees' breaks from work	BS Start End Total Paid 01 9:30 10:00 0.5hrs Y 02 12:00 1:00 1.0hrs N
Period work schedule	Combinations of different daily work schedules (including working and non-working schedules) linked together to map an employee's planned working time for a week or a rolling roster	PWS DWS 01 00A 02 00A 03 00B 04 00B 05 00B 06 OFF 07 OFF

Table 2.9 Work Schedule Components

Object	Description	Example					
Work schedule rule	Combines a period work schedule with a public holiday calendar and then applies it to a specific period of time to map an actual period of work	Day	Month	Year		PWS	DWS
		22	Jan	2009		01	00A
		23	Jan	2009		02	00A
		24	Jan	2009		03	00B
		25	Jan	2009		04	00B
		26	Jan	2009		05	00B
		27	Jan	2009		06	OFF
		28	Jan	2009		07	OFF
Personal work schedule	An employee's actual working time, taking into account the planned working time from the work schedule and absences, attendances, and substitutions						

Table 2.9 Work Schedule Components (Cont.)

Figure 2.7 shows an employee's work schedule details.

Personnel No	20177		Name	Ms Cath Whitaker		
EE group	A	ABC Active	Pers.area	ABCS South		
EE subgroup	AP	ABC Permanent	Cost Center	CCHR	Human Resources	
Start	08/01/2008	To	12/31/9999	Chg.	08/25/2008 GREGN	

Work schedule rule

Work schedule rule	40.00HRS	40 hours
Time Mgmt status	0 - No time evaluation	
☐ Part-time employee		

Working time

Employment percent	100.00
Daily working hours	8.00
Weekly working hours	40.00
Monthly working hrs	173.33
Annual working hours	2080.00
Weekly workdays	5.00

Figure 2.7 Employee Work Schedule

Work schedules are also the main source of information in the SAP HCM Time and Attendance functionality, and are discussed in more depth in Chapter 7.

Now that we have reviewed what we can store in Employee Administration and how this information is stored, we need to look at what we do with the data.

What Can You Do with the Data?

One of the main purposes of Employee Administration is to streamline and automate the basic processes related to personnel and employee information management. SAP ERP HCM does this by providing tools that support the core tasks related to Employee Administration, including master data maintenance.

Master Data Maintenance

SAP ERP HCM provides a central employee maintenance transaction that can be used across many of the components to create, display, edit, copy, and delete master data. The maintenance transaction (called *Maintain HR Master Data*) allows you to quickly view all of an employee's data, including employee history, in an overview or detail mode.

As we discussed earlier, all employee master data is stored in infotypes. Each infotype is defined with a *time constraint* that applies a specific validity rule to the infotype. An example of these rules is a time constraint that determines if an infotype record must always exist for an employee while he is active at the company. Time constraints also determine if an infotype can exist multiple times for the same period for an employee and whether the infotype can have overlapping records, or if records must be sequential with no time gaps in between records.

Master data entry is further enhanced by the provision of the *object manager*. This tool appears on the side of the data maintenance screen and allows you to select groups of employees via a search tool. You can then switch quickly between them as you perform your data

The object manager allows you to search your data easily

maintenance. In addition, commonly used employee searches can be stored for quick access, further speeding up data maintenance.

Another feature is the *personnel file* function, which allows you to scroll through an employee's virtual file and displays all of an employee's infotype records in chronological order.

When significant employee lifecycle changes such as hiring, promotions, or transfers take place, in order to record all of the details of the changes, HR administrators often have to maintain multiple infotypes. Personnel actions are used to control the editing of multiple infotype records.

Personnel Actions

Personnel actions link infotypes together to speed up processing

SAP ERP HCM uses a system called *personnel actions* to link together strings of infotypes so that they can be performed sequentially. Personnel actions are used to speed up common processes such as hiring employees, performing organizational reassignments, and processing terminations. Each personnel action contains all of the infotypes required for that specific action, allowing the user to proceed sequentially through the screens for inputting all of the required information. Different versions of the same action can be defined for different types of employees and for different countries, which allows you to tailor them to specific requirements and speed up data entry tasks.

Ex Example

When an employee is transferred from one regional office to another, the following infotypes are likely to be processed as part of a Transfer action:

0000 Actions

0001 Organizational Assignment

0006 Address

0007 Planned Working Time

0008 Basic Pay

Figure 2.8 shows an example of a set of commonly used actions for a company.

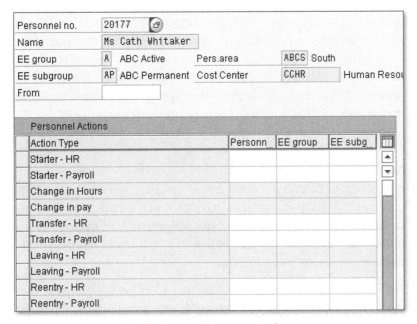

Figure 2.8 Actions Available for Process Changes to Employees

Master Data Fast Entry

This tool is designed to speed up the process of bulk data entry. It allows you to process infotype updates for multiple employees simultaneously. Employees can be selected dynamically using a set of reporting tools to select only the employees you require, based on your own search criteria. In *fast entry* only the fields that you require for input are displayed, depending on the infotype you have selected. This tool provides valuable time savings when you need to process bulk employee updates such as bonus payments, increases in recurring allowances, or the termination of a specific payment to a range of employees.

Reporting

Recognizing that any HR system is only as good as the information that can be retrieved from the system, over 200 reports are delivered as standard. For ultimate flexibility, two standard reporting tools are delivered that allow users to create their own reports. These tools are *InfoSet Query* and *SAP Query*. The two tools offer differing levels of complexity and power, allowing users to work with a simple click and drag report producer or a more complex reporting tool with more input and output options. All of the data stored in the Employee Administration infotypes is also available for reporting from external reporting tools such as SAP Business Intelligence (BI) without having to spend time on programming. More information on SAP ERP HCM's reporting capabilities can be found in Chapter 8.

Audit Information

The amount of audit information you collect is fully configurable

As a standard function defined during system implementation, master data entry can be automatically checked as it is entered to ensure it is correct and valid. Any changes to employee-related data are stored in the audit log clusters to ensure that all activities can be tracked and traced.

The level of audit tracking is able to be defined by the company during system implementation. Single fields or entire infotypes can be set to have changes logged. This flexibility allows audit reporting to focus on key pieces of information and ignore non-essential data changes.

The audit log report can be run for the following combinations of audit searches by:

> Employee

> Infotype

> Time and/or date

The report output then shows the following information:

> The user responsible for the change

> The time and date of the change

> The type of change (creation, change, deletion)

> A field-by-field breakdown of all changes made

A similar report is available for reporting on changes to Personnel Development infotypes.

Archiving

With most large SAP ERP HCM systems, the question eventually becomes not *if* you are going to archive your data but *when*. Most multinational SAP ERP HCM systems reach a point where the databases are getting too large, or a large portion of the data is obsolete for day–to–day requirements, but the data is still required for long-term access requirements and legal reporting purposes. Large volumes of data slow down system response times and make the system inefficient— not to mention frustrating. Data archiving is facilitated in SAP ERP HCM using SAP NetWeaver technology. The process for archiving in the SAP ERP HCM components is consistent with the process used in other parts of SAP ERP.

Employee Administration's standard archiving solution makes archiving and retrieval stress free

Within SAP ERP HCM, you can choose which pieces of information you archive and from what time they are archived. The archiving decision can be made based on several criteria including the following commonly used objects:

> Personnel Administration records

> Payroll results

> Time evaluation results

> Payroll posting documents

> Time sheet data

The SAP ERP archiving process allows you to determine a proactive archiving and retrieval process so you can balance system response against reporting requirements to ensure you get the best of both worlds.

Authorizations

Authorization and security controls within SAP ERP are an area of specialty all on their own. The ability to view, edit, or delete employee data is a critical component of any SAP ERP HCM system, so it's good to know that SAP ERP's authorization control for SAP ERP HCM is

Authorizations allow you full control of who sees what and when they see it

built around the standard logic used across all SAP ERP components. Authorizations and accesses can be controlled at an employee, infotype, wage type, personnel area, subarea, employee group, employee subgroup, or organizational level, providing significant flexibility in maintaining control of your employee data. Authorizations can be built around role authorizations, where the authorizations for a user are dependent on the user's job, and via structural authorizations, where the authorizations are assigned depending on where the employee works in the company.

In addition to the ability to control access to employee data, SAP ERP HCM also gives you the ability to control your users' access to transactions and reports, allowing you to create authorizations that meet the specific requirements of your company. Employees can be authorized to run payroll, but only in test mode; they can be allowed to access their own data, but only in display mode, or in maintain mode for some infotypes and display for others.

SAP ERP HCM also contains a tool called the *Profile Generator*, which allows you to maintain authorizations for people who have different job roles and perform the same functions for the same position but in different company areas. This gives you the ability to create custom authorizations where required and the ability to reuse the same authorizations across the company.

Integration

Employee Administration is seamlessly integrated with all of the other SAP ERP HCM components

As mentioned earlier, Employee Administration is the core of the SAP ERP HCM product. Employee Administration is fully integrated with all of the other SAP ERP HCM components, either directly through the data stored in PA infotypes or via links and relationships between this data and data stored in PD infotypes or even other SAP application areas, such as cost centers (which are stored in Finance/Controlling). This means that, for example, changes to an employee's cost center are picked up instantly by payroll, and a change to an employee's marital status will have an instant impact on which employee benefits he is entitled to in the Benefits function. Employee Administration draws finance information, such as cost centers and company codes, straight from the SAP ERP Financials component; therefore, any creations or changes to a cost center done there will be instantly visible in Employee Administration. The seamless integration capability of SAP ERP HCM has always been one of its main benefits.

So let's take a look at a British satellite company to see Employee Administration at work.

Case Study

Table 2.10 provides you with a quick overview of a case study before we explain it in more detail.

Company	British Satellite Company
Existing Solutions	SAP R/3 for Finance and Controlling
Challenges	Replace and consolidate separate MS Excel- and Access-based HR administration system and separate legacy payroll system
SAP Solutions	SAP Employee Administration and Payroll
Benefits	Centralized employee information storage Increased process efficiency Divulged data ownership

Table 2.10 SAP Employee Administration Case Study

This relatively small British company manages a highly qualified workforce spread across the globe. The company owns and operates a global satellite network offering global communication services. The company has 600 employees spread over eight countries.

The Challenges

Running two employee data management systems, the HR and Payroll departments operated in a totally autonomous manner with no automatic interface between these two independent systems. Employee master data changes from the HR side (for example, new hires and terminations) were often not communicated to the payroll team, resulting in an unreasonably high error rate in payroll. Similarly, employee data changes such as pay increases or adjustments in allowances and benefits were often only updated in the payroll system, meaning the HR system was frequently looking at incorrect data.

The SAP Solution

Over an eight-month period, the implementation team replaced the separate HR and payroll systems with Personnel Administration, Organizational Management, Benefits, and Payroll. Significant time was taken to understand the business processes of both the HR and payroll teams, which were widely different despite large overlaps in responsibility. The new system integrated the requirements of both departments into one set of consistent and efficient processes. Automatic integration with the existing finance system was also introduced to streamline the payroll process. Numerous master data conflicts were encountered during the data cleanse and upload process; employees terminated in one system but not the other, differences in employee salary and benefits data, and even ghost employee records all needed to be investigated and resolved before they could be uploaded.

The Benefits

The biggest benefits the company received were related to the centralizing of their Employee Administration systems. For example, now when new employees are hired, they are instantly available to both the HR and Payroll departments. All of the errors and omissions related to the double entry of employee data are instantly removed by the single centralized system. Both teams save considerable amounts of time in data entry because data only has to be entered once.

Through the maintenance of a single employee data system, the company was able for the first time to allocate distinct areas of responsibility and authorization between the two departments, ensuring that employee data is only maintained by the responsible teams, reducing data entry errors.

Having a centralized Employee Administration system also allows the company to effectively control its employee absence data. The central system allows them to assign leave quotas, and for the first time all unpaid leave is guaranteed to be correctly calculated and deducted from employee payroll results.

The creation of a centralized organizational structure through the use of Organizational Management also had immediate benefits, giving the team the ability to quickly get an overview of the company's structure rather than relying on manually created and maintained PowerPoint documents.

One of the small but surprisingly important benefits of the system from the user's point of view was the access to up-to-date correct finance information, such as new cost centers and cost objects, one of the great benefits of integration with the Finance component.

Summary

Employee Administration gives you a system that efficiently and effectively manages your employee data, freeing up your HR administrators' time to focus on the more strategic (and interesting) parts of their roles.

In this chapter:

> We discussed the wide range of information that can be stored in Employee Administration, how that information is managed, how it is stored, and most important, what we can do with it.

> We were introduced to some of the key concepts in SAP ERP HCM including infotypes, wage types, pay structures and work schedules.

> We discussed the many tools available for maintaining, updating, and reporting on employee data and how this data is integrated with other SAP ERP HCM components.

> Reflecting on the importance of keeping employee data safe and secure, we discussed the security controls and options for managing the critical and sensitive data that we store and manage in Employee Administration.

> We reviewed a case study demonstrating some of the benefits received by one company from centralizing all of its employee data into one database.

In the next chapter we will learn about another key component of SAP ERP HCM: Organizational Management. This component creates the foundation for company organizational structure views, manager and employee self-services, workflow, and integration with other Personnel Development functions such as Performance Management, Career and Development Planning, Succession Planning, Recruiting, and Learning Solution.

3

SAP ERP HCM Organizational Management

One of the first things people want to know when they start a new job is what the structure of their company is. To whom do they report? How is their team structured? Where does their new team fit in the department? Where does the department fit into the company as a whole? Defining a company's organizational structure is always a challenge. Reporting lines, managerial lines, team structures, and other issues make mapping a company's structure a real challenge for many companies.

Organizational Management is the SAP ERP HCM tool that allows you to create a graphical representation of your company's structure. Creating and maintaining your company's structure has always been a large task for HR departments. Traditionally, it has been done manually using PowerPoint or Visio or even written by hand. Now, using Organizational Management, you can maintain, view, edit, and model your organizational structure. Because Organizational Management is fully integrated into your other SAP ERP HCM components, you always have a seamless, integrated, real-time view of your organizational structure.

You can create many different views of your company within Organizational Management, and these structures then form the backbone for many other HR processes, including performance management, compensation management, workflow management and, of course, organizational reporting.

How Organizational Management Fits into an Enterprise

The Organizational Management function gives your HR department the ability to quickly create and maintain hierarchies that represent the various structures in your company.

The whole SAP ERP HCM solution is anchored by the structures that are defined in this function. Organizational Management gives companies the ability to map their regions, countries, legal entities, locations, departments, teams, and employees so that they really are the heart of the company. This structure, once defined, is then used heavily in many other components but especially for reporting, workflow, manager self-service, and budgeting. It represents an up-to-date, real-time view of your company's structure, so it is key to many decision-making processes within your HR team and all of its departments. In the most recent versions of SAP ERP HCM, seamless integration with SAP Talent Visualization by Nakisa (TVN) is available and provides a simple, visual user interface for Organizational Charting and Modeling.

A Closer Look at Organizational Management

At the beginning of any SAP ERP HCM implementation, Organizational Management is one of the components that generates excitement among HR team members. The chance to define your company's structure and maintain it in an integrated and user-friendly way, where changes to employee data are instantly reflected in the organizational structure and all members of the HR team can work on it simultaneously, makes Organizational Management one of the most eagerly anticipated functions. In reality, the amount of work involved in defining the "true" organizational structure can be quite overwhelming. Fortunately, Organizational Management gives users the ability to develop multiple versions of their company's organizational structure so that all users' needs are met.

Let's look at what the organizational structure is and what it is used for.

What Is It?

Organizational Management is essentially a set of building blocks you use to define your company.

These building blocks are known as objects; some examples of standard objects are organizational units, positions, and jobs. These objects are linked together using a concept known as relationships. Relationships determine which type of link the objects have.

The building blocks of Organizational Management are objects and relationships

 Example

> A person is linked to a position via a holder relationship; generally only one person can *hold* a position.

All of these objects and their relationships are stored in infotypes. So let's explore objects, relationships, and infotypes in more detail, beginning with objects.

Objects

Organizational Management is based on the concept that each element of a company is defined as a stand-alone object with individual characteristics. These objects are created and maintained individually and then linked together via relationships to map out the organizational structure. SAP HCM delivers more than 38 standard objects to use in building your organizational structure.

38 standard objects allow you to define your structure in many ways

To help illustrate this concept, let's look briefly at the most commonly used objects:

> **Organizational units**
> For example, your company's departments such as Finance, Human Resources, and Payroll

> **Positions**
> These are held by employees and define a person's place in the organization; examples are Finance Director and Human Resource Administrator.

> **Persons**
> Using employee records as a base, employees are assigned to the organizational structure as the holders of positions. This process occurs when using Personnel Administration functions instead of Organizational Management functions.

> **Jobs**
> These are a set of skills or an occupation, such as Accountant or Secretary, used to define the skills required to fulfill a position.

> **Work centers**
> These define a physical place of work, for example, as general as an office building or as specific as Desk 120, Fifth Floor.

> **Tasks**
> A set of tasks is used to define a specific job or position.

> **Cost centers**
> These elements are maintained in financial accounting, but are available as objects in Organizational Management to assist financial reporting.

These are only the most commonly used of the over 38 types of standard objects you can use. These objects allow you to define your company from a wide range of perspectives—from profit centers and business partners all the way through to value driver trees (used to display areas of the organizational structure that are focused on delivering great value). The minimum objects you need to build and maintain your organizational structure are organizational units and positions.

Figure 3.1 shows a company organizational structure defined in Organizational Management with some of the key objects.

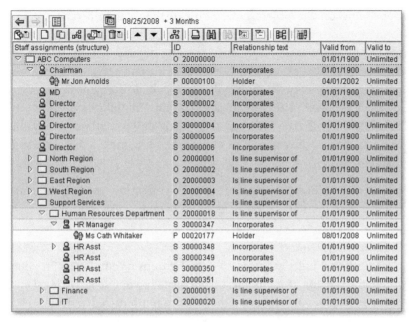

Figure 3.1 The Organizational Structure with Organizational Units, Positions, and Employees Assigned

In addition to the standard objects, you can also define your own custom objects, if your company has an organizational structure requirement that isn't provided.

Ex Example

Some examples of previously created custom objects include faculty, school, and census categories.

Upon creation, objects are assigned a unique eight-digit numeric code. This code and the name of the object are both searchable. This is important because one of the benefits of objects is that once they are created, they can be used as many times as required across the company. For example, you only need to define one job Secretary, and this can then be assigned to every position in the company, cutting down on maintenance and allowing further changes to be quickly applied throughout the whole company.

Once you create objects, they are reusable

Depending on the object type, you can then assign a range of information to the object to help define its purpose and details. Some object attributes are then inherited by any objects that are related to the object, so for example, if you assign a cost center to an organizational unit, this cost center will be defaulted to any positions that are then assigned to the organizational unit. The inherited value can be overridden if required, but this trickle-down method of default value assignment saves a lot of effort when it comes to ongoing data maintenance.

Now let's look in more detail at the most commonly used objects and the information that can be assigned to them:

Organizational units

Organizational units are used to define groups of employees in your company, starting at the highest level, usually your separate legal entities, and then working down the structure into each department, all the way down to specific teams of employees.

In your organizational unit, you can define standard company codes, working hours, and set rules regarding which types of employee groups and subgroups can be assigned to the organizational unit. You can also assign an address or location and a default cost center. Figure 3.2 shows the finance and personnel area detail associated with an organizational unit.

Once you have placed your employees in organizational units, you can go down another level to *positions*.

Positions

To determine where an employee fits in your organization, you assign him to a position, which is a single instance of an entity that is described by a job. Every employee who works for your company is assigned to a position. Usually, the position-to-person relationship is 1 to 1, but sometimes in the case of job sharing or other business scenarios, a position may have multiple holders at a single time. Positions are assigned to organizational units to define the organizational hierarchy.

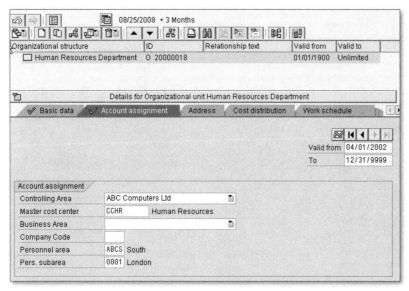

Figure 3.2 Account Assignment Details for an Organizational Unit

 Tip

A position generally outlasts its holder and can be made vacant, and then a new employee can be assigned as the holder of the position.

You can define positions (an example is shown in Figure 3.3) as occupied (by a person), vacant, or obsolete if the position currently has no one assigned to it. You can make it a chief position, which indicates that it's the head of its organizational unit. The defaults for company code, cost center, employee group, subgroup, and work schedule can be inherited from the parent organizational unit and then, if required, overwritten with information specific to this position. For example, you can assign specific reporting relationships to positions, and link the position a manager holds to other positions, even if the positions are outside of the managers' organizational unit. Jobs are assigned to positions so that the job skills required to hold the position can be determined and reported.

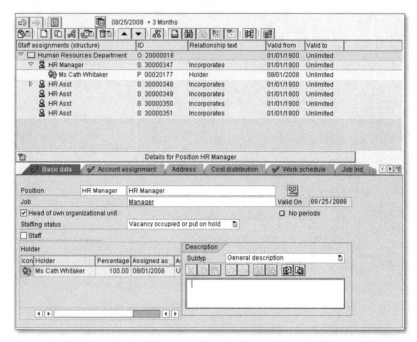

Figure 3.3 The Organizational Structure Showing Some of the Detail Assigned to the HR Manager Position

So now that you can define all of the positions that make up your company, you need to define the people who hold them. In the OM component these are called persons.

Persons

Persons are the Organizational Management objects that represent your employees. Every employee in your system is available in Organizational Management as a person to be assigned to positions within organizational units. The person record cannot be created or maintained in Organizational Management, because these processes are enabled though Personnel Administration functions in Employee Administration. In most cases a person can only hold only one position at a time, and one position is only occupied by one person at a time. Next, we will look at the job object.

Jobs

A job defines a set of skills or an occupation, such as accountant or secretary, and is used to define the specific skills or tasks required to fulfill a position. So if only one set of skills is required to define a job, such as a carpenter or welder, you only need to define this job once in Organizational Management, and you can assign this job to all of the positions in your company that require these skills, using a relationship in Organizational Management. So your one welder *job* could define 50 separate welder *positions* that your company employs. Defining all of the jobs for your organization can be a large initial task, but the ongoing benefits of maintaining an accurate job catalog are many.

 Example

> The jobs you define here are used in many other parts of the SAP ERP HCM solution. For example, you can record information relating to planned compensation, cost planning, job evaluation results, and salary survey results, which are then utilized by the different components.

More information on each of these subjects can be found in Part Two of the book, Talent Management.

Cost Centers

Cost centers are used for reporting financial results, and can be assigned to organizational units or positions, or the default cost centers can be inherited from superior objects higher in the organizational structure. Cost centers are only maintained in Financial Accounting, although you can see them and assign them in Organizational Management, but you can't edit them there.

Work Centers

These represent where employees do their actual work. When defining your work centers, you can be as specific or as general as your company requires. Some companies define each cubicle or desk as an individual work center. Other companies that do not require this level of detail (or do not want the overhead of maintaining all that information) use broader work centers such as floors of an office building or even just the buildings themselves.

A wide variety of information can be stored relating to a work center. Examples include information relating to shift group, required health examinations, standard working hours, standard cost distribution for employees, and postal and physical addresses.

Tasks

Tasks are the individual duties and responsibilities carried out by an employee. A set of tasks can be grouped together into a task group. Tasks are then assigned to a job or position to define that object. A task can be:

> Responding to telephone queries

> Answering customer emails

> Refilling the printer and copier

A set of tasks that are commonly performed together can then be assigned to a task group. The advantage of task groups is that you only need to assign the group to the object rather than each individual task.

By defining your tasks and assigning tasks to positions and jobs, you start to build up information on the required skills and qualifications in your company. These can then be used within the Talent Management function. Tasks are also used to manage the processing of workflows; more information on their use in this area is covered in Part Three of the book, Workflow.

When you create a task, you can define what type of task it is. The following categories of tasks are available:

> **Rank**
Classify tasks as planning, completion, or control tasks.

> **Phase**
Classify how tasks fit into a business process.

> **Purpose**
Identify tasks that directly contribute to the products or services that a company provides.

Now that we have identified our objects, we need something to link them together to form our organizational structure. These links between objects are stored as relationships.

Relationships

To make maintaining relationships within your company straightforward, Organizational Management comes with more than 180 standard relationships to help define the most common relationships within your company. Relationships between objects can either be reciprocal or one way. In SAP ERP the superior object is known as the *Parent* object, and the inferior object is known as the *Child* object. When a reciprocal relationship is required, it will be automatically created by the system. Some examples of common relationships and their reciprocal relationships are listed in Table 3.1. An example of the how this is displayed in an infotype record is shown in Figure 3.4.

Relationship	Direction	Relationship Description	Explanation
Org to Org	Parent	Is Line Supervisor of	Org Unit 1 is line supervisor of Org Unit 2
Org to Org	Child	Reports to	Org Unit 2 Reports to Org Unit 1
Position to Org	Child	Belongs to	Position 10 belongs to Org Unit 1
Org to Position	Parent	Incorporates	Org Unit 1 incorporates Position 10
Job to Position	Child	Describes	Job 100 describes Position 10
Position to Job	Parent	Is Described by	Position 10 is described by Job 100
Cost Center to Org Unit	One Way	Cost Center Assignment	Cost center 999 is assigned to Org Unit 10

Table 3.1 Common Organizational Relationships

Organizational unit	HR			Human Resources Department				
Planning Status	Active							
Relationships	01 O 20000018 1							

Start	End	R	Rel	Relat.text	R	Rel'd object ID	Abbr.	% Rate
01/01/1900	12/31/9999	A	002	Reports (I	O	20000005	Supp Serv	0.00
04/01/2002	12/31/9999	A	011	Cost cente	K	CCHR ABC1	Human Resour	0.00
01/01/1900	12/31/9999	B	003	Incorporat	S	30000347	HR Manager	0.00
01/01/1900	12/31/9999	B	003	Incorporat	S	30000348	HR Asst	0.00
01/01/1900	12/31/9999	B	003	Incorporat	S	30000349	HR Asst	0.00
01/01/1900	12/31/9999	B	003	Incorporat	S	30000350	HR Asst	0.00
01/01/1900	12/31/9999	B	003	Incorporat	S	30000351	HR Asst	0.00
02/18/2008	12/31/9999	B	012	Is managed	S	30000347	HR Manager	0.00

Figure 3.4 An Organizational Unit and the Related Organizational Objects

In relationships, one of the key concepts and most important benefits of Organizational Management is the concept of inheritance. This means that an attribute assigned to an object is automatically assigned to specific related objects. For example, some of the settings defined in a job are automatically inherited by any position with that job assigned to it. When objects are arranged in a hierarchical order, the attributes of the higher object are automatically inherited by lower-level objects. This inheritance can be overwritten, but is an invaluable time saver. Let's say, for example, you have 100 carpenter positions with the same job in your company. You only need to update the one job record, and it will be reflected in all 100 positions. The inheritance principle is standard only on specific, SAP-delivered object attributes.

In addition to the many standard relationships, Organizational Management allows you to define company-specific relationships to meet your specific requirements.

 Example

> Examples of these *custom relationships* could include things such as "fire warden responsible" and "assigned union representative."

Infotypes

As mentioned in Chapter 2, infotypes are one of the key concepts in SAP ERP HCM. We talked a lot about infotypes already, but let's have a brief refresher on them.

Infotypes are used to store logical pieces of data together. They provide a structure, facilitate data entry, and enable maintenance. Infotypes are typically valid only for a certain period of time, so as time moves on and data is changed, we build up a chain of date-based records showing a history of changes. Each infotype is defined by a four-digit key. Infotypes fall into two categories:

> **Personnel Administration infotypes**
> These were covered in the Employee Administration chapter, but the main difference between Personnel Administration and Personnel Development infotypes is that the Personnel Administration infotypes are always created for a single employee, whereas Personnel Development infotypes are linked to objects in Personnel Development and Organizational Management.

> **Personnel Development infotypes**
> Although similar in name, these infotypes are used for very different tasks in the Personnel Development and Organizational Management functions. Personnel Development infotypes are used to store the details of many types of information, from holding the details of different departments for organizational units to defining a specific task or job.

In other components outside Organizational Management, these infotypes are used to record details of qualifications, career and succession planning, and development plans.

Because Personnel Development infotypes are used to record such a wide range of information, their organization and structure is quite different from Personnel Administration infotypes. Some of them are very generic, and their name and use does not relate to a specific component. Others are designed for a very specific piece of information specific to a certain object or component, for example, the infotypes listed in Table 3.2 are used across all of the components. Others are designed for a very specific piece of information specific to a certain object or component.

Infotype	Name	Description
1000	Object	The anchor record for an object; gives the object a name, validity period, and a brief description
1001	Relationships	Lists all of the related objects for an object; for example, for a specific position it may list the organizational unit and manager, cost center, and holder of the position
1002	Description	A longer description of the object for informational purposes

Table 3.2 Generic PD Infotypes

To help you identify to which type of object the infotype is related, the objects are given a one- or two-digit key to identify the object type relationships on Infotype 1000 (which holds all of the relationships).

Examples of commonly used object keys include:

> O – Organizational units

> S - Positions

> P - Persons

> C –Jobs

> K – Cost centers

Other Personnel Development infotypes are more tailored to their functions within a component. The most commonly used infotypes within Organizational Management and their uses are listed in Table 3.3.

Infotype	Name	Object Type	Description
1003	Department/ Staff	Organizational unit or position	If used for an organizational unit, then this organizational unit is a Department.
			If it has been defined for a position, then this position reports outside the normal hierarchy.
1007	Vacancy	Position	Here you can identify positions that are currently vacant or will be vacant in the future for reporting purposes.
1008	Account Assignment	Organizational unit or position	Allows you to assign an appropriate cost center and personnel area and subarea for costing and reporting purposes. This can then be inherited by all objects below this one.
1011	Work Schedule	Organizational unit or position	Here you define the planned working hours for employees related to this object.
1013	Employee Group/ Subgroup	Position	Allows you to determine which type of employee can hold this position.
1018	Cost Distribution	Organizational unit or position	Determines how costs are to be split between several cost centers and what percentages each split represents.
1028	Address	Organizational unit, position, work center	The physical address of the object; used for reporting purposes.

Table 3.3 Organizational Management-Specific Infotypes

These are only a few of the many infotypes that you can use to build up a picture of your company in Organizational Management.

What Can You Do with It?

This can be a really useful component. It enables you to:

> Depict your companies' organizational structure, its reporting structures, and your current organizational plan

> Use your organizational structure to analyze your current organizational plan utilizing different evaluation paths and then use this information to plan workforce requirements and personnel costs

> Use your current organizational structure as a base to simulate new structures, allowing you to model large organizational changes

> Use your reporting structure as a framework for creating workflow-based processes, allowing business processes to be automated and streamlined

> Define employees' access and authorizations based on their position in the organizational structure, controlling their ability to view, maintain, and report on employee data

Organizational Management is built around a set of key objects that are related via different types of relationships to allow you to define your company's HCM-related structures. These structures can include the following:

> **Organizational structure**

- A hierarchical view of your company, showing the arrangement of your organization from an administrative point of view

> **Organizational plan**

- A functional view of your organization showing departments, positions, holders, tasks, jobs, and work centers

> **Reporting structure**

- Defining the lines of responsibility within your company: who reports to whom, and who manages what

> **Matrix organizations**

- Allowing non-hierarchical views of the company, for example, project teams made up of employees from many departments

> **Job index**

- Lists all of the jobs performed in your company

> **Work center index**

- Lists all of the locations where employees physically work in your company

> **Task catalog**

- A complete listing of all of the tasks performed by your employees

How Do You Maintain It?

As any HR expert knows, maintaining an up-to-date and accurate version of the organizational structure is a task not to be underestimated. However, the benefits of having an up-to-date and relevant organizational structure that you can rely on and quickly access are also significant. Next we will look at the ways you can maintain the organizational structure and some of the key features of it.

You can view your organizational structure forward or backward in time

Loading the Organizational Structure

All of the objects that make up your structure can be loaded into the system using a standard program that allows you to upload each object type and then the relationships that link them together.

Maintenance via the Visual Mode

Figure 3.5 shows the visual mode of maintaining the organizational structure. This is the view of the organizational structure that most of your users will use; the visual mode allows users to see the full organizational structure visually arranged in its hierarchy. Users can swap views between the hierarchical organization structure, the matrix structure, and workflow structures as required. They can drill down on organizational units to see the positions assigned to them and then down to see which employee hold the position.

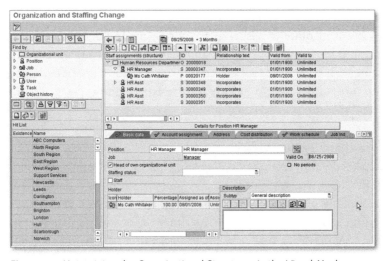

Figure 3.5 Maintaining the Organizational Structure via the Visual Mode

Users can view the organizational structure using several completely different views including:

> Organizational structure

> Organizational assignments

> Staff assignments in the form of a list or a tree structure

> Reporting hierarchy

> Job assignments

> Task assignments

> Task hierarchy

> Workflow agents

> Account assignments

Drag and drop employees from one department to another

The visual mode allows the users to drag and drop objects from one part of the organizational structure to another. For example, if an employee is moving from one department to another, it's a simple case of selecting the effective date, selecting the employee, and then dragging them into their new organizational unit. This then triggers a master data update in employee administration, performing the required personnel action, and updating both the organizational structure and personnel administration side all in one go.

Maintenance via the Expert Mode

This view isn't quite as visual as the visual mode, but expert users performing more than ordinary maintenance on their organizational structure, can quickly see all of the information for a specific object. This in turn allows you to quickly resolve issues, and it gives experienced users more maintenance options.

Historical and Future Views

To help keep your system up to date and current, everything stored in SAP ERP HCM Organizational Management is stored as a date-based record. So when you perform any sort of maintenance on your structure—for example, if you close a department as of today's date or terminate an employee, as you would expect—that data will disappear from your organizational structure tomorrow. But if in a month or a year, you want to know what your organizational structure looked like, all you need to do is set the view date as you require, and you get a complete view of your organization at that date. The same works for the future. If you know that a department is being moved in two months, there is no reason why you can't make the change today with an effective date in the future. Everyone's view of the organizational structure will remain unchanged until that key date, when the structure will reflect the changes.

Plan Versions

Planning large-scale reorganizations can be a very complex and time-consuming task. Traditionally, modeling was done using PowerPoint or Visio, but with SAP ERP HCM Organizational Management, you can create a complete copy of your current organizational structure and assign a new plan version to it. This new plan version can then be changed, deleted, edited, and maintained however you need to model your organizational changes. Once you've created your perfect new organizational structure, you can replace the existing plan version with your new version. As well as performing organizational planning directly in Organizational Management, customers can purchase the SAP Talent Visualization by Nakisa (SAP TVN) function, which provides a simple user interface for modeling and creating organizational structure versions based on reorganizations, mergers, and acquisitions.

Create a copy of your organizational structure to use for modeling changes

Matrix Organizations

Sometimes the traditional top-down hierarchical view of a company does not provide for complex cross-departmental teams and projects. For example, a project to develop a new product or to conduct the annual graduate recruitment process may require resources from all across the company. You don't want to reorganize your existing organizational structure just to be able to report for the limited duration of the project, but you do need to track costs and people for day-to-day project reporting.

Matrix structures allow you to group employees in cross-departmental teams

Organizational Management allows users to create matrix structures to meet these requirements that use existing data such as positions and cost centers, and assign them to a second structure that will provide for the project's needs without disrupting the day-to-day reporting requirements of the rest of the company. As you can now appreciate, having seen the capabilities of the organizational structure, having an accurate, detailed, and representative organizational structure relies on a lot of information from other parts of SAP ERP HCM. We will next look at how this integration is managed.

SAP Talent Visualization by Nakisa

In 2007 SAP signed a global reseller arrangement with Nakisa Inc. to provide enhancement tools for the Organizational Management function. Known as SAP Talent Visualization by Nakisa (SAP TVN), this application complements and enhances the Organizational and Talent Management functionality of SAP ERP HCM by providing easy-to-use and quick-to-learn visual tools for Organizational Management. These tools include (Figure 3.6):

> **SAP TVN OrgChart**
> Allows users to create, visualize, and print dynamic organization charts based on position, department, cost center, or any other logical structure, along with access to employee roles, groups, salaries, relationships, reporting structure, and other human capital information. An example of the Nakisa OrgChart screen layout is shown in Figure 3.6

> **SAP TVN OrgModeler**
> Gives users the ability to quickly model organizational changes by creating simulated organizational structures to assess the human impact of hierarchy and human capital changes.

> **SAP TVN Directory**
> Allows users to organize and view employee directory and contact information to find up-to-date phone and fax numbers, email addresses, reporting hierarchy, and other human capital information.

> **SAP TVN FloorPlan**
> Lets users produce high-quality detailed maps of employees and

equipment such as faxes and printer locations to map offices, conferences, and so on.

> **Nakisa SAPExtractor**
Helps users and extract data for external applications or reporting tools.

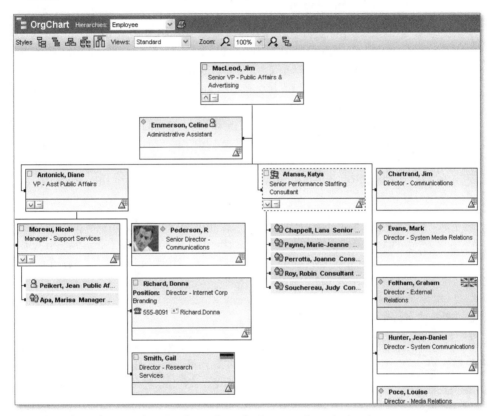

Figure 3.6 The Nakisa OrgChart Displaying Part of a Company Organizational Structure

Integration

One of the great advantages of having your organizational structure defined in SAP ERP HCM is that all of the information you need to create and report on your structure is integrated throughout SAP and reflected in a single system view. If you need to assign a cost center to a new organizational unit, you see the list of cost centers straight from the finance system. If you need to choose an employee to assign to a position, the list you see contains exactly the same values that you would see if you went straight into the Employee Administration function. All new hires and organizational reassignments performed in Employee Administration become effective immediately in Organizational Management.

This real-time availability of key data means that your organizational structure is always up to date. If, for example, your finance department closes a cost center at the end of the month, then at that date the cost center will no longer be available in Organizational Management. The same applies if you terminate an employee in Employee Administration. As of the date he is terminated, he will disappear from your organizational structure, and his old position will be flagged as vacant. Alternatively, you can assign the position as obsolete, or end the position, meaning that position disappears from the structure.

Your organizational structure is as real-time and current as the rest of your SAP ERP HCM data. Having taken the time to define your organizational structure makes the best use of its full integration with other components. The next thing most HR administrators want to do is start reporting on it.

Reporting

Changes to employee data are immediately transferred to the organizational structure

By defining your organization's various structures in Organizational Management, you are building your own reporting engine. The more detail you put into your structures, the more reporting possibilities you have. For example, most SAP ERP HCM reports can be run for a specific organizational unit or position or a range or selection of them, if that is required, so the greater level of detail you put into your structure, the better information you can get out of it.

You can run any SAP ERP HCM report using objects in your organizational structure

SAP ERP HCM Organizational Management provides numerous standard reports, giving you the ability to report on almost any aspect of your organization. Some examples of standard reports include:

> Organizational Structure with Persons

> Organizational Structure with Work Centers

> Descriptions of all Jobs
> Staff Functions for Positions
> Vacant Positions

Being able to quickly and simply print, display, and publish your organizational chart has always been a highly rated requirement of any SAP ERP HCM system. In addition to the agreement with Nakisa to provide a visualization layer for Organizational Management SAP has partnered with other third-party suppliers of organizational chart software to develop a standard interface allowing Organizational Management data to be published quickly and efficiently through the third parties' specialist charting tools. The interface allows third-party vendor's applications to extract all of the Organizational Management objects, relationships, and attributes from SAP ERP HCM. The data is then automatically ready for publishing via the third parties' specialist tools (no duplication, no convoluted extraction and conversion processes) straight from SAP ERP HCM into the specialist software.

 Tip

For a full list of accredited suppliers of organizational charting solutions for SAP ERP HCM, please contact SAP directly.

It is important to remember that the organizational structure is more than just a passive tool for reporting and viewing. It is the backbone that Workflow uses to move leave requests, new employee approvals, and other communications around your company.

Workflow

The SAP ERP Workflow solution is designed to speed up your business processes by directing tasks to the appropriate person at the right time to ensure that tasks are processed as efficiently as possible. Tasks requiring approvals and actions by other employees are routed via the organizational structure for approvals, actions, and notifications. These workflows can be as simple as one-step approvals such

Workflow allows you to automate approval processes based on your organizational structure

as getting a manager to approve a new payment for an employee or as complex as multilevel workflows generating subsequent workflows with conditional decisions involving many people across the company. Workflows can also be used to respond to errors and exceptions within the system. For example, you can start a workflow when a predefined event occurs, such as the generation of an error message.

Workflows are used throughout the SAP ERP solution and are available as standard for most components. In the SAP ERP HCM component, some examples of commonly used workflows include vacation and leave approvals, approvals for pay increases and bonus payments, and organizational reassignment approvals for transferring employees within the company.

The approval of a payment or a salary increase is an example of a workflow task. These workflow tasks can be single or multistep tasks. Obviously, if only a single approval is required, this is defined as a single-step task, and if multiple approvals are required, the workflow will be defined as a multistep task. A person who can approve this task is defined as an agent. Agents for specific workflows are identified by assigning tasks to either jobs or positions. As we discussed earlier, tasks can be grouped together into task groups so that only one relationship between a job or position needs to be maintained. A task group for workflows may include several approval tasks for different workflow scenarios.

What this means for Organizational Management is that because workflow approval hierarchies can differ from reporting and other HR hierarchies within Organizational Management, you can define a separate organizational plan specifically for processing approvals. This separate organizational plan allows you to keep your business process approval hierarchy separate from your personnel planning and reporting-focused plans.

Authorizations and Security

General SAP ERP HCM authorizations allow you to control your users' access to the system and limit their access to transactions and data based on security roles assigned to their user IDs.

By implementing Organizational Management, you can also implement structural authorizations that allow you to control users' access based on their locations in the organizational structure. Structural authorizations are a great tool for controlling which employee data users can see. For example, you can assign structural authorizations to a position, which means that any employees who hold that position will be able to see all of the employee data of employees below them in the organizational structure, but only to a maximum of three organizational units below their own organizational unit. A manager's position could be set up to allow the manager to see all of the telephone numbers of employees underneath him, but only the salary details of those employees who directly report to him.

A great example of the benefits of structural authorizations over general authorizations is in the scenario where a manager has the ability to maintain the data of employees in his organizational unit. If the manager is moved out of that position into a new position, he will automatically lose the maintenance authorizations of the first position and the ability to maintain those employees' data, and gain the ability to maintain the data of the employees in his new position.

In practice, authorizations are normally maintained using a combination of general authorizations limiting users' access to screens and transactions along with structural authorizations controlling the users' access to employees.

So let's take a look at a case study of a company that implemented SAP ERP HCM Organizational Management so they could have an up-to-date view of its organizational structure, among other benefits.

Case Study

Table 3.4 provides a brief overview of a case study before we explain it in more detail.

> Access and authorizations can be assigned to the position and the holder

Company	European Telecommunications Company
Existing Solutions	SAP ERP Finance system
Challenges	> Lack of visibility of the company structure > Maintaining stand-alone organizational structure on PowerPoint > Organizational structure not in sync with HR data
SAP Solutions	SAP ERP HCM including organizational management
Benefits	> Fully integrated and up-to-date organizational structure > Project teams mapped and monitored via matrix structure > Organizational structure published automatically on company intranet

Table 3.4 Global Employee Management Case Study

This globally active French-owned telecommunications company implemented SAP ERP HCM initially for its British operations. The solution covered 12,000 employees.

The Challenges

Coming from a legacy payroll system with very limited HR management capabilities, this company had never had an up-to-date view of its organizational structure. Finance had its own view of the organizational structure, representing their requirements. Similarly, HR kept its own version of the organizational structure on a set of PowerPoint files. Any employee transfers, hires, terminations, or organizational restructuring had to be manually updated in the PowerPoint file. Different HR offices even kept their own versions of the organizational structure.

The SAP Solution

As part of a larger SAP ERP HCM implementation bringing all of the core components to the company, Organizational Management was implemented. The function required little in terms of customization, with all of the company's requirements being met by the standard offering. The company also purchased a third-party organizational charting software to help quickly print and publish the organizational structure on their intranet.

The Benefits

Before the company could receive the many benefits of an integrated single-source organizational structure, a lot of work needed to be done defining the company's real organizational structure. Weeks were spent going through reports from the legacy payroll and HR systems matching employees to jobs, positions, and departments. Issues relating to reporting hierarchies and even defining members of teams and dependents all had to be sorted out before the structure could be signed off (by the CEO) and then loaded into SAP ERP HCM.

Once these challenges were overcome, the company instantly began to receive the benefits of having a truly integrated organizational structure. Now cost centers are assigned directly from Finance, ensuring that all employees are costed correctly. The organizational structure can be printed at will, with 100% certainty that the data being presented is up-to-the-minute correct. The organizational structure is also published directly onto the company intranet; an overnight program ensures that it was updated daily.

Summary

Organizational Management is one of SAP ERP HCM's most interesting functions. The numerous options available for creating, maintaining, and publishing your company's organizational structures makes it an incredibly powerful tool.

In this chapter we looked at:

> What information can be stored in Organizational Management, how it is stored, how access to it is controlled, and what you can do with it once you have it in SAP ERP HCM.

> The possibilities for modeling the organizational structure with plan versions, allowing your HR team to prepare for impending or proposed organizational changes by graphically modeling their impact on the company.

> The capabilities of maintaining matrix structures to represent your company's special projects and custom reporting relationships in addition to the traditional hierarchical organization structure.

> We saw how Nakisa and other third-party tools enable companies to quickly view, print, publish, and make accessible all of the different views of their company's organizational structure.

One of the great advantages of using Organizational Management is the ability to define, view, and edit your company's structure, not just nationally but internationally as well. This global view will prove very useful in the next chapter, where we look at Global Employee Management.

4

Global Employee Management

As companies expand and grow internationally, the need to effectively manage the transition of employees between countries has become a top priority. Moving employees between countries is stressful for the employees and their families (and also the HR departments that manage the process). So the Global Employee Management (MGE) function gives you a framework to ensure that the processes relating to moving employees between countries is as painless as possible—for both the employee and the company.

The Global Employee Management function is a set of predefined processes to help manage the most common processes relating to international transfers. It also contains a set of infotypes that allow you to record all of the required information and manage the tasks relating to the transfers. Perhaps most important, it provides a comprehensive process for managing the compensation package—a key issue for all potential expatriates. Once an employee is overseas, this function is used to check the impact on the employee of ongoing policy changes and to efficiently apply policy changes for groups of employees. The component also allows you to generate all of the required forms, notifications, and documents that enable you to communicate with your expatriates. The enhancement for payroll, which is known as Global Employee Payroll, can also be utilized to help with the payroll implications of having employees based in another country.

How Global Employee Management Fits into an Enterprise

Manage your expatriate employees before, during, and after their overseas experience

Global Employee Management is at its most basic level a set of actions, infotypes, forms, and reports that allow you to manage your expatriate employees before, during, and after their overseas experience. It allows you to manage all of the processes related to expatriates, from helping the employee and the home and destination countries decide if the move is a good idea, to managing the transfer, monitoring the employee while he is overseas. You can also manage changes to his situation while overseas, and manage his return to ensure he fits back into his home country smoothly. The component is fully integrated with SAP ERP HCM Payroll and Organizational Management, and utilizes the SAP ERP Business Workflow to facilitate the required data exchanges between departments and countries.

A Closer Look at Global Employee Management

Enables key processes for effective expatriate management

Global Employee Management focuses on the key phases that enable expatriates to be efficiently managed and monitored before during and after their expatriate experiences:

> Relocation preparation
> Global assignment planning
> Assignment activation
> Global assignment
> Repatriation

These processes are managed via a set of special actions that allow the relevant data to be input as quickly and easily as possible.

Actions

As we discovered in Chapter 2, Employee Administration, actions are used to link logical sets of infotypes together so that they can be processed as efficiently as possible.

Infotypes

As discussed in Chapter 2, infotypes are used to store pieces of employee data in logical groups. Infotypes provide a structure, facilitate data entry and maintenance, and enable you to store data for specific periods. The following infotypes were created to store expatriate employee information in a logical and efficient manner; they are either maintained individually or used in one of the Global Employee Management–specific actions.

> Specific infotypes are specially created for recording global employee data

Global Assignment Details

Infotype 0710 (Figure 4.1) is the main infotype for this function, providing an overview of the employee's international assignments. In this infotype you can store information relating to the employee's assignment including the following information:

Future Assignment Details

This section is for recording details of impending assignments before they begin. It stores information on the expected duration of the assignment, if the assignment results in the employee being promoted such as if the employee's family is joining him, and details of the HR administrator who is managing his assignment from both his home and destination country. You can also record details of the career sponsor who is the official point of contact for the employee while he is away.

Assignment Attributes

If your employee is working in more than one role while on assignment, this section allows you to assign the appropriate percentages to the different roles.

Current Assignment Details

Because your employee will need to be hired as a new employee in the destination country, this section is used to link the employee's various personnel numbers.

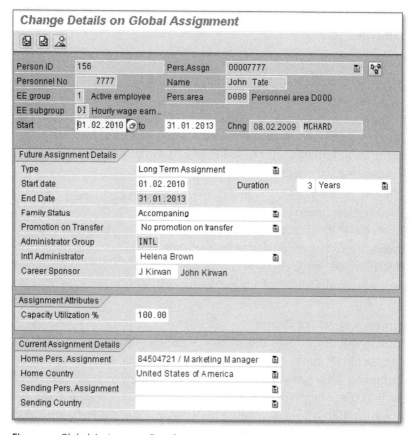

Figure 4.1 Global Assignment Details

Global Assignment Status

Get instant information on your global employees' status

Infotype 0715 (Table 4.2) Global Assignment Status allows you to track the entire expatriate process.

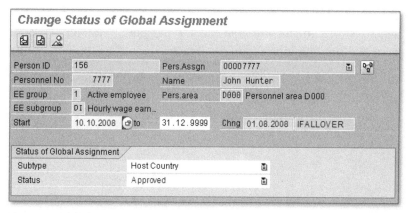

Figure 4.2 Global Assignment Status

The infotype uses the statuses shown in Table 4.2 to show the current state of the process.

Status	Description
Planned	The initial stage of the process.
Submitted	The terms and conditions of the assignment have been submitted for approval by the host country.
Approved	The terms and conditions have been approved by the home and the host line managers.
Declined by manager	The compensation package has been rejected by either of the line managers.
Accepted	The employee has accepted the compensation package.
Declined by employee	The employee has declined the package.
To be activated	All of the necessary information has been gathered in the relevant infotypes.

Table 4.1 Possible Status of a Global Assignment

Documents

Almost all international transfers require numerous documents to be applied for, produced, verified, or copied during the preparation phase. Infotype 0702 allows you to store copies of these documents

A central repository of your employees' key documents

97

against an employee record for easy access. Common types of documents stored in this infotype include passports, visa applications, work permits, and inoculation certificates.

The process for applying for and receiving some of these documents can be quite lengthy, so the infotype allows you to record the processing status of the document, for example, recording if the document is currently:

> Posted

> In progress

> On hold

> Accepted

> Rejected

Once the document has been produced, and an electronic copy of the document stored in the digital personnel file, you can also store information pertaining to the document such as:

> Document type

> Issue details including location

> Document number

> Expiration date

> Status

Information on Dependents

Keep all of the information you need on your employee and his dependents in one central place

A key part of any international assignment, Infotype 0704 (Figure 4.3) is used to record the details of an assignees family and dependents. A separate infotype record is created for each dependent. This record can be based on the information already stored in the existing Infotype 0021 Family/Related Persons. Once the records are linked, you can then record if the dependent is going to join the employee on his assignment or remain in their home country. If the dependent will be attending school while overseas, you can record the level of schooling required.

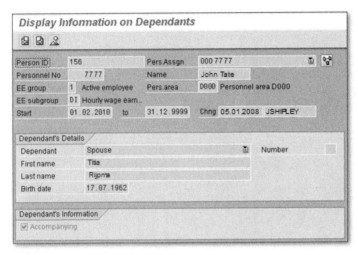

Figure 4.3 Dependent Information

Documents on Dependents

Much like Infotype 0702 Documents, Infotype 0703 allows you to record all of the details of the documents required for an employee's dependents who are joining the employee overseas. You can create a separate record for each dependent, tracking the processing status of their respective documents and all of the details of the documents when they are received.

Checklist Information

Infotype 0705 is designed to help the HR administrator ensure that he does not miss any of the key steps in the expatriate process. This infotype allows the HR administrator to define his own checklist of key steps or tasks that need to be completed to ensure that the transfer is successful. This could include tasks such as booking accommodations, booking air tickets, confirming school enrollments, booking language training, and so on.

Users can create their own checklists to ensure nothing is forgotten

The HR administrator can define his own tasks and then compile a task list based on these tasks. Lists and tasks can differ from employee to employee and help the HR administrator ensure that nothing is forgotten.

Compensation Package Offer

Manage all of the parts that make up an expatriate employee's package

One of the key parts of any expatriate program, Infotype 0706 (Figure 4.4) is used to bring together all of the parts that make up the compensation package the employee will receive while on assignment.

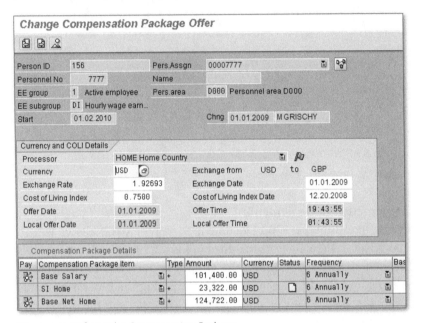

Figure 4.4 Defining the Compensation Package

This infotype allows you to define the individual elements of the compensation package that you are offering the employee and how they are calculated.

Compensation Package Items

The individual elements that are combined into the compensation package might include the following types of payments:

> Base salary

> Relocation allowance

> Housing allowance

> Remote location allowance

> Expatriate allowance

> School fees allowance

> Repatriation allowance

Of course, depending on your company's requirements, different elements can be defined as required. All items can be defined as being paid and controlled by either the home or host assignment countries. This assignment of elements to specific countries ensures that neither the home nor host parties can see the total package unless authorized to.

Calculation Rules

Once you have defined the payments, you can define the rules that are used to control their values. These are generally related to currency rules and cost of living rules:

> **Currency rules**

Often when employees are sent overseas, some of the payments they receive are paid in the local currency and some are paid in their home currency. To work out the value of these payments, you can either use an exchange rate as of a set date, or you can define your own artificial rate if you prefer. Another aspect of SAP ERP's broad integration is that you can use the same foreign currency exchange rates that the finance team already maintains in their part of the system, rather than having to define your own HR-specific table of exchange rates.

Split payments between home and host currencies, and process them automatically

> **Cost of living**

Often when an employee is sent somewhere that is more expensive to live in than the home country, a cost of living factor is applied to some or all of the payments. Individual items in the compensation package can be determined as being cost-of-living-factor relevant or not. The cost of living factor can then be assigned as of a certain date so that all of the elements are increased by this factor. As with all of the other parts of the compensation offer, this is a date-based field, allowing ongoing changes in the cost of living factor to be quickly added without affecting historical records.

Establish rules and calculations for cost of living adjustments

Payroll Integration

All of this information is integrated straight into payroll

Once all parties agree on a compensation package, the elements that make up the package can then be mapped to payroll wage types so that, depending on the elements and country assignment, they can be paid automatically through payroll in either the home or host country.

Assignment Activation Details

When you agree to pay an employee in a local currency, the actual value of these payments can fluctuate based on the prevailing exchange rate. Infotype 0707 is used to control these fluctuations by assigning currency fluctuation protection to some or all of the individual elements of the compensation package.

Ex **Example**

If your employee is being sent to France, you could determine that his expatriate premium allowance is paid 100% in the host country currency (in this case Euros) at the prevailing exchange rate. However, his salary, which was negotiated as a value in Euros, should be paid as 50% Euros, and the other 50% should be converted to U.S. dollars and paid at the prevailing rate.

Instant access to exchange rate data from the Finance component

These payments will then be transferred to payroll processing, where the calculation will take place automatically each period, checking prevailing exchange rates and adjusting the employee's pay automatically each period that he is overseas.

This powerful tool also allows you to ensure that deductions such as tax or social security that need to be paid in the home country can be set up in the home currency, ensuring that regardless of what happens to the exchange rate, the correct deduction is always made.

Global Commuting Types

Keep track of key data to manage your employee's tax status

Many countries' tax laws are dependent on the number of days that a person is present in the country. Infotype 0708 is used to track an employee's absences so that they can be used to determine the employee's tax residence. For example, if you work more than a certain number of days in the United States, you are legally obliged to report your worldwide income and have it taxed in the United States. This infotype (Figure 4.5) allows you to track all of an employee's absences, and record the duration of the absence, and determine which country it relates to and whether it is tax-relevant or not.

This information can then be reported on and used in year-end reporting to determine an employee's tax liabilities or be used before the end of the tax year to monitor an employee's absences to manage his potential tax liabilities.

Figure 4.5 Global Commuting Record

Actions

A set of actions are delivered within this component that allow the completion of the key processes used to manage global employees.

Specific actions to manage the key steps of the expatriate process

 Actions

An action is a set of linked infotypes that are processed together to record major changes to employee data.

Help your employee manage all of the steps in organizing his relocation

The actions in Global Employee Management are used to perform the following processes:

1. Relocation preparation phase
2. Planning Global Assignment phase
3. Assignment activation
4. Global assignment phase
5. Repatriation phase

Let's look at each of these actions in more detail to understand what they are used for and what they do.

Relocation Preparation Phase

This action is used to signal that a business need for a global assignment has been identified, and the tasks involved in organizing the relocation are underway. Once this need has been identified, the skills required to fulfill the need have to be matched against potential employees to find the correct employee. Global Employee Management is designed to follow after this matching process has been completed. Typical tasks involved in this phase include booking flights, arranging accommodations, enrolling dependents in local schools, and beginning the process of arranging local visas and documents.

 Note

> The matching of job requirements to employees can be done through Career and Succession Management (covered in Chapter 11) functions, which can identify employees against requirements criteria such as qualifications, skills, and experience, depending on the requirements for the role.

When the employee's compensation package and all of the other details of the assignment have been agreed upon, the system can generate a formal offer letter. This functionality reads the information relating to the compensation package from the employee's master data and uses a preformatted layout to produce a letter that can be generated as either an Adobe or Word document that can then be sent to the employee and the host manager for formal sign off.

Planning for Global Assignment Phase

Once you have identified your potential international assignee, the action is executed during the period in which the conditions of the assignment are being discussed, the discussions regarding compensation packages are finalized, and the decision on transferring family members is being made. The planning phase action is essentially used to record that the planning of the employee's international assignment is currently underway.

Assignment Activation

The employee and all other parties have now agreed to the formal offer detailing the terms of the assignment, and the start of the employee's transfer is imminent. The assignment activation action is now used to record that the assignment is technically active.

This step is generally used as the trigger for the final steps in the host country such as hiring the employee as a new employee in the local company, and setting the employee up for processing in the local payroll.

Global Assignment Phase

Now that the employee is overseas, this action is used by the HR administrator to record any changes to employee details during the assignment. This infotype is typically used to record changes in pay, promotions, changes to family status, and changes in duration and conditions of the assignment.

Two important actions are delivered to help you manage your employee while he is away and when he returns

Repatriation phase

The term of the assignment is now almost complete, and the process needs to be begun to reintegrate the employee back into his home country. This action is used to trigger the list of steps that need to be taken to ensure that the employee's return is managed smoothly. Typical tasks that would be included in this phase include setting a date for the employee's return to work, identifying the role he will perform when he has returned to work, and managing the relocation of his belongings.

Processing Policy Changes

Test the impact of policy changes on your global employees

When your employees are away on international assignment, it is important that any changes to your expatriate HR policies that may impact their compensation are carefully managed to minimize the impact on this important group of employees.

Global Employee Management gives you a tool that allows you to test the impact of policy changes relating to expatriate compensation packages before they are applied to the production system. This tool, known as *Policy Tracking*, allows you change your policies in your test system and then use the real employee data from your production system to compare the current compensation package values with the new values after the new policy is applied.

Once you have analyzed the impact on your employees, you can decide if the policy is going to be acceptable to them or if you need to review your policies again. When you are happy with your revised policy and its impacts on your expatriates, you can move the new policy into your production client and use a standard report known as *Mass Activation* to apply the policy changes to all expatriate employees, automatically creating new compensation package offer infotype records for the effected employees and making the changes instantly available to payroll.

Use the automatic letter generator to generate notification for your employees of policy changes and the impact on them

Global Employee Management also provides a standard tool for generating notification letters for employees when policy changes affect them. Much like the automatic letter generation used to generate the compensation package confirmation letter mentioned earlier, SAP ERP HCM provides you with the ability to generate a *Global Employee Compensation Calculation Overview* (GECCO). This document, which can be created as an Adobe PDF or Microsoft Word document, can be generated automatically according to a predetermined format for all affected employees when their compensation package changes. These notifications can then be emailed or posted to the employees, quickly and efficiently informing them of the impacts of the policy changes.

Payroll for Global Employees

Using the strong integration between the Human Resources and Payroll components is one of the key benefits of the HCM offering; this is probably no better illustrated than in the link between management of global employees and payroll processing through *Payroll for Global Employees*. It is often the case that when employees are sent on international assignments, they will still have obligations such as social security (in the U.S.) and superannuation (in Australia) contributions that they need to keep making in their home country. Payroll for Global Employees allows payments and deductions to be calculated for the employee in the home payroll system, and then these payments and deductions can be paid or deducted through the employee's host country payroll results.

Strong payroll integration allows payments and deductions to be processed in both countries

For example, an employee who normally lives in Britain has been transferred to New Zealand for a three-year contract. The employee is legally obliged to continue his National Insurance contributions in England and still wants to contribute to his superannuation fund while he is away. So when payroll is run for him in his home country, the amounts of National Insurance and superannuation that he needs to contribute for each period are calculated by the British payroll. These results are stored in special wage types and are then transferred to the employee's New Zealand employee record, where they are picked up in the next payroll run and deducted from the employee's pay in New Zealand. The employee's deductions are processed as normal in Britain, and the employee is able to keep up his vital contributions with the minimum of fuss and no manual adjustments or awkward international cross-charges.

It is also worth noting that you can run Payroll for Global Employees without using the full-blown Management of Global Employees and vice versa.

Integration

Management of Global Employees is seamlessly integrated with the other SAP ERP HCM components such as Employee Administration and Organizational Management, allowing your internationally as-

Manage all of your employee data in both the home and host countries' systems

signed employees to be maintained and managed in both their home and host countries. Using payroll for Global Employees allows you to link the payments from the employee's host country with their home country payroll results. Like any of the other components that feed into payroll, once payroll results are generated, it is then fed straight into finance for up-to-the minute reporting and analysis.

Let's wrap up this chapter by reviewing a case study of a company using a global SAP ERP HCM system.

Case Study

Table 4.2 provides a quick overview of the case study before we explain it in more detail.

Company	Global chemicals manufacturer
Existing Solutions	Global SAP ERP HCM system
Challenges	> Reduction in global HR barriers > Decrease in redundant activities > Reduce processing time for key processes
SAP Solutions	Global Employee Management
Benefits	Centralized employee information storage, increased process efficiency, divulged data ownership

Table 4.2 Global Employee Management Case Study

This large chemicals and manufacturing company already used SAP ERP HCM to manage its human resources. The company has over 8,000 employees working in nine languages across 45 locations around the world.

The Challenges

The process for managing global employees was a paper-based process using internal mail to process all of its global tasks. Each country maintained a separate HRMS system limiting, visibility of an international view of the company. Any task related to internationally mobile employees took an average of 10 days to complete using this process.

The SAP Solution

As part of implementing an integrated single-instance global HR solution, the company was able to use Global Employee Management to create an integrated, electronic, workflow-driven solution for managing global employees. The solution empowered line managers to make new employee requests via the portal, and the HR teams in both home and host countries to enter changes directly into the central database. Confirmations and notifications were delivered electronically using workflow and email.

The Benefits

The centralization of HR information into a single instance instantly solved numerous duplication and consistency issues that the company had faced. HR managers are now able to quickly access a global view of their human resources, and HR departments around the world are able to instantly access a global pool of potential talent.

Managers are able to monitor the progress of global employee requests online, track progress, and be involved in the process.

The HR departments from both the home and host countries can view employee data from a single source. The new system can automatically handle all issues regarding changes in languages and currencies, and monitor the progress and status of each globally mobile employee. As a result of the use of Global Employee Management, the processing time has been reduced to just three days from ten.

Summary

As we learned in this chapter, by using the Global Employee Management function of SAP ERP HCM, HR departments can handle the entire process of negotiating, transferring, and repatriating employees using a combination of infotypes, actions, and processes.

In addition, the vital time when the employee is on assignment is also managed, and the key information for both the home and host countries' HR departments is all available for them to see. And, the link into payroll processing allows payments and deductions from the host country payroll to be transferred into the home payroll, ensuring that key payments and deductions are never missed.

The fact that employees who are willing to move internationally for their work are often hard to find means that managing your pool of global employees is always going to be a top priority, and this function ensures it always is.

In the next chapter, we will cover the Concurrent Employment function available of SAP ERP HCM.

Concurrent Employment

An ever changing workforce leads to an ever changing set of demands for effectively managing working relationships. This is perhaps best demonstrated by the growing demand for companies to be able to effectively manage concurrent or multiple employment situations for their employees. Concurrent employment is a scenario where an employee works in two or more separate employment engagements within the company. Where traditionally, employees had just one full-time job or a part-time job, now flexible working requirements (from both the employee and employer) have led to many situations where employees work for a company in two or more completely unrelated positions on separate contracts at the same time.

Concurrent employment was traditionally only a requirement in the public health care and education sectors, but increasingly the need to be able to manage flexible working arrangements that result in multiple employment engagements for employees is becoming a priority in many sectors.

How Concurrent Employment Fits into an Enterprise

Having an employee working in two positions in your company can initially sound very appealing and perhaps not that complicated, but when we get into the details of managing concurrent employment, the reality can be far from simple. Let's begin by looking at an example.

Ex   Example

Pat Connell is a part-time receptionist at a pharmaceutical company. Pat has worked for 18 years as a receptionist, working Monday to Wednesday, leaving two days a week to raise her children. Now that her children have grown up and left home, Pat decides she wants to work the remaining days of the week. We already have someone working reception on Thursday and Friday, so Pat takes a job working in the canteen two days a week.

This is all pretty simple so far, but what happens to Pat's personnel record? Pat's reception position requires more skills, and she has 18 years experience, so she is paid $19,000 per year for her three days a week as receptionist. Her work in the canteen, however, is not as well paid and is paid hourly, at a rate of $11.00 an hour. She is a member of two different unions because of her two unrelated jobs, so she has two completely different sets of entitlements: different leave entitlements, sick pay entitlements, allowances, and deductions. In many countries, having a second job also leads to complications in the calculation of taxes and other statutory deductions.

This example is rather complicated, but fortunately, it is manageable with SAP ERP HCM. As a company, you may also have to consider what impact having multiple contracts will have on entitlements to benefits. However, by using Concurrent Employment, you can effectively manage a situation like Pat's by having two separate contracts rather than trying to combine both into one full-time contract which does not really reflect the reality of the employment situation.

Mulitple active employee records in a single system – the HR alarm bells start ringing!

Traditionally, managing employees who work in two positions in the company was a nightmare for HR departments. For example:

> How do you manage the process when an employee leaves one of his jobs but not the other?

> How do you keep personal data in sync, e.g., marriages, address changes, tax code changes, and so on?

> How do you process back-dated tax code changes—potentially affecting both payroll processes?

> How can you process an employee on a weekly and a monthly payroll and ensure the tax is correct?

Being able to employ existing employees on concurrent employment contracts can be extremely beneficial to the company. For example, you already know the employee and his performance and capabilities, so there isn't as much potential risk as hiring a new employee.

Effectively managing all of the tasks related to handling an employee's multiple contracts with the minimum of fuss is exactly what this function is designed to assist. The Concurrent Employment function delivers a framework to support business processes that covers all of the key areas, including personnel administration, benefits, time management, payroll, and reporting.

A Closer Look at Concurrent Employment

Let's now look at the main parts of Concurrent Employment that allow us to maintain multiple employee records for single employees.

The Central Person

The key to concurrent employment is allowing an employee to have multiple records within the system. Traditionally, maintaining multiple records for single employees within an HR system has been avoided because of the potential issues related to keeping the multiple records in sync. Concurrent Employment overcomes these issues by using what is known as a *central person*. A central person is the initial or main employee record; all subsequent employee records are linked to this record and are thus kept connected and in sync. Figure 5.1 provides an example of the look and feel of the concurrent employment solution, with a central person and her two assignments shown.

Control multiple active employee records through a central person

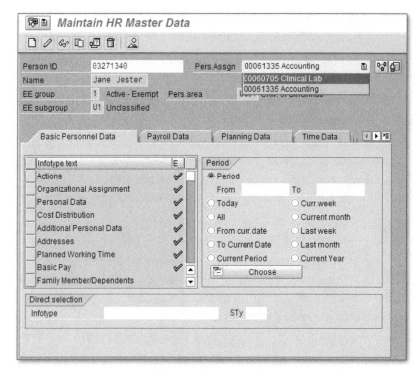

Figure 5.1 A Central Person with Her Two Personnel Assignments

Each employment record has its own employee number, and all of the required information relating to employment is stored on an individual record. Let's look at an example to illustrate this concept in Table 5.1:

Employee Number	Position	Work Schedule	Salary
199227	Receptionist	Mon-Wed 8 hrs a day	$59,000 per annum
192718	Canteen Assistant	Thu-Fri 7 hrs a day	$11.00 per hour

Table 5.1 Concurrent Employment Example

When hiring a new person, the system automatically checks to see if he is already active in the company

Each record is totally independent, and shows different start dates, positions, and jobs; different managers and supervisors; different payments and deductions; and even different bank accounts if required. However, both records are linked through the central employee number, so administrators can simply move between the records to facilitate effective maintenance. The recording of multiple linked records means that if Pat from our earlier example leaves one of her jobs, that employment record can be terminated, and the other record remains active.

Depending on your company's requirements, an employee may have even more active records than just the two we illustrated. Concurrent Employment can handle as many assignments as your company and your employee requires. If the unique record used as the central person employment record is terminated, then a subsequent record takes over as the central person.

When your HR administrators hire an employee who is already active within the system, the system will use key information such as name, date of birth, social security number, and so on to match the new hire to an existing personnel record (Figure 5.2). Once the records are matched, the administrator can speed up the hiring process and reduce the chance of keying errors by copying the data already assigned to the employee, such as address, family, and bank details, and assign it to the new employee record.

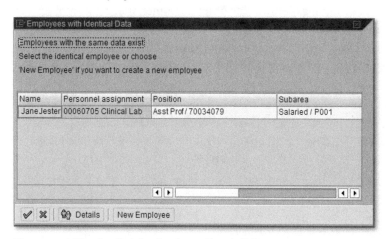

Figure 5.2 A Warning that the Employee Already Exists

The central person (sometimes known as the main personnel assignment record) is the key record in the employee's data; it is stored on Infotype 0712 Main Personnel Assignment. The central person is the

Key employee data is only stored on the central person and displayed in the linked records

main employee record. This is where the key personal information for the employee is centrally stored. For example, you can centrally record employee name, address, social security number, family details, emergency contacts, and so on. This central storage means that key information for the employee only needs to be maintained once. It is then displayed in all of the employee's other assignments, and will always be up to date because it is drawn from the central record.

Grouping Personnel Assignments

Grouping personnel assignments allows you to link areas of your company so concurrent employee records are processed together

In larger companies and government organizations, it is not uncommon for an employee to work in roles spread across several different legal entities within the company. In most countries, employment within a legal entity must be reported at a legal-entity level. Concurrent Employment uses a solution called *grouping of personnel assignments* to manage these scenarios.

Groupings of personnel assignments can be used to divide and group your company's offices and locations into logical groups for employee processing. These groups are commonly used to control decision-making and processing control points at country-specific or intercountry levels to group legal entities or other customer-specific groupings for reporting and payroll processing. To illustrate, let's look at an example of an employee who works for a local city. The employee (Cath Whitaker) has four part-time jobs and four personnel records (Table 5.2).

Employee Number	Entity	Employer	Position
356215	Dept. of Schools	Nelson High School	Part-Time History Teacher
457523	Dept. of Schools	Wynumm State School	Part-Time English Teacher
645831	Dept. of Recreation	Riverside Pool	Part-Time Swim Coach
582732	Dept. of Recreation	Manly Pool	Part-Time Life Guard

Table 5.2 Concurrent Employment Across Separate Legal Entities

By using the grouping of personnel assignments, the multiple employ-ment contracts in the separate legal entities (in this case the depart-ment of schools and the department of recreation) can be processed and reported together. Processing decisions and calculation rules can be applied to different groups as required and all of your processing rules assigned correctly.

This means that when the system processes the employee, it consid-ers, processes, and collates the results for the employee based on the department, location, country, and legal entity he is working in at the time. So at the end of the year, the employee in the above example will receive just two end of year income statements—one for each of the departments, not one for each employment contract. This ability to roll up employment contracts is a great time saver where tradi-tionally, a statement would have been created for each employment contract and then the results manually collated into legal–entity-level summaries.

Automatically create a single merged end of year summary statement for multiple employment contracts

Processing Benefits for Concurrent Employment

Many employee benefits entitlements are based on length-of-service or hours-worked calculations to determine employee eligibility. The integration between Concurrent Employment and the Benefits Man-agement function means that employee eligibility for benefits can be calculated taking into account multiple employment records. Figure 5.3 shows an employee with two contracts being processed for ben-efits. Her benefits entitlements are based on combining both her con-tracts.

A periodic report is used to check employee eligibility for benefits such as health care entitlement or pension contributions based on a criteria such as actual hours worked or employee length of service. When the report is run, each employee's records are checked to see if they qualify for the entitlement. This check will run against all of their active employee records and calculate as necessary.

Process dynamic benefits eligbilty checks across multiple employee contracts

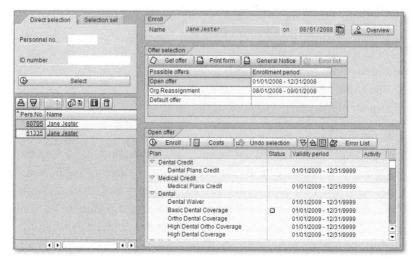

Figure 5.3 Processing Benefits for Concurrent Employment

For example, if entitlement to a medical care benefits plan is based on 200 hours of service over three months, the report will count the actual hours worked against all of the employee's records for the period and flag the employee as entitled to the medical care. Every time the report is subsequently run, it will recount the actual hours worked for the employee and retain or remove the entitlement as required. Because all data entered against any of the employee records will have a time and date stamp, accurate calculations can be determined. Similarly, if your company wanted to count each employment record as an individual record for calculating benefits entitlement and not aggregate the data from all of the employee records, this can also be configured.

Processing in Time Management

Time management allows multiple employee contracts to be compared and checked against working time rules

Managing and planning the working time for employees who have multiple employment contracts can be a processing and administration nightmare, especially in terms of planning and coordinating working times and then in evaluating them to ensure that they are paid correctly.

The integration between Concurrent Employment, Time Management, and Payroll takes away most of these time-consuming manual tasks and automates them through the application of a complex yet flexible set of processing rules and decision points. Combining this processing capability with the ability to set rules for specific combinations of employment scenarios through the use of groupings of personnel assignments within a single legal entity or group of companies gives you the ability to effectively manage the complex employment arrangements in your company and keep within all relevant employment laws and regulations.

Some examples where time management has been enhanced to allow for concurrent employment include the following specific areas:

> **Planning working times and availability**
Concurrent Employment gives you the ability to plan and manage an employees' working and shift times, taking into account all of their work obligations on their different employment records. This means employees are not double-booked for shifts or, even worse, missed completely. It also takes into account absences such as sickness and holidays to ensure that you always have a full picture of your employees' availability and obligations.

Centrally control employee working time across multiple contracts

> **Checking employment laws and regulations**
In some countries the laws regarding maximum and minimum working times, the duration of breaks and down times, and the control of overtime are set at an employee level rather than a contract level. Concurrent employment allows you to monitor and control your employees' working time across all of their employment contracts.

> **Managing absence and attendance quotas**
Controlling how much leave and sick time and other absence and attendance entitlements an employee with multiple contracts is allowed is always complex. Concurrent Employment allows you to set rules controlling the accrual of leave entitlement and ensure that employees always have the correct entitlement based on their combined employment contracts. This allows you to assign quotas for sick leave or holidays to be assigned, deducted, and controlled

Manage complex absence entitlement rules automatically

over all of an employee's contracts rather than based on each contract individually.

> ### Calculating and valuating payments

Automatically
calculate overtime
and bonus payments
across multiple
employment
contracts

The rules for the calculation and valuation of payments such as overtime and shift allowances are often controlled at a union or state level. When you try to apply these rules to employees with multiple contracts, determining which contracts count toward these rules and how they should be paid (valuated) can be a real challenge. For example, if overtime should be paid after eight hours of work, which contracts should count toward these eight hours, and on which contract should the overtime be paid based? The Concurrent Employment function uses the full processing power of the time evaluation and payroll components to ensure that all of your processing requirements can be defined and automated to ensure efficient processing.

The rules that define employment laws and regulations, quota accrual rules and balances, and the checks and error messages that you need to monitor your Time Management are defined in *Time Evaluation Business Subjects*. These are used to define the rules for your company and decide how they are computed, checked, and calculated. They are then assigned to your Personnel Assignment groupings, which can then apply or ignore the rules for different employment contracts. All of this information is then fed through to Payroll processing, where it is processed and paid to the employee.

Processing in Payroll

The processing of concurrently employed persons through SAP ERP HCM Payroll can, in large part thanks to the amazing array of processing possibilities in the Payroll component, be complex. The possibilities are probably best illustrated by working through an example, so let's take our employee Catherine Whitaker, who we used earlier in the chapter, to explain the payroll process. Here are Cath's vital details with regard to payroll (Table 5.3).

Employee Number	Employer	Position	Payroll Period
356215	Nelson High School	Part-Time History Teacher	Monthly – Calendar based
457523	Wynumm State School	Part-Time English Teacher	Monthly – Calendar based
645831	Riverside Pool	Part-Time Swim Coach	Weekly – Monday–Friday
582732	Manly Pool	Casual Life Guard	Weekly – Sunday–Monday

Table 5.3 Vital Payroll Details

We can see that our employee is employed in three different payroll periods — one monthly and two different weekly payrolls. The concurrent employment process allows employee records that are in the same period and the same grouping of personnel assignments to be processed in synchronization. This means that although Cath works for two different schools as a teacher, she is only employed by one legal entity. Because both of the payroll periods for her two teaching jobs are the same, both of these employments can be processed by payroll in synchronization. This means she will only get one check at the end of the payroll run.

> Process multiple contracts in payroll together or separately depending on your requirements

For her two other employments, the dates of the payroll periods are different, so she must be run through both payrolls separately. However, because they are both within one grouping of personnel assignments, she will only have one check generated for both of these employments as well.

> Process employees correctly even if they are on different pay cycles

From a payroll perspective, the integration between the different employments is necessary for the correct calculation and collection of taxes and deductions. For example, if the employee is obliged to pay National Insurance or Social Security contributions based on her earnings, it is necessary to add up all of her earnings across the three different payrolls to ensure that her contributions are correct. This is further complicated by the fact that she is on both monthly and weekly payrolls, so the calculations need to take all of these factors into account to calculate the right figures.

Another issue that frequently arises in these situations is retroactive adjustments. For example, let's imagine that Cath got a back-dated pay bonus for one of her jobs. This increase in taxable pay and the net increase in pay would be automatically calculated and brought into the current period by the payroll system. However, if the bonus was to move her into a higher tax bracket, it would necessitate the recalculation of all of her other employments in the previous periods to ensure that all of her payroll results were correct. If you then imagine other possible scenarios such as back-dated periods of unpaid leave or back-dated hourly rate increases, you can see that the Concurrent Employment Payroll solution needs to be a well-developed and robust solution — which it definitely is.

Automatically recalculate tax code changes across multiple contracts

The Concurrent Employment function automatically handles all of these processes, allowing you to be sure that your employees' pay is correct and that they are paying the right taxes and deductions no matter how complex their employment assignments are. The Concurrent Employment solution also seamlessly and automatically handles the processing of payments to employees through bank transfers or check payments and the resulting postings of payroll data to finance.

Figure 5.4 shows the summarized payment summary for an employee with multiple contracts, showing payments from both of the contracts.

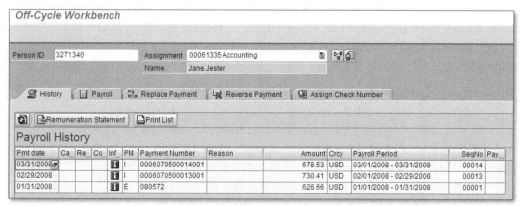

Figure 5.4 Off-Cycle Workbench for a Concurrent Employee

Summary

The Concurrent Employment solution gives your company the ability to effectively and efficiently manage employees on multiple contracts within your company. There are many things you can do with this tool, but the key things to remember include:

> You can manage all employee-related HR processes in an efficient manner.

> The *central person* functionality allows you to have a central control person to anchor the different employee records, so you can centrally store key data and maintain separate data for contract-specific records such as salary, location, manager, and so on.

> The Grouping of Personnel Assignments function allows you to determine which parts of your company have similar processing requirements and are statutorily linked and need to be processed together and therefore which employee contracts can be processed together and which can be processed independently.

> The full integration with Time Management means employees on multiple contracts can be automatically monitored to ensure that they do not exceed working time limits. Similarly, employees who are working shifts on different contracts can have their working times combined for automatically evaluating and paying overtime and other shift-related payments.

> Automatic payroll integration means that tax and other statutory calculations are processed automatically even if the employee is working on monthly, weekly, and biweekly contracts.

The Concurrent Employment function is definitely one of SAP ERP HCM's most powerful components, but it is important to note that it is still being developed and enhanced by SAP. Some of the functionality is not available for all countries, and prospective users should check with SAP to ensure that Concurrent Employment and all of its related processing is available for their country.

For countries for which the solution is fully active, it provides an end-to-end solution ensuring that your employees on multiple contracts can be correctly processed through Administration, Time Management, and Payroll with the minimum of manual intervention.

In the next chapter, we're going to talk about Benefits Management.

Benefits Management

Being able to offer your employees competitive benefits as part of their total package is becoming an increasingly important aspect of HR management. The SAP ERP HCM Benefits Management function offers a flexible framework for creating, maintaining, and reporting on benefits packages for employees. Standard integration with payroll, employee self-service, strong reporting capabilities, and automatic letter and form generation means that your benefits solution allows you to streamline the administrative processes and gives you up-to-date information on your benefits package.

How Benefits Management Fits into an Enterprise

As employee compensation packages become more complex, effectively managing employee benefits is also becoming more important. With the increasing size of many companies and the simultaneously increasing complexity of their benefits offerings, HR or specialized benefits departments need a benefits management solution that allows them to perform the key tasks of benefits management.

A Closer Look at Benefits

For companies to effectively manage their benefits commitments, the Benefits Management function provides solutions to manage the five core parts of Benefits administration:

> **Benefits plans**
  How they are set up, stored, and updated

> **Employee data**
  How employee benefits data is stored

> **Benefits Administration**
  How benefits are administered

> **Reporting**
  How to monitor your benefits plans

> **Employee Self-Service**
  How benefits allow employees to administer their own benefits

> **Country-specific functionality**
  A quick look at the country-specific benefits solutions that SAP ERP offers

Benefits Plans

Be sure you know your benefits inside out before you try to map them into SAP ERP HCM

As with most parts of an implementation, the first step in setting up Benefits Management is usually done outside the system. Identifying all of your employee benefits, defining who is entitled to which of them, and then clarifying the individual rules of the benefits is a large job, but is essential in mapping your benefits program to Benefits Management.

Benefits Areas and Benefits Programs
To ensure that your company's benefits program can be mapped into SAP ERP HCM, Benefits Management allows you to define many different benefits programs, first at the highest level, known as a benefits area, and then down into the different subsets depending on your

company's requirements. Because each benefits area can only use a single currency, a benefits area is often set at a country level. However, if different areas within your company have completely separate benefits pools, you would use separate benefits areas within a single country to separate them.

As illustrated in Figure 6.1, in each benefits area you define all of your benefit programs; a benefits program is a set of benefits that are offered to a specific group of employees. depending on your company's requirements, you may have many or just a few separate benefits programs. Benefits programs are mapped to different types of employees. The entry requirements for a benefits program can be determined for many variables including length of service, type of employee, contract type, and employee age. Let's look at an example of a Benefits Area and its separate benefits programs.

 Example

USA Benefits Area

Executive Benefits
Executives with 20 years of service and longer

Executives with 10–19 years of service

Executives with less than 10 years of service

Regular Employee Benefits
Full-time employees

Part-time Employees

Hourly Paid Employee Benefits
Employees age 50 and above

Employees age 30–49

Employees age 20–29

Employees age less than 20 years

Once you have defined your benefits programs, it's time to create your individual benefits.

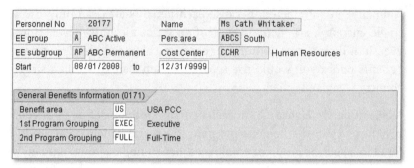

Figure 6.1 An Employee Record Showing Benefits Area and Benefits Groupings

Benefits Plans

SAP ERP HCM offers five standard plan types providing for the most common types of employee benefits and one miscellaneous benefits plan that can be used to handle most other benefits requirements.

The five standard benefits plans are:

> **Health plans**
>
> For storing details of employees' private health care selections, including coverage options, limits, dependent coverage, and coverage periods. Figure 6.2 shows an overview of an example health plan.

> **Insurance plans**
>
> Used for storing the details of employees' insurance choices. This can include their life, disability, and travel insurance; details of their coverage rules; and information relating to beneficiaries.

> **Savings plans**
>
> This infotype is used to store information relating to an employee's choice of savings plans, contributions, investments, and possible beneficiaries of that plan.

> **Stock purchase plans**
>
> When an employee is entitled to purchase company stocks, this infotype manages all of the required information including contributions and beneficiaries.

> **Credit plans**

Credit plans allow employees to receive the money in their benefits pots that they do not spend on benefits.

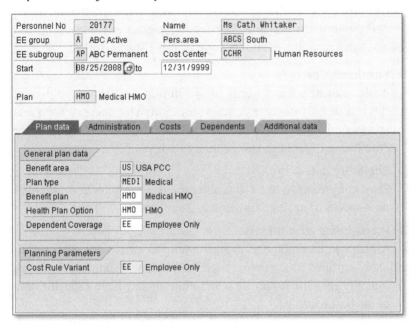

Personnel No	20177		Name	Ms Cath Whitaker
EE group	A	ABC Active	Pers.area	ABCS South
EE subgroup	AP	ABC Permanent	Cost Center	CCHR	Human Resources
Start	08/25/2008 to		12/31/9999

Plan   HMO   Medical HMO

Plan data | Administration | Costs | Dependents | Additional data

General plan data

Benefit area	US	USA PCC
Plan type	MEDI	Medical
Benefit plan	HMO	Medical HMO
Health Plan Option	HMO	HMO
Dependent Coverage	EE	Employee Only

Planning Parameters

| Cost Rule Variant | EE | Employee Only |

Figure 6.2 An Employee with an Example Medical Plan Assigned

With the benefits areas defined, the specific benefits areas and programs are set up for different groups of employees. The individual benefits are then assigned to the areas and programs. Like the rest of SAP ERP HCM, the validity of individual plans is fully configurable. For example, an insurance plan can be created, made valid for two years, and then terminated. Similarly, a benefits plan can be created and then at some point made no longer available to new members. The existing members can keep receiving the benefit, but it will no longer be included in a program. Plans can be reused across several different programs, so a base level of life insurance can be offered as part of all of the benefits programs. Similarly, a plan can be made available only to some or one of the benefits areas.

Benefits Offer

The benefits that are available for an employee to select within a benefit program on a specific date are called the benefits offer. What makes up a benefits offer and their rules and characteristics are determined by your customizing. The following customizing settings can be used to determine eligibility for plans in a specific offer:

> **Enrollment periods**
  A plan can be set to be only joined during a specific time period; this can be only once, (e.g., for a stock purchase plan), or for a certain period each year, (e.g., for medical coverage that is open for enrollment in January and February each year).

> **Eligibility dates**
  Plans can be made to be available only for enrollment or changes on a specific date, e.g., on January 1 each year.

> **Prerequisite enrollments**
  A plan can be defined as available only to employees who are already enrolled in another related benefit. For example, employees can only get a life insurance plan if they already have a specific type of medical coverage.

> **Employee eligibility**
  The type of employee, the length of service, the employee's age, and many other factors can be used to determine an employee's eligibility for a specific plan.

> **Dependent and beneficiary eligibility**
  As well as controlling employees' eligibility, the system can also set eligibility rules for dependents and beneficiaries of a specific plan. This could, for example, be used to say that only employees' children under age 10 can be included in a health care plan, or only employees over 25 can be included as beneficiaries of a life insurance plan.

> **Adjustment permissions**
  Adjustments allow the maintenance of benefits data for specific scenarios such as an employee's promotion, marriage, or retirement. (Adjustments are covered in more detail in the next section.)

So now we understand that a benefits area (usually defined at the country level) is made up of various benefits programs (for different types of employees) with individual benefits plans (for example, a specific brand of health insurance) made available in them. We know that a benefits offer describes which plans are available for an employee at a specific time and that adjustments can be used to control the maintenance of an employee's benefits data.

Benefits areas are made up of benefits programs that contain the actual plans that employees choose

We will now look at the different types of offers delivered in Benefits Management:

> **Automatic offer**

  The simplest type of offer. As the name suggests, benefits plans in this type of offer are automatically assigned to employees as soon as they are assigned to the benefits program. A benefit that is defined as automatic might be something straightforward like entitlement to a base level of life insurance, with no choices for the employee to make and at no cost to the employee

> **Open offer**

  In an open offer benefits, plans can be adjusted at any time as long as the benefit is flagged as open for enrollment. An example of a benefit that could be assigned to an open offer is a savings plan that an employee can join or leave at anytime during the year.

> **Default offer**

  This type of offer is usually used as an intermediate benefits selection, assigned by default to employees while they make their own benefits selections. An example of default offer is the minimum level of health coverage, provided at minimum cost to the employee.

> **Adjustment offer**

  An adjustment is one of a predefined lists of scenarios that your company has recognized as requiring the adjustment of benefits entitlements. Common adjustments include the employees' initial enrollment, which may be valid for three months from the employee's start date, and the annual adjustment window that is valid in August and September each year. Adjustments can also be defined for major employment and lifestyle changes that often drive benefits changes, such as promotions, marital status changes, births, and moves. Adjustments are made available by creating an adjustment infotype for an employee to allow them to open a specific benefit and make the required adjustments they want.

Benefits Management can generate adjustment reasons for either a single employee or groups of employees. The group adjustment generation functionality is an invaluable tool for triggering benefits adjustments when the employees' benefits are affected by company restructuring.

Employee Data

As with the other functions, infotypes are used to store employee data

Like all other employee information in SAP ERP HCM, employee benefits information is stored in infotypes. Infotypes allow date-based record keeping, creating a complete history of employee benefits selections. More information on the infotype concept is available in Chapter 9, Employee Administration

Benefits information is stored in a set of benefits-specific infotypes and also draws information from other more generic infotypes.

 Infotypes

> As a reminder, infotypes are used to store pieces of employee data together in logical groups. Infotypes provide a structure, facilitate data entry and maintenance, and enable you to store data for specific periods.

A set of international infotypes provide for the most commonly used benefits types around the world. A set of country-specific benefits infotypes is also available for the United States, UK, and Asia. More information on these infotypes is available in the later section on country-specific processing.

All of the infotype records are date based, and track the details of an employees' enrollment, further adjustments, and eventual termination of their participation in each plan. If an employee has multiple insurance plans active at a time, these plans will be stored in multiple infotype records. Thanks to SAP ERP HCM's strong integration, the information stored in these infotypes is used as the source of all benefits-related payroll processing, so any changes made to benefits data is instantly reflected in payroll processing.

Benefits-Specific Infotypes

The following infotypes are used for storing benefits information:

> **Infotype 0171 General Benefits Information**
> This is the first infotype record created when an employee is set up in benefits. It holds the details of the employees' benefits area, the details of the employees' first and second level of benefits selection, and the start and end date of eligibility. The combination of these groupings then determines which benefits program is available to the employee. The first and second program grouping is generally defaulted into this record based on the employee eligibility. This can then be overwritten if a different benefits program is required.

> **Infotype 0378 Adjustment Reasons**
> Because most benefits programs have strict rules regarding when employees can join and make changes to their selections, this infotype is used to control adjustments to benefits selection. For example, an adjustment reasons record may be created when an employee gets married or has a child. This then opens the benefits system up for this employee, allowing him to make further benefits selections based on his change of family status.

> **Infotype 0167 Health Plans**
> As its name suggests, this infotype holds the details of the health care plans in which the employee is enrolled. The infotype contains information on the plans costs to both employer and employee and details of tax-free status and employee deduction amounts and any overrides required. The infotype can also show evidence of insurability, a list of the dependents who are covered by the plan, and details of the provider and policy number. Figure 6.3 shows the detail of an example health plan.

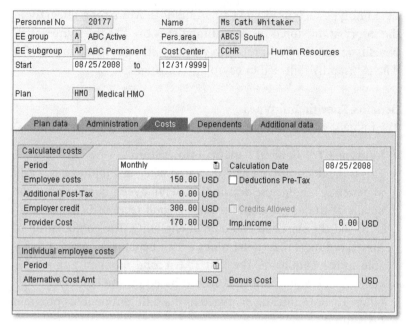

Figure 6.3 Cost Details of a Health Plan Stored on Infotype 0167

> **Infotype 0168 Insurance Plans**
> This infotype stores details of an employees' insurance coverage along with administrative data regarding evidence of insurability. The levels of coverage are also shown on the infotype, calculated automatically based on the defined calculation rules, as are the costs associated with the coverage. Employer and employee costs, tax-free contributions, and any overrides of regular figures are also shown here. This infotype also gives the user the ability to record details of the possible beneficiaries of the plan and the amounts or percentages of payment chosen by the employee.

> **Infotype 0169 Savings Plans**
> This infotype is used to store the details of an employee's savings plans. The details of these plans vary widely from country to country, but in general, the following information can be stored in this infotype: details of the employees' selected plan with details of the contributions, vesting, and investments options available within the plan; the amounts or percentages of employee regular and bonus contributions (any employer contributions are stored here for

payroll processing); the employees' choice of investments for the plan and their spread of percentages; details of possible beneficiaries of the plan and their payouts. An example entry of a U.S. 401k savings plan is shown in Figure 6.4.

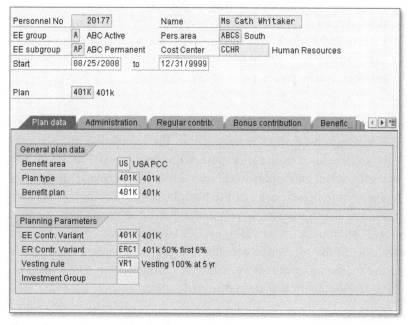

Figure 6.4 401k Savings Plan for the United States

> **Infotype 0379 Stock Purchase Plans**
> The details of an employee's stock options and other stock purchases plans are stored here. Matching the type of information generally required to record stock purchases, this infotype stores details of the plan type and contribution rules, the employee's regular and bonus contributions, and the possible beneficiaries of the plan and their respective payouts.

> **Infotype 0236 Credit Plans**
> This infotype stores the details of any credit plan in which the employee is enrolled. Information stored in this infotype includes the details of the credit plan, administrative data as required, and details of the calculated credit value and any override.

> **Infotype 0377 Miscellaneous Plans**
> This infotype allows you to add any other employee benefit not provided in the standard infotypes. Depending on the configuration of the miscellaneous plan, this infotype can include a wide range of information, including details of the plan, administrative data, details of costs, credits, coverage, and contributions (both regular and bonus). This infotype also allows the storage of information relating to possible beneficiaries and investment choices as required by the plan type.

Benefits are dependent on data stored in other infotypes

Integration with Other Infotypes

The integration of other infotypes into the calculation and the creation of benefits data is a great time-saving tool in SAP ERP HCM. For example, when an employee chooses a life insurance plan and wants to specify the beneficiaries of the plan, instead of having to maintain a separate list of the employee's dependents, the dependents already stored on the standard Infotype 0021-Family/Related Persons are available in the respective benefits infotype. This integration extends to the following infotypes available for entitlement decision making, data creation, and calculation of contributions:

> 0000 Actions

> 0001 Organizational Assignment

> 0002 Personal Data

> 0006 Addresses

> 0007 Planned Working Time

> 0008 Basic Pay

> 0009 Bank Details

> 0014 Recurring Payments and Deductions

> 0021 Family/Related Persons

> 0041 Date Specifications

> 0019 Monitoring of Tasks

> 0219 External Organizations

Benefits Administration

Like most of the HCM functions, Benefits has been built with a focus on streamlining administration-focused tasks and moving employees onto more strategic tasks. Let's look at the major functions within Benefits Administration and how Benefits Management makes them as efficient as possible.

Enrollment and Adjustment

The enrollment function allows you to enroll and adjust the benefits for employees either singularly or in groups. Enrollment can be used for an initial enrollment for new starters to the company and it is also used to process ongoing changes such as annual updates to benefits, and to process employees whose change of circumstances such as promotions means they are entitled to a new set of benefits.

As illustrated in Figure 6.5, to process an individual employee, you simply select the employee's record, generate an offer for him (containing all of the available plans for the employee), and process it, choosing the appropriate plans and adding dependents and beneficiaries as required. All of the steps required to process the enrollment are included in one process. Once it is complete, you can automatically print out the pre-formatted confirmation letters.

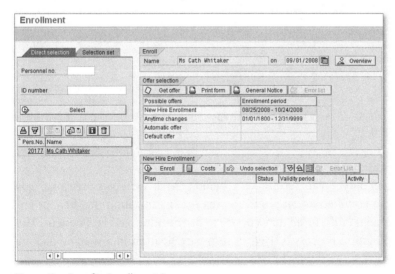

Figure 6.5 Benefits Enrollment Screen

137

As illustrated in Figure 6.6, groups of employees can be enrolled in their available default and automatic plans in one simple step. To do this, you simply select the employees you want to process and then execute the offer. You will be presented with a list of employees to enroll, which you can then action.

All of the required checks of prerequisite plans, combined contribution or coverage limits, and evidence of insurability that are required for the plan will be checked during processing, and warnings and errors generated as required to notify you of the requirements. Evidence of insurability can be set up as an immediate requirement or with a predetermined grace period, allowing initial enrollment, but dependent on evidence being provided at a later date.

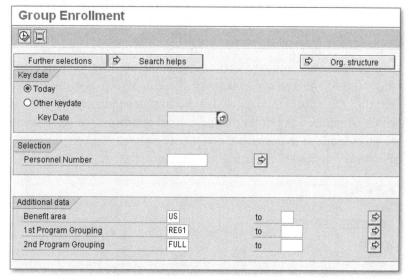

Figure 6.6 Selection Screen for Processing Groups of Employees and Specific Benefits Areas

Termination

An employee can terminate a benefit for a variety of reasons. For example, when an employee leaves the organization, his benefit entitlement ends, or he may choose to discontinue a certain benefit. The termination process is used to stop participation in a specific plan or all of an employee's plans. The termination process is similar to the enrollment process. The employee's current plans are displayed, and they can then be individually or collectively terminated. The rule for determining the date of termination for a specific plan can be set in Customizing so benefits can be set to finish at the end of the month, the end of the year, or on a specific day. As shown in Figure 6.7, a termination date can also be manually entered allowing benefits to be continued as long as required after termination.

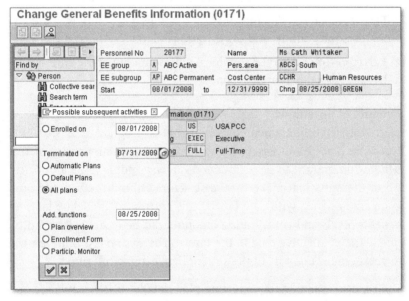

Figure 6.7 Processing a Future-Dated Termination of Benefits Plans for a Terminated Employee

When an employee's entitlement to a benefit continues after he has left the company, Benefits Management has a functionality called pre-deduction, which is integrated with Payroll and allows the cost of the ongoing benefit to be taken from the employee's final pay. This automatic processing ensures that all of the loose ends around employees' entitlements and obligations are taken care of before they leave the company, rather than trying to catch up with them after they have left.

Participation Overview

To be able to respond to employee and provider queries for up-to-date benefits information, you can perform a quick participation overview report for a specific employee. This report gives you all of the information you need relating to the employee's benefits selections including:

> **Employee selections:** The plans in which the employee is enrolled

> **Costs:** Both employee and employer costs for the plans

> **Employee's data:** Key information relating to the employee including personal, family, and organizational data

> **Participation history:** A graphical representation of the employee's benefits participation over time.

Benefits Maintenance

All benefits plans are date based, ensuring that ongoing maintenance is always independent of the current benefits

Once you have implemented your benefits program into SAP ERP HCM, the speed and ease with which ongoing maintenance of the benefits programs can be maintained is always going to be a priority. All of the parts that make up the structure behind the benefits program are designed with date-based table entries, so annual updates to benefits levels and contribution amounts can be done well ahead of time with an effective date in the future. There is no last-minute rush to get the new amounts in the system between payroll runs.

The reports available for reporting plan details such as coverage options and costs allow you to quickly analyze your benefits program and change it as required to ensure it continues to meet your employees' needs.

Participation Monitoring and Evidence of Insurability

Once you have enrolled your employees in their benefits selection, two ongoing reporting requirements are critical to good benefits management. The enrollment process ensures that employees are offered benefits that they are entitled to on the day of joining. Once an employee is participating in the benefits program, it is important that all employees are regularly checked to ensure that they are still entitled to participate in their benefits plans. It is also important to monitor employees' evidence of insurability to ensure that any evidence promised upon initial enrollment is later provided.

Promotions, changes in working hours, and transfers can lead to an employee having an incorrectly assigned set of benefits. Likewise, changes to the eligibility rules of the benefits themselves can mean that employees are incorrectly assigned. Benefits Management provides a standard reporting tool to monitor employee participation and resolve issues as they arise.

This report (called participation monitoring) can be run at the current date or as of a future date to ensure that employees' participation is correct. Errors and incorrect assignments can be resolved within the reporting tool. When an error is identified, you can withdraw the employee from the plan, change the details of a plan assignment, or move the employee to another more appropriate plan.

Participation monitoring ensures that your employees' benefits are always up to date

Many forms of insurance allow employees to enroll in the plan immediately, based on the requirement to provide evidence of insurability at a later date. Benefits Management allows you to set rules defining if evidence needs to be provided before an employee can join a benefit and then set rules relating to how soon evidence needs to be provided. Benefits Management also provides you with a standard evidence of insurability report that allows you to monitor all of your employees' plans with outstanding evidence of insurability, registering receipt of evidence of insurability, or stopping participation in the plan if the required evidence of insurability is not provided.

Form Printing

Informing employees of their enrollment choices and confirming those choices and any adjustments to their entitlements is made simpler and faster by the built-in automatic printing functionality within Benefits Management. This functionality allows you to print individualized enrollment forms or confirmation letters for a single employee as part of the individual enrollment process. If a large number of employees are being processed, individualized letters can be printed in bulk, ready for distribution.

Automatically generate confirmation forms for employees as soon as they are enrolled

Transferring Data to Providers

Now that we have set up our benefits, assigned them to our employees, monitored their participation, and notified the employees of their choices with our automatic form generation, it's time to pass all of this information on to the benefits providers and third-party administrators. Each provider can be individually defined within Benefits Management, their contact details, representatives, provider numbers, and addresses all stored for quick access and contact. If you are also running payroll on an SAP system, a standard report is provided to help reconcile the payments for each provider. At the end of each payroll period, you can generate a payment list detailing the total amount your finance department needs to pay to each provider. The report also allows you to analyze the differences between this period and the last period and any amounts brought forward into this period from retroactive processing.

Benefits Management also provides you with standard report formats that can be used as the basis for any interface files that need to be developed. This information is provided in the form of IDocs. These contain predefined layouts for all of the information required by providers relating to employee benefits, as well as details of employee plan selections. The information also includes all of the required personal and organizational information that providers generally require.

Depending on what your provider requires, you can either send all of the benefits-related information for all of your employees each time, or if you have Infotype Change Logging enabled, you can just send the information for employees who have had their records created, changed, or deleted within the period.

It is also worth noting that to help with the processing of retirement plans, which are generally the most complex type of employee benefit, the system has been enhanced to allow interfaces to be sent out from SAP ERP and to be received into SAP ERP. These inbound IDocs allow third-party administrators to send changes in employee details such as service date calculations and accumulations of employee entitlements that can be automatically interfaced both out of and into Benefits Management.

Reporting

As with all the other SAP ERP HCM functions, Benefits Management is fully integrated with SAP ERP Business Warehouse. Benefits information stored as either employee data in infotypes or as payroll results in payroll clusters is stored in a logical format that makes it simple to report on from third-party reporting tools. Benefits Management data can also be reported on using the two SAP ERP HCM report-writing tools—SAP Query and ABAP Query—so users can quickly write, run, and save their reports to meet their own reporting requirements. More information on these tools is provided in Chapter 8, Payroll and Legal Reporting. Benefits Management also comes equipped with a set of standard benefits reports that provide for the most common reporting requirements. These include the following key reports:

> Employee Participation Summary

> Changes in Benefits Elections

> Changes in Employee Eligibility

> Benefits Plan Cost Summaries

> Benefits Plan Contribution Summaries

> Contribution Limit Checks

> Employee Demographics

> Benefits Selection Analysis

> Enrollment Analysis

In addition to employee-focused reports, you are also provided with several reports that allow you to analyze your company's whole benefits offering, look at costs, take-up, and other critical information.

Integration

As mentioned previously, SAP ERP HCM offers seamless integration that is always one of its strongest selling points, and the integration of

Changes to
employee data are
automatically picked
up by payroll

Benefits Management is no exception. From a day-to-day perspective, the most important integration point is between benefits administration and payroll. The fact that administrators from both the benefits and payroll teams know that any changes made to employee benefits data can be automatically picked up and included in payroll processing is a tremendous improvement over separate systems. Changes including new starter enrollments, existing benefits changes, and pre-deductions are picked up immediately and included in the next payroll automatically. Because all of the benefits records are date based and because of the SAP ERP HCM payroll concept of retroactive accounting, back-dated benefits changes are also automatically included and automatically calculated, with any under- or over-contributions processed in the current pay period.

Benefits Management is also fully integrated with Employee Administration, so the benefits enrollment for new starters can be integrated into the initial new starter hiring action. Your new employees can have their automatic benefits entitlements assigned to them the moment they are hired into the system.

Benefits Management is also fully integrated with Employee Self-Service, giving employees the ability to manage their own benefits program and removing most the administration burden completely from your benefits team and empowering the employee. Employee Self-Service and Benefits Management is covered in more detail in the following sections.

Employee Self-Service

Employee Self-
Service puts the
data maintenance
responsibility back
onto the employee

Adding another facet to the already strong integration capabilities of SAP ERP HCM's, Employee Self-Service (ESS) (covered in more detail in Chapter 15) is also fully integrated with Benefits Management, allowing you to move the responsibility for many day-to-day benefits administration tasks and processes onto the employees, freeing up your benefits team's time to focus on more strategic goals.

ESS allows employees to manage their own benefits data through the SAP ERP portal. Employees can access their own data, seeing in real time their benefits selections, and perform the following functions via the portal.

Participation Overview

This is the most used function in the benefits part of the portal. It allows employees to view and edit the details of their benefits selections. They can see an overview and a detailed plan-by-plan breakdown of their benefits, showing costs, contributions, investments, details of enrolled dependents, and the nominated beneficiaries of their plans. Employees can also print individualized enrollment confirmation forms when required.

Enrollment

Either for a new employee to the company, as part of annual benefits updates, or as a result of a change in employment or personal circumstances, the enrollment function allows employees to view their own benefits options, including costs, contributions, investments, dependents, and beneficiaries. They can then choose the plans they want to enroll in, print a simulated pay slip to see the impact on their pay packet, and (depending on your customizing choices) either print an enrollment form or enroll directly in the plan via the portal. Once enrolled, employees can print individualized confirmation of enrollment forms.

As with any other changes made through Benefits Management, any changes the employee makes in the portal are immediately reflected in the system and can be automatically picked up by Employee Administration, Payroll, and other SAP ERP HCM components.

Country-Specific Functionality

Benefits Management offers enhanced processing options for the United States, UK, and Asia to enable standard processing of the most common types of benefits offered in these areas. We will now take a brief look at the extra functionality for each of these areas.

Enhanced processing is offered for UK, U.S., and Asian requirements

United States

Benefits Management for U.S. customers has been enhanced in three areas where the United States has specific requirements.

Flexible Spending Account Claims Administration

Flexible spending accounts are used in the United States to allow employees to set aside pretax income to cover anticipated medical or dependent care costs. The total value the employee has contributed is stored as a balance, and when an employee incurs a cost, he can claim against this balance to recover his costs. This system is totally integrated into ESS to allow employees to review their contributions, display their balances, and submit and monitor claims for processing. Workflow is used to manage the claims process, allowing administrators to monitor, approve, and reject claims as required.

COBRA Administration

Benefits Management is fully developed to provide for all of your COBRA maintenance and reporting requirements. It allows you to record COBRA details and beneficiary details. It also allows you to process changes in eligibility including new dependents, marriages, and divorces and manage COBRA flexible spending accounts, health plans, and payments.

Highly Compensated Employees

The ability to determine and record employees as highly compensated is required as part of U.S. 401(k) processing. Benefits Management provides a specific infotype for recording this information and the gives you the ability to identify these employees via the standard 401(k) nondiscrimination test report.

Tax-Sheltered Annuity Plans

If your employees made contributions to 403(b) savings plans prior to your implementing SAP ERP HCM, you can record details of these contributions on a dedicated infotype. This infotype holds all of the details of contribution dates and catch ups as required by law.

United Kingdom

Responding to the high level of demand in the UK for a process to manage flexible benefits, SAP ERP HCM now includes a UK-specific set of customizing that enables flexible benefits management. Flexible benefits gives the employees the ability to choose their own benefits up to a set level of entitlement. This entitlement, which is held as a monetary value, can be determined based on various factors depending on your company's requirements.

Three types of flexible benefits plans are provided for:

No Additional Funding

This type of plan is used when your company pays your employees a salary and has a set value of benefits entitlement for each employee that can be spread across a pre-determined set of benefits programs. For example, an employee could have the following benefits available:

> Private medical insurance

> 22 days holiday per year

> Life insurance at three times their annual salary

> 6% employer pension contribution

So in addition to getting their salaries, employees can choose the level of options within each of these benefits categories to reflect their personal life choices. For example, an employee could reduce his life insurance coverage and increase the level of employer pension contribution. The total value of the benefits selection is determined by the company at the beginning of the process, so if the employee chooses benefits options that go above that value, the employee must cover that extra cost.

Additional Funding

This type of plan is based on the provision of a flex fund or pot of money that the employee can use to purchase benefits. This is set in addition to the salary. The value of the flex fund can be determined using various calculations including a set value based on the employee's position or grade, a percentage of the salary, or the value of the previous benefits package. All of the benefits that are then offered have a flexed value, so employees can choose whatever benefits they require, and any surplus or deficit can then be either deducted from the employees' pay, credited to their pay, forfeited, or paid in part as the company determines appropriate.

Total Packages Funding

Sometimes considered the holy grail of benefits packages, the total package plan is used when your employees total remuneration package is included in the flexible benefits pot, including salary, benefits, pension contributions, etc. As with the other plans, your company defines a set of benefits that the employee can choose from. The employees can then choose the amount of their pot that they want paid as salary and then choose whatever benefits they think necessary with the remainder of the pot. An employee could choose to have a very low salary, few holidays, and a large employer pension contribution or any other combination of benefits.

National Insurance Cost Neutrality

In the U.K., when an employee chooses to take benefits such as selling part of his holiday entitlement and taking it instead as part of his salary, this increase in the employee's salary can trigger an increase in the amount of National Insurance that the employer is required to pay. The cost neutrality function within GB flexible benefits allows you as the employer to charge this extra national insurance contribution back to the employee, ensuring that employee benefits choices do not cost your company extra. This National Insurance claw back functionality is fully integrated into both Benefits Management and GB Payroll.

Asia

Because many companies in Asia provide private medical coverage to their employees, Benefits Management has been enhanced to allow the input, processing, and reporting of medical claims data with benefits. The functionality has also been provided to allow for claims to be input into the system, with a separate approval process required before it is processed through payroll.

This concludes our coverage of Benefits Management and its functionality.

Summary

As we learned, SAP ERP HCM's Benefits Management function provides a flexible framework for developing complex benefits programs that can meet all of your benefits requirements. We looked at:

> The structure of benefits within SAP ERP HCM, how they are defined, and how they are maintained.

> The processes built into the solution that allow you to efficiently process your employee benefits data and the reporting capabilities that are built into this.

> Employee Self-Service, which allows your benefits team members to concentrate on strategic goals rather than the day-to-day transactional changes to the system.

> The country-specific enhancements to Benefits Management and how those solutions ensure that the system provides for all of your company's needs.

In the next chapter we will switch focus and explore the area of time management, another key area in SAP ERP HCM.

7 Time and Attendance

Starting time, ending time, vacation time, time sheet entry, evaluating time recording, planning working time, managing employee time recording: That crucial word *time* impacts companies in a wide range of areas and is one of the key pieces of information that companies need to effectively manage. As a result, the SAP ERP HCM Time and Attendance (Time and Attendance) function is the largest function in SAP ERP HCM. It encompasses every aspect of time recording and administration, including recording employees' contracted working hours when they are first hired, tracking their actual working times against their planned times, recording working time and vacations, monitoring leave balances, matching employees' work times against business requirements, evaluating their working times, and generating payments based on this information. It also allows you to provide a summary of all this information to HR, payroll, finance, plant management, customer relationship management, and many other parts of your company.

Time and Attendance is one of the most complex and powerful components in SAP ERP HCM. Employees can complete their time sheets online, and managers can approve or reject these entries online as well. The Time Manager's Workplace (TMWP) gives your time administrators a central control panel where they can manage employees' working times, correct data entry errors, and process adjustments in a powerful and customizable user-friendly interface. Shift planning also gives your company the ability to quickly match your employee working times to your changing demands, while incentive wages allow you to automatically generate payments to employees based on production and sales figures. Time Evaluation allows you to feed in simple start and end times for an employee. Time Evaluation can then compare these clock entries against employees' normal working hours and work out when and how many hours overtime and how much shift allowance and any other payments the employee is entitled to and transfer this information straight to payroll for processing.

How Time and Attendance Fits into an Enterprise

The recording of working and non-working time impacts every employee in every company

Effective time and attendance management has an impact on all employees in a company, from the hourly waged gardener to the salaried CEO and president. Whereas time management is often considered an issue that is most important for waged employees, bad time and attendance management can also have a large impact on salaried employees. Examples of areas where salaried employees feel the impact include the calculation and storage of leave and sickness entitlements, payment of overtime and penalty payments, and the calculation of sales and production and related bonuses. Nobody thanks you when your time and attendance systems are working properly, but everyone will tell you when they are not.

The Time and Attendance function gives you the ability to effectively and efficiently plan, record, and maintain all aspects of your company's time data. This information then needs to be correctly evaluated and interpreted so it is available for all of the other SAP ERP HCM and SAP ERP components such as Payroll, Finance, and Plant Management to use as they require.

A Closer Look at Time and Attendance

Time and Attendance is another area of SAP ERP HCM that is so large it could have its own book explaining the many parts of the solution and the myriad ways they interact. In this chapter we will focus on describing the core parts of Time and Attendance, what they are used for, and how the information they generate is stored and accessed.

For more information see *Time Management with SAP ERP HCM* also from SAP PRESS.

The six core parts of Time and Attendance that we will be looking at are:

> **Time Recording**
The aim of the Time Recording function is to give you the ability to quickly and efficiently record your employees' working time. It gives you the ability to record when your employees were supposed to work, when they actually worked, what they were working on, and to where it should be costed. It also records when your employees were not at work, recording details of their absences (vacations, sickness, etc.), managing their leave balances, and recording other work-related attendances such as training courses.

> **Cross Application Time Sheets**
Moving responsibility for time sheet entry and approval to employees and managers, Cross Application Time Sheets (CATS) ensure that time recording can be completed quickly and efficiently, correctly assigned to projects and costing details, and then approved and made ready for payment and provided where required for other components.

> **Time Evaluation**
One of the most complex of the SAP ERP HCM functions, Time Evaluation takes your raw time recording from numerous possible sources and then according to your company's rules and procedures, it processes and interprets the data. The resulting output is then available in the form of time recording results that can be paid to the employee via payroll.

> **Incentive Wages**
This function is designed for companies that pay their employees based on incentive wages such as piece work, premiums, and pro-

duction results. The Incentive Wages function is used to pull production, maintenance, customer service, and project systems data from other components and interpret it for paying through payroll.

> **Shift Planning**
> This function allows you to plan and schedule your employee working time to meet your business needs. Combining employee information such as skills, locations, and qualifications with demand information from the Logistics component, Shift Planning ensures that you have the right people in the right place at the right time to keep production running.

> **Time Manager's Workplace (TMWP)**
> Designed for organizations in which time recording is decentralized out to time administrators, the TMWP provides you with a simple user interface that allows you to complete all of the tasks involved in Time Recording and Time Evaluation. It meets all of your time reporting requirements as well.

Time Recording

Record and store all of the required time information to meet your organizational, payroll, production control, accounting, and legal requirements

SAP ERP HCM has evolved over numerous versions to become a complete time recording solution. The Time Recording function allows you to record and store all of the required information to meet your organizational, payroll, production control, accounting, and legal requirements, ensuring that you always have up-to-date and accurate time information at your fingertips. The rest of the Time and Attendance functions are built around some key concepts that we will explore next.

Being able to define your company and your employees in terms of the different time recording rules and agreements is one of the most important steps in setting up Time and Attendance in SAP ERP HCM. Recognizing the variances between locations, departments, and groups of employees within your company in terms of rules for time recording and managing absences and attendances, and then defining the rules and logic for turning this time recording into correct payroll results is a large task. Getting this information ready before you begin to build your system ensures a much easier implementation process.

Grouping Your Employees

The first step in setting up Time Recording is working out how many types of employees you have in terms of determining rules for time and attendance calculations and payments and then documenting how these calculations are made. Some common groupings and decision points used to define employees in Time Recording include:

> The most important part of the time solution is defining all of your different types of employees

> **Positive time recording**

These are the employees in your company who are only paid when they have time recorded, for example, casual employees are only paid when working time is entered into the system for them. If no time is entered, the employee receives no pay.

> **Negative time recording**

These are the employees who are paid a salary every pay period with no requirement to enter working time to generate pay. These employees are only affected by time recording when an exception (or negative event) is triggered. For example, a period of unpaid leave may reduce their normal salary.

> **Shift workers and standard hours**

What determines if an employee is shift worker? How do you define "standard hours" in your company? Is it 9 to 5, Monday to Friday? How many versions of standard hours does your company have?

> **Extra hours, weekend work, and overtime**

Defining when your employees get paid above their normal hours and at what rates overtime is paid is an important part of Time and Attendance setup. Under what circumstances are employees entitled to time and a half, double time, triple time, and so on? How does an employee qualify for extra pay. Is it based on the number of hours worked in a shift, a day, a week, or a month?

> **Flexible working time**

How late can an employee be before his time is docked? How flexible can employees be with the timing of breaks and start and finish times. How do you calculate deductions from pay for breaking the rules?

> **Annual leave, vacation, and time off in lieu**
> How much leave are your different types of employee entitled to? Is it accrued per year, per quarter, or every day? How many rules for time off in lieu of leave (TOIL) do you have? Can your employees sell their vacation or buy extra days?

> **Sick, maternity, paternity, and adoption leave**
> How much sick leave can your employees take in a year? How is it paid? How much unpaid sick leave can they take? What are the leave rules when employees become pregnant? How long can they have off? How are they paid when they are off? What is your policy if an employee adopts a child, or if an employee's child is sick?

> **Part-time employees**
> How do the rules for part-time, casual, and job-share employees work? Are they separate groups with totally separate rules, or are they just a percentage of the full-time equivalent?

> **Local and work place agreements and union rules**
> How many union or work agreements does your company have for your different types of employees? Do work rules vary by location, state, or even floor?

These are just some of the areas that you need to analyze to define your employee groupings and the calculation for rules for Time Recording. Ensuring that you can group your employees in a way that allows you to apply these rules correctly is a large task in any SAP ERP HCM implementation. Some of these areas may not be relevant to your company or country, but chances are you may have some peculiar rules of your own. Companies often think their time recording requirements are quite simple until they really start looking at them. Historical agreements, local working practices, company mergers, and acquisitions are just some of the things that can complicate your time recording requirements.

Time and Attendance gives you a wide range of ways of dividing your employees into time processing groups

As a result of the many possible complexities in time recording and calculation, the Time Recording function gives you many ways of grouping your employees to ensure that you get the right blend of flexibility and structure. These sometimes overlapping groups mean that rules can be applied correctly, decisions made, entitlements awarded, and eventually that everyone's pay results are correct.

Table 7.1 lists the most common employee groupings for Time Recording, and what they group employees for, and an example of where they are used.

Employee Grouping	Used to Group Employees For	Example of Use
Employee Subgroup Grouping (ESG)	Time quota types	Assigning annual leave entitlements
	Work schedules	Determining available working times
	Personnel calculation rules	Making payroll calculation decisions
Personnel Subarea Grouping (PSG)	Attendances and absences types	Allowing employees to use different absences
	Time quota types	Time evaluation processing rules
	Work schedules	Defining the allowed period work patterns
	Daily work schedules	Defining the allowed daily work patterns
	Substitution and availability types	Determining if employees can be substituted
	Attendance and absence counting	To value how much an absence is worth
	Time recording	To determine which type of time recording an employee can do
	Premiums	Entitlement for different premium calculations
Employee Groupings for Time Evaluation	Time wage type selection	For time-related calculations in Time Evaluation

Table 7.1 Employee Groups for Time Management

Employee Grouping	Used to Group Employees For	Example of Use
	Time type determination	For time-related calculations in Time Evaluation
	Automatic quota accrual	Determining how quotas are accrued
Time Management-Related Employee Groupings for Payroll	Absence valuation	Calculating how absences are paid

Table 7.1 Employee Groups for Time Management (Cont.)

Defining your Company Calendar

Calendars represent the working arrangements of your sites and offices

After defining your employee groupings based on their working arrangements, the next most important grouping of employees is based on the calendars that different offices, factories, locations, and countries follow. For example, public holidays can change from state to state or even town to town, and factories and offices can have their own local rules regarding company holidays and annual plant shutdowns and different rules for determining how public holidays are treated. The Time Recording function provides you with two tools to help you define all of your public holidays and company holidays:

> **Holiday calendars**
> As shown in Figure 7.1, holiday calendars are used to define the public holidays for each personnel subarea in your company. Calendars are defined for 12-month periods, and public holidays are then assigned to them. Public holidays can be defined as fixed or movable or have their own custom logic for how they are determined each year.

> **Factory calendars**
> A factory calendar is a subset of a holiday calendar and defines, in addition to the public holidays, which days your location considers working days. Factory calendars are especially important in production environments and seasonal operations where they take into account maintenance and planned shutdowns of locations.

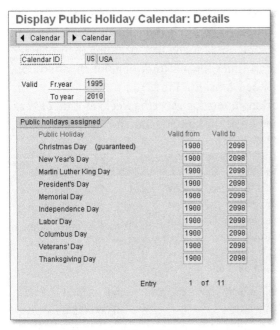

Figure 7.1 An Example Public Holiday Calendar for the United States

So if your company has factories and offices in two U.S. states and two European countries, you would need to define at least four separate holiday calendars, and then, depending on the working arrangements in your factories and offices, you may need to define a separate factory calendar for each of your locations. Of course, if separate locations share the same holiday and factory rules, the calendars can be shared across multiple sites.

Defining your holiday and factory calendars provides important background information to the Time Recording and Time Evaluation functions so they can evaluate employee working times and record and calculate the data correctly.

Calendars provide important background information for later processing

Mapping Your Working Times

As already explored in Chapter 2 Employee Administration, work schedules are one of the key components to an employee's record. Because they are so important, let's quickly recap the key concepts behind work schedules.

Work schedules
record your
employees' planned
working time, down
to the minute if
necessary

SAP ERP HCM uses work schedules to record your employees' planned or contracted working times. A work schedule allows you to view an employee's planned working time for any day including their planned start time (or range of start times) breaks (morning, lunch, afternoon, or as required), and planned finishing time. You can quickly see the employee's planned working hours for a specific week, month, or year. Work schedules are made up of the components shown in Table 7.2.

Object	Description	Example
Daily work schedule	Define the authorized working times and break times for a single day; can provide for fixed working times, flextime, and days off	DWS Start End Total 00A 8:00am 5:00pm 7.5hrs 00B 9:00am 6:30pm 8.0hrs OFF 0.0hrs
Break Schedule	Used within a daily work schedule to define the employee's breaks from work	BS Start End Total Paid 01 9:30 10:00 0.5hrs Y 02 12:00 1:00 1.0hrs N
Period work schedule	Combinations of different daily work schedules (including working and nonworking schedules) linked together to map an employee's planned working time for a week, or rolling roster	PWS DWS 01 00A 02 00A 03 00B 04 00B 05 00B 06 OFF 07 OFF
Work schedule rule	Combines a period work schedule with a public holiday calendar and then applies it to a specific period of time to map an actual period of work	Day Month Year PWS DWS 22 Jan 2009 01 00A 23 Jan 2009 02 00A 24 Jan 2009 03 00B 25 Jan 2009 04 00B 26 Jan 2009 05 00B 27 Jan 2009 06 OFF 28 Jan 2009 07 OFF

Table 7.2 Work Schedule Components

Object	Description	Example
Personal work schedule	An employee's actual working time, taking into account the planned working time from the work schedule and absences, attendances, and substitutions	

Table 7.2 Work Schedule Components (Cont.)

Figure 7.2 shows the detailed view of an employee work schedule including the details of the employee's time management groupings, holiday calendar assignment, and work schedule for a month.

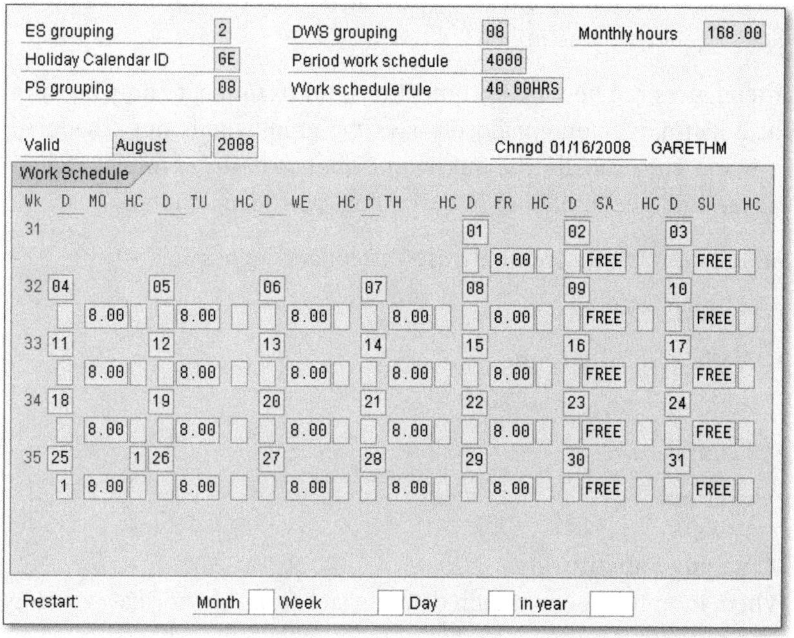

Figure 7.2 Detail View of an Employee Work Schedule

The complexity of your work schedules depends on the complexity of your business. For example, if you are a professional services firm, you may only have a few work schedules. If you operate numerous factories around the country, you might have thousands of work schedules to cover all of your employment scenarios.

Recording Attendances

Define attendance types to find out what your employees are doing during work

Now that you have identified when your employees are planned to be working, you need to be able to record when they actually work and what they are doing. Time and Attendance uses *attendances* to record when an employee is at work. Of course, not every moment at work is spent "working." Employees spend work time in meetings, attending training, and traveling, so attendances are used to record an employee's general activity while at work.

Different attendances can have different rules assigned to them, for example, to control the eligibility of the attendance, or the person who can use this type of attendance. They can control the effect the attendance has on payroll. Is it paid at normal or overtime rates, or does it generate time in lieu?

Attendances can be set with time limits, for example, to only be valid for a half-day or only valid on days the employee is not scheduled to work. They can also be linked to a quota, so, for example, an employee could be limited to five "training" attendances in any year.

Some examples of commonly used attendance types are:

> Productive hours

> Works council meeting

> Union meeting

> Business travel

> Overtime

Managing Substitutions

Substitutions allow employees to record short-term changes to employee working arrangements

When an employee is required to deviate from his normal working time or is required to work in a different position or office for a limited time, this process is managed via a *substitution*. Substitutions are used in Time and Attendance to allow employees to work different times and or be paid at a different rate or on a different basis while they are performing tasks outside their normal tasks. This process means you can assign an employee to another employee's position, and the employee will then be paid according to the rules applicable to the employee for whom they are performing the tasks. Figure 7.3 shows an employee substitution being maintained.

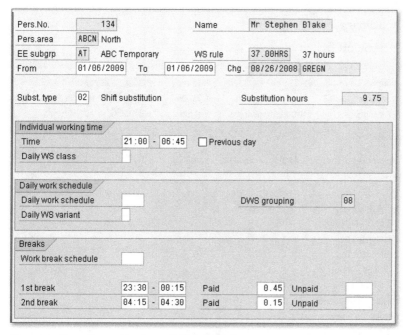

Pers.No.	134		Name	Mr Stephen Blake
Pers.area	ABCN	North		
EE subgrp	AT	ABC Temporary	WS rule	37.00HRS 37 hours
From	01/06/2009	To 01/06/2009	Chg. 08/26/2008 GREGN	

| Subst. type | 02 | Shift substitution | | Substitution hours | 9.75 |

Individual working time

| Time | 21:00 - 06:45 | ☐ Previous day |
| Daily WS class | | |

Daily work schedule

| Daily work schedule | | DWS grouping | 08 |
| Daily WS variant | | | |

Breaks

Work break schedule					
1st break	23:30 - 00:15	Paid	0.45	Unpaid	
2nd break	04:15 - 04:30	Paid	0.15	Unpaid	

Figure 7.3 Recording an Employee Shift Substitution

Recording Absences

In addition to knowing what employees are doing when they are at work, it's important to know why employees are not at work. Absences are used to record the reasons that employees are absent. They are also used to control how these absences effect payroll and control how much leave an employee is entitled too. Absences can be configured with payment rules that set the number of paid days of absence, with any additional days being unpaid, or they can be set so that additional days will be removed from the next years' entitlement. Absences can also be configured so that additional information is required for the absence before it is processed, so for sickness absences, medical evidence is required for the absence to be approved.

Use absence types to record and report on key absence data

Some examples of commonly used absence types are:

> Sick leave (as shown in Figure 7.4)

> Unpaid leave

> Maternity leave

> Military leave

> Time off in lieu

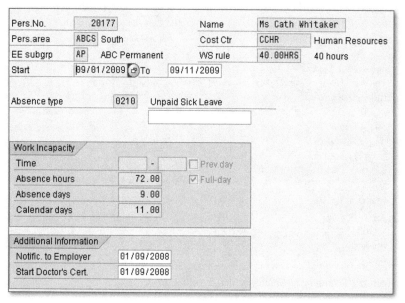

Pers.No.	20177		Name	Ms Cath Whitaker
Pers.area	ABCS	South	Cost Ctr	CCHR	Human Resources
EE subgrp	AP	ABC Permanent	WS rule	40.00HRS	40 hours
Start	09/01/2009	To	09/11/2009

Absence type 0210 Unpaid Sick Leave

Work Incapacity

Time	-	☐ Prev.day
Absence hours	72.00	☑ Full-day
Absence days	9.00	
Calendar days	11.00	

Additional Information

| Notific. to Employer | 01/09/2008 |
| Start Doctor's Cert. | 01/09/2008 |

Figure 7.4 Recording an Unpaid Sick Absence for an Employee

Managing Leave Quotas

Leave quotas allow you to automaticaly track vacation and sick leave entitlements

Quotas can be used for both attendances and absences to manage the entitlements for these types of time. Quotas can be defined with set values of either hours or days of entitlement. They can be set to be either accrued over a set period of time or given automatically on a specified day. You can configure an absence so that the quota can be exceeded or so that its value is strictly limited. Quotas can be determined as valid for a set period of time, for example, a year, or for the entire length of the employee's employment. Assigning quotas to employees gives you the ability to instantly view employees' quota entitlements, the remainder of their entitlements, the value of their quotas that have been requested (but not approved), and the amounts of their quotas that have been used for any period of time. Figure 7.5 shows an employee's quota overview, with the two quotas showing the employee's entitlement and the number of days taken for the leave quota period.

Pers.No.		20177		Name		Ms Cath Whitaker			
Pers.area	ABCS	South		Cost Ctr	CCHR		Human Resources		
EE subgrp	AP	ABC Permanent		WS rule	40.00HRS		40 hours		
Choose	07/01/2008	To	09/30/2008	STy.					

Absence Quotas (2006)

	Start Date	End Date	Ab.	Quota text	Start ded	End ded.	Number	Deduction
	08/26/2008	08/26/2009	10	Vacation	08/26/2008	08/26/2009	24.00000	12.00000
	08/01/2008	08/01/2009	01	Paid time off in lieu	08/01/2008	08/01/2009	50.00000	10.50000

Figure 7.5 Employee Absence Quota Overview

Some examples of commonly used quota types are:

> Paid vacation

> Unpaid vacation

> Paid maternity leave

> Paid paternity leave

> Onsite training

> Self-directed training

Cross Application Time Sheets (CATS)

CATS is a cross-component tool for recording working times and tasks completed. It is a one-stop shop for recording employee working time, developed for use by the employees themselves or for decentralized data input. In addition to inputting time recording, CATS enables allocating this time to other components such as Project Systems and Plant Maintenance and is also linked to Controlling, allowing you to assign internal activity allocation and statistical data to employee working time. Utilizing the powerful Xapps cross-application tool, employees can even submit their own time recordings while on the go using mobile devices. Figure 7.5 shows a CATS time entry screen with employee start and end times.

CATS provides a powerful time sheet entry tool to meet all your data entry requirements

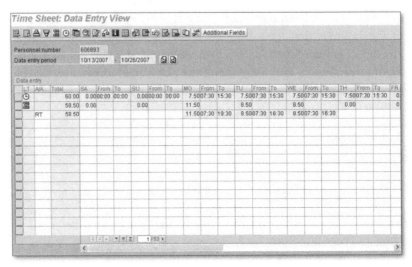

Figure 7.6 The CATS Data Entry Screen

CATS is probably one of the best examples of SAP ERP's powerful integration. Let's look at the main features of CATS that exploit this integration.

Time Recording

CATS gives you the ability to record time sheet data, either as a whole day, if that is the level that's required, or with the working period broken into parts if further granularity is required. Although referred to as time recording, the data input section of CATS allows for much more than just recording working time. CATS gives you the ability to record three distinct types of data on the time sheet:

Payroll Data

CATS gives you the ability to record your employees' working time, such as normal hours, overtime hours, and travel time using attendance and absence types. It also gives you the ability to record payments and deductions using wage types. For example, employees can put in payments for cash-based clothing allowances or units.

Controlling and Billing Data

All of the attendances, absences, and wage types can be allocated to orders, projects, or work breakdown structures so that these costs can be directly assigned in finance and controlling, allowing you to automatically interface time data to projects and cost objects. You can also record details of non–hours-related data by using *statistical key figures* such as kilometers or units to record such details as kilometers driven so that this information can be used in customer billing and expenses management.

CATS allows you to enter and interface costing and project billing information into your time entries

External Employees

In addition to recording these details about your employees, CATS can be used for recording the time of external employees. When external employees complete their time recording in CATS, their working hours can be allocated to activity numbers, allowing quick and efficient invoice verification.

CATS can also be used for external employees

Integrated Approval Processes

Allowing your employees to record their own time recording usually requires an approval process before the time recording data is transferred to other components such as controlling and payroll for payment. Using SAP ERP's integrated workflow processes, you can assign approval rights to line managers, team leaders, and project managers, so that when an employee submits a time recording, an approver has the ability to approve or reject it.

Use workflows to trigger time sheet approval and rejection

As with other workflows, approval hierarchies can be assigned according to your organizational structure, ensuring that approval hierarchies always reflect the current state of the company.

Not all elements of a time sheet have to be configured to require approval. Elements can be set to be automatically approved, and for those that require approval, managers can assign messages to their rejections, giving employees input into the rejection reason and the ability to resubmit corrected entries.

Once a time sheet has been approved, it can be transferred to other components ready to be paid via payroll. In situations where time sheets do not require approval, for example where they are centrally input, the approval step can be switched off completely; the data transfer can be started immediately after input.

Time Sheet Control and Management

Simple reports are available to monitor time sheet entries (or the lack of them)

Now that we understand just how much information is stored in CATS, it's good to know that Time and Attendance provides you with numerous reporting options to analyze this wealth of information. Some of the most regularly used reports are:

> **Time-Leveling Report**
> A favorite report among time administrators, this report provides users with a quick graphical display of employees who have entered either too few or too many hours for a period. Automatic email notifications can be triggered for employees with time sheet inconsistencies, and users can drill down from the report straight into the CATS line entries to correct errors where required.

> **Display Time Sheet Data**
> A simple report for displaying the time entered for employees and the costing details assigned to that time, this report can be run by an employee or organizational unit, allowing quick access to time sheet information.

> **Display Working Times and Task Details**
> A more detailed version of the above report, this report gives the full details of all information entered into the time sheet.

Time Manager's Workplace (TMWP)

TMWP is a specialized tool for managing groups of employees' time data

If specific people in your company are responsible for completing the time recording for relatively small groups of employees, then TMWP is just the tool for your company.

As time recording technology becomes more flexible, the responsibility for time data entry is often being decentralized away from large teams of data entry clerks to shift supervisors, team leaders, or secretaries who complete the time recording for the people in their team. TMWP is designed to speed up time recording by providing a specially designed interface that is easy to learn and quickly customizable for individual users.

TMWP is quick to learn and use because it is focused on the following key concepts:

> **Fast access to all employee data**
All employees' data are automatically listed and ready for instant access.

> **Easy and quick selection of time data**
Using a scrollable calendar view, administrators can choose between annual, monthly, weekly, or daily views of either individual or multiple employees' time data.

> **All data available in one view**
The screen layout allows all information to be displayed on one screen, from a basic annual overview of employee data to the full detail of a specific day with clock in and out times and all of the costing information for the time recorded. Views of time data can then be tailored to individual requirements.

> **No cryptic codes to learn**
There are no additional codes for users to remember.

> **A specialized tool for managing groups of employees' time data**
Resolving a common complaint in almost all new systems, TMWP allows users to assign their own logical time data IDs to the SAP ERP HCM codes, bringing instant familiarity to time recording and speeding up the learning process.

TMWP is the central place where all of the time and attendance data is drawn together from all of the other parts of the component, allowing it to be accessed and processed in one place. The coordination of all of this information is completed through the following tasks, which are the most common time recording scenarios.

Users can create their own time entry codes that are relevant to them

Maintaining Time Data

Time administrators can quickly enter, edit, and review time data for their employees. This could be as simple as recording a one-day attendance of a training course or editing the cost assignment for a piece of work that has been completed. TMWP is designed to ensure that all aspects of data administration can be performed as quickly and as simply as possible. The availability of copy-and-paste, drag-and-drop, and drill-down controls improve the speed and flexibility of the tool.

Enter data for one employee or a group, by day or by week

Time administrators can choose to enter multiple pieces of time recording for a single employee, for example, completing a weeks' worth of time recording for one employee. Alternatively, they can edit multiple employees' data all at once, for example, entering the whole teams' time recording for a whole day on a single screen.

The amount of information displayed and entered can be determined by time administrators. If they prefer to see all of the time recording detail (day, start time, end time, break time, duration, position, cost center or costing assignment) in a single line, they can do that. If they only need basic information, they can tailor the view to their own requirements. Users can drill down into screens from summary annual views, right down to individual time recordings. Because TMWP is fully integrated with the rest of the SAP ERP HCM functions, all of the employees' information is also available on the screen. Users can check an individual employees' position, employee group, and planned working time without having to switch screens. Figure 7.7 shows a half-day absence entered for an employee in TMWP.

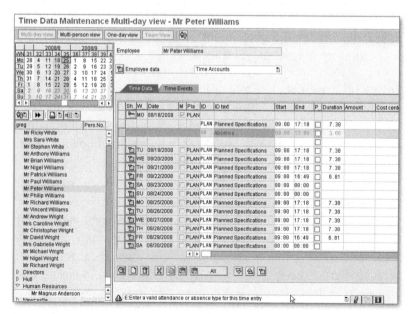

Figure 7.7 Maintaining a Half-Day Absence for an Employee in TMWP

Checking and Monitoring

In addition to entering time data, TMWP is a useful and speedy tool for checking employee data, such as attendance and absence records and quota entitlements. For example, when a manager asks where an employee was on a certain day, the administrator can quickly find the day and check the employees' time recordings for the day. Similarly, if an employee wants to know how much vacation he has left for the remainder of the year or how many sick days he's had this year, he can find this information in one central and up-to-date location.

Providing rapid access to frequently needed key pieces of employee time data

Processing Messages

When Time Evaluation has been run, TMWP presents all of the errors, warnings, and information messages that were generated during the evaluation process for each of the employees being administered. The messages for the employees can then be viewed in TMWP, and the related data is automatically displayed, allowing changes and corrections to be instantly made to the data, ready for reprocessing by Time Evaluation.

Some examples of Time Evaluation messages that could be displayed are warnings that an "employee is not at work" when they are expected to be or notifying you that the employee is "at work on a public holiday" when not expected to be. These messages can then be reviewed and addressed where appropriate, and any required changes to the data can be made in the same screen and saved instantly.

Incentive Wages

If your company rewards employees or groups based on production output figures measured in terms of time spent, quality or quantity of work, or piecework rates, then Incentive Wages can be used to automate much of the related processing.

Manage piecework and project-, quality-, and time-related payments automatically

Incentive Wages uses individual employee or group production figures transferred from the Logistics component and evaluates these results against specified targets and goals to allocate the appropriate rewards for employees or groups. This information can then be evaluated and turned into payments by payroll.

The Logistics Component

The Logistics component is used to process and handle the details of an operation such as order processing or delivery. The Logistics component is broken into the following subcomponents:

Materials Management

Plant Maintenance

Production Planning

Production Processing

Quality Management

Sales and Distribution

Service Management

Warehouse Management

Processing Options

Incentive Wages can be used to process any combination of the following types of standard incentive wages calculations:

> **Piecework wages**
  Payment made based on the number of units produced.

> **Time wages**
  The amount of time spent completing a set job.

> **Quality or quantity wages**
  Known in SAP ERP HCM as *premium wages*, these are used when payment is based on the quality or quantity of the work completed.

These calculation methods can then be applied to either individuals, groups, or a combination of both. The raw data for these calculations is stored as *time tickets*, which are recording and maintenance documents for Incentive Wages data. Information concerning work performed and to be compensated is stored on the time tickets. We will now look at the different types of time tickets used for individual and group calculations.

Individual Calculations

These are used when incentive wages are applied to an employee based solely on the employees' own performance:

> **Premium time tickets**
> Time tickets are created to store information relating to the employee's quantity or quality of work completed over a set period of time compared to expected quantity and quality levels.

> **Time-based time tickets**
> These are created to record the actual time taken to complete a task. This is then used to build a picture of the average processing times for the employee and compare actual versus average processing times.

Group Calculations

Many companies calculate incentive wages based on the performance of work groups. These groups can be defined ahead of time and then adjusted at the time recording (for example, to allow for substitutions). The work of all of the individual members of the group is then anonymously aggregated into a group figure that is used to calculate the incentive wages. The following types of calculations can be used for groups of employees:

Calculate incentive wages for individuals and employees

> **Quantity time tickets**
> The actual amounts of time taken by individual employees to complete tasks are compared to the target times for the tasks for the period. The success of the entire group in meeting or exceeding the group targets are then evaluated.

> **Person time tickets**
> The incentives are determined by comparing the actual times of the group to the target times for the group. The individual times of the group members are then multiplied by the group result, and each member is remunerated with his percentage of the group result.

> **Foremen time tickets**
> These time tickets are useful when you have a foreman or team leader who though not actually responsible for physical production is to be included in the calculation of incentive wages. Foremen

time tickets can be assigned to both individual and group remuneration, thus allowing the foremen to be remunerated on two separate bases: their own performance and their teams' performance.

Sources of Data

Source data directly from Production Planning, Logistics, and other components to aid automatic calculations

The Incentive Wages function is mainly used by companies that also use one or more of the Logistics subcomponents to control their Production Planning, Production Control, Plant Maintenance, and Project Systems. You can use incentive wages without implementing Logistics, but it is most commonly used with Logistics because it allows for the automatic generation of production figures.

The input data can come from plant data collection systems. It can be loaded directly into the Logistics component or entered into Time Management and then stored in the form of time tickets. These dual entry methods are very useful when some of the time has been missed in Logistics and only picked up by the time administrator.

Processing Incentive Wages

The Incentive Wages function takes the raw results from Logistics and stores them as different types of time tickets. Time tickets are then picked up by Time Evaluation and evaluated based on the rules defined by the company. For example, employees could be paid for each unit they produce, or a bonus could be paid for every 100 units produced by a group of employees within a specified time frame.

Output and Integration

Once evaluated by Time Evaluation, the time tickets are calculated in payroll, and the monetary amounts are allocated to the different production figures and individuals or groups of employees.

Shift Planning

Shift Planning allows you to quickly create rosters and schedules to meet your ever-changing demands

The *Shift Planning* function has been part of the SAP ERP HCM solution for many years. Shift Planning focuses on ensuring that you can find the right employees to meet your company's demands. And

used with the increasing integration of the SAP Customer Relationship Management (CRM) component, customers who need access to current sales figures and demand projections to predict and model workforce demands are utilizing the Workforce Deployment component to manage their workforce planning. Of course, customers who do not need this type of integrated information to perform their shift planning can still use traditional Shift Planning. You can find out more about the Workforce Deployment components at *www.sap.com*.

Before SAP CRM made measuring and predicting demand a more exact science, it was difficult to match your business requirements to your staffing levels. So this process was traditionally performed based on a mix of experience and luck. With the *Shift Planning* function you can bring a bit more science to your resource planning, allowing you to quickly find the types of employees your company requires to meet its operational needs. Shift Planning also allows you to create every conceivable planning scenario your company may face, model staffing plans to meet those needs, and measure their impacts.

Processing Options

Shift Planning gives you the chance to create shift planning scenarios, and then using the integrated functionality from Time Evaluation, your planners can run a simulated evaluation of the impacts of the scenario. Once a shift planner is happy with a shift plan, the status of the plan is defined as the *target plan*. This plan is then finalized and will remain unaltered. Of course, minor adjustments can be made to the plan. These changes are reflected in a second version of the plan, known as the *actual plan*.

Sources of Data

Using strong integration with the other SAP ERP HCM function, shift planners can take into account qualifications requirements for their plans and find suitably qualified employees. Shift Planning can check employees' daily work schedules and see if they are available to be rostered on the days required or if they are on leave or have called in sick. Because there is only one source for all of this employee data,

Use detailed profiles to match your employees to the right shifts

shift planners are guaranteed to always see the most up-to-date and current data every time they look.

Similarly, changes to rostering performed in Shift Planning are instantly available to all of the other users of the SAP ERP HCM system, so managers can see their employee's roster changes, and employees can see their own rosters instantly on Employee Self-Service.

Performing Shift Planning

The *Requirements Matchup function* allows you to schedule employees' shifts and working times according to your needs. You can define *personnel requirements*, which represent individual requirements within your company. The personnel requirements list the following information:

> The organizational unit that has the open requirement

> The shift to be filled and the working times of the shift

> The job description of the role to be filled

> The qualifications required to fulfill the requirements profile

Figure 7.8 shows Shift Planning being used to define requirements for a day.

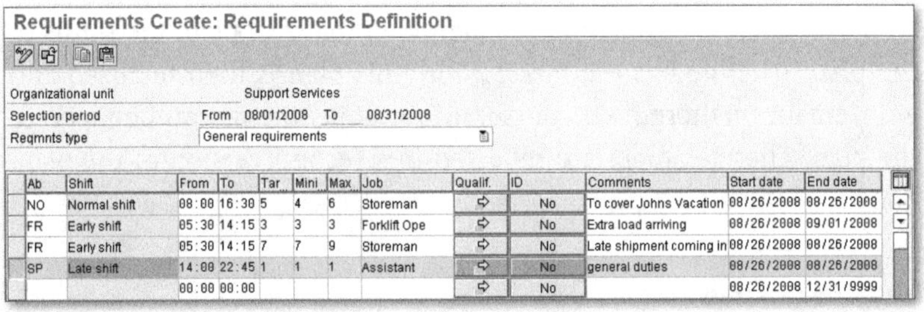

Requirements Create: Requirements Definition

Organizational unit			Support Services									
Selection period		From	08/01/2008	To	08/31/2008							
Reqmnts type			General requirements									

Ab	Shift	From	To	Tar	Mini	Max	Job	Qualif.	ID	Comments	Start date	End date
NO	Normal shift	08:00	16:30	5	4	6	Storeman	⇨	No	To cover Johns Vacation	08/26/2008	08/26/2008
FR	Early shift	05:30	14:15	3	3	3	Forklift Ope	⇨	No	Extra load arriving	08/26/2008	09/01/2008
FR	Early shift	05:30	14:15	7	7	9	Storeman	⇨	No	Late shipment coming in	08/26/2008	08/26/2008
SP	Late shift	14:00	22:45	1	1	1	Assistant	⇨	No	general duties	08/26/2008	08/26/2008
		00:00	00:00					⇨	No		08/26/2008	12/31/9999

Figure 7.8 Defining the Required Resources for a Day Through Shift Planning

Automatically match employees to shifts based on defined criteria

The *Proposal Determination feature* is a utility for matching employees to personnel requirements automatically. This feature can take into account location, qualifications, planned working hours, and seniority. It creates proposed matches based on the requirements and available employees. The shift planner can then accept the proposed employees or assign his own selections.

If a suitable employee cannot be found within the available resources, the shift planner can use the *Assignment Assistant* to request a temporary transfer of a qualified employee from another part of the company.

The integration of Shift Planning and Time Evaluation means that shift planners can instantly see the impact on employees of their proposed shift plan. This includes the ability to see the total number of hours that will need to be paid during the plan, including overtime and bonuses, and the effects on employee leave quotas. The shift planner can keep running scenarios until he is happy with the results, in terms of providing resources to the company and in terms of the costs and impacts on employees.

> Use scenario planning to model potential shift plans and measure their impacts and costs

Once the shift plan has been finalized, it can be printed for distribution, and employees can check their shift plans online using Employee Self-Service.

Output and Integration

Changes to shift plans are instantly updated in all of the employees' master data records. Changes to working hours are, therefore, instantly reflected, and other HR users will see the changes as soon as they are made.

When an employee's costs need to be allocated to a different area, for example, if the employee was brought in from a different team to cover an emergency, the costs of the employee can be automatically allocated to the temporary team through Shift Planning. This cost allocation will be processed through payroll and posted automatically to finance.

> Shift schedules are instantly updated in employee data, so everyone can see it instantly

Time Evaluation

Time Evaluation is best thought of as a calculation engine similar to the payroll process. It is the final step in the Time Time and Attendance process. It takes into account all of the functions we have looked at in this chapter and evaluates the information they provide. It starts off by looking at the different types of employees that have been defined for the company and collecting information on how each group

> Time Evaluation automates all of your complex time calcualtions and evaluations

should be processed — who should be paid hourly, who is entitled to overtime, who gets 10 days of paid holidays, and who gets 20 days. It then looks at the company's calendars, evaluating all of the days for the period to see if they are working days, public holidays with extra payments, or shutdown periods. It then uses all of these rules and calculations to evaluate the employee working times entered in CATS and adjusted in TMWP.

Time Evaluation compares planned versus actual working time and interprets this data according to your company rules. It processes time tickets from Incentive Wages and calculates the piecework rates and production bonuses based on production figures. Shift Planning adjustments are taken into account, and working hours are adjusted; overtime hours are calculated, and absences and attendances included. All of this information is evaluated to create *time wage types* that are then used in payroll to calculate the employees' pay for the pay period.

Time Evaluation integrates data from all of the other parts of Time and Attendance

Because of the complex requirements that customers define regarding their time and attendance rules, Time Evaluation is one of the most complex parts of SAP ERP HCM. To better understand Time Evaluation, we will look first at the processing options for Time Evaluation, the processing options you can choose, where it gets its data, how it processes the data, and where this data goes after it is processed. Finally, we will look at the reporting options for Time Evaluation data.

Processing Options

Most companies implement Time Evaluation using one of the following two types of processing. Some companies with large and complex workforces implement both types of Time Evaluation.

Time Evaluation without Clock Times

Also known as positive Time Evaluation, this method is used when all time data for an employee needs to be recorded to generate results. In this method of Time Evaluation, if no time data was recorded for a working day, the employee would have no clock entries, and thus no wage types generated and eventually no pay.

Let's go through a quick example to illustrate how this works.

 Example

> The employee clocks in at 10:52 a.m. and clocks out again at 11:27 p.m.
>
> The Time Evaluation rules for his department state that employees can start or finish their shifts within 10 minutes of their planned start or end time without any change in pay. Our employee is entitled to a 15-minute paid break every 3 hours and a 30-minute unpaid lunch break every shift. The first eight hours of work are paid at the normal rate. The first two hours of work after the first eight are paid at time and half. Any hours beyond 10 in a day are paid at triple time. If a shift starts after 10:30 a.m. but before 3:00 p.m., employees are entitled to a late-start shift payment.
>
> You simply record employee start and end times and leave the rest up to Time Evaluation. Time Evaluation will produce the following time wage types for our employee:
>
> Normal hours   8.00
>
> Overtime @ 1.5   2.00
>
> Overtime @ 3.0   1.45
>
> Late Start Shift Allow   1.00

These results will then be processed by payroll to generate the payment amounts based on the figures payroll calculates for the employee's hourly rate and the preset amount for late-shift allowance.

Time Evaluation with Clock Times

Clock times (also known as negative time reporting) are used when we assume the employee has worked his normal planned working hours according to his work schedule, and we only adjust his pay according to clock times that are entered for the day. Time wage types are produced on the basis of both the planned work schedule and the exceptions. If an employee is scheduled to work 40 hours per week and no time data is recorded, the employee is still paid for those 40 hours. If, however, extra hours were recorded for a day or an unpaid absence is recorded, the employee's normal pay may be increased or decreased.

Sources of Data

Integrate time data
from both SAP and
non-SAP systems

Depending on your company's requirements, Time Evaluation can get time data from a variety of sources. We have already looked at some of the sources including CATS timesheets, TMWP, Incentive Wages, and Shift Planning. Some other common sources of Time Evaluation data are:

> **Third-party time-recording systems**
> If your company already has a time-recording, -clocking, -punching system, this can be interfaced into Time and Attendance to be used in Time Evaluation. SAP ERP provides a certified interfacing program called the HR-PDC interface. This interface was developed with clocking systems in mind, and over 60 clocking machine systems are certified for interfacing into Time and Attendance.

> **Web applications**
> Similar to CATS, employee time data can be entered, edited, and approved via the Enterprise Portal for instant processing in Time Evaluation.

> **Time and HR administrators**
> Data can be entered by dedicated time administrators or by your HR team members. This information can be input via CATS, entered into the TMWP, or entered directly into the Employee Administration function.

Evaluating the Time Data

Time Evaluation uses a schema very similar to the payroll schema; it also uses rules and functions to control the processing. Time Evaluation can be run as an overnight job or executed manually. It can be run for a single employee, for all employees, or for any group of employees that the administrator chooses.

Automate
calculations and
build processing
logic for every time
scenario anywhere
in your company

It can be run in test mode for evaluation purposes and then run in real mode to create real Time Evaluation results. As with SAP ERP HCM payroll, Time Evaluation can be run as many times as required to get the results right, and can be run for past periods, ensuring that all changes in previous periods are brought into the current period for processing.

Time Evaluation enables you to automatically accrue absence entitlements (for example, time off in lieu) dependent on an employee's actual working times.

To help you ensure that your Time Evaluation results are correct, it issues messages when specific situations occur, for example, if an employee's working times fall outside working time regulations. As with payroll, you can define your own messages for any situation that is required in your company. You can also make corrections (through TMWP) and rerun Time Evaluation as many times as necessary to get the results as you require. Figure 7.9 shows the Time Evaluation log for an employee.

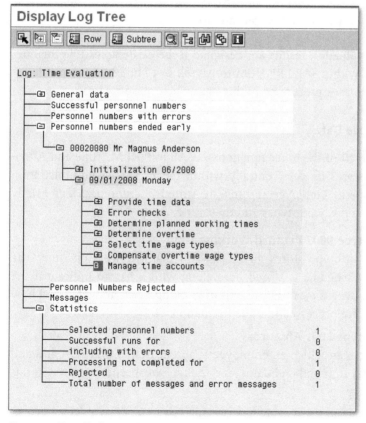

Figure 7.9 Time Evaluation Processing Log

Output and Integration

Time Evaluation (like payroll) stores its results in *clusters*. Clusters can be read by standard and custom reports and SAP internal reporting tools, are available for interrogation by SAP NetWeaver BI, and, most important, are interrogated as part of the payroll process.

There are four Time Evaluation clusters:

> **ZL** contains all of the time wage types.

> **C1** contains the information on cost assignment for the working times.

> **AB** contains details of employee absences during the period.

> **ALP** is used to store information on different payments, for example, when substitutions are used.

Time Evaluation results are designed to be easily accessible for integration within SAP ERP HCM to payroll or to be readily available for extraction for processing in third-party payroll software.

Employee Data

As with all of the other functions in SAP ERP HCM, Time and Attendance stores its data centrally within the Personnel Administration component. Employee records are stored in infotypes, let's briefly look at the key infotypes and their uses:

> **Infotype 0007 Planned Working Time**
This infotype stores an employee's planned working time. The work schedule is stored here along with a flag to indicate if the employee is part time, details of working hours and days, and how they are processed in Time Evaluation.

> **Infotype 2001 Absences**
Periods in which an employee is absent from work, start and end times, start and end dates, and the type of absence is stored in this infotype.

> **Infotype 2002 Attendances**
> If employees are required to record all of their working times, their attendances at work are stored here.

> **Infotype 2003 Substitutions**
> When an employee deviates from his planned working time, this is recorded here. Information regarding the working time can be stored, including information created if a substitution generates a different payment rule.

> **Infotype 2004 Availability**
> This infotype is used to record an employee's availability for work outside his normal working pattern, for example, for on-call duties.

> **Infotype 2005 Overtime**
> When an employee works overtime, it is stored here. Start and end times of overtime and the type of overtime can also be stored here.

> **Infotype 2006 Absence Quotas**
> Entitlement balances for annual leave, Time Off in Lieu of Leave (TOIL), and unpaid and paid absences are stored here. You can view an employee's remaining leave balances on this infotype.

> **Infotype 0416 Time Quota Compensation**
> When an employee has unused quota balances remaining, they can be automatically paid out via payroll. This payment is triggered by an entry in this infotype.

> **Infotype 2007 Attendance Quotas**
> When employees are given entitlement quotas for work-related attendances such as training or overtime, the balances of entitlement are stored here.

> **Infotype 2010 EE Remuneration Info**
> When time recording is required that is not covered by any of the other time infotypes, it is entered here. This could include hazardous work payments or irregular bonuses.

> **Infotype 2011 Time Events**
> Time entries such as clock in and out times received from clock-ing machines and third-party clocking systems are stored in this infotype.

> **Infotype 2012 Time Transfer Specifications**
> When adjustments need to be made to an employee's Time Evalu-ation balances, they are stored here.

> **Infotype 2013 Quota Corrections**
> Time Evaluation calculates and adjusts absence and attendance quotas. If necessary, these figures can be overwritten through this infotype.

Reporting

The reporting tools match the wide variety of reporting requirements needed for effective time management

As with all of the other parts of SAP ERP HCM, the design of the Time and Attendance function enables reporting to be simple and straight-forward. The use of infotypes to store employee data and clusters to store Time Evaluation results ensures that Time and Attendance data can be quickly reported on with a wide variety of standard reports. Two custom reporting tools give users the ability to quickly create and save their own report layouts. As with all other functions, the data from Time and Attendance can also be reported on from the Business Warehouse component, allowing integrated cross-component report building.

As we saw in the CATS section, CATS provides users with a full suite of reporting and monitoring tools to ensure that you can quickly check the progress of your employee time recording, and, when needed, adjust and correct the values.

TMWP is solely designed to speed up and centralize the time-record-ing process. It contains many reports that allow time administrators to monitor time-recording entries, correct Time Evaluation errors, and report on the results.

Although Time Evaluation is really just one step in a larger process—ensuring that employees are paid correctly—it is still important that you can report on the results of Time Evaluation processing. Time

Evaluation uses a tool called a *time statement* to provide users with a summary form of Time Evaluation results.

The time statement is much like a payslip. It provides you with a fully configurable form to display the results of Time Evaluation that you consider important. Different versions of the time statement can be created for different audiences, including a very technical version for your time administrators, providing them with all of the information regarding an employee's results, and a simple summary of Time Evaluation results for employees to view via Employee Self-Service. Some examples of information that can be displayed on a time statement include:

> Daily start and finish times from clocking machines

> Wage type totals for normal, overtime, and other payments

> Bonuses achieved within the period

> Information on cost assignment

> Leave balances and quotas such as vacation and sick pay

It is important to note that the Time Evaluation results do not include monetary values. Turning these into monetary values is the responsibility of the Payroll component. Time Evaluation only calculates the hours and units for employees based on their time recording.

Integration

There are numerous integration points between the Time and Attendance functions that ensure that your data is always up to date, that duplication and double entry are avoided, and that all system users can report on the information they need in an efficient and timely manner. We will now look at some of the main integration points between Time and Attendance and other parts of SAP ERP.

Strong integration solves duplicate data entry, storage, and interface issues

> **Personnel Administration**
One of the great advantages of Time and Attendance and its integration with Personnel Administration is that the data you see in Time and Attendance is actually being instantly stored in Personnel Administration. This central storage of data works both ways. HR

administrators can see employee absences such as holidays or sickness the moment they are entered into the software, and time administrators instantly see the most up-to-date version of employee data. Changes in positions and departments and new hires and terminations are instantly updated in, ensuring that everyone sees the most recent data instantly.

> **Organizational Management**
Being able to see the whole company graphically in Time and Attendance helps time administrators quickly manage their employees. Administrators can view employees and their organizational assignments, instantly view reporting hierarchies, and determine the right manager to talk to when time recording problems arise. Similarly, when employees are reassigned within the company, their changes in location, employee groupings, and working hours are instantly and seamlessly reflected in the Time and Attendance data.

> **Payroll**
Probably the most important aspect of the Time and Attendance integration points, the seamless integration between this function and payroll is one of the great labor saving aspects of SAP ERP HCM. When a time administrator performs any sort of time adjustment for an employee, this change will be automatically picked up by Time Evaluation and passed onto payroll, or if your company does not run Time Evaluation, the changes will be automatically picked up by payroll and included in the next payroll run.

> **Controlling**
Finance uses the Controlling function to monitor costs across the company. Through Payroll, Time and Attendance sends information regarding the costing allocation of employee working times, such as time allocated to production orders, and process orders, sales document items, and cost object IDs. Controlling can also receive information relating to statistical key figures such as kilometers travelled for costing purposes.

> **Plant Maintenance and Customer Service**
The Plant Maintenance function is used to monitor maintenance on technical facilities such as machinery and hardware. You can use CATS to transfer employees' hours allocated to plant maintenance

and customer service tasks, for example, time allocated to maintenance or service orders and goods movements.

> **Project Systems and Collaboration Projects (cProjects)**
If your company uses the Project Systems or cProjects to manage large and technical projects, you can use CATS to allocate employee time to the key units of your projects' systems such as work breakdown structures and individual activities that are used to track projects.

> **Materials Management**
Materials Management is an SAP ERP component used for managing both the procurement process and inventory management. Within CATS time recordings, employee time can be allocated to sending purchase orders, and within those orders, individual items of the purchase orders can be allocated.

> **Logistics**
The production and sales results stored in the Logistics component are a key part of Incentive Wages calculation and processing. Production figures, team results, and sales figures can all be transferred into Time and Attendance for inclusion in the Incentive Wages calculations.

Well as we said at the beginning of the chapter, Time and Attendance is the largest function in SAP ERP HCM, so we covered a lot of information in this chapter. At this point, it would be helpful to take a look at a company that is actually using it, so let's move on to our case study about a European Automobile Manufacturer who needed to realign and standardize their HR, time management, and payroll processes.

Case Study

Table 7.3 provides a quick overview of the case study before we explain it in more detail.

Company	European Automobile Manufacturer
Existing Solutions	Legacy HR and payroll systems
Challenges	> Realign and standardize HR, time management, and payroll processes > Shift decision-making responsibility to business units > Reduce processing time for key processes
SAP Solutions	SAP ERP HCM including Time Management
Benefits	> Optimized and standardized HR, time management, and payroll processes > Eliminated multiple interfaces to streamline data management process > Empowered business reps to make staffing decisions locally

Table 7.3 Time Management Case Study

This large automobile maker based in Germany has over 120,000 employees and 75,000 pensioners on their HR system. The company is famous for its flexible working conditions (with over 10,000 separate work schedules), and it has impressive production statistics.

The Challenges

With a large workforce and numerous 24-hour production facilities, the company needed a solution that could replace the legacy HR and payroll systems, replace numerous interfaces, and unify them into one core integrated solution. The company also had to provide for its famously flexible working conditions, allowing both the company to meet its production requirements and employees to keep their right to flexible working arrangements.

The SAP Solution

During a project lasting nearly two years the company implemented the whole SAP ERP HCM suite of applications, including Time and Attendance and TMWP. The new solution has nearly 8,000 users across the HR, payroll, and time management departments.

The Benefits

The new fully integrated solution processes over 750,000 transactions per day. By creating a fully integrated solution the company removed many interfaces and sped up and increased the quality of data in the system.

TMWP allowed the company to move its entire time sheet entry process out of a centralized department to the production plants.

Even with so many employees, the company can meet all of its time recording, absence, and attendance management requirements through Time and Attendance.

Conclusion

Time and Attendance is a large and complex function. It is capable of developing solutions ranging from automatically calculating how to pay maternity pay to part-time casual employees to integrating production figures from Plant Maintenance into calculations of incentive wages. Some important points to remember from this chapter include:

> Time and Attendance is a highly developed function giving companies access to a powerful set of tools for grouping employees and defining time-recording and calculation requirements, speeding up data input and error checking, planning resource requirements, and, possibly most important, automating complex calculations.

> Companies need to spend a lot of time confirming their requirements before embarking on a Time and Attendance implementation. Defining your requirements in terms of grouping employees and documenting how your company calculates all of its time-related data is a large task.

> Once this task is completed, your company can benefit from time-saving tools such as CATS that allow you to move responsibility for

time recording to employees and the responsibility for approvals to the managers.

> The Time Manager's Workplace (TMWP) gives your time administrators an easy-to-learn and simple tool to enable them to quickly and efficiently manage all aspects of time recording.

> Time Evaluation brings all of this data together, enabling your company to automatically calculate employee time data. Taking results from clocking machines, it can automatically determine how many standard hours, overtime hours, paid and unpaid breaks, and late start penalties each employee should receive. Using your employee groupings allows you to develop completely different calculations for each part of your business.

In the next chapter we will see how all of this time data is processed and turned into employee payroll results and key data for finance and other departments to use.

8

Payroll and Legal Reporting

Payroll is often the largest single expense for a company, so ensuring that your company's payroll is handled efficiently and legally is always a top priority.

Because many companies look at centralizing, globalizing, and outsourcing their HR and payroll departments, the focus on streamlining and automating the payroll processes to create efficiencies and ensure accuracy is becoming increasingly important. Large multiple-country payroll solutions incorporating highly mobile global employees and the complex legal, statutory, and organizational reporting requirements that come with globalization are also becoming more common—and more and more complex.

Based on these evolving demands, the SAP ERP HCM payroll solution is continually being refined to ensure that it keeps up to date with ever-evolving organizational and legislative demands.

Within the SAP ERP HCM Payroll component, legal reporting is also delivered as a country-specific solution tailored to the requirements for each country supported by the payroll solution. The SAP ERP HCM Payroll solution ensures that the software is legally and statutorily compliant in the way that it processes and pays employees and that it provides the required interfaces and reports so that the company can produce the necessary reports when required by local laws.

In this chapter we will give you an overview of the concepts behind the payroll solution along with an overview of the SAP ERP HCM legal reporting capabilities. Although these two areas are grouped together by SAP, in practice they are generally quite separate processes, payroll being the much larger portion of the solution. So the chapter has been divided into two sections: Payroll and Legal Reporting.

Let's begin with Payroll.

How the SAP ERP HCM Payroll Solution Fits into an Enterprise

As anyone who gets a pay check will tell you, ensuring that people are paid correctly and on time is a top priority for all companies, so the payroll system is always going to be close to the heart (and possibly the wallet) of any company.

Where the SAP ERP HCM payroll function differentiates itself from other standalone payroll systems is that when a company has the full suite of SAP components, the number of automatic and standard data flows going into and out of the payroll system can be quite staggering.

A Closer Look at the SAP ERP HCM Payroll Function

The SAP ERP HCM Payroll function supports all of the processes required to remunerate all of the different types of employees you have in your company. Like any other payroll system, the payroll function takes the various payroll inputs and uses the information to calculate the gross and net payments and deductions for an employee for a pay period. The results are then posted to finance, transferred to the employee, and made available for reporting, and interfaces are triggered to various parties as required.

So let's talk about the various inputs you have to consider during payroll processing (Figure 8.1).

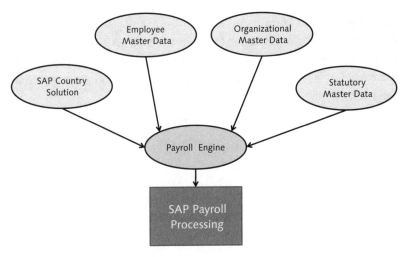

Figure 8.1 Inputs into SAP Payroll Processing

SAP Country Solutions

SAP supplies and supports payroll solutions for over 50 countries and has partnerships with local companies to offer payroll solutions for many other countries. The list of countries currently supported is constantly growing as SAP expands its coverage. However, even if a country is not included in these standard solutions, you can still process payroll for the country in SAP ERP HCM, but keep in mind that the amount of work required to set up, maintain, and support the custom solution will be more than for a standard solution.

Payroll solutions for over 50 countries

Payroll Inputs

Three key types of data are required to process payroll in SAP ERP HCM:

> Employee master data

> Organizational master data

> Statutory master data

All key employee data is sourced from related and fully integrated components

We will look at all three of these areas to see what is required for SAP ERP HCM payroll processing and how they are used.

Employee Master Data

Based on your employee data stored in the SAP ERP HCM Personnel Administration function, Payroll uses information stored in infotypes as a basis for the processing and calculation of payroll. This information normally includes the following:

> **Employee's personal details including**
> - Name
> - Age
> - Gender
> - Address

> **Employee's work details**
> - Employing organization
> - Position in organization
> - Payroll area and frequency
> - Contracted working days and hours

> **Employee's payment and deduction information**
> - Salary or wage details, for example, annual salary or hourly rate. Figure 8.2 shows Infotype 0008, where salary and wage data is stored.
> - Recurring and one-time payments, for example, meal allowances and annual bonus payment. Figure 8.3 shows examples of payments and deductions assigned to an employee.
> - Recurring and one-time deductions, for example, union dues and social club membership fees.
> - Pension or voluntary social security contributions.

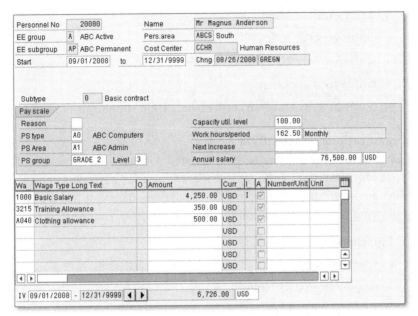

Figure 8.2 Infotpye 0008 Basic Pay

Personnel No	20080		Name	Mr Magnus Anderson		
EE group	A	ABC Active	Pers.area	ABCS	South	
EE subgroup	AP	ABC Permanent	Cost Center	CCHR		Human Resources
Choose	01/01/1800	to	12/31/9999	STy.		

Wage type	Wage Type Long Text	From	To	O	Amount	Crcy	Number/	U	L
A050	Luncheon vouchers	09/01/2008	12/31/9999		0.00	USD	10.00	Day	
D010	Union dues	09/01/2008	12/31/9999	A	25.00	USD	0.00		
D020	Sports and social club	09/01/2008	12/31/9999	A	35.00	USD	0.00		

Figure 8.3 Recurring Payment and Deduction Wage Types on Infotype 0014

> **Time recording information**

- Work schedule, planned working hours for the employee for the pay period

- Attendances including actual worked hours, start and end times, in-house training courses attended

- Absences (e.g., vacation, sickness, unpaid leave)

> **Statutory Information**

- Employees tax code
- Social Security/National Insurance number
- Employee's tax office
- Garnishments and court orders, e.g., child support

Organizational Master Data

Organizational data is key for making correct calculation decisions

For your employees' pay to be calculated correctly, the structure of your organization and the organizational rules for payments and deductions need to be configured in the system. This can include the following type of information that will be set up in your SAP system:

> **Enterprise structure**

- Legal entities
- Organizational divisions
- Types of employees
- Organizational reporting requirements

> **Payroll length and frequency**

- Payroll periods
- Pay days and pay day rules
- Specific *payroll area*

> **Salary and Wage information**

- Rules regarding pay bands and levels
- Payment and deduction calculation
- Overtime and extra payment rules
- Part-period calculation logic

Statutory Master Data

All of the legal and statutory information the system needs to calculate taxes and deductions correctly

When the Payroll solution offers a standard country solution, all of the legal and statutory requirements for processing payroll for employees in that country are stored in the software. This information varies from country to country but typically includes the following information either delivered by SAP or configured as part of the implementation process:

> **Labor laws**

- Rules and calculation logic for minimum and maximum working hours, work duration, and other working time regulations

- Rules for minimum wages or annual salary

- Sickness, maternity, and absence payment logic

> **Taxes and garnishments**

- Calculation logic for local, state, and federal taxes

- Calculation logic for the processing of court orders, child support, and other employee garnishments

> **Employee Benefits**

- Retirement fund and pension contribution calculation rules

- Employee medical contribution calculation rules

- School fees and other employee benefits paid via payroll

If a standard country solution you need is not offered, you'll need to include the required configuration and processing logic to enable statutory processing during your SAP ERP HCM Payroll implementation.

Building an SAP ERP HCM Payroll solution effectively from scratch is usually a very large task and should be undertaken only with careful consideration. Often it's not practical to develop a custom payroll solution for a non-standard country because the ongoing overheads of maintaining the solution, for example, providing for changes to tax laws, are too large for a single organization to bear. In these cases SAP ERP HCM can still be used to process the gross part of payroll (which is often less country specific), and the gross payroll results can then be transferred via an interface to a third-party supplier for the calculation of net payroll. SAP provides the *Payroll Interface Toolbox* to enable the design and execution of interfaces of payroll results to third-party suppliers.

The Payroll Interface Toolbox helps you quickly create complex payroll interfaces

Now that you have an understanding of the key inputs to the SAP ERP HCM Payroll system, we'll look at the processing engine.

The Payroll Engine

The payroll engine takes all of these payroll inputs and processes them according to your national and regional legislation and your company's own payroll rules.

A payroll engine is provided for each country, enabling totally separate national solutions

The SAP ERP HCM payroll processing logic is based on a country-specific payroll driver that is used to determine the required payroll processing logic. The payroll driver is configured via a *schema* and sets of *functions, operations,* and *rules.* The schema gives the payroll system a structure, and the rules and associated operations and functions are used to perform the calculations required to determine the employees' net pay as illustrated in Figure 8.4.

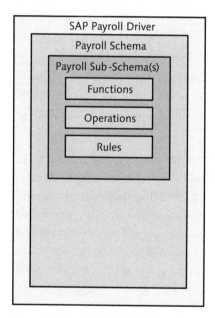

Figure 8.4 The SAP ERP HCM Payroll Engine

Payroll Schema

An organization running an SAP ERP HCM Payroll system will generally have just one schema per payroll country. However, when an organization has very diverse sets of rules and requirements across geographical or organizational processing units within a single country, then multiple schemas may be required. The maintenance of multiple schemas for a country leads to larger overhead for ongoing maintenance.

> **Functions**
> The schema uses functions to access and interpret payroll inputs from employee, organizational, and statutory data. A schema has numerous functions built into it.
>
> An example of the processing of a function is the determination of an employee's correct tax basis, taking into account such things as the employee's age, location, marital status, and other disparate pieces of information.

> **Rules**
> Rules are used for the actual mathematical calculation of employee payments and deductions. They are the finest level of processing granularity and allow very specific calculations to be made based on a wide range of data.
>
> An example of a calculation processed by a rule is the amount of salary to reduce an employee's pay in a period when the employee has taken unpaid leave for a week in the period.

> **Operations**
> An operation is a small piece of code for processing specific logic. An operation can be called within a function or a rule. It gives the schema the ability to process more complex calculations requiring specific coding.
>
> An example of an operation is to create the employees' hourly rates by dividing their annual salaries by their normal working hours.

Payroll Periods

The SAP ERP HCM Payroll solution uses the term *payroll period*, to identify different payroll durations. The duration of a payroll period can be weekly, fortnightly, monthly, lunar monthly, quarterly, or whatever duration the client requires.

Payroll Areas

The *payroll area* is a further definition of a company's payroll. A payroll area is defined by a set payroll period (for example, monthly), by its payday (the day employees in the payroll area are paid every period), and by the legal entity that the payroll area represents. Figure 8.5 shows an example payroll area with its assigned payroll periods.

Many companies require a range of payroll periods and payroll areas to represent the different payroll frequencies, pay day rules, and legal entities that make up their company.

Now that we have seen the key inputs to the SAP ERP HCM Payroll solution and the key parts that make up the payroll engine, let's look at the most important payroll outputs.

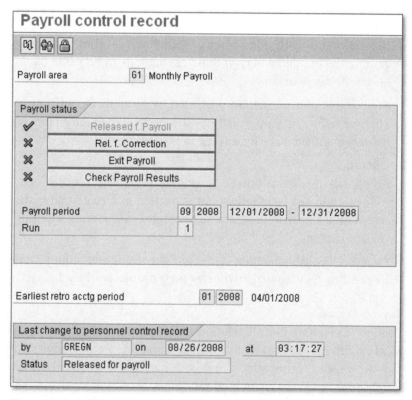

Figure 8.5 Payroll Control Record for a Monthly Payroll

Payroll Outputs

Once payroll has been run, the employees' final payroll results are stored as *wage types* in the *payroll clusters*. This information is then used to create a file to transfer the employees' pay to the bank and to transfer the results to the finance system. Let's look at each of these outputs.

Wage Types

These are effectively buckets for storing the amount, rates, and numbers relating to individual payments and deductions. Wage types are identified by a four-digit code (either alpha or numeric) and a long text name field.

Wage types – a key concept in the SAP ERP HCM payroll solution

Wage types are divided into two groups: SAP standard and customer specific. The SAP standard wage types include some example wage types but are mainly used for storing results from the more technical parts of payroll processing. Some examples of SAP standard wage types are:

> /001 Employee Hourly Rate

> /010 Daily Rate

> /100 Monthly Rate

> /501 Tax Paid

The names and numbers for customer wage types are customer dependent, allowing them to be tailored to individual customers' needs. Some examples of customer wage types to illustrate the concept are:

> 1000 Salary

> 2010 Overtime @ 1.5

> 3000 Union Deduction

Clusters

Payroll results including wage types are stored in objects called payroll clusters. These can be read by custom reports, SAP standard reports,

Clusters store results for later processing, access, and storage

and reporting tools available for interrogation by SAP NetWeaver Business Intelligence (BI) and other reporting interfaces.

There are two payroll cluster data tables:

> **PCL1 clusters** are used for storing master data and time data.

> **PCL2 clusters** store the actual payroll results for the employee. These are stored as wage types in the payroll results tables. Figure 8.6 shows the employee results table for an employee with a selection of customer and SAP standard wage types generated during payroll processing.

```
Settlement Result
Personnel No.     100 Mr Jon Arnolds - United States
Sequential No     00005 - accounted on 07/15/2008 - current result
For-Period        01.2007 (04/01/2007 - 04/30/2007)
In-Period         01.2007 (Fin.: 04/30/2007)

Table RT - Results Table

PCR1Gr Wage salary type              WC  C1 C2 C3  Assign: AltPa  CA  BT Abs.
Var s. Unit      Rate                    Number        Amount

 *      /101 Total gross
                                                              31,727.91
 *      /105 Working net pay
                                                              18,335.13
 *      /111 Pensionable pay
                                                              17,500.00
 *      /121 Taxable pay
                                                              30,827.91
 *      /124 Pre-tax deductions
                                                                 900.00-
 *      /250 Salary summarized
                                                              17,500.00
 *      /501 Tax paid
                                                              11.942.20
 *      /550 Statutory net pay
                                                               4,007.41
 *      1005 Directors' Basic Salary  01
                                                              17,500.00
 *      3000 Bonus                    01
                                                              14,227.91
```

Figure 8.6 Payroll Results Table

Data Medium Exchange File

The *Data Medium Exchange file* (DME file) is the source file used to create a file of the appropriate format to send to a company's bank to generate employee payments. It contains the payment amount and bank details of every employee paid in a period. The DME file is a standard file type generated by the SAP system. This file is then tailored for each SAP ERP HCM payroll country to meet their local data transfer rules and processes.

Posting to Finance

The posting to the finance process is a great example of the integration within SAP ERP. The posting of costing information to the SAP ERP Financials component can be performed as a test run, allowing payroll team members to ensure that when the posting documents are finally transferred into the SAP finance system, they go through with no errors or warnings.

Automatically post payroll results into the finance system

Integration

The numerous standard data flows allowing the movement of data between components are one of the big selling points of SAP systems. To explain the many points of integration, we will break them into incoming and outgoing flows. Some of these flows are not direct into payroll, but occur via another SAP ERP HCM component.

Inbound Integration
> Employee Self-Service to Personnel Administration
  - Changes to personal details including name, address, family members, etc.
> Employee Self- Service to Benefits
  - Employee benefits selection
> Employee Self-Service to Time Management
  - Employee leave requests,
  - Employee time recording
> Manager Self-Service to Personnel Administration
  - Personnel change requests, (e.g., employee organizational reassignments)

> Manager Self-Service to Time Management
  - Approved employee leave requests,
  - Employee attendance data
> Cross Application Time Sheets to Time Management
  - Employee working start and end times
  - Employee breaks
  - Employee costing assignments
  - Payment and deduction information
> Benefits Management to Personnel Administration
  - Employee benefits selections, (e.g., health plans and pension fund selections
> Shift Planning to Time Management
  - Employees' rostered planned working times
> Compensation Management to Personnel Administration
  - Details of incentive reward programs
  - Salary increases and wage rate increases
> Time Management to Time Evaluation
  - Employees' actual working times
  - Absences and attendances
  - Overtime and extra time recording
> Time Evaluation to Payroll
  - Summarized employee time data, ready for payment, including:
    - Normal hours
    - Overtime hours
    - Absence and attendance hours
> Personnel Administration to Payroll
  - Employee master data
  - Organizational assignment data
  - Costing information

Outbound

Once payroll has processed all of the input data, the information is sent out from payroll to the following integrated components.

> Payroll to Finance

- Full posting information for each employee for transfer into relevant financial accounts. This information can be drilled down right to individual payments and deductions, allowing rapid analysis and interpretation.

> Payroll to *Data Medium Exchange* (DME)

- DME is the SAP standard interface generating flat files or XML files for transferring payment information to financial institutions.

> Payroll to Payslips

- Payslips are known in the SAP ERP HCM Payroll system as *remuneration statements*. Payroll can trigger the printing of remuneration statements, the generation of Adobe PDF payslips, the generation of electronic payslips for online viewing through Employee Self-Service, and the generation of print files for external printing.

> Payroll to Legal Reporting

- Payroll stores all of the required information in the payroll clusters for the creation of all necessary legal reports per period, quarterly, annually, or as required.

> Payroll to Internal Reporting

- Either via standard reports, reporting tools, or custom ABAP reports, any reporting requirements can be handles.

> Payroll to external reporting

- Payroll results can be mapped to BI reporting cubes for flexible BI reporting. This enables payroll results to be reported on with SAP ERP Financials or other components' data.

- Other external interfaces and extracts can also draw on the payroll results clusters.

Payroll Process

The SAP ERP HCM payroll process is anchored by the *payroll control record*. Every payroll area has its own payroll control record; this allows separate payroll areas to be processed independently. The payroll control record determines which step in the payroll process is currently being processed and what the overall processing status is.

Steps in the Payroll Process

Table 8.1 lists the steps required to process an SAP ERP HCM Payroll:

Process Step	Description
Data input	The system is open for input, master data changes, and corrections. Data is input into the various SAP ERP HCM components.
Payroll Released	All employee records are effectively locked for editing so the existing information can be used to generate payroll results.
Payroll Run	Payroll is physically processed.
Results Analysis	Using a set of standard reports, payroll results are analyzed; errors and warnings are analyzed to determine solutions.
Released for Correction	Employee records are available for editing, allowing corrections to be made to fix highlighted errors and warnings.
Payroll Run, Analysis, and Correction Loop	These three steps can be repeated as many times as necessary to get the payroll results right.
Generate DME Files	Bank files are generated first in test mode and then checked. If errors are detected, the payroll run loop can be entered again to fix them.

Table 8.1 The SAP ERP HCM Payroll Process

Process Step	Description
Generate Posting to Finance	Finance posting documents are produced based on the latest payroll results. These results can be generated in test mode and checked. If errors are detected, the payroll processing loop can be entered again and issues resolved. Once all errors are resolved, the payroll results are posted to Finance.
Exit Payroll	When the payroll is processed and all of the results are correct for payroll, DME, and posting, the period is closed for processing.

Table 8.1 The SAP ERP HCM Payroll Process (Cont.)

Payroll Process Status

The flow of the payroll process is controlled by the payroll control records status. The statuses listed in Table 8.2 are used to control payroll processing:

Payroll Status	Description
Released For Payroll	All employee records are effectively locked for editing so the existing information can be used to generate payroll results. Payroll is physically processed in this status.
Released For Correction	Employee records are available for editing to allow corrections to be made to fix highlighted errors and warnings.
Exit Payroll	When the payroll is processed and the results are correct, this closes a period for processing.

Table 8.2 Payroll Statuses

SAP allows an individual payroll period to be run and rerun as many as times as required to get the correct results. This means you never finish a payroll run until you are happy with 100% of the payroll results. Payroll can also be run in simulation mode (without saving any

Keep running and re-running payroll until you get your results 100% correct

payroll results into the clusters) or in real mode at any time during the payroll period. This ability means the error analysis process can begin as soon as the pay period is opened, so on the day of the final pay run you can be assured of error-free processing.

Process both regular and off-cycle payroll runs as and when you need them

SAP ERP HCM Payroll systems can be configured to process both regular payroll runs, such as a normal monthly payroll run, and off-cycle payroll runs. These are irregular payroll runs such as annual bonus runs or runs to process leavers. The SAP system stores the results of both types of payrolls in payroll clusters, allowing integrated reporting of both regular and off-cycle payroll results.

Automate many steps in your payroll process with the HR Process Workbench

SAP enables the automated run of payroll via the *HR Process Workbench*. This is a tool that allows users to define a processing template for executing payroll runs and initiating subsequent activities such as posting results to SAP ERP Financials, generating payslips to employees, and triggering bank files for payments.

Reporting

Over 200 standard payroll reports

The best system in the world is rendered useless if its users cannot access data with minimum fuss and maximum flexibility. SAP payroll reporting tools allow the payroll results (stored in payroll clusters) to be accessed via over 200 standard international and country-specific reports and external reporting tools.

Standard International Reports
SAP provides a set of key reports that are used throughout the world, so let's explore the most commonly used of these reports.

Wage Type Reporter
This report details the wage types generated during payroll processing for an employee for a period. The report integrates the payroll results with employee data and organizational data stored in the infotypes to provide numerous ways of reporting on payroll results, for example, to report on a single pay period or across multiple periods. It allows period-to-period comparisons for variance analysis to filter the results

based on individual wage types or on many master data fields, for example, to produce a report of employees' net pay only for a single cost center or organizational unit.

Because payroll results are stored with a reference to the period in which they were paid and the period in which they were earned, the report gives users the choice of reporting on results created both those periods. This functionality is very useful for reporting on payments that were earned in one tax year and paid in another.

Payroll Journal

The Payroll Journal is designed to be used for reconciling payroll results from gross to net. It is also known as the *Gross to Net Report* and it lists all of the wage types used to build up the gross side of payroll and all of the deductions used to build up the net payroll. The report indicates if the gross to net does not balance, and highlights master data errors and SAP customizing errors. It can be run for a single employee or for any other grouping within the organization and is normally used to confirm that payroll is correct prior to the generation of the payment file and posting of results to finance. The report allows cross-period comparisons, and is used to reconcile the amount of taxes paid to the government each period.

Payroll Exception Report

During payroll processing any number of situations may occur that are not technically payroll errors but still require investigation before payroll is completed. The Payroll Exception Report is used to highlight the errors, warnings, and exceptions that have been triggered from payroll processing.

The Payroll Exception Report delivers all of your errors and warnings in one efficient report

Many standard warnings and errors are built into the SAP ERP HCM Payroll function, but custom messages specific to an organization's requirements can also be built into the report. Standard messages may include such things as notification of employees being paid below the minimum wage, employees with no net pay, employees missing bank details, and employees with unusually large payments.

Wage Type Statement

This report is very similar to the Wage Type Reporter but allows results to be read from both the results table (RT) (for a per payroll period analysis) and the cumulated results table (CRT) (for multiple period reporting, for example, year to date, quarter to date, or a longer period as configured).

Assignment of Wage Types to GL

This report displays the mapping of wage types to the SAP ERP Financials General Ledger accounts. It is an invaluable tool for reconciling issues involving posting of payroll results.

These are the key international payroll reports, but many other international payroll reports are available as standard within the payroll function, meeting all of a payroll manager's reporting needs.

Logged Changes in Infotype Data

Infotype change logging helps quickly track the cause of payroll errors

The SAP audit trail allows every change to employee master data to be logged for audit and error checking purposes. A complete history of creations, changes, and deletions of employee master data and the fact that the report can be run by individual SAP users by employee, by infotype or wage type, or by date and time of change ensures that all changes are available and reportable for error resolution and security audits during the payroll process.

Country-Specific Reports

Every national report you require to run payroll for a country

In addition to the large suite of international reports, for each country for which SAP provides a payroll solution, all of the required country-specific reporting requirements are also met as standard. The topic of legal reporting is covered in more detail in the second section of this chapter, but some examples of country-specific reports that are available as standard are listed in Table 8.3.

Report	Use
NC-9901 – Report of Organization (USA)	A report to submit payroll data to the Bureau of the Census for each calendar year
P45 – Leavers details (GB)	A report to produce the statutory form required with details of leavers payments and tax paid for the year
HNZLSCS0 – Quarterly Labor Cost Survey for Superannuation Costs (NZ)	As required by New Zealand labor law, a report for the costs of superannuation provisions

Table 8.3 Examples of Standard International Reports

External Reporting Tools

To provide for the ever-increasing demands and complexity of reporting requests, payroll results are stored in a format that is easily accessible for both SAP reporting tools such as BI and for external reporting tools and interfaces. For example, the Interface Tool Box covered earlier in this chapter is a standard SAP solution for creating automated interfaces and reports to be transferred to external organizations.

Other Key Concepts

There are three other key concepts that it is important to understand when working with the SAP ERP HCM Payroll function: retroactive accounting, support packs, and ongoing maintenance.

Retroactive Accounting

Payroll uses a process called *retroactive accounting* to recalculate previous payroll results, allowing the automatic adjustment and inclusion of late payments and other payroll adjustments into previous payroll periods. Retroactive accounting also allows retrospective adjustments to employees' work details such as position, job, salary, and start date.

Automatically calculate adjustments for previous periods' payroll figures

This process is based on the concept of *for period* and *in period*. The in period is the period in which a payment is paid or deducted from the employee's pay. This is usually the current payroll period. The *for* period is the period in which a payment, deduction, or change to employee data should have been made.

By using retroactive accounting, the SAP ERP HCM Payroll function ensures that all master data changes and payroll adjustments can be entered into the system with accurate dates. SAP automatically adjusts the employees' payroll results for previous periods, bringing forward adjustments to the employees' net pay into the current period.

For example, if an employee's unpaid absence was not recorded two months ago, the SAP system users simply enter the absence record into the system with the actual start and end dates. Retroactive accounting will automatically process the deduction from the employee's pay. The deduction will be attributed to the correct *for* period but will be taken from the employee's net pay in the current *in* period.

This solution proves invaluable when large-scale changes such as back-dated pay changes (e.g., pay awards, federal increases, or cost center assignments) are required. The SAP system allows the master data changes to trigger these changes to be input efficiently and processed automatically.

Support Packs

SAP delivers your statutory changes and bug fixes through support packs

Support packs are the standard SAP method for the delivery of important system changes such as statutory updates and software changes and bug fixes. Support packs are released as required, generally quite frequently. From an SAP ERP HCM Payroll perspective there are two types of support packs:

Bug Fixes

These are released to fix to a known problem, for example, an error in tax calculation logic for a specific country. The issues are usually reported by the SAP user community and resolved by SAP developers. The support packs contain examples of the problem and details of the resolution.

New Functionality

These support packs, now called Enhancement Packages, contain new functionality or improvements in existing functionality or facilitate the implementation of changes to statutory legislation.

Enhancement packages are generally SAP-version specific. Some are country specific, for example, to update the tax rates for a country. Others are country independent, for example, to correct a code error in a report or program.

In other SAP components, enhancement packages can be downloaded from *www.service.sap.com* and applied by the basis team with a minimum level of testing, but the enhancement packages for payroll are a quite different story.

You can apply enhancement packages as often as your company wants

Due to the complex nature of the payroll engine and the statutory rules concerning payroll, the application of enhancement packages that can potentially impact the payroll schema, functions, operations, and rules require detailed analysis and interpretation before application. Often after application, they also require manual configuration by SAP to apply the SAP-suggested changes to a customer's version of the payroll engine.

Any changes delivered in enhancement packages that could impact employees' payroll results or statutory reporting then require a detailed testing regime including functional, regressive, and negative and positive testing to ensure that the enhancement package solves the problem or makes the required changes to the system, but also that it does not have a negative impact on other parts of the system. This type of testing typically involves first the technical team for the interpretation and application of the enhancement packages and then business users for detailed testing of the changes.

There is no hard and fast rule for how often enhancement packages should be applied, but some key enhancement packages need to be applied immediately to fix serious errors. Some organizations opt for one large application of Payroll enhancement packages just prior to the end of the payroll year; others apply them monthly or quarterly. The decision about the scheduling of the application of enhancement packages and the associated testing regime is often a balance between business need and resource availability.

Increasingly, organizations are using automated testing tools to analyze and test enhancement packages, ensuring that the testing regime

Many companies use automated testing tools to test their enhancement package changes

213

is as rapid as possible and that, where possible, the tests are reusable. This cuts down on system downtime and allows packs to be applied more frequently, thus reducing risk to the system.

Ongoing Maintenance

Payroll is different from most other SAP components in that there is normally a sizable requirement for ongoing support and development to keep the system up to date with organizational and statutory requirements that change and develop over time. Compared to "set and forget" SAP ERP HCM components such as Organizational Management, which can require little ongoing maintenance (apart from master data maintenance), Payroll, especially when multi-country solutions are implemented, has ongoing overheads for system maintenance that need to be considered and evaluated. Remember that these overheads are not specifically an SAP issue but are more a result of the dynamic nature of payroll rules and legislation and their effect on payroll software.

That is all we can cover regarding the Payroll function, so let's move on to look at the closely related area of legal reporting.

How Legal Reporting Fits into an Enterprise

Legal reporting gives you the tools you need to meet your legal reporting obligations

For many companies, *legal reporting* is a necessary evil. Historically, the reporting of end-of-year results and preparing data for national statistics submissions can be a time-consuming and frustrating trial and error process. With the Payroll legal reporting functions, however, some, if not all, of these headaches disappear.

Requirements for legal reporting vary widely between countries in terms of data required and the frequency of reporting. Usually, legal reporting revolves around three areas: employee master data (age, gender, race, disability), employee payroll results (year-to-date earnings, taxes paid, garnishments, and employee contributions), and employer data and contributions.

A Closer Look at Legal Reporting

When SAP develops a Payroll solution for a country, it considers the current legal reporting requirements for that country and works to build these requirements into the solution. The legal reporting functions use data from three sources in SAP ERP HCM to produce the required legal reports.

> If SAP provides a payroll solution for a country, it also provides all of the necessary legal reports

> Employee master data

> Payroll results

> Employer data

You need to understand the processing of the legal reporting requirements so that you can understand all of the capabilities. Let's start with employee master data.

Employee Master Data

When looking at employee master data in the legal reporting process, we can divide the data into two areas.

Shared Employee Data

This includes employee information that is held in the system for a variety of uses including Legal Reporting. Some examples of this type of shared data are employee name and address, tax code, and national identification number. This data is used by other SAP ERP HCM components such as data inputs in payroll processing and calculation. Because this single source of data is used for many purposes, any changes to this data for the purpose of legal reporting must consider the potential impact on the other SAP ERP components that use the information.

Information Specifically Held for Legal Reporting

 Example

> Some examples of this sort of data are employees' company car information, veteran and national service history, and the recording of an employee's race or ethnicity (according to national reporting characteristics).

When a piece of information is required solely for legal reporting, it will either be included in an existing screen or infotype, or, if a large amount of information is required in a specific area, a new infotype will be defined to hold the data. Where possible, SAP integrates the requirements into existing screens, sometimes providing country-specific versions of infotypes. If this is not possible, a separate country-specific infotype will be developed.

An example of country-specific information being integrated into an international infotype is Infotype 0077 Additional Personal Data. This infotype has country-specific layouts allowing things such as the recording of race and military service, information specific to the United States. These fields are not available for other countries.

A country-specific infotype is Infotype 0222 Superannuation Australia, which is used to record details of employee superannuation and pension contributions. Another is Infotype 0088 Maternity Data Recording for Great Britain, used to record the details of an employee's maternity in that country.

Employee Payroll Results

Payroll clusters are grouped and organized for easy legal reporting access

When Legal Reporting data is required at an individual employee level, the payroll results stored in the payroll clusters are the most commonly used source for data. When only summarized results, for example, organization-wide information rather than individual employee-level data, are required, the payroll results posted to SAP ERP Financial can be used for legal reports.

Payroll clusters are divided into international payroll clusters and country-specific payroll clusters. The country-specific clusters are often used to record information relevant for legal reporting. Some examples are listed in Table 8.4.

Cluster	Use	Country
TAXR	Residence and unemployment tax details	United States
CNIC	Cumulative National Insurance contributions	United Kingdom
NS	Details of night shifts spent working in heavy labor	Austria
Q4	Details of payment advances given to employees	Australia
VC_T5KEEA,	Employment Equity Act Reporting details	Canada

Table 8.4 Country-Specific Clusters Used in Legal Reporting

International clusters commonly used for legal reporting are shown in Table 8.5.

Cluster	Use
WPBP	Work Place/Basic Pay – data relating to an employees' organizational assignment and work location
RT	Results Table – payroll results for an individual period
CRT	Cumulated Results Table – payroll results accumulated over a period, for example annually, quarterly, employment period
BENTAB	Benefits – accumulations for certain employee benefits plans
AVERAGE	Frozen Average – details of stored averages, for example, average rate of pay, average net pay

Table 8.5 International Clusters Commonly Used in Legal Reporting

Employer Data

In addition to employee data and payroll results, the legal structure of organizations, their physical locations, registered head offices, registration numbers, permit details, and other organizational information is often required for legal reporting. As with employee data, SAP

Key employer data is stored in this function for reporting access

217

works to integrate this information into the system, allowing for a single source of data where possible.

Details of benefits the employer provides to the employee and of payments and deductions the organization makes on the employees' behalf are often used in legal reporting processes.

 Examples

> Some examples of these types of data are employer retirement savings contributions, company cars, and health care payments.

In the SAP ERP HCM Payroll function, any payment or deduction that affects an employee's net pay is stored against the employee in a payroll cluster and is available for legal reporting.

Legal Reporting Requirements

SAP works proactively to keep its systems up to date with legal reporting requirements

As new legal requirements are released by statutory organizations such as the local tax office or revenue department, SAP proactively works to account for these changes and deliver new legal reporting solutions for the system. As with other SAP ERP HCM system changes, these changes are delivered via enhancement packages. As discussed earlier, these changes can then be applied immediately or as part of a prearranged process, depending on their impact on the system.

Producing Legal Reports

The legal reporting functions are almost entirely country specific, so depending on your company's federal, state, local, and other statutory reporting requirements, you can produce all of the required legal reports to ensure that your organization is statutorily compliant. SAP works to ensure that enhancements and changes to statutory reporting are built into the solution before you need them.

Legal reports are also delivered in the style and format required by the statutory bodies, whether they are paper-based reports or electronic files. The reports can also be automatically transmitted to the statutory body using one of the middleware products available with the software.

 Note

Version 4.7 included the SAP Business Connector, a tool to integrate SAP systems with external applications and third parties such as statutory bodies. This has since been replaced by SAP NetWeaver Process Integration (PI). SAP NetWeaver PI is designed to make the process of electronically sending and receiving files over the Internet simpler and faster. SAP NetWeaver PI is optimized to support file transmission over all of the most common file transfer protocols including MQ, JMS, HTTP, HTTPS, FTP/FTPS, batch file, and Web service.

Table 8.6 lists some of the statutory reports currently produced.

Report	Format	Country	Category
W2 – Employee Wage and Tax Statement	Paper or via Employee Self-Service	United States	End of year
NC-9901: Report of Organization	Electronic for submittal	United States	End of year
P60 – Employee Summary of YTD Earnings	Paper	Great Britain	End of year
P35 – Employers Annual Return	Electronic submittal via Business Connector	Great Britain	End of year
P46 _ Company Car	Paper or electronic submittal via Business Connector	Great Britain	Quarterly

Table 8.6 Examples of SAP Legal Reports

Now that we have seen all of the key areas of both Payroll and legal reporting, we will look at a case study illustrating some of many benefits a company can receive after implementing these tools.

Case Study

Table 8.7 provides with a quick overview of the case study before we explain it in more detail.

Company	British Manufacturing and Construction Company
Existing Solutions	SAP R/3 for some parts of the business; basic SAP ERP HCM modules already in place
Challenges	> Replace three existing payroll systems and merge 17 payroll areas into three on an SAP system > Ensure minimum disruption to weekly, fortnightly, and monthly payroll operations
SAP Solutions	SAP ERP HCM Payroll function and CATS
Benefits	Increased process efficiency, centralized reporting, faster processing time, three fewer IT systems to maintain

Table 8.7 SAP Payroll Case Study

This large British organization operates a range of companies involved in many heavy industries including quarrying, manufacturing, and building roads over 700 sites in the UK. The company has a workforce of over 25,000.

The Challenges

The company had grown through numerous mergers and acquisitions and was now supporting three payroll systems requiring a large overhead in terms of processing and supporting the systems.

Employment contracts, terms of employment, payment rules, and calculation logic varied widely within the organization, and there was little clarity of the overall picture.

The company had to use a third-party tool to centralize payroll results for reporting and maintained many interfaces between the payroll systems, production systems, time sheeting systems, external interfaces, and the SAP ERP Financials component.

The SAP Solution

The implementation project took 18 months, with staggered go-lives after the initial 12 months of system build. Three legacy payroll systems were replaced with the SAP ERP HCM Payroll function, and 17 payroll areas were merged into three on the SAP system. A significant amount of the time on this project was spent confirming the requirements for the new payroll system, and union agreements and work contracts that had not been analyzed for many years were compared to current practices and with agreement from all parties were made consistent in the SAP system. The payroll team of 26 people and over 200 data input clerks were trained in the new Payroll and CATS system.

In addition to the implementation, the team integrated the new payroll system into the existing SAP ERP Financials and HCM systems, implemented CATS for time recording at over 200 time-recording sites, and realigned the existing HR system to provide for the requirements of the new SAP Payroll solution.

The Benefits

In additional to experiencing improvements in the speed of payroll processing, the company realigned its processes for more efficient data entry and error resolution. Their IT operation has fewer systems to maintain and support, and their knowledge can now be concentrated on the one system. Through the centralization of payroll into the SAP system, their ability to access and analyze payroll data more rapidly has given them a greater understanding of their whole business and laid the foundation for future growth by adding further SAP ERP HCM components into their system for even greater operational efficiencies.

Summary

You could easily fill a book just on SAP ERP HCM Payroll and Legal Reporting, because they are definitely some of the most complex and fascinating solutions. In this chapter, we outlined these solutions for you. The key things to remember include:

> How SAP ERP HCM Payroll and Legal Reporting fits in your enterprise, including the main data flows into and out of payroll.

> The key concepts behind the SAP Payroll solution and an overview of the SAP legal reporting capabilities.

Finally, the case study gave you an idea of some of the challenges faced in an SAP ERP HCM Payroll implementation and the benefits to be gained.

In the next chapter we will explore the SAP ERP HCM capabilities for the maintenance and production of SAP ERP HCM Processes and Forms.

HCM Processes and Forms

The HCM Processes and Forms function provides a great view of the future of SAP ERP HCM systems. This function is designed to allow you to move your common HR processes (such as hiring and transfers) onto the Web, allowing a powerful combination of web-based forms, online document storage, organizational structure-based decision making, and workflow. This allows you to streamline and optimize the processing of your most common pieces of organizational data.

Employees can also download forms from Employee Self-Service (ESS) and fill them in electronically while offline, or print them out and post them back to the HR department.

In addition to HR requirements, forms can be created for other departments, such as for finance approvals and even for external bodies such as health care providers. An electronic record of all of these processes is then stored in the digital personnel file and all parties can track the progress of the request.

Example

> Your complex multistep processes such as those involved in managing an employee transfer are processed via the Internet using electronic forms. After being informed of the transfer request by the employee, the employee's current manager can raise the transfer request via an interactive web-based form. HR and the employee's new manager can then review and approve or reject the transfer based on the information contained in the electronic form. When the approval or rejection decision is made, this notification is again transferred online via workflow, and the HR administrator and the employee can work together through a shared form to complete all of the steps required to make the move possible. All of these tasks can be completed online, without generating or touching a single piece of paper.

How Processes and Forms Fit into an Enterprise

Move forms out of your "in" tray and onto your desktop

Use the digital personnel file to create an electronic filing cabinet for each employee

HCM Processes and Forms uses the enterprise portal to manage your most complex SAP ERP HCM processes via the Web. *SAP Interactive Forms by Adobe* allows you to create complex user-input forms that are delivered via the enterprise portal and are directly linked to SAP ERP HCM. Changes entered onto the form can be sent for approval, for further processing and subsequent input, or stored directly in the system. Using the SAP ERP HCM organizational structure as a backbone, workflow allows tasks and steps in processes to be directed to the appropriate team member or manager for input or approval. The *HR administrator portal* allows your HR team members to do the bulk of their day-to-day processing via the portal using custom-designed forms and processes. The *digital personnel file* gives you the ability to keep an electronic copy of all of an employee's documents (from both online and offline sources), ensuring that there is no duplication and all documents are readily available.

Reduce data entry errors by sourcing data directly from your HR system

HCM Processes and Forms and its integrated technologies allows you to reduce the amount of duplication of HR data and cut down on the chance of incorrect data entry by using your SAP ERP HCM system as the source of all information. It allows you to create media bridges to bring online and offline documents together in a single file. Most important, it brings employees, HR administrators, business decision makers, managers, and required approvers together in one discreet process for optimal processing.

A Closer Look at HCM Processes and Forms

Processes and Forms are really two separate but closely related tools within SAP ERP HCM. The processes part allows you to automate your HR processes over the Internet using the SAP ERP enterprise portal. The forms part of this function allows you to create complex online multistep forms that link separate approvers and those who input the data together to collaboratively complete HR processes.

Automate both processes and forms and then link them for even greater efficiencies

As with all SAP ERP HCM functions, this function can be configured to match your business-specific requirements, but it is important that you first identify all of your HR processes and then highlight which are suitable for online processing. For these suitable processes you then need to fully explore your requirements and detail all of the necessary steps and the required information at each step, and then identify the appropriate people within your company to process approvals and rejections, manage and monitor the processing, and handle any errors within these processes. The more time you spend initially mapping, testing, and verifying these processes before you start configuring them in SAP ERP HCM, the easier the implementation will be.

HCM Processes and Forms has four important aspects that we will now explore to gain a full understanding of the power of this component.

> Forms
> Processes
> HR Administrators
> Employees' digital personnel files

Let's look at each of these areas in detail to gain an understanding of the capabilities of HCM Processes and Forms.

Forms

SAP Interactive Forms by Adobe creates interactive error handling forms for employees

SAP and Adobe have partnered to enable companies to create web-delivered PDF-based forms that are customizable and reusable to support business processes. These forms can be delivered over the Internet and integrated into the enterprise portal or simply emailed to employees like normal PDF files.

The forms have the familiar look and feel of regular PDF forms, but they are fully integrated into SAP ERP HCM. This integration means the form can be pre-populated with employee-specific details, saving the employee from filling in the entire form. The form can have fields designated as compulsory or optional, and the PDF can be saved locally and edited offline as well as being edited within the portal. Figure 9.1 shows an example of an interactive form used by a manager to process an employee transfer via Manager Self-Service (MSS).

Figure 9.1 Interactive Form for Processing an Employee Transfer via MSS

Because the form is integrated into SAP ERP HCM, it can make calculations, be refreshed, and instantly display the results of SAP ERP HCM calculations as the user inputs data. Once completed, the offline form can be digitally signed by the employee and submitted back into SAP ERP HCM via the portal, or, if the employee prefers, the form can be printed and submitted offline.

Include automatic calculations and costs in your benefits selections forms

In practice, this means an employee could log onto his ESS portal and open a PDF version of the same health care benefits selection form that he has been using to make his annual health care benefits choices for many years. However, this form is now totally interactive, allowing the employee to either fill it in online or save a local copy offline to complete later. As the employee fills in the form, he can instantly see the total updated cost of his health care selections for the year. Once the employee has chosen his health care selections and possibly added a new child to the plan details, he can digitally sign the form and submit it electronically for processing or print it out and submit it offline.

The fields in the PDF benefits selection form are mapped to the required fields in the employee's benefits infotype, and the employee's master data is instantly updated in SAP ERP HCM and ready to be processed by payroll. The fields can be pre-populated with employee data, and they can include calculations, validations, and error checking. The employee can even attach an electronic sticky note to the form if he has a question about the form. A copy of the form is also added to the employee's digital personnel file (which we will explore later in this chapter).

Map data directly from your form into your HR system

The Adobe forms can also be integrated into multistep processes, allowing forms to have input from a range of people or require approvals and sign offs before being approved and submitted into the backend system. Let's look at the process side of the system to see how these complex processes can be mapped into the system.

Create processes and forms that manage multistep approval and action steps

Processes

SAP ERP HCM processes allow companies to integrate the simple look and feel of Adobe forms with the processing and calculation power of the background system and the routing and decision-making power of the SAP ERP workflow system. This integration means that detailed multistep HR related processes, such as applying for and approving an increase in headcount for a department or team, can be mapped into SAP ERP HCM and largely automated.

Integrate these forms into ESS and MSS for even simpler access

If, for example, a manager wanted to request the creation of a new position for his team and begin the recruitment process to hire an employee, the manager could execute his part of the process using an Adobe form via MSS. After logging on to the portal, the manager would fill in the new-employee request form. This form, when checked and completed, could then be electronically routed via workflow to the managers' HR representative for approval or rejection. Each step of the process is mapped out in the *process roadmap*, a multistep process that can be divided into smaller processes (Figure 9.2).

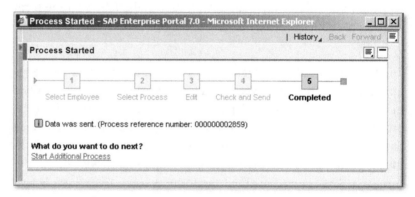

Figure 9.2 Part of a Large Process Roadmap

This approval could then be routed to the relevant cost center manager, who after reviewing the details of the new position could give the final approval. This approved request would then appear in the relevant HR administrators' list of action items, indicating that the administrator can begin the recruitment process. Different pieces of information can be made available to different approvers, so sensitive information can be hidden from some approvers and displayed to others.

Each process is made up of three interlinked parts: defining your process, forms, and workflow.

Defining Your Processes

Defining all of the steps involved in each of your HR business processes is a key part of automating the processes. For example, if we look at an everyday process such as awarding an annual bonus to your team members, we can automate a large part of this routine using HCM Processes and Forms, but we first have to define each step in the process in these terms:

> What triggers this process?

> Who is involved in this process?

> What information is needed at each step?

> Who should be able to see which pieces of data?

> What data needs to be input at each step?

> Who can approve or reject the result?

> Who should monitor this process?

Once you have answered all of these questions, you can set up your process in the system. Using the standard SAP Workflow, you can use your company's organizational structure as the basis for your approvals and escalations, or you can define your own hierarchy for approvals.

Defining your processes can take longer than building the forms

Using *SAP Interactive Forms by Adobe*, you can create complex interactive forms that ensure you get the right pieces of information from all of the required parties. Processes can be linked into Microsoft® Outlook so that notifications and reminders are delivered straight into employee's inboxes. Full analytics of all of the processes currently under way are also available, allowing you to collect statistics on things such as average processing times and highlight processing bottlenecks. This sort of detailed information allows you to monitor and constantly enhance your processes to ensure that they are as efficient as possible.

Forms

We looked at the detail of the SAP-delivered Adobe forms in the earlier part of this section, but to recap, Adobe forms allow you to create interactive and tailored forms that can be delivered electronically as part of a process. For example, you can define a form for recording changes to an employee's family status. So when an employee has a new child or gets married, he can access the form via the portal and fill in all of the required details. This completed form can then trigger a workflow that is delivered to the employee's HR administrator, and a notification can be triggered advising the employee's manager that his family status has changed.

Another example is employee travel requests. Figure 9.3 shows a simple travel approval form that an employee is editing online.

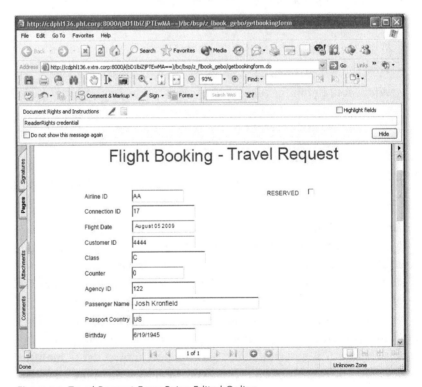

Figure 9.3 Travel Request Form Being Edited Online

Once the employee edits the form, the administrator can approve the changes so they can be automatically loaded into the system, creating new infotype records and ensuring that the information is picked up automatically by the next payroll run. The HR administrator's approval of a change in family circumstances can then trigger a separate process whereby the employee benefits team is automatically notified of the change via a summary form. The benefits team can then trigger a benefits enrollment process for the employee or whatever else is required by the business.

Workflow

HCM Processes and Forms is fully integrated into the SAP ERP Business Workflow tool, which is the central tool for controlling information flows within SAP ERP. We have looked at business workflow and its impact on other SAP ERP HCM functions, so by now you should be aware of the capabilities of workflow. Let's look at some of the most important aspects of workflow with regard to processes and forms.

Integrate forms and processes with workflow to move the entire integrated process online

A workflow represents all of the tasks involved in running a process. A workflow is used to identify the position in the company that should act on the task. The person who holds that position can then approve a request (such as a leave request) or change of details (such as a change of address) as required. Figure 9.4 shows the flow of an example workflow for a manager requesting a change to employee data.

Workflows determine who the correct person is to execute a task by using the organizational structure or a custom mapping table. If that person does not implement the task in a predetermined time frame (because the employee is on leave or the position is currently vacant), the workflow can redirect the task to the next level or a colleague to ensure that the process continues. Mapping who is authorized to approve a request is a large part of setting up workflows. Defining appropriate processing time frames and establishing who should monitor the process and handle errors and problems are also key areas to define.

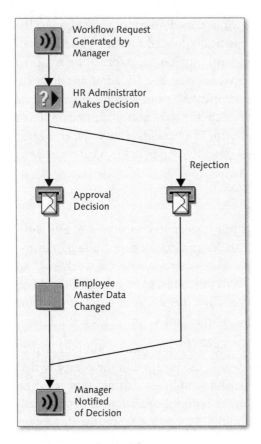

Figure 9.4 Example Workflow

Workflows can be delivered via the portal or integrated emails, ensuring that even employees who do not regularly use the SAP ERP portal can still be fully involved in processing workflows.

That wraps up the three parts of creating your processes, so let's move on to the HR Administrator role.

HR Administrators

The *HR administrator role* in HCM Processes and Forms is a web-based portal role tailored specifically to the work of a typical HR administrator. Using the Web as its interface, this role allows users to perform all of their normal tasks without logging onto the SAP system. Examples of common tasks that can be performed by the HR administrator include managing SAP ERP HCM processes and performing data maintenance.

Managing SAP ERP HCM Processes

You create, manage, complete, and monitor your processes through the *Universal Worklist* (Figure 9.5). The universal worklist is a screen that allows HR administrators to track all of the processes currently being undertaken that relate to the employees for whom they are responsible.

Universal Worklist provides administrators with an overview of their tasks

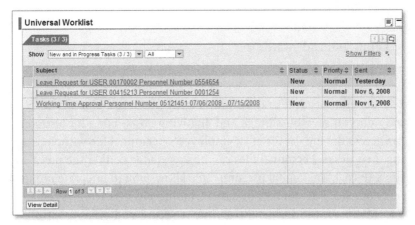

Figure 9.5 The Universal Worklist

Performing Data Maintenance

HR administrators can perform all of the normal data maintenance tasks to complete their jobs via the enterprise portal. They can view and display employee data, perform tasks such as hiring new employees, perform personnel appraisals, edit organizational data, and create statements and reports.

The interface for the personnel administration portal is set up to make the maintenance of employee data as efficient as possible. The screen allows users to create lists of favorite employees and infotypes, search for employees, and view the data for specific periods of time. The portal also allows the HR administrator to view employees' digital personnel files.

Employee Digital Personnel File

A virtual filing cabinet for each employee, with every form and document stored forever

The digital personnel file is simply the electronic version of your more traditional filing-cabinet-based personnel file. Users can manually add electronic copies of physical records such as contracts or notifications of salary increases to an employee's digital personnel file. If HCM Processes and Forms is used, any resulting documents and forms are automatically added to the employee's file. If it's not used, the HR administrator can manually add files and documents to employee records. The document types that can be added to the digital personnel file include:

> Employee resumes

> Contracts of employment

> Certificates and awards

> Legal documents

Access through either the portal or the SAP GUI

The benefits of electronic records management are significant: Not only do you save on storage and archiving costs, but administrators can access the full details of an employee's personnel file without leaving their desks. Personnel files can be accessed via either the portal or the SAP GUI. The digital personnel file allows you to integrate numerous non–SAP ERP sources of data including physical HR files, emails, and Microsoft office documents into a secure and access-controlled central repository.

Electronic personnel files also give you control over who accesses the files. You can give virtual lending rights to other administrators or employees and managers to give them access to limited versions of the files for limited periods of time.

The electronic personnel file has strong access built in, and you can't lose the keys!

With digital files, you have better control over access and compliance by using standard SAP ERP authorizations and control objects. You'll have no more worries about people accessing filing cabinets you might forget to lock, because your personnel files are now as securely controlled as the rest of your electronic employee data.

Because the electronic personnel file is built around the standard SAP ERP records management technology, you also have full control over archiving and deleting old and obsolete records.

Now let's have a look at HCM Processes and Forms in a real-world scenario.

Case Study

Table 9.1 provides you with a quick overview of our case study before we explain it in more detail.

Company	European Bank
Existing Solutions	SAP ERP including HCM
Challenges	› Need to minimize data entry and accuracy issues › Slow paper and internal mail-based processes › Complex and ad hoc processes slowing down HR function › Reduce the cost of maintaining forms and eliminate paper forms
SAP Solutions	SAP Interactive Forms by Adobe and e-Recruiting
Benefits	› Faster more efficient data processing › Improved communications › Fully integrated, standardized processes

Table 9.1 SAP Interactive Forms Case Study

This case study involves a large retail bank with over 50,000 employees spread over multiple subsidiaries operating in 10 European countries.

The Challenges

Hiring new employees is always a complex processes. The sourcing, short listing, reviewing, selecting, and interviewing of employees involves many parties and is a traditionally document-heavy process. The bank needed to standardize its processes across multiple countries to gain efficiencies in the recruitment process. A paper-based process with several electronic interfaces led to large amounts of duplicate data entry and resulting errors and omissions.

The SAP Solution

The project implemented SAP Interactive Forms by Adobe and e-Recruiting with full workflow and email integration over a set of standardized processes over three months. The project team and business representatives created company-specific interactive forms for internal communications and allowed forms and memos to be preloaded with employee data and quickly edited and transferred between departments.

The Benefits

The company reduced its recruitment paper flow to virtually zero by automating and controlling the process via e-Recruiting and workflow. Standardized processes allowed the use of standard forms, and data quality improved dramatically in those forms because of the preloading of data already stored in the system. Overall, time to hire was reduced by the combination of the all of the individual benefits.

Summary

HCM Processes and Forms allow you to move your HR data maintenance into the 21st century.

> It gives your HR team the ability to complete all of their HR processes via the Internet through the enterprise portal.

> Employees get the power to maintain their own data online, relieving your HR department of the task.

> Electronic forms allow you to input data online and offline with built-in calculations and error handling and reduce your error rates and processing times.

> The digital personnel file signals the end of the masses of filing cabinets that one usually associates with HR departments. Docu-

ments can be stored and accessed electronically in a secure and efficient manner.

> Workflow is used to tie all of these steps together to ensure that the correct forms are approved and implemented by the right people in the minimum amount of time.

In the next chapter we will look at other new technology solutions that allow you to manage your employees and the work they do using all of the new tools that SAP provides.

PART II
Talent Management

Finding the right employees, helping employees manage their careers, planning potential succession paths within your company, managing employee learning, fostering employee performance, and effectively managing employee compensation are all parts of the Talent Management solution. This wide-ranging function enables companies to deliver solid solutions to effectively manage some of the most complex HR processes.

Anyone who works in HR will recognize the many challenges for a company to develop effective programs around recruitment, motivation, learning, career management, and employee compensation. This function uses cutting-edge technology to give companies a framework in which to develop and manage their individual way of handling these processes.

This section of the book explores Talent Management by explaining the capabilities of SAP ERP HCM in the following chapters:

> *Recruitment*
  SAP has developed two solutions for companies that want to better manage their recruitment processes. For companies that want their own online recruitment presence, E-Recruiting delivers a so-

lution to manage every step from vacancy advertising to employee applications to HR and management involvement and interfacing with third-party recruiters and websites. E-Recruiting also provides companies with a tool to manage their resource pool—not just external applicants, but also internal applicants and unsolicited applicants—to help fill new vacancies faster. Traditional recruitment allows companies that do not need their own web portal to manage all of the steps of employee recruitment in a simple fuss-free tool.

> *Career and Succession Management*
This function enables your company to work with employees to develop career and succession management plans that benefit both the employee and the company. Career plans help keep employees motivated and focused by showing them potential paths of advancement in the company that match their skills and experiences. The succession management part of the solution allows companies to match potential successors from within the company (or the talent pool) to key roles to minimize the impact of sudden changes in company staffing.

> *Enterprise Learning Management*
Taking advantage of the flexibility and power of the web, the Enterprise Learning Management function enables companies to create and maintain a centralized database of all of their training materials. They can develop and manage both traditional and web-delivered training programs using new technology tools to enable employees and customers to participate in fully interactive learning and collaboration programs to the benefit of all parties. A powerful authoring tool allows companies to create and share online content for training, from web seminars to interactive online classroom presentations.

> *Compensation Management*
Starting with development and disbursement of a compensation budget, or cutting straight to reviewing employee benefits, this function enables companies to create and manage complex global compensation programs. From allocating the budget across the company to developing long-term incentives programs and tying performance management into the compensation process, this

function provides companies with all of the tools needed to build an effective, fair, and cost-efficient compensation program.

This part of the book covers a set of very powerful tools that build on the core of the system covered in Part 1, enabling companies to gain great benefits from their SAP ERP HCM investment. We will begin by looking at the first part of Talent Management, the recruitment process.

10

Recruitment

In the past 10 years no area of HR has changed as dramatically as the recruitment process. The growth of Internet-based recruitment tools has allowed potential employees to quickly and efficiently access jobs and employers without the traditional tedium of hand-written applications and mail-delivered application forms. From an employer's point of view, the benefits have also been great, but many companies have struggled to fully utilize the benefits of Internet-based recruitment.

In SAP ERP HCM, the recruitment processes are based on the e-Recruiting solution, which is designed to optimize your company's online recruitment processes. This flexible global solution fully integrates your online recruitment portal with existing business processes, covering all aspects from vacancy creation and approval, advertising, application screening, and selection, right through to the hiring process. The use of the SAP Workflow and the Manager Self-Service (MSS) portal brings all of the involved parties together to ensure that the recruitment process is as automated, streamlined, and efficient as possible. The portal allows you to develop your own company-specific recruitment site with all of the branding, look and feel, and usability controls that users of your company's website expect.

In addition to automatically integrating your recruitment processes with recruitment agencies and external recruitment websites, the solution takes the technology a step further by creating a talent warehouse that allows you to group all of your current and potential employees together in one powerful central, searchable recruitment database.

For companies that do not need a full-blown online recruitment tool, SAP also offers the more traditional offline recruitment management solution that allows you to manage all of the steps of the recruitment process, from creating vacancies to loading and maintaining applicants and all aspects of the selection and hiring processes.

How Recruitment Fits into an Enterprise

Recruitment is a traditional HR function, and in larger companies it is the responsibility of a dedicated recruitment team. Business involvement is key to good recruitment processes. Getting good information from the business about potential vacancies and then having their input in the selection and interview process enables the recruitment team to deliver candidates who exactly meet the business' requirements.

The recruitment team has two potential pools of candidates when trying to fill vacancies: external candidates, who do not currently have any relationship with the company, and internal candidates who already work within the company but are looking for a new role. Both pools of resources need to be fully utilized because both bring different benefits to the company.

Internal candidates can be a lower risk because they already understand the company culture, and their performance is a known entity. External candidates can bring more risk because they are largely unknown to the company, but they also bring new ideas and ways of thinking. Any recruitment system needs to serve the needs of all of the parties involved in the process: the recruitment team, company management, and internal and external candidates.

A Closer Look at Recruitment

The SAP ERP HCM e-Recruiting solution consists of two possible solution implementation approaches. The first, known as e-Recruiting, is an end-to-end solution that starts with an online recruitment tool and a candidate management solution, and then moves all the way to transferring newly hired employees into the company. The second solution is simply called Recruitment. It is an offline SAP ERP–based solution used by companies that do not require their own web-based solution to manage their recruitment requirements. We will now look at both of these solutions and how they are used.

Choose between two solutions depending on your company's needs

E-Recruiting

E-Recruiting takes advantage of the power of the Internet to create a recruiting solution that manages every step of the recruitment process, from publishing vacancies online, to managing relationships with external recruitment suppliers, to managing all types of potential employees (both internal and external). The solution helps you process all of the steps required to turn a new candidate into an onboarded and working employee. So it's look at each of the parts of this solution.

e-Recruiting manages every step of the recruitment process

The Online Solution

E-Recruiting allows you to develop and manage a truly global recruitment solution. This function is designed to handle multiple languages, support different legislative requirements, and to handle national requirements for data protection and storage. E-Recruiting allows you to create a web portal that external and internal candidates can use to search for vacancies. Applicants can maintain their own profiles, apply for advertised vacancies, and register their interest in working for the company if there are no current vacancies in their area.

Create a global system providing for national and regional requirements through one central solution

E-Recruiting allows you to quickly and efficiently post new vacancies to your intranet and to your company's external job website and to publish jobs via third-party websites and job boards. It delivers a set of tools to enable your recruitment team to do their job in a stream-lined, automated, efficient, and effective manner. One of the key concepts utilized in e-Recruiting is the idea of a talent pool, which gives you access to a large group of potential employees to ensure that you always have access to a strong candidate pool. To understand how e-Recruiting fits together, let's start by looking at the portal.

Recruitment Portal

Tailor your portal view to the needs of your candidates, creating a more personalized service

To provide for the different requirements that different groups of candidates have, e-Recruiting allows you to develop separate *context* views of the recruitment portal. A context is used to tailor content toward the target applicant group. Depending on the role or type of job being advertised, your company could develop simple or elaborate contexts to ensure that you get the right amount of information from your candidates while not frustrating them with too many or two few questions.

Contexts can also be applied at a regional or national level, ensuring that your company complies with all employment legislation when it comes to requesting information about subjects such as age, gender, race, marital status, and so on. For example, a context could be defined for your Australian portal that does not ask applicants their age. In Germany, where a candidate's age is a legitimate question, a different context can include that question. Each of the questions and requests for information in the portal can also be defined as optional, required, hidden, visible, or invisible in each context, allowing you to create flexible yet detailed screens to gather candidate information.

Internal versus External Candidates

Include both internal and external candidates in your recruitment pool

Your portal can be divided to offer different vacancies to internal and external applicants. Vacancies can be advertised on your internal portal context to your existing employees before later being advertised more widely on your external portal. E-Recruiting also delivers interfaces that allow you to automatically post new vacancies to external third parties such as job boards, job websites, and recruiters and then automatically receive and integrate applications posted from them.

Candidates

There are three ways that potential candidates can access the vacancies listed on your recruitment portal:

> **Registering**

By registering, candidates can upload their resumes and provide information about themselves, their qualifications, their experience, and their interests. Once they are registered, this information can be used to match them to jobs and notify them of a potential match. Figure 10.1 shows the employee registration screen.

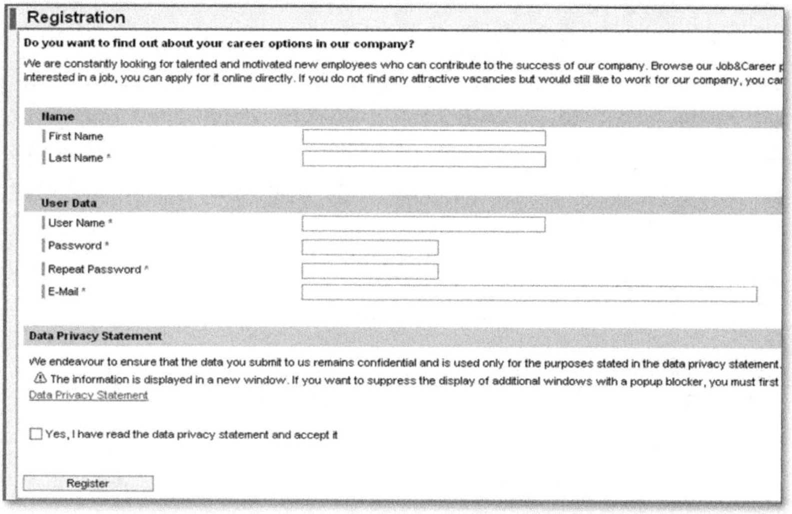

Figure 10.1 Employee Registration Screen

> **Logging in**

Once registered, returning candidates can update their current resume, view and update their previously entered information, search for new jobs, and check the progress of existing applications.

> **Unregistered access**

Candidates who don't want to register can anonymously search and apply for jobs without registering (Figure 10.2).

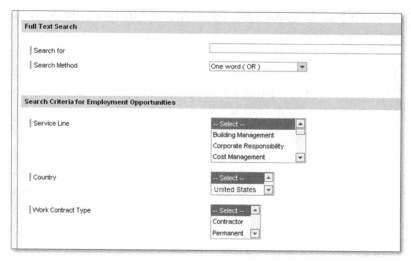

Figure 10.2 Searching for a Vacancy

Candidates can record all of the information required to help your recruitment team evaluate their fit to your company's requirements. You can ask an applicant for the following types of data. This is known as a *candidate profile* (Figure 10.3):

> **Personal data**
> Name, date of birth, nationality, and so on.

> **Communication data**
> Telephone numbers, addresses, email addresses.

> **Work experience**
> The applicant's employment history.

> **Education and training**
> Courses and training received to date.

> **Qualifications**
> The candidate's qualifications with a proficiency rating if required.

> **Desired job**
> The roles an applicant is interested in can be listed so that unsolicited applicants can be matched to potential vacancies.

> **Desired work location**
> The applicant's preferred work locations.

Candidates can create and maintain their own profiles on your company portal

Integrate privacy and release statements into your candidate's profile

> **Release statement**
  When a privacy statement and release form is required, employees can agree with the terms of these statements. These can be used to control if a candidate is applying for a specific vacancy or wants to be added to the talent pool.

> **Attachments**
  Electronic copies of resumes, certificates, and so on can be uploaded by the candidate and stored in the profile.

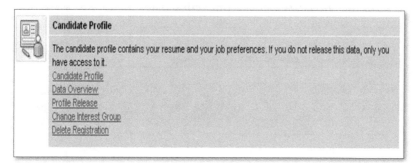

Figure 10.3 *Maintaining a Candidate Profile*

Internal candidates can also apply for vacancies through your company's recruitment portal. Integration with the Personnel Administration function allows employees' details (such as personal data, contact details, address, and qualifications) to be automatically transferred from the Personnel Administration component when they apply for new jobs on the intranet. This saves employees from having to retype their own details.

Recruiter Tools

After ensuring that your e-Recruiting system is easy to use and efficient, the next most important group to satisfy is your internal recruiters. Through the *recruiter tool*, recruiters can quickly view and search the candidate database. When a potential candidate has been identified, they can view and edit the candidate's profiles, including application history, resume, and any notes made by other recruiters. The recruiter tool aims to increase speed and efficiency throughout the recruitment process. It includes a dashboard-type layout that pro-

Recruiter tools ensure that your recruitment system is an asset, not a hindrance, to the recruitment process

vides all of the information in one central place, including the following key information:

> An overview of the recruitment task currently in progress (Figure 10.4)

> New applications received and a list of all external candidates currently being administered

> Publications that are nearing their expiration date

> Tasks that are nearing their completion date

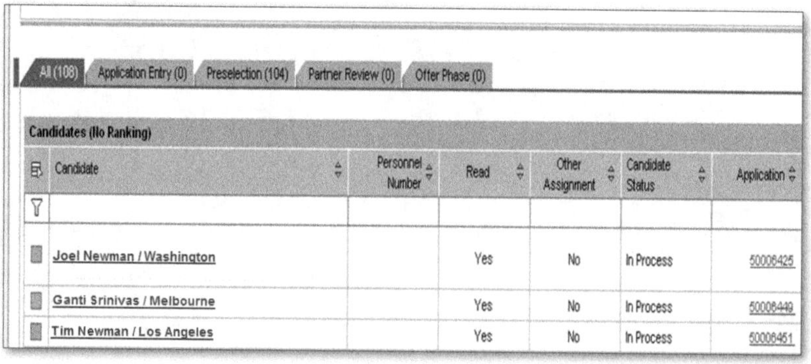

Figure 10.4 Recruiter's Inbox Showing Tasks in Progress

Integration with Manager Self-Service means managers are fully involved in the recruitment process

The requisition management process in e-Recruiting moves the responsibility for creating new employee requisitions to the managers of the team where the vacancies exist, freeing up the recruiters' time for doing what they do best—finding good candidates and getting them into the company.

The entire requisition to recruitment process takes place online; no more messy paper trails to keep track of

The new employee requisition process is fully integrated with workflow, allowing all of the tasks related to recruiting new employees to be quickly and automatically moved to the responsible people with little or no manual intervention. From the moment the manager raises a new employee requisition, it is automatically routed to the designated recruiter, who sees the new requisition on his dashboard. Because of the creation of the talent warehouse (which we will look at in the next section), the recruiter can search a detailed pool of potential candidates before they even raise a new job advertisement.

If suitable candidates cannot be found in the talent warehouse, the recruiter can post the requisition internally, externally, and directly onto third-party external websites without any need for messy paper-based forms or emails. The recruiter can then monitor and appraise the process of new applications through the *applicant tracking tool*. This tool allows recruiters to create and track each step of the recruitment process, ensuring that applicants are never lost in the system and that recruitment deadlines and time frames are always kept a top priority.

When suitable candidates have been identified, the recruiter can create a candidate short list and pass them directly back to the manager. Once the manager chooses the candidates he wants to interview, he notifies the recruiter via workflow. The recruiter can then contact the candidates, generating rejections, invitations to attend interviews, and interview appointments, all through the e-Recruiting recruiter tool.

The applicant tracking tool ensures that applicants are not lost in the system and all deadlines are met

Talent Warehouse

One of the greatest functions of e-Recruiting is the way it provides easy access to your company's talent pool (Figure 10.5). The *talent pool* is the collection of all of the people who have expressed an interest in working for your company; they may be candidates who have applied for specific positions in the past, candidates who have sent unsolicited applications, or your current active employees. By combining all three types of potential candidates, you have created a very broad database for finding and quickly filling your company's vacancies.

The talent warehouse redefines the way you look at your candidates

Candidates in your talent pool are a high-quality source of potential employees. They have already proactively sought out your company to find employment, demonstrating some degree of enthusiasm for working for you. The talent warehouse is designed to enable your company to make the most of these potential employees by giving you a set of tools to manage your talent pool.

Figure 10.5 Searching the Talent Pool

Divide your talent into groups that make it easier to find the right people quickly

The talent warehouse gives your administrators the ability to identify, track, rank, and manage potential employees. Recruitment administrators can search the talent pool for potential candidates when new vacancies are created. The talent pool can be divided into subsets known as *talent groups* to group candidates with similar attributes together into logical groups that reflect your company's recruiting needs. For example, you could define your talent pool into the following talent groups:

> Senior management

> Sales force

> Finance and administration

> Canteen staff

> Candidates living in the northwest region

Talent groups do not need to reflect qualitative judgments about your candidates. They are normally created simply to group your talent pool into groups that make your administrators' jobs easier. Candidates can be assigned to multiple talent groups if required.

You can also divide your candidates into *application groups*. This type of grouping is used for managing candidates who apply for work in the company but are not responding to a specific job advertisement. Application groups help your recruitment administrators divide the unsolicited applicant pool into more meaningful groups and speed up the process of finding good candidates.

Candidates can choose if they want to be included in the talent pool. Some candidates are only interested in applying for a specific job and may not want to be considered for any future jobs. These candidates can elect to not be included in the talent pool.

Because of the integration of e-Recruiting with third parties such as recruitment agencies and external head hunters, you can also open your talent groups and application groups up so that external recruiters can access and manage these groups. Allowing these external recruiters to complete the process of adding new candidates and screening, searching for, and allocating candidates to these groups and then searching the groups for candidates for advertised vacancies frees up your own recruitment team from these tasks.

> Move responsibility for managing your talent pool to head hunters and external recruiters

Once you have defined your talent groups, you can proactively market to these groups to raise awareness of specific jobs and the overall potential of your company. Because of the level of information stored in the talent warehouse, these marketing campaigns can be very specific (for example, you could create a talent group for potential chefs and bakers). You then keep the members of the talent group up to date with happenings at your company, keeping up their interest and increasing the chance of matching high-quality candidates to vacancies in your company.

> Create marketing campaigns that target specific groups of your talent pool to keep them up to date and engaged with your company

Each talent group can have its own designated administrator. Authorizations can be added to control who can access these groups, and documents relating to the group, such as recruitment policies, can be attached to the groups for ease of access.

Integration

As with all other components of SAP ERP HCM, the ability to fully integrate with other SAP ERP HCM functions is one of e-Recruiting's best assets. A great example of this integration is that recruiters can download the requirements for a new vacancy straight from a position in a succession plan created in the succession management function. This allows the requirements for a new vacancy to be quickly defined. Information such as required education, experience, and qualifications can be transferred instantly into a talent pool search with no manual transcribing of requirements or waiting for slow paperwork and emails to arrive.

Candidate Ranking

When you build up a large talent pool, it is important to be able to find the best candidates quickly, so ranking can be applied to candidates. High-potential candidates can be ranked higher, making searching the talent groups and identifying high-potential candidates simpler. Rankings can be performed relative to a specified requisition or in terms of a candidate's responses to questionnaires. They can be ranked by more than one recruiter. The system takes an average of the rankings if multiple rankings exist for a single candidate on a specific scale. Different rankings can be assigned weightings, so more important rankings can count for more points overall than less important ranking scales.

Candidate Searches

To ensure that searches of your talent pool always find the best possible candidates, e-Recruiting uses a search machine known as TREX (Text Retrieval and Information Extraction) to search your candidate and resume data (Figure 10.6). TREX enables fast and accurate searches by allowing searches to be performed on multiple search criteria at once. It can also take into account rankings applied to candidates to ensure that you find the best-qualified and highest-ranked candidates in every search.

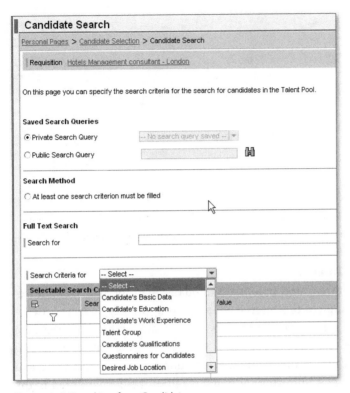

Figure 10.6 Searching for a Candidate

Candidate Communication

Recruiters can communicate with candidates through automatic email generation. The email address on the candidate's profile can be used automatically to generate follow-up correspondence. Recruiters can also generate correspondence based on preconfigured HTML and PDF templates. They can automatically generate tailored versions of standard templates for a variety of notification purposes. For example, templates can be created to notify employees of an invitation to an interview (Figure 10.7), to ask them to attend an assessment center, request further information, or extend an offer of employment. An attachment can be added, for example, to give the employee directions to the interview.

Pre-formatted candidate communication templates speed up communication

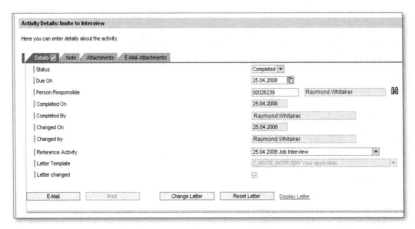

Figure 10.7 Inviting an Applicant to an Interview with Integrated Letter Generation

Candidate Transfer

Seamlessly transfer successful candidates into your Employee Administration system

Once you have found potential candidates, had the manager and recruiters complete the interview and testing process, selected a candidate and completed the process of offer and acceptance, the final step in the recruitment process is to turn the candidate into an employee. Because of the seamless integration between e-Recruiting and the Personnel Administration function, all of the details stored in the recruitment data are automatically available for the HR administrator to transfer the candidate into the employee side of the system. Candidate information such as position, job, start date, reports to, salary, contact details, address, qualifications, and education history are all available to be instantly transferred into the employee master data in Personnel Administration. This seamless integration eliminates the painful process of rekeying the information. Figure 10.8 shows the transferred candidates ready to be updated or loaded into the employee side of the system.

The Audit Trail

With automated snapshots, the audit trail is always visible

To provide a simple and secure audit trail of an applicant's progress through the recruitment process, a snapshot of the candidate profile is automatically taken at key stages of the process. When an applicant is moved to "in process," "rejected," or "to be hired" are some of the stages when snapshots are taken. These snapshots can then be viewed to see what data was used to make the decision at each step of the process.

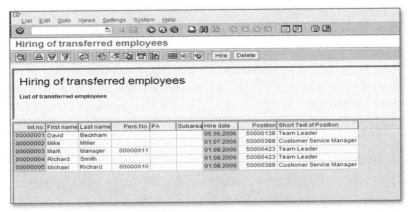

Figure 10.8 List of Successful Internal and External Candidates Ready To Be Updated in the Core Personnel Administration Component

The Manager's View

One of the aims of this function is to increase managers' access to and involvement in the recruitment process. Managers have their own portal view of key recruitment information via MSS, which is fully integrated with e-Recruiting and allows managers to be involved in the recruitment process by performing the following recruitment-related actions:

Create Requisitions

Managers can create hiring requests for jobs or positions. They simply select the job or position from the organizational structure and specify all of the details of the type of person they want to hire. Then workflow sends the requisition to the recruitment department to approve and take further action. The manager's requisition overview screen is shown in Figure 10.9.

Managers can create their own online requisitions and monitor them electronically

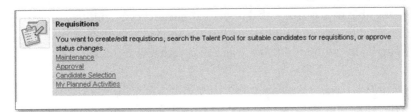

Figure 10.9 Manager's Requisition Overview Screen

Managing Candidates

Once a requisition has been approved, candidates' profiles are presented to the manager for his consideration. A short list of potential candidates can be viewed as well. Once the candidate list has been viewed, the manager can invite candidates for interviews, reject them, or ask for more information from the recruitment team using interactive Adobe forms.

Status Overview

The status of requisitions currently in progress can be quickly checked with this up-to-the minute view of their progress.

Linking to External Job Websites

E-Recruiting provides you with an external interface solution that allows you to quickly configure links to external job boards and websites. Numerous job boards and aggregators have already been certified as being compliant with e-Recruiting, allowing your company to quickly and simply post new vacancies from your intranet and company job site to external providers.

This link is a two-way automated link allowing resumes and applications received on third-party websites to be quickly transferred into your company's e-Recruiting system for consideration by your recruitment team. The technology delivers a standard interface for resume parsing integration. Therefore, your systems will be able to quickly extract data from external systems in the form of complete resumes or packages of data from individual fields, eliminating the need to re-enter candidate data.

Recruitment Master Data

Being able to access a global pool of applicants can definitely increase the quality of your applicants, but it can also raise issues regarding compliance with local privacy and data protection rules.

Data Protection

When dealing with a global talent pool, local legislation can vary widely regarding the protection of candidate data. Sometimes the one country's national legislation can contradict the legislation for another country. The SAP ERP HCM e-Recruiting solution allows you to work around these issues by issuing a standardized international privacy statement incorporating the national requirements for each country.

Equal Employment

Many countries require employers to collect and report on data relating to local diversity and equality legislation. The e-Recruiting function uses country-specific questionnaires to ensure that the right amount of information is collected from every applicant to satisfy Equal Employment Opportunities (EEO) and diversity legislation. As with the other SAP ERP HCM functions, access to employee data relating to EEO and diversity are strictly controlled using authorizations and security.

Data Storage and Purging

Different rules exist around the world regarding the storage and purging of candidate data. Some countries such as the United States have legislated to ensure that candidate data is kept up to two years after an application. Other countries such as Germany require that candidate data be deleted after only four months. These widely varying requirements are provided for in this component by the definition of *business rules*. These can be applied to a country or region as required to control the storage and purging of candidate data.

Document storage via an electronic document management system is also fully supported by e-Recruiting. Resumes, interview transcripts, and contracts can be linked directly to candidate and employee records and then stored and archived according to your company's archiving policy. More information on document storage and archiving can be found in Chapter 2, Employee Administration.

Keep electronic copies of all your recruitment paperwork and archive it automatically

Reporting

As with all the other components of SAP ERP HCM, reporting is a key focus of e-Recruiting. A set of standard reports is provided, and several reporting tools are supplied to ensure that recruiters, managers, and HR team members can get all of the information they require

Standard reports and reporting tools ensure that you always have the information you need right at hand out of the recruitment function. E-Recruiting is also linked to SAP NetWeaver Business Intelligence for integrated reporting across multiple components. Examples of commonly used reports include:

> Average time to hire (open to filled)

> Applications by education and training

> Number of applicants hired or rejected

> Outstanding vacancy list

> Offer versus acceptance rate

> All rejected EEO applicants

> All applicants with EEO data

> Source of hires

> My current requisitions

Figure 10.10 shows a recruiter's reporting list.

Reporting for SAP E-Recruiting

Title	Variant
Activities with Requisition and Candidate	My Due Activities
Activities with Requisition and Candidate	My Activities
Applications with Posting and Requisition	My New Applications Today
Applications with Posting and Requisition	My Applications
EEO Data (Compact Format)	All Rejected EEO Applicants
EEO Data (Compact Format)	My Requisitions with EEO Data
EEO Data (2-Question Format)	All Rejected EEO Applicants
EEO Data (2-Question Format)	My Requisitions with EEO Data
Requisitions and Postings	My Requisitions
Requisitions and Postings	My Current Postings

Figure 10.10 Recruiter's View of the Standard Reports

Traditional Recruitment

A full recruitment solution for companies that don't need a new web presence

The SAP ERP HCM e-Recruiting function has evolved over many releases to become a full recruitment solution for companies that require an online presence. Since this approach is one of the most common in today's global market, it is the approach that SAP recommends. However, it could be that your company already has an established online presence through third-party software or that your company works in an industry in which online recruitment is not a priority. Interfacing with third-party software is possible, as is using non portal-enabled recruitment functions in SAP ERP HCM from a more administrative management approach. So let's briefly look at what is included in this function.

Workforce Requirements and Advertising

Without a direct link to e-Recruiting, this function focuses on defining your vacancies and recording and managing the details of the advertisement that is used to publicize the vacancy.

Vacancies

Recruitment gives you the ability to create a new vacancy and display and manage existing vacancies. You can record all of the required details to describe the vacancy, such as position, job, department, and expected remuneration.

Efficiently manage your vacancies and advertisements in one place

Advertisements

Recruitment uses the terms recruitment instrument and recruitment medium to describe the different methods of advertising. These could include newspapers, external websites, the company notice board, or head hunters and job agencies. Once you have defined your recruitment instruments, you can record details of your company's advertisements and assign them to these instruments and media to track their progress.

Administering Applicants

After applications are received by your recruiters, they can be recorded and tracked in the recruitment function. Applicants can be grouped into external, internal, solicited, and unsolicited. These groups can then be used to search and classify applicants.

Data entry is facilitated via two steps. The data is stored on a set of infotypes tailored for recording applicant data. The first step is to perform the initial entry of master data. Once this is complete, any further information that needs to be recorded can be entered as additional data. By

Applicants can be stored and managed with the minimum of fuss

dividing the process into two parts, initial data entry for large numbers of applicants can be quickly completed, with additional data recorded at a later stage. The initial entry also contains the key data needed to make recruitment classification decisions, so you do not needs to waste time entering data on candidates who do not fit your requirements.

Applicants can be searched and sorted by all the required means to help recruiters make their decisions. Recruiters can track which vacancies applicants have applied for and watch their progress through the process.

All of the steps required to process a candidate from applicant to employee can be defined and the candidate moved through all of the required stages to ensure that the process is always followed correctly. These are referred to as applicant activities. Recruiters can monitor a candidate's applicant activities and quickly spot candidates who are stalled in the process.

Correspondence templates make communication with candidates quick and simple

Templates can be set up for generating correspondence to candidates, notifying them of their progress through the process and inviting them in for interviews or rejecting their applications.

Selecting Applicants

Unlike e-Recruiting, traditional recruitment is more a tool for recording the progress of the recruitment process, rather than the core tool for managing that process. So whereas the process of matching applicants to vacancies can be done via a qualification and requirements profile match-up, the process of informing the manager of the short list and managing his feedback is completed outside the system.

After an applicant has been selected for interview and the interview process has been completed, unsuccessful applicants can be notified via correspondence generated from the recruitment template. The recruitment functions do not support email and short message service (SMS) communication with applicants; this is only provided in the e-Recruiting solution. The successful applicant and all of his stored data can then be automatically transferred to the Personnel Administration component, where the responsible administrator can process the record and set him up as a full employee.

Reporting

A full suite of reports is available for applicants, vacancies, and advertisements. Recruiters can pull all of the required information to fulfill all of the standard recruitment reporting requirements.

Infotypes

E-Recruiting and Recruitment use fundamentally different methods to store and manage applicants. E-Recruiting data is not stored in the central SAP ERP HCM component until the end of the recruitment process. Traditional Recruitment, however, stores applicants very similarly to the way employee records are stored in the HCM system. Both e-Recruiting and Recruitment store applicant data in infotypes, but each has its own separate group of infotypes specific to the needs of the solution. First, we will look at the most important e-Recruiting infotypes:

> **Infotype 5102 Candidate Information**
> All of the key information regarding an applicant is stored in this infotype, including the candidate's overall status, self-description, and personal homepage on the recruitment portal and details of any rankings that have been applied to the candidate

> **Infotype 5103 Work Experience**
> When a candidate adds his work history in the portal, each employment period is created as a separate infotype record for the employee in this infotype. Details relating to employer, location, description of activity, end of employment, and so on are stored here.

> **Infotype 5104 Education**
> Data concerning a candidate's education is stored in this infotype, including details of each of his education courses.

> **Infotype 5105 Qualifications**
> All of a candidate's qualifications-related information is stored here. This includes the type of qualification and the proficiency awarded.

> **Infotype 5106 Desired Employment**
> In the portal, candidates can store information relating to their desired employment. This might be as specific as a particular job or position or as general as working hours per week, size of company, amount of personal responsibility, and expected salary. This information is transferred to this infotype.

Infotypes ensure that all employee and candidate data is stored logically and efficiently

> **Infotype 5107 Desired Location**
>
> When a candidate expresses specific preferences regarding location of employment, this is logged in this infotype. This could include specific branches or offices of the company or more general location and country information. Details of a candidate's work permits are also stored here.

> **Infotype 5108 Availability**
>
> The period during which a candidate is available to start or finish his employment is stored here.

> **Infotype 5126 Job Description**
>
> When a requisition is turned into a firm job vacancy, the details of the job including its title, hierarchy level, location, city, span of control, minimum and maximum salary level, start date, and other key fields that define a vacancy are stored here.

> **Infotype 5128 Education Requirements**
>
> When a vacancy has educational requirements, the type, field, subject, and degree or certificate level required to fill the vacancy are recorded in this infotype.

> **Infotype 5129 Required Qualifications**
>
> Some vacancies require an applicant to hold specific qualifications. All of the details required to define the qualification are stored in this infotype.

Here is a brief overview of the most important traditional Recruitment infotypes:

> **Infotype 4000 Applicant Actions**
>
> Much like an action performed on an employee, applicant actions are used to store an overview of all of the processing steps carried out for an applicant. This might include initial entry of master data, processing, on hold, invitation for interview, rejected, and so on.

> **Infotype 4001 Applications**
>
> Every time an applicant applies for a specific vacancy, a record is created in this infotype to record the event.

> **Infotype 4002 Vacancy Assignment**
>
> This infotype links the applicants with the vacancies for which they have applied. Each new vacancy creates a new record here.

> **Infotype 4003 Applicant Activities**
> Each activity carried out in the process of hiring or rejecting a candidate is recorded here with details of what was involved.

> **Infotype 4005 Applicant's Personnel Number**
> When an applicant is already an employee in your company, this infotype stores his personnel number so that the applicant and the employee are always linked.

This concludes the review of the relevant infotypes and our overview of SAP ERP HCMs recruiting capabilities. So let's look at a company that needed to address an increase in demand for an online recruiting activity.

Case Study

Table 10.1 provides a quick overview of the case study before we explain it in more detail.

Company	Indian Chemicals Company
Existing Solutions	SAP CRM, SAP NetWeaver Portal and SAP ERP HCM
Challenges	› React to increasing demand for effective online recruitment solution › Replace manual paper-based processes › Include internal and external communications with candidates and agencies
SAP Solutions	SAP ERP HCM e-Recruiting
Benefits	› Automation of previously manual tasks › Increase in transparency of process for both candidates, agencies, and business › Ability to get new vacancies advertised faster › Decrease in turnaround time for recruitment process

Table 10.1 E-Recruiting Case Study

This fast-growing chemical company produces paints for the domestic market. Based in India, the company has over 4,500 employees.

The Challenges

The company's rapid growth had stretched their old paper- and telephone-based systems to the breaking point. Because of the high demand for potential candidates, the company had to manage relationships with many external recruitment agencies. Valuable time was being wasted communicating with both candidates and external agencies. The flow of information from external agencies was a constant problem and was slowing down the already inefficient recruitment process.

The SAP Solution

By implementing e-Recruiting in seven months, the company was able to develop a fully web-enabled solution that managed the entire recruiting processes through a single integrated platform. External agencies and candidates were able to take proactive roles in their respective parts of the recruitment process via the portal.

The Benefits

In the competitive recruitment market in which the company operates, it has developed a clear competitive advantage by speeding up the recruitment process via the portal. The company automated its recruitment process, using workflow and email to involve all parties in the process and reducing the time taken at each step. The company also increased the visibility of the recruitment process, benefitting both internal and external parties, and gained valuable market information thanks to the analytical reporting tools available.

Summary

The recruitment capabilities of SAP ERH HCM provide two solutions that cater to each end of the recruitment system spectrum. Traditional

Recruitment provides you with a place to record your recruitment information and manage your candidates. E-Recruiting provides a full end-to-end solution that allows you to develop your own recruitment portal and use it to manage a global online recruitment program.

> E-Recruiting allows you to quickly develop different contexts of your portal so you can tailor the look, feel, and content of your portal for different locations and different types of candidates.

> It allows you to attract both internal and external candidates.

> The talent warehouse gives your company the ability to proactively manage groups of potential candidates, ensuring that they are always informed of what's happening at your company and maintaining their interest in joining your company until you need them to fill a vacancy.

> The integration with MSS makes managers and business representatives fully involved in the recruitment process. Managers can create their own new employee requisitions, and the process of advertising for, selecting, interviewing, and hiring a new employee can be entirely managed online through one integrated system.

> Full integration with Personnel Management and Organizational Management allows new employees to be instantly transferred and activated in your employee management system.

> With date-based control, new employees can be transferred ahead of time. There's no need to wait for a new employee's first day to do the transfer; it can be done as soon as the contracts are signed.

> The e-Recruiting solution fulfills all of your company's requirements for protecting candidate data, complying with equal employment opportunity legislation, and complying with data storage and purging requirements.

> Integration with NetWeaver Business Intelligence gives you the ability to create reports that integrate recruitment data with all of the other SAP ERP components. Standard reports and reporting tools in the ECC backend also allow you to get the information you need when you need it, giving you up-to-the minute information on all aspects of your recruitment program.

> Traditional Recruitment gives you a set of tools to manage all of the offline aspects of your recruitment process. Vacancies, candidates, and applicants are all administered in a process-oriented way that ensures that all key tasks are completed and the recruitment process is as smooth as possible.

In the next chapter we will be looking at career and succession management.

11

Career and Succession Management

Career paths within a company are often a murky and dark world. Few employees have a clear idea of their own career path, and even fewer companies have spent the time to work with their employees to help them develop their career plans. From a company perspective, the topic of succession management is becoming increasingly important. Having succession plans for the key positions in your company can have enormous benefits because it ensures that you have a continuous supply of qualified employees to fill the most important positions in your company.

Career and succession management also allows you to identify and track your employees, while working proactively to develop a career path that is both rewarding and motivating, and that matches your company's internal succession plans.

Having an automated and process-oriented career and succession management function also allows you to move the responsibility to managers and business representatives. Managers can then run career and succession management scenarios themselves, calculate the employees' potential, analyze gaps in skills and experience, and use the built-in integration within SAP ERP HCM to fill qualification deficits through the qualifications function.

How SAP ERP HCM Career and Succession Management Fits into an Enterprise

Career and Succession Management touches all areas of your company, because most employees like the idea that they are not just doing a job but are working toward a career goal. The goal doesn't have to be high—not everyone wants to be the CEO—but employees work better and are more motivated if they know that a career path is mapped out for them. The *Career Management* process of SAP ERP HCM therefore is a key tool in the management and motivation of employees. It can be used both by the HR department and by line managers, by making an employee's potential to move within the company visible.

Succession Management is a tool most often used by the HR department as part of their planning process. Again, the potential impact on the company stretches all the way from the factory floor to the president's office, because employees don't have to be highly paid to be vital to your company. So having a succession management plan for your company's key roles gives your company the ability to react quickly and effectively to organizational changes.

A Closer Look at Career and Succession Management

This function is broken into two separate yet interrelated areas: career management and succession management. These areas can be implemented separately, but in practice they are exponentially more beneficial when they are implemented and used in parallel.

> **Career Management**

This function helps your employees define and develop their careers by allowing managers to look at the employees' personalities, abilities, skills, and qualifications. Based on this information, you can help them identify future positions toward which they can work. You can develop career paths that help employees understand their potential within the company. By taking the time to develop these plans, you can ensure that your company is developing employees with the right skills, abilities, and qualifications to benefit both your employees and your company. Progress toward an employee's career goals is then managed and enhanced by the creation and monitoring of development plans that allow the employee to manage his own career goal.

Career management has employees and their needs as the central focus

> **Succession Management**

Succession management has two sides. The first is identifying key positions within your company that are either new or vacant. The next step is to define the skills, competencies, qualifications, and abilities required to fill these roles. You can use the matching tools in this component to find employees who have the right or nearly right qualifications to fill these positions. Therefore, rather than starting the search after the vacancy has been created, you can work proactively with these high-potential employees to ensure that you always have the right people available to fill vacancies as they arise.

Succession Management focuses on your business needs

Career and Succession Management is delivered either via SAP ERP or via the Enterprise Portal. More and more companies are using the Enterprise Portal because it provides a more user-friendly and familiar view for users. Both HR administrators and managers can access Career and Succession Management via the portal.

Figure 11.1 shows an example of the HR administrators' Succession Management portal dashboard.

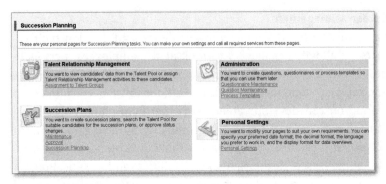

Figure 11.1 Succession Management Portal View

Let's take a closer look at both of these areas to see what they can do, what they are used for, and what their major features are.

Career Management

Today, employees, line managers, and HR professionals are becoming more focused on effectively managing their own and their employees' career paths. Creating and maintaining potential career paths, tracking employees, measuring their progress against their career paths, and turning this information into employee development equally benefits the employee and the company.

In SAP ERP HCM the Career Management process consists of three steps:

1. Defining the careers in your company
2. Running career planning scenarios that move employees through various career paths
3. Measuring the fit between an employee and a potential career path to ensure the employee's suitability for the career

Let's start by looking at what is involved in defining career paths.

Defining Careers

In all companies there are usually a few easily recognizable careers that have evolved over time (usually with no external control or management). An example of a common career path is an employee who

272

starts off working in the mail room, is promoted to the switchboard, and from there to working as a receptionist. Another example is the career path toward becoming the director of human resources; the expected career path could be defined as human resource administrator to senior administrator to employee benefits administrator to human resource manager, and regional human resources manager to the final step of director of human resources.

 Note

In Chapter 3, Organizational Management, we looked in detail at the jobs and positions used in your company's organizational structure, but as a quick refresher let's look at these two object types and what information they contain and what they are used for (see Table 11.1).

Object Type	Description
Positions	To determine where employees fit in the organization, we assign every employee to a position. A position is a single instance of a job. Usually the position-to-person relationship is 1 to 1, but sometimes in the case of job sharing or other business scenarios a position can have multiple holders at a single time. Positions are assigned to organizational units to define the organizational hierarchy.
Jobs	Jobs define sets of skills or occupations, such as accountant or secretary, and are used to define the skills required to fulfill a position. So if only one set of skills is required to define a job, such as a carpenter or welder, you only need to define this job once in Organizational Management and you can assign this job to all of the positions in your company that require these skills.

Overview of Positions and Jobs

A career path is used to map the progress an employee should take to move toward a career goal. Career paths are usually based on a linear collection of positions or jobs, but sometimes career path progression is not always directly upward. Successful career paths can also involve sideways moves and sometimes even downward steps (if reskilling is required). Your career path can stretch as far your company stretches.

A career path doesn't always have to be a linear progression; sideways steps can be just as important

You can include positions from anywhere in your company—any office, country, or location that is defined in your organizational structure.

Although you could define an unlimited number of career paths, it's simply not practical for a company to define a career path for every employee and position in the company. However, it's important to keep in mind that defining career paths has three main benefits:

1. They are the basis of employee career development that is included as part of the employee review process.

2. They are useful for succession planning and determining who has the potential to fill roles in your company.

3. They are useful as an HR demonstration tool, allowing your HR department to demonstrate potential career paths in the company to existing or potential employees. They are also a great tool to use if you have a graduate recruitment process because they focus the graduate's attention on the long-term benefits of joining and staying with your company.

Use career paths to educate and motivate your current employees and attract new ones

To get the most out of career paths you need to identify the key career paths in your company—paths that will justify the time and effort of defining and maintaining them by delivering benefits in the three areas just described.

Creating a career path in SAP ERP HCM is a simple process: You create a name for your career path and a validity date, and then simply select and insert the positions into the path as required, creating a progression from an entry-level job to the highest level of career development in the path.

The steps can be vertical or horizontal, representing the forward, backward, or sideways movement required to progress through the career path. You can also develop separate paths within a career path to represent different career options. Career paths can include occupied and vacant positions in your organization.

Performing Career Management

Once you have identified and created the key career paths for your company, you can use them to measure the suitability of employees for potential careers. Because of SAP ERP HCM's strong integration with other SAP ERP components, you can perform these match-ups for internal and external applicants and partners such as freelance or contract employees and agency workers.

Measuring Employees' Suitability for Careers

As you will see in the next chapter on Enterprise Learning Management, one of the main benefits of defining jobs and positions in your company is that they can then be integrated with your company's qualification's catalog. Therefore, the skills and qualifications required to complete a job or position can be formally linked to the object. This integration is one of the key benefits of this component because you can now map an employee (whose skills and qualifications are stored in his personnel record) against the skills and qualifications stored in positions and jobs that make up the career path. You can then evaluate the following employee criteria to measure suitability:

> Qualifications

> Preferences

> Potentials

> Likes and dislikes

> Potential career(s)

> Designations

 Note

Information regarding all of these criteria can be stored against employee records via the Enterprise Learning Management and Employee Performance Management functions. More information on the capabilities of these components can be found in their respective chapters.

By comparing the employee's qualifications and other information with the requirements stored in a career or position, we can measure the employee's fit to a potential a career. The result of this comparison is provided in the form of a table displaying the suitability percentage of the employee on each of the defined objects.

Use statistical measures to assess an employee's suitability to a potential career

Booking Training to Address Qualification Deficits

When you measure an employee's suitability for a certain career, you can display the missing qualifications that the employee would need to acquire to follow the career path. Because this functionality can be fully integrated with the Training and Events functions, you can highlight any qualifications deficits and automatically trigger a training proposal to book the employee into the training course (at the next convenient date) to gain the required qualification.

Designating Potential Candidates

If you find that the person (or object as they are sometimes referred to in SAP ERP HCM) whom you are performing career planning for has a good match to the career path, you can designate him for that career. Being *designated* means the employee has been formally highlighted as suitable for the position or career path. Therefore, when a position in that career path becomes vacant, the person can be considered for the role. To provide for all possible scenarios, you can create more than one designation for an employee, thereby highlighting him as available for multiple possible positions.

Finding Careers for Potential Employees

Compare potential employees' skills to the career paths in your company to measure their fit to your needs

If your company also chooses to use the e-Recruiting function, you will be storing the details of your potential employees within SAP ERP HCM as well. Once you have entered an applicant's details, qualifications, skills, and other pertinent information, you can run him through Career Management to find suitable careers in your company. This is a great tool when you are talking to potential employees, because you can quickly and professionally demonstrate a range of potential careers based on the match between their skills and your company's needs. You can also demonstrate some of the qualifications they could acquire working with your company by showing the qualifications required in the career path.

Transferring an Employee

Completing career plans can open up a potential career path that is too good for the employee and company to pass up. If this happens, you can immediately transfer the employee directly into his new position. All of these changes are date based, so you can make the date of transfer some time in the future to allow all of the appropriate paperwork to be completed, but in this functionality the link between career planning and actual career change is definite and immediate.

Succession Management

Whereas Career Management is focused on ensuring that the employee gets a career that most benefits his skills and preferences, Succession Management looks at similar information but from the point of view of the company. The aim of Succession Management is to ensure that your company always has the right people available to fulfill roles in your company when organizational or personnel changes create vacancies in key positions.

> Succession Management ensures that you always have the right people ready to fill vacant positions quickly

The first step in Succession Management is identifying which positions or jobs in your company are so vital to your company's operations that you need to have succession plans in place. In a perfect world you would have a succession plan for all of your positions, but the amount of work involved in creating such a plan and the ongoing maintenance of it means most companies are limited to identifying key positions and just planning for these.

 Example

> If you were running an orchestra, you would probably identify the conductor as a key position. You could afford to lose one trumpeter without a large impact on your overall performance, but if you lose your conductor, it's the end of the show.

The same kind of thinking needs to be applied to your company before you embark on Succession Management. What are the key roles in your company, which if an unexpected vacancy occurs would cause your organization to feel an immediate and dramatic impact. Obvious examples include the chief executive officer or president, but different companies have different priorities, and no two companies will be quite the same.

For example, if your company identified the chief executive officer position as a key role, the following *criteria* might be defined against the role:

> 20 years experience in the industry

> Previous experience in the public sector

> Master' degree in business administration

> Fluent in English and Spanish

> Member of the League of CEOs

Figure 11.2 shows the requirements defined in Succession Management for an example position.

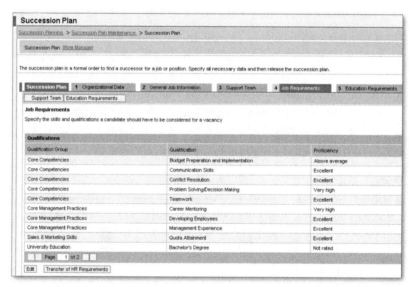

Figure 11.2 Requirements Defined in Succession Management

Succession Management works by matching the criteria defined for the role with the skills, qualifications, and preferences of your potential candidates. Depending on your company's requirements, these candidates could be employees, employment candidates, and even external employees who you record in your system. There are several different methods of performing succession management, so let's explore them in more detail.

Defining the Requirements

Once you have identified the key roles in your company, you need to ensure that they are well enough defined to find the right candidate to fill them. The more specific your definition of the role, the better chance you have of finding a candidate with the same qualities. You can use the criteria listed in Table 11.2 to define a position or a job.

Criterion	Explanation
Qualifications	As defined in your company's qualifications catalog, these could be a mix of formal qualifications, industry qualifications, and internal qualifications.
Preferences	These could include a preference for the holder to speak Portuguese, have worked in a specific job in the company already, or be working toward a specific qualification.
Potentials	Defines that the person could have the potential to fulfill a certain position or job in the future.
Designations	Designations are used in Career Planning to indicate that a person has been designated as working a specific career path within the company.
Dislikes	These can be used to highlight the dislikes of a certain position, for example, travel or long hours
Career(s)	Indicates that a position or job is included in a career path or paths in your company.

Table 11.1 Criteria Defining a Position

Succession Planning for a Single Position

This is the most common form of Succession Management, and it involves identifying key positions in your company and identifying candidates for them. You do this by running the Succession Management transaction for your selected position or job. The system looks at the criteria you have defined for this role (made up of any combination of skills, qualifications, preferences, etc. that define the role). The program analyzes all of the candidates in your system and shows you a ranked list of those who have the closest profiles.

Match the requirements of key jobs with your employees' skills to find good candidates and start prepping them for their next career step

279

The output has several views including:

> A list of all of the criteria for the position and the number of people who meet each of the criteria, so the same person may appear multiple times, if he meets more than one of the criteria

> The people who meet *all* of the criteria—your most obvious candidates for succession planning

> Ranked lists showing all of the potential candidates with suitability percentages based on various criteria

> Figure 11.3 shows a list of potential successors ranked on their response to a questionnaire

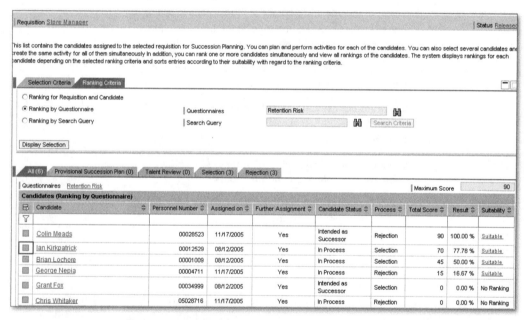

Figure 11.3 Ranking Potential Successors

You can double-click on individual candidates to see more detail on their profiles. When you have selected your ideal candidate, you can formally link the potential successors to the position as a potential candidate, a designated successor, or someone having a preference for the position. All of these forms are recorded against the employees' personal records so they can be included in the employee's career and development planning.

Finding a Successor with Immediate Effect

If your succession need is immediate, for example, if the position has just become vacant or it's a newly created position, you can identify and transfer the employee into the new role immediately.

When you run Succession Management for a position, you can display the employees who are already assigned as designates for the position. Being a designate means the employee has already been identified (possibly as part of the Career Management process) as having all or most of the skills and qualifications required to fulfill the position.

The standard integration with the SAP ERP HCM Personnel Administration and Organizational Management components ensures that the employee is successfully transferred into the new position and that all necessary records are immediately updated.

> You can use Succession Management to quickly find suitable replacements for key vacancies

 Tip

The transfer is a one-stop process; of course, if you want to trigger workflow notifications or approval requests, this too can be built into the solution.

Help Potential Successors Upgrade Their Skills

If you don't find a potential successor with exactly the right qualifications, you can highlight the specific skill deficits of potential successors and help them create development plans to address the skills deficit. Alternatively, you can link directly into the training component and either book the employee into the required training course or notify the training department of the deficit so that they can make an action plan.

> Identify qualification gaps and link into Enterprise Learning Management to address the deficit

Succession Planning for Groups

In addition to looking at specific positions, you can perform the same tasks for a whole organizational unit or a group of jobs. As discussed in Chapter 3, Organizational Management, an organizational unit is a grouping of positions in your company, for example, your finance department or a group of shift workers in a production plant. You can run succession planning for all of the positions in a specific organizational unit, a group of organizational units, or a group of jobs (known as a job family). You'll then be presented with an overview of the number of potential successors for each position in the organizational unit based on the selection criteria (Figure 11.4).

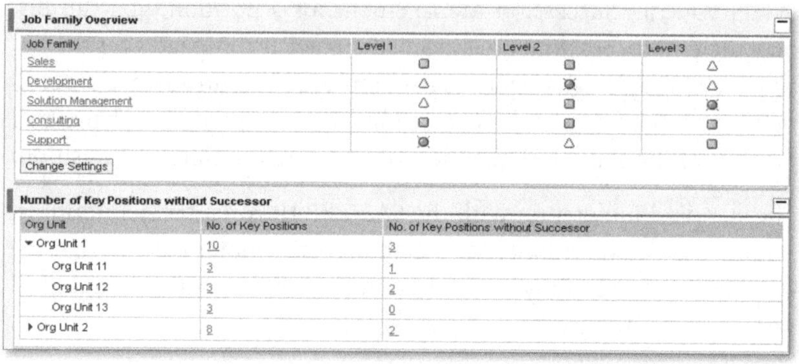

Figure 11.4 Overall View of Your Succession Planning Status

This allows you to evaluate how thorough your succession planning has been. Gaps in your succession plans will be highlighted to show where no employee has the right capabilities to fill a position. You can also see a breakdown of the number of people who meet each of the individual criteria for a position and the number of people who meet all of the criteria.

Analyzing the Effects of Your Succession Planning

Quickly establish the potential effects of succession-related movements

Being able to quickly and effectively identify and move an employee into the next step in his career path allows you to fill key positions in your company, but moving an employee from one position to another obviously leaves a vacancy in the employees' original position. Fortunately, the Career and Succession Management function gives you a tool that allows you to analyze the effects of moving employees.

The program allows you to simulate a change to one position and view the potential career movements that will be required to fill the vacancies that are created as a result. You can see all of the steps in the chain, analyze the matches between candidates and positions, and ensure that the benefits gained from moving the employee at the top of the chain do not outweigh the potential impacts further down the chain.

Summary

The Career and Succession Management function of SAP ERP HCM gives you the tools to tackle one of the most complex and difficult tasks in HR management. The benefits that come from spending the time developing career and succession plans are well recognized, but the amount of effort involved in creating and then maintaining these plans must also be recognized. Here are some key points to remember from this chapter:

> Career and Succession Management gives you the ability to create career paths that formalize the common career paths in your company. These career paths can then be used to demonstrate the potential for employee development in your company and to motivate current employees and attract potential employees to your company.

> The Succession Management function ensures that your company has the right people available with the right skills, qualifications, experience, and preferences to fill key roles.

> Having succession plans in place for your key positions gives you the comfort of knowing that no matter what sudden employee-related surprises occur, you have the plans in place to ensure a rapid transition, minimizing the negative impact of employee changes on your company.

> Career and Succession Management uses qualifications and skills catalogs, among other things, to define the positions in your company.

In the next chapter, Enterprise Learning Management, we'll look at how your company can manage learning and use it to your best advantage.

Enterprise Learning Management

Today's knowledge economy demands skilled workers, yet studies show that 80% of a knowledge worker's skills are obsolete within five years. The Enterprise Learning Management function enables companies to provide a learning environment for their employees (and external delegates) that can deliver training quickly and efficiently over a wide variety of media. It is a truly blended learning offering. It enables companies to deliver traditional classroom-based training, web-based training, virtual classroom training, and online collaborative environments to ensure that learners get the most out of their learning experience.

This function delivers a set of tools to ensure that all of the key participants in the learning process get the most out of the learning process. Learners can access their personal learning portal. Instructors have their own instructor portals to manage their work, and administrators are provided with a set of tools to streamline and optimize the organization of the training program.

A fully developed content creation and management solution allows content authors to quickly and efficiently develop and publish a range of content, from traditional paper training materials to the latest technology, such as Macromedia and Flash training materials, to online tests and surveys. The solution also allows the integration of training materials from third-party suppliers and the direct integration of third-party content into your course catalog.

How SAP ERP HCM Enterprise Learning Management Fits into an Enterprise

The days of your training department sitting quietly back in their corner of the HR department are long over. New technology such as web-delivered training can have a dramatic effect on your company's ability to deliver learning in an efficient, timely, and cost-effective manner. The Internet helps employees find, book, and attend learning events. This saves companies large amounts of money in their training budget by removing the need for centralized and time-based classroom-style training courses. When you add the ability for instructors and tutors to manage their learning commitments online using real-time data, you start to see great savings and optimization of the training course.

The use of online learning and collaboration tools allows users spread over wide geographical ranges to participate and collaborate in online training courses. Learners, managers, and training administrators can also all be kept up to date with real-time information and communication. Traditional classroom-based training is also enhanced by the use of demand planning and efficient booking management systems, ensuring that your classroom training is always well attended and provided only when a real demand exists.

A Closer Look at Enterprise Learning Management

Enterprise Learning Management is conducted in the SAP Enterprise Learning Solution

Enterprise Learning Management in HCM is enabled by the SAP *Enterprise Learning Solution (LSO)*. In keeping up with increasing customer demand for web-based training, this component is focused on online portal access rather than more traditional direct SAP ERP access. Because the content and management interfaces are delivered via the portal, companies can tailor and customize the look and feel of the solution more than they can with the more direct SAP ERP access components.

The SAP Enterprise Learning Solution is made is up of a set of related components that manage all aspects of enterprise learning management, from employee access and course booking to online course creation tools and the newest technology in online collaboration and virtual learning. The functions of the SAP Enterprise Learning Solution that we will look at in this chapter are:

> **Authoring and Publishing Content**
Tools and functions to help your training department and instructors quickly create both online and offline training materials and publish them for use.

Create and manage all of your learning content

> **Content Management**
You can have the best content in the world, but if your instructors can't access it, it's worthless. Content Management ensures that your content is always available and up to date.

> **Training Management**
This function gives you all of the tools you need to manage your learning program, course schedule, demand planning, learner, instructor, and resource management tools, and the ability to charge and recover costs associated with learning provision.

Manage your companies learning with the minimum of fuss

> **Learning Portal**
The Learning Portal is an employee-tailored view of your company's training program. It allows employees to view their history, make new bookings, and view course content.

> **Content Player**
Designed for the effective delivery of online content, the Content Player delivers and monitors web content, allowing employees to learn and the training team to monitor their progress.

Content Player, Virtual Learning Rooms, and Collaboration Rooms allow you to deliver training wherever your employees are located

> **Virtual Learning Rooms**
Utilizing cutting edge technology, Virtual Learning Rooms provide an interactive platform for the efficient delivery of online learning. Instructors can deliver web cam training and course handouts, and

learners can engage in question and answer and chat sessions to ensure the best learning environment.

> **Collaboration Rooms**
After a training course has been completed, these online rooms allows learners, instructors, and tutors to work together to get the most benefit out of the learning process

> **Instructor Portal**
This function is designed to cut down on administration and maximize instructors' training time by providing them with all of the information they need in one efficient and up-to-date location.

> **Integration**
The full integration between the Enterprise Learning Solution, other SAP ERP HCM functions, and other SAP ERP components ensures that your training department always has up-to-date information and can provide information to all interested parties, from finance to compensation management.

Let's look at all of these functions in more detail to understand their potential.

Authoring and Publishing Content

Authors can create all types of training materials in one streamlined tool

The creation of good course content such as training materials, tests, and handouts is a large part of ensuring the success of the learning process. The *Authoring Environment* is an application that is installed separately from the SAP ERP installation on authors' machines. It is designed to allow authors to quickly and efficiently create or upload course content. In addition to allowing uploading of pre-prepared course content, it contains tools and wizards to allow course authors to create, maintain, test, and publish content. It allows authors to create course materials using a large variety of applications including Microsoft PowerPoint and FrontPage, Adobe Flash, Macromedia DreamWeaver, and Authorware. Content can be created and maintained in many formats including .html, .pdf, and .swf.

Companies that run large learning and training programs naturally have a large volume of learning materials and therefore an ongoing requirement for the creation and maintenance of course materials. Some companies choose to outsource the creation of training materials, others create their own, and some choose a mix of both. Either way, if your company is creating its own training materials or outsourcing, you will use the Authoring Environment to prepare the content to be released into the Content Management system (which we will learn about in the next section).

Creating and Organizing Content

The content that is created and maintained in the Authoring Environment is described by its own SAP ERP–specific terms, which we will now explain:

Learning Nets

A *learning net* represents a complete course. It is a collection of individual learning objects that combined provide the course content. Complex courses contain subnets representing training course subunits within a larger course.

Learning Objects

These are the individual units of training. The aim of creating *learning objects* is to break a training course into discrete parcels of content that can then be reused in other training courses.

By defining your content in small chunks, you can reuse pieces across many courses

Instructional Elements

These are the smallest unit of the content structure. *Instructional elements* impart the actual content of the learning. Instructional elements can be combined to create learning objects or stand-alone elements. The point of defining these at such a low level is so the elements can be used across multiple learning objects and learning nets. Instructional elements contain content and a delivery method. Examples of instructional elements are shown in Table 12.1.

Orientation	Practical Instruction	Explanation	Reference Material
History	Rule	*Why* explanation	Background document
Scenario	Procedure	*What* explanation	Explanation PowerPoint
Facts	Checklist	Definition	Excel Checklist
Summary	Principle	Example	Summary document
Overview	Strategy	Example	Strategy overview document

Table 12.1 Types of Instructional Elements

Delivery methods define how the content is delivered to the learner. They can be either passive, as in a presentation, or interactive (Table 12.2).

Passive	Interactive
Text	Compound/form
Graphic	Virtual learning room
Image	Collaboration room
Animation	None
Audio	None
Film/video	None

Table 12.2 Instructional Element Delivery Methods

All content has full version control, ensuring that users always see the latest versions of learning materials

Once created, instructional elements are stored with version control. When a new version of an element is created, for example, to include updated instructions, the newest version of the element is automatically used in all of the learning nets and objects to which it is related.

Follow-up activities can be allocated to content. This could include completion surveys, tests, or the awarding of qualifications to those who successfully complete the course. Automatically awarding quali-fications upon completion is useful for web-delivered content, but for more traditional classroom-based content, qualifications can be set to be awarded upon the specific action of the course instructor or train-ing administrator.

Test Elements

A *test element* is a form of element used for performing different types of tests as part of a learning program. Examples of the types of test elements include:

> Final test

> Self-assessment test

> Exercise

> Placement test

Measure the effectiveness of your training by creating online tests and exercises

So the combination of instructional and test elements representing the content of courses and tests to evaluate understanding are com-bined into a learning object that represents the parts of a training course. The training course itself is represented by the learning net. This is a lot to understand and may be best illustrated with an exam-ple. For our example, let's imagine what content elements you would need to create a web-delivered food handling course for new starters at a hypothetical food company (Table 12.3).

Title	Description	Technical Term
Introductory Food Handling Training	A two-hour online training course teaching food handling rules for new starters	Learning Net
Part A: Introduction and Skills Assessment	An introduction to web-delivered training and a test of existing knowledge	Learning Object 1
Introduction	Generic PowerPoint presentation introducing delegates to online training	Instructional Element 1

Table 12.3 Hypothetical Enterprise Learning Course

Title	Description	Technical Term
Food Safety Introduction	A PowerPoint explanation of what will be covered in the training course	Instructional Element 2
Skills Assessment	An online test of food handling knowledge	Test Element 1
Part B: Food Handling Training Delivery	The details of the training course and a test of learner comprehension	Learning Object 2
Basic Food Handling Safety Training	A web-delivered film on food handling rules	Instructional Element 3
Comprehension Test	An online test of understanding	Test Element 2
Take-Home Materials	A PDF document explaining food safety rules	Instructional Element 4

Table 12.3 Hypothetical Enterprise Learning Course (Cont.)

Authoring Tools

Now that you have seen what goes into defining learning content, we will look at the tools used to create the content.

Instructional Design Editor

The instructional design editor centralizes all of your authoring and design tools

This tool is the main editor for content. It allows you to create, edit, and maintain the elements of the content we explored above. The course author tags the elements with a *knowledge category* in the *Instructional Design Editor*. A knowledge category is used to group similar elements together so that they can be efficiently stored, searched, and sorted. A knowledge category could be "orientation documents." In this case, all of the elements that have been created that orient trainees in a specific subject are grouped in this knowledge category. Defining these categories gives your content its structure.

Inside the editor you link your elements together to form your learning objects and learning nets. You create relationships between the elements to link them together. For example, a generic video introduction to web-based course (which is stored as an instructional element) could have relationships to all of the web-delivered training courses (stored as learning nets), because it used as the generic introduction to all of them.

The tool for creating learning nets and objects is a graphical display (Figure 12.1), making it simple to arrange course content in a layout that represents the order in which it will be presented. Being able to reuse your content across many training courses is a good way of defraying the cost of developing content.

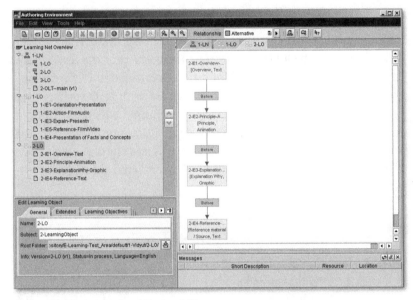

Figure 12.1 The Instructional Design Editor

The Instructional Design Editor also contains an area for displaying information, warnings, and help messages. These messages provide all of the information a content author needs to create the required content and speeds up the learning process. There is also an area called the *Learning Strategy Preview*, which is used for validating content before it is released into the Content Manager.

Test and Questionnaire Author

Once an author has created a training course or imported one into the system, he can add tests or questionnaires to the course to measure learner understanding. These tests and surveys can be added to the

Create detailed tests to automatically decide who passes and fails a course

293

course wherever they are required using the *Test Author*. A test or a learner survey could be added at the start of the course to test initial understanding midway through the course to ensure learners are keeping up with the content, and at the end to ensure that learners have learned and determine which learners have successfully completed the course and should receive the qualification. Tests can also be created outside any course. Stand-alone tests can be created where required and added to the Learning Solution.

Create interactive tests with videos and web content built into the questions

Tests can be configured as multiple choice, question and answer, or multiple answer formats. Graphics, screen prints, videos, and other web content can be added to improve the content of the test. Different scoring models can be used for different calculation requirements. Conditions and parameters can be associated with tests such as time limits for completing the test and setting required pass rates. You can set tests so that they can be retaken multiple times or only attempted once. You can also provide feedback about test results via workflow. Figure 12.2 shows a questionnaire being delivered through the Virtual Learning Room.

Figure 12.2 A Quiz Question Being Asked in a Virtual Learning Room

Repository Explorer

The *Repository Explorer* is used to administer course content. You can perform all of the functions required to manage your content. You can create, copy, delete, check, and transport your content here. The explorer allows you to store content on your local PC via the *Local Repository*. Authors can then make changes to course content while offline, and then when they are online, they can transport this content back into the *Master Repository*. The Local and Master Repositories are integrated with version management, allowing you to control different versions of a specific piece of content while switching from online to offline maintenance. After content has been stored in the Master Repository, it is available for other authors to view, edit, and collaborate on. The Repository Explorer gives you the ability to create folder structures to store your content in a way that is logical and meaningful to your course authors.

Automatically synchronize your local and networked content

Publishing

Publishing is the final step in creating course content. Until the content is published, it is only stored in the authoring environment. Once it is published, it is made available for training administrators to use in the Enterprise Learning Solution and is available in the Content Management system. Part of the release process requires the author to identify the type of course he has created. This course type is then used in content administration to correctly assign the course in the Content Management system.

Content Management System

The *Content Management System* (CMS) is designed to allow you to effectively and efficiently manage your company's Learning Solution content. Once the author publishes and releases his content, it is stored as reusable content. The content is controlled by the CMS so that version control is applied and the link between the course and the resulting qualification is established.

Store your own content and third-party content in one central system

Create and store
SCROM- and AICC-
compliant content

Quickly import and
export content to
third-party suppliers

The CMS is designed to be an open storage and management system for any content—not just content created in the SAP ERP Authoring Environment. The CMS is certified as compliant with the Shareable Content Object Reference Model (SCORM) and the Aviation Industry Computer-Based Training Committee (AICC) web-delivered training standards. These are the two most commonly used standards for the creation of web-delivered training content, and the CMS system is designed to quickly and efficiently import and export content that is compliant with both of these standards.

Content can be pushed via the organizational structure to parts of your company that require the training. For example, new management training programs can be pushed directly into the Learning Portals of employees who are identified as holding management positions.

Training Management

Administer your
Learning
Management
program with
minimum fuss and
maximum efficiency

Now that we have our content, it's time to start developing training plans to deliver it. This is where the *Training Management* function comes into play. Training Management is the administrative side of the SAP Learning Solution. It is used to plan the company curricula, manage course participants, allocate and manage training costs, manage training resources such as rooms and equipment, as well as the company's course catalog. Let's look at these areas in more detail to understand how they work.

Course Catalog

The course catalog
makes all of your
content available to
all potential learners

Having a well-structured *course catalog* is important to ensure that learners, instructors, and administrators can find the courses they need with the minimum of fuss. The course catalog divides the content into *course groups, course types,* and *courses.* Let's look at an example of a small course catalog to illustrate how these terms are used (see Table 12.4).

The course catalog includes all of the formats of training that your company or third parties provide. This could include web-based training, classroom training, and virtual classroom training. Users who are browsing the course catalog can view all of the information on the courses to help them evaluate the courses they are interested in.

Course Groups	Computer Courses	Language Courses
Course Group 1	Software Training	Portuguese Courses
Course Types	Basic SAP training	Beginners Portuguese
	Advanced SAP training	Business Portuguese
Course Group 2	Hardware Installation	Spanish Courses
Course Types	PC installation	Beginners Spanish
	Network installation	Business Spanish

Table 12.4 Course Groups and Course Types in a Course Catalog

Your training administrators can define the courses in ways that make them easier to categorize and ensure that they are easily available to the relevant parties. Administrators can add course descriptions detailing the course contents, objectives, target groups, compulsory and optional content, prerequisite courses, and qualifications. They can link the imparted qualifications and any fees and charges.

Define your catalog with categories and target groups and link to qualifications

Courses can also be defined as time dependent or independent. Time-independent courses can be taken at any time. They do not need to be run according to a specific schedule. These are usually web-delivered courses because time-dependent courses are normally more traditional classroom-based classes. They need to be scheduled and booked before they can be delivered.

Delivering web-based training introduces a whole new set of course parameters that need to be defined such as expected course durations, if the course is always available or only for specified periods, and to whom it is available. Figure 12.3 displays an example course catalog, as viewed by a learner.

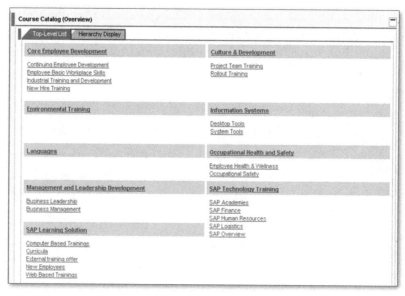

Figure 12.3 Example Course Catalog

Publish your catalog with automatic brochure-creation tools

Training administrators can create course brochures listing the company's entire course catalog or specific sections of the catalog targeted at specific groups of employees. Brochures can be either downloaded or posted on the portal for learners to access.

Seamless integration of your content and third-party external learning content

Once a learner has found a course he wants to attend, he can register for the course from the course catalog. Of course, some bookings require approval before a delegate can attend them. This requirement can be assigned to the course in the catalog, and the employee's registration will be forwarded to the correct approver via workflow. As soon as the approval is received, the employee can register for the course.

In addition to managing your course catalog, you can automatically connect to third-party training catalogs to integrate their content into your company's offerings. When an employee selects a course from a third-party supplier, the employee is then taken to the external providers system to view the content.

The training administrator can also use the course catalog for reporting on learning management. For example, an administrator can select a specific course and run reports for course demand, participation and sales statistics to provide important information for course planning.

Curricula

The curricula of your company's Learning Solution system represents the combination of courses into larger programs of learning. Sometimes a training course is presented on its own to deliver a specific goal, but often a goal such as a new qualification or promotion can only be achieved by attending a range of courses. An example of a curriculum could be your company's graduate intake training curriculum, as shown in Table 12.5.

> Curricula allow you to link multiple courses into a comprehensive training program

Course	Content	Format
Introduction	Introduction to the graduate program	Classroom
Company History	Presentation on the history of the company	Web-delivered video
Course Overview	Explanation of the graduate program	PowerPoint presentation in the virtual classroom
Sales and Marketing Training	Introduction to sales and marketing	Class and web-delivered training
HR Training	Introduction to human resources	External classroom training
Finance Training	Introduction to finance operations	Web-delivered training

Table 12.5 Graduate Intake Training Curriculum

Defining curricula allows your company to provide truly *blended learning* that allows you to combine traditional classroom courses with virtual classroom and web-based training to provide an integrated training platform that delivers the best possible training results. You can define prerequisite qualifications or training courses for specific curriculum, so that learners can book themselves onto a curriculum only when they achieved all of the prerequisites.

> Curricula give you the ability to provide multi-format blended training programs

Creating a Course Calendar

Demand planning helps you optimize your training delivery, ensuring that you only provide training when real demand exists

After you have defined your courses and created your curricula, you need to create your learning calendar. Within Training Management you have all of the tools required to efficiently manage your company's learning program. Training administrators can manually schedule face-to-face training courses for set times, dates, languages, and locations, or schedule them to take place at fixed intervals or spread over a planning period. Courses can be scheduled automatically by the system per date, location, and language based on demand for the course.

The scheduling of courses takes into consideration time constraints such as local public holidays, factory calendars, factory working days, and fixed start dates. The Enterprise Learning Solution can automatically propose learning resources such as rooms and instructors based on the requirements defined on the course and the availability of the resources.

Person Management

Automatic integration with Personnel Administration and Time Management means you always see the most up-to-date data on learners

The training administrator can manage both internal and external participants. External participants can be set up as basic human resource records so they can be booked into courses, their participation monitored, and their results and qualifications reported back to third-party organizations. All of the relevant employee data stored in SAP ERP HCM can be made available to training administrators so they can make informed decisions when managing employees. Information such as location, position, job, employment, and qualifications history can be viewed by the training administrators and help them allocate employees to the right courses and events. Training administrators can carry out the following activities to manage participants:

> **Prebook**
> When an employee expresses an interest in attending a course, but a direct booking cannot be made, a prebooking can be made that can then be used to measure future demand.

> **Book**
> Individual learners or groups of learners such as teams or organizational units can be quickly booked into specific courses or curricula.

> **Rebook**
Participants can have an existing booking moved to an earlier or later session using the automatic rebooking functionality.

> **Replace**
Individual participants or groups of participants can be replaced with different participants or groups if required.

> **Cancel**
The cancel function allows you to remove booked participants.

The training administrator can also manage the course instructors and tutors. Being able to view potential instructors' and tutors' locations, qualifications, experience, and costs helps the administrator allocate the appropriate instructor to each course. Because the SAP Learning Solution is fully integrated with all of the other functions of SAP ERP HCM, training administrators can always be sure that the employee data they are using is up to date and consistent.

In addition to managing learners, you can manage your instructors to maximize their use

Resource Management

The *Resource Management* area gives the training manager the ability to effectively manage all of the resources involved in training provision. Objects such as rooms, training equipment, and training materials and devices can all be logged in the system and then matched and allocated against course requirements. The resources identified in the Learning Solution can also be linked to the Materials Management component for tracking purposes. Training managers view a training course, check the list of required resources for the course, and then can ensure that all training courses have been allocated the right resources, for example, rooms have adequate capacities and are free at the time required and the right equipment and training materials are available on the day required.

Links to the Materials Management component avoids duplicating resource lists and maintenance

Recurring Activities

This function is focused on making the administration of learning as simple and efficient as possible. Activities that commonly reoccur including course follow-up activities such as awarding qualifications and cancellation processes are managed through the *Recurring*

Automate your routine tasks such as reminders, booking confirmations, and cancellations

Activities function. This allows common processes to be allocated to specific training team members and automated where possible. The generation of training correspondence such as course notifications, reminders, status updates, and other activities can be efficiently processed using Adobe templates. The templates can then be sent to the appropriate learners, instructors, and managers via workflow, printed media, email, or SMS. Automatic notifications can be triggered when courses are cancelled, changed, or other notifications are required.

Budgeting and Cost Allocation

Links to Finance, Payroll, and Sales and Distribution allow you to keep your learning costs well under control

As we will see later in Chapter 14, Compensation Management, the use of budgets to estimate and measure actual costs is an important part of SAP ERP HCM. Budgets can also be used in this component to allocate and track training courses costs against a set budget limit at organizational unit or individual employee levels. Managers can then monitor budget burn rates, tracking both training costs and cancellation fees against their own budgets.

In addition to managing training budgets, this function also provides four methods for allocating training costs. The link to the Sales and Distribution component allows your training team to charge attendance and cancellation fees to external customers via Sales and Distribution customer management. Attendance and cancellation fees and instructor costs can also be charged to the cost centers, internal orders, and projects of internal attendees via an interface to SAP ERP Financials' controlling function.

The costs of providing training equipment such as computers and training rooms can also be allocated back to the correct department via cost allocation to controlling. When a course is led by an instructor (as opposed to being web delivered), the actual cost of the instructors' time can be derived via the integration between the Learning Solution and Payroll from the instructors' payroll results. This cost can then be used to measure the costs and the effectiveness of the training.

Reporting

The Enterprise Learning Solution along with its full integration with NetWeaver BI provides all of the reporting functionality you would expect to manage the learning process. The range of reports includes delegate and attendee lists for offline courses, delegate lists, start and end times, and completion times for web-delivered training. Reports for pass and fail rates and all other statistics relating to testing are also available so you can measure the success of your training. Resource reports allow you to ensure that all of the required resources are available when needed and that there are no clashes in requirements for resources or instructors.

Get instant access to learning statistics and view pass and fail rates, attendance records, and so on as soon as the course is completed

Learning Portal

Once a course or curricula has been released by the training manager, the employee can use the *Learning Portal* to view the available courses and then apply for or book directly on a training course. When an employee accesses his personal Learning Portal, he sees content that is tailored to him. This tailoring may be personal to the individual or based on his job, position, organizational unit, or whatever other group is used to define learning requirements and needs.

Learners see a personalized web-delivered view of their learning past and future

The employee can instantly see the course catalog and what is known as his *learner account*. A learner account details the employee's full learning history including courses attended and future course bookings, qualification information, and *preferred learning strategy*. The preferred learning strategy is used to match employees with the kind of learning that they respond best too. Types of learning strategies include explanation-oriented, task-oriented, and example-oriented training.

The portal also allows the training management team to communicate with the employee. This might be done to highlight to the employee any required training courses, for example, because of a skills gaps analysis, missing or expired qualifications, or an overview of current learning activities.

The Learning Portal is designed to empower employees to manage their own learning and training. Employees can use a variety of search tools to find learning and training courses that they can then inves-

Powerful search tools empower learners to find, book, and manage their own learning

tigate. Employees can also perform *profile matchups*, which are used to compare the employees' skills, qualifications, and experience with the requirements for a new job, position, or development plan. The profile matchup displays the qualifications that the employee would need to acquire to move into the new job of position.

Once an employee finds a course he is interested in attending, he can view the details of the course, the scheduling of the course, its location, and any costs associated with it. If the employee wants to attend the course, depending on the setting of the course itself and the employee's privileges, the employee can enroll in a training course or notify a manager via workflow that he wants approval to attend the course.

Automatic integration with Time Management means employees are only booked in courses when it suits their roster and working times

When an employee is booked in a specific training course, the automatic integration with Time Management allows the system to automatically check the employee's work schedule and planned working times to ensure that the employee is actually available to attend the course and does not have any conflicting time bookings such as other training or holidays.

Figure 12.4 shows an employee Learning Portal/ Messages displayed across the top. Underneath that is the employees' training activities including booked and in progress courses. On the left side of the screen, the course catalog can be accessed.

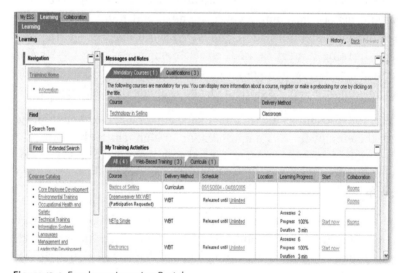

Figure 12.4 Employee Learning Portal

Content Player

When an employee has been scheduled to receive web-based content (for example, a training course or online test), the course content is delivered to the employee via the *Content Player*. The Content Player is an application that allows the learner to view the content and receive the training. The content player monitors the learner's progress through the content and feeds progress information back into the learner account.

The Content Player can be used online or offline, so the learner can download the content onto his own machine and view the content at a convenient time. The learner can then synchronize the content, updating all of the information about progress and completion.

After an employee has completed the content, he can attach a date-stamped digital signature to the content registering that he has completed the course and any tests associated with the content. All of this information is then automatically updated in the employee's master data. If a qualification is to be awarded based on the course completion, this will be automatically awarded upon completion, or a training administrator can be notified to award the qualification.

> The Content Player allows employees to watch web-delivered content on- and offline and monitors them to ensure that the course was really completed

Virtual Learning Rooms

Virtual Learning Rooms are a great illustration of the future of learning delivery. Using Adobe Connect software and fully integrated with SAP ERP, Virtual Learning Rooms are a web-communication system that allows you to deliver interactive training courses, presentations, online collaborations, and conferences via the web.

Instructors create Virtual Learning Rooms that can then be used to upload, collate, and present materials relating to courses. Once set-up and linked to a training course or curriculum a virtual learning room can be reused each time a course is run. Virtual Learning Rooms can use web cams and voice pods to share live video and audio files. Chat and question and answer sessions can be run through the virtual learning room, allowing instructors to present content and take questions at the end—or during the presentation. The instructor or tutor can

> Virtual Learning Rooms: all of the benefits of classroom training, without the associated commuting time

also produce ad hoc surveys and questionnaires in the virtual learning room that can be presented to attendees during the training course. Documents, presentations, and handouts can be made available for learners to download at the end of or during a learning session.

Figure 12.5 shows an example of a virtual learning room with four attendees. In this figure, a chat is going on between two learners. We can see the current slide of the PowerPoint presentation and the slides to come. The handout document is attached in the bottom right corner for learners to download.

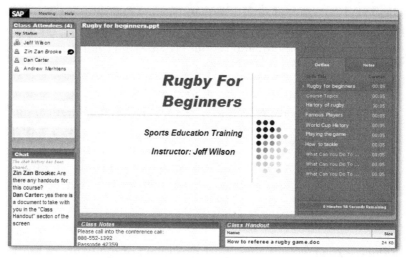

Figure 12.5 Virtual Learning Rooms in Action

Collaboration Rooms

Collaboration Rooms allow web-based chat, discussions, and document sharing before, during, and after a learning session

The actual training content of courses is only one of the benefits of attending training courses. The group learning experience of attending training is enhanced by interactions that naturally occur as part of the training. *Collaboration Rooms* are designed to enhance the direct training benefits by providing attendees with a forum for collaborating further. The Collaboration Rooms can be accessed either as part of a specific training course or as part of a broader curriculum. They can be set up to be ongoing so future and past attendees of a course or curriculum can share their experiences. Trainers, attendees, and experts can share information relating to the course through instant messenger chats, posted white papers, discussion forums, calendars, news forums, and document sharing to ensure that the learning experience is as effective as possible.

Instructor Portal

The *Instructor Portal* (Figure 12.6) delivers all of the functionality and services that instructors need to help them maximize their time delivering training and minimize the time they spend on administration. The Instructor Portal provides an up-to-the-minute, reliable, and personalized view of all of the information instructors need to perform their jobs. It enables them to view the courses they are scheduled to deliver, review delegate lists, add and remove delegates from courses, and confirm delegates to ensure that they attend.

The Instructor Portal ensures that instructors spend more time instructing and less time doing administration

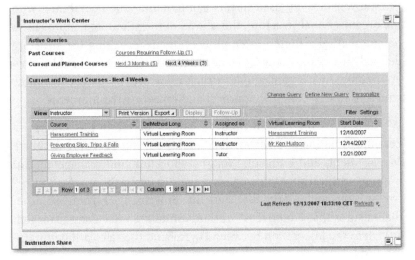

Figure 12.6 The Instructor Portal

Instructors can launch Virtual Classroom sessions directly from their portals, enabling them to prepare for and deliver virtual learning immediately and participate and monitor collaboration rooms, and deliver tutoring. At the end of a course, the instructor can be prompted to assess delegates' performance, evaluating their pass or fail status and awarding marks and perform appraisals. These appraisals are directly linked to the appraisals completed in the Employee Performance Management function. The Enterprise Learning Solution appraisals can then form part of the employee's overall Performance Management program.

Integration with other Components

The Enterprise Learning Solution leverages the strong integration with other SAP ERP components. With full integration, when employees receive new qualifications, the information is instantly available in the employees' master records. When employees are booked into training courses, shift planners can instantly see that the employees are no longer available to work at that time. Costs associated with attending training courses are accounted for and transferred automatically to the correct financial areas for accounting purposes.

Workflow is heavily used in this component. When combined with the organizational structure, this allows notifications and approvals to be automatically routed to employees' managers using the structure defined in Organizational Management. This structure could follow your company's organizational structure or use a separate workflow structure to fulfill specific approval and reporting requirements.

We also explored the integration points between the Enterprise Learning Solution and Materials Management for Learning Resource Management, and budgeting for the allocation and management of training and learning budgets. And we discussed the integration between Time and Attendance and the Enterprise Learning Solution that ensures that employees' working times are effectively managed, as well as the integration between Payroll and the calculation of training costs.

Enterprise Learning Management can even be installed without SAP ERP HCM

In addition, the SAP Enterprise Learning Solution can also be installed as a stand-alone component in companies that do not use the other functions of SAP ERP HCM. A third-party vendor can be integrated into the solution, and data can be stored in the SAP ERP HCM functions, though it can only be accessed through the Learning Solution interface.

Key Infotypes

Many infotypes are related to Enterprise Learning Solution, so let's look at the most important ones and see what they are used for.

> **Infotype 1001 Relationships**
This infotype is used throughout SAP ERP HCM to link courses and curricula to course groups to create a hierarchically arranged catalog.

> **Infotype 1002 Description**
This key infotype holds the details of courses including Extended Course Text, Course Content, and Notes.

> **Infotype 1026 Course Info**
This infotype stores information that defines if the course is being presented internally or externally, lists the language in which the course is presented, and shows if the course is to be locked or deleted (to stop future bookings).

> **Infotype 1035 Schedule**
When you define the schedule for your course, the details of the dates, start and end times, and duration are stored here.

> **Infotype 1036 Costs**
Here is where you allocate the costs of conducting a course, either divided per course, per time unit of course, or per participant.

> **Infotype 1063 Course Group Info**
This infotype is used to store the top levels of your course groups. Each record here represents a new separate group of courses.

> **Infotype 5003 Course Content Static**
This infotype links the courses stored in Content Management with the web addresses called from the Learning Portal and Content Player.

> **Infotype 5004 Curriculum Type Info**
When you define a curriculum made up of a set of courses, this infotype is used to define if follow-up learning can be done after the whole curriculum or just some of the courses are completed.

> **Infotype 5006 Course Type Content**
> The link between a course and its content (such as training materials, PowerPoint slides, etc.) is stored here.

> **Infotype 5007 Delivery Method**
> This infotype shows how the course is delivered. For example, web-delivered or classroom training is recorded here for each course.

> **Infotype 5008 Completion Specifications**
> When a course has rules regarding its completion, those are stored here. Examples include the maximum and optimum completion time. When the course includes third-party web content, you can store how long the license for the content is valid and how many times it can be accessed.

> **Infotype 5009 Course Content**
> This infotype stores links to the most recent versions of all of the content linked to a course. Each time content is revised, the new version in Content Management is linked to this infotype.

> **Infotype 5042 External Catalog Connection**
> When content is provided by an external provider, this infotype stores the link to the content on the external system and records the delivery language and method.

> **Infotype 5045 Collaboration Room**
> When you assign a collaboration room to a course or curriculum, the two are linked via this infotype.

> **Infotype 5047 Follow-Up Control**
> When you define a course, you define what follow-up steps should be taken at the end of the course. This infotype stores details of all the follow-up activities associated with the course.

> **Infotype 5048 Correspondence Control**
> Correspondence that is automatically generated as part of a course is stored here. This could include booking-confirmation emails, course cancellations SMSs, and so on.

> **Infotype 5049 Versioning Options**
> When new versions of course content are created, this infotype controls when the update is released, how it is released, and what category of change it is.

This concludes the overview of the Enterprise Learning Solution offered in SAP ERP HCM, so let's take a look at a case study illustrating how this function can be put to use in a real-world setting.

Case Study

Table 12.6 provides a quick overview of the case study before we explain it in more detail.

Company	German Manufacturing company
Existing Solutions	SAP ERP including HCM
Challenges	› Rapid increase in learning and training requirements due to technological changes › Managing a broad range of training suppliers and training materials › Increase return on investment of existing SAP ERP HCM components
SAP Solutions	SAP Enterprise Learning Solution
Benefits	› Access to key training results and data › Increase in knowledge transfer › Reduced training management costs › Ability to offer training courses online and worldwide

Table 12.6 Enterprise Learning Management Case Study

This global manufacturing company is based in Europe and employees 40,000 people.

The Challenges

Rapid technological advances had changed the products that this company produced, so they needed a way to deliver a broad range of training courses to employees worldwide. Continual changes to products meant that a large variety of training courses needed to be quickly developed and deployed then kept available for later reference. The company needed to deliver employee performance enhancements via an inexpensive, effective, globally accessible training medium.

The SAP Solution

The company implemented the SAP Enterprise Learning Solution to create a central Learning Portal that could be easily integrated into the company's operations. The Learning Solution delivered classroom-style training anywhere in the world, taking into account local requirements and languages.

The company partnered with two external training companies to help them quickly develop and publish online learning materials.

The Benefits

By switching to an online (and externally accessible) Learning Portal, the company transformed its training department from a liability to a revenue generator. Training courses can now be delivered to employees spread across multiple countries. Employees can download training and complete it when it suits them or complete the training online. Being able to share training materials across the world dramatically reduced the cost of developing the materials. Management uses the powerful reporting tools to evaluate training courses and identify areas where training needed to be performed.

Summary

The Enterprise Learning Solution provides a total learning management solution for even the most complex learning requirements. This is a powerful solution that offers numerous options:

> The Authoring and Publishing solution ensures that companies can quickly create, collaborate on, and publish learning materials and tests using the most up-to-date technology.

> The Content Manager ensures that you derive the most benefit from your valuable content by making all of your courses accessible

to your audience. Content is managed so that it can be reused and shared, ensuring that it is not just used once and forgotten.

> Training Management takes care of recurring tasks such as course follow-up activities and helps the training team generate correspondence to free up their time from administration.

> The Learning and Instructor Portals give personalized and directed content to learners and instructors, saving them precious time and making their learning experience much richer.

> The Content Player and Virtual Learning and Collaboration Rooms move training and learning into the next century, allowing learners to receive and participate in high-quality, well-organized online training with two-way communications and collaboration tools that ensure that learners receive much more than just a handout and a free lunch.

In the next chapter we will look at the Employee Performance Management function, which can be directly integrated with the Enterprise Learning Solution so that results of employee learning, including test results and appraisals, can be fed directly into Employee Performance Management. Similarly, the output of employee development such as training and development requests can be fed straight into this function.

Employee Performance Management

It's not enough to just hire good people. Once you've hired them, your company needs them performing at their optimum level. For a long time employee performance management has been a rather hit-and-miss affair where career development planning and performance appraisals were performed in a well-intentioned but ad-hoc manner with little or no follow through. Taking the time to develop an effective employee performance management program can have massive benefits for your employees and your company. Working with your employees to develop personal career management plans helps keep them motivated and working toward their development goals. Creating a performance appraisal program that includes regular employee appraisals with multiple input sources measured against specific development objectives allows you to monitor your employee performance and ensure that appraisals are performed in a consistent, structured, and fair manner. The SAP HCM Performance Management function enables you to develop an effective system of employee development and performance monitoring, appraisal, and feedback that keeps your employees involved and motivated.

How Performance Management Fits in an Enterprise

Move responsibility
for performance
management out of
the HR office

Even if your company's performance management program is as simple as an annual review for all your employees, this SAP ERP HCM function can help improve the process. If your company currently has or is looking to develop a full employee performance management program, this function can help by providing you with the tools and processes needed to ensure that you create an efficient, manageable, and objective performance management program that will benefit both your employees and your company. Through use of the Enterprise Portal, this function gives employees and managers the ability to perform the majority of the performance management tasks themselves, freeing up time for your HR department to concentrate on more important issues than chasing managers and employees for feedback.

A Closer Look at Performance Management

Performance management, though a very general and common term, translates very differently depending on the company and organization. Everyone agrees that developing your employees to help them meet their potential benefits both the employees and the employer. However, turning this vision into a practical, efficient, and objective process is usually a significant challenge.

SAP HCM Performance Management is a powerful and flexible function that allows you to create performance management tools that are tailored to your company's unique needs. As with other SAP ERP HCM functions, it is tightly integrated with other functions to ensure that the process is as effective and efficient as possible. SAP HCM Performance Management allows the use of the following key processes:

> **Development Plans**
> Development plans are structured paths that move employees toward development goals. A goal may be as simple and short term as attaining a qualification or as complex as managing an appren-

ticeship or college hire program. Once developed, goals are used as road maps for managing employee development.

> **Objective Setting**
> Objectives are the building blocks of good appraisal management. By defining good reusable objectives, you provide a measurable and independent basis on which to assess your employees' performance.

> **Appraisals**
> This is often one of the most contentious parts of managing employees, but by creating effective appraisal templates you can make formal and standardized evaluations of employee performance based on your company's specific needs.

Development Plans

Development plans are a way of giving structure and control to an employee's growth in personal and professional competencies that support the organizational strategic and financial goals. Development plans are created as reusable development templates that formalize personnel development plans as they are used to document specific employee growth and development tasks and goals. You can create development plans for common events that reoccur in your company. The reoccurrence could be in terms of multiple employees progressing through a specific plan at the same time, for example, a development plan for qualifying employees to use a new piece of machinery, or it could be reused periodically, for example, a development plan for an annual new hire or college hire program.

Create development templates to map common development paths

Development plans can be used to define all of the most common employee development scenarios including:

> **Formal training programs**
> For example, apprenticeship training, school leaver training programs, and rehabilitation training courses

> **Further education and training**
> Training courses aimed at increasing the skills of existing employees, for example, first aid training and management training

› On-the-job training

Training delivered in working time, usually on site rather than formal classroom-based training

All of these different development tasks and processes are then used to create individual employee development plans. An employee development plan is created by picking and choosing the appropriate tasks and processes for the specific employee and his goals, and is usually based on mutual agreement between the employee and his manager.

Development plans can be as simple or as complex as your company needs require. An example of a simple development plan is one for getting a forklift driving qualification. As we discussed in the previous chapter, defining the qualification is quite straightforward. We define when the qualification is valid (the effective date), the criteria on which it is awarded (for example, pass or fail or a letter grade), and how long it is valid. So the qualification for forklift driver might be valid from 2008 onward, awarded on a pass/fail basis, and valid for two years.

The more complex part of the process is the development side, for example, how we decide who should be able to become a heavy forklift driver, how they earn that right, how we measure their suitability, what prior qualifications or experience they require, and so on. Some criteria that we could include in the development plan could therefore be:

› Must be working in the dispatch or freight forwarding organizational units

› Must have a clean driving record

› Must have completed the training course on operating the Bristol GF929 Heavy Forklift in the past year

› Must have two years' experience working with the Bristol GG929 Light Forklift

All of these requirements can then be built into the development plan for gaining the heavy forklift qualification.

Taking the time to create a development plan for this qualification has two main benefits. First, because you have defined the criteria for measuring the eligibility of an employee for the development plan, you can quickly, logically, and impartially measure an employee's suitability for the development plan. Second, after you have identified an employee as being a good fit for the plan and have agreed with the employee on the tasks in the development plan, you can track the employee's progress toward the goal. Each step in the development plan is defined, and the progress toward each step is measured and recorded.

Development plans help employees quickly gain qualifications in a structured and efficient program

The Activities of a Development Plan

The steps involved in completing a development plan can be as simple as working in the correct department and then attending a two-day training course to attain a basic qualification. However, most companies need much more complex development plans. For example, a development plan for a college hire program might have tasks that require a three-year period to complete. A development plan can be made up of a series of *activities* or *goals* that define how a qualification is achieved. These activities may include items such as having to hold a specific position in the company, attending a training course, and holding a related qualification. The activities in a development plan can be completed sequentially or in parallel. For example, an employee may have to take a vision test before taking a driving test, or an employee may be required to attend seven unrelated training courses that can be taken in any order.

Development plans can be as short term as a day or as long term as decade

Development Plan Catalog

Once defined, a development plan template is stored centrally in the *plan catalog*. This plan catalog is often confused with the qualification catalog, which we looked at in Chapter 11, Career and Succession Management, but it is a different data structure in SAP HCM. Whereas a qualification catalog records the details of all of the qualifications employees can acquire, the plan catalog stores templates with

Use the development catalog to centrally sort, store, and manage all of your development plans

requirements, goals, or objectives that determine how an employee works toward a qualification or any other development goal. The plan catalog gives you a central repository for any number of development plan templates that the company requires and creates. Storing your development plans centrally has the advantage of reducing duplication and thus increasing efficiency. The catalog gives you the ability to create new plans, copy and change existing plans, and archive plans that are no longer relevant.

As with all of the other parts of SAP ERP HCM, the plan catalog and its entries are date based, so you can make new plans effective as of a certain date (such as at the beginning of the year), and when a development plan is no longer required you can delimit it so that it no longer is available for use. By delimiting rather than deleting the record, the plan is still stored for historical reference and reporting.

Because they are all stored centrally, you can organize your company's development plans into logical and relevant templates, so employees in your accounts department do not need to look at development plans for welders and brick layers.

Use your catalog to track the success of your plans. Which plan are employees completing most often?

Having all of your company's development plans formalized and stored in a central location gives you a wealth of information on the success of your company's employee development planning. For example, you can search the catalog for specific development plans, and with one click you can get a list of all of the employees who are working on or have completed the plan.

Quickly find out which employees are interested in a specific development plan, and get them started on it

Without a centralized development plan system, it has always been challenging for a company to get an understanding of how many employees are working toward development goals and what their progress is. Using development plans allows you to quickly see how many employees have embarked on any development plan and how many actually completed the plan. This kind of information on failure rates can help you quickly highlight problems with your development plans. A high incompletion rate could indicate that the plan is too hard, badly structured, or no longer relevant to your employees.

You can also quickly find employees who have been assigned to a specific development plan, those who are currently working on a plan, and those who have completed a plan. This kind of information is invaluable when making decisions around employee career and succession planning.

When all of the development plan templates for your company have been documented and defined in this function, you can use these as building blocks to create an employee's individual development plan. We will now look at developing and utilizing individual development plans.

Individual Development Plans

Many companies are becoming more proactive in the management of their employees' development. Employees are also increasingly seeing the benefit of taking an interest in their own career development. Until recently the management of an employee's development was a fairly ad hoc process where the manager and the employee worked together (usually during the annual review) to formulate a development plan that would benefit both the employee and, they hoped, the company. Now, using the broad and flexible solution provided by the SAP HCM Performance Management function, it is much simpler for companies to work with their employees in a structured and measured way to enhance employees' careers by focusing on *individual development plans*.

Help employees create their own development plans, and then track and measure their progress toward their development goal

In addition to planning the development of your existing employees, this function allows you to create development plans for potential employees.

A development plan can mean very different things to different employees. For a shop floor worker, a development plan can be straightforward with a short duration and benefit realization. For a senior manager, a development plan can be a complex multileveled plan with activities spread over many years. Increasingly, the need to work out effective development plans for all sorts of employees means that even shop floor employees can benefit from well-thought-out, individually focused and monitored development plans.

SAP HCM Performance Management allows you to create individual development plans that help employees identify and work toward development goals using training and further education opportunities. Let's look at a hypothetical development plan for a machine operator. The development plan, which is created when the employee is hired and then regularly monitored and updated, could look like Table 13.1.

Objective or Goal Type	Objective Description	Status
Obtain Qualification	Basic Health and Safety	Complete
Complete Training Course	Curtain Pole Extractor Machine Operations	Complete
Complete Training Course	Fire and Hazard Recognition	In Progress
Obtain Qualification	Curtain Rail Machine Maintenance	Not Started
Complete Training Course	Team Leadership and Management	Not Started

Table 13.1 Machine Operator Development Plan

From this example we can see that in a perfect world an employee's development plan is begun as soon as the employee starts. It is then added to and adjusted as the employment timeframe progresses. The development plan is made up of all the items the employee has completed, is working on now, and is scheduled for or has shown interest in completing in the future. The validity date and the status of each objective of the development plan can be created in the template and used for monitoring progress of the employee.

Schedule regular meetings to measure progress toward a development goal

Once created, an employee's development plan can be monitored and adjusted as necessary. This monitoring and updating can be included in the employee's annual performance review, or more regular monitoring can be scheduled for the employee's manager and the HR department. The development plan can then be changed to allow for the employee's changing development goals. For example, a change of job, a promotion, or a change in working times can change an employee's development plan.

At any time, the employee's manager and or the HR team can track the employee's progress against the objectives or activities of the development plan, updating statuses on tasks, and making changes as required. The template can be created to allow an employee's plan to contain job or position requirements that are missing from the employee's qualification profile. When the qualifications are obtained by the employee via specific development or training tasks, their profile will be updated to indicate that he now holds the qualification. As the employee progresses through his career with your company, he builds up a development history that is accessible to him and his manager.

Working with employees to manage their development can have many facets. Although strictly work-related development is normally the core of an employee's development plan, the chance is also there to add less directly work-related development goals to a development plan. Examples of development goals that are not directly work related but may be of benefit to a company include learning new languages, joining industry groups, clubs, and societies to increase the employee's business network, and taking advanced driver training or working on health and fitness, both of which can have an impact on corporate insurance rates and thus have an indirect benefit to the company.

The Link with Enterprise Learning Management

The two-way integration between Performance Management and Enterprise Learning (covered in the previous chapter) means that when an employee's development plan calls for training, there is a direct link to the specific training course stored in Enterprise Learning. With this integration, you can instantly see all of the details of the training course including the schedule, the number of spaces remaining, and the location, cost, and other details. You can book the employee in the training course or, alternatively, using workflow technology and the organizational structure, notify the training department, the employee's manager and the employee that the training course would be beneficial for the employee.

Directly link employee development plans to training events and vice versa

Similarly, if an employee is booked in a training course from within the Enterprise Learning function, a corresponding entry can be added automatically to the employee's development plan.

Objective Setting

Employee objectives need to meet both the employees' and the company's goals

By developing performance-related objectives for your employees, you can create measurable statistics to monitor their performance. Traditionally *objective setting* has been done at a local level by the employee and his line manager. The local nature of this objective setting process often ignores the company's stated aims and goals. By using the objective setting part of SAP HCM Performance Management and taking the time to develop structured performance objectives, you can integrate the goals of the company with the goals of the employee, ensuring that both parties benefit from the objective management process.

Once the employee's performance goals have been defined as a set of objectives, the employee's progress toward these goals can be measured against the objectives. The information gathered in the objective setting and measurement process can then be used as part of the employee appraisal process and eventually feed into the Enterprise Compensation Management function. Creating a concrete link between objective setting and Enterprise Compensation Management provides you with the performance information you need to make objective and consistent compensation decisions. Creating structured objectives that are used across your company increases the transparency that is often lacking in the appraisal process.

The link to Strategic Enterprise Management allows you to directly link company objectives to employee objectives

The objective setting function used in a development plan ensures that employees' objectives meet their own development goals and are tied in with the company's goals. The link between the company's goals and individual goals is strengthened by integration with the *Strategic Enterprise Management* function, which we will look at shortly. All of this information is then used as the basis for the appraisal process.

Developing Employee Objectives

Employee objectives vary as widely as your employees themselves. The key part defining them is that they should be measurable. There is no sense in developing an objective that simply states, "Catherine should improve sales in her region." This objective does not contain enough information to accurately measure her performance. A discussion should take place with Catherine, and a sales target should be developed in agreement with her manager and the company's wider goals. A much smarter goal would be "Catherine is to increase her sales of products X and Y by 10 - 20% by the end of July this year." This objective allows a much more analytical measurement. Sales figures can be transferred from the Sales component of SAP ERP and her performance measured against the target. The success or failure of her meeting this objective can be used in Catherine's performance appraisal, and the information then used in her compensation review.

The SAP HCM Performance Management function gives you a framework with templates to help employees and managers define both qualitative and quantitative objectives and then measure employee performance against them. The function allows the employee and manager to move through the three stages of objective setting:

> Give your performance management process some real structure – structure that can be tracked and measured

> **The planning stage**
> As part of an employee's development review, or as a separate performance review step, the manager and employee assess what qualifications or development goals the employee will be working toward in the review period. Based on these goals and plans, the objectives that need to be achieved within the period are set. In this stage the objectives are created in the system and stored in the employee record.

> **The review stage**
> After the manager and employee agree on the objectives and create them in the planning stage, the review stage allows them to enter periodic input on progress toward goals and objectives.

> **The appraisal stage**
> As discussed in more detail in the next section, the appraisal stage involves the employee and manager reviewing the employee's

progress toward the specified objectives and making final input, comments, and ratings against the objectives. The manager can attach notes to the objectives describing why the employee did or did not meet the objectives for the period. The process of identifying objectives for an employee can be quite difficult for some managers and employees, but because of the integration with Personnel Development, standard objectives that have already been defined for positions and qualifications can be transferred into an employee's objectives profile and used as basis for the development of objectives.

Strategic Enterprise Management and the Balanced Scorecard

Directly link your broad company goals with your individual employees' goals to ensure that your company is actually working toward its stated goals

Strategic Enterprise Management (SEM) is one of the finance components of SAP ERP. It is used to define company strategies, scorecards, objectives, measures, and initiatives. It allows you to formulate different strategic goals for your company and then assign responsibility for the goals across your company. One of the key parts of this component is the *Balanced Scorecard*, a tool that allows you to set up a dashboard-style view of your company's main strategic goals and monitor performance toward those goals. This information and monitoring can be integrated into the organizational structure and then into Performance Management.

The ability to assign scorecards to organizational structures, create performance overviews, and calculate personal scores for employees means the company's goals are spread across the organization. The Balanced Score Card allows you to create complex calculations of employee and team performance, taking into account information from many other SAP ERP components such as sales figures, production results, and SAP CRM data, all integrated into NetWeaver Business Intelligence for warehousing and reporting purposes. For example, it allows you to evaluate teams' performances against weighted performance scales, such as sales by region adjusted for the market conditions in each region. The results of these calculations and scoring are calculated for each employee within SEM and then integrated into employee objectives.

Appraisals

Employee performance appraisals are an area of HR that is continually developing, and the effectiveness of the appraisal process is improving. Whereas only five or ten years ago, most companies were happy with a fairly informal annual appraisal process, companies are increasingly seeing the benefit of investing more time and effort on their employee appraisals.

The Appraisals function allows you to develop as complex or simple an appraisal program as your company requires

In addition to a core annual appraisal, the process for many organizations now often includes 360-degree input, part appraisals from multiple reviewers, and self-appraisals. The appraisals function of SAP HCM Performance Management is designed to give you the ability to create and manage all of these types of appraisals and deliver a planned, formalized, and standardized yet flexible appraisal program that meets your company's specific needs.

Types of Appraisals

Now let's look at the most commonly used types of appraisals in the Performance Management module.

Individual Appraisals

The traditional method of appraising an employee is usually conducted by the employees' manager. This type of one-on-one appraisal leads to the completion of just one appraisal document. Individual appraisals are most commonly used for annual performance reviews and *business event appraisals*. A business event appraisal is used when an employee is appraised following the completion of a specific business event, for example an IT implementation project.

Include individual, anonymous, part, multisource, and 360-degree appraisals into your program

Multisource Appraisals

These are also known as 360-degree appraisals because they include multiple appraisal inputs, not just from an employee's manager, but also from other employees both above and below the employee in the company hierarchy. These appraisals can be set to be anonymous if this is preferred. The final appraisal is made by collating the results of multiple appraisals and a final appraisal by the employee's manager.

Part Appraisals

Part appraisals allow a single appraisal to be created by assigning different sections of the appraisal document to different persons for input. For example, an employee can be assigned responsibility for completing part of his own appraisal. A manager, a coworker, and subordinate can all complete different parts of a single employee's appraisal.

Appraisal Templates

Appraisal templates save your appraisers from having to reinvent the wheel

Appraisal templates form the basis of the employee appraisal. They are the predefined appraisals that are used to process the different types of appraisals your company performs. Examples of different types of appraisal templates are:

> Senior manager annual appraisal

> Senior manager quarterly progress appraisal

> Graduate half-yearly appraisal

> General objective-setting appraisal

> End of probation appraisal

Depending on your company's requirements, many appraisal templates could be defined to provide for the different purposes and processes of your company's appraisals program. Identifying who the appraisee and appraiser are for an appraisal template can be largely automated using evaluation paths within the organizational structure. For example, the annual appraisal form can be defined for each employee in a position belonging to an organizational unit, and the appraiser can be defined as the manager of the organizational unit to which the employee belongs.

The Appraisal Catalog

All of these appraisal templates are stored in the *appraisals catalog*. Each template contains criterion groups and criterions, and these two groupings allow you to logically order the goals and objectives and measures in your appraisal. A central catalog gives you a single source of appraisal templates for your company. This allows appraisals to be reused across your entire company (even internationally if required), saving time and focusing your efforts on creating and maintaining a standard, reusable, and consistent appraisal program.

Processing Appraisals

Once you have taken the time to create your development plans, identify your objectives, and tie them together into appraisals, it's finally time to actually perform some employee appraisals.

Let's look at some of the most important parts of performing personnel development through appraisals and examine how they are facilitated by this function.

Planning and Preparation

The first step in preparing your appraisal is determining who is going to be appraised, by whom, and on what basis. You can use the organizational structure to find both your appraisee and appraiser (of course with multipart and 360-degree appraisals, you can name multiple appraisers). Then you choose your appraisal template (for example, senior manager annual appraisal). You then determine when the appraisal must be completed. This can be a period of time or a specific date as your company practice dictates.

Once you have identified the appraisee and appraiser, all parties can be notified by workflow that the process has begun. If you are performing a similar appraisal for multiple employees, you can copy an existing appraisal and quickly set it up for other users. A specific manager portal view provides managers a list which identifies all of the appraisals they are responsible for and tracks the progress and status of each appraisal.

Performing and Following Up

Appraisals can be performed by the employees' manager or any other named part appraiser; they are performed online through the portal. The SAP HCM Performance Management function also provides an offline capability which allows appraisal data to be entered offline and then uploaded back into the SAP HCM system.

Appraisals can be completed by the manager online, directly in SAP ERP, or on preprinted paper forms

If an appraisal is set up as a multisource appraisal, individual appraisers can complete their sections or sub-appraisals independently of each other.

Completing and Approving (Status Archived)

Once all of the parts of the appraisal have been completed, all appraisers have agreed on the appraisal, and the overall final result has been determined and entered, the appraisal document is automatically set to complete and the status of the document reflects this change. Once the document has been set to complete, the data in the appraisal cannot be changed or edited. It is then added to the employee record.

Following Up on Appraisal Results

Once completed, appraisals can be compared, ranked, standardized, and analyzed to ensure consistency

The completed appraisal can be passed back to the employee for his review. Alternately, the template can be designed to allow for employee input into the final rating before the document is set to complete and changes are no longer permitted.

Comparison and analysis of the results of the appraisal process is a source of very useful HR information. SAP NetWeaver BI gives you the tools and reports required to complete complex and detailed analysis of your appraisals. You can determine which appraisals have not been completed or were not completed in the set time. You can analyze specific appraisal types, or appraisers or compare the different appraisals performed on a single employee. You can identify employees who achieved certain results and identify benchmark appraisals and determine the variance from the norm. You can determine averages and complete ranked lists of appraisal results. Based on your comparisons and analysis, you can re-edit and correct appraisals to ensure that they are fair and consistent across all of your company's scales and measures.

Once the entire process is complete, employees and managers can be automatically informed of the final results of the appraisal process via workflow, and the information is then available for use in other components. Frequently, companies integrate the results of annual performance appraisals into the Enterprise Compensation Management process to help calculate a proposed employee merit increase.

Performance Management via the Portal

SAP HCM Performance Management is integrated with both the Employee and the Manager Self-Services in the SAP Enterprise Portal. This integration gives both the employee and the manager the ability to process and display all of the information stored in the system relating to their specific tasks and responsibilities. By providing the employee and manager with the tools to manage aspects of the performance management process, such as completing and viewing appraisals online, SAP ERP HCM frees up more of the HR department's time, allowing them to focus on more strategic and value-adding tasks.

Employees can view their appraisals online, and managers can complete them online

Let's conclude this chapter with a case study of a company using SAP HCM Performance Management effectively.

Case Study

Table 13.2 provides a quick overview of the case study before we explain it in more detail.

Company	European Food and Beverage Producer
Existing Solutions	SAP ERP
Challenges	› Minimal visibility and tracking of performance appraisal process › Low visibility of company-wide performance appraisal results › Reduce processing time for key processes › Reduce manual processes
SAP Solutions	SAP ERP HCM suite including Performance Management
Benefits	› Consistent and efficient objective setting and appraisal process › Better insight into workforce capabilities › Increased visibility of performance management process › Standardized processes

Table 13.2 Performance Management Case Study

The company is a rapidly expanding food producer based in Europe, with customers throughout the world. Currently, the company has 400 employees.

The Challenges

This company is relatively small but growing fast. A small HR department worked using mainly manual paper-based processes and needed to automate and drive these processes online. Though currently running an annual review process, the results of this process were often stored in a filing cabinet and received no follow-up or monitoring.

The SAP Solution

As part of a broad SAP ERP HCM implementation (including e-Recruiting and core HCM functions), the company implemented Performance Management, enabling them to store performance management information centrally and effectively manage tasks related to the monitoring and feedback processes.

The Benefits

By storing all of their HR data in a centralized database, the company gained a clear picture of their organization and all of the information they required to support effective performance management evaluations. This information allowed the company to quickly react to highlighted performance gaps at an individual or group level.

Through e-Recruiting, the company moved its entire recruitment process online, enabling fast responses and communication using automatic email generation, all at the click of a button.

By implementing SAP ERP HCM, the company built a scalable and stable solution that will support the HR department as the company continues to grow and expand.

Summary

The SAP HCM Performance Management function gives your company the framework it needs to develop a new performance management process or enhance and improve your existing processes. By taking the time to develop and document your company's common development plans, you create a useful tool for informing employees of potential development goals in your company. There are some important factors to keep in mind when considering SAP HCM Performance Management:

> Development plans are a proven way of keeping your employees motivated and focused on achieving goals that benefit both them and the company.

> Having predefined development plans to use as a basis for employee development is a great time saver and a good motivational tool; employees can quickly see their potential in the company.

> Being able to directly link employees' development plans with qualifications and find and book training courses to meet these goals straight from Enterprise Learning means that your development plans are always integrated and relevant and will not merely be filed away somewhere until next year.

> Objective setting is again another area of Performance Management where having pre-defined objectives and structured measurement and tracking methods is a great step forward for many companies. Having information, examples, and structures available at the start of the objective setting process rather than the traditional blank sheet of paper makes working with employees to define objectives much simpler and faster.

> Similarly, having a structure within which you can create, manage and store your company's appraisals is a great tool to help you standardize your appraisals process.

> Online access to the appraisal process helps to shift responsibility onto the manager and the employee and away from the HR department.

> Following the completion of your appraisals, the reports and tools available to compare and measure the results of the appraisals process provide your company with a wealth of information to ensure that your employee performance management process is efficient, consistent, fair, and relevant to your company's needs.

In the next chapter we will look at Enterprise Compensation Management, a topic that is closely linked to Performance Management. These two components can be integrated if it is appropriate for your company requirements, providing you with more information to make better-informed compensation decisions.

14

Enterprise Compensation Management

Planning for and managing your employees' compensation can have great benefits for your company. Having a complete picture of your compensation commitments gives you the information you need to make informed compensation decisions. In addition, many other benefits come from having a centralized, integrated, and optimized process, which ensures that you are always in control of your salaries, wages, and benefits — usually company's largest overhead cost.

Enterprise Compensation Management is one of the most integrated products within SAP ERP HCM. It contains tools that allow you to plan and model your employee costs. You can also design an effective performance-based compensation program involving both HR professionals and line management in the decision and approval process. Depending on your company's requirements, this function can include the use of a budgetary framework to enable rigorous control of the awarding of annual, variable, and long-term incentives to employees. It also allows you to use salary surveys and internal compensation data to ensure that your company is competitive with regard to employee compensation. Its built-in processes and procedures ensure that your company can quickly and sensibly react to environmental changes that affect employee compensation management.

Enterprise Compensation Management is also fully integrated into Manager Self-Service (MSS). This helps you ensure that, where possible and practical, the basic tasks and processes are automated, and employees and managers are empowered to manage their own tasks, leaving HR team members to concentrate on more strategic priorities.

How Compensation Management Fits into an Enterprise

Manage your compensation without resorting to Excel- and paper-based calculations

Enterprise Compensation Management broadens the traditional responsibilities for compensation management by drawing management into the compensation process. Because of the integration with MSS, managers can be made responsible for drawing up, approving, and allocating budgets. They can then make compensation decisions for individuals and groups of employees. These decisions are made straight into SAP system through the portal, so there is no paperwork to shuffle about and misplace, all of the input, control, and activation of the compensation process is completed inside the HR system.

This one-stop shop for compensation management frees up considerable amounts of time for your HR or compensation management professionals. The integration of workflow into the function also means that decisions made by the compensation team can be approved and implemented automatically after management's electronic notices are sent. The total integration with other SAP ERP HCM functions such as Employee Administration, Organizational Management, Payroll, and eventually, Finance means that the entire compensation management process can be completed in real time online in SAP ERP HCM, from initial budget preparation through to the employees pay check.

A Closer Look at Enterprise Compensation Management

Enterprise Compensation Management is made up of five separate but related sections, all of which can be implemented independently based on your company's requirements. We will look at each of the sections in more detail, but first let's take a quick look at what they are and what they can do for your company:

> **Personnel Cost Planning (PCP)**
> PCP allows you to calculate how much your employees cost your company. This gives you the total cost of your employees — not just their salary and payments, but also costs associated with training, education, and the provision of employee benefits. You can use this information to model different organizational scenarios to measure the potential impact on your employees and your company.

> **Budgeting**
> One of the most contentious and complicated parts of compensation management, determining your budget and allocating it across your company. Once the overall budget pot has been agreed on, the Budget function helps you develop a view of your company specifically for the budgetary process and then allocate your budget (or budgets) across your company using several criteria.

> **Long-Term Incentives**
> Long-term incentives are becoming increasingly popular because they reward longer periods of service, and their value can be related to the company's performance. This functionality allows you to efficiently set up, award, and administer all of the most common types of long-term incentives.

> **Job Pricing**
> This function allows you integrate multiple sources of salary information, from external salary surveys to internally sourced information, and use it to effectively evaluate your compensation packages. This evaluation can include salaries, wages, and variable payments. All of the information is presented in a concise yet detailed layout to help in the decision-making process.

> **Compensation Programs**
>
> This component provides you with a wide range of compensation tools and frameworks to ensure that you deliver the most effective compensation package to the right groups of employees as and when required. From highly complex executive compensation plans to simple annual salary increases, there is scope to develop a compensation package that meets your company's requirements no matter how complex or simple. Useful tools ensure that compensation packages can be applied with the minimum of fuss.

So now let's look at the different parts of Enterprise Compensation Management in more detail and explore their capabilities.

Personnel Cost Planning (PCP)

PCP – working out exactly how much your employees cost you

PCP gives you the ability to calculate the total cost to your company of your employees, including the obvious costs such as salary and wages, employer costs such as taxes and social insurance, employee benefits such as medical coverage and other insurance, and costs that are not directly employee related, such as the costs of providing training and education. You can measure these costs in several ways, for example, based on project pay, basic pay, or actual payroll results.

Automatically send your cost planning results to the controlling team for inclusion in company budgets

Once you have a complete picture of your employee costs and the potential costs of vacant positions, you can use your organizational structure to build complex scenario-based models of how planned organizational changes or compensation adjustments will impact your personnel costs. PCP can then be integrated into your budget preparation process and can be transmitted to the controlling component, so your cost plans are integrated into the finance budgeting system.

The PCP solution involves several steps, including defining your costs, sourcing your data, creating your scenarios, and integrating with other SAP ERP components. Let's look at each of these individually.

Defining your Costs

PCP divides your costs into two types depending on where the cost is to be allocated:

Cost Items

Cost items are used to store the values of the different types of costs associated with employees. Cost items include employee payments such as salaries and wages, bonuses, overtime payments, and employer costs such as employer pension contributions, social security payments, and health care provisions.

Cost elements are made up of two types of data:

1. Wage types are used for recording amounts for employee payments and are sourced directly in employee master data in infotypes.

2. Wage elements are used only for PCP to record employer costs that are not generally stored as amounts in employee master data. The values stored in wage elements can either be maintained centrally or entered as an employee-by-employee value.

So the total cost of an employee is calculated by adding up all of the values stored in the wage types and wage elements associated with that employee. You can choose which wage elements and wage types are associated with a specific employee.

Cost Objects

A cost object allows you to allocate costs that are not specifically employee related. Commonly used cost objects include organizational units and work centers as well as positions, jobs, and employees. Therefore, as well as allocating your costs against your individual employees, when specific costs are allocated to teams or departments as wage elements, you can assign wage elements to specific organizational units, jobs, and so on to ensure that the cost is correctly allocated.

Sourcing Your Data

The intent of PCP is to allow you to develop and compare different costing scenarios so you can make better costing decisions. Different companies, however, have different requirements for what information should be used as the basis of this planning. PCP provides three methods of calculating the costs.

> Cost planning allows you to calculate the total cost of your employees, not just their salaries and bonuses

> You can base your cost planning on previous payroll results or employee salary figures or use a future projection

Payroll Results

Perhaps the most detailed of the three costing options, payroll results use actual payroll results as the basis of your cost planning. You can use either historical payroll results (from one or more stored payroll periods) or future payroll results based on simulations of future periods. Having actual payroll results gives you the most information to base your analysis on, but it also takes the most time to process. It is worth noting that this option only works as a view of your company as it is at the time of the payroll run. It does not provide for future changes such as new hires or planned organizational changes.

Basic Pay

The simplest way of getting your costing information, this option simply takes the values stored in wage types on your employees' Infotype 0008 Basic Pay record, which normally only includes main payments such as salary or wages. It does not take into account all of the payments an employee may receive such as overtime and bonuses. It also takes into account information from the wage elements such as employer costs. Although not as accurate as a full payroll result, this option is often chosen because it is the fastest for creating costing data.

Projected Pay

This is probably the most detailed method of gathering cost planning data. To create projected pay data, you assign all of your costing information to positions and jobs via the cost planning infotype. This costing data can contain direct personnel costs such as a wages and salaries, higher-level costs such as those associated with retraining a team of employees, or the costs associated with providing a work bus service.

By using projected pay, you can also include costs associated with currently vacant positions. For example, if you are currently trying to hire a new HR manager, you can add the expected costs for the new position onto the position so they are included in cost planning.

Creating Your Scenarios

Once you have defined and allocated your costs to your employees and organizational structure objects using one of the three described methods, you can create scenarios to model the impact of changes on your organization. Scenarios represent a set group of employees for a set period of time. In a scenario you can also define scenario groups that give you the ability to apply different adjustments to subsets of your larger scenario. PCP provides you with a graphical drill-down tool that facilitates the process. The basic process works as follows:

You can apply different rules to different parts of your company

1. Select which employees you want to model. This could be a single employee, a job (e.g., all of the accountants in the company), or organizational units (e.g., Finance, HR, and IT). Then select the period that you want to model. This can be any time period from a single pay period to a year or more.

2. Select the cost objects you want to change. You can add, increase, decrease, or delete each of your cost items as you require. For example, you may want to decrease basic salaries by 20%, so you would select the wage type salaries and apply a percentage increase. The system will recalculate the salaries for all employees, reducing them by this percentage. You could also try increasing your pension contributions by 3% to see what the overall cost would be for your organization. The options are only limited by the number of cost objects you have defined.

3. Once you have finished modeling your changes, you can compare the changes to a reference scenario (where no changes have been made), or you can load external salary survey data to compare to your changes.

Because this is potentially very sensitive information, you can control access to each scenario with passwords and delete scenarios at the end of the planning period. You can also keep the scenarios and compare them later to actual results to measure your success.

Integration with Other Components

One of the key benefits of implementing an SAP system is the standard integration between components; this is well demonstrated here in PCP, where your HR planning scenarios can be sent directly to Finance to be integrated into the company's financial planning process. The Controlling component of Finance is the part of the software that is used to create and manage company budgets. PCP scenarios can be developed and finalized in Enterprise Compensation Management and then, when agreed upon by all relevant parties, they can be electronically transferred to the controlling department for integration into their overall financial plans and budgets. This ability of HR to develop their own detailed budgets that can be added to the controlling budget without any duplication of effort is one of the best examples of SAP systems' built-in integration.

Let's move on to talk about setting up your compensation budgets.

Budgeting

The first step in managing compensation is determining how much money you have available and then assigning it across your company. The Budget function within Enterprise Compensation Management gives you the ability to allocate cash and other types of incentives (such as share options) to the different parts of your organization. The level of detail that you go into when dividing the budget across your organization is up to you. You can simply define one budget pot for the whole company, or break the pot down into individual portions for each team or organizational unit within your company. Your budget can be defined globally if required. Therefore, multiple currencies can be assigned to your budget, and the amounts can be displayed in the local currencies. All of the local currency amounts will be rolled up to a single budget reference currency so that it can be reconciled at the highest level of your company.

Defining your Budget Units

After determining how much cash is available for compensation management, the next step is defining your budgeting structure, that is, how your company is divided for allocating the budget. To do this, you generate a budget structure, which is composed of *budget units*. Each unit is assigned a portion of the budget, and it is then shared among the members of the unit.

Depending on your company's requirements, the budget structure can be identical to, or very similar to your existing organizational structure, or can be completely different.

You can define a budget structure hierarchy to give your budget units a structure. This hierarchy can match your organizational structure, or you can create your own budget-specific structure.

Each budget unit contains the key information shown in Table 14.1.

Field	Definition
Name	Identifies the budget unit.
Budget Type	Determines for which type of budget this unit is relevant, for example, salary, bonus, or stocks.
Budget Period	Each budget is valid for a set duration; this field shows the validity of this budget unit.
Plan Version	When multiple budget plans are being developed and tested, this field identifies to which budget this unit belongs.
Status	Determines the stage of the budget process: planned, approved, rejected, or released.
Budgeted Amount	The cash amount allocated to this unit.
Budgeted Units	The number of shares or other types of non-monetary rewards allocated to this unit.

Table 14.1 Key Budget Items

To create the budget units, the Enterprise Compensation component provides a budget generation function that allows you to simply link organizational units or groups of organizational units into generated budget units.

Once you have defined your budget units, you can reuse them for each new budget period. All you need to do is extend the validity of the budget unit, and then you revalue the amounts in the budget — either by a percentage increase or decrease or by a flat amount. Figure 14.1 shows the budget for a group of organizational units.

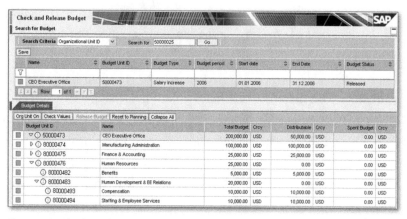

Figure 14.1 Checking the Budget Allocation for a Group of Organizational Units

A standard report is also provided for uploading budget data from the PCP application into Enterprise Compensation Management.

Several different budget models can run at once, so by assigning a plan version to each of the budgets you can model different scenarios and plans until you are satisfied with the overall budget. Once everyone has approved the budget, it moves from planned to released and becomes available for distribution to employees.

The next part of Enterprise Compensation Management to consider is long-term incentives.

Long-Term Incentives

Long-Term Incentives is designed for creating, processing, and awarding complex employee benefit programs

As employees become more mobile, it is important that a company can provide benefits programs that are earned and exercised based on longer terms of service to help increase retention. The Long-Term Incentives part of the Enterprise Compensation Management function allows you to create benefits such as incentive stock options, performance shares, and restricted stock options that can then be awarded to specific types of employees. The compensation can be defined with whatever vesting period is required and then exercised by employees according to their own requirements. Stock options and shares can then be linked back into the SAP Treasury component to your actual securities.

Types of Long-Term Incentives

This feature has been designed around the most commonly used long-term incentives (known as *awards* in Enterprise Compensation Management) including:

> Incentive stock options (SOs)

> Non-qualifying stock options (NQSOs)

> Performance shares

> Performance units

> Restricted stocks

As with most parts of SAP ERP HCM, you can define your own awards if the standard ones do not meet your company's requirements. Awards can be defined with a specific start date and a term of duration in which the employee can exercise the award that is granted. As with all of the other parts of Enterprise Compensation Management, this date-based functionality allows you to use date-based controls to manage all of your compensation components.

Long-Term Incentive Plans

Individual awards are built into *long-term incentive plans*. These are created by combining one or more awards into a plan and then determining the numbers of units of shares or stocks for each award and validity period. Determining which employees are entitled to the incentives is also a key part of long-term incentive plans, so as with the other parts of Enterprise Compensation Management, all of the required criteria such as seniority, length of service, or location are available as decision points. Rules relating to when the incentives can be exercised and vested can also be built into the plan according to your company's requirements.

Based on these inputs, for example, an incentive plan could be created that is valid for the next financial year. The plan could be applicable for senior management who have been with the company for more than 12 years and made up of parcels of restricted stock options and performance shares that can be exercised within the next financial year and vested in five years time.

Maintaining Long-Term Incentives

After you have defined incentive plans, they can then be assigned to employees using the Compensation Administration functionality.

> **Granting**
>
> Granting determines which employees are entitled to incentives. This can be a wide range of criteria including the type of employee, length of service, and position in the organization.

> **Vesting**
>
> This allows you to create rules for when employees can exercise their rights to long-term incentives. For example, you can specify to which employees the rule applies, and then specify the duration that they are allowed to exercise the award. This duration can be fixed dates or a set duration. You can then link your exercising rule to one or more of your awards.

> **Exercising**
>
> When employees are allowed to purchase the stock options they have been awarded, this is referred to in SAP ERP HCM as *exercising*. When employees want to exercise their options, the current fair market value can be automatically derived if your system is linked to the Treasury component. If no link has been set up, you can manually enter the fair market value. The status of the options is then updated from awarded to exercised, with a date and value stored against them for future records. Additionally, when employees decide to exercise their awards, the details of the transaction are retrieved and can be exported to your bank or broker via a standard report.

❯ Ongoing Maintenance

Given the months and years over which these types of incentives are spread, it is important that the system can efficiently handle all of the changes that can occur to long-term incentives. This function is designed to efficiently handle the following scenarios:

– Changing life events

Over time an employee's position in the company may change, for example, through promotion or demotion or changes to their personal circumstances, through births, marriages, and so on. Any of these changes can have an impact on the employee's entitlement to long-term incentives. Through configuration you can define which of these life events trigger a change in employee long-term incentives and can link these changes to actions such as immediate vestment of options, immediate cancellation of options, or an increase in options within a certain time frame.

The processing of life events can be linked via workflow so that as soon as an HR administrator makes the change to the employee record, the benefits administrator is automatically notified and can process the changes in the Enterprise Compensation Management function. This largely automated processing allows your HR and benefits administrators to concentrate on more important tasks knowing that SAP ERP HCM will take care of the more routine ones.

– Expiring, Forfeiting, and Canceling

When an employee fails to exercise his options, or changes in circumstance such as retirement or organizational changes force cancellation or forfeit, the system allows you to quickly terminate the awards. You can also selectively cancel the awards, for example, leaving vested shares but cancelling unvested shares or cancelling only some of an employee's long-term compensation plan items.

Figure 14.2 shows an employee being administered a long-term incentive of stock options.

Figure 14.2 An Employee Being Awarded Stock Options

Job Pricing

Combine multiple salary surveys with internal data to create a detailed baseline to compare your company's benefits against

The Job Pricing function allows you to compare and benchmark the salaries paid in your company against external market data based on multiple salary surveys or internal job evaluation results. You can use this comparative information to build a competitive compensation policy in your company and react rapidly to changes in the job market. Depending on your compensation policy, you can then price your jobs so that they "lead" or "lag" or are "at" the market rate compared to data from other companies based on your industry, geographical location, or size.

You can use external salary surveys (such as Towers Perrin and Mercer) to help evaluate your employees' salaries and wages. You can automatically upload provider salary survey data into SAP ERP HCM, and then map the survey data to existing jobs in your SAP system. You can then adjust this information as you require by weighting the market data and ageing it and then compare market data with actual values of your internal jobs and employee compensation data. Salary structures and employee salaries can then be adjusted as required.

Positions and jobs are key parts of an organizational structure, so it is worth refreshing ourselves about them before we carry on.

 Positions and Jobs

> Positions are held by employees and define an employee's place in the company (e.g., finance director or human resource director).
>
> Jobs define a set of skills or an occupation, such as accountant or cleaner. They define the higher-level attributes of positions that are linked to them.

Sourcing Job Pricing Data

Many companies use external salary survey information or in-house job evaluation systems (or a combination of both) to determine the relative worth of positions and jobs within their company.

Automatically import and export salary survey data – from providers and for providers

Enterprise Compensation Management allows seamless integration between multiple salary survey sources, enabling you to quickly upload the salary survey information from disk, Excel file, or test files into your system. Companies can also produce their own salary survey information using in-house job evaluation systems and upload this information to SAP ERP HCM.

More important, the solution gives you a standard reporting tool for exporting your own salary data to provide to third-party survey providers. Figure 14.3 shows newly imported salary survey data.

The Job-Pricing Process

Salary survey data consists of a job, a job description, and salary information. This information is usually supplied based on groupings such as industry or location. The first step of the job-pricing process is to import the data and match the jobs in the survey with jobs in your own company. Some companies match every job; others mark a selection of jobs and use them as a benchmark.

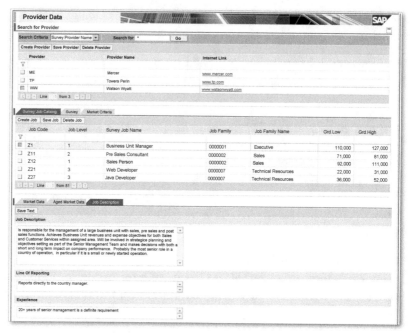

Figure 14.3 Imported Salary Survey Data

Enterprise Compensation Management is totally integrated with the Enterprise Portal, allowing the entire process to be completed online, either by your HR administrators or by compensation specialists. The entire process from uploading the salary survey information to matching the survey jobs to jobs in your company and analyzing specific employees is completed online.

Once you have loaded your salary survey information into the system, you use this as the basis for generating your new salary structure. You can include information such as average salary and average bonus for specific roles and currencies. As with all of the other SAP ERP HCM data, all of this information is stored as date-based entries, giving you the ability to "age" the market data and give priority to more current results.

You can match the salary survey information against a set of benchmarked jobs. These jobs can be from multiple salary survey providers, and weightings can be applied to different surveys depending on your requirements. You can establish market composite results for jobs and compare internal salaries against blended and weighted survey data.

Updating Your Salary Structure

Now that you have mapped the salary survey and internal information to your company's jobs, you can analyze your employees and make adjustments as required.

The portal-based maintenance tool allows the person responsible for administering salary adjustments (either a line manager or an HR administrator) to view all of the salary survey information required to decide on an employee's compensation. This compensation adjustment could be in the form of a salary or wage increase or bonus and performance-related payments. The information presented typically includes the following details:

> Employee's current job

> Current salary, wage, or bonus

> Compa ratio to reference salary

> Position within salary range

> Employee's employment percentage

The administrator can then view the following information from the salary survey:

> Minimum salary for job

> Reference salary

> Maximum salary

> Spread of salaries over a percentile range

It is worth noting that this comparison information can be either from a single salary survey, from composite data from multiple surveys, or based on the company's own data.

The administrator can then adjust the salary by amounts or percentages, attach notes and comments, and then either submit the adjustment for approval or make the changes immediately effective. All changes are date based and can be set to become effective in the future.

Defining Your Compensation Program

Create a compensation program that allows you to deliver compensation adjustments as effectively as possible

The process of applying compensation adjustments to your employees can be as simple or as complex as your company's processes demand. In the simplest solution, you do not even need to define an overall budget. You can simply work through your list of employees, adding adjustments to their compensation as you see fit. In the most complex scenarios, the budget is spread across the company based on a several rules of determination.

Employees or groups of employees are then compensated on a range of compensation types based on complex criteria mixing performance management, production output, length of service, and many other potential categories. The provisional distribution of compensation can then be automatically managed via workflow, allowing several levels of review and approval prior to the compensation being applied to the employees. Because this is SAP ERP HCM, as soon as your compensation adjustments have been through their final level of approval, they are instantly available for payroll processing and then finance reporting.

We will now review the major components of the compensation administration process and explain how they fit together.

Defining Your Compensation Packages

Include elements such as salary, wages, bonus, merit pay, commission, profit share, and stocks and shares in your compensation program

As employee compensation gets more complex, the effective management of compensation is also becoming more complex. Whereas compensation management used to be just about annual bonuses and salary increases, compensation management now involves managing many different types of rewards with different rules for deciding the amounts of the rewards. Compensation management now commonly includes at least the following types of compensation:

> Base pay, including salary and wages

> Merit pay — extraordinary payments rewarding employee merit

> Bonuses and one-time awards of payment
> Commissions — payment based on employee efforts and results
> Profit sharing — rewards based on team or company performance
> Nonmonetary rewards such as stocks and shares

Enterprise Compensation Management allows you to define as many *compensation categories* as your company requires. These compensation categories are then defined as one of the following types of compensation component, which controls how they are awarded:

Fixed Compensation
Compensation is defined as fixed when it is awarded to an employee as part of his basic pay. So once awarded, it's fixed for the compensation period and is paid every pay period. This type of compensation is stored on Infotype 0008 Basic Pay.

Variable Compensation
The opposite of fixed compensation, this compensation component is used to define compensation types such as bonus payments, sales commissions, and performance-related pay, which is paid on a more variable basis. This type of compensation is typically stored on Infotype 0015 Additional Payments as a one-time payment.

Long-Term Incentives
Aimed at tying employees into the company by providing rewards over a set period of time, long-term awards include stock options, performance shares and units, and restricted stocks. They are generally earned and paid out over a set period of time. They are stored in Infotype 0761 LTI Granting.

Defining Employee Eligibility
Now that you have defined the different types of compensation to be awarded, you can define which of your employees are entitled to these rewards. Typical bases for these decisions include length of service or specific jobs or teams within the company. You do this by creating *eligibility rules*, which have *eligibility groups* assigned to them.

Enterprise Compensation Management gives you the ability to define benefits as available to only selected groups of employees

Eligibility Rules

Eligibility rules give you the flexibility to define any of the different groups of employees you need to reward. For example, you can define an eligibility group based on some of the following common categories:

> Length of service with company, for example, employees with more than one years' service

> A fixed date, for example, employees who started before 2008

> Minimum working time per week, for example, employees who work more than n hours per week

> Salary, for example, only employees earning under $200,000 per year

> Performance, for example, only employees who were awarded at least the average score in Performance Management

Figure 14.4 shows the eligibility rules for a fixed-salary adjustment. You can also determine your own company-specific rules.

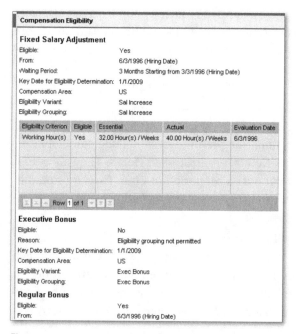

Figure 14.4 Determining an Eligibility Rule

Eligibility Groups

Eligibility groups are a further subset of an eligibility rule based on your organizational structure. For example, you could define that in addition to having an eligibility rule stating that only employees who started before 2008 are entitled to a particular type of compensation, for the northwest region (based on your organizational structure), only employees who are defined as manager are entitled to this type of compensation.

You can override these rules by using Infotype 0760 Compensation Eligibility Override. For example, if an employee fails the length of service check but has extra service with an overseas office that is not recorded on the system, you can still award him the length-of-service-based compensation.

Defining Guidelines

So now that we understand how to define our compensation types and we have discussed who is entitled to these rewards, we need to look at how much they are entitled to. The rules regarding the amounts or units of compensation for different groups of employees are controlled using *compensation guidelines*. Three types of guideline can be used to set rules.

Fixed Guidelines

Compensation adjustments that are deemed to be fixed are calculated based on a fixed percentage, a fixed number of units, or a fixed amount. For example, a fixed percentage may be used to deliver a 7% increase in basic salary, or a range of units may be used for a delivering a long-term incentive such as a share option package of between 1,000 and 1,500 shares per employee. An example of a fixed amount guideline is the awarding of a flat-amount bonus of 1,000 Great Britain Pounds per employee.

Matrix Guidelines

A matrix guideline takes this to the next step by enabling you to create multidimensional calculations for compensation adjustments. For example, you might say that compensation adjustments are calculated

Combine different performance indicators to create a matrix showing employee eligibility for benefits

355

based on an individual employee's performance, combined with his length of service and his number of working hours per week. All three parts of the matrix can be given different weightings to determine the amount of an employee's compensation adjustment.

User-Defined Guidelines

Giving you ultimate flexibility, compensation guidelines also allow for the creation of totally custom-made calculations. Using the user defined criteria, the only limit to the complexity of the calculation guidelines is the talent of your programmer. The user-defined criteria can be used, for example, to bring in data from external systems and include it in the calculation.

It is worth noting that defining guidelines is an optional part of Enterprise Compensation Management. If your company does not require guidelines to control the compensation adjustment process, you can skip this step and leave the determining of amounts of units to the HR administrator or manager responsible.

Processing Your Compensation Program

We have seen how to define our compensation budget, we have determined the different types of compensation we want to distribute through compensation packaging, and we have identified who we will be administering through the eligibility rules. We then looked at how much employees can potentially receive through the setting of guidelines. Now we need to actually process the adjustments to compensate the employees.

Compensation adjustments can be processed either on an employee-by-employee basis or for groups of employees using the Compensation Planning iView in the Enterprise Portal.

Individual Employee Processing

Editing an individual employee is simply a matter of selecting the employee, selecting the benefit period that you want to administer, and then if you have built-in guidelines, applying these to the employee (Figure 15.5). If you do not use the guidelines, you can apply your compensation types such as bonus or salary increases as required. A simple yet effective function integrated here allows you to automatically apply rounding rules to the calculated amounts to round them to the nearest full unit to keep the figures tidy.

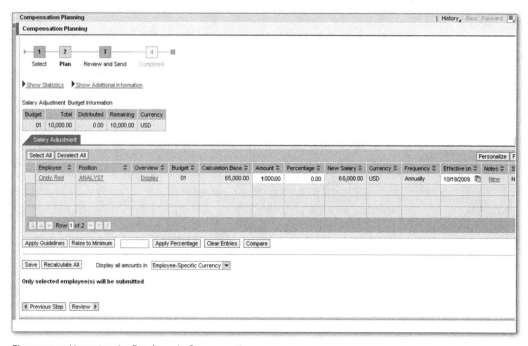

Figure 14.5 Managing An Employee's Compensation

Mass Data Maintenance

The HR administrator can handle compensation based on information provided by the business or by the managers themselves using MSS. For example, if you as a manager want to administer the adjustments for a team of employees, or all of your shift workers, you can use the Compensation Planning iView to adjust your group of employees using the organizational structure and the budget defined earlier to find the right employees. To help you make your adjustment decision, you can then choose what information you want to display about these employees on the adjustment screen. For example, you can show the start dates, or working hours for the period to be compensated. You can then apply the guidelines you have defined for all of the employees or manually compensate them.

Process compensation adjustments for individual employees or for groups of employees as required

357

A manager has the ability at any point to override any amounts that are suggested by applied guidelines. Notes can be added to the adjustments explaining why the override was made, and this adjustment information is stored against the employee record, available for any audit or review process.

After all of the employees have had their compensation adjusted, if you have chosen to integrate the compensation management process with workflow, you can submit the adjustments for approval by the manager's manager and/or the HR or compensation departments. Using workflow, approvals or rejections can be automatically forwarded to the correct role to approve manager adjustments or to reject them and send them back to the manager for re-planning.

When the entire approval process is finished and all records have been adjusted, the records are set to active and are thus ready to be automatically picked up by payroll in the next pay run. No messy upload files or interfaces are required to move your compensation adjustment results into the payroll system. Once again, the integration is seamless and largely automated.

Figure 14.6 shows a graphical overview report of an organizational unit's salaries versus the salary survey average market rate.

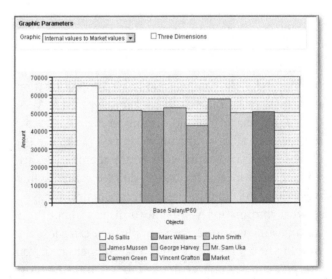

Figure 14.6 Overview of an Organizational Unit's Salaries Compared to the Market Value

ESS and MSS

The integration of employee and manager functions into the portal ensures that your employees and managers are fully involved in all aspects of compensation.

Employee Self-Service

The main function an employee can use within Enterprise Compensation Management is the *total compensation statement*. This PDF form is designed to be accessed through ESS and contains details of all of an employee's compensation elements including salary and bonuses, other incentives such as long-term incentives, employee benefits, and personnel development details for the current year.

Full integration of Enterprise Compensation Management with the Enterprise Portal gives managers access wherever they are working

The form is designed for the employees to generate themselves as and when they need it and it can be used for providing details of salary and benefits to banks and financial institutions. The form is totally configurable and can be tailored to your company's requirements. The total compensation statement can also be generated and printed centrally when required, for example, to notify all employees of changes made at the end of the annual compensation adjustment program.

Manager Self-Service

There are three separate roles in MSS that relate to Compensation Management. The first allows a manager or HR administrator who is the *compensation planner* to plan the various award amounts for the employees for whom he is responsible. This compensation planning iView within the portal contains all of the information from compensation management in a set of easy-to-follow screens and tables (Figure 15.6). Information relating to the compensation budget, the employee's existing compensation, job pricing and salary survey results, and other relevant information is available to help the manager make a logical and consistent compensation decision. The planning manager can also enter notes for the approver, indicating why he has given a specific award amount to an employee.

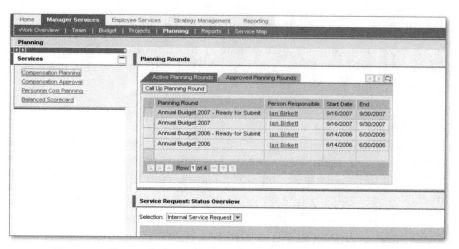

Figure 14.7 Manager's View of Budget Planning

When the compensation planner has finished his compensation planning, the status of the plan is changes and is then available to the approver (who is generally the manager's ,manager). This could be also be a more senior manager or an HR professional. The approver approves or rejects the planned compensation amount and can include notes and comments about why the award is approved or rejected. If rejected, the plan is then sent back via workflow to the compensation planning manager to adjust the data and resubmit.

Once the approving manager approves the planned amounts, the HR or compensation department is notified, the final version of the compensation plan is activated, and all of the changes to master data are automatically made. As soon as the changes are made, they are available for payroll processing and payment.

One of the great advantages of the MSS-driven compensation management process is that it turns what was traditionally a very labor-intensive paper-based process into a highly automated and process-driven project. As with any other workflow-driven process, all of the involved parties have access to reporting and monitoring functionality, allowing deadlines to be monitored and delays automatically escalated to the relevant parties.

Compensation Management Infotypes

Many infotypes are used in Enterprise Compensation Management to group the information into logical parcels of information. There are two groups of compensation infotypes: employee focused and organizational structure focused. We will now look at the most important ones and briefly outline what they are used for.

Compensation-specific infotypes gives you all of the information in clear, logical, and sensible parcels of data

Employee-Specific Infotypes

Infotype 0758 Compensation Program

The highest-level infotype for an employee's compensation management, this infotype is used to determine to which compensation areas and plans an individual employee is entitled. For example, you can assign an employee to the executive compensation program and determine that he is entitled to the combined bonus and share options plan. If an employee works across multiple countries or you have an international compensation area, an employee could have multiple records of this infotype active at a time.

Because this infotype is compulsory to run Compensation Management, it can be set for automatic creation based on the type of employee, location, salary, and so on, and changes and updates can be processed automatically for large groups of employees via a standard report.

Infotype 0759 Compensation Process

This is the main infotype for recording and tracking the details of an employee's compensation change. It has two key parts. First, it displays the amounts or percentages of the different compensation awards for the employee such as long-term incentives, bonuses, and salary awards. Second, it allows you to determine at which stage of the compensation process the employee is. For example, when all of the compensation changes for a group of employees have been proposed by an HR administrator and then approved by the relevant line manager, a report is used to apply the physical changes to the employee records. This infotype monitors the status of these changes and tracks their progress from in planning to approved to active.

This infotype is also used to store the amount of the compensation budget that has been allocate to an employee.

Infotype 0760 Eligibility Override

Through Enterprise Compensation Management, you try to determine a process that meets your exact organizational requirements. Employees are assigned the correct type of compensation awards based on complex hierarchies and decision-making processes. However there are always going to be cases of employees who don't quite fit into the standard structure. This infotype is used to create individual overrides of the entitlement rules, for example, allowing employees who do not have long enough service to be entitled to long-term employee's incentives, or the opposite, removing entitlement for a specific employee for reasons that are too complex or rare to record in the compensation process.

Infotype 0761 Long-Term Incentives Granting

Each time an employee is awarded a new long-term incentive through the compensation management process, a new Infotype 0761 record is created, allowing you to easily view the award date, the award type, and the expiration date.

Infotype 0762 Long-Term Incentives Exercising

When long-term incentives such as stock options mature, they can be exercised by the employee. This infotype is used to store the related information:

> Number of exercised awards

> Fair market value

> Exercise price

> Number of sold awards

> Tax advance (to be deducted in payroll)

> Imputed income (if required)

Infotype 0763 Long-Term Incentives Participant Data

Because the awarding of shares and options needs to be handled in an open and transparent manor, this infotype is used to flag if an employee is a company director or insider. It records the details of the shares the employee owns as part of the long-term incentives program.

Organizational-Structure-Related Infotypes

Infotype 1005 Planned Compensation

This infotype is attached to a job or position via the organizational structure and is used to store the details of the planned compensation for the position or job. For example, employee Mark Donald holds the position of Chief Accountant – Textiles and Fabrics. Mark's job is defined as Accountant. As part of the compensation management process, it is determined that the salary range for the job Accountant should be $55,000 to $62,000, so this range is entered in the planned compensation infotype.

The link from job to position to employee means that when an administrator gives Mark a pay raise on Infotype 0008 Basic Pay, the SAP ERP HCM system will generate either a warning or an error if the salary is outside the range of $55,000 to $62,000 per annum.

Because a job such as an accountant could be used in several countries, you can define a different planned compensation infotype record for each country/currency required.

Infotype 1015 Cost Planning

The cost planning infotype is used to store the amounts from PCP against an object in the organizational structure such as a position, job, or in some cases an organizational unit. It stores for a set period of time, the details of wage elements, amounts, currencies, and time frames, for example, a monthly or annual figure.

Infotype 1271 Composite Survey Result

Once you have imported your survey data from several sources and combined this information into composite results (if collective results are required), this information is stored in the survey result infotype for each internal benchmark job. You can then compare market pay and your company pay for employees, positions, or jobs. In this infotype you can create multiple composite results, so you can compare different market movement assumptions, provider weightings, and market data aging factors to build up as many views of a job or position as you require to determine its worth to your company.

Infotype 1520 Budget Amounts

When you allocate your budget across your organizational structure, this infotype holds the individual amount that has been allocated to each organizational unit, allowing simple reporting and information gathering.

Compensation Management Reporting

Enterprise Compensation Management provides you with a fully integrated set of reports that provide for all your reporting needs in all areas of Compensation Management. Reports are provided for reporting details of budgeting, long-term incentives, compensation administration, and all other parts of the process. The function is fully provided through integration with the NetWeaver Business Warehouse, allowing compensation-management-related data to be included in reports combining information with Human Resource, Finance, and any other components' data.

Now let's look at a few of the key reports in Enterprise Compensation Management:

> **Planned Labor Costs Report**
> This report allows you to see the planned labor costs for your organizational units. It uses the information stored in Infotype 1005 Planned Compensation as the basis for its calculations.

> **Actual versus Planned Compensation Report**
> This report compares the actual base salary that an employee receives to the salary range assigned to the job or position that the employee holds. Figure 14.8 shows the planned salary data versus the actual figures for a range of pay scales.

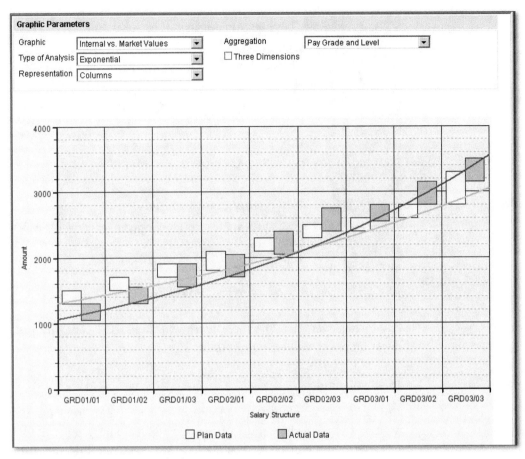

Figure 14.8 Planned versus Actual Salary Figures

We covered a lot of information in this chapter, so let's look at a case study to see how a real company used Enterprise Compensation Management effectively.

Case Study

Table 14.5 provides a quick overview of the case study before we explain it in more detail.

Company	US Chemicals Manufacturer
Existing Solutions	SAP ERP including Financials, Project Management, Production Planning, Plant Maintenance, and existing HCM solution
Challenges	> Local compensation and budget control has led to inconsistent program delivery > Lack of global oversight of costs of program
SAP Solutions	Enterprise Compensation Management
Benefits	> Global view of compensation data > Integration with BI provides powerful reporting capabilities > More consistent compensation program

Table 14.2 Compensation Management Case Study

Employing over 18,000 people worldwide, this U.S. company produces high-tech and chemical products.

The Challenges

This company employees a wide range of employees, from manual workers to high-tech scientists. It needed a global integrated SAP ERP HCM system to replace its separate local systems. The company managed its global compensation through a set of local budgets and spent a lot of time consolidating the information and then judging its impact.

The SAP Solution

As part of a broader SAP ERP HCM implementation including ESS and MSS, the company also implemented Enterprise Compensation Management for it operations worldwide.

The Benefits

The company developed a global and consistent compensation management program with an internationally standardized planning process. The integration between Enterprise Compensation Management and Business Warehouse allowed the company to perform extensive analysis of data and provide broad-based reporting, giving clarity and definition to areas that were previously only estimated. All of these changes allowed them to rapidly get accurate information to support strategic decision making and ensure that compensation management is performed more quickly, efficiently, and accurately.

Summary

Enterprise Compensation Management is a fully developed set of tools that allows you to develop a comprehensive compensation management program for your company. It encompasses all aspects of compensation management, including cost planning, budgeting, long-term incentives, job pricing, and all other aspects of planning that give you the ability to ensure effective compensation management.

The entire package may seem to be somewhat overwhelming in its breadth and scope, but the compartmental structure of the component allows you to pick and choose which parts you implement depending on your company's requirements. The key things to remember about this tool include:

> It is a flexible tool, and you have many options for how to implement it. For instance, you can implement only long-term incentives if that is what your company requires. Or you can implement the compensation adjustment process without implementing budgeting, if this area is not important to your company.

> Integration with ESS and MSS and a complete portal-based delivery approach has made SAP ERP HCM Enterprise Compensation Management a cutting-edge, user-friendly, and up-to-date function. It can help you enhance your company's effectiveness when it comes to compensation management and ensure that your company always knows where it stands in terms of compensation management, so you can act both proactively and reactively, depending on your operating environment.

In the next chapter we will be exploring the important area of Employee Self-Service.

PART III
End-User Service Delivery

Around the world, HR departments are being faced with a requirement to cut costs and focus on the provision of strategic services while also improving the day-to-day service they deliver to their customers, the company's employees. Balancing these sometimes conflicting challenges is made much easier by this SAP ERP HCM function, which empowers both employees and managers to take responsibility for their own HR-related tasks via self-service applications and provides a powerful tool for enabling excellent customer service to employees using SAP Customer Relationship Management technology. There are three chapters in this section:

> *Employee Self-Service*
  This function gives employees quick access to their own data using a simple-to-learn employee-specific portal. Employees can maintain their own data, check their payslips online, process leave requests, complete forms and checklists, and check their benefits entitlements. Changes to employee data completed via Employee Self-Service can be instantly reflected in the core HR system or sent for approval from either the HR team or the employee's manager.

> *Manager Self-Service*
> Again using the benefits of the SAP Enterprise Portal, this function empowers managers to take control of their own teams, giving them ability to manage employee-related transactions such as recruitment requests, team budgets, and project management tasks and produce their own reports.

> *Employee Interaction Center*
> For companies wanting to offer a centralized or outsourced employee customer service program, this function provides an integrated tool enabling administrators to manage employee requests via phone, email, chat, or fax. It uses a sophisticated call tracking and monitoring tool to ensure that employees get excellent, correct, and consistent service no matter from where in the world the service is provided.

We will explain each of these topics in their own chapter, beginning with the most important one: Employee Self-Service.

15

Employee Self-Service

When HR was a paper- and filing-cabinet based operation, the idea of employees maintaining their own records was unimaginable. Even when HR data first moved onto computer systems and was transferred to electronic records, there was no sensible way employees could access the system to maintain their own data. However, HR departments always knew a time would come when the burden of day-to-day tasks such as address changes, holiday quota balance checks, and benefits queries could be handled automatically with little or no input from the HR team.

That time has now truly arrived. The SAP ERP HCM Employee Self-Service function empowers employees worldwide to view and maintain their own data. All manner of tasks from simple address changes to applying for a new job or completing a performance appraisal can be completed online. The required consistency checks, authorization, and security controls are all in place to ensure that employees do not do more damage than good when maintaining their own data. HR departments and managers of employees find themselves freed of the time-consuming repetitive tasks of data maintenance and can concentrate more fully on realizing the company's more strategic goals.

How Employee Self-Service Fits into an Enterprise

Employee Self-Service (ESS) fits into every corner of a company. Whether an employee needs to get a reprint of a payslip, to inform the HR department of the birth of a child so that benefits can be adjusted accordingly, or to enter his working time, ESS is there. Employees with ready access to a computer can access their personal ESS work area via the company intranet through the Enterprise Portal. Employees who don't have access to a computer as part of their normal job such as factory workers or outdoor workers can be provided with access to a dedicated ESS machine, allowing whole shifts of employees access to a shared computer to manage their own data. ESS has a simple-to-use, easy-to-learn web interface that uses strong data validation and security controls to manage data entry and reduce mistakes and errors.

HR administrators freed of the responsibility to perform manual, and often repetitive, data entry tasks can focus their time instead on proactive tasks and work toward more strategic goals.

A Closer Look at ESS

ESS is a powerful SAP ERP HCM application, delivered as part of the Enterprise Portal. It uses the latest SAP NetWeaver architecture to deliver flexible and configurable functionality to employees via the Internet. The concept behind ESS doesn't take much explaining. Employees have access to view, edit, and maintain a large amount of their own data. Employees can also view company information such as training schedules and recruitment opportunities and interact with the relevant department straight through the portal. To better understand the capabilities of ESS, we will look at how ESS works and what is available on it.

How ESS Works

How ESS really works is a very technical but important subject. However, for most people, how the system works is not really important.

All that matters is that it does. In this section we will take just a brief look at the structure behind ESS so people involved with it have an overview of the key parts of the architecture.

SAP NetWeaver Portal

ESS is delivered via the *SAP NetWeaver Portal*, which offers companies a single point of access to SAP and non-SAP applications, information repositories, databases, and services from both internal and external sources. In practice, this means users can access a multitude of programs, reports, applications, and websites through a single portal.

The SAP NetWeaver Portal allows the SAP system and external content to be centrally managed and presented

SAP offers many solutions tailored for delivery through the portal, as well as ESS and Manager Self-Service (MSS), which we cover in the next chapter. SAP also delivers tools for many other situations including managing projects, collaborating on product design and higher education and research projects, customer relationship management, professional services, and retail and financial services. The portal provides the means to deliver the content of ESS, which is made up of many iViews.

iViews

An *iView* is any kind of application, information, or service that is delivered via the portal. iViews are self-contained web documents that are used to perform specific tasks within the portal. They are not just web links to other websites. They are small self-contained programs that can display data, perform tasks, or offer some form of content.

iViews are used to present information and perform tasks within the portal

 Example

Some iViews that are commonly used in ESS include:

Change own data (e.g., address or name)

Record working times (e.g., enter start and finish times)

Application status (e.g., check the status of a new job application)

When defining the look and feel of ESS in the portal, you can pick and choose which SAP iViews you include in your version of the portal. Most companies customize existing iViews to meet their specific requirements, so the standard iViews should be thought of as just a starting point for developing a perfect solution rather than a finished product. In addition to the standard iViews, you can include iViews created by third parties and use them to create an ESS solution that really meets the needs of your company.

Creating Your ESS Layout

The ESS layout allows you to tailor your content to your company's specific needs

Once you have a portal and you have decided which iViews you want your employees to access, you need to arrange them on the screen. A simple hierarchy is used to explain how the layout is set up. Table 15.1 explains the hierarchy, the SAP terms used to describe them, and how they are related.

Object	Description	Example
Role	The highest component, it contains one or more worksets	One role may be defined for regular permanent employees, another for casual employees.
Workset	Used to group pages and other worksets	Several worksets will be used to divide the portal layout into logical groups (pages).
Page	A logical collection of iViews	A page is used to group specific iViews together; for example, the personal information iViews are usually stored on one page.

Table 15.1 Components of a Portal Layout

In addition to the terms used to define the layout, the portal itself and iViews are the two main concepts that regular users of ESS need to understand. We will now look at what employees can do via ESS using the iViews we have just learned about.

What Employees Can Do via ESS

SAP delivers a massive set of iViews that can be integrated into your company's version of ESS. The solution is divided into logical groupings to organize the iViews:

> Life and work event management

> Personal information management

> Time management

> Benefits management

> Payment administration

> Internal opportunities

> Corporate learning

> Business travel and expenses

> Corporate information

> Procurement

> Work environment

A wide range of iViews empower employees and remove the administration from your HR team

Let's look at each of the groupings and some of the iViews contained within them to understand their potential.

Life and Work Event Management

From the moment new employees start with your company, the life and work event management iViews allow them to update and maintain key information regarding life and work events.

My First Days

Designed to provide and capture information for new starters, this iView allows you to manage all of the steps associated with new starters. For example, you can present them with important documents and policies to read and download. You can also ask new employees to record key data such as home address and emergency contacts.

New employees can start using ESS on their first day at work and complete all of the normal new starter tasks directly online

Benefits

This iView allows employees to maintain their own benefits selections during the annual benefits registration process, a task that was traditionally a significant source of overhead for HR benefits administrators. Employees can also be presented with benefits-related documents such as brochures, contracts, checklists, and links to contacts for questions and queries.

Changes in Employment Status

When an employee has been transferred to a new position, this iView allows you to move responsibility for some of the related details back to the employee. Employees can update key information such as office location, communication data, and their own skills profiles. Documents relating to the impacts of contract changes and required training courses can also be attached.

Termination

Use the termination iView to ensure that your leavers complete all of the required tasks before they leave the company

When an employee leaves your company, this iView can be used to help the employee complete the termination process. It can include a list of tasks the employee is required to complete prior to leaving, such as confirming that address and bank details are correct and updating benefits information. Policy documents and checklists can also be provided for the employee to access.

Marriage, Divorce, Birth, and Adoption

These iViews allow employees to perform all of the tasks required to update the system with details of their change of marital or family status. The names and addresses of family members and emergency contacts can be updated. Documents relating to the impacts on benefits and taxes of the marital or family status change can also be presented.

Personal Information Management

Covering some of the most common tasks in Employee Administration, these iViews allow employees to carry out key changes to their personal data such as address, bank, and dependent data changes. Changes are automatically reflected in the employee's infotypes, ensuring that anyone viewing the employee records will always see the most recent up-to-date data.

Personal Data

Employees can maintain their own personal data such as name, marital status, nationality, and birth data. Which of these key pieces of information you allow your employees to update is up to your company to decide (Figure 15.1).

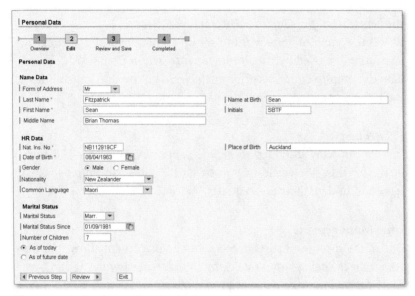

Figure 15.1 An Employee Changing his Personal Details

Address

Changes in employee addresses can be quickly updated. Employees can update their permanent, postal, and emergency address records as and when required.

Bank Information

One of the first things most HR or payroll departments ask for, this iView allows employees to view and update their main bank, travel expenses bank, and any secondary bank accounts that the employee requires.

Employees can quickly update their bank details online with instant effect

It is important to note that this information is checked for consistency and correctness upon input, minimizing the chance of employees inadvertently entering incorrect data.

Family Data

Employees can update data on their spouses and children as and when required. This information can then be automatically picked up in the Benefits Management function.

Authentication for Employee Interaction Center

This iView enables employees to set up authentication questions and answers to be used by the Employee Interaction Center (EIC) to validate the employee for security purposes. The use and capabilities of the EIC is explained in more detail in Chapter 17.

EIC Request

If your company provides employee support through the EIC portal interface, this iView allows you to create a link so employees can track and update their EIC requests.

Time Management

The Time Management iViews allow employees to manage their own time online

One of the most used parts of ESS, Time Management allows employees to check their planned working hours, record working time, and apply for and manage leave requests.

CATS Regular/Record Working Time

With a view that can be set to either daily or weekly, employees can use all of the functionality of the CATS time recording tool to enter their working time and absences via the portal (Figure 15.2). Employees can enter time in advance and in the past. Standard error checking and approval processes are all built into this iView. An overview of time recording shows days or weeks where the employees have not yet entered enough time and the approval status of their time sheets.

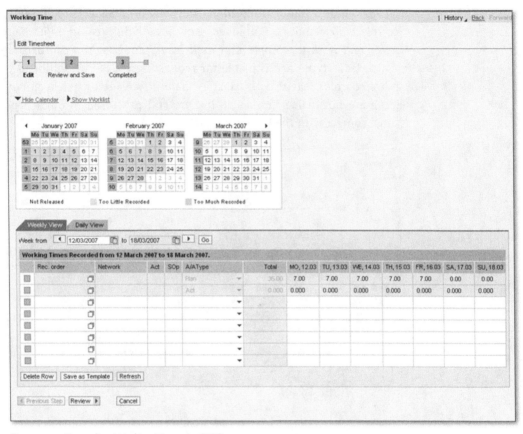

Figure 15.2 Recording Working Time via CATS

Clock-In and Clock-Out Corrections

If your company uses time-recording machines such as punch cards or clocking machines, this iView can be used to correct data entry errors such as duplicate entries or missing entries. An approval process can be linked to these changes, ensuring that no changes are made without being reviewed and approved.

Employees can check and correct their time recording entries, correcting errors before they cause payroll errors

Leave Request

Using the Leave Request iView (Figure 15.3), employees can create and manage periods of leave. This can be used for any time of employee absence including vacation, sickness, unpaid leave, and study

Create and manage leave requests and approvals without any paper forms or processes

leave. Requests can be directed via workflow to managers to approve or reject the requests. Employees can view their existing quota balances and track the progress of their leave requests. You can decide which leave types are available for requesting via ESS. Traditionally, more complex leaves types such as maternity leave or bereavement leave are not managed via ESS but are still processed through personal contact with the HR team.

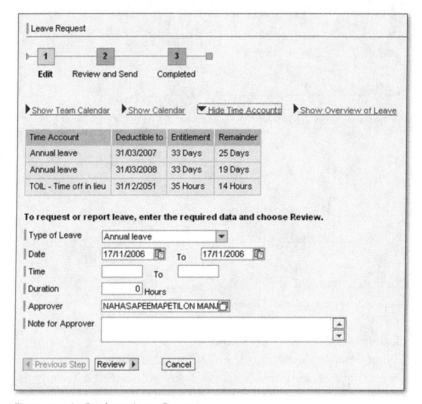

Figure 15.3 An Employee Leave Request

Time Accounts

In addition to being able to see their quota balances in the Leave Request iView, this specialized iView allows employees to see the details of all their quotas. This could include overtime, training, and time off in lieu entitlements.

Time Statement

As we discovered in the Time and Attendance chapter, the time statement is like an employee payslip, but only displays the details of the employee's time recording as processed in Time Evaluation. Employees can use this statement to ensure that all of their working time has been processed and calculated properly rather than waiting for a resulting error to appear in a payslip after their pay has gone to the bank.

Benefits Management

Based on data stored in the Benefits Management function, employees can get instant overviews of their benefits participation and change their existing benefits selections. This information reflects your current benefits program and could include health care, dental, investments, and life insurance benefits.

Employees can get an overview of their benefits enrollments and process adjustments online

Participation Overview

After selecting a key date, employees can view the benefits selections in which they are enrolled. They can drill down to a specific benefit, reviewing costs, dependent assignments, coverage options, and beneficiaries. Because most benefits are only open for adjustment at specific periods, this iView is a display-only iView. Any errors or omissions that the employee spots here need to be fixed outside ESS by communicating with the HR or benefits department.

Benefits Enrollment

When your benefits program is open for enrollment, such as during the annual adjustment period or for new starters or status changes, employees can access their benefits data and complete all of the required information for a new or changed enrollment. To ensure correct data entry, the three-step process involves plan selection, review, and confirmation.

Payment Administration

Employees can access reprints of their payslips or a total compensation overview.

Payslip Printing

Potentially a great time and money saver for many companies, this iView gives employees the ability to print current or historic payslips. Companies can choose to use the same payslip layout as employees already receive, or develop a custom layout just for ESS access. This iView reads directly from the employees' payroll results, so payslips are available online the moment payroll is processed. This iView is very popular with employees, allowing them to quickly access reprints of payslips that are often required by banks or finance companies.

Total Compensation Statement

This form is a PDF statement detailing all of the employee's benefits in a summary form. It includes salary and wage information, other compensation elements such as allowance or bonuses, details of employee benefits entitlements, and any personnel development benefits such as training courses provided. You can choose which elements you want included in this statement to meet your company's needs.

Internal Opportunities

With a direct link to the e-Recruiting component, these iViews allow employees to search, apply for, and monitor any applications they have made. Because this information is directly linked to e-Recruiting, employees are assured of an up-to-date and accurate view of the company's vacancies. Among the iViews available here for employees, the following are the most important.

Search for Jobs

Employees can search the vacancy database to find jobs they are interested in.

Candidate Profile

Employees can create their own candidate profiles, which are used to apply for jobs. Employees can maintain copies of their resumes, their contact data, and their job preferences.

Profile Release

If employees want to apply for specific jobs or make their profiles visible to recruiters when they are searching for potential candidates, they can release their profiles through this iView.

Apply Directly

When employees find a vacancy they want to apply for, this iView takes their candidate profile data and directly submits it for consideration.

Applications

This is an overview iView that allows employees to directly monitor the status of their applications.

Corporate Learning

The SAP Learning Solution is integrated into ESS here, so employees can view their personal skills profiles, browse the learning catalog, and make new training requests to address skills deficits. Training approvals are also tracked through this iView.

Allow employees to view and book training courses, with approval mechanisms built in to the process

Skills Profile

Employees can display and edit their own skills profiles, comparing their current skills with the skills required to perform a different role within the company. Employees can also add new skills, and when skills are found to be lacking, employees can specify the skills they want to acquire and link directly to the Learning Solution to create training requests and bookings (Figure 15.4).

Business Travel and Expense Management

Companies that implement Travel and Expense Management can use these iViews to allow employees to manage all aspects of their corporate travel and expense reimbursement processes. Many iViews are available in this section, so we will just cover the most commonly used ones.

Take travel and expense approvals online, allowing quick processing and making both Finance and employees happier

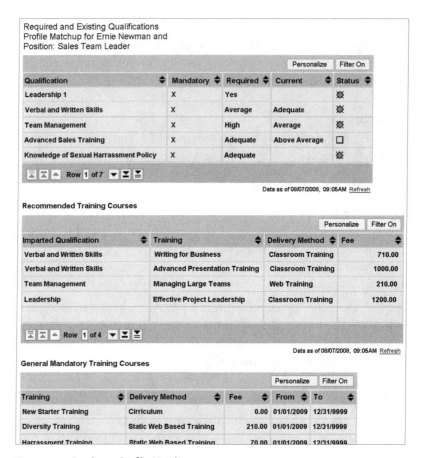

Figure 15.4 Employee Profile Matchup

My Travel Profile

Employees can maintain travel related preferences such as car, rail, and flight preferences and their credit card information for easy access.

All My Trips and Expenses

The central iView of travel and expenses, this iView displays an overview of all of an employee's trips and expenses, showing their approval status and allowing employees to edit or delete entries.

Create/Delete Travel Request

Linked with a workflow for manager approval, this iView allows employees to quickly create or delete a travel request, detailing the reason for the travel, the destination, the cost distribution, and the amount of cash advance required. This is sent to the employee's manager for approval.

Create/Cancel Travel Plan

Integrated with the SAP Internet Graphic Server, these iViews allow employees to create and edit travel bookings including flights, rental cars, trains, and hotels. Employees can use the interactive maps to search for hotels and airports to effectively plan their work-related travel.

Route Planning

This iView gives employees an overview of the expected distance they will cover on a work trip. After entering the start and end points of a trip, the interactive service displays a travel map with a calculated distance that can be used for expense reimbursement.

Employees can see graphical views of their travel plans including maps

Create/Delete Travel Expense Report

When an employee wants to be reimbursed for a work-related trip, these iViews allow the employee to create (Figure 15.5) and edit expense reports, including the reasons for the trip and the expenses incurred, and linking this information to a credit card receipt.

Assign Credit Card Receipts

As part of Travel and Expense Management, credit card receipts can be imported into the travel system. Using this iView, employees can then link credit card receipts with the related trips.

Travel Management Forms

Any standard travel-related forms can be linked to this iView, allowing employees ready access to forms such as airline rewards plan applications, travel policies, and preformatted claim forms.

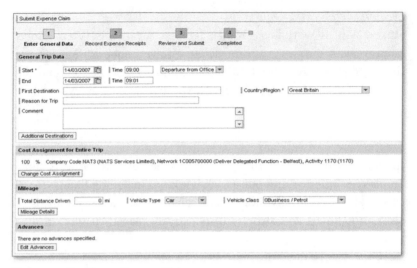

Figure 15.5 Creating an Expense Claim

Alerts

When part of an employee's travel expenses have been rejected or more information is required, the employee is notified of the reason for the alert in this iView.

Corporate Information Management

Provide employees with easy access to corporate documents and forms. Adobe interactive forms can be loaded here, allowing employees to read, complete, and submit electronic forms online.

Code of Business Conduct

This iView is used to display your corporate code of business conduct. Employees can review it and check a box to confirm that they have read it and agree with the terms and conditions.

Procurement

Using SRM, employees can complete work-related purchases online, with all of the approvals and security built in

If your company uses the SAP Supplier Relationship Management (SRM) component to manage purchasing and suppliers, employees can purchase goods and services related to their work.

Procurement iView

Employees can directly access your company's suppliers through this iView and purchase and track any work-related objects. This iView is commonly used for small day-to-day purchases such as office supplies, and because it uses the core SRM functionality, approvals can be used to verify purchases before sales are completed.

Work Environment

Companies that use the Plant Maintenance, Asset Accounting, or Objects on Loan functionality within SAP ERP HCM can use the Work Environment iView to enable employees to manage their own work environments.

When an employee needs a new chair or computer, he can log the problem online

Equipment Overview

Employees can quickly see an overview of all of the company assets assigned to them and use the iView to request repairs, changes, or the loss of items assigned to them. Traffic lights can be used to inform employees that the assets they have are incorrectly assigned, located, or costed.

More iViews are available from the portal, but we have focused on the most important and commonly used here. These iViews cross into many other components of SAP ERP, so let's look at some of the topics surrounding integration within ESS.

Integration

ESS is designed to simplify and streamline numerous common employee processes. Therefore, the integration with other SAP ERP HCM functions and other SAP ERP components is necessarily strong in this area. As we saw when we looked at the potential capabilities of ESS, data is pulled and pushed between ESS and many other components. Once set up, this integration allows immediate and up-to-date information to be displayed. Workflow is also heavily used in this component. Approvals and rejections are managed and processed using the organizational structure to find the correct approver and transfer approval and rejection notifications.

It is important to remember that your ESS solution is a user interface extension of your core SAP ERP HCM implementation, so you can't

ESS can only perform functions already delivered in your core SAP ERP HCM implementation do things in ESS that you aren't going to be doing in the core of your SAP ERP HCM implementation. For example, you can't enable leave requests in ESS without spending the time to create the required absence types and quotas in the Time and Attendance function. Similarly, you can't manage your employee assets unless you are using one of the components enabled to manage these assets.

The processes that you define as standard in your core implantation should be the same processes that you enable in your ESS and MSS solutions. If you have a process for internal applicants to apply for vacancies in e-Recruiting, you don't want to maintain a separate process for employees to do this via ESS. For the sake of efficiency and ongoing maintenance, both these processes should be the same.

We hope you now have a good understanding of the ESS function offered with SAP ERP HCM. It has truly evolved into an effective and useful option for companies, so let's wrap up the chapter with a case study illustrating ESS at work.

Case Study

Table 15.2 provides a quick overview of our case study before we explain it in more detail.

Company	European Engineering and Construction Operator
Existing Solutions	SAP ERP including HCM
Challenges	› Numerous paper-based processes › Majority of workforce not regular computer users
SAP Solutions	ESS, MSS, and EIC (Employee Interaction Center)
Benefits	› Significant cost savings resulting from reduced HR workload › Wide acceptance by factory workers › Rapid company-wide communication

Table 15.2 ESS Case Study

This large European company employees 110,000 employees spread over numerous locations. The company produces technological and engineering products in over 30 separate locations.

The Challenges

The company operated in an environment where most employees did not have access to computers or email. All employee data updates were processed centrally using paper-based forms and processes. All employee communication was done via company magazines and notice boards.

The SAP Solution

Leveraging the existing investment in SAP ERP HCM technology, the company installed ESS, MSS, and EIC over its existing HR software. At the same time, it also centralized its HR operations into a shared service center. ESS largely automated the flow of HR transactional data from employees into the HR system. The company provided dedicated shop floor terminals, allowing all employees access to ESS.

The Benefits

The first and most dramatic benefit was the removal of most of the paper-based forms and processes through online automation. This resulted in the HR team no longer spending time manually entering and checking data. All data is now entered directly by employees. Shop floor workers found the ESS portal easy to use, and data accuracy and completeness has dramatically improved by removal of double keying requirements and the built-in data validations within ESS.

The company also uses the ESS solution to manage all of its employee communications. Employee notices and company newsletters are provided online, so employees can access the information online if they want or download and print it for later access.

Summary

In many ways, ESS represents one of the greatest benefits of operating a truly integrated HR system, giving employees the ability to manage many aspects of their own information, from changes of address to travel bookings to creating a request for a new desk or computer. The impact on the HR team, who are freed from many mind numbing repetitive data entry and validation tasks, is dramatic.

In this chapter we have briefly explored the ESS solution. We have looked at the following areas:

> **How ESS works**
> We explored the key parts of the ESS architecture including the portal, iViews, and the structure used to control how they fit together.

> **What employees can do with ESS**
> We looked at a broad range of iViews that demonstrate the amazing array of capabilities of ESS, from entering time data to updating key data following a birth or marriage to applying for a new job.

> **Integration**
> We noted key points, to consider regarding the integration of ESS: ESS can only reflect the functionality already implemented in your core ERP SAP HCM system, and workflow manages the approval process within ESS.

We also saw the impressive benefits that one company using ESS received from empowering its workforce to maintain its own data, creating a new employee communication interface, and allowing HR team members to focus on more strategic and value-adding goals. In the next chapter we will look at another great value-adding and empowering tool: SAP ERP HCM Manager Self-Service.

16

Manager Self-Service

The days of giant central HR departments controlling every aspect of employee administration and management are seemingly numbered. More and more companies are moving to empower their managers and free up their HR departments' time by moving key decision-making powers to the managers on the front line. This decentralization of the decision-making process means that managers need ready access to all of the information required to make effective decisions.

The SAP *Manager Self-Service (MSS)* function is designed to assist this process by providing managers with the tools to effectively manage their employees. It also helps with a wide variety of tasks that are better managed at the front line with local knowledge than in some remote HR department miles and perhaps continents away from those affected by these decisions. MSS allows managers to control and manage processes from their team to budgets, project management, planning, and reporting all through the easy-to-use, quick to learn SAP NetWeaver Enterprise Portal.

How MSS Fits into an Enterprise

MSS can be accessed anywhere your managers can access the Internet

Much like the ESS function that we looked at in the previous chapter, MSS can also be deployed wherever your employees are working. As long as Managers have access to the Internet, they have the tools to effectively manage their teams and many of their other responsibilities through the portal.

Because of the full integration between MSS and a wide range of SAP ERP components and other SAP ERP HCM functions, managers always have the most up-to-date information instantly at hand. From the progress of recruitment requests to checking attendance and absence levels to compensation planning, MSS enables managers to make good decisions fast.

A Closer Look at MSS

MSS empowers your managers to take control of the decision-making process by giving them all of the information they need

MSS empowers your managers to make decisions affecting their teams and departments. These decisions cover all of the major aspects of a typical manager's role including budgeting, cost management, employee compensation, and leave and absence management. Where traditionally managers had to ask HR or finance for access to key analytical information, MSS gives managers access to unprecedented levels of information and reporting from many sources at once, allowing them to make better-informed decisions faster and helping the company work toward its strategic goals.

Empowering managers with MSS also has a dramatic impact on many other parts of the company, but especially on your HR and finance departments, which are relieved of many tedious and time-consuming tasks. These are now taken care of at the front line by managers with access to the best and most up-to-date information.

To understand the capabilities of MSS and what it could do for your company, let's first look at how the solution works and then what it can do.

How MSS Works

The technology that runs MSS is exactly the same as for ESS. In the previous chapter we covered the major parts of this technology, but let's quickly recap the most important points before we look at what MSS can do for your company.

SAP NetWeaver Portal

ESS and MSS are delivered via the *SAP NetWeaver Portal*, which offers companies a single point of access to SAP and non-SAP applications, information repositories, databases, and services from both internal and external sources. In practice, this means that users can access a multitude of programs, reports, applications, and websites through a single portal.

The SAP NetWeaver Portal allows SAP and external content to be centrally managed and presented

SAP offers many solutions tailored for delivery through the portal, including project management, collaborative design on products, higher education and research projects, customer relationship management, professional services, and retail and financial services. The portal provides the means to deliver the content of MSS. This content is made up of many iViews that we will explore in the next section.

iViews

As mentioned earlier in the book, an *iView* is any kind of application, information, or service that is delivered via the Enterprise Portal. iViews are self-contained web documents that are used to perform specific tasks within the portal. They are not merely a web link to another website. They are small self-contained programs that can display data, perform tasks, or offer some form of content.

iViews are used to present information and perform tasks within the portal

 Example

Some iViews that are commonly used in MSS include:

Headcount: Quickly get an accurate count of your employees.

Illness Rate: Instantly get statistics on your employees' sick leave rates.

Critical Vacancies: Monitor the status of key vacancies.

When defining the look and feel of MSS within the portal, you can pick and choose which SAP iViews you include in your version of the portal. Most companies customize the existing iViews to meet their specific requirements, so the standard iViews should be thought of as starting points for developing a perfect solution rather than as finished products. In addition to the standard iViews, you can include iViews created by third parties and use them to create an MSS solution that really meets the needs of your company.

Creating your MSS Layout

The MSS layout allows you to tailor your content to your company's specific needs

Once you have a portal and you have decided which iViews you want your employees to access, you need to arrange them on the screen. A simple hierarchy is used to explain how the layout is set up. Table 19.1 explains the hierarchy, the SAP terms used to describe the items in the hierarchy, and how they are related.

Object	Description	Example
Role	The highest component, it contains one or more worksets	One role can be defined for senior managers and another for shift managers.
Workset	These are used to group pages, and other worksets.	Several worksets will be used to divide the portal layout into logical groups (pages).
Page	A page is a logical collection of iViews.	A page is used to group specific iViews together; for example, absence information iViews are usually stored on one page.

Table 16.1 Components of a Portal Layout

Adobe Interactive Forms

Interactive forms allow you to quickly develop forms that support the process rather than just holding information

One of the key tools that make MSS so useful is the integration of Adobe interactive forms. This technology allows companies to develop fully interactive forms for presenting and gathering information and managing processes. Examples of interactive forms that companies have developed and used through MSS include custom performance-appraisal feedback forms. These forms are sent to appraisers to complete. When an appraiser receives the form, all of the input data is already loaded, such as the candidate for appraisal and the appraisal method. The appraiser simply has to enter the appraisal results, which are checked against appraisal master data for keying errors and mistakes. The completed form can then be routed via workflow back to the appraisal manager for evaluation.

Interactive forms make creating meaningful, targeted employee-specific forms a simple task, increasing data accuracy, usability, and, most important, the amount of time taken in completing form filling and processing.

In addition to Adobe interactive forms, the portal itself, iViews, and layout controls, we have now seen the main concepts of MSS that regular users need to understand. So let's look at what employees can do via MSS using iViews.

What Managers Can Do via MSS

SAP delivers a comprehensive set of iViews that you can use to create the perfect view of MSS for your company. As we noted in the previous chapter, the standard iViews are best viewed as starting points for automating processes and tasks in a way that matches your company's requirements. Few companies can take all of these iViews straight out of the box. Most require tinkering with and tailoring to meet their own data entry and process requirements.

Over 50 standard iViews are available in MSS, and they cover a wide range of topics, so we will only look at the most commonly implemented ones in this chapter. For ease of use, the MSS iViews are divided into *worksets*. Worksets allow the iViews to be grouped into logical process- and task-oriented groupings. The MSS function is made up of the following worksets:

> **Work Overview**
> This workset contains iViews that help managers get overviews of what is going on in their areas of control.

Over 50 standard iViews are available in MSS

> **Team**

Managing employees is just one of the tasks possible in MSS. This workset allows managers to process all of the tasks relating to managing their teams.

> **Budget**

This workset provides managers with all of the budget related information they need to effectively manage their team or department budgets.

> **Projects**

When a manager is responsible for the whole or part of an ongoing project, his responsibilities can be managed here.

> **Planning**

This workset enables managers to perform planning tasks such as compensation management, budget control, and balanced scorecard function.

> **Reports**

Providing key up-to-the minute information to managers when they need it, the reporting workset gives managers tools to analyze and report on their areas of control.

Let's look a little deeper into these worksets and discuss some of the most important iViews contained in them.

Work Overview

This workset includes the following key iViews that help managers control their tasks and outstanding tasks.

Universal Worklist

The Universal Worklist centrally stores all of a manager's outstanding tasks, notifications, and reminders

This iView is one of the key parts of MSS. It provides managers with a unified and centralized view of all of their responsibilities including outstanding workflows such as leave requests, alerts (for example, of employees who have not submitted their time sheets on time), Knowledge Management notifications (for example, ongoing discussions and notifications), and collaboration tasks from project management. Managers can also process any of these tasks directly from the universal worklist.

Attendance Overview

One of the most popular iViews, this simple iView enables managers, with the click of a button, to view their team members' work status for the current day. They can quickly see which employees are at work, absent, or have a leave request currently awaiting approval.

See which employees are at work today, with the click of a button

Reminder of Dates

Another simple but useful iView, the Reminder of Dates overview allows managers to display the key dates coming up for their employees including birthdays, service anniversaries, and outstanding Monitoring of Tasks records such as reminders to complete performance appraisals or disciplinary reviews.

Figure 16.1 shows the Reminder of Dates and the Attendance Overview iViews.

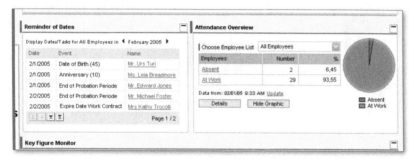

Figure 16.1 Reminder of Dates and Attendance Overview

Team

The Team workset is the largest of the worksets and contains many powerful iViews to help managers effectively manage their most important resource—their employees. Let's look at some of the key iViews.

General Data and Personal Data

These two iViews (Figure 16.2) give managers a work-related or personal overview of their team members' details from information stored in the Personnel Administration component. The General Data

Provide access to key employee personal data to help managers do their jobs without interrupting your HR department

397

iView provides the manager with information relating to where the employee works in the company and how he can be contacted. The Personal Data iView shows employee information such as name, date of birth, marital status, and home address. If this information is not required for a manager, fields can be hidden.

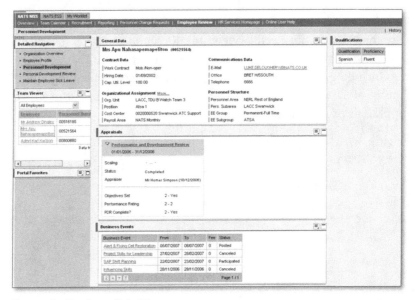

Figure 16.2 Employee Data iViews

Absence Days

This iView lets a manager display the absence history for an individual employee for the past two months by reading information straight from the Time and Attendance function. Additional months can be viewed by scrolling through the calendar. This report is a great tool for establishing patterns of absence and working with the employee to address any absence-related issues.

Work and Absence Approvals

Workflow-enabled leave approvals mean the end of paper-based leave request forms

These two iViews allow managers to review and approve or reject time recording and leave requests created by their team members in ESS. Managers can view details of remaining leave quotas and pass comments back to the employees along with their leave approval or rejections.

Salary Data

This set of iViews allows a manager to view all salary and wage information for an employee. Information for these iViews is sourced from both the Personnel Administration and the Enterprise Compensation Management functions. This could include the average salary survey results for the employee's job or position and the employee's actual salary figure. The manager can quickly create a graph comparing the two figures. Managers can also compare an employee's salary to the average salary in their team and other reference figures. The manager can display any long-term incentives assigned to the employee and view their current status.

Find out how much your employee costs you compared to up-to-date salary survey data

Profile and Qualifications Matchup

This iView (Figure 16.3) allows a manager to quickly compare an employee's existing skills and qualifications against the requirements for the employee's job or position. This can lead to the development of a training plan or other actions through the Learning Solution.

Figure 16.3 Matching an Employee Skills to Position Requirements

Training Activities

A manager can use this iView to get a detailed overview of an employee's training history from the Enterprise Learning Management function, the classes the employee has attended, qualifications gained, and any training events booked in the future. The manager can then see the location, cost, and status of the training courses.

Recruitment Activities

Perform all of the recruitment activities required to request and approve a new employee in one place

With a direct link to the e-Recruiting function, this set of iViews allows managers to perform the full range of recruitment activities, from creating a new employee requisition request and sending it via workflow to the nominated recruiter, to viewing a candidate shortlist, viewing recruiter comments and assessments, and the status of the overall recruitment process. Figure 16.4 shows a manager's view of current requisitions.

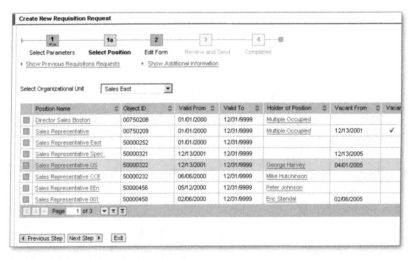

Figure 16.4 Requisitons for New Employees

Object and Data Provider

Although not strictly part of the Team workset, the Object and Data Provider iView is used to view employee data. This iView allows managers to quickly view the company's organizational structure from Organizational Management. Managers can view all of the data available in the organizational structure, analyzing the assignment of employees, positions, chief positions, organizational units, and costing details straight from the Organizational Management function.

Budget

Utilizing the full integration with the Controlling component, the Budget workset allows managers to view the financial situations of the profit centers, cost centers, and internal orders for which they are responsible. Some of the critical iViews for this are described next.

Critical Postings and Variances

Linking to the posting monitor, this iView allows a manager to display posting elements such as line items and internal orders that have exceeded specified threshold levels or are raised as exceptional variances. Once reviewed, these critical postings and variances can be sent to the controlling team via internal service requests or flagged as acceptable to the manager.

Get instant notification of budget and project financial variances and fix them fast

Equipment Monitor

Using the Equipment Monitor iView, managers can quickly get overviews of the assets and equipment for which they are responsible. This could include computers, furniture, company cars, and even whole buildings. Managers can then allocate these objects to specific cost centers and manage depreciation settings. Managers can also report equipment as requiring repair, requiring replacement, or lost. All of this information is stored in the Asset Accounting and Plant Maintenance components.

Control the assignment of your team's assets and manage depreciation of them

Projects

Integrated with the SAP cProjects, Controlling, and Service Relationship Management components, this set of iViews gives managers the ability to effectively create and manage projects within their areas of responsibility, from creating new projects to monitoring costs and requesting additional resources.

Create a Project

When a manager embarks on a new project, such as an IT software implementation or the construction or renovation of a new office, this iView links the manager directly to the creation templates contained in cProjects. Managers can assign details to the project such as a description or expected completion date and assign resources.

Plan and Budget Consumption

Create and manage projects, from resource allocations to budget allocations and tracking

When a project's costs are allocated to an internal order or project in Controlling, the manager can plan how these funds will be consumed during the project. Managers can get an overview of their rates of consumption and graphical views of their remaining budgets.

Request and Monitor External Service

Request external resources to assist in your project and monitor their status

When linked with the SAP Service Relationship Management component, managers can automatically create requests for external services such as consultancy or training resources to assist with the project. This request is then auctioned by the Service Relationship Management team, and the manager can monitor the progress of the request.

Enter Invoice or Credit Memo

When linked with the SAP Service Relationship Management component, managers can enter invoices and credit memos for processing relating to the costs incurred in their projects.

Planning

The Planning workset gives you the ability to monitor budgets, consumption, and balanced score cards

The planning iViews aim to give managers more information to help with corporate planning. This could be planning budgets, sales targets, or spending levels.

Planning Rounds

As part of the overall budgeting process, the portal uses collaboration rooms to help manage the creation, approval, and monitoring of a budget. A planning round is part of this overall process, where team members work toward defining and agreeing on the budget.

This iView allows managers to receive notification of an impending planning round.

Budget Consumption Overview

Based on information stored in cProjects or Controlling, managers can track the consumption of the budget for the projects for which they are responsible or in which they are involved.

Balanced Scorecards Elements

Companies that use SAP Strategic Enterprise Management to develop a balanced scorecard of company performance can use this iView to help managers track performance against these targets. Though managers cannot edit the targets in the scorecard, they can enter comments and appraisals.

Reports

The reporting functionality of MSS is really flexible. Any reports currently being used in SAP can be integrated into the MSS reporting section. This can include reports from SAP ERP HCM, Business Intelligence, and even the traditional Managers Desktop reporting suite. Companies can also develop their own reports using a variety of report-writing tools such as SAP Query, and NetWeaver Business Intelligence. As standard, the following reports are also included for MSS reporting:

Add any SAP report to your managers' reporting menus, and let them create their own as well

> Headcount

> Full Time Equivalents

> Starters and Leavers

> Illness Rate

> Overtime Rates

> Overtime Costs

This list shows just some of the tasks, processes, and reports that managers can execute through MSS. Next we will take a brief look at the integration that makes all of this possible.

Integration

In this chapter we have seen the numerous points of integration between MSS and other SAP components including Organizational Management, Enterprise Compensation Management, Time and Attendance, Personnel Administration, the SAP Learning Solution, CATS, SAP Strategic Enterprise Management, and Business Intelligence. This massive standard integration and the information it provides makes MSS a truly powerful tool for increasing manager effectiveness.

Use the organizational structure to map your workflow and approval processes

Among the integration points, MSS uses the organizational structure heavily to control which employees a manager is responsible for and in turn which managers are notified when employees' process tasks require approvals. It is therefore vital that your company's organizational structure meets both the requirements of your HR department for managing the organization and your MSS requirements.

Sometimes if the two sets of requirements are vastly different, companies will maintain two versions of the organizational structure or use a matrix organizational structure or custom relationships to meet their needs. More information on these topics can be found back in Chapter 3, Organizational Management.

Remember that MSS can only perform tasks supported by configurations in your core SAP system

Like ESS, MSS can only perform tasks and complete processes that are already configured in your core SAP ERP system. For example, you can't manage team budgets unless you are using the relevant component in your company's system.

As we mentioned earlier, the standard iViews are best thought of as a foundation to which your company can apply its own rules and peculiarities. For example, if you need the approval of at least two managers before an employee can take leave, you are going to need to enhance the standard iViews that control leave requests and approvals to meet your company's requirements.

This concludes our review of the MSS function. As with ESS, this is a powerful and efficient tool that will benefit your HR department greatly. Let's take a look at a case study to see how it can work.

Case Study

Table 16.1 provides a quick overview of the case study before we explain it in more detail.

Company	Middle Eastern Automobile Manufacturing Plant
Existing Solutions	SAP R/3 for Finance and Controlling
Challenges	❯ Replace costly legacy HR systems Numerous paper-based forms and processes
SAP Solutions	SAP ERP HCM including ESS, MSS, and SAP NetWeaver Enterprise Portal
Benefits	❯ 25% decrease in the processing time for key processes ❯ Increased visibility of employee data for managers ❯ Decentralized control of time recording and leave management to managers ❯ Stable platform for further HR initiatives

Table 16.2 SAP MSS Case Study

This large automobile manufacturer manages operations in 26 countries from its base in the Middle East.

The Challenges

The company had many paper-based forms and processes based on its legacy HR and payroll system. The processes were slow and inefficient. The company wanted to automate these processes and decentralize responsibility for approvals to business managers.

The SAP Solution

As part of a larger SAP ERP HCM implementation project, the company implemented MSS. They were impressed that many of the tools provided worked out of the box, with little or no customization required. This contributed to the 19-week implementation time.

The Benefits

In addition to reducing the processing time of key HR processes by 25%, reducing HR-based forms and empowering managers to make decisions increased the speed of its payroll processing by 35%. Managers were instantly able to manage working time, leave, and overtime and conduct performance appraisals online. Keeping the system as standard as possible made it possible to easily integrate the system into the company's global SAP system, and increase reporting capabilities.

Summary

MSS is one of the tools customers want to see demonstrated first when they choose to implement SAP ERP HCM. Its ease of use and the powerful range of processes that can be managed through it make it an appealing tool to both HR teams wanting to divest tasks and managers wanting to regain central control of their teams and their work.

In this chapter we saw the underlying technology that makes MSS possible. We looked at Adobe interactive forms and how they can help make traditional processes faster, more targeted, and less error prone.

We looked at the major worksets and iViews that deliver the tools managers can use to make their teams work better and more efficiently. Among the tools we saw, some of the highlights were:

> **The universal worklist**
Allows managers to centrally view and complete their outstanding tasks.

> **Work and leave approvals**
This workflow-based tool allows managers to review employee working time and leave requests, consult leave balances, and approve or reject requests with comments attached.

> **Salary Data**
We saw how managers can quickly compare an employee's salary

to salary survey information and team averages to help make compensation adjustment decisions.

We also saw how through integration with non-SAP ERP HCM components, managers can control budgets, request resources, and monitor their teams' progress against the company's balanced scorecard. In the next chapter we will see how the SAP NetWeaver Enterprise Portal powers the Employee Interaction Center and allows central staff to quickly and efficiently handle HR-related employee requests.

Employee Interaction Center

The mantra of treating your employees like customers is an often-repeated but not often-practiced management slogan. Customers traditionally get treated better than employees, probably because they lead directly to sales and therefore income and revenue, whereas employees are often regarded as an expense and an overhead. HR departments have traditionally struggled to create a real customer-focused service. Failing to deal in a structured manner with high volumes of phone calls and email requests, peak periods of demand such as benefits enrollment periods or after annual salary reviews have been implemented can also affect HR service levels.

Another common problem with HR customer service is inconsistency of service. Inconsistent information regarding company policies and procedures, inconsistent employee communication channels, hard-to-reach telephone contacts, and ever-changing email addresses are just some of the communications problems employees face.

The Employee Interaction Center (EIC) addresses these problems by allowing your HR team to bring real customer-relationship management technology to better manage your company's relationship with your most important asset—your employees.

The EIC allows you to streamline and standardize the provision of employee-focused services through a centralized, single point of contact delivery channel. This channel can be controlled and managed as either an internal or external shared services center. Using customer relationship technology, HR resources and staffing levels can be tailored to demand so that companies can deliver a cost-efficient service.

How the EIC Fits into an Enterprise

From an employee's perspective, the EIC is a single point of contact that allows employees to contact their HR department via phone, email, fax, or chat to find answers to HR-related questions and access HR services. You can quickly measure employee satisfaction with your service using an integrated survey tool.

Managers can also use the EIC to get quick information or resolve simple HR problems without taking up the valuable time of your HR professionals.

From an HR point of view, the EIC helps deliver employee and manager queries and questions straight to HR team members' desktops via an easy-to-learn, simple-to-use web-based interface. HR team members are then provided with a set of tools to let help them effectively handle employee queries or problems. They can quickly and simply edit HR master data, review employee history, and respond to employee queries promptly because all of the required information is centrally stored and right at hand.

The EIC integrates human resources data with customer-relationship management tools to ensure that employees receive the service they deserve and the company can operate its HR team at optimum levels. The EIC delivers increased employee satisfaction and HR credibility through a consistent, quality, and tailored service. It also decreases HR costs and improves productivity by providing a simple and effective tool to quickly solve employee queries.

A Closer Look at the EIC

The EIC combines the best parts of the SAP ERP HCM and SAP Customer Relationship Management (CRM) components to enable your HR team members (known as *agents* in EIC) to deliver excellent service to your employees. At its most basic level the EIC enables agents to complete the following tasks:

> Rapidly access employee data

> Manage employee contacts and relationships

> Conduct knowledge searches

> Review employee interaction history

Treat your employees like customers and give them the service they deserve

The aim of the EIC is to deliver a unified and effective face of the HR department through consistent messaging of HR policies and procedures, streamline HR processes, and leverage technology to benefit employees and the company. We will now look at how the EIC can be implemented at your company.

Implementation Considerations

The EIC solution can be installed in two way, as part of either an SAP ERP Customer Service Management (CRM) or SAP ERP HCM installation. The reason for these two options is to provide for differing client requirements. We will look at both of these options and reasons customers may choose one over the other.

The EIC can be installed as part of SAP ERP CRM or HCM

The EIC via SAP ERP HCM

Companies that have run their HR service in-house using a centralized HR shared service center and are using the SAP ERP HCM component usually use the EIC as part of their SAP ERP HCM solution. Running SAP ERP HCM and the EIC together enables seamless linking between the EIC and employee data. Employee data changes are therefore immediately reflected in the core SAP ERP HCM system.

The EIC via SAP CRM

Generally, companies that use an outsourced HR provider to provide their HR support use the EIC via SAP CRM. These companies usually do not use SAP ERP HCM, or if they do, the solution is maintained by a third-party company and hosted by the third-party provider. If this is the case, changes to employee data may need to be interfaced back into the third-party HR system from the EIC, employee data changes will not be reflected immediately.

Both solutions allow you to realize all of the benefits of the EIC solution, and both provide the same view of the solution from an employee's perspective.

The Employee's View

Deliver HR services to all of your potential HR customers

In addition to the most obvious customers, your employees other potential users of the EIC include former employees, potential employees (applicants), pensioners, contract workers, temps, and even employees' family members. The EIC provides employees with multiple access channels but always a single point of contact. The access channels enable phone, email, fax, letter communication, and chat applications.

Link directly from ESS to the EIC for super quick service

Employees can also interact with the EIC from their own ESS portals, launching the EIC interaction center directly from their ESS menus. This ensures that employees can always find the correct way to contact the EIC. When employees contact the EIC with a query using any of the contact channels, they are assigned a ticket number (discussed in more detail in the next section). This ticket is then the employees' reference for any future contacts. If employees lose or forget their tickets, the powerful search facilities in EIC allow agents to quickly find the employees' problems and continue working on them.

The Manager's View

You can also provide the EIC to your managers, enabling them to get HR information and fix HR-related problems quickly efficiently

In addition to being a point of contact for employees, the EIC can be used to deliver excellent HR services to your management team. Managers can use the EIC to get answers to day-to-day queries such as finding out employee details, getting salary survey information to make compensation decisions, or checking employee leave balances. More complex HR-related problems such as employee performance management or payroll- and benefits-related queries can also be directed first through the EIC, with the agents then forwarding the queries or problems to the appropriate HR, payroll, or benefits team member. Using EIC to manage all of your HR queries saves your HR professionals from wasting time on low-level queries and frees them up to deliver real service to managers and employees.

Next, let's look at the agent's end of the system and what they can do from within the EIC.

The Agent's View

The EIC helps deliver standardized support for both employees and management. By making the employee-related tasks as effective and streamlined as possible, the HR team is freed up to concentrate on more strategic objectives. The EIC's single point of contact also enhances collaboration between employees and agents to ensure proper levels of response to problems.

Serve your employees effectively so you can spend more time on strategic goals

Because employee data and company processes are controlled and managed centrally, EIC agents can be based anywhere in the world. The central control and standard processes ensure that no matter where the EIC is located, employees get consistent service and information.

Communication

One of the aims of the EIC is to enable employees and other users to quickly access its services through a single point of contact, via a range of communication channels. The EIC enables employees to communicate by phone, email, chat, letter, or fax.

Employees can contact you via phone, email, or chat via a central point of contract

Ticket-Based Service

To effectively manage employee interactions, the EIC uses service tickets to track and effectively manage the process.

When an employee contacts the EIC with a new request, the EIC automatically creates a service ticket to store the information relating to the request. The ticket information includes the details of the request including employee name, reason for inquiry, and channel of inquiry (for example, phone or email). The time and date that the ticket was

Log and track every employee request with a ticket to help tracking and resolution

created and the agent assigned to the ticket are also automatically recorded.

All further contacts between the agent and the employee are then logged and tracked on this ticket. These tickets help organize the employee interaction history, allowing HR team members to quickly track causes, resolutions, and the communication history of a problem.

Manage complex multipart problems with a linked structure to ensure that problems don't get lost or dropped

Many employee tickets require multipart solutions. Resolving these complex problems may involve contacting external agencies or different teams within the company. An example of this could be an employee contacting the EIC to report a payroll error. The agent may then have to contact an external payroll provider to find the cause of the problem and then the employee's manager to resolve a problem with the employee's time recording.

To provide for multistep resolutions, a *master service ticket* can have subsequent tickets assigned to it. This master ticket is the only ticket the employee needs to concern themselves with; subsequent tickets are only relevant to the EIC agents.

A centralized and shared ticket in box allows agents and managers to manage and prioritize incoming tasks to meet service delivery levels according to service-level agreements (SLAs).

Knowledge Management

Solve queries faster by searching for existing solutions and advice

Using technology from SAP CRM, agents can search resolution databases using the Text Retrieval and Information Extraction (TREX) search engine to execute searches from their desktops. Agents can quickly search for resolutions from corporate policies and procedures, frequently asked questions databases, and third-party knowledge bases (such as benefits suppliers' FAQs). This ability to search for solutions quickly also speeds up problem resolution for employees.

Employee Surveys

Survey your employees to find out what they really think of your service

Have you ever wanted to know what your employees where thinking but didn't have the tools to find out? The EIC provides you with access to the *Appraisal Evaluation and Survey tool* (AES), which allows you to measure employee's satisfaction when they have had tickets closed in the EIC. An email can be automatically sent to the employee with details of the ticket and a link to an online survey to complete. The survey can be tailored to ask the questions you need to understand the employees' satisfaction with the EIC experience. Survey results can be analyzed using the Business Intelligence tool.

Alerts

Managers can quickly communicate with their agents using alerts and broadcast messages. These immediate notifications are automatically displayed on the agents' desktops, allowing immediate communications and updates. *Alerts* are used to communicate open tickets, updates on employee status, urgent priorities, or other business goals from within the EIC. *Broadcast messages* are used to update agents on changes to policies and other HR information.

HR managers can communicate with their agents using instant broadcast messages

Transaction Launcher

The *transaction launcher* is used to launch SAP ERP HCM transactions or third-party applications to enable agents to perform employee data maintenance tasks.

In addition to making it possible for agents to access the core ERP SAP HCM system to directly update employee records, the EIC also allows agents to execute "on-behalf-of" transactions in ESS, directly assisting employees in changing and correcting data entry errors in their own ESS portal.

Solve queries in SAP ERP HCM, ESS or even external systems with ease

The transaction launcher can also be linked to external applications to enable agents to perform key tasks that are controlled outside the company's systems. This can include maintaining employee benefits data in benefits supplier systems or directly interacting with an outsourced payroll provider.

Workflow

Using workflow technology and your company's organizational structure, the EIC enables employee queries, escalations, and approvals to be directed to the appropriate person. Queries can be directed to nominated agents, and agents can find and communicate with superi-

Workflow allows messages to be automatically sent to the best person to solve the problem

ors, specialists, or the employees' managers using the organizational structure and workflow to find and process messages.

Service Level Agreements

Define and monitor SLAs to ensure high-quality service

To ensure consistent and high-quality service to your customers, the EIC enables you to define SLAs and report on them using the strong reporting functionality.

Reporting

Reporting can be performed on either the master ticket alone or the master ticket and all of the subsequent tickets to gain a better understanding of average processing time per step and identify areas for improvement.

The EIC is furnished with powerful reporting tools to allow managers to pull key information out of the system to analyze both the quality and cost of the service.

Powerful reporting allows you to report by problem, by region, or by response time

Using the EIC reporting (from NetWeaver BI), managers can easily identify trends in requests and employee data, breaking employee data into logical reporting groups such as locations or employee types. This access to real-time data allows the company to proactively address recurring problems and employee concerns. The EIC team can then proactively address these problems by communicating with the employees through ESS or direct employee contact.

The cycle of service improvement is continuous, with reports being run regularly to assess both employee data and ticket throughput and success rates to ensure that the EIC team is always reacting in an optimum way to problems and concerns.

Integration

As we have seen, the EIC relies on a wide range of technologies to deliver well-rounded and complete solution. As a result, the following integration problems need to be included as part of the EIC solution.

Search Functionality

The Search and Knowledge Management functionality relies on the TREX search engine, which is also used by e-Recruiting to enable fast searches and high-quality results. This engine is an extra SAP product that needs to be installed separately to the EIC product.

Third-Party Computer Telephony Integration

To enable all of the contact methods, companies have to integrate the EIC with integrated computer and technology software to manage all of the channels of communication.

Let's review a case study of the EIC in use at an information technology company.

Case Study

Table 17.1 provides a quick overview of the case study before we explain it in more detail.

Company	European Information Technology Company
Existing Solutions	Various SAP ERP products
Challenges	› HR departments spread across multiple locations › Error-prone and inconsistent service levels
SAP Solutions	SAP CRM, SAP ERP HCM, and EIC
Benefits	› Benefits from multichannel, single point of contact interface › Rapid resolution of employee problems › 70% of issues resolved on first contact › "Extraordinary HCM success story"

Table 17.1 SAP EIC Case Study

This worldwide information technology company has over 400,000 employees worldwide and operates in a range of industries from information technology to healthcare and manufacturing.

The Challenges

As part of wider plan to centralize its support services, the company wanted to create a central service to deal with HR-related inquires coming from employees and managers.

The SAP Solution

In addition to centralizing HR support, the project delivered an EIC solution that allowed over 30,000 employees to access EIC via phone or email. The EIC configuration and initial rollout was completed in just 12 weeks.

The Benefits

The company is easily able to process inquiries from around 30,000 employees over several communication channels. Employee inquiries are rapidly completed owing to a totally integrated source of employee data. Higher-quality service to all employees has resulted from standardized processes and the resulting shorter processing times.

Summary

The EIC is the final step in building a perfect HR system. After implementation of the full SAP ERP HCM system covering every aspect of employee management, maintenance, and reporting, the EIC solution sits above all of these components to ensure that all communication with employees is dealt within an efficient, consistent, and customer-focused manner.

The EIC can also be implemented without an SAP ERP HCM system through the CRM component. Interfacing HR master data via a third-party HR system, the EIC gives you or your outsourcing partner an excellent framework to ensure great customer service to your employees.

In looking at the EIC solution we discussed the following points:

> The two options for installing the EIC, depending on your companies' situation.

> The employees' view of the EIC enables them to use multiple channels to access a single consistent point of contact for all of their HR queries.

> Managers can also use the EIC to get rapid response to their HR requirements.

> The many tools that make the EIC a great tool for HR administrators to deliver consistently high levels of service to HR customers, including employees, family members, candidates, and even former employees.

> The EIC solution stores all of the key information required for fast and detailed reporting on all aspects of employee interactions. This information can then be analyzed and reported using NetWeaver BI to ensure that you always deliver world-class human service to all your customers.

This concludes our overview of the SAP ERP HCM solution. We covered a lot of information throughout this book, but, hopefully, you now have a good sense of the power and possibilities offered with this complete HR solution. When you are ready to implement or upgrade to SAP ERP 6.0 HCM, be sure to establish a team, plan well, and use all the resources available, including a number of other SAP PRESS titles on all of the key areas of HR.

A   Glossary

ABAP   Advanced Business Programming Language. The SAP programming language used in SAP ERP.

ABAP Query   A standard report-writing tool that enables users to create and maintain their own reports and queries with no programming required.

Action   See Personnel Action

Adobe Interactive Forms   Using Adobe PDF files as their base, interactive forms allow companies to develop interactive electronic forms that include calculations, workflow, and tools to streamline and automate the process of creating and using online forms.

Application link enabling (ALE) Enables data to be transferred and synchronized across multiple SAP and non-SAP systems. For example, finance master data such as cost centers can be application-link-enabled into a separate HR system to save duplicate entry.

Appraisals   A way of measuring employee performance used with employee performance management. Potential appraisal methods include individual, multisource, part, and anonymous appraisals.

Authorization   The authority to execute a particular action, transaction, or task in the SAP system.

Background processing   Scheduling a process to happen without coming onto the screen, thus speeding up processing. For example, the payroll calculation can be performed in the background while other functions are being carried out in parallel on the screen.

Benefits   The SAP ERP HCM solution for managing all aspects of employee benefits, from health care to stock options, and all of the necessary back office processing.

Benefits area   A national or regional grouping used to define and control a set of employee benefits that are available in a company.

Benefits plan   The individual benefits such as health coverage or stock purchase plans that are combined into a benefits program in a benefits plan.

Budget   An approved cost structure for an action or project in a particular period of time.

Budget category   Classification of the budget of a capital investment program such as capital expenditure or expenses.

Business area   An organizational unit of financial accounting that represents a separate area of operations or responsibilities in an organization.

Business forecast Part of Retail Scheduling, it uses information from sales figures, traffic counters, and financial plans and BI information to accurately predict your business demand in retail environments.

Business process A process in a company that uses resources and can involve the activities of different departments.

Career Management The SAP ERP HCM solution that enables companies to develop standard career paths that represent commonly used careers in their company and then map and manage these against employees' requirements and aspirations.

Catalog Catalogs are used in SAP ERP HCM to manage, organize, and store large groups of related information. Examples include the qualifications catalog, the development catalog, and the learning catalog.

Career and Succession Management An overall solution allowing HR departments, managers, and employees to be involved in managing of an employee's career and a company's succession requirements.

Central person An anchoring central record that controls the shared data between multiple employee records in concurrent employment situations, ensuring that employee data remains in sync.

Chart of accounts A classification scheme consisting of a group of general ledger accounts.

Client A self-contained SAP ERP system with separate master data records and its own set of tables and configuration. Examples include the development, testing, and production clients.

Cluster Clusters are used in Time Management and Payroll to efficiently store processing results for easy access for reporting and further processing. The results are stored in tables known as clusters.

Collaboration Rooms Part of the Learning Solution. These virtual rooms are used by course attendees and instructors after or during course delivery to gain the benefits of post-learning collaboration with other attendees, instructors, and tutors.

Company code The smallest organizational unit of Financial Accounting for which a complete self-contained set of accounts can be drawn up for purposes of external reporting.

Compensation Management Enabling companies to effectively manage all aspects of an employee compensation plan, from budget creation and allocation to performance pay, long-term incentives, and performance management.

Compensation package All of the elements that combined represent an employee's total compensation. This could include salary and wages, bonuses, commission profit sharing, stocks and shares, and so on. Compensation packages are defined and allocated to different types of employees in Enterprise Compensation Management.

Concurrent employment   The SAP ERP HCM solution enabling companies to manage all aspects of employee data and payroll processing for employees with multiple simultaneous employment contracts with one company.

Content Player   A tool developed to provide for the effective delivery of training and learning content to employees and training administrators over the Internet.

Controlling   The SAP component that enables companies to plan, report, and monitor the financial aspects of their operations.

Controlling area   An organizational unit in a company, used to represent a closed system for cost accounting purposes.

Cost center   An organizational unit in a controlling area that represents a defined location of cost incurrence.

Cross Application Time Sheets (CATS)   A sophisticated and integrated time sheet solution enabling fast time data entry, cost and work allocation, and integrated approval and release procedures enabled via SAP ERP or through the portal.

Customer Relationship Management (CRM)   SAP solution focused on managing the numerous relationships between a company and its customers, including marketing planning, sales and transaction management, and customer service.

Data Medium Exchange (DME) file   The standard program used to generate bank transfer files to facilitate the payment of employee net pays into employees' bank accounts.

Delimit   The term used in SAP ERP HCM to describe replacing the existing end date of an infotype record with a new date.

Development plan   Part of Employee Performance Management. It enables companies to work with their employees to create individual development plans based on a mix of predetermined plans and employee requirements.

E-Recruiting   The SAP ERP HCM solution for creating and maintaining a web recruitment portal and managing all of the related recruitment processes.

Employee digital personnel file   An electronic record of all of the forms completed by and on behalf of an employee and any other forms stored by the company for an employee, including resumes, contracts, sick forms, and benefits information, stored electronically for rapid access and archiving.

Employee group   Used to define different types of employees in a company for making payroll, time evaluation, and benefits decisions.

Employee Self-Service (ESS) A web-delivered solution allowing employees to access their own personnel files online and view and edit their own data, create training requests, view their payslips, and perform a wide range of functions online.

Employee subgroup A subset of an employee group, used to define the lowest level of different types of employees in a company.

Employee Interaction Center (EIC) A tool that enables companies to effectively manage all types of interactions between employees, managers, and the HR department, giving consistent cost-effective service to users irrespective of where the HR department is situated.

Employee Performance Management The SAP ERP HCM solution for effectively managing the performance of your employees, from development plans and objective setting through to performance appraisals and linking into compensation management.

Enhancement Packages Method for delivery of important system changes, corrections, and new system functionality so it can be tested and applied to your own SAP system. Previously called support packs.

Enterprise Compensation Management The SAP ERP HCM solution for all aspects of your company's employee compensation program.

Enterprise Resource Planning (ERP) An application that is used to integrate all the data and processes of a business or organization, with the goal of maximizing the efficiency of operations.

Enterprise structure Used to show how your company is set up in the SAP system. It integrates legal, physical, reporting, and geographic requirements into a defined structure. Includes clients, company codes, personnel areas, subareas, and organizational keys.

Functions Used in payroll processing to access, interpret, and process calculations on employee data. For example, a tax function is used to calculate taxes for an employee.

Global Employee Management A total solution for managing the processes and data for employees with international assignments.

Groupware Integration The SAP solution for integrating email and calendar entries from the SAP system with third-party tools such as Microsoft Exchange and Lotus Domino Servers.

GUI (or SAPGUI) The tool used to provide users with the screens that enable them to view the SAP ERP system.

iView A self-contained application, service, or piece of information used in ESS and MSS to perform specific tasks in the portal. The tool for allowing employees to update their own bank details is an example of an iView.

iTime Clock   A web-delivered integrated tool that allows employees and managers to efficiently manage working time in the Retail Scheduling component.

Implementation Guide (IMG)   The hierarchical structure used to organize all of the tasks associated with configuring the SAP ERP system.

Incentive wages   The facility to pay employees based on production and sales figures instead of, or in addition to, hours worked.

Infotype   A container used to store and group logically related pieces of employee or organizational data, for example, Infotype IT0008 basic pay or Infotype IT2001 Absences.

Intermediate document (Idoc)   The container used to transfer packets of data (such as employee records or cost centers) between separate SAP and non-SAP systems.

Internal order   An instrument used to monitor costs and, in some instances, the revenues of an organization.

Job   A general classification of skills that defines the role carried out by an employee in a position. For example, the position of Internal Auditor could be defined by the job Auditor, which is defined by the set of skills, experience, and qualifications required to perform the job.

Job Pricing   Part of Enterprise Compensation Management, this tool enables companies to benchmark their employees' salaries and wages against salary survey data from third-party suppliers and determine where they currently are compared to their competitors either by sector or location.

Journal   A list of all Financial Accounting postings in a period.

Learning Portal   Part of the Learning Solution, this is an employee-specific web-delivered portal that enables employees to manage all aspects of their own learning, from course bookings and training reminders to online course participation and collaboration.

Learning Solution   The SAP ERP HCM solution that delivers and manages all aspects of a company's learning and training requirements, including course creation, content management, course scheduling, allocation, and web delivery of training.

Leave Request   Used in ESS, this iView manages the process of employees requesting different types of leave and keeps track of their leave quotas. It includes an approval process.

Legacy System Migration Workbench   The standard SAP solution for loading data from legacy systems. It can also be used post-go-live to record and automate data loading processes.

Legal Reporting   The part of SAP ERP HCM dedicated to meeting all aspects of a company's legal reporting obligations, ensuring that data is available in the format required for statutory reporting including payroll results, tax and social security data, and EEO reporting.

Long-term incentives   Employee benefits that are tied into a long duration of either earning or paying out to encourage long-term loyalty. Delivered as part of the Enterprise Compensation Management solution.

Manager Self-Service   Delivered over the Internet via the Enterprise Portal, this tool gives managers the ability to manage many of their own tasks and processes using an intuitive tool that is fully integrated with numerous SAP components.

Matrix organizations   Used to map nonlinear and cross-department reporting relationships such as project teams and cross-functional departments.

Nakisa   An SAP partner product that enables companies to use their SAP organizational structure and employee data to create visual models of their companies.

Objects   All of the items that when combined make up your organizational structure are known as objects. These could include organizational units, positions, jobs, and so on. They are held together via relationships.

Off-cycle payroll run   A payroll run that is carried out in addition to the regular payroll run for a specific day and for individual employees.

Operations   A small piece of code used in payroll processing to perform complex calculations, such as determining a salaried employee's hourly rate.

Organizational Assignment   The link between an employee (stored in Personnel Administration) and his place in the company's organizational structure (stored in Organizational Management).

Organizational key   A customer-definable key allowing companies to create unique keys to group employees by combining other standard system keys to meet local reporting requirements.

Organizational Management   The SAP solution for managing a company's various organizational hierarchies and structures.

Organizational plan   The functional view of your organization showing organizational units, positions, holders, tasks, jobs, and work centers.

Organizational structure   Mapping the various hierarchies of a company, this could include the traditional organizational structure represent the reporting hierarchy of the company and other nontraditional and nonlinear reporting and management structures such as project teams and cross-functional departments that are mapped using a matrix structure.

Organizational unit   Used throughout SAP ERP HCM, an organizational unit defines a group of employees that work together and carry out similar functions. For example, the finance department might be one organizational unit.

Payment method   A method that specifies how payment is to be made: check, bill of exchange, or bank transfer.

Pay scales   Used to define and group employees into their salary and wage bands and groups. They can be used to default amounts that can then be set to be edited or unchangeable as required.

Payroll area   A group of employees with the same pay period duration, pay day, and legal reporting requirements processed together in the same payroll run.

Payroll control record   The central control point for administrating a payroll area, setting its processing status, and controlling the payroll period.

Personnel action   A set of linked infotypes processed sequentially to complete all of the changes and creations required to process major changes in employee data, for example, the hiring action, promotion action, and termination action.

Personnel Administration   The core part of SAP ERP HCM. A broad solution for storing and managing all types of employee data including both personal data and organizational data relating to an employee's work.

Personnel area   An organizational unit representing an area in an enterprise delimited according to personnel administration, time management, and payroll accounting criteria.

Personnel Cost Planning   Enables companies to calculate the entire cost of employing their employees, including salary, taxes and social insurance, employee benefits including medical coverage, and so on to derive a total cost of each employee.

Personnel structure   Defines all of the different types of employees in your company, determining how and when they are employed and how their time management and payroll results are calculated. This includes employee group and subgroup, payroll area, and organizational key.

Personnel subarea   An organizational entity that represents part of a personnel area, used for determining appropriate personnel administration, time management, and payroll decisions.

Plan version   A tool that enables different data to be run in parallel for the same object. For example, a new plan version of the organizational structure could be created to enable changes to be modeled.

Plant Maintenance   Enables companies to effectively monitor, schedule, and manage the maintenance of all types of plants and equipment to minimize downtime and maintenance costs.

Position   Defined by a job and held by an employee, a position represents a specific role in a company, for example, Finance Director or Vice President of Sales. Positions represent specific concrete roles held by employees, and jobs define the skills required to perform the roles.

Processes and Forms   A solution for automating and web-delivering your company's most common HR-related processes. This includes the use of workflow for task automation and interactive forms for designing customer-specific interactive forms.

Processing class   Wage type characteristic that determines how processing is conducted during the payroll run.

Procurement   See SAP Supplier Relationship Management.

Profit center   An organizational unit in accounting that reflects a management-oriented structure of the organization for the purpose of internal control.

Project version   The status of a project at a particular time or during a particular action.

Project Resource Planning   Enables project and resource managers to effectively manage their company's resources across all of their project requirements.

Quota   Used in Time Management related for tracking employee absences and attendance to compare to allowed quotas.

Recruitment   An offline version of E-Recruitment for companies that need a recruitment solution but don't need an online portal.

Relationship   Used in Organizational Management to link objects together. For example, a position and an organizational unit would be linked by a "belongs to" relationship, and a job would be linked to a position by a "describes" relationship.

Remuneration statement   The SAP ERP HCM term for an employee payslip, created after payroll processing and either printed or made available online through ESS.

Reporting structure   Defines the lines of responsibility in your company: who reports to whom, and who manages what.

Resource and Program Management   A high-level tool that gives companies an overview of all of their projects and the projects' progress and status. This information can be used to allocate resources (such as employees) to projects that most need them.

Requisition   The MSS process that allows managers to request, recruit, and manage the entire process of finding new employees.

Results table   One of the payroll clusters. It's used to store payroll results at the end of the payroll calculation process. Results are stored as wage types.

Retail Scheduling An integrated tool allowing companies to forecast demand (using CRM Data) and schedule retail employees according to skills and competencies, location, and availability using information from the SAP ERP HCM component.

Rules Used in payroll to complete mathematical calculations of employee payments and deductions. For example, the process of generating part-period payments for employee is controlled in a rule.

SAP All-in-One An integrated software system built on business SAP Best Practices for the small to midsize company.

SAP Business One SAP's offering for the smaller end of the mid-market.

SAP Business Suite A comprehensive business solution from SAP that includes SAP ERP, SAP Customer Resource Management, SAP Product Lifecycle Management, SAP Supply Chain Management, and SAP Supplier Relationship Management.

SAP Collaboration Folders (cFolders) Delivered via the Enterprise Portal, this set of tools enables team members working on new product development or projects to work together in a collaborative online space.

SAP Collaboration Projects (cProjects) A total project management suite delivered via the SAP NetWeaver Enterprise Portal. It enables project managers, administrators, and team members to be involved in all aspects of the project planning and execution, from budgets to time management and reporting.

SAP Composite Applications (xApps) A set of powerful software tools that integrate the processing power from a range of existing applications to enable users to receive more accurate information faster, using the best parts of many other applications.

SAP Enterprise Buyer (SAP EB) An e-procurement solution enabling companies to manage their buying and sourcing processes using SAP Supplier Relationship Management.

SAP Financials The SAP solution that helps companies improve their processing and interpretation of financial and business data, their handling of financial transactions, and communication with their shareholders.

SAP Human Capital Management A cross-industry solution that delivers key strategic, analytic, and enabling facilities for human resource management, administration, payroll, organizational management, learning, training, time management, resource and project planning, and legal reporting.

SAP Materials Management Ensures that companies have the right materials available at the right time, in the right quantities and at the right cost to maximize efficiencies in materials management.

SAP NetWeaver   SAP's technology platform for most of its solutions that allows for the integration of various application components and composing services using a model-based approach.

SAP NetWeaver Business Intelligence (SAP NetWeaver BI)   A component of the SAP NetWeaver platform that offers data warehousing functionality via repositories of data and tools for information integration.

SAP NetWeaver Exchange Infrastructure (SAP NetWeaver XI)   A feature in SAP NetWeaver that allows you to integrate processes, thereby allowing applications to communicate with each other.

SAP NetWeaver Portal   The web-based interface used throughout SAP systems to provide a portal infrastructure and enable companies to manage processes and actions online with full integration with their backend systems.

SAP Query   A report-writing tool that enables users with no knowledge of programming to quickly create complex reports of employee and organizational data.

SAP R/3   The SAP client/server–architecture-based software introduced in 1992, which was a predecessor of SAP ERP.

SAP Strategic Enterprise Management   The SAP solution for companies to develop high-level strategies, scorecards, and objectives to measure their performance. It integrates with Employee Performance Management to help managers and employees integrate these company-wide objectives into their own objectives.

SAP Supplier Relationship Management (SRM)   An application that enables companies to enhance their e-procurement processes, evaluate procurement strategies, and allow vendors to connect and integrate with the procurement process.

Schema   The framework on which payroll calculations are based. It controls all aspects of payroll calculation, from gathering master data to creating data for bank transfer, payslip generation, and financial posting.

Shift planning   Part of time management designed to enable companies to allocate employees based on skills, qualifications, and locations to meet work force planning requirements.

Structural authorizations   Automatically assigning users' access and editing rights for data based on where they are positioned in the organizational structure.

Subtype   A subdivision on an infotype. For example, the address infotype has subtypes that allow home address, mailing address, and permanent residence details to be stored.

Succession Management   A tool used by companies to define and manage the succession requirements for their key positions to ensure that an appropriate resource is available to fill key positions when a vacancy is created.

Symbolic account   A customizing object used for posting payroll results and data from personnel cost planning and simulation to accounting.

Substitution   The process of changing an employee's work hours or location to cover for short-term increases in demand or staffing changes.

Support packs   See Enhancement Packages.

Talent Pool   See Talent Warehouse.

Talent Warehouse   A solution for managing your company's relationships with all of its potential recruitment candidates, including external candidates, interested externals, and internal resources. The talent warehouse allows your company to manage, communicate, market to, and search a group of potential candidates, known as the talent pool.

Task   Used in Organizational Management to define the individual work duties done by job, position, person, or organizational unit.

Text Retrieval and Information Exchange (TREX)   The SAP tool used in numerous applications (including E-Recruitment to search candidate databases) to enable rapid and accurate searching of large amounts of data.

Time Evaluation   The automated process of interpreting employee time recording, including clock in and out times, absence and attendance records, company and legal working time rules and calculating employees' entitlements to normal, overtime, shift pay, and other types of time-related payments used for valuation in payroll processing

Time management   A set of tools and processes that enable companies to effectively manage all aspects of employee time recording, evaluation, and reporting.

Time Manager's Workplace (TMWP)   An integrated solution enabling time administrators to complete all of their time recording and management tasks in one central, customizable solution.

Time statement   Produced as part of Time Evaluation, the time statement provides a summary of all of an employee's time inputs and time evaluation results for a period of time.

Total compensation statement   A PDF-based form used in ESS to provide employees with a form they can print or download summarizing all of their benefits and compensation elements.

Universal Worklist   Used in ESS, MSS, and EIC, this simple tool allows users to quickly view the status of and take action on any outstanding tasks for which they are responsible.

431

Virtual learning rooms All of the benefits of a classroom environment without the travel, logistics, and costs associated with them, virtual learning rooms provide a method of delivering interactive instructor-led learning and training courses over the Internet.

Wage type Object in Payroll and Personnel Administration in which the user or the system stores amounts, numbers, rates, and time units that are used, for example, for entering master data, calculating pay, and as a source for reporting.

WBS element A structural element in a work breakdown structure representing the hierarchical organization of a project.

Work areas Used in retail scheduling to define physical locations where an employee is available to work.

Work center A physical location where employees do their work; used in organizational management to define the company.

Work schedule Used to define an employee's planned working time, including start and end times, paid and unpaid work breaks, and working days for a set period of time including public and company holidays; used heavily in time and payroll processing.

Workforce Management Core A tool for finding employees with the right skills, qualifications, experience, and availability and matching them to project resource requirements.

Workflow A messaging and approval tool that uses your organizational structure to automatically manage the individual tasks and find the appropriate person(s) to approve, reject, or do tasks and processes.

Index

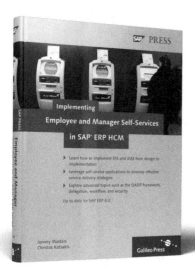

Provides an overview of ESS and MSS

Covers the fundamentals of implementing SAP ESS/MSS

Provides an overview of Duet™ focusing on key areas, and provides a roadmap of future releases/functionality.

Uses ECC 6.0 and SAP NetWeaver Portal 7.0

Jeremy Masters, Christos Kotsakis

Implementing Employee and Manager Self-Services in SAP ERP HCM

Written for HR managers, power users, IT professionals, and consultants, this is the first comprehensive guide to what Employee and Manager self services (ESS & MSS) are all about. Not only does it explain ESS & MSS, but it also teaches how to implement an effective strategy in SAP ERP HCM. The book details the baseline ESS/MSS functionality in SAP's latest release (ECC 6.0) using NetWeaver Portal (EP 7.0. It also covers more advanced topics like developing self-service applications with the Floor Plan Manager, authorization management (i.e., security), workflow, and delegation. In addition, Duet™ is used as the example of an intuitive (and familiar) user interface. The book concludes with real-world case studies as examples of effective ESS/MSS applications currently in use.

approx. 431 pp., 69,95 Euro / US$ 69.95
ISBN 978-1-59229-188-5, Nov 2008

>> www.sap-press.de/1682

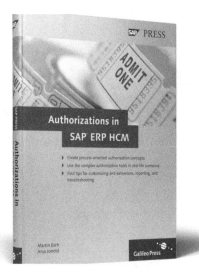

Learn how to create and implement a process-oriented authorization strategy for your company

Discover how to use the complex authorization tools of SAP ERP HCM in real-life scenarios

Explore practical customizing and extensions, reports, and error analyses examples

Martin Esch, Anja Junold

Authorizations in SAP ERP HCM

Design, Implementation, Operation

This book describes how you can create and implement an appropriate authori–zation strategy for your company in SAP ERP HCM. It answers all of your potential questions, from the differences and areas of usage for general, structural, and context-sensitive authorization checks to the specific challenges involved in using performance management functions. In addition, you'll learn about the typical problem areas and discover how to resolve them. The book contains many useful tips that support you in implementing the authorization system for the first time or in your daily work.

336 pp., 2008, 69,95 Euro / US$ 69.95
ISBN 978-1-59229-165-6

>> www.sap-press.de/1602

Provides a complete guide to
Organizational Management (OM)
with SAP ERP HCM

Teaches all functions of OM from a
global perspective

Includes practical integration and
customizing tips and techniques

Sylvia Chaudoir

Mastering SAP ERP HCM
Organizational Management

This book teaches the HCM team how to maximize the organizational management (OM)
component of SAP ERP HCM. It takes readers beyond the basics, by delving into all aspects
of the component as well as the little-known concepts. It teaches all of the key OM
functions, their purpose, and how to use and customize them. Numerous examples from
customers are used to provide context for decisions and to explain the benefits of the choices
that can be made. And in-depth explanations and practical examples are used to help readers
leverage the many available organizational objects to get the most out of their SAP HR
implementation.

348 pp., 2008, 69,95 Euro / US$ 69.95
ISBN 978-1-59229-208-0

>> www.sap-press.de/1796

Learn how to set up the Time Management to meet your business needs

Explore configuration and customization options

Find out how to use Infotypes and BAdIs to streamline and integrate cost-intensive processes

Brian Schaer

Time Management with SAP ERP HCM

This book provides a detailed guide to understanding, implementing, and configuring the Time Management component of SAP ERP HCM. It teaches readers the core topics of Time Management and provides the foundational information they need for implementing and configuring the business requirements. It also provides insight into some of the more advanced topics, such as process flows.

approx. 500 pp., 69,95 Euro / US$ 69.95
ISBN 978-1-59229-229-5, Dec 2008

>> www.sap-press.de/1848

Provides a complete guide to configuring CATS

Covers all essential CATS enhancements and User-Exits

Includes user-exit sample code, a sample program for loading external CATS data, and a configuration assistant tool on the website

Manuel Gallardo

Configuring and Using CATS

SAP PRESS Essentials 51

This Essentials is a complete guide to effectively configuring CATS to meet your business needs. It provides detailed explanations of items to consider before beginning an implementation, along with steps for setting up CATS to fulfill the many complex configuration requirements. It also includes details about each CATS user-exit and tips on what functionality can or cannot be accomplished with particular user-exits. In addition, explanations for how to prevent and correct performance problems, answers to frequently asked questions, and tips for audit report development are provided.

approx. 160 pp., 68,– Euro / US$ 85
ISBN 978-1-59229-232-5, Oct 2008

>> www.sap-press.de/1864

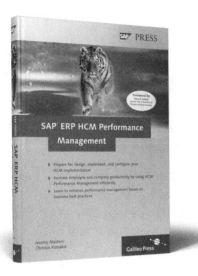

Prepare for, design, implement, and configure your HCM implementation

Increase employee and company productivity by using HCM Performance Management efficiently

Learn to enhance performance management based on business best practices

Jeremy Masters, Christos Kotsakis

SAP ERP HCM Performance Management

From Design to Implementation

This comprehensive book is an indispensable reference for HR professionals, analysts, and consultants learning how to implement SAP ERP HCM Performance Management. The book teaches you everything you need to know about the Objective Setting and Appraisal (OSA) module within SAP so that you can identify and retain key talent within your organization. You'll take a step-by-step journey through the design and implemen–tation of your own performance management application that will help you improve your companies' performance and talent management processes.   The book covers all the latest releases, including the R/3 Enterprise Release (4.7), SAP ERP 2004 (ECC 5.0) and SAP ERP 2005 (ECC 6.0).

302 pp., 2008, 69,95 Euro / US$ 69.95
ISBN 978-1-59229-124-3

>> www.sap-press.de/1421

Solves difficult US Payroll-related problems

Create custom wage types and learn about the schemas and rules specific to US Payroll

Discover advanced topics, such as overpayments, accruals, payroll interfaces, garnishments, and more

Satish Badgi

Practical SAP US Payroll

„Practical US Payroll" has everything you need to implement a success–ful payroll system. Readers will learn how to create custom wage types, process deductions for benefits and garnishments, handle accruals, report and process taxes, and process retroactive payrolls.
From the hands-on, step-by-step examples to the detailed wage type tables in the appendix, this book is your complete guide to the US Payroll system.

332 pp., 2007, 69,95 Euro / US$ 69.95
ISBN 978-1-59229-132-8

>> www.sap-press.de/1450

Covers standard SAP reports, queries, SAP NetWeaver BI, and the creation of customer reports

Provides practical examples for report creation in the different SAP ERP HCM components

Examines reports in area menu, HIS, MDT, and SAP NetWeaver Portal formats

Up-to-date for SAP ERP 6.0

Hans-Jürgen Figaj, Richard Haßmann, Anja Junold

HR Reporting with SAP

This comprehensive book describes how you can use the powerful reporting tools of the SAP system efficiently and in a goal-oriented manner. You will first get to know the details of the reporting tools, Standard SAP Report, Query, SAP NetWeaver BI, and Customer Report. The book then describes various real-life examples in order to demonstrate how you can use the tools in the different HCM modules in the best-possible way. You will get to know selected standard reports as well as the SAP NetWeaver BI Standard Content for each module. In addition, you will learn how you can make the reports available to users. The book is based on SAP ERP 6.0 and can be used with Release R/3 Enterprise or higher.

435 pp., 2008, 69,95 Euro / US$ 69.95
ISBN 978-1-59229-172-4

>> www.sap-press.de/1638

Provides a complete guide to
the functionality of E-Recruiting

Teaches how to configure and
use E-Recruiting with other
HCM components

Uses a real-world workflow
approach

Ben Hayes

E-Recruiting with SAP ERP HCM

This book provides a practical guide to configuring and using SAP E-Recruitment effectively
in the real-world. It is written to teach SAP ERP HCM users and the implementation team
what the E-Recruiting tool is so that they can use it effectively in their recruitment process
and integrate it easily with other HCM components. Beginning with an overview, the book
progresses through the configuration process from a real workflow perspective. And all of
the processes are covered in the order in which they are used in a real recruiting project.
The book also details how to integrate E-Recruiting with other SAP components, and, as
applicable, examples of companies using E-Recruiting successfully will be integrated
throughout.

approx. 320 pp., 69,90 Euro / US$ 69.95
ISBN 978-1-59229-243-1, Jan 2009

>> www.sap-press.de/1957

MCTS
Windows Server® 2008
Active Directory Configuration
Study Guide

MCTS
Windows Server® 2008
Active Directory Configuration
Study Guide

Will Panek
James Chellis

Wiley Publishing, Inc.

Acquisitions Editor: Jeff Kellum
Development Editor: Stef Jones
Technical Editor: Rodney Fournier
Production Editor: Eric Charbonneau
Copy Editor: Rebecca Rider
Production Manager: Tim Tate
Vice President and Executive Group Publisher: Richard Swadley
Vice President and Executive Publisher: Joseph B. Wikert
Vice President and Publisher: Neil Edde
Media Project Supervisor: Laura Atkinson
Media Development Specialist: Josh Frank
Media Quality Assurance: Angie Denny
Book Designer: Judy Fung
Compositor: Craig Johnson, Happenstance Type-O-Rama
Proofreaders: Steve Johnson; Jen Larsen, Word One
Indexer: Nancy Guenther
Cover Designer: Ryan Sneed

Sybex®
An Imprint of
WILEY

Dear Reader,

Thank you for choosing *MCTS: Windows Server 2008 Active Directory Configuration Study Guide (70-640)*. This book is part of a family of premium quality Sybex books, all written by outstanding authors who combine practical experience with a gift for teaching.

Sybex was founded in 1976. More than thirty years later, we're still committed to producing consistently exceptional books. With each of our titles we're working hard to set a new standard for the industry. From the paper we print on, to the authors we work with, our goal is to bring you the best books available.

I hope you see all that reflected in these pages. I d be very interested to hear your comments and get your feedback on how we re doing. Feel free to let me know what you think about this or any other Sybex book by sending me an email at nedde@wiley.com, or if you think you ve found a technical error in this book, please visit http://sybex.custhelp.com. Customer feedback is critical to our efforts at Sybex.

Best regards,

Neil Edde
Vice President and Publisher
Sybex, an Imprint of Wiley

This book is dedicated to my wife, Crystal, and my two daughters, Alexandria and Paige. This book would not have been possible without their love and support.

—Will Panek

Acknowledgments

First and most important I would like to thank my wife, Crystal, and my two daughters, Alexandria and Paige. This book would not have been possible without their love, support, and understanding.

Thanks to my mother and all three of my brothers, Rick, Gary, and Bob. Special thanks to my father, Richard, for who without his extra help financially and his endless motivation, I would not have made it through college many, many, many years ago.

Thanks to my extended family, Bud, Diane (who we lost recently but will be with us forever), Gene, Jen, and Denise. Your love and support has helped make me the person I am today.

Thanks to my friend and business partner Tylor Wentworth for his friendship and laughter. He is always there whenever I need a smile. Thanks to all my friends down at the FD. The best group of brothers and sisters a firefighter could have.

Thanks to my Stellacon family, Jeremy, Jim, Lisa, Mike, Julie, Jesse, and Travis. All of your support over the years has made it fun to go to work everyday.

Thanks to James Chellis for giving me the opportunity to work with him on this project. It is an honor to have my name next to his on this book.

Thanks to Jeff Kellum for helping me through this process and always being there when I needed guidance. Thanks to Stef Jones for the endless hours of editing. It was a pleasure to work with her on this project. Thanks to Rodney Fournier (another geek like me) who is one of the best Tech Editors a writer could ask for, and to Eric Charbonneau for guiding me through to the finish line. Also, I would like to thank all the other editors and staff at Wiley who helped to make this book better. I feel fortunate to have been able to work with all of you.

Finally, I would like to thank one of the funniest and most knowledgeable individuals (even though he's a Cisco guy) that I have ever had the pleasure to work with and call a friend, Todd Lammle. Without Todd's help and guidance, this book would not have been possible.

—Will Panek

About the Authors

William Panek (MCP®, MCP+I®, MCSA®, MCSA® W/SECURITY & MESSAGING, MCSE – NT (3.51 & 4.0)®, MCSE – 2000 & 2003®, MCSE W/SECURITY & MESSAGING, MCDBA®, MCT®, MCTS® (Windows Server 2008 Active Directory: Configuration, Windows Server 2008 Applications Infrastructure: Configuration, Windows Server 2008 Network Infrastructure: Configuration, Microsoft Windows Vista: Configuration, SQL Server 2005), MCITP®, CCNA®, CHFI®).

After many successful years in the computer industry and a degree in computer programming, William Panek decided that he could better use his talents and his personality as an instructor. He started teaching for The Associates – instructing at such schools as Boston University, Clark University, and Globalnet, just to name a few. In 1998 William started Stellacon Corporation. Stellacon has become one of New England's leading training companies. He brings years of real world expertise to the classroom and strives to ensure that each and every student has an understanding of the course material. William has helped thousands of students get certified over his 10 years of teaching experience.

William currently resides in New Hampshire with his wife and their two daughters. In his spare time he is a commercially rated helicopter pilot and volunteer fire fighter.

James Chellis, MCSE, has co-authored more than 30 IT certification titles in print. He is currently CEO of Comcourse, Inc., an online education provider.

Contents at a Glance

Contents

Table of Exercises

Introduction

Microsoft has recently changed its certification program to contain three primary series: Technology, Professional, and Architect. The Technology Series of certifications are intended to allow candidates to target specific technologies and are the basis for obtaining the Professional Series and Architect Series of certifications. The certifications contained within the Technology Series consist of one to three exams, focus on a specific technology, and do not include job-role skills. By contrast, the Professional Series of certifications focus on a job role and are not necessarily focused on a single technology, but rather a comprehensive set of skills for performing the job role being tested. The Architect Series of certifications offered by Microsoft are premier certifications that consist of passing a review board consisting of previously certified architects. To apply for the Architect Series of certifications, you must have a minimum of 10 years of industry experience.

When obtaining a Technology Series certification, you are recognized as a Microsoft Certified Technology Specialist (MCTS) on the specific technology or technologies that you have been tested on. The Professional Series certifications include Microsoft Certified IT Professional (MCITP) and Microsoft Certified Professional Developer (MCPD). Passing the review board for an Architect Series certification will allow you to become a Microsoft Certified Architect (MCA).

This book has been developed to give you the critical skills and knowledge you need to prepare for the exam requirement for obtaining the MCTS: Windows Server 2008 Active Directory, Configuring (Exam 70-640).

The Microsoft Certified Professional Program

Since the inception of its certification program, Microsoft has certified more than 2 million people. As the computer network industry continues to increase in both size and complexity, this number is sure to grow—and the need for *proven* ability will also increase. Certifications can help companies verify the skills of prospective employees and contractors.

Microsoft has developed its Microsoft Certified Professional (MCP) program to give you credentials that verify your ability to work with Microsoft products effectively and professionally. Several levels of certification are available based on specific suites of exams. Microsoft has recently created a new generation of certification programs:

Microsoft Certified Technology Specialist (MCTS)   The MCTS can be considered the entry-level certification for the new generation of Microsoft certifications. The MCTS certification program targets specific technologies instead of specific job roles. You must take and pass one to three exams.

Microsoft Certified IT Professional (MCITP)   The MCITP certification is a Professional Series certification that tests network and systems administrators on job roles, rather than only on a specific technology. The MCITP generally consists of passing one to three exams, in addition to obtaining an MCTS-level certification.

Microsoft Certified Professional Developer (MCPD) The MCPD certification is a Professional Series certification for application developers. Similar to the MCITP, the MCPD is focused on a job role rather than on a single technology. The MCPD generally consists of passing one to three exams, in addition to obtaining an MCTS-level certification.

Microsoft Certified Architect (MCA) The MCA is Microsoft's premier certification series. Obtaining the MCA requires a minimum of 10 years of experience and requires the candidate to pass a review board consisting of peer architects.

How Do You Become Certified on Windows Server 2008 Active Directory?

Attaining a Microsoft certification has always been a challenge. In the past, students have been able to acquire detailed exam information—even most of the exam questions—from online "brain dumps" and third-party "cram" books or software products. For the new generation of exams, this is simply not the case.

Microsoft has taken strong steps to protect the security and integrity of its new certification tracks. Now prospective candidates must complete a course of study that develops detailed knowledge about a wide range of topics. It supplies them with the true skills needed, derived from working with the technology being tested.

The new generations of Microsoft certification programs are heavily weighted toward hands-on skills and experience. It is recommended that candidates have troubleshooting skills acquired through hands-on experience and working knowledge.

Fortunately, if you are willing to dedicate the time and effort to learn Windows Server 2008 Active Directory, you can prepare yourself well for the exam by using the proper tools. By working through this book, you can successfully meet the exam requirements to pass the Windows Server 2008 Active Directory exam.

This book is part of a complete series of Microsoft certification Study Guides, published by Sybex Inc., that together cover the new MCTS, MCITP, MCPD exams, as well as the core MCSA and MCSE operating system requirements. Please visit the Sybex website at www.sybex.com for complete program and product details.

MCTS Exam Requirements

Candidates for MCTS certification on Windows Server 2008 Active Directory must pass one Windows Server 2008 Active Directory exam. Other MCTS certifications may require up to three exams. For a more detailed description of the Microsoft certification programs, including a list of all the exams, visit the Microsoft Learning Web site at www.microsoft.com/learning/mcp.

The Windows Server 2008 Active Directory, Configuring Exam

The Windows Server 2008 Active Directory exam covers concepts and skills related to installing, configuring, and managing Windows Server 2008 Active Directory. It emphasizes Active Directory support and administration.

This exam is quite specific regarding Windows Server 2008 Active Directory requirements and operational settings, and it can be particular about how administrative tasks are performed within Active Directory.

Microsoft provides exam objectives to give you a general overview of possible areas of coverage on the Microsoft exams. Keep in mind, however, that exam objectives are subject to change at any time without prior notice and at Microsoft's sole discretion. Please visit the Microsoft Learning Web site (www.microsoft.com/learning/mcp) for the most current listing of exam objectives.

Types of Exam Questions

In an effort to both refine the testing process and protect the quality of its certifications, Microsoft has focused its newer certification exams on real experience and hands-on proficiency. There is a greater emphasis on your past working environments and responsibilities and less emphasis on how well you can memorize. In fact, Microsoft says that certification candidates should have hands-on experience before attempting to pass any certification exams.

Microsoft will accomplish its goal of protecting the exams' integrity by regularly adding and removing exam questions, limiting the number of questions that any individual sees in a beta exam, limiting the number of questions delivered to an individual by using adaptive testing, and adding new exam elements.

Exam questions may be in a variety of formats: Depending on which exam you take, you'll see multiple-choice questions, as well as select-and-place and prioritize-a-list questions. Simulations and case study–based formats are included as well. You may also find yourself taking what's called an *adaptive format exam*. Let's take a look at the types of exam questions and examine the adaptive testing technique, so you'll be prepared for all of the possibilities.

The Microsoft Windows Server 2008 exams provided a detailed score breakdown. This is because of the various and complex question formats. Previously, each question focused on one objective. Recent exams, such as the Windows Server 2008 Active Directory exam, however, contain questions that may be tied to one or more objectives from one or more objective sets. Therefore, grading by objective is almost impossible. Also, Microsoft no longer offers a score. Now you will only be told if you pass or fail.

Multiple-Choice Questions

Multiple-choice questions come in two main forms. One is a straightforward question followed by several possible answers, of which one or more is correct. The other type of multiple-choice question is more complex and based on a specific scenario. The scenario may focus on several areas or objectives.

Select-and-Place Questions

Select-and-place exam questions involve graphical elements that you must manipulate to successfully answer the question. For example, you might see a diagram of a computer network, as shown in the following graphic taken from the select-and-place demo downloaded from Microsoft's website.

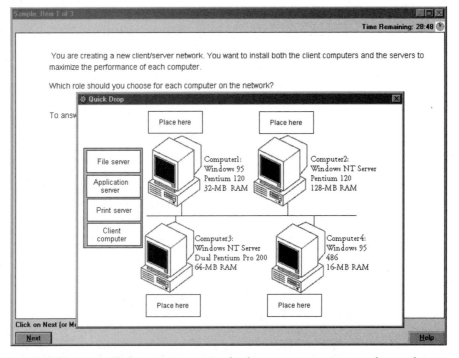

A typical diagram will show computers and other components next to boxes that contain the text "Place here." The labels for the boxes represent various computer roles on a network, such as a print server and a file server. Based on information given for each computer, you are asked to select each label and place it in the correct box. You need to place *all* of the labels correctly. No credit is given for the question if you correctly label only some of the boxes.

In another select-and-place problem you might be asked to put a series of steps in order, by dragging items from boxes on the left to boxes on the right, and placing them in the correct order. One other type requires that you drag an item from the left and place it under an item in a column on the right.

For more information on the various exam question types, go to
www.microsoft.com/learning/mcpexams/policies/innovations.asp.

Simulations

Simulations are the kinds of questions that most closely represent actual situations and test the
skills you use while working with Microsoft software interfaces. These exam questions include
a mock interface on which you are asked to perform certain actions according to a given scenario. The simulated interfaces look nearly identical to what you see in the actual product, as
shown in this example:

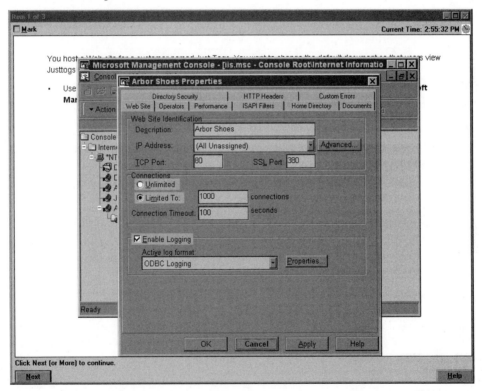

Because of the number of possible errors that can be made on simulations, be sure to consider the following recommendations from Microsoft:

- Do not change any simulation settings that don't pertain to the solution directly.

- When related information has not been provided, assume that the default settings are used.

- Make sure that your entries are spelled correctly.

- Close all the simulation application windows after completing the set of tasks in the simulation.

The best way to prepare for simulation questions is to spend time working with the graphical interface of the product on which you will be tested.

Case Study–Based Questions

Case study–based questions first appeared in the MCSD program. These questions present a scenario with a range of requirements. Based on the information provided, you answer a series of multiple-choice and select-and-place questions. The interface for case study–based questions has a number of tabs, each of which contains information about the scenario. At present, this type of question appears only in most of the Design exams.

Microsoft will regularly add and remove questions from the exams. This is called *item seeding*. It is part of the effort to make it more difficult for individuals to merely memorize exam questions that were passed along by previous test-takers.

Tips for Taking the MCTS: Windows Server 2008 Active Directory, Configuring Exam

Here are some general tips for achieving success on your certification exam:

- Arrive early at the exam center so that you can relax and review your study materials. During this final review, you can look over tables and lists of exam-related information.

- Read the questions carefully. Don't be tempted to jump to an early conclusion. Make sure you know *exactly* what the question is asking.

- Answer all questions. If you are unsure about a question, then mark the question for review and come back to the question at a later time.

- On simulations, do not change settings that are not directly related to the question. Also, assume default settings if the question does not specify or imply which settings are used.

- For questions you're not sure about, use a process of elimination to get rid of the obviously incorrect answers first. This improves your odds of selecting the correct answer when you need to make an educated guess.

Exam Registration

You may take the Microsoft exams at any of more than 1,000 Authorized Prometric Testing Centers (APTCs) around the world. For the location of a testing center near you, call Prometric at 800-755-EXAM (755-3926). Outside the United States and Canada, contact your local Prometric registration center.

Find out the number of the exam you want to take, and then register with the Prometric registration center nearest to you. At this point, you will be asked for advance payment for the exam. The exams are $125 each and you must take them within one year of payment. You can schedule exams up to six weeks in advance or as late as one working day prior to the date of the exam. You can cancel or reschedule your exam if you contact the center at least two working days prior to the exam. Same-day registration is available in some locations, subject to space availability. Where same-day registration is available, you must register a minimum of two hours before test time.

> You may also register for your exams online at www.prometric.com.

When you schedule the exam, you will be provided with instructions regarding appointment and cancellation procedures, ID requirements, and information about the testing center location. In addition, you will receive a registration and payment confirmation letter from Prometric.

Microsoft requires certification candidates to accept the terms of a Non-Disclosure Agreement before taking certification exams.

Is This Book for You?

If you want to acquire a solid foundation in Windows Server 2008 Active Directory, and your goal is to prepare for the exam by learning how to use and manage the new operating system, this book is for you. You'll find clear explanations of the fundamental concepts you need to grasp and plenty of help to achieve the high level of professional competency you need to succeed in your chosen field.

If you want to become certified as an MCTS, this book is definitely for you. However, if you just want to attempt to pass the exam without really understanding Windows Server 2008 Active Directory, this Study Guide is *not* for you. It is written for people who want to acquire hands-on skills and in-depth knowledge of Windows Server 2008 Active Directory.

What's in the Book?

What makes a Sybex Study Guide the book of choice for hundreds of thousands of MCPs? We took into account not only what you need to know to pass the exam, but what you need to know to take what you've learned and apply it in the real world. Each book contains the following:

Objective-by-objective coverage of the topics you need to know Each chapter lists the objectives covered in that chapter.

> The topics covered in this Study Guide map directly to Microsoft's official exam objectives. Each exam objective is covered completely.

Assessment Test   Directly following this introduction is an Assessment Test that you should take. It is designed to help you determine how much you already know about Windows Server 2008 Active Directory. Each question is tied to a topic discussed in the book. Using the results of the Assessment Test, you can figure out the areas where you need to focus your study. Of course, we do recommend you read the entire book.

Exam Essentials   To highlight what you learn, you'll find a list of Exam Essentials at the end of each chapter. The Exam Essentials section briefly highlights the topics that need your particular attention as you prepare for the exam.

Glossary   Throughout each chapter, you will be introduced to important terms and concepts that you will need to know for the exam. These terms appear in italic within the chapters, and at the end of the book, a detailed Glossary gives definitions for these terms, as well as other general terms you should know.

Review questions, complete with detailed explanations   Each chapter is followed by a set of Review Questions that test what you learned in the chapter. The questions are written with the exam in mind, meaning that they are designed to have the same look and feel as what you'll see on the exam. Question types are just like the exam, including multiple choice, exhibits, and select-and-place.

Hands-on exercises   In each chapter (with the exception of Chapter 1, which is more an introduction to Active Directory) you'll find exercises designed to give you the important hands-on experience that is critical for your exam preparation. The exercises support the topics of the chapter, and they walk you through the steps necessary to perform a particular function.

Real World Scenarios   Because reading a book isn't enough for you to learn how to apply these topics in your everyday duties, we have provided Real World Scenarios in special sidebars. These explain when and why a particular solution would make sense, in a working environment you'd actually encounter.

Interactive CD   Every Sybex Study Guide comes with a CD complete with additional questions, flashcards for use with an interactive device, and the book in electronic format. Details are in the following section.

What's on the CD?

With this new member of our best-selling Study Guide series, we are including quite an array of training resources. The CD offers bonus exams and flashcards to help you study for the exam. We have also included the complete contents of the Study Guide in electronic form. The CD's resources are described here:

The Sybex E-book for Windows Server 2008 Active Directory   Many people like the convenience of being able to carry their whole Study Guide on a CD. They also like being able to search the text via computer to find specific information quickly and easily. For these reasons, the entire contents of this Study Guide are supplied on the CD, in PDF. We've also included Adobe Acrobat Reader, which provides the interface for the PDF contents as well as the search capabilities.

The Sybex Test Engine   This is a collection of multiple-choice questions that will help you prepare for your exam. There are four sets of questions:

- Two bonus exams designed to simulate the actual live exam.

- All the questions from the Study Guide, presented in a test engine for your review. You can review questions by chapter, or you can take a random test.

- The Assessment Test.

Here is a sample screen from the Sybex Test Engine:

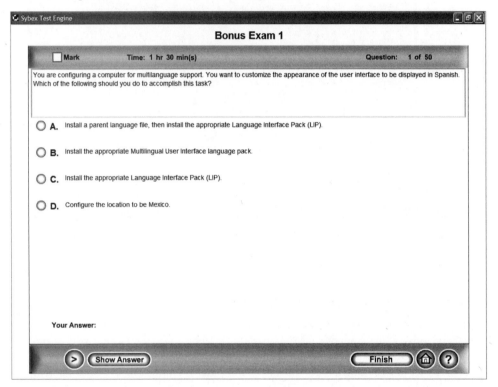

Sybex Flashcards for PCs and Handheld Devices   The "flashcard" style of question offers an effective way to quickly and efficiently test your understanding of the fundamental concepts covered in the exam. The Sybex Flashcards set consists of 100 questions presented in a special engine developed specifically for this Study Guide series. Here's what the Sybex Flashcards interface looks like:

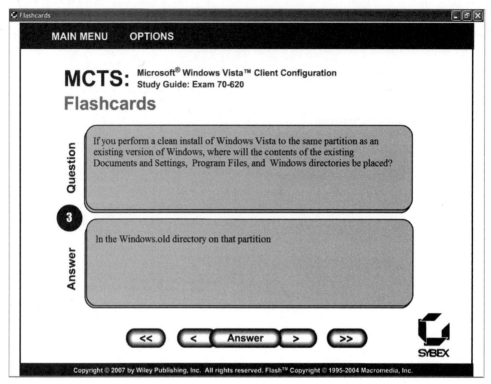

Because of the high demand for a product that will run on handheld devices, we have also developed, in conjunction with Land-J Technologies, a version of the flashcard questions that you can take with you on your Palm OS PDA (including the PalmPilot and Handspring's Visor).

Hardware and Software Requirements

You should verify that your computer meets the minimum requirements for installing Windows Server 2008 as listed in Chapter 2, "Domain Name System." We suggest that your computer meets or exceeds the recommended requirements for a more enjoyable experience.

The exercises in this book assume that your computer is configured in a specific manner. Your computer should have at least a 20GB drive that is configured with the minimum space requirements and partitions. Other exercises in this book assume that your computer is configured as follows:

- 20GB C: partition with the NTFS filesystem
- Optional D: partition with the NTFS filesystem
- 15GB or more of free space

Of course, you can allocate more space to your partitions if it is available.

The first exercise in the book assumes that you have installed Windows Server 2008 and that your partitions have already been created and formatted as previously specified.

Contacts and Resources

To find out more about Microsoft Education and Certification materials and programs, to register with Prometric, or to obtain other useful certification information and additional study resources, check the following resources:

Microsoft Learning Home Page

www.microsoft.com/learning

This website provides information about the MCP program and exams. You can also order the latest Microsoft Roadmap to Education and Certification.

Microsoft TechNet Technical Information Network

www.microsoft.com/technet

800-344-2121

Use this website or phone number to contact support professionals and system administrators. Outside the United States and Canada, contact your local Microsoft subsidiary for information.

Prometric

www.prometric.com

800-755-3936

Contact Prometric to register to take an exam at any of more than 800 Prometric Testing Centers around the world.

MCP Magazine Online

www.mcpmag.com

Microsoft Certified Professional Magazine is a well-respected publication that focuses on Windows certification. This site hosts chats and discussion forums and tracks news related to the MCTS and MCITP program. Some of the services cost a fee, but they are well worth it.

WindowsITPro Magazine

www.windowsITPro.com

You can subscribe to this magazine or read free articles at the website. The study resource provides general information on Windows Vista, Server, and .NET Server.

Assessment Test

1. Which of the following operations is not supported by Active Directory?

   A. Assigning applications to users

   B. Assigning applications to computers

   C. Publishing applications to users

   D. Publishing applications to computers

2. Which of the following single master operations apply to the entire forest? (Choose all that apply.)

   A. Schema Master

   B. Domain Naming Master

   C. RID Master

   D. Infrastructure Master

3. Which of the following is *not* a valid Active Directory object?

   A. User

   B. Group

   C. Organizational unit

   D. Computer

   E. None of the above

4. Which of the following pieces of information should you have before you begin the Active Directory Installation Wizard? (Choose all that apply.)

   A. Active Directory domain name

   B. Administrator password for the local computer

   C. NetBIOS name for the server

   D. DNS configuration information

5. Which of the following is *not* considered a security principal?

   A. Users

   B. Security groups

   C. Distribution groups

   D. Computers

6. Which of the following is a valid role for a Windows Server 2008 computer?

   A. Stand-alone server

   B. Member server

   C. Domain controller

   D. All of the above

7. Trust relationships can be configured as which of the following? (Choose all that apply.)

   A. One-way and transitive

   B. Two-way and transitive

   C. One-way and nontransitive

   D. Two-way and nontransitive

8. Which of the following should play the *least* significant role in planning an OU structure?

   A. Network infrastructure

   B. Domain organization

   C. Delegation of permissions

   D. Group Policy settings

9. Which of the following file extensions is used primarily for Windows Installer setup programs?

   A. `.msi`

   B. `.mst`

   C. `.zap`

   D. `.aas`

10. How can the Windows NT 4 file and printer resources be made available from within Active Directory?

   A. A systems administrator can right-click the resource and select Publish.

   B. A systems administrator can create Printer and Shared Folder objects that point to these resources.

   C. The Active Directory Domains And Trusts tool can be used to make resources available.

   D. Only resources on a Windows 2000 or above server can be accessed from within Active Directory.

11. An Active Directory environment consists of three domains. What is the maximum number of sites that can be created for this environment?

   A. 2

   B. 3

   C. 9

   D. Unlimited

12. Which of the following statements regarding auditing and Active Directory is false?

   A. Auditing prevents users from attempting to guess passwords.

   B. Systems administrators should regularly review audit logs for suspicious activity.

   C. Auditing information can be generated when users view specific information within Active Directory.

   D. Auditing information can be generated when users modify specific information within Active Directory.

13. A systems administrator wants to allow a group of users to add Computer accounts to a specific organizational unit (OU). What is the easiest way to grant only the required permissions?

    A. Delegate control of a User account.

    B. Delegate control at the domain level.

    C. Delegate control of an OU.

    D. Delegate control of a Computer account.

    E. Create a Group Policy object (GPO) at the OU level.

14. A Group Policy object (GPO) at the domain level sets a certain option to Disabled, while a GPO at the OU level sets the same option to Enabled. All other settings are left at their default. Which setting will be effective for objects within the OU?

    A. Enabled

    B. Disabled

    C. No effect

    D. None of the above

15. The process by which a higher-level security authority assigns permissions to other administrators is known as which of the following?

    A. Inheritance

    B. Delegation

    C. Assignment

    D. Trust

16. What is the minimum amount of information you need to create a Shared Folder Active Directory object?

    A. The name of the share

    B. The name of the server

    C. The name of the server and the name of the share

    D. The name of the server, the server's IP address, and the name of the share

17. Which of the following is a benefit of using Active Directory? (Choose all that apply.)

    A. Hierarchical object structure

    B. Fault-tolerant architecture

    C. Ability to configure centralized and distributed administration

    D. Flexible replication

18. Which of the following features of the Domain Name System (DNS) can be used to improve performance? (Choose all that apply.)

    A. Caching-only servers

    B. DNS forwarding

    C. Secondary servers

    D. Zone delegation

19. Which of the following tools can be used to create Group Policy object (GPO) links to Active Directory?

    A. Active Directory Users And Computers

    B. Active Directory Domains And Trusts

    C. Active Directory Sites And Services

    D. Group Policy Management Console

20. What is the name of the list that shows removed certificates from a certificate server?

    A. Certificate removed list

    B. Certificate revocation list

    C. Certificate revoke list

    D. Certificate released list

21. A systems administrator suspects that the amount of RAM in a domain controller is insufficient and that an upgrade is required. Which of the following Performance Monitor counters would provide the most useful information regarding the upgrade?

    A. Network Segment/% Utilization

    B. Memory/Page Faults/Sec

    C. Processor/% Utilization

    D. System/Processes

22. Which of the following are considered security principals?

    A. User accounts and groups

    B. Sites

    C. Trusts

    D. Group Policy objects (GPOs)

23. Which of the following single master roles do *not* apply to every domain within an Active Directory forest? (Choose all that apply.)

    A. PDC Emulator Master

    B. RID Master

    C. Infrastructure Master

    D. Schema Master

24. Which of the following types of server configurations *cannot* be used within a single DNS zone?

    A. A single primary server with no secondary servers

    B. Multiple primary servers

    C. A single primary server with a single secondary server

    D. A single primary server with multiple secondary servers

    E. A single primary server and multiple caching-only servers

25. A Group Policy object (GPO) at the domain level sets a certain option to Disabled, whereas a GPO at the OU level sets the same option to Enabled. No other GPOs have been created. Which option can a systems administrator use to ensure that the effective policy for objects within the OU is enabled?

    A. Block Policy Inheritance on the OU

    B. Block Policy Inheritance on the site

    C. Set No Override on the OU

    D. Set No Override on the site

26. Which of the following are *not* types of backup operation that are supported by the Windows Server 2008 Backup utility? (Choose all that apply.)

    A. Normal

    B. Incremental

    C. Weekly

    D. Differential

27. Which of the following are generally true regarding the domain controllers within a site? (Choose all that apply.)

    A. They are generally connected by a high-speed network.

    B. They may reside on different subnets.

    C. They are generally connected by reliable connections.

    D. They may be domain controllers for different domains.

28. Which of the following types of servers contains a copy of Active Directory?

    A. Member server

    B. Stand-alone server

    C. Domain controller

    D. Certificate server

29. You need to place a domain controller in a non-secure location. What type of domain controller would you use?

   A. Read-only domain controller

   B. Primary domain controller

   C. Backup domain controller

   D. No access domain controller

30. Which of the following protocols may be used for intrasite replication?

   A. RPC

   B. IP

   C. SMTP

   D. NNTP

Answers to Assessment Test

1. D.   Applications cannot be published to computers, but they can be published to users and assigned to computers. See Chapter 8 for more information.

2. A, B.   There can be only one Domain Naming Master and one Schema Master per Active Directory forest. The purpose of the Domain Naming Master is to keep track of all the domains within an Active Directory forest. The Schema Master defines the Active Directory schema, which must be consistent across all domains in the forest. The remaining roles apply at the domain level. See Chapter 4 for more information.

3. E.   All of the choices are valid types of Active Directory objects, and all can be created and managed using the Active Directory Users And Computers tool. See Chapter 7 for more information.

4. A, B, C, D.   Before beginning the installation of a domain controller, you should have all of the information listed. See Chapter 3 for more information.

5. C.   Permissions and security settings cannot be made on Distribution groups. Distribution groups are used only for sending email. See Chapter 7 for more information.

6. D.   Based on the business needs of an organization, a Windows 2008 Server computer can be configured in any of the above roles. See Chapter 1 for more information.

7. A, B, C, D.   All of the trust configurations listed are possible. A one-way trust means that Domain A trusts Domain B, but not the reverse. A two-way trust means that both Domain A and Domain B trust each other automatically. Transitive trusts are implied, meaning that if Domain A trusts Domain B, and Domain B trusts Domain C, then Domain A trusts Domain C. See Chapter 4 for more information.

8. A.   In general, you can accommodate your network infrastructure through the use of Active Directory sites. All of the other options should play a significant role when you design your OU structure. Permissions and Group Policy can both be applied at the domain or OU level. See Chapter 7 for more information.

9. A.   .msi files are native Windows Installer files used with Windows Installer setup programs. The other file types do not apply to this situation. See Chapter 8 for more information.

10. B.   Printer and Shared Folder objects within Active Directory can point to Windows NT 4 file and printer resources, as well as Windows 2000, 2003, and Server 2008 resources. See Chapter 7 for more information.

11. D.   The number of sites in an Active Directory environment is independent of the domain organization. An environment that consists of three domains may have one or more sites, based on the physical network setup. See Chapter 5 for more information.

12. A.   The purpose of auditing is to monitor and record actions taken by users. Auditing will not prevent users from attempting to guess passwords (although it might discourage them from trying, if they are aware it is enabled). See Chapter 9 for more information.

13. E. In order to allow this permission at the OU level, the systems administrator must create a GPO with the appropriate settings and link it to the OU. See Chapter 8 for more information.

14. A. Assuming that the default settings are left in place, the Group Policy setting at the OU level will take effect. See Chapter 8 for more information.

15. B. Delegation is the process by which administrators can assign permissions on the objects within an OU. This is useful when administrators want to give other users more control over administrative functions in Active Directory. See Chapter 7 for more information.

16. C. The name of the server and the name of the share make up the UNC (Universal Naming Convention) information required to create a Shared Folder object. See Chapter 7 for more information.

17. A, B, C, D. All of the options listed are benefits of using Active Directory. See Chapter 1 for more information.

18. A, B, C, D. One of the major design goals for DNS was support for scalability. All of the features listed can be used to increase the performance of DNS. See Chapter 2 for more information.

19. D. In Windows Server 2008 you can create GPOs only by using the Group Policy Management Console. See Chapter 8 for more information.

20. B. The certificate revocation list (CRL) is the list that shows all certificates that have been revoked. See Chapter 6 for more information.

21. B. A page fault occurs when the operating system must retrieve information from disk instead of from RAM. If the number of page faults per second is high, then it is likely that the server would benefit from a RAM upgrade. See Chapter 10 for more information.

22. A. User accounts and groups are used for setting security permissions, whereas OUs are used for creating the organizational structure within Active Directory. See Chapter 7 for more information.

23. A, B, C. Of the choices listed, only the Schema Master applies to every domain in the forest. All of the other roles listed are configured individually for each domain within the Active Directory forest. See Chapter 4 for more information.

24. B. DNS does not allow you to use more than one primary server per zone. See Chapter 2 for more information.

25. A. By blocking policy inheritance on the OU, you can be sure that other settings defined at higher levels do not change the settings at the OU level. However, this will only work if the No Override option is not set at the site level. See Chapter 8 for more information.

26. C, D. The Windows Server 2008 Backup utility does not support weekly or differential backups. Weekly and differential backups can be performed if using a third party utility. See Chapter 10 for more information.

27. A, B, C, D. All of the descriptions listed are characteristics that are common to domain controllers within a single site. See Chapter 5 for more information.

28. C.   Only Windows Server 2008 computers configured as domain controllers contain a copy of the Active Directory database. See Chapter 3 for more information.

29. A.   Windows Server 2008 has a new domain controller type called a read-only domain controller (RODC) that is a good choice for non-secure locations. See Chapter 6 for more information.

30. A.   Remote Procedure Calls (RPCs) are used for intrasite replication. See Chapter 5 for more information.

Chapter

1

Overview of Active Directory

Managing users, computers, applications, and network devices can seem like a never-ending process. As a result, you need to be organized, especially when it comes to some of the most fundamental yet tedious tasks you perform every day. That's where the concept of directory services comes in.

Microsoft's Active Directory is designed to store information about all of the objects within your network environment, including hardware, software, network devices, and users. Furthermore, it is designed to increase capabilities while it decreases administration through the use of a hierarchical structure that mirrors a business's logical organization.

You've probably also heard that a great deal of planning and training is required to properly implement Active Directory's many features. In order to reap the true benefits of this technology, you must be willing to invest the time and effort to get it right. From end users to executive management, the success of your directory services implementation will be based on input from the entire business. That's where the content of this book—and the Microsoft exam for which it will prepare you—comes in.

It's difficult to cover the various aspects of Windows Server 2008's most important administrative feature—Active Directory—even in a whole book. Microsoft's main goal in Exam 70-640: Microsoft Windows Server 2008 Active Directory is to test your understanding of the features of Active Directory. The problem is that it doesn't make much sense to begin implementing Active Directory until you understand the terms, concepts, and goals behind it.

Once you have determined exactly what your Active Directory design should look like, it's time to implement it. Throughout this book, you'll learn about the various methods you can use to implement the tools and features of Windows Server 2008 based on your company's business and technical requirements. Despite the underlying complexity of Active Directory and all of its features, Microsoft has gone to great lengths to ensure that implementation and management of Active Directory are intuitive and straightforward; after all, no technology is useful if no one can figure out how to use it.

In this chapter, you'll look at some of the many benefits of using directory services and, specifically, Microsoft's Active Directory. You'll explore basic information regarding the various concepts related to Microsoft's Active Directory. The emphasis will be on addressing the concepts of a directory service, why directory services are needed, the different Active Directory models, and how you can use one to improve operations in your environment. You'll then look at the various logical objects created in Active Directory and the ways in which you can configure them to work with your network environment. We will look at some of the new Windows Server 2008 server roles and how they can be implemented in your company. Finally, you'll learn the details related to how Identity and Access (IDA) in Windows Server 2008 can strengthen the security of your directory services.

The Industry before Active Directory

Many production networks today are still operating without a single unified directory service. A number of small businesses and large global enterprises still store information in various disconnected systems instead of a centralized, hierarchical system such as Active Directory. For example, a company might record data about its employees (such as home addresses, phone numbers, and locations within the corporate entity) in a human resources database while network accounts reside on a Windows NT 4 Primary Domain Controller (PDC).

Other information, such as security settings for applications, resides within various other systems. And there are always the classic paper-based forms.

The main reason for this disparity was that no single flexible data storage mechanism was available. Implementing and managing many separate systems is a huge challenge for most organizations. Before you look at some potential solutions, you should examine Windows NT 4 further.

The Windows NT 4 Domain Model

The Windows NT 4 platform met many of the challenges of the networked world. However, like any technical solution, it had its limitations. First and foremost, questions regarding the scalability of its rudimentary directory services prevented some potential inroads into corporate data centers.

Windows NT used the concept of a *domain* to organize users and secure resources. A Windows NT 4 domain is essentially a centralized database of security information that allows for the management of network resources. A Windows-based domain is a logical grouping of computers that shares common security and user account information for the purpose of centralized security and administration. A domain is a logical entity applied to help secure and administer resources on your network. A domain is stored on a Domain Controller (DC). On an NT 4 system, it is called either a PDC (Primary Domain Controller) or a BDC (Backup Domain Controller), even though they are no longer used except in NT 4–based configurations. With advancements in Windows 2000 and beyond, all servers that participate in sharing domain information are just called DCs.

A single domain constitutes a single administrative unit, and you can have multiple domains located within your organization (multiple domains mean a more complex administrative scenario).

The domain database in Windows 2000, Windows 2003, and Windows Server 2008 is now stored in Active Directory. The domain controllers are now peers in an Active Directory configuration. They all replicate to each other so as to build reliability and high availability into the design.

As just mentioned, domains are implemented through the use of Windows NT 4 Server computers that function as either PDCs or BDCs. Every domain has exactly one PDC and may have one or more BDCs depending on your needs. All network security accounts are stored within a central database on the PDC. To improve performance and reliability in distributed environments, this database is replicated to BDCs. Although BDCs can help distribute the load of network logon requests and updates, there can be only one master copy of the accounts database. This primary copy resides on the PDC, and all user and security account changes must be recorded by this machine and transmitted to all other domain controllers. Figure 1.1 provides an example of such a topology.

FIGURE 1.1   A Windows NT 4 domain topology using PDCs and BDCs

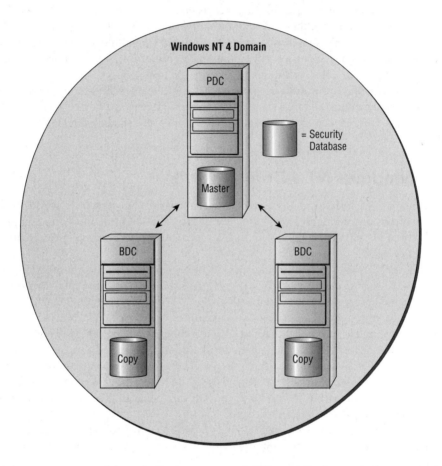

In order to meet some of these design issues, several different Windows NT domain models have been used. Figure 1.2 provides an example of a *multiple-master domain topology*. In this scenario, user accounts are stored on one or more master domains. The servers in these domains are responsible primarily for managing network accounts. BDCs for these user domains are stored in various locations throughout the organization. Network files, printers, databases, and other resources are placed in resource domains with their own PDC and BDCs. The organization itself can create and manage these domains as needed, and it often administers them separately. In order for resources to be made available to users, each of the resource domains must have a trust relationship with the master domain(s). The overall process places all users from the master domains into *global groups*. These global groups are then granted access to network resources in the resource domains.

FIGURE 1.2   A multiple-master domain topology

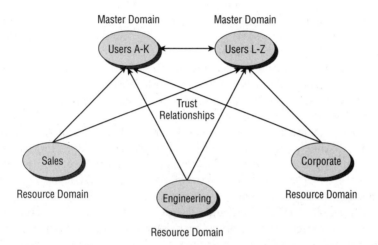

The Windows NT domain model worked well for small to medium organizations and even some large-sized organizations. It was able to accommodate thousands of users fairly well, and a single domain could handle a reasonable number of resources. However, the network traffic created to keep domain controllers synchronized and the number of trust relationships to manage can present a challenge to network and systems administrators—especially on networks that are low on bandwidth. As the numbers of users grow, it can get much more difficult for the domains to accommodate numbers of changes and network logon requests.

The Limitations of Windows NT 4

The Windows NT 4 domain model has several limitations that hinder its scalability to larger and more complex environments. One was already alluded to—this domain model is not recommended when you need to accommodate the number of users supported by large organizations. When it comes to Windows NT 4, the larger the deployment, the more difficult and all-encompassing it is to design and implement it. With Active Directory, design and implementation of a large network is easier.

Although Windows NT 4 allows multiple domains to be set up to ease administration and network constraint issues, administering these domains can quickly become quite complicated and management intensive. For example, trust relationships between the domains can quickly grow out of control if they are not managed properly, and providing adequate bandwidth for keeping network accounts synchronized can be a costly burden on the network. When working with Windows NT 4, you must make sure that you have the appropriate bandwidth on your network to satisfy the needs of the BDCs to synchronize with and replicate to PDCs.

Excessive traffic on wide area network (WAN) links that are undersized can cause a *bottleneck*—an area within your network in which, because of poor design or excessive traffic, the transfer of data is dramatically slowed or, worse, stopped. When you have a bottleneck, there is slow traffic, and you may even see KCC (Knowledge Consistency Checker) errors in your Event Viewer logs showing you replication problems. Either way, you find errors.

Consider a plumbing job where water needs to flow through four pipes to get from point A to point B. Three of the four pipes have the same diameter, but the pipe by point B is much smaller than the others. When water is flowing from point A to point B, pressure builds because the water is being forced from a bigger pipe into a smaller one. Now, apply this to network communication media and the data that flows across it. What if you transferred a 200MB file across a 56K WAN link? You can start to see where any excessive traffic on undersized links can create problems.

It is very important to consider network bandwidth and the ability of your Windows servers to synchronize and replicate to each other to maintain convergence of the centralized database so that bottlenecks and associated errors never occur in the first place. Too many problems on your network with your PDC and BDCs trying to communicate—and not being able to—are surefire ways to trigger corruption in your directory and cause even more problems for your users. Consider a situation where the PDC and BDC can't replicate and, as a result, account information becomes incorrect while you are trying to log in. Not only is this hard to pinpoint and diagnose, but it's also frustrating if you can't log in and do your work—or worse, if many users can't log in and do their work.

Bottlenecks can appear almost anywhere in the network infrastructure for a variety of reasons. To avoid misdiagnosing performance issues, it is imperative that you determine where these bottlenecks are before you deploy a directory services infrastructure. A network topology map can help you to locate bottlenecks easily, especially if transmission media speeds are listed in the documentation. For instance, you see that your whole network runs on Fast Ethernet (at 100Mbps) and then you find out that all your server Network Interface Cards (NICs) operate at Ethernet speed (10Mbps). In this scenario, the servers' NICs are the bottleneck because they force 100Mbps down to 10Mbps. By upgrading your NICs to 100Mbps, you relieve this particular type of bottleneck. This is only one example; a more common example would be when you have a WAN link that is saturated or has failed altogether and you have no backup link to the headquarters site.

It is common for bottlenecks to occur with WAN links. A slow or unreliable link can cause network traffic to bog down to a point where data is prevented from flowing from its source to its intended destination. Now, consider what happens if that same WAN link connects one of your branch offices to a main site (the company headquarters) where the BDC is located. This BDC is used to authenticate users in the branch office so that they can log in and access resources on the server. What if this link becomes saturated to the point where data can no longer travel across it? Nobody in that branch office is able to work with resources on the server in the headquarters location because there is no way to communicate with the BDC that would have allowed the access to the resources. Once you can identify (and correct) the bottleneck, you can continue with your normal operations, although you should continue to keep an eye on the Event Viewer for more errors, as well as possibly use network-monitoring gear to help find and locate other bottlenecks that you may already have or that may occur.

Another limitation of Windows NT, in addition to its being a bandwidth hog, is that the directory in use is completely flat and does not scale well in very large organizations. Because Windows NT domains are flat entities, they do not take into account the structure of businesses and cannot be organized in a hierarchical fashion (using subdomains for administrative purposes) the way Active Directory can. Therefore, systems administrators are forced to place users into groups that cannot be nested (that is, cannot have subgroups). In a large organization, it might be necessary to manage hundreds of groups within each domain. In this scenario, setting permissions on resources (such as file and print services) can become an extremely tedious and error-prone process.

As far as security is concerned, administration is often delegated to one or more users of the Information Technology (IT) department. These individuals have complete control over the domain controllers and resources within the domain itself. This poses potential security and technical problems. Because the distribution of administrator rights is extremely important, it is best to assign (or delegate) only essential permissions to each area of the business.

However, the delegation options available in the Windows NT 4 network operating system (NOS) are either difficult to implement or do not provide enough flexibility. All of this leads to a less-than-optimal configuration. For example, security policies are often set to allow users more permissions than they need to complete their jobs.

If you have ever worked with Windows NT 4 domains in a medium- to large-sized environment, you are probably familiar with many of the issues related to the domain model. Windows NT 4 provided an excellent solution for many businesses and offered security, flexibility, and network management features unmatched by many of its competitors at the time. As with almost any technical solution, however, there are areas in which improvements can be made. Now that you've gone over the basics of Windows NT 4 and its directory structure, you can move on and examine how Windows Server 2008's Active Directory addresses some of these challenges.

The Benefits of Active Directory

Most businesses have created an organizational structure in an attempt to better manage their environments and activities. For example, companies often divide themselves into departments (such as Sales, Marketing, and Engineering), and individuals fill roles within these departments (such as managers and staff). The goal is to add constructs that help coordinate the various functions required for the success of the organization as a whole.

The IT department in these companies is responsible for maintaining the security of the company's information. In modern businesses, this involves planning for, implementing, and managing various network resources. Servers, workstations, and routers are common tools of the infrastructure connecting users with the information they need to do their jobs. In all but the smallest environments, the effort required to manage these technological resources can be great.

That's where Windows Server 2008 and Microsoft's Active Directory come in. In its most basic definition, a *directory* is a repository that records and stores information and makes it available to users. Active Directory allows you to create a single centralized (or decentralized with multiple domain controllers) repository of information with which you can securely manage a company's resources. User account management, security, and application usages are just a few of the solutions Active Directory offers. Many features of this directory services technology allow it to meet the needs of organizations of any size. Specifically, Active Directory's features include the following:

Hierarchical organization   Active Directory is based on a hierarchical layout. Through the use of various organizational components (or *objects*), a company can create a network management infrastructure and directory structure that mirrors the business organization. For example, if a company called Stellacon.com had several departments (such as Sales and Human Resources), the directory services model can reflect this structure through the use of various objects within the directory (See Figure 1.3). Stellacon.com could then organize its users into the appropriate department containers.

The directory structure can efficiently accommodate the physical and logical aspects of information resources, such as access to other databases, user permissions, and computers. Active Directory also integrates with the network naming service, the *Domain Name System (DNS)*. DNS provides for the hierarchical naming and location of resources throughout the company and on the public Internet.

Extensible schema   One of the foremost concerns with any type of database is the difficulty you encounter when you try to accommodate all types of information in one storage repository. That's why Active Directory has been designed with extensibility in mind. In this case, extensibility means the ability to expand (or extend) the directory schema. The *schema* is the actual structure of the database—what data types it contains and the location of their attributes. The schema is important because it allows applications to know where particular pieces of information reside. You cannot delete any portion of the schema, but you can change, modify, or alter it. The information stored within the structure of Active Directory can be expanded and customized through the use of various tools. One such tool is the Active Directory Service Interfaces (ADSI).

ADSI provides objects and interfaces that can be accessed from within common programming languages such as Visual Basic, Visual C#, and Active Server Pages (ASP). This feature allows Active Directory to adapt to special applications and to store additional information as needed. It also allows all of the various areas within an organization (or even among several organizations) to share data easily.

Centralized data storage   All of the information within Active Directory resides within a single, distributed, data repository. Users and systems administrators must be able to easily access the information they need wherever they may be within the company. This is one of the most important design goals of the directory service—to provide a secure and centralized location for all of your data. The benefits of centralized data storage include reduced administrative requirements, less duplication, higher availability, and increased visibility and organization of data.

FIGURE 1.3   Directory services model

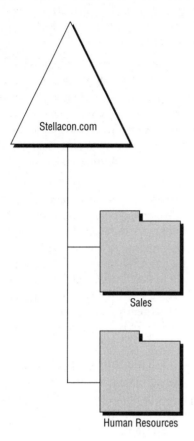

Replication   If server performance and reliability were not concerns, it might make sense to store the entire Active Directory on a single server. In the real world, however, accessibility of remote sites and cost constraints may require that the database be replicated throughout the network. Active Directory provides for this functionality. Through the use of replication technology, Active Directory's database can be distributed among many different servers in a network environment. The ability to define sites allows systems and network administrators to limit the amount of traffic to and from remote sites while still ensuring adequate performance and usability. Reliable data synchronization allows for multimaster replication—that is, all domain controllers can update information stored within Active Directory and can ensure its consistency at the same time.

Ease of administration   In order to accommodate various business models, Active Directory can be configured for centralized or decentralized administration. This gives network and systems administrators the ability to delegate authority and responsibilities throughout the organization while still maintaining security. Furthermore, the tools and utilities used to add, remove, and modify Active Directory objects are available with all Windows Server 2008 domain controllers (except read-only domain controllers).

Network security   Through the use of a single logon and various authentication and encryption mechanisms, Active Directory can facilitate security throughout an entire enterprise. Through the process of *delegation,* higher-level security authorities can grant permissions to other administrators. For ease of administration, objects in the Active Directory tree inherit permissions from their parent objects. Application developers can take advantage of many of these features to ensure that users are identified uniquely and securely. Network administrators can create and update permissions as needed from within a single repository, thereby reducing chances of inaccurate or outdated configuration.

Client configuration management   One of the biggest struggles for systems administrators comes with maintaining a network of heterogeneous systems and applications. A fairly simple failure—such as a hard disk crash—can cause hours of work in reconfiguring and restoring a workstation, especially an enterprise-class server. Hours of work can also be generated when users are forced to move between computers and they need to have all of their applications reinstalled and the necessary system settings updated. Many IT organizations have found that these types of operations can consume a great deal of IT staffers' time and resources. New technologies integrated with Active Directory allow for greatly enhanced control and administration of these types of network issues. The overall benefit is decreased downtime, a better end-user experience, and reduced administration.

Scalability   Large organizations often have many users and large quantities of information to manage. Active Directory was designed with scalability in mind. Not only does it allow for storing millions of objects within a single domain, it also provides methods for distributing the necessary information between servers and locations. These features relieve much of the burden of designing a directory services infrastructure based on technical instead of business factors.

Search functionality   One of the most important benefits of having all your network resources stored in a single repository is that it gives you the ability to perform accurate searches. Users often see NOSs as extremely complicated because of the naming and location of resources, but they shouldn't be that complicated. For example, if we need to find a printer, we should not need to know the name of the domain or print server for that object. Using Active Directory, users can quickly find information about other users or resources, such as printers and servers, through an intuitive querying interface.

The technical chapters of this book cover the technical aspects of how Windows Server 2008 delivers all of these features. For now, keep in mind the various challenges that Active Directory was designed to address. This chapter introduces the technical concepts on which Active Directory is based. In order to better understand this topic, you'll now see the various areas that make up the logical and physical structure of Active Directory.

Understanding Active Directory's Logical Structure

Database professionals often use the term *schema* to describe the structure of data. A schema usually defines the types of information that can be stored within a certain repository and special rules on how the information is to be organized. A schema can be manipulated with the right tools, such as ADSI, mentioned earlier in the chapter. Within a *relational database* or Microsoft Excel spreadsheet, for example, we might define tables with columns and rows. Similarly, the Active Directory schema specifies the types of information that are stored within a directory.

The schema itself also describes the structure of the information stored within the Active Directory data store. The Active Directory data store, in turn, resides on one or more domain controllers that are deployed throughout the enterprise. In this section, you'll see the various concepts used to specify how Active Directory is logically organized.

Components and Mechanisms of Active Directory

In order to maintain the types of information required to support an entire organization, Active Directory must provide for many different types of functionality. Active Directory is made up of various components. Each of these components must work with the others to ensure that Active Directory remains accessible to all of the users that require it and to maintain the accuracy and consistency of its information.

In the following sections, you'll see each of the components that make up Active Directory.

Data Store

When you envision Active Directory from a physical point of view, you probably imagine a set of files stored on the hard disk that contain all of the objects within it. The term *data store* is used to refer to the actual structure that contains the information stored within Active Directory. The data store is implemented as a set of files that resides within the file system of a domain controller. This is the fundamental structure of Active Directory.

The data store itself has a structure that describes the types of information it can contain. Within the data store, data about objects is recorded and made available to users. For example, configuration information about the domain topology, including trust relationships, are contained within Active Directory. Similarly, information about users, groups, and computers that are part of the domain are also recorded.

The Active Directory data store is also commonly referred to as the Active Directory database.

Schema

The Active Directory schema consists of rules on the types of information that can be stored within the directory. The schema is made up of two types of objects: attributes and classes.

- An *attribute* is a single granular piece of information stored within Active Directory. First Name and Last Name, for example, are considered attributes, which may contain the values of Bob and Smith respectively.

- A *class* is an object defined as a collection of attributes. For example, a class called Employee could include the First Name and Last Name attributes.

It is important to understand that classes and attributes are defined independently and that any number of classes can use the same attributes. For example, if we create an attribute called Nickname, this value could conceivably be used both as part of a User class and as part of a Computer class.

By default, Microsoft has included several schema objects. In order to support custom data, applications developers can extend the schema by creating their own classes and attributes. The entire schema is replicated to all of the domain controllers within the environment to ensure data consistency among them.

The overall result of the schema is a centralized data store that can contain information about many different types of objects—including users, groups, computers, network devices, applications, and more.

Global Catalog

The *Global Catalog* is a database that contains all of the information pertaining to objects within all domains in the Active Directory environment.

One of the potential problems with working in an environment that contains multiple domains is that users in one domain may want to find objects stored in another domain, but they may not have any additional information about those objects.

The purpose of the Global Catalog is to index information stored in Active Directory so that it can be more quickly and easily searched. The Global Catalog can be distributed to servers within the network environment. That is, network and systems administrators specify which servers within the Active Directory environment will contain copies of the Global Catalog. This decision is usually made based on technical considerations (such as network links) and organizational considerations (such as the number of users at each remote site).

You can think of the Global Catalog as something like a universal phone book. Much like the local phone book you may keep in your house, the Global Catalog is quite large and bulky, but just like the phone book, it is also very useful in helping you locate information. Your goal (as a system administrator) would be to find a balance where you are maintaining enough copies in enough locations so that users can quickly and easily access it, without it taking up too much space.

This distribution of Global Catalog information allows for increased performance of company-wide resource searches and can prevent excessive traffic across network links. Because the Global Catalog includes information about objects stored in all domains within the Active

Directory environment, its management and location should be an important concern for network and systems administrators.

Searching Mechanisms

The best-designed data repository in the world is useless if users can't access the information stored within it. Active Directory includes a search engine that users can query to find information about objects stored within it. For example, if a member of the Human Resources (HR) department is looking for a color printer, they can easily query Active Directory to find the one located closest. Best of all, the query tools are already built into Windows Server 2008 operating systems and are only a few mouse clicks away.

Replication

Although it is theoretically possible to create a directory service that involves only one central computer, there are several problems with this configuration. First, all of the data is stored on one machine. This server would be responsible for processing all of the logon requests and search queries associated with the objects that it contained. Although this scenario might work well for a small network, it would create a tremendous load on a single server in a very large environment. Second, clients that are located on remote networks would experience slower response times due to the pace of network traffic. If this server became unavailable (due to a failed power supply, for example), network authentication and other vital processes could not be carried out.

To prevent these problems, Active Directory has been designed with a replication engine. The purpose of *replication* is to distribute the data stored within the directory throughout the organization for increased availability, performance, and data protection. Systems administrators can tune replication based on their physical network infrastructure and other constraints.

An Overview of Active Directory Domains

As mentioned earlier, in a Windows Server 2008 Active Directory deployment, a domain is considered a logical security boundary that allows for the creation, administration, and management of related resources.

You can think of a domain as a logical division, such as a neighborhood within a city. Although each neighborhood is part of a larger group of neighborhoods (the city), it may carry on many of its functions independently of the others. For example, resources such as tennis courts and swimming pools may be made available only to members of the neighborhood, whereas resources such as electricity and water supplies would probably be shared between neighborhoods. So, think of a domain as a grouping of objects that utilizes resources exclusive to its domain, but keep in mind that those resources can also be shared between domains.

Although the names and fundamental features are the same, Active Directory domains are quite different from those in Windows NT. As we mentioned earlier, an Active Directory domain can store many more objects than a Windows NT domain. Furthermore, Active Directory domains can be combined together into trees and forests to form more complex hierarchical structures.

Before going into the details, let's discuss the concept of domains. If you think of a domain as a neighborhood, you can think of a group of similar domains (a *tree*) as a suburb and a group of disparate domains that trust each other (a *forest*) as a city. This is in contrast to Windows NT domains, which treat all domains as peers of each other (that is, they are all on the same level and cannot be organized into trees and forests).

Within most business organizations, network and systems administration duties are delegated to certain individuals and departments. For example, a company might have a centralized IT department that is responsible for all implementation, support, and maintenance of network resources throughout the organization. In another example, network support may be largely decentralized—that is, each department, business unit, or office may have its own IT support staff. Both of these models may work well for a company, but implementing such a structure through directory services requires the use of logical objects.

A domain is a collection of computers and resources that share a common security database. An Active Directory domain contains a logical partition of users, groups, and other objects within the environment. Objects within a domain share several characteristics, including the following:

Group Policy and security permissions   Security for all of the objects within a domain can be administered based on policies. Thus, a domain administrator can make changes to any of the settings within the domain. These policies can apply to all of the users, computers, and objects within the domain. For more granular security settings, however, permissions can be granted on specific objects, thereby distributing administration responsibilities and increasing security.

Hierarchical object naming   All of the objects within an Active Directory container share a common namespace. When domains are combined together, however, the namespace is hierarchical. For example, a user in one department might have the object name `willp@engineering`
`.stellacon.com`, while a user in another department might have the name `wpanek@`
`sales.stellacon.com`. The first part of the name (in these examples, the usernames `willp` and `wpanek`) is the name of the object within the domain. The suffix (in this case `engineering`
`.stellacon.com` and `sales.stellacon.com`) is determined by the organization of the domains. The hierarchical naming system allows each object within Active Directory to have a unique name.

Hierarchical inheritance   Containers called *organizational units (OUs)* can be created within a domain. These units are used for creating a logical grouping of objects within Active Directory. The specific settings and permissions assigned to an OU can be inherited by lower-level objects.

For example, if we have an OU for the North America division within our company, we can set user permissions on this object. All of the objects within the North America object (such as the Sales, Marketing, and Engineering departments) automatically inherit these settings. The proper use of hierarchical properties allows systems administrators to avoid inconsistent security policies and makes administration easier, but it's important to remember how inheritance works when implementing and administering security, because it results in the implicit assignment of permissions.

Trust relationships   In order to facilitate the sharing of information between domains, trust relationships are automatically created between them. The administrator can break and establish trust relationships based on business requirements. A trust relationship allows two domains to share security information and objects, but it does not automatically assign permissions to these objects. *Trusts* allow users who are contained within one domain to be granted access to resources in other domains. To make administrating trust relationships easier, Microsoft has made transitive two-way trusts the default relationship between domains. As shown in Figure 1.4, if Domain A trusts Domain B and Domain B trusts Domain C, Domain A implicitly trusts Domain C.

FIGURE 1.4   Transitive two-way trust relationships

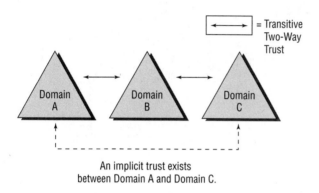

An implicit trust exists
between Domain A and Domain C.

Generally, triangles are used in network diagrams to represent Active Directory domains (thereby indicating their hierarchical structure), and circles are used to represent flat domains (such as those in Windows NT).

Overall, the purpose of domains is to ease administration while providing for a common security and resource database.

Overview of an Active Directory Forest

Although the flexibility and power afforded by the use of an Active Directory domain will meet the needs of many organizations, there are reasons for which companies might want to implement more than one domain. It is important to know that domains can be combined together into domain trees.

Domain trees are hierarchical collections of one or more domains that are designed to meet the organizational needs of a business (see Figure 1.5).

FIGURE 1.5   A domain tree

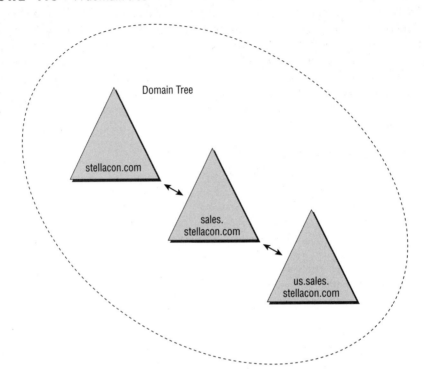

Trees are defined by the use of a contiguous namespace. For example, the following domains are all considered part of the same tree:

- `stellacon.com`
- `sales.stellacon.com`
- `research.stellacon.com`
- `us.sales.stellacon.com`

The first domain that gets installed in your Active Directory forest is the most important domain. The first domain is called the *root domain*. Notice that all of these domains are part of the `stellacon.com` domain, which is the root domain for this tree. Domains within the same tree still maintain separate security and resource databases, but they can be administered together through the use of trust relationships. By default, trust relationships are automatically established between parent and child domains within a tree.

Although single companies will often want to configure domains to fit within a single namespace, noncontiguous namespaces may be used for several reasons. Domain trees can be combined together into noncontiguous groupings. Such a grouping is known as a *forest* (see Figure 1.6). A forest can consist of a single domain, but a forest often contains multiple noncontiguous namespaces—domains that are kept separate for technical or political reasons.

FIGURE 1.6   An Active Directory forest

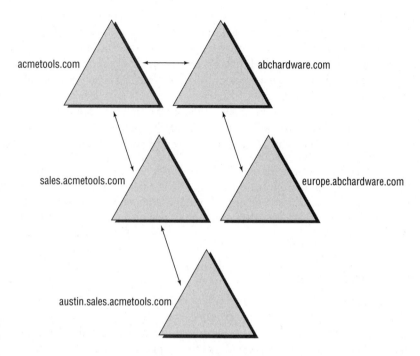

Trust relationships (which facilitate shared resources) can be created among the following entities:

- Among domains within a tree
- Among trees within a forest
- Among forests (Windows Server 2008 only)

Understanding Active Directory Objects

The Active Directory database is made up of units called *objects*. Each object represents a single unique database entry.

Names and Identifiers of Objects

Objects are uniquely identified within your database in the following ways:

- Each object has a globally unique identifier (GUID) or security identifier (SID).
- Each object has a distinguished name (DN).

GUIDs and SIDs

Globally unique identifiers are security identification numbers placed on applications by Active Directory. These numbers are not guaranteed to be unique, but the number generated is very large, so the odds are very low that two applications will end up with the same GUID.

Security identifiers are security identification numbers placed on objects (for example, users, groups, and printers) by Active Directory. All rights and permissions are placed on the SID and not the account name. For example, let's say we have an IT manager named Maria who is going on maternity leave. John is temporarily replacing Maria. By renaming Maria's account and having John change the password, we give John all the rights and permissions that Maria had; this is because the SID on the account did not change, even though the name did.

Microsoft likes to ask questions on the exam about switching rights and permissions from one user to another. Understanding how the rights and permissions are associated with the SID will help you answer these questions correctly.

Distinguished Names

A fundamental feature of Active Directory is that each object within the directory has its own unique name, as well as a unique SID. For example, your organization may have two different users named John Smith (who may or may not be in different departments or locations within the company). There should be some way for us to distinguish between these users (and their corresponding user objects).

Within Active Directory, each object can be uniquely identified using a long name that specifies the full path to the object. Generally, this long name for an object is called the *distinguished name (DN)*. Following is an example of a DN:

`/O=Internet/DC=Com/DC=Stellacon/DC=Sales/CN=Managers/CN=John Smith`

In this name, we have specified several different types of objects:

- *Organization* (O) is the company or root-level domain. In this case, the root level is the Internet.

- *Domain component* (DC) is a portion of the hierarchical path. Domain components are used for organizing objects within the directory service. The three domain components in the example DN specify that the user object is located within the `sales.stellacon.com` domain.

- *Common name* (CN) specifies the names of objects in the directory. In this example, the user `John Smith` is contained within the `Managers` container.

Together, the components of the DN uniquely identify where the user object is stored.

Instead of specifying the full DN, you might also choose to use a *relative distinguished name (RDN)*. This name specifies only part of the object's path relative to another object. For example, if your current context is already the `Managers` group within the `sales.stellacon.com` domain, you could simply specify the user as `CN=John Smith`.

Functions of the SID and the DN

The difference between the DN and the SID is this: If you change the structure of the domain—for example, by renaming one of the containers or moving the user object—the DN of this object also changes, but its SID does not. This type of naming system allows for flexibility and the ability to easily identify the potentially millions of objects that might exist in Active Directory.

Using Organizational Units (OUs) in Active Directory

As we mentioned earlier, one of the fundamental limitations of the Windows NT 4 domain organization is that it has a flat structure—all users and groups are stored as part of a single namespace. Real-world organizations, however, often require further organization within domains. For example, we may have 3,000 users in one domain. Some of these should be grouped together in an Engineering group. Within the Engineering group, we might also want to further subdivide users into groups (for example, Development and Testing). Active Directory supports this kind of hierarchy. Figure 1.7 depicts the differences between the structure of a Windows NT 4 domain and that of an Active Directory domain.

FIGURE 1.7   Flat Windows NT 4 domain vs. hierarchical Active Directory domains

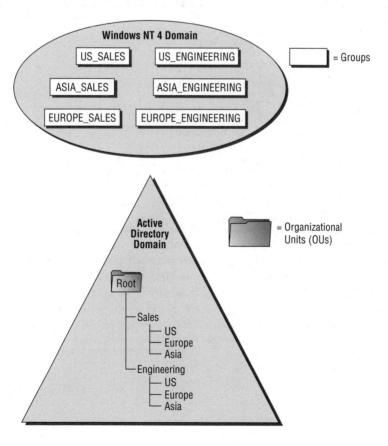

The fundamental unit of organization within an Active Directory domain is the OU. OUs are container objects that can be hierarchically arranged within a domain. Figure 1.8 provides examples of two typical OU setups. OUs can contain other objects such as users, groups, computers, and even other OUs.

FIGURE 1.8 Two different OU hierarchy models

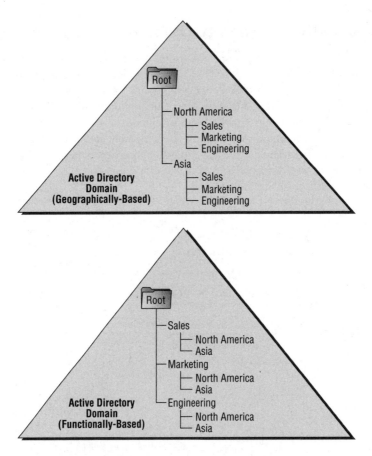

OUs are the objects to which security permissions and group policies are generally assigned. This means that proper planning of OU structure is important. A well-designed OU structure can allow for efficient administration of Active Directory objects.

OUs can be organized based on various criteria. For example, we might choose to implement an OU organization based on the geographic distribution of our company's business units or based on functional business units (see Figure 1.8).

Security Features of User, Computer, and Group Objects

The real objects that you will want to control and manage with Active Directory are the users, computers, and groups within your network environment. These are the types of objects that allow for the most granular level of control over permissions and allow you to configure your network to meet business needs.

- *User accounts* enforce security within the network environment. These accounts define the login information and passwords that individuals using your network need to enter to receive permissions to use network objects.

- *Computer objects* allow systems administrators to configure the functions that can be performed on client machines throughout the environment.

Both user account objects and computer objects enable security to be maintained at a granular level.

Although security can be enforced by placing permissions directly on user and computer objects, it is much more convenient to combine users into groups for the purpose of assigning permissions.

For example, if three users will require similar permissions within the Accounting department, you can place all of them in one group and assign permissions to the group. If users are removed or added to the department, you can easily make changes to the group without having to make any further changes to security permissions. Figure 1.9 shows how groups can be used to easily administer permissions.

FIGURE 1.9   Using groups to administer security

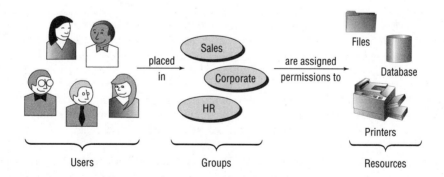

There are two main types of groups within Active Directory:

- *Security groups* are used to administer permissions. All members of a security group receive the same security settings and are able to send email and other messages to several different users at once.

- *Distribution groups* are used only to send email and other messages to several different users at once. You don't have to maintain security permissions when using distribution groups, but they can help you handle multiple users.

Overall, using groups properly really helps you implement and manage security and permissions within Active Directory.

Delegation of Administrative Control

An OU is the smallest component within a domain to which administrative permissions and group policies can be assigned. (Administrative permissions and group policies are covered in Chapter 5, "Configuring Server Roles," and Chapter 6, "Administering Active Directory.") Now, we take a look at specifically how to set administrative control on OUs.

Delegation occurs when a higher security authority assigns permissions to a lower security authority.

As a real-world example, assume that you are the director of IT for a large organization. Instead of doing all of the work yourself, you would probably assign roles and responsibilities to other individuals.

For example, if you worked within a multidomain environment, you might make one systems administrator responsible for all operations within the Sales domain and another responsible for the Engineering domain. Similarly, you could assign the permissions for managing all printers and print queues within your organization to one individual user while allowing another individual user to manage all security permissions for users and groups.

In this way, you can distribute the various roles and responsibilities of the IT staff throughout the organization. Businesses generally have a division of labor that handles all of the tasks involved in keeping the company's networks humming. Network operating systems, however, often make it difficult to assign just the right permissions, or in other words, they have very granular permissions. Sometimes, this complexity is necessary to ensure that only the right permissions are assigned.

A good general rule of thumb is that you should provide users and administrators the minimum permissions they require to do their jobs. This way you can reduce the risk that accidental, malicious, and otherwise unwanted changes will occur.

You can also use auditing to log events to the Security Log in the Event Viewer. Doing so ensures that if accidental, malicious, and otherwise unwanted changes do occur, they are logged and traceable.

In the world of Active Directory, you use the process of delegation to define permissions for OU administrators. As a system administrator you will occasionally need to delegate responsibility to others—you can't do it all (although sometimes some administrators believe that they can!). If you do need to delegate, remember that Windows Server 2008 was designed to offer you the ability to do so.

Simply, delegation allows a higher administrative authority to grant an individual or a group specific administrative rights for containers and subtrees. This feature eliminates the need to assign any one individual administrator sweeping authority over large segments of the user population. You can break up this control over branches within your tree, within each OU you create.

To understand delegation and rights, you should first understand the concept of access control entries (ACEs). ACEs grant specific administrative rights on objects in a container to a user or group. The container's access control list (ACL) is used to store ACEs.

When you are considering implementing delegation, there are two main concerns to keep in mind:

Parent-child relationships   The OU hierarchy you create will be very important when you consider the maintainability of security permissions. OUs can exist in a parent-child relationship, which means that permissions and group policies set on OUs higher up in the hierarchy (parents) can interact with objects in OUs lower on the hierarchy (children). When it comes to delegating permissions, this is extremely important. You can allow child containers to automatically inherit the permissions set on parent containers. For example, if the North America division of your organization contains 12 other OUs, you could delegate the same set of permissions to all of them by placing security permissions on the North America division. By doing the task only once, you save time and reduce the likelihood of human error. This feature can greatly ease administration, especially in larger organizations, but it is also a reminder of the importance of properly planning the OU structure within a domain.

You can delegate control only at the OU level and not at the object level within the OU.

Inheritance settings   Now that you've seen how you can use parent-child relationships for administration, you should consider *inheritance*, the actual process of inheriting permissions. When you set permissions on a parent container, all of the child objects are configured to inherit the same permissions. You can override this behavior, however, if business rules do not lend themselves well to inheritance.

Introducing Windows Server 2008 Server Roles

Windows Server 2003 had many tools an administrator could use to configure the services they needed to make a network run efficiently. Some of these tools included the Manage Your Server, Configure Your Server, and the Add/Remove Windows components.

Windows Server 2008 includes a new feature called *Server Manager*. Server Manager is a Microsoft Management Console (MMC) snap-in that allows an administrator to view information about server configuration, the status of roles that are installed, and links for adding and removing features and roles (see Figure 1.10).

FIGURE 1.10 Windows Server 2008 server roles

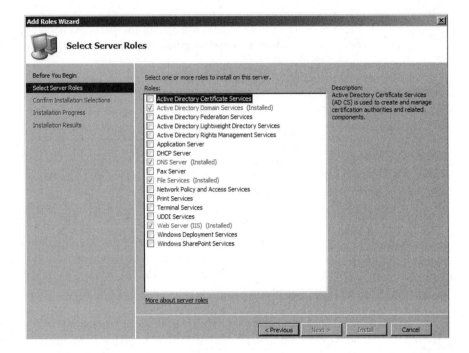

The following are some of the roles that you can install and manage using Server Manager.

- Active Directory Certificate Services
- Active Directory Domain Services
- Active Directory Federation Services
- Active Directory Lightweight Directory Services
- Active Directory Rights Management Services

This is not the complete list of roles. These are some of the roles that directly affect Active Directory. All Active Directory server-based roles are discussed in detail in Chapter 5.

Active Directory Certificate Services

Active Directory Certificate Services (AD CS) allows administrators to configure services for issuing and managing public key certificates. Companies can benefit from AD CS security by combining a private key with an object (such as users and computers), devices (such as routers), or services. When using Server Manager, you can configure the following components of AD CS:

Web enrollment   This feature allows users to request certificates and retrieve certificate revocation lists (CRLs) through the use of a web browser.

Certification authorities (CAs)   Enterprise Root CAs and Stand Alone Root CAs are the two types of CAs. Enterprise Root CAs (automatically integrated with Active Directory) are the topmost trusted CAs of the hierarchy. They hold the certificates that you issue to the users within your organization. The Stand Alone Root CAs hold the CAs that you issue to Internet users.

CAs below the Enterprise and Stand Alone Root CAs in the hierarchy are referred to as Subordinate CAs. The Enterprise or Stand Alone Root CAs give certificates to the Subordinate CAs, which in turn issue certificates to objects and services

Network Device Enrollment Service   The Network Device Enrollment Service allows network devices (such as routers) to obtain a certificate even though they do not have an account in the Active Directory domain.

Online Responder Service   Some applications such as Secure/Multipurpose Internet Mail Extensions (S/MIME), Secure Sockets Layer (SSL), Encrypting File System (EFS), and smart cards may need to validate the status of a certificate. The Online Responder service responds to certificate status requests, evaluates the status of the certificate that was requested, and answers the request with a signed response containing the certificate's status information.

Active Directory Domain Services

In Windows Server 2008, you can use Active Directory Domain Services (AD DS) to manage objects (users, computers, printers, etc.) on a network. Many new features have been added to AD DS that were not available in previous versions of Windows Server Active Directory. Thanks to these new features, now organizations can securely deploy and administer AD DS more efficiently.

User interface improvements   The updated Installation Wizard for AD DS allows it to be installed more easily. Administrators are able to locate domain controllers anywhere throughout the enterprise, and due to the improved AD DS user interface (UI), domain controllers have new options during the installation process. One of these is the ability to set up *read-only domain controllers (RODCs)*.

Read-Only Domain Controllers   Windows Server 2008 has a new type of domain controller called a read-only domain controller (RODC). This gives an organization the ability to install a domain controller in an area or location (on or offsite) that has limited security.

Let's imagine a hospital running Microsoft Windows Server 2003. This hospital has many affiliated physicians' offices located near it. Most likely these remote locations would not have domain controllers at their offices because administrators usually do not like to put a writable domain controller in an unsecured location. If the staff at these offices wanted to log into the hospital system, they would have to go across the WAN to be authenticated.

Now let's imagine the same hospital running Microsoft Windows Server 2008. The hospital can now place RODCs at these remote physicians' offices, which greatly improves performance for these sites.

Auditing   In previous versions of Microsoft Windows Server, you had the ability to audit Active Directory by watching for successes or failures. If an individual made a successful or unsuccessful change to an Active Directory object, the attempt was logged in the Security Log. The problem with this was that, although you could view the Security Log and notice that someone accessed an object, you could not view what they might have changed in that object's attributes.

In Microsoft Windows Server 2008, you can view the new and old values of the object and its attributes.

Fine-Grained Password Policies   In Microsoft Windows Server 2000 and 2003, when an organization implemented a domain-based password policy, it applied to all users in that domain. There was no inexpensive way to have individuals or groups use a different password policy. The same limitation applied to the account lockout policy. Fine-grained password policies allow an organization to have different password and account lockout policies for different sets of users in the same domain.

Restartable Active Directory Domain Services   Microsoft Windows Server 2008 gives an administrator the ability to stop or restart Active Directory Domain Services. For example, administrators can do an offline defragmentation of the Active Directory database or apply security updates without needing to restart the machine. This allows other services not dependent on Active Directory (DNS, DHCP, etc.) to continue to operate while Active Directory is offline.

Database Mounting Tool   In previous versions of Active Directory, if an object got deleted, an administrator had to load multiple online backups until they found the object to restore. The Windows Server 2008 Active Directory database mounting tool (`Dsamain.exe`) allows an administrator to view Active Directory data that was backed up online or through the Volume Shadow Copy Service (snapshot) at different times and then decide which online backup or snapshot to restore. This allows an administrator to quickly find and restore the data that they need.

Active Directory Federation Services

Active Directory Federation Services (AD FS) provides Internet-based clients a secure identity access solution that works on both Windows and non-Windows operating systems.

Let's imagine a user who logs into their domain when arriving at work in the morning. An authentication box asks the user for their credentials (username and password). The same user then tries to access an Internet application that operates on another network. Normally when a user from one network tries to access an application in another network, they must have a secondary username and password.

AD FS gives users the ability to do a *single sign-on (SSO)* and access applications on other networks without needing a secondary password. Organizations can set up trust relationships with other trusted organizations so a user's digital identity and access rights can be accepted without a secondary password.

 Real World Scenario

AD FS in Use

Two companies have decided to work together. CompanyA is a retail shop that gets all of its supplies from CompanyB. Once these two companies decided to become partners, if they use AD FS, they can work together as if they were one company.

The companies might set up their operations so that a manager from CompanyA can log into an inventory database in CompanyB's network and order as many products as they need without approval. A lower-level employee in CompanyA can also log into the inventory database and place an order, but the order first has to be approved (since this level of employee does not have the rights to automatically order) by someone with the appropriate rights.

If these companies decided to use AD FS, they can now share resources easily.

Active Directory Lightweight Directory Services

Active Directory Lightweight Directory Services (AD LDS) is a *Lightweight Directory Access Protocol (LDAP)* directory service. This type of service allows directory-enabled applications to store and retrieve data without needing the dependencies AD DS requires.

To fully understand AD LDS, you must first understand the LDAP. LDAP is an application protocol used for querying and modifying directory services.

Think of directory services as an address book. An address book is a set of names (your objects) that you organize in a logical and hierarchical manner (names organized alphabetically). Each name in the address book has an address and phone number (the attributes of your objects) associated with it. LDAP allows you to query or modify this address book.

Active Directory Rights Management Services

Active Directory Rights Management Services (AD RMS), included with Microsoft Windows Server 2008, allows administrators or users to determine what access (open, read, modify, etc.) they give to other users in an organization. This access can be used to secure email messages, internal websites, and documents.

To secure documents, Microsoft Office 2003 Professional (Word, Excel, PowerPoint, and Outlook) or Microsoft Office 2007 Enterprise, Professional Plus, or Ultimate is required.

Organizations can use AD RMS for confidential or critical information. They can design usage policy templates that can be applied directly to the confidential information.

AD RMS requires an AD RMS–enabled client. Windows Vista includes the AD RMS client by default. If you are not using Windows Vista or Windows Server 2008, you can download the AD RMS client for previous versions of Windows from Microsoft's Download Center.

An advantage of AD RMS is its easy installation and administration. You can install AD RMS easily through Server Manager and administer it through the MMC snap-in. AD RMS has created three new administrative roles to allow for its easy delegation throughout an organization:

- AD RMS Enterprise Administrators
- AD RMS Template Administrators
- AD RMS Auditors

Another advantage of AD RMS is its integration with AD FS, which allows two organizations to share information without needing to install AD RMS in both organizations.

We will discuss the advantages of AD RMS in Chapter 5. Chapter 5 also shows the step-by-step installation of all the server roles we have discussed in this section.

Introducing Identity and Access (IDA) in Windows Server 2008

In today's complex business world, users may have to access resources on different types of hardware, software, and devices. Because many of these systems and devices do not always communicate with each other, it is not unusual for users to have multiple identities on multiple systems.

If you have worked in the computer industry for even a short period of time, you understand that users having multiple identities and passwords for multiple systems can cause many problems. This practice can actually increase security risks due to the errors that end users can encounter by having multiple accounts.

> ### Real World Scenario
>
> #### How Users Deal with Multiple Accounts and Passwords
>
> In today's technical world, we all have multiple usernames and passwords. I recently watched a morning news program that stated that the average person has eight sets of these. Think about it. Credit card logons, online banking, websites that we visit, and many others.
>
> Now many of us (me included) write down all the different website usernames and passwords we use. At home, this is normally not an issue because we do not have 100 employees walking by our computer or office. The problem occurs when we use the same method at the office.
>
> Let's say my company, Stellacon Corporation, decides to hire a good sales person. Now when I say a good sales person, I mean someone you can give a list of names and phone numbers to and they can make sales happen. But now they must use a computer to do their job.
>
> This new sales person has a username and password to log into the Microsoft Windows domain, a username and password to log into a lead-generating website, and other usernames and passwords to do their job. So what do they do? Well if you have been in this industry long enough, you know the stories of what users do with their credentials—they write them down and tape them to their monitor or maybe under the keyboard. My favorite story is of the person who put all their credential information on a Rolodex card and made it the first card in their Rolodex holder.
>
> The Information Technology (IT) department needs to train their users on the importance of user credential security. If users tape their credentials to their monitor, it's our fault as IT managers; we did not train them properly. It's up to us to help make our users safe and secure.

Users' identities are an ongoing concern for most companies. This is where Identity and Access (IDA) solutions can help an organization. Through technologies and products specifically designed for IDA, organizations can manage user identities and associated access privileges. IDA solutions can be categorized into five distinct areas:

- Directory services
- Strong authentication
- Federated Identities
- Information protection
- Identity Lifecycle Management

In the following sections, we will explain these five distinct areas in more detail. Because IDA is so tightly integrated with Windows Server 2008, some of these categories were covered in the previous section, "Introducing Windows Server 2008 Server Roles." Here we will explain how these previously discussed concepts interact with IDA.

Using Directory Services

As discussed earlier in this chapter, in Windows Server 2008, AD DS can be used by organizations to manage objects (users, computers, printers, etc.) on a network.

One of the advantages of using AD DS with IDA solutions is that directory services is deployed in many organizations worldwide. The chances are very good that when you work with other companies, they will also be using Microsoft directory services.

Also, by default, directory services is integrated with certificates, rights management, and Federation Services. As discussed earlier in this chapter, directory services gives you the following benefits:

- Read-Only Domain Controllers
- Auditing
- Fine-Grained Password Policies
- Restartable Active Directory Domain Services
- Database Mounting Tool

Strong Authentication

You can strengthen your network in many ways. One of the major ways to use strong authentication is with two-factor authentication. The most common two-factor authentication method uses the *smart card*. Windows XP has built in smart-card support, but Windows Vista has taken this to a higher level. Smart cards look like bank ATM cards or hotel room key cards. To use a smart card, you place it into a smart card reader and put in a personal identification number (PIN).

Another form of strong authentication uses the certificate. Certificate authority is fully integrated with Active Directory. Active Directory Certificate Services (AD CS) allows administrators to configure services for issuing and managing public key certificates. Companies can benefit from AD CS security by combining a private key with an object (such as users and computers), devices (such as routers), or services. With AD CS you get the following benefits:

- Web enrollment
- Certificate authorities (CAs)
- Network Device Enrollment Service
- Online responder

Strong authentication helps strengthen your IDA. Remember that IDA tries to minimize the number of usernames and passwords that users have to remember. When using a form of strong authentication, users keep track of fewer credentials (usernames and passwords) while still keeping security a top priority.

 Another easy way to help with strong authentication is to enforce a strong password policy (minimum password lengths, unique characters, a combination numbers and letters, and mixed capitalization).

Federated Identities

As we discussed earlier, AD FS gives users the ability to do a single sign-on (SSO) and access applications on other networks without a secondary password. Organizations can set up trust relationships with other trusted organizations so users' digital identity and access rights can be accepted without a secondary password.

Federated Identities enables new models for cross-over SSO systems between organizations. SSO can be used for Windows and non-Windows environments.

The full implementation of Federation Identities Claims–based architecture is based on the Web Services Federation (WS-Federation). The Federation Identities models support groups, roles, and rules-based models.

This works well as part of the IDA architecture because users who can use SSO authentication require fewer password resets and make fewer errors while entering credentials.

Information Protection

Active Directory Rights Management Service (AD RMS) is what information protection is all about. Information protection is included with Microsoft Windows Server 2008 automatically once the AD RMS service is installed. This service allows administrators or users to determine what access (open, read, modify, etc.) they give to other users in an organization. This access can be used to secure email messages, internal websites, and documents.

Information protection supports Microsoft Office 2003 (Word, Excel, PowerPoint, and Outlook) and Microsoft Office 2007.

 If you are not using Microsoft Office 2003 (Word, Excel, PowerPoint, and Outlook) or Microsoft Office 2007, users can always use basic information protection in the form of encryption. (Encryption is only available if the file structure is NTFS).

Information protection prevents unauthorized users from opening files, email messages, and internal websites if they do not have appropriate access. It also allows email to be tracked.

This information protection and tracking will help organizations stay compliant with local, state, or federal regulations for data privacy requirements.

 Real World Scenario

Unauthorized Opening and Tracking of Emails

WXY Corporation is an organization that deals with many classified pieces of data and information. A manager in WXY Corporation sends out a classified email, but accidentally sends it to the wrong address. An individual at Company 123 gets the classified email. They open it, read the data, and see the text at the bottom of the email; it states, "This is classified email. If you received this email by error, please delete immediately." The problem is that the individual at Company 123 has already read the email.

Now if WXY Corporation was using information protection along with Outlook, the unauthorized individual would not have had the rights to even open the email. Second, the sender would have had the ability to see where the email was sent, who opened it, and to where it was forwarded.

Some companies have designed information protection solutions to support PDF, Blackberry, and CAD formats.

Identity Lifecycle Management

The goal of Identity Lifecycle Management (ILM) version 2 (ILM 2007 is the previous version) is to take some of the basic administration work (resetting passwords, managing groups and distribution lists, managing resource access, and policy creation) out of the hands of administrators and put it into the hands of users.

 Helpdesk support technicians reportedly spend an average of one-third of their workdays resetting passwords.

Now I understand that many of you felt a burning in the pit of your stomach when I stated that the goal was to allow users to do administrator's tasks. For most of us, this just seems like an impossible goal. But it's not.

ILM allows you to set up policies that allow users to do specific tasks. Let's say a user goes to log into their network but they forget their password. Instead of calling IT or helpdesk, they can check a box labeled "Forgot Password." A portal opens and the user is asked several security questions. If the answers are correct, the user can reset their password.

Think about a policy that allows managers to keep track of their own groups and distribution lists. Let's say a new sales person is hired in your company. The sales manager can add that individual to the sales group and the sales distribution list. The new sales person will now have access to all the resources every other sales person has.

You may be thinking, "how does this help the IT department?" Well, first it helps IT save money. If administrators and IT professionals did not have to spend unproductive time doing some of these basic tasks, they could focus on important tasks.

Let's say we have an administrator who makes $70,000 a year. For a 40-hour workweek, that's about $35 an hour. Let's say that administrator spends 10 to 15 hours a week on group management and resetting passwords. That's a lot of money to pay someone to do a task that a basic user can now accomplish.

If users and managers could do some of the small day-to-day tasks that take up so much of our time, that would free us up to do some of the more important tasks we need to accomplish:

- System architecture
- System deployments
- System administration and auditing
- Creating security policies

Another advantage of ILM is that over 20 *connectors* are included with the installation. Connectors are software add-ons that allow different applications and servers to communicate with each other. Many other add-on connectors are also available and will allow you to connect a wide range of systems and applications quickly and easily.

Summary

In this chapter, we covered Active Directory fundamentals. We gave you a high-level overview of many concepts related to Active Directory and how it is logically laid out. We covered the benefits of deploying Active Directory, including its hierarchical organization, extensible schema, centralized data storage, replication, ease of administration, network security, client configuration management, scalability and performance, and its searching functionality.

You also learned about how the Active Directory compares to Windows NT's domain model. As you might recall, Windows NT 4 uses a flat domain model, whereas Active Directory is robust, hierarchical, and scaleable and can grow far beyond NT 4's limitations.

We went on to cover the logical components of Active Directory, such as forests, domains, trees, and objects, and how you can create multiple Active Directory domains and why you might do so. (For example, you can keep two companies' internal system models separate if you have a merger and acquisition). We also covered the importance of how you name Active Directory objects and how domain naming affects the planning of Active Directory.

You then learned about the Windows Server 2008 server roles that are integrated with Active Directory. We covered the five main Windows Server 2008 Active Directory server roles (Active Directory Certificate Services, Active Directory Domain Services, Active Directory Federation Services, Active Directory Lightweight Directory Services, and Active Directory Rights Management Services).

Finally, we covered identity and access (IDA) solutions and how IDA can help an organization's users stay safe and secure while entering their credentials.

In the next chapter, we will cover the Domain Name System (DNS).

Exam Essentials

Understand the problems that Active Directory is designed to solve.   The creation of a single, centralized directory service can make network operations and management much simpler. Active Directory solves many shortcomings in Windows NT's domain model.

Understand Active Directory design goals.   Active Directory should be structured to mirror an organization's logical structure. Understand the factors that you should take into account, including business units, geographic structure, and future business requirements.

Understand Windows Server 2008 server roles.   Understand what the five Active Directory Windows Server 2008 server roles—AD CS, AD DS, AD FS, AD LDS, and AD RMS—do for an organization and its users.

Understand identity and access (IDA) solutions.   Understand how IDA can help organizations solve the problems associated with multiple usernames and passwords. Understand how the Active Directory Windows Server 2008 server roles work with and affect IDA.

Review Questions

1. Which of the following is not a feature of Active Directory?

   A. The use of LDAP for transferring information

   B. Reliance on DNS for name resolution

   C. A flat domain namespace

   D. The ability to extend the schema

2. Domains provide which of the following functions?

   A. Creating security boundaries to protect resources and ease of administration

   B. Easing the administration of users, groups, computers, and other objects

   C. Providing a central database of network objects

   D. All of the above

3. You are the administrator for a large organization with multiple remote sites. Your supervisor would like to have remote sites log in locally to their own site but he is nervous about security. What type of server can you implement to ease their concerns?

   A. Domain controller

   B. Global Catalog

   C. Read-only domain controller

   D. Universal Group Membership Caching Server

4. Which of the following objects is used to create the logical structure within Active Directory domains?

   A. Users

   B. Sites

   C. Organizational units (OUs)

   D. Trees

5. Which of the following is *false* regarding the naming of Active Directory objects?

   A. Active Directory relies on DNS for name resolution.

   B. Two objects can have the same relative distinguished name.

   C. Two objects can have the same distinguished name.

   D. All objects within a domain are based on the name of the domain.

6. Which of the following are *true* regarding Active Directory trust relationships?

   A. Trusts are transitive.

   B. By default, trusts are two-way relationships.

   C. Trusts are used to allow the authentication of users between domains.

   D. All of the above.

7. Which of the following protocols is used to query Active Directory information?

    A. LDAP

    B. NetBEUI

    C. NetBIOS

    D. IPX/SPX

8. You are the administrator for a large organization. Your organization currently has a Windows Server 2003 domain. Your company has set up a domain-based password policy but the organization is unhappy with the requirement to have a single policy for all users. Your company is considering upgrading to Windows Server 2008. What feature will solve the problem of only one policy for all domain users?

    A. Microsoft Windows Server 2008 multi-password policy

    B. Fine-grained password policy

    C. Certificate server policy

    D. None of the above

9. What Windows Server 2008 server role allows a user to have a single sign-on (SSO) to access multiple applications?

    A. Active Directory Domain Services

    B. Active Directory Federation Services

    C. Active Directory Lightweight Directory Services

    D. Active Directory Rights Management Services

10. What are some of the advantages of using Windows Server 2008 Active Directory Certificate Services?

    A. Web enrollment

    B. Network Device Enrollment Service

    C. Online Responder

    D. All of the above

11. What Windows Server 2008 server role allows a user to secure an email while using Microsoft Office 2007 Outlook?

    A. Active Directory Domain Services

    B. Active Directory Federation Services

    C. Active Directory Rights Management Services

    D. Active Directory Lightweight Directory Services

12. Identity and access (IDA) has five distinct categories. What are they?

    A. Directory services, strong authentication, Federated Identities, information protection, and Identity Lifecycle Management

    B. Directory services, strong certificates, Federated Identities, data protection, and LDAP

    C. LDAP, strong authentication, Federated Identities, information protection, and Identity Lifecycle Management

    D. Directory services, basic authentication, Federated Identities, data protection, and Identity Lifecycle Management

13. You are the administrator for your company. Another administrator has changed a user's group settings. What is the easiest way to get the original setting back for the user?

    A. Restore tapes.

    B. Perform auditing.

    C. Use a recovery disk.

    D. Enter safe mode and then restore from tape.

14. Which of the following features of Active Directory allows information between domain controllers to remain synchronized?

    A. Replication

    B. The Global Catalog

    C. The schema

    D. None of the above

15. Jane is a system administrator for a large, multidomain, geographically distributed network environment. The network consists of a large, central office and many smaller remote offices located throughout the world. Recently, Jane has received complaints about the performance of Active Directory–related operations from remote offices. Users complain that it takes a long time to perform searches for network resources (such as shared folders and printers). Jane wants to improve the performance of these operations. Which of the following components of Active Directory should she implement at remote sites to improve the performance of searches conducted for objects in *all* domains?

    A. Data store

    B. Global Catalog

    C. Schema

    D. None of the above

16. What is the name of the server that is a repository of Active Directory topology and schema information for Active Directory?

    A. Domain Partition

    B. Schema Master

    C. Global Catalog

    D. None of the above

17. You need to install the Active Directory Federation Services. What application do you use to do the install?

   A. Server Set-Up

   B. Role Manager

   C. Server Manager

   D. Add/Remove Programs—Services

18. What term is used to refer to the actual structure that contains the information stored within Active Directory?

   A. Schema

   B. Data store

   C. Global Catalog

   D. NTDS Storage group

19. You are the administrator for your company's domain. You need to subdivide groups in your organization within Active Directory. If you wanted to separate Sales from Marketing, for example, what could you do to create a system of organizing this subdivision and any others that you need to divide?

   A. Create OUs.

   B. Use Users and Groups.

   C. Create a Sites and Services subnet grouping.

   D. Build a container in LM Manager.

20. You are the network administrator for a 200-node network. You are currently looking at creating software packages to roll out to your network users. When the users log in, they will automatically install needed updates. You need to roll out a specific set of updates to 30 of those nodes. What could you create so that you can separate those 30 from the 200 and roll out updates only to that group?

   A. A policy that deploys only to those 30 members

   B. A group assignment through Administrative Tools

   C. An organizational unit (OU) for those 30 users

   D. None of the above

Answers to Review Questions

1. C. Active Directory uses a hierarchical namespace for managing objects.

2. D. All of these options are features of domains and are reasons for their usefulness.

3. C. Windows Server 2008 has a new type of domain controller called a read-only domain controller (RODC). This gives an organization the ability to install a domain controller in an area or location (on or offsite) where security is a concern.

4. C. OUs are used for creating a hierarchical structure within a domain. Users are objects within the directory, sites are used for physical planning, and trees are relationships between domains.

5. C. The distinguished name of each object in Active Directory must be unique, but the relative distinguished names may be the same. For example, we might have a User object named Jane Doe in two different containers.

6. D. Trusts are designed for facilitating the sharing of information and have all of these features.

7. A. LDAP is the Internet Engineering Task Force (IETF) standard protocol for accessing information from directory services. It is also the standard used by Active Directory.

8. B. Fine-grained password policies allow an organization to have different password and account lockout policies for different sets of users in the same domain.

9. B. Active Directory Federation Services gives users the ability to do a SSO and access applications on other networks without a secondary password.

10. D. Web enrollment, certification authorities (CAs), the Network Device Enrollment Service, and the Online Responder are four advantages of Active Directory Certificate Services.

11. C. Active Directory Rights Management Services (AD RMS) is included with Microsoft Windows Server 2008. This service allows administrators or users to determine what access (open, read, modify, etc.) they give to other users in an organization. This access can be used to secure email messages, internal websites, and documents. Organizations can use AD RMS for confidential or critical information.

12. A. Directory services, strong authentication, Federated Identities, information protection, and Identity Lifecycle Management are the five categorizes for IDA.

13. B. With the Microsoft Windows Server 2008 auditing feature, you have the ability to view the new and the old values of the object and its attributes. After viewing the old values, you can restore them.

14. A. Replication ensures that information remains synchronized between domain controllers

15. B. The Global Catalog contains information about multiple domains and additional Global Catalog servers can greatly increase the performance of operations such as searches for shared folders and printers. The other options are features of Active Directory, but they are not designed for fast searching across multiple domains.

16. C. The Global Catalog is a repository of the Active Directory topology and schema information. The Global Catalog contains information about multiple domains. Adding more Global Catalog servers can greatly increase the performance of operations such as searches for shared folders and printers. The other options are features of Active Directory, but they are not designed for fast searching across multiple domains.

17. C. Server Manager is a Microsoft Management Console (MMC) snap-in that allows an administrator to view information about server configuration, status of roles that are installed, and links for adding and removing features and roles.

18. B. The term *data store* is used to refer to the actual structure that contains the information stored within Active Directory.

19. A. An OU is an organizational unit and is a container object that is an Active Directory administrative partition. OUs can contain users, groups, resources, and other OUs. You can use OUs to help build organization into your directory so that you can roll out software updates to groupings of users and computers. OUs enable the delegation of administration to very distinct subtrees of the directory. OUs can be departments or groups. They are used to structure and manage your network in a way that reflects a company's business organization.

20. C. An OU is a container object that is used for administering an Active Directory database. OUs contain Active Directory objects. You can use OUs to help build organization into your directory so that you can roll out software updates to groupings of users computers. OUs enable the delegation of administration to very distinct subtrees of the directory. OUs can be departments or groups. They are used to structure and manage your network in a way that reflects a company's business organization.

Chapter

2

Domain Name System (DNS)

MICROSOFT EXAM OBJECTIVES COVERED IN THIS CHAPTER:

✓ **Configuring Domain Name System (DNS) for Active Directory**

- Configure zones. May include but is not limited to: Dynamic DNS (DDNS), Non-dynamic DNS (NDDNS), and Secure Dynamic DNS (SDDNS); Time to Live (TTL); GlobalNames; Primary, Secondary, Active Directory Integrated, Stub; SOA; zone scavenging; forward lookup; reverse lookup

- Configure DNS server settings. May include but is not limited to: forwarding; root hints; configure zone delegation; round robin; disable recursion; debug logging; server scavenging

- Configure zone transfers and replication. May include but is not limited to: configure replication scope (forestDNSzone; domainDNSzone); incremental zone transfers; DNS Notify; secure zone transfers; configure name servers; application directory partitions

The Domain Name System (DNS) is one of the most important topics that you need to know about if you are planning on taking any of the Microsoft administration exams (70-640, 70-642, etc.). It's also imperative that you understand DNS in order to work with Active Directory, because Active Directory requires DNS to function properly.

DNS is a requirement of Active Directory and many important system functions (including Kerberos authentication and finding domain controllers) are handled through DNS lookups. Windows 2000, XP, and Vista clients use DNS for name resolution and to find Kerberos key distribution centers (KDCs), Global Catalog servers, and other services that may be registered in DNS.

By the time you finish this chapter, you will have a deeper understanding of how DNS works and how to set up, configure, manage, and troubleshoot DNS in Microsoft Windows Server 2008.

Introducing DNS

The Domain Name System (DNS) is a service designed to resolve Internet Protocol (IP) addresses to hostnames. One of the inherent complexities of working in networked environments is working with multiple protocols and network addresses. Thanks largely to the tremendous rise in popularity of the Internet, however, most environments have transitioned to use TCP/IP (Transmission Control Protocol/Internet Protocol) as their primary networking protocol. Microsoft is no exception when it comes to supporting TCP/IP in its workstation and server products. All current versions of Microsoft's operating systems support TCP/IP, as do most other modern operating systems. Since the introduction of Windows NT 4, TCP/IP has been the default protocol installed with Microsoft operating systems.

TCP/IP is actually a collection of different technologies (protocols and services) that allow computers to function together on a single, large, heterogeneous network. Some of the major advantages of this protocol include widespread support for hardware, software, and network devices; reliance on a system of standards; and scalability. TCP handles tasks such as sequenced acknowledgments. IP involves many issues such as logical subnet assignment and routing.

It is beyond the scope of this chapter to fully describe the intricacies of working with TCP/IP; full details are covered in stand-alone volumes.

The Form of an IP Address

To understand DNS, you must first understand how TCP/IP addresses are formed. Since DNS is strictly on a network to support TCP/IP, understanding the basics of TCP/IP is very important.

Microsoft exams are going to cover TCP/IP in depth. For more information on IPv4 and IPv6, read *MCTS Windows Server 2008 Network Infrastructure Configuration (Exam 70-642, with CD)* by Will Panek, Tylor Wentworth, and James Chellis (Sybex, 2008).

An IP address is a logical number that uniquely identifies a computer on a TCP/IP network. TCP/IP allows a computer packet to reach the correct host. Windows Server 2008 works with two versions of TCP/IP: IPv4 and IPv6. An IPv4 address takes the form of four octets (eight binary bits), each of which is represented by a decimal number between 0 and 255. The four numbers are separated by decimal points. For example, all of the following are valid IP addresses:

- 128.45.23.17
- 230.212.43.100
- 10.1.1.1

The dotted decimal notation was created to make it easier for users to deal with IP addresses, but this idea did not go far enough. As a result, another abstraction layer that used names to represent the dotted decimal notation was developed—the domain name. For example, the IP address 11000000 10101000 00000001 00010101 maps to `192.168.1.21`, which in turn might map to `server1.company.org`—how the computer's address is usually presented to the user or application.

As stated above, IPv4 addresses are made up of octets or the decimal (base 10) representation of 8 bits. It takes four octets to add up to the 32 bits required. IPv6 expands the address space to 128 bits. The address is usually represented in hexadecimal notation, like this:

`2001:0DB8:0000:0000:1234:0000:A9FE:133E`

You can tell the implementation of DNS will make life a lot easier for everyone, even those of us who like to use alphanumeric values (for example, some of us enjoy pinging the address in lieu of the name). Fortunately, DNS already has the ability to handle IPv6 address using an AAAA record. An A record in IPv4's addressing space is 32 bits, and an AAAA record (4 A's) in IPv6's is 128 bits.

Nowadays, most computer users are quite familiar with navigating to DNS-based resources, such as www.microsoft.com. In order to resolve these "friendly" names to TCP/IP addresses that the network stack can use, you must have some method for mapping them. Originally, ASCII flat files (often called HOSTS files, as seen in Figure 2.1) were used for this purpose.

In some cases, they are still used today in very small networks, and they can be used to help troubleshoot name resolution problems.

As the number of machines and network devices grew, it became unwieldy for administrators to manage all of the manual updates required to enter new mappings to a master HOSTS file and distribute it. Clearly, a better system was needed.

FIGURE 2.1   Sample HOSTS file

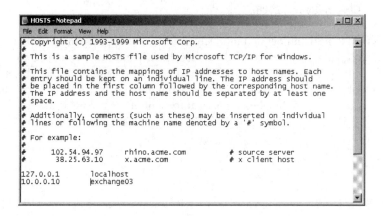

As you can see from the sample HOSTS file in Figure 2.1, you can conduct a quick test of the email server's name resolution.

1. Open the HOSTS file <C:\Windows\Systems32\drivers\etc>.

2. Add the IP address–to–hostname mapping.

3. Try to ping the server using the hostname to verify that that you can reach it using an easy-to-remember name.

Following these steps should drive home the concept of DNS for you because you can see it working to make your life easier. Now you don't have to remember 10.0.0.10; you only need to remember exchange03.

You can also see how this method can become unwieldy if you have many hosts that want to use easy-to-remember names instead of IP addresses to locate resources on your network.

When dealing with large networks, both users and network administrators must be able to locate the resources they require with minimal searching. Users don't care about the actual physical or logical network address of the machine; they just want to be able to connect to it using a simple name that they can remember. From a network administrator's standpoint, however, each machine must have its own logical address that makes it part of the network on which it resides. Therefore, some scalable and easy-to-manage method for resolving a machine's logical name to an IP address and then to a domain name is required. DNS was created for this purpose.

DNS is a hierarchically distributed database. In other words, its layers are arranged in a definite order, and its data is distributed across a wide range of machines, each of which can exert control over a portion of the database. DNS is a standard set of protocols that defines the following:

- A mechanism for querying and updating address information in the database

- A mechanism for replicating the information in the database among servers

- A schema of the database

NOTE   DNS is defined by a number of RFCsCommon Knowledge, though primarily by RFC 1034 and RFC 1035.

DNS was originally developed in the early days of the Internet when the Internet (called ARPAnet at the time) was a small network created by the Department of Defense for research purposes. Before DNS, computer names, or hostnames, were manually entered into a HOSTS file located on a centrally administered server. Each site that needed to resolve hostnames outside of its organization had to download this file. As the number of computers on the Internet grew, so did the size of this HOSTS file, as well as the problems with its management. The need for a new system that would offer features such as scalability, decentralized administration, and support for various data types became more and more obvious. DNS, introduced in 1984, became this new system.

With DNS, the hostnames reside in a database that can be distributed among multiple servers, decreasing the load on any one server and providing the ability to administer this naming system on a per-partition basis. DNS supports hierarchical names and allows registration of various data types in addition to the hostname–to–IP address mapping used in HOSTS files. Database performance is ensured through its distributed nature as well as through caching.

The DNS distributed database establishes an inverted logical tree structure called the domain namespace. Each node, or domain, in that space has a unique name. At the top of the tree is the root. This may not sound quite right, which is why the DNS hierarchical model is described as being an inverted tree, with the root at the top. The root is represented by the null set " ". When written, the root node is represented by a single dot ".".

Each node in the DNS can branch out to any number of nodes below it. For example, below the root node are a number of other nodes, commonly referred to as top-level domains (TLDs).

These are the familiar com, net, org, gov, edu, and other such names. Table 2.1 lists some of these TLDs.

TABLE 2.1   Common Top-Level DNS Domains

Common Top-Level Domain Names	Type of Organization
com	Commercial (for example, stellacon.com for Stellacon Training Corporation
edu	Educational (for example, gatech.edu for the Georgia Institute of Technology)
gov	Government (for example, whitehouse.gov for the White House in Washington, D.C.)
int	International organizations (for example, nato.int for NATO). This top-level domain is fairly rare.
mil	Military organizations (for example, usmc.mil for the Marine Corps). There is a separate set of root name servers for this domain.
net	Networking organizations and Internet providers (for example, hiwaay.net for HiWAAY Information Systems). Many commercial organizations have registered names under this domain, too.
org	Noncommercial organizations (for example, fidonet.org for FidoNet)
au	Australia
uk	United Kingdom
ca	Canada
us	United States
jp	Japan

Each of these nodes then branches out into another set of domains and they combine to form what we refer to as domain names, such as microsoft.com. A domain name identifies the domain's position in the logical DNS hierarchy in relation to its parent domain by separating each branch of the tree with a period. Figure 2.2 shows a few of the top-level domains, where the Microsoft domain fits, and a host called Tigger within the `microsoft.com` domain. If someone wanted to contact that host, they would use the fully qualified domain name (FQDN), `tigger.microsoft.com`.

An FQDN includes the trailing dot (`.`) to indicate the root node, but it's commonly left off in practice.

FIGURE 2.2   The DNS hierarchy

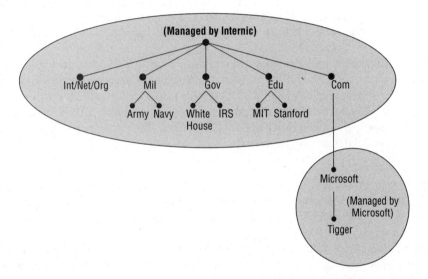

As previously stated, one of the strengths of DNS is the ability to delegate control over portions of the DNS namespace to multiple organizations. For example, the Internet Corporation for Assigned Names and Numbers (ICANN) assigns the control over the TLDs to one or more organizations. Those organizations in turn delegate portions of the DNS namespace to other organizations. For example, when we register a domain name—let's call it `example.com`—we control the DNS for the portion of the DNS namespace within `example.com`. The registrar controlling the `.com` TLD has delegated control over the `example.com` node in the DNS tree. No other node can be named `example` directly below the `.com` within the DNS database.

Within the portion of the domain namespace that we control (`example.com`), we could create host records and other records (more on these later). We could also further subdivide `example.com` and delegate control over those divisions to other organizations or departments. These divisions are called subdomains. For example, we might create subdomains named for the cities in which the company has branch offices and then delegate control over those

subdomains to the branch offices. The subdomains might be named
`losangeles.example.com`, `chicago.example.com`, `portsmouth.example.com`, and so on.

Each domain (or delegated subdomain) is associated with DNS *name servers*. In other words, for every node in the DNS, one or more servers can give an authoritative answer to queries about that domain. At the root of the domain namespace are the root servers. More on these later.

> Domain names and hostnames must contain only characters *a* to *z*, *A* to *Z*, 0 to 9, and - (hyphen). Other common and useful characters, like the & (ampersand), / (slash), . (period), and _ (underscore) characters, are not allowed. This is in conflict with NetBIOS's naming restrictions. However, you'll find that Windows Server 2008 is smart enough to take a NetBIOS name, like `Server_1`, and turn it into a legal DNS name, like `server1.example.com`.

DNS servers work together to resolve hierarchical names. If a server already has information about a name, it simply fulfills the query for the client. Otherwise, it queries other DNS servers for the appropriate information. The system works well because it distributes the authority over separate parts of the DNS structure to specific servers. A DNS zone is a portion of the DNS namespace over which a specific DNS server has authority (DNS zone types are discussed in detail later in this chapter).

> There is an important distinction to make between DNS zones and Active Directory (AD) domains. Although both use hierarchical names and require name resolution, DNS zones do not map directly to AD domains.

Within a given DNS zone, resource records (RRs) contain the hosts and other database information that make up the data for the zone. For example, an RR might contain the host entry for `www.example.com` pointing it to the IP address 192.168.1.10.

Understanding Servers, Clients, and Resolvers

You will need to know a few terms and concepts in order to manage a DNS server. Understanding these terms will make it easier to understand how the Windows Server 2008 DNS server works:

DNS server   Any computer providing domain name services is a *DNS name server*. No matter where the server resides in the DNS namespace, its still a DNS name server. For example, 13 root name servers at the top of the DNS tree are responsible for delegating the TLDs. The root servers provide referrals to name servers for the TLDs, which in turn provide referrals to an authoritative name server for a given domain.

The Berkeley Internet Name Domain (BIND) was originally the only software for running the root servers on the Internet. However, a few years ago the organizations responsible for the root servers undertook an effort to diversify the software running on these important machines. Today, root servers run multiple kinds of name server software. BIND is still primary, however, and it is the most popular for Internet providers as well. None of the root servers run Windows DNS.

Any DNS server implementation supporting Service Location Resource Records (see RFC 2782) and Dynamic Updates (RFC 2136) is sufficient to provide the name service for any operating system running Windows 2000 software and above.

DNS client A *DNS client* is any machine that issues queries to a DNS server. The client hostname may or may not be registered in a DNS database. Clients issue DNS requests through processes called resolvers. You'll sometimes see the terms client and resolver used synonymously.

Resolver *Resolvers* are software processes, sometimes implemented in software libraries, that handle the actual process of finding the answers to queries for DNS data. The resolver is also built into many larger pieces of software so that external libraries don't have to be called in order to make and process DNS queries. Resolvers can be what you'd consider client computers or other DNS servers attempting to resolve an answer on behalf of a client.

Query A query is a request for information sent to a DNS server. Three types of queries can be made to a DNS server: recursive, inverse, and iterative. We'll discuss their differences in the following section.

Understanding the DNS Process

To help you understand the DNS process, we will start by covering the differences between Dynamic DNS and Non-Dynamic DNS. During this discussion you will learn how Dynamic DNS populates the DNS database. You'll also see how to implement security for Dynamic DNS. We will then talk about the workings of different types of DNS queries. Finally we will discuss caching and time to live (TTL). You'll learn how to determine the best setting for your organization.

Dynamic DNS and Non-Dynamic DNS

To understand Dynamic DNS and Non-Dynamic DNS, you must go back in time (here is where the TV screen always used to get wavy). Many years ago when we all worked on NT 3.51 and NT 4.0, most networks used *Windows Internet Name Service (WINS)* to do their TCP/IP name resolution. Windows versions 95/98 and NT 4.0 Professional were all built on the idea of using WINS. This worked out well for administrators because WINS was *dynamic* (which meant that, once it was installed, it automatically built its own database). Back then, there was no such thing as Dynamic DNS; administrators had to manually enter DNS records into the server. This is important to know even today. If you have clients still running any of these older operating systems (95/98 or NT 4) these clients cannot use Dynamic DNS.

Now let's move forward in time to the release of Windows Server 2000. Microsoft announced that DNS was going to be the name resolution method of choice. Many administrators (me included) did not look forward to the switch. Because there was no such thing as Dynamic DNS, most administrators had nightmares about manually entering records. But luckily for us, when Microsoft released Windows Server 2000, DNS had the ability to be dynamic.

Now, when you're setting up Windows Server 2008 DNS, you can choose what type of dynamic update you would like to use, if any. Let's talk about why you would want to choose one over the other.

The *Dynamic DNS (DDNS) standard*, described in RFC 2136, allows DNS clients to update information in the DNS database files. For example, a Windows Server 2008 DHCP server can automatically tell a DDNS server which IP addresses it has assigned to what machines. Windows 2000, 2003, 2008, XP Pro, and Vista DHCP clients can do this, too—but for security reasons it's better to let the DHCP server do it. The result: IP addresses and DNS records stay in sync so that you can use DNS and DHCP together seamlessly.

Because DDNS is a proposed Internet standard, you can even use Windows Server 2008's DDNS-aware parts with Unix/Linux (*nix)-based DNS servers.

Non-Dynamic DNS (NDDNS) does not automatically populate the DNS database. The client systems do not have the ability to update to DNS.

If you decide to use Non-Dynamic DNS, an administrator will need to populate the DNS database manually. Non-Dynamic DNS is a reasonable choice if your organization is small to mid-sized and you do not want extra network traffic (clients updating to the DNS server), or if you need to manually enter the computer due to strict security measures.

Dynamic DNS has the ability to be secure, and the chances are slim that a rogue system (a computer that does not belong in your DNS database) could update to a secure DNS server. Nevertheless, some organizations have to follow stricter security measures and are not allowed to have dynamic updates.

The major downside to manually entering records into DNS occurs when the organization is using the *Dynamic Host Configuration Protocol (DHCP)*. When using DHCP, it is possible for users to end up with different TCP/IP addresses every day. This means that an administrator has to manually update DNS daily to keep it accurate.

If you decide to allow Dynamic DNS, you need to decide how you want to set it up. When setting up dynamic updates on your DNS server, you have three choices (see Figure 2.3):

- None—This means your DNS server is Non-Dynamic.

- Nonsecure and secure—This means that any machine (even if it does not have a domain account) can register with DNS. Using this setting could allow rogue systems to enter records into your DNS server.

- Secure only—This means that only machines with accounts in Active Directory can register with DNS. Before DNS registers any account in its database, it checks Active Directory to make sure that account is an authorized domain computer.

FIGURE 2.3   Setting the Dynamic Updates option

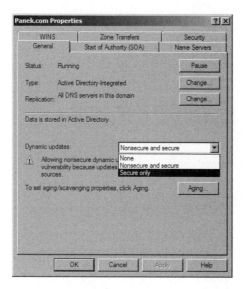

How Dynamic DNS Populates the DNS Database

On a Microsoft Windows Server 2008 network, TCP/IP is the protocol used for network communications. Users have two ways to receive a TCP/IP number:

- Static (administrators manually enter the TCP/IP information)
- Dynamic (using DHCP)

When an administrator sets up TCP/IP, DNS can also be configured.

Once a client gets the address of the DNS server, if that client is allowed to update with DNS, the client sends a registration to DNS or requests DHCP to send the registration. DNS then does one of two things, depending on which Dynamic Updates option is specified:

- Check with Active Directory to see if that computer has an account (Secure Only updates) and if it does, enter the record into the database
- Enter the record into its database (Nonsecure and Secure updates)

What if you have clients (95/98 and NT 4) that cannot update DNS? Well there is a solution—DHCP. In the DNS tab of the IPv4 Properties window, check the option labeled "Dynamically update DNS A and PTR records for DHCP clients that do not request updates (for example, clients running Windows NT 4.0)" (See Figure 2.4).

FIGURE 2.4 DHCP settings for DNS

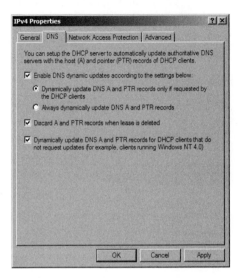

DHCP, along with Dynamic DNS clients, allows an organization to dynamically update its DNS database without the time and effort of having an administrator manually enter DNS records.

DNS Queries

As stated earlier, a client can make three types of queries to a DNS server: recursive, inverse, and iterative. Remember that the client of a DNS server can be a resolver (what you'd normally call a client) or another DNS server.

Iterative Queries

Iterative queries are the easiest to understand: A client asks the DNS server for an answer, and the server returns the best answer. This information likely comes from the server's cache. The server never sends out an additional query in response to an iterative query. If the server doesn't know the answer, it may direct the client to another server through a referral.

Recursive Queries

In a recursive query, the client sends a query to a name server, asking it to respond either with the requested answer or with an error message. The error states one of two things:

- The server can't come up with the right answer.
- The domain name doesn't exist.

In a recursive query, the name server isn't allowed to just refer the client to some other name server.

Most resolvers use recursive queries. In addition, if your DNS server uses a forwarder, the requests sent by your server to the forwarder will be recursive queries.

Figure 2.5 shows an example of both recursive and iterative queries. In this example, a client within the Microsoft Corporation is querying its DNS server for the IP address for www.whitehouse.gov. Here's what happens to resolve the request:

FIGURE 2.5   A sample DNS query

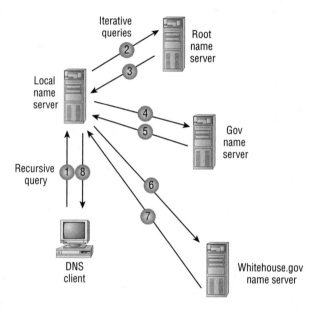

1. The resolver sends a recursive DNS query to its local DNS server asking for the IP address of www.whitehouse.gov.

    The local name server is responsible for resolving the name and cannot refer the resolver to another name server.

2. The local name server checks its zones and finds no zones corresponding to the requested domain name.

3. The root name server has authority for the root domain and will reply with the IP address of a name server for the .gov top-level domain.

4. The local name server sends an iterative query for www.whitehouse.gov to the Gov name server.

5. The Gov name server replies with the IP address of the name server servicing the whitehouse.gov domain.

6. The local name server sends an iterative query for www.whitehouse.gov to the whitehouse.gov name server.

7. The whitehouse.gov name server replies with the IP address corresponding to www.whitehouse.gov.

8. The local name server sends the IP address of www.whitehouse.gov back to the original resolver.

Inverse Queries

Inverse queries use pointer (PTR) records. Instead of supplying a name and then asking for an IP address, the client first provides the IP address and then asks for the name. Because there's no direct correlation in the DNS namespace between a domain name and its associated IP address, this search would be fruitless without the use of the in-addr.arpa domain. Nodes in the in-addr.arpa domain are named after the numbers in the dotted-octet representation of IP addresses. But because IP addresses get more specific from left to right and domain names get less specific from left to right, the order of IP address octets must be reversed when building the in-addr.arpa tree. With this arrangement, administration of the lower limbs of the DNS in-addr.arpa tree can be given to companies as they are assigned their Class A, B, or C subnet address or delegated even further down thanks to Variable Length Subnet Masking (VSLM).

Once the domain tree is built into the DNS database, a special PTR record is added to associate the IP addresses to the corresponding hostnames. In other words, to find a hostname for the IP address 206.131.234.1, the resolver would query the DNS server for a PTR record for 1.234.131.206.in-addr.arpa. If this IP address is outside the local domain, the DNS server would start at the root and sequentially resolve the domain nodes until arriving at 234.131.206.in-addr.arpa, which would contain the PTR record for the desired host.

Caching and Time to Live

When a name server is processing a recursive query, it may be required to send out several queries to find the definitive answer. Name servers, acting as resolvers, are allowed to cache all the received information during this process; each record contains information called time to live (TTL). The TTL specifies how long the record will be held in the local cache until it must be resolved again. If a query comes in that can be satisfied by this cached data, the TTL that's returned with it equals the current amount of time left before the data is flushed.

There is also a negative cache TTL. The negative cache TTL is used when an authoritative server responds to a query indicating that the record queried doesn't exist and indicates the amount of time that this negative answer may be held. Negative caching is quite helpful in preventing repeated queries for names that don't exist.

The administrator for the DNS zone sets TTL values for the entire zone. The value can be the same across the zone or the administrator can set a separate TTL for each RR within the zone. Client resolvers also have data caches and honor the TTL value so that they know when to flush.

⊕ **Real World Scenario**

Choosing Appropriate TTL Values

For zones that you administer, you can choose the TTL values for the entire zone, for negative caching, and for individual records. Choosing an appropriate TTL depends on a number of factors, including the following:

- Amount of change you anticipate for the records within the zone

- Amount of time that you can withstand an outage that might require changing an IP address

- Amount of traffic that you feel the DNS server can handle

Resolvers query the name server every time the TTL expires for a given record. A low TTL, say, 60 seconds, can burden the name server, especially for popular DNS records. (DNS queries aren't particularly intensive for a server to handle, but they can add up quickly if you mistakenly use 60 seconds instead of 600 seconds for the TTL on a popular record.) Set a low TTL only when you need to quickly respond to a changing environment.

A high TTL, say, 604,800 seconds (that's 1 week), means that if you need to make a change to the DNS record, clients might not see the change for up to a week. This consideration is especially important when making changes to the network, and it's one that's all too frequently overlooked. We can't count the times we've worked with clients who have recently made a DNS change to a new IP for their email or website, only to ask why it's not working for some clients. The answer can be found in the TTL value. If the record is being cached, then the only thing that can solve their problem is time.

You should choose a TTL that's appropriate for your environment. Take the following factors into account:

- The amount of time that you can afford to be offline if you need to make a change to a DNS record that's being cached

- The amount of load that a low TTL will cause on the DNS server

In addition, you should plan well ahead of any major infrastructure changes and change the TTL to a lower value in order to lessen the effect of the downtime by reducing the amount of time that the record(s) can be cached.

Introducing DNS Database Zones

As we mentioned earlier in this chapter, a DNS zone is a portion of the DNS namespace over which a specific DNS server has authority. Within a given DNS zone there are resource records

(RRs) that define the hosts and other types of information that make up the database for the zone.

You can choose from several different zone types. Understanding the characteristics of each will help you choose which is right for your organization.

The DNS zones discussed in this book are all Microsoft Windows Server 2008 zones. Non-Windows (e.g., Unix) systems set up their DNS zones differently.

In the following sections, we will discuss the different zone types and their characteristics.

Understanding Primary Zones

When you're learning about zone types, things can get a bit confusing. But it's really not difficult to understand how they work and why you would want to choose one type of zone over the other.

Zones are databases that store records. By choosing one zone type over another, you are basically just choosing how the database works and how it will be stored on the server.

The *primary zone* is responsible for maintaining all of the records for the DNS zone. It contains the primary copy of the DNS database. All record updates occur on the primary zone. You will want to create and add primary zones whenever you create a new DNS domain.

There are two types of primary zone:

- Primary zone
- Primary zone with Active Directory Integration (Active Directory DNS)

From this point forward, we refer to a primary zone with Active Directory Integration as an Active Directory DNS. When we just use the term primary zone, Active Directory is not included.

To install DNS as a primary zone, first you must install DNS using the Server Manager MMC. Once DNS is installed and running, you create a new zone and specify it as a primary zone.

The process of installing DNS and its zones will be discussed later in this chapter. In addition, we've included step-by-step labs that walk you through how to install these components.

Primary zones have advantages and disadvantages. Knowing the characteristics of a primary zone will help you decide when you need the zone and when it fits into your organization.

Local Database

Primary DNS zones get stored locally in a file (with the suffix .dns) on the server. This allows you to store a primary zone on a domain controller or a member server. In addition, by loading

DNS onto a member server, you can help a small organization conserve resources. Such an organization may not have the resources to load DNS on an Active Directory domain controller.

Unfortunately the local database has many disadvantages:

Lack of fault tolerance   Think of a primary zone as a contact list on your cell phone or hand-held. All of the contacts in the list are the records in your database. The problem is that if you lose your phone or the phone breaks, you lose your contact list. Until your phone gets fixed or you swap out your phone card, the contacts are unavailable.

It works the same way with a primary zone. If the server goes down or you lose the hard drive, DNS records on that machine are unreachable. An administrator can install a secondary zone (explained later in this section) and that provides temporary fault tolerance. Unfortunately, if the primary zone is down for an extended period of time, the secondary server's information will no longer be valid.

Additional network traffic   Let's imagine that you are looking for a contact number for John Smith. John Smith is not listed in your cell phone directory, but he is listed in your partner's cell phone. You have to contact your partner to get the listing. You cannot directly access your partner's cell contacts.

When a resolver sends a request to DNS to get the TCP/IP address for Jsmith (in this case Jsmith is a computer name), and the DNS server does not have an answer, it does not have the ability to check the other server's database directly to get an answer. So it forwards the request to another DNS. This causes additional network traffic. When DNS servers are replicating zone databases with other DNS servers, this causes additional network traffic.

No security   Staying with the cell phone example, let's say you call your partner looking for John Smith's phone number. When your partner gives you the phone number over your wire-less phone, someone with a scanner can pick up your conversation. Unfortunately wireless telephone calls are not very secure.

Now a resolver asks a primary zone for the Jsmith TCP/IP address. If someone on the network has a *packet sniffer*, they can steal the information in the DNS packets being sent over the net-work. The packets are not secure unless you implement some form of secondary security. Also, the DNS server has the ability to be dynamic. A primary zone accepts all updates from DNS servers. You cannot set it to accept secure updates only.

Understanding Secondary Zones

In Windows Server 2008 DNS, you have the ability to use *secondary DNS zones*. Secondary zones are non-editable copies of the DNS database. You use them for *load balancing* (also referred to as load sharing)—a way of managing network overloads on a single server. A secondary zone gets its database from a primary zone.

A secondary zone contains a database with all the same information as the primary zone and can be used to resolve DNS requests. Secondary zones have the following advantages:

- A secondary zone provides fault tolerance, so if the primary zone server becomes unavail-able, name resolution can still occur using the secondary zone server.

It is a good general practice to ensure that each zone has at least one second-ary zone server to protect against failures.

- Secondary DNS servers can also increase network performance by offloading some of the traffic that would otherwise go to the primary server.

  Secondary servers are often placed within the parts of an organization that have high-speed network access. This prevents DNS queries from having to run across slow wide area network (WAN) connections. For example, if there are two remote offices within the `stellacon.com` organization, you may want to place a secondary DNS server in each remote office. This way, when clients require name resolution, they will contact the near-est server for this IP address information, thus preventing unnecessary WAN traffic.

Having too many secondary zone servers can actually cause an increase in network traffic due to replication (especially if DNS changes are fairly fre-quent). Therefore, you should always weigh the benefits and drawbacks and properly plan for secondary zone servers.

Understanding Active Directory Integrated DNS

In Windows Server 2000, Active Directory Integrated DNS was introduced to the world. This zone type was unique and was a separate choice during setup. In Windows Server 2003, this zone type became an add-on to a primary zone. In Windows Server 2008, it works the same way. After choosing to set up a primary zone, you check the box labeled "Store the zone in Active Directory" (See Figure 2.6).

FIGURE 2.6   Setting up an Active Directory Integrated Zone

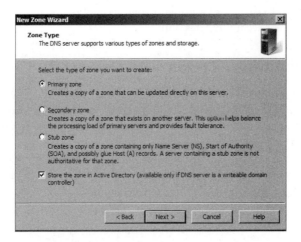

Microsoft covers Active Directory Integrated DNS on most of the DNS-related exams. Knowing the characteristics of this zone type will help you answer many exam questions. Remember, this is an Active Directory Exam (70-640), so you can bet that the Active Directory portion of DNS will be covered in depth.

Disadvantages of Active Directory Integrated DNS

The main disadvantage of Active Directory Integrated DNS is that it has to reside on a domain controller because the DNS database is stored in Active Directory As a result, you cannot load this zone type on a member server, and small organizations might not have the resources to set up a dedicated domain controller.

Advantages of Active Directory Integrated DNS

The advantages of using an Active Directory Integrated DNS zone well outweigh the disadvantage just discussed. The following are some of the major advantages to an Active Directory Integrated zone:

Full fault tolerance   Think of an Active Directory Integrated zone as a database on your server that stores contact information for all your clients. If you need to retrieve John Smith's phone number, as long as it was entered, you can look it up on the software.

If John Smith's phone number was stored only on your computer and your computer stopped working, no one could access John Smith's phone number. But since John Smith's phone number is stored in a database that everyone has access to, if your computer stops working, other users can still retrieve John Smith's phone number.

An Active Directory Integrated zone works the same way. Since the DNS database is stored in Active Directory, all Active Directory DNS servers can have access to the same data. If one server goes down or you lose a hard drive, all other Active Directory DNS servers can still retrieve DNS records .

No additional network traffic   As previously discussed, an Active Directory Integrated zone is stored in Active Directory. Since all records are now stored in Active Directory, when a resolver needs a TCP/IP address for Jsmith, any Active Directory DNS server can access Jsmith's address and respond to the resolver.

When you choose an Active Directory Integrated zone, DNS zone data can be replicated automatically to other DNS servers during the normal Active Directory replication process.

DNS security   An Active Directory Integrated zone has a few security advantages over a primary zone:

- An Active Directory Integrated zone can use secure dynamic updates.
- As explained earlier, the Dynamic DNS standard allows secure-only updates or dynamic updates, not both.

- If you choose secure updates, then only machines with accounts in Active Directory can register with DNS. Before DNS registers any account in its database, it checks Active Directory to make sure it is an authorized domain computer.

- An Active Directory Integrated zone stores and replicates its database through Active Directory replication. Because of this, the data gets encrypted as it is sent from one DNS server to another.

Background zone loading   *Background zone loading* (discussed in more detail later in this chapter) allows an Active Directory Integrated DNS zone to load in the background. As a result, a DNS server can service client requests while the zone is still loading into memory.

Understanding Stub Zones

Stub zones work a lot like secondary zones—the database is a non-editable copy of a primary zone. The difference is that the stub zone's database contains only the information necessary (three record types) to identify the authoritative DNS servers for a zone (see Figure 2.7). You should not use stub zones to replace secondary zones, nor should you use them for redundancy and load balancing.

FIGURE 2.7   DNS stub zone type

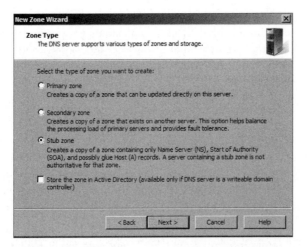

 Stub zone databases only contain three record types: name server (NS), start of authority (SOA), and glue host (A) records. Knowing about these records will help on the Microsoft Certification Exams. Microsoft asks many questions about stub zones on all DNS related exams.

Real World Scenario

When to Use Stub Zones

Stub zones become particularly useful in a couple of different scenarios.

Consider what happens when two large companies merge: example.com and example.net. In most cases, the DNS zone information from both companies must be available to every employee. You could set up a new zone on each side that acts as a secondary for the other side's primary zone, but administrators tend to be very protective of their DNS databases and they probably wouldn't agree to this plan.

A better solution is to add a stub zone to each side that points to the primary server on the other side. When a client in example.com (which you help administer) makes a request for a name in example.net, the stub zone on the example.com DNS server would send the client to the primary DNS server for example.net without actually resolving the name. At this point it would be up to example.net's primary server to resolve the name.

An added benefit is that even if the administrators over at example.net change their configuration, you won't have to do anything because the changes will automatically replicate to the stub zone, just as they would for a secondary server.

Stub zones can also be useful when you administer two domains across a slow connection.

Let's change the example above a bit and assume that you have full control over example.com and example.net, but they connect through a 56k line. In this case, you wouldn't necessarily mind using secondary zones because you personally administer the entire network, but it could get messy to replicate an entire zone file across that slow line. Instead, stub zones would refer clients to the appropriate primary server at the other site.

Zone Transfers and Replication

DNS is such an important part of the network that you should not just use a single DNS server. With a single DNS server you also have a single point of failure, and, in fact, many domain registrars encourage the use of more than two name servers for a domain. Secondary servers or multiple primary Active Directory Integrated servers play an integral role in providing DNS information for an entire domain.

As previously stated, secondary DNS servers receive their zone databases through zone transfers. When you configure a secondary server for the first time, you must specify the primary server that is authoritative for the zone and that will send the zone transfer. The primary server must also permit the secondary server to request the zone transfer.

Zone transfers occur in one of two ways: full zone transfers (AXFR) and incremental zone transfers (IXFR).

When a new secondary server is configured for the first time, it receives a full zone transfer from the primary DNS server. The full zone transfer contains all of the information in the DNS database. Some DNS implementations always receive full zone transfers.

After the secondary server receives its first full zone transfer, subsequent zone transfers are incremental. The primary name server compares its zone version number with that on the secondary server and sends only the changes that have been made in the interim. This significantly reduces network traffic generated by zone transfers.

Windows NT 4 does not support incremental zone transfers.

Zone transfers are typically initiated by the secondary server when the refresh interval time for the zone expires or when the secondary or stub server boots. Alternatively, you can configure notify lists on the primary server that send a message to the secondary or stub servers whenever any changes to the zone database occur.

When you consider your DNS strategy, you must carefully consider the layout of your network. If you have a single domain with offices in separate cities, you want to reduce the number of zone transfers across the potentially slow or expensive WAN links, although this is becoming less of a concern as bandwidth seems to multiply daily.

Active Directory Integrated zones do away with traditional zone transfers altogether. Instead, they replicate across Active Directory with all of the other AD information. This replication is secure since it uses the Active Directory Security.

How DNS Notify Works

Windows Server 2008 supports *DNS Notify*. DNS Notify is a mechanism that allows the process of initiating notifications to secondary servers when zone changes occur (RFC 1996). DNS Notify uses a push mechanism for communicating to a select set of secondary zone servers when their zone information is updated. (DNS Notify does not allow you to configure a notify list for a stub zone.)

After being notified of the changes, secondary servers can then start a pull zone transfer and update their local copies of the database.

Many different mechanisms use the push/pull relationship. Normally one object pushes information to another and that other object pulls the information from the first. Most applications push replication on a change value and pull it on a time value. For example, a system can push replication after 10 updates or it can be pulled every 30 minutes.

To configure the DNS Notify process, you create a list of secondary servers to notify. List the IP address of the server in the primary masters Notify dialog box (See Figure 2.8). The Notify dialog box is located under the Zone Transfers tab, which is located under the Zone Properties dialog box (See Figure 2.9).

FIGURE 2.8   DNS Notify dialog box

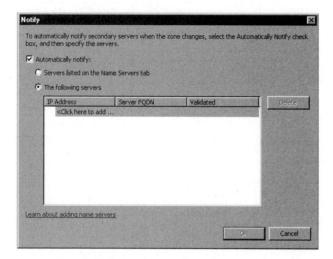

FIGURE 2.9   DNS Zone Transfers tab

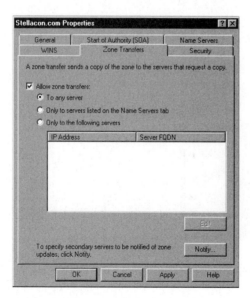

Configuring Stub Zone Transfers with Zone Replication Scope

In the preceding section, we talked about how to configure secondary server zone transfers. What if you wanted to configure settings for stub zone transfers? This is where zone replication scope comes in.

Only Active Directory–integrated primary and stub zones can configure their replication scope. Secondary servers do not have this ability.

You can configure zone replication scope configurations in two ways. An administrator can set configuration options through the DNS snap-in or through a command-line tool called Dnscmd.

To configure zone replication scope through the DNS snap-in, follow these steps:

1. Click Start ➢ Administrative Tools ➢DNS.

2. Right-click the zone that you want to set up.

3. Choose Properties.

4. In the Properties dialog box (see Figure 2.10), choose the Change button next to Replication.

FIGURE 2.10   DNS zone replication scope

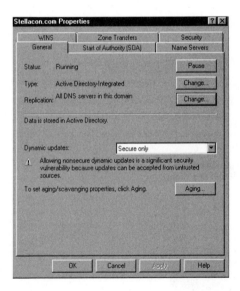

5. Choose the replication scope that fits your organization.

New Functionality in Windows Server 2008 DNS

Microsoft Windows Server 2008 has improved their version of DNS in many different ways. This section covers this new functionality. Here are some of the new DNS features we will discuss:

- Background zone loading
- Support for TCP/IP version 6 (IPv6)
- Read-only domain controllers
- GlobalName zone

Background Zone Loading

If an organization had to restart a DNS server with an extremely large Active Directory Integrated DNS zones database in the past, DNS had a common problem with an Active Directory Integrated DNS zone. After the DNS restart, it could take hours for DNS data to be retrieved from Active Directory. During this time, the DNS server was unable to service any client requests.

Microsoft Windows Server 2008 DNS has addressed this problem by implementing background zone loading. As the DNS restarts, the Active Directory zone data populates the database in the background. This allows the DNS server to service client requests for data from other zones almost immediately after a restart.

Background zone loading accomplishes this task by loading the DNS zone using separate threads. This allows a DNS server to service requests while still loading the rest of the zone. If a client sends a request to the DNS server for a computer that has not loaded into memory yet, the DNS server retrieves the data from Active Directory and updates the record.

Support for IPv6 Addresses

Over the past few years, the Internet has starting running into a problem that was not foreseen when the it was first created—it started running out of TCP/IP addresses. As you probably already know, when the Internet was created, it was used for government and academic purposes only. Then, seemingly overnight, it grew to be the information super highway. Now, asking someone for their email address is almost as common as asking for their phone number.

In the past, the common version of TCP/IP was version 4 (IPv4). The release of TCP/IP version 6 (IPv6) has solved the lack of IP addresses problem. IPv4 addresses were 32 bits long, but IPv6 addresses are now 128 bits. The longer lengths allow for a much greater number of globally unique TCP/IP addresses.

Microsoft Windows Server 2008 DNS has built in support to accommodate both IPv4 and IPv6 address records (DNS records are explained later in this chapter). DHCP can also issue IPv6 addresses, which lets administrators allow DHCP to register the client with DNS, or the IPv6 client can register their address with the DNS server.

Support for Read-Only Domain Controllers

As mentioned in Chapter 1, "Overview of Active Directory," Windows Server 2008 has introduced a new type of domain controller called the read-only domain controller (RODC). This is a full copy of the Active Directory database without the ability to configure Active Directory. The RODC gives an organization the ability to install a domain controller in a location (on or offsite) where security is a concern

Microsoft Windows Server 2008 DNS has implemented a new type of zone to help support an RODC. A primary read-only zone allows a DNS server to receive a copy of the application partition (including ForestDNSZones and DomainDNSZones) that DNS uses. This allows DNS to support an RODC due to the fact that DNS now has a full copy of all DNS zones stored in Active Directory.

A primary read-only zone is just what it says—"a read-only zone"; so to make any changes to it, you have to change the primary zones located on the Active Directory Integrated DNS server.

GlobalName Zones

Earlier in this chapter we talked about organizations using the Windows Internet Name Service (WINS) to resolve NetBIOS names (also referred to as computer names) to TCP/IP addresses. Many organizations, even today, still use WINS along with DNS for name resolution. Unfortunately, WINS is slowly becoming obsolete.

To help organizations move forward with an all-DNS network, Microsoft Windows Server 2008 DNS supports GlobalName zones. These use single-label names (DNS names that do not contain a suffix such as .com, .net, etc.) the same way WINS does. Unlike WINS, GlobalName zones are not intended to support peer-to-peer networks and workstation name resolution, nor do they support dynamic DNS updates.

GlobalName zones were designed to be used with servers. Since GlobalName zones are not dynamic, an administrator has to manually enter the records into the zone database. In most organizations, the servers have static TCP/IP addresses and this works well with the GlobalName zone design. GlobalName zones are normally used to map single-label CNAME (Alias) resource records to an FQDN.

Introducing DNS Record Types

No matter where your zone information is stored, you can rest assured that it contains a variety of DNS information. Although the DNS snap-in makes it unlikely that you'll ever need to edit these files by hand, it's good to know exactly what data is contained there.

As stated previously, zone files consists of a number of *resource records (RRs)*. You need to know about several types of resource records to effectively manage your DNS servers. They are discussed in the following sections.

Part of the resource record is its class. Classes define the type of network for the resource record. There are three classes: Internet, Chaosnet, and Hesoid. By far, the Internet class is the most popular. In fact, it's doubtful that you'll see either Chaosnet or Hesoid classes in the wild.

 The following are some of the more important resource records in a DNS database. For a complete listing of records in a Microsoft DNS database, visit Microsoft's website.

Start of Authority (SOA) Records

The first record in a database file is the start of authority (SOA) record. The SOA defines the general parameters for the DNS zone, including the identity of the authoritative server for the zone.

The SOA is in the following format:

```
@ IN SOA primary_master contact_e-mail serial_number
refresh_time retry_time expiration_time time_to_live
```

Here is a sample SOA from the domain example.com:

```
@ IN SOA win2k3r2.example.com. hostmaster.example.com. (
                    5              ; serial number
                    900            ; refresh
                    600            ; retry
                    86400          ; expire
                    3600       ) ; default TTL
```

Table 2.2 lists the attributes stored in the SOA record.

TABLE 2.2   The SOA Record Structure

Field	Meaning
Current zone	The current zone for the SOA. This can be represented by an @ symbol to indicate the current zone or by naming the zone itself. In the example, the current zone is example.com. The trailing dot (.com.) indicates the zone's place relative to the root of the DNS.
Class	This will almost always be the letters IN for the Internet class.
Type of record	The type of record follows—in this case it's SOA.

TABLE 2.2 The SOA Record Structure *(continued)*

Field	Meaning
Primary master	The primary master for the zone on which this file is maintained.
Contact email	The Internet email address for the person responsible for this domain's database file. There is no @ symbol in this contact email address since @ is a special character in zone files. The contact email address is separated by a single dot (.). So the email address of root@example.com would be represented by root.example.com in a zone file.
Serial number	The "version number" of this database file. This increases each time the database file is changed.
Refresh time	The amount of time (in seconds) that a secondary server will wait between checks to its master server to see if the database file has changed and a zone transfer should be requested.
Retry time	The amount of time (in seconds) that a secondary server will wait before retrying a failed zone transfer.
Expiration time	The amount of time (in seconds) that a secondary server will spend trying to download a zone. After this time limit expires, the old zone information will be discarded.
Time to live	The amount of time (in seconds) that another DNS server is allowed to cache any resource records from this database file. This is the value that is sent out with all query responses from this zone file when the individual resource record doesn't contain an overriding value.

Name Server (NS) Records

Name server (NS) records list the name servers for a domain. This record allows other name servers to look up names in your domain. A zone file may contain more than one name server record. The format of these records is simple:

```
example.com.    IN     NS       Hostname.example.com
```

Table 3.3 explains the attributes stored in the NS record.

TABLE 2.3 The NS Record Structure

Field	Meaning
name	The domain that will be serviced by this name server. In this case we used example.com.

TABLE 2.3   The NS Record Structure *(continued)*

Field	Meaning
AddressClass	Internet (IN)
RecordType	Name server (NS)
Name Server Name	The FDQN Name of the server responsible for the domain

 Any domain name in the database file that is *not* terminated with a period will have the root domain appended to the end. For example, an entry that just has the name `sales` will be expanded by adding the root domain to the end, whereas the entry `sales.example.com.` won't be expanded.

Host Record

A *host record* (also called an A record for IPv4 and AAAA record for IPv6) is used to statically associate a host's name to its IP addresses. The format is pretty simple:

```
host_name optional_TTL IN  A  IP_Address
```

Here's an example from our DNS database:

```
www   IN   A   192.168.0.204
SMTP IN   A   192.168.3.144
```

The A or AAAA record ties a hostname (which is part of an FQDN) to a specific IP address. This makes these records suitable for use when you have devices with statically assigned IP addresses; in this case, you create these records manually using the DNS snap-in. As it turns out, if you enable DDNS, your DHCP server can create these for you; that automatic creation is what enables DDNS to work.

Notice that an optional TTL field is available for each resource record in the DNS. This value is used to set a TTL that is different from the default TTL for the domain. For example, if you wanted a 60-second TTL for the www A or AAAA record, it would look like this:

```
www 60 IN  A  192.168.0.204
```

Alias Record

Closely related to the host record is the alias or canonical name (CNAME) record. The syntax of an alias record looks like the following:

```
alias optional_TTL  IN  CNAME  hostname
```

Aliases are used to point more than one DNS record toward a host for which an A record already exists. For example, if the hostname of your web server was actually `chaos`, you would likely have an A record like this:

`chaos IN A 192.168.1.10`

Then you could make an alias or CNAME for the record so that `www.example.com` would point to chaos:

`www IN CNAME chaos.example.com.`

Note the trailing dot (.) on the end of the CNAME record. This means the root domain is not appended to the entry.

Pointer (PTR) Record

A or AAAA records are probably the most visible component of the DNS database because Internet users depend on them to turn FQDNs like `www.microsoft.com` into the IP addresses that browsers and other components require to find Internet resources. However, the host record has a lesser-known but still important twin: the *pointer (PTR) record*. The format of a PTR record looks like the following:

reversed_address.in-addr.arpa. optional_TTL IN PTR *targeted_domain_name*

The A or AAAA record maps a hostname to an IP address, and the PTR record does just the opposite—mapping an IP address to a hostname—through the use of the `in-addr.arpa` zone.

The PTR record is necessary because IP addresses begin with the least-specific portion first (the network) and end with the most-specific portion (the host); whereas hostnames begin with the most specific portion at the beginning and least specific at the end.

Consider the example 192.168.1.10 with a subnet mask 255.255.255.0. The portion 192.168.1 defines the network and the final .10 defines the host, or the most specific portion of the address. DNS is just the opposite: The hostname `www.example.com.` defines the most-specific portion, `www`, at the beginning, and then traverses the DNS tree to the least-specific part, the dot (.), at the root of the tree.

Reverse DNS records, therefore, need to be represented in this most-specific-to-least-specific manner. The PTR record for mapping 192.168.1.10 to `www.example.com` would look like this:

`10.1.168.192.in-addr.arpa. IN PTR www.example.com.`

Now a DNS query for that record can follow the logical DNS hierarchy from the root of the DNS tree all the way to the most-specific portion.

Mail Exchanger (MX) Record

The mail exchanger (MX) record is used to specify which servers accept mail for this domain. Each MX record contains two parameters—a preference and a mail server—as shown in the following example:

domain IN MX *preference mailserver_host*

The MX record uses the preference value to specify which server should be used if more than one MX record is present. The preference value is a number. The lower the number, the more preferred the server. Here's an example:

```
example.com.     IN   MX   0   mail.example.com.
example.com.     IN   MX   10  backupmail.example.com.
```

In the example, `mail.example.com` is the default mail server for the domain. If that server goes down for any reason, the `backupmail.example.com` mail server is used by mailers.

Service (SRV) Record

Windows Server 2008 depends on some other services, like the Lightweight Directory Access Protocol (LDAP) and Kerberos. Using a service record, which is another type of DNS record, a Windows 2000, XP, or Vista client can query DNS servers for the location of a domain controller. This makes it much easier (for both the client and the administrator) to manage and distribute logon traffic in large-scale networks. For this approach to work, Microsoft has to have some way to register the presence of a service in DNS. Enter the *service (SRV) record*.

SRV records tie together the location of a service (like a domain controller) with information about how to contact the service. SRV records provide seven items of information. Let's look at an example to help clarify this powerful concept (Table 2.4 explains the fields in the following example):

```
ldap.tcp.example.com.   86400 IN SRV   10   100   389   hsv.example.com
ldap.tcp.example.com.   86400 IN SRV   20   100   389   msy.example.com
```

TABLE 2.4   The SRV Record Structure

Field	Meaning
Domain name	Domain for which this record is valid ldap.tcp.example.com.
TTL	Time to live (86,400 seconds).
Class	This field is always *IN*, which stands for Internet.
Record Type	Type of record (SRV).
Priority	Specifies a preference, similar to the preference field in an MX record. The SRV record with the lowest priority is used first (10).
Weight	Service records with equal priority are chosen according to their weight (100).

TABLE 2.4   The SRV Record Structure *(continued)*

Field	Meaning
Port number	The port where the server is listening for this service (389).
Target	The FQDN of the host computer (hsv.example.com and msy.example.com).

You can define other types of service records. If your applications support them, they can query DNS to find the services they need.

Configuring DNS

In the following section, we are going to start the explanation of the actual DNS server. We will start with an exercise to install DNS. Then we will talk about different zone configuration options and what they mean. We will follow this by completing a lab that covers configuring Dynamic DNS, delegating zones, and manually entering records.

Installing DNS

Let's start by installing DNS.

EXERCISE 2.1

Installing and Configuring the DNS Service

1. Open the Configure Your Server wizard by selecting Start ➤ Administrative Tools ➤ Server Manager.

2. Under Roles Summary, click the link to the right labeled Add Role.

3. Click the DNS Server Item in the Server Role list and click Next to continue.

4. Click Next on the Summary page to complete the DNS installation. You may need to insert the Windows Server 2008 CD into the CD-ROM drive, regardless next click Install.

5. If your computer is configured with a dynamic IP address, you are prompted to use a static address. At this point, the Local Area Connection Properties dialog box automatically appears. Once you have made the necessary changes, click OK.

6. The Configure A DNS Sever wizard automatically appears. Click Next to dismiss the Welcome screen.

7. Select the Create Forward Lookup Zones radio button and click Next.

8. Select Yes, Create A Forward Lookup Zone Now and click Next.

9. Select the Primary Zone option. If your DNS server is also a domain controller, do not check the box to store the zone in Active Directory. Click Next when you are ready.

10. Enter a new zone name in the Zone Name field and click Next.

11. Leave the default zone filename and click Next.

12. Select the Do Not Allow Dynamic Updates radio button and click Next.

13. Select No, Don't Create A Reverse Lookup Zone Now and click Next.

14. Click Finish to end the wizard. The Configure Your Server wizard reappears and informs you that the DNS service was successfully installed. Click Finish.

Load Balancing with Round Robin

Like other DNS implementations, the Windows Server 2008 implementation of DNS supports load balancing through the use of round robin. Load balancing distributes the network load among multiple network hosts if they are available. You set up round robin load balancing by creating multiple resource records with the same hostname but different IP addresses for multiple computers. Depending on the options that you select, the DNS server responds with the addresses of one of the host computers.

If round robin is enabled, when a client requests name resolution, the first address entered in the database is returned to the resolver and is then sent to the end of the list. The next time a client attempts to resolve the name, the DNS server returns the second name in the database (which is now the first name) and then sends it to the end of the list, and so on. Round robin is enabled by default.

Configuring a Caching-Only Server

Although all DNS name servers cache queries that they have resolved, caching-only servers are DNS name servers that only perform queries, cache the answers, and return the results. They are not authoritative for any domains, and the information that they contain is limited to what has been cached while resolving queries. Accordingly, they don't have any zone files, and they don't participate in zone transfers. When a caching-only server is first started, it has no information in its cache; the cache is gradually built over time.

Caching-only servers are very easy to configure. After installing the DNS service, simply make sure that the root hints are configured properly.

1. Right-click your DNS server and choose the Properties command.

2. When the Properties dialog box appears, switch to the Root Hints tab (see Figure 2.11).

FIGURE 2.11   The Root Hints tab of the DNS server's Properties dialog box

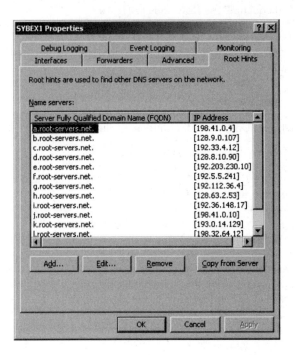

3. If your server is connected to the Internet, you should see a list of root hints for the root servers maintained by ICANN and the Internet Assigned Numbers Authority (IANA). If not, use the Add button to add root hints as defined in the cache.dns file.

    You can obtain current cache.dns files on the Internet by using a search engine. Just search for "cache.dns" and download one (I always try to get cache.dns files from a university or a company that manages domain names.

Setting Zone Properties

There are six tabs on the Properties dialog box for a forward or reverse lookup zone (see Figure 2.10 earlier in this chapter). You use the Security tab only to control who can change properties and make dynamic updates to records on that zone. The other tabs are discussed in the following sections.

Secondary zones don't have a Security tab and their SOA tab shows you the contents of the master SOA record, which you can't change.

General Tab

The General tab (see Figure 2.10) includes the following:

- The Status indicator and the associated Pause button lets you see and control whether this zone can be used to answer queries. When the zone is running, the server can use it to answer client queries; when it's paused, the server won't answer any queries it gets for that particular zone.

- The Type indicator and its Change button allow you to select the zone type. The options are standard primary, standard secondary, and AD-integrated. (See "Introduction to DNS Database Zones," earlier in this chapter.) As you change the type, the controls you see below the horizontal dividing line change too. For primary zones, you'll see a field that lets you select the zone filename; for secondary zones, you'll get controls that allow you to specify the IP addresses of the primary servers; but the most interesting controls are the ones you see for AD-integrated zones When you change to the AD-Integrated zone, you have the ability to make the dynamic zones secure only.

- The Replication indicator and its Change button allow you to change the replication scope if the zone is stored in Active Directory. You can choose to replicate the zone data to any of the following:

  - All DNS servers in the Active Directory forest

  - All DNS servers in a specified domain

  - All domain controllers in the Active Directory domain (required if you use Windows 2000 domain controllers in your domain)

  - All domain controllers specified in the replication scope of the application directory partition

- The Dynamic Updates field gives you a way to specify whether or not you want to support Dynamic DNS updates from compatible DHCP servers. As you learned earlier in the section "Dynamic DNS and Non-Dynamic DNS," the DHCP server or DHCP client must know about and support Dynamic DNS in order to use it, but the DNS server has to participate too. You can turn dynamic updates on or off, or you can require that updates be secured.

Start Of Authority (SOA) Tab

The following options in the Start Of Authority (SOA) tab control the contents of the SOA record for this zone:

FIGURE 2.12   The Start Of Authority tab of the zone Properties dialog box

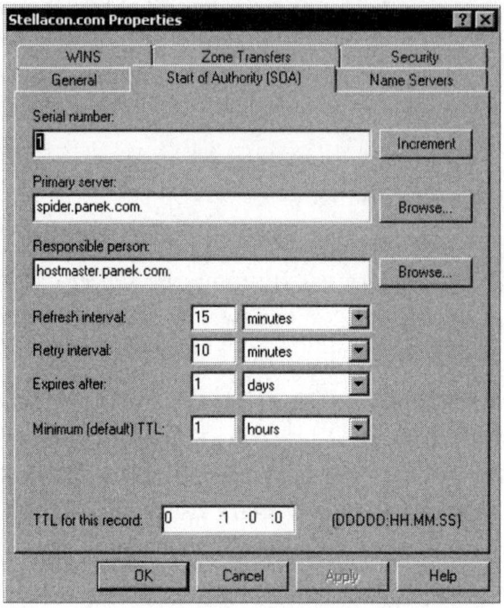

- The Serial Number field indicates which version of the SOA record the server currently holds; every time you change another field, you should increment the serial number so that other servers will notice the change and get a copy of the updated record.

- The Primary Server and Responsible Person fields indicate the location of the primary NS for this zone and the email address of the administrator responsible for the maintenance of this zone, respectively. The standard username for this is the "hostmaster."

- The Refresh Interval field controls how often any secondary zones of this zone must contact the primary zone server and get any changes that have been posted since the last update.

- The Retry Interval field controls how long secondary servers will wait after a zone transfer fails before they try again. They'll keep trying at the interval you specify (which should be shorter than the refresh interval) until they eventually succeed in transferring zone data.

- The Expires After field tells the secondary servers when to throw away zone data. The default of 1 day (24 hours) means that a secondary server that hasn't gotten an update in 24 hours will delete its local copy of the zone data.

- The Minimum (Default) TTL field sets the default TTL for all RRs created in the zone; you can assign specific TTLs to individual records if you want.

- The TTL For This Record field controls the TTL for the SOA record itself.

Name Servers Tab

The name server (NS) record for a zone indicates which name servers are authoritative for the zone. That normally means the zone primary server and any secondary servers you've configured for the zone (remember, secondary servers are authoritative read-only copies of the zone). You edit the NS record for a zone using the Name Servers tab (Figure 2.13). The tab shows you which servers are currently listed, and you use the Add, Edit, and Remove buttons to specify which name servers you want included in the zone's NS record.

FIGURE 2.13   The Name Servers tab of the zone Properties dialog box

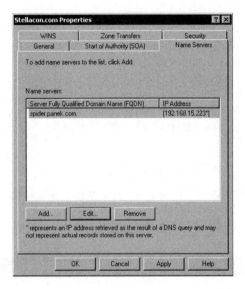

WINS Tab

The WINS tab allows you to control whether this zone uses WINS forward lookups or not. These lookups pass on queries that DNS can't resolve to WINS for action. This is a useful setup if you're still using WINS on your network. You must explicitly turn this option on with the Use WINS Forward Lookup checkbox in the WINS tab for a particular zone.

Zone Transfers Tab

Zone transfers are necessary and useful because they're the mechanism used to propagate zone data between primary and secondary servers. For primary servers (whether AD-integrated or not), you can specify whether or not your servers will allow zone transfers (See Figure 2.9, earlier in this chapter) and, if so, to whom.

You can use the following controls on the Zone Transfers tab to configure these settings per zone:

- The Allow Zone Transfers checkbox controls whether or not the server answers zone transfer requests for this zone at all—when it's not checked, no zone data is transferred. The Allow Zone Transfers selections are as follows:

  - To Any Server allows any server anywhere on the Internet to request a copy of your zone data.

  - Only To Servers Listed On The Name Servers Tab (the default) limits transfers to servers you specify. This is a more secure setting than To Any Server because it limits transfers to other servers for the same zone.

  - Only To The Following Servers controls allows you to specify exactly which servers are allowed to request zone transfers. This list can be larger or smaller than the list specified on the Name Servers tab.

- The Notify button is for setting up automatic notification triggers that are sent to secondary servers for this zone. Those triggers signal the secondary servers that changes have occurred on the primary server so that the secondary servers can request updates sooner than their normally scheduled interval. The options in the Notify dialog box are similar to those in the Zone Transfers tab. You can enable automatic notification and then choose either Servers Listed On The Name Servers Tab or The Following Servers.

Configuring Zones for Dynamic Updates

In Exercise 2.2, you will modify the properties of a forward lookup zone, configuring the zone to use WINS to resolve names not found by querying the DNS namespace. In addition, you'll configure the zone to allow dynamic updates.

EXERCISE 2.2

Configuring a Zone for Dynamic Update

1. Open the DNS management snap-in by selecting Start ➤ Administrative Tools ➤ DNS.

2. Click the DNS server to expand it and then expand the Forward Lookup Zones folder.

3. Right-click the zone you want to modify (which may be the one you created in the previous exercise) and choose the Properties command.

4. Switch to the WINS tab and click the Use WINS Forward Lookup checkbox.

5. Enter the IP address of a valid WINS server on your network, click Add, and then click OK.

6. Click the General tab.

7. Change the value of the Allow Dynamic Updates control to Yes. Click OK to close the Properties dialog box. Notice that there's now a new WINS Lookup RR in your zone.

Delegating Zones for DNS

DNS provides the ability to divide the namespace into one or more zones, which can then be stored, distributed, and replicated to other DNS servers. When deciding whether to divide your DNS namespace to make additional zones, consider the following reasons to use additional zones:

- A need to delegate management of part of your DNS namespace to another location or department within your organization

- A need to divide one large zone into smaller zones for distributing traffic loads among multiple servers, for improving DNS name resolution performance, or for creating a more fault-tolerant DNS environment

- A need to extend the namespace by adding numerous subdomains at once, such as to accommodate the opening of a new branch or site

Each new delegated zone requires a primary DNS server just like a regular DNS zone. When delegating zones within your namespace, be aware that for each new zone you create, you need to place delegation records in other zones that point to the authoritative DNS servers for the new zone. This is necessary both to transfer authority and to provide correct referral to other DNS servers and clients of the new servers being made authoritative for the new zone.

In Exercise 2.3, you'll create a delegated subdomain of the domain you created back in Exercise 2.1. Note that the name of the server to which you want to delegate the subdomain must be stored in an A or CNAME record in the parent domain.

EXERCISE 2.3

Creating a Delegated DNS Zone

1. Open the DNS management snap-in by selecting Start ➢ Administrative Tools ➢ DNS.

2. Expand the DNS server and locate the zone you created in Exercise 2.1.

3. Right-click the zone and choose the New Delegation command.

4. The New Delegation wizard appears. Click Next to dismiss the initial wizard page.

5. Enter **ns1** (or whatever other name you like) in the Delegated Domain field of the Delegated Domain Name page. This is the name of the domain for which you want to delegate authority to another DNS server. It should be a subdomain of the primary domain (for example, to delegate authority for huntsville.example.net, you'd enter **huntsville** in the Delegated Domain field). Click Next to complete this step.

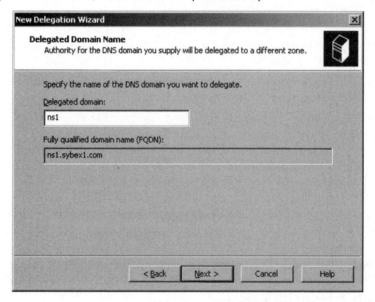

6. When the Name Servers page appears, use the Add button to add the name and IP address(es) of the servers that will be hosting the newly delegated zone. For the purpose of this exercise, enter the zone name you used in Exercise 2.1. Click the Resolve button to automatically resolve this domain name's IP address into the IP address field. Click OK when you are done. Click Next to continue with the wizard.

7. Click the Finish button. The New Delegation wizard disappears and you'll notice the new zone you just created appear beneath the zone you selected in step 3. The newly delegated zone's folder icon is drawn in gray to indicate that control of the zone is delegated.

Manually Creating DNS Records

From time to time you may find it necessary to manually add resource records to your Windows Server 2008 DNS servers. Although Dynamic DNS frees you from the need to fiddle with

A and PTR records for clients and other such entries, you still have to create other resource types (including MX records, required for the proper flow of SMTP email) manually. You can manually create A, PTR, MX, SRV, and many other record types.

There are only two important things to remember:

- You must right-click the zone and use either the New Record command or the Other New Records command.

- You must know how to fill in the fields of whatever record type you're using.

    For example, to create an MX record, you need three pieces of information (the domain, the mail server, and the priority), but to create an SRV record, you need several more.

In Exercise 2.4, you will manually create an MX record for a mailtest server in the domain you created back in Exercise 2.1.

EXERCISE 2.4

Manually Creating DNS RRs

1. Open the DNS management snap-in by selecting Start ➤ Administrative Tools ➤ DNS.

2. Expand your DNS server, right-click its zone, and use the New Mail Exchanger (MX) command.

3. Enter **mailtest** in the Host Or Child Domain field, and enter **mailtest.*yourDomain.com* (or whatever domain name you used in Exercise 2.1) in the Fully Qualified Domain Name (FQDN) Of Mail Server field and then click OK. Notice that the new record is already visible.

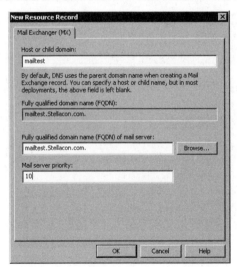

4. Next, create an alias (or CNAME) record to point to the mail server. (It is assumed that you already have an A record for mailtest in your zone.) Right-click the target zone and choose Other New Records. When the Resource Record Type dialog box appears, find Alias (CNAME) in the list and select it.

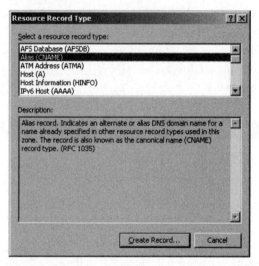

5. Click the Create Record button. The New Resource Record dialog box appears.

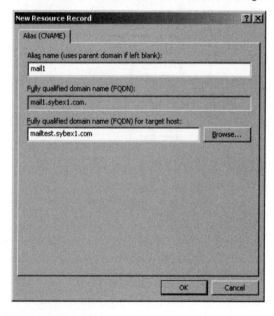

6. Type **mail** into the Alias Name field.

7. Type **mailtest.*yourDomain.com*** into the Fully Qualified Domain Name (FQDN) For Target Host field.

8. Click the OK button, then click Done.

Monitoring and Troubleshooting DNS

Now that you have set up and configured your DNS name server and created some resource records, you will want to confirm that it is resolving and replying to client DNS requests. A couple of tools allow you to do some basic monitoring and managing. Once you are able to monitor DNS, you'll want to start troubleshooting.

The simplest test is to use the `ping` command to make sure the server is alive. A more thorough test would be to use `nslookup` to verify that you can actually resolve addresses for items on your DNS server.

In the following sections, we'll look at some of these monitoring and management tools, as well as how to troubleshoot DNS.

Monitoring DNS with the DNS Snap-In

You can use the DNS snap-in to do some basic server testing and monitoring. More importantly, you use the snap-in to monitor and set logging options. On the Event Logging tab of the server's Properties dialog box (Figure 2.14), you can pick which events you want logged. The more events you select, the more log information you'll get. This is useful when you're trying to track what's happening with your servers, but it can result in a very, very large log file if you're not careful.

FIGURE 2.14 The Event Logging tab of the server's Properties dialog box

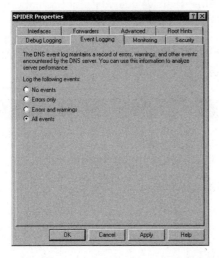

The Monitoring tab (Figure 2.15) gives you some testing tools. When the checkbox labeled A Simple Query Against This DNS Server is checked a test is performed that asks for a single record from the local DNS server; it's useful for verifying that the service is running and listening to queries, but not much else. When the checkbox labeled A Recursive Query To Other DNS Servers is checked, the test is more sophisticated—a recursive query checks whether forwarding is working okay. The Test Now button and the Perform Automatic Testing At The Following Interval checkbox allow you to run these tests now or later, as you require.

FIGURE 2.15   The Monitoring tab of the server's Properties dialog box

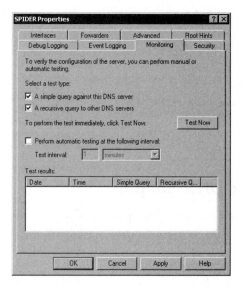

 If the simple query fails, check that the local server contains the zone 1.0.0.127.in-addr.arpa. If the recursive query fails, check that your root hints are correct and that your root servers are running.

In Exercise 2.5, you will enable logging, use the DNS MMC to test the DNS server, and view the contents of the DNS log.

EXERCISE 2.5

Simple DNS Testing

1. Open the DNS management snap-in by selecting Start ≻ Administrative Tools ≻ DNS.

2. Right-click the DNS server you want to test and select Properties.

3. Switch to the Debug Logging tab, check all the debug logging options except Filter Packets By IP Address, and enter a full path and filename in the File Path And Name field.

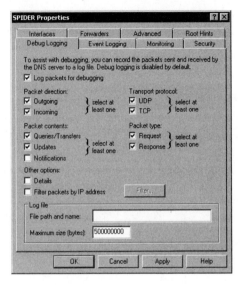

Click the Apply button.

4. Switch to the Monitoring tab, and check both A Simple Query Against This DNS Server and A Recursive Query To Other DNS Servers.

5. Click the Test Now button several times and then click OK.

6. Using Windows Explorer, navigate to the folder that you specified in step 3 and use WordPad to view the contents of the log file.

Troubleshooting DNS

When troubleshooting DNS problems, ask yourself the following basic questions:

- What application is failing? What works? What doesn't work?

- Is the problem basic IP connectivity, or is it name resolution? If the problem is name resolution, does the failing application use NetBIOS names, DNS names, or hostnames?

- How are the things that do and don't work related?

- Have the things that don't work ever worked on this computer or network? If so, what has changed since they last worked?

Windows Server 2008 provides several useful tools, discussed in the following sections, that can help you answer these questions:

- Nslookup is used to perform DNS queries and to examine the contents of zone files on local and remote servers.

- DNSLint is a command line utility used for troubleshooting many common DNS issues.

- Ipconfig allows you to perform the following tasks:

  - View DNS client settings.

  - Display and flush the resolver cache.

  - Force a dynamic update client to register its DNS records.

- The DNS log file monitors certain DNS server events and logs them for your edification.

Using Nslookup

Nslookup is a standard command-line tool provided in most DNS server implementations, including Windows Server 2008. Windows Server 2008 gives you the ability to launch nslookup from the DNS snap-in.

When launching nslookup from the DNS snap-in, a command prompt window opens automatically. You enter nslookup commands in this window.

Nslookup offers the ability to perform query testing of DNS servers and to obtain detailed responses at the command prompt. This information can be useful for diagnosing and solving name resolution problems, for verifying that resource records are added or updated correctly in a zone, and for debugging other server-related problems. You can do a number of useful things with nslookup:

- Use it in non-interactive mode to look up a single piece of data.

- Enter interactive mode and use the debug feature.

- Perform the following from within interactive mode:

  - Set options for your query.

  - Look up a name.

  - Look up records in a zone.

  - Perform zone transfers.

  - Exit nslookup.

When you are entering queries, it is generally a good idea to enter FQDNs so you can control what name is submitted to the server. However, if you want to know which suffixes are added to unqualified names before they are submitted to the server, you can enter nslookup in debug mode and then enter an unqualified name.

Using Nslookup on the Command Line

To use nslookup in plain old command-line mode, enter the following in the command prompt window:

`nslookup DNS_name_or_IP_address server_IP_address`

This command will look up a DNS name or address using a server at the IP address you specify.

Using Nslookup in Interactive Mode

Nslookup is a lot more useful in interactive mode because you can enter several commands in sequence. Entering **nslookup** by itself (without specifying a query or server) puts it in interactive mode, where it will stay until you type **exit** and press Enter. Before that point, you can look up lots of useful stuff. Following are some of the tasks you can perform with nslookup in interactive mode:

Setting options with the `set` command   While in interactive mode, you can use the `set` command to configure how the resolver will carry out queries. Table 2.5 shows a few of the options available with `set`.

TABLE 2.5   Command-Line Options Available with the `set` Command

Option	Purpose
`set all`	Shows all the options available.
`set d2`	Puts nslookup in debug mode so you can examine the query and response packets between the resolver and the server.
`set domain=`*domain name*	Tells the resolver what domain name to append for unqualified queries.
`set timeout=`*timeout*	Tells the resolver how long to keep trying to contact the server. This option is useful for slow links where queries frequently time out and the wait time must be lengthened.
`set type=`*record type*	Tells the resolver which type of resource records to search for (for example, A, PTR, or SRV). If you want the resolver to query for all types of resource records, type **set type=all**.

Looking up a name   While in interactive mode, you can look up a name just by typing it: *stellacon.com*. In this example, *stellacon* is the owner name for the record you are looking for, and *.com* is the server that you want to query.

You can use the wildcard character (*) in your query. For example, if you want to look for all resource records that have *k* as the first letter, just type **k*** as your query.

Looking up a record type   If you want to query for a particular type of record (for instance, an MX record), use the set type command. The command set type=mx tells nslookup that you're only interested in seeing MX records that meet your search criteria.

Listing the contents of a domain   To get a list of the contents of an entire domain, use the ls command. To find all the hosts in the apple.com domain, you'd type **set type=a** and then type **ls -t apple.com**.

Troubleshooting zone transfers   You can simulate zone transfers by using the ls command with the -d switch. This can help you determine whether or not the server you are querying allows zone transfers to your computer. To do this, type the following: **ls -d *domain_name*.**

Nslookup Responses and Error Messages

A successful nslookup response looks like this:

```
Server: Name_of_DNS_server
Address: IP_address_of_DNS_server
Response_data
```

Nslookup might also return an error message. Some of the common messages are listed in Table 2.6:

T A B L E 2.6   Common Nslookup Error Messages

Error message	Meaning
DNS request timed out. Timeout was *x* seconds. *** Can't find server name for address *IP_Address*: Timed out *** Default servers are not available Default Server: Unknown Address: *IP_address_of_DNS_server*	The resolver did not locate a PTR resource record (containing the hostname) for the server IP address you specified. Nslookup can still query the DNS server, and the DNS server can still answer queries.
*** Request to Server timed-out	A request was not fulfilled in the allotted time. This might happen, for example, if the DNS service was not running on the DNS server that is authoritative for the name.
*** Server can't find *Name_or_IP_address_queried_for*: No response from server	The server is not receiving requests on UDP (User Datagram Protocol) port 53.

TABLE 2.6   Common Nslookup Error Messages

Error message	Meaning
`*** Server can't find` *Name_or_IP_address_queried_for*: `Non-existent domain`	The DNS server was unable to find the name or IP address in the authoritative domain. The authoritative domain might be on the remote DNS server or on another DNS server that this DNS server is unable to reach.
`*** Server can't find` *Name_or_IP_address_queried_for*: `Server failed`	The DNS server is running but is not working properly. For example, it might include a corrupted packet, or the zone in which you are querying for a record might be paused. However, this message can also be returned if the client queries for a host in a domain for which the DNS server is not authoritative. You will also receive the error if the DNS server cannot contact its root servers, it is not connected to the Internet, or it has no root hints.

In Exercise 2.6, you'll get some hands-on practice with the nslookup tool.

EXERCISE 2.6

Using the `nslookup` Command

1. Open a Windows Server 2008 command prompt by selecting ➢Start ➢ Command Prompt.

2. Type **nslookup** and press the Enter key. (For the rest of the exercise, use the Enter key to terminate each command.)

3. Try looking up a well-known address: Type **www.microsoft.com**. Notice that the query returns several IP addresses (Microsoft load-balances Web traffic by using multiple servers in the same DNS record).

4. Try looking up a nonexistent host: type **www.example.ccccc**. Notice that your server complains that it can't find the address. This is normal behavior.

5. Type **Exit** at the prompt. Type **Exit** again to leave Command Prompt.

Using DNSLint

Microsoft Windows Server 2008 DNS can use the DNSLint command line utility to help diagnose some common DNS name resolution issues and to help diagnose potential problems of incorrect delegation. You need to download DNSLint from the Microsoft Download Center.

DNSLint uses three main functions to verify DNS records and to generate a report in HTML:

- dnslint /d helps diagnose reasons that cause "lame delegation" and other related DNS problems.

- dnslint /ql helps verify a user-defined set of DNS records on multiple DNS servers.

- dnslint /ad helps verify DNS records pertaining to Active Directory replication.

Here is the syntax for DNSLint:

```
dnslint /d domain_name | /ad [LDAP_IP_address] | /ql input_file
[/c [smtp,pop,imap]] [/no_open] [/r report_name]
[/t] [/test_tcp] [/s DNS_IP_address] [/v] [/y]
```

The following are some sample queries:

```
dnslint /d stellacon.com
dnslint /ad /s 192.168.36.201
dnslint /ql dns_server.txt
dnslint /ql autocreate
dnslint /v /d stellacon.com
dnslint /r newfile /d stellacon.com
dnslint /y /d stellacon.com
dnslint /no_open /d stellacon.com
```

Table 2.7 explains the command options.

TABLE 2.7   DNSLint Command Options

Command option	Meaning
/d	Domain name that is being tested.
/ad	Resolves DNS records that are used for Active Directory forest replication.
/s	TCP/IP address of host
/ql	Request DNS query tests from a list. This switch sends DNS queries specified in an input file.
/v	Turns verbose mode on.
/r filename	Allows you to create a report file.
/y	Overwrites an existing report file without being prompted.
/no_open	Prevents a report from opening automatically.

Using Ipconfig

You can use the command-line tool ipconfig to view your DNS client settings, to view and reset cached information used locally for resolving DNS name queries, and to register the resource records for a dynamic update client. If you use the ipconfig command with no parameters, it displays DNS information for each adapter, including the domain name and DNS servers used for that adapter. Table 2.8 shows some command-line options available with ipconfig.

TABLE 2.8   Command-Line Options Available for the ipconfig Command

Command	What It Does
ipconfig /all	Displays additional information about DNS, including the FQDN and the DNS suffix search list.
ipconfig /flushdns	Flushes and resets the DNS resolver cache. For more information about this option, see the section "Configuring DNS" earlier in this chapter.

TABLE 2.8 Command-Line Options Available for the `ipconfig` Command *(continued)*

Command	What It Does
`ipconfig /displaydns`	Displays the contents of the DNS resolver cache. For more information about this option, see "Configuring DNS" earlier in this chapter.
`ipconfig /registerdns`	Refreshes all DHCP leases and registers any related DNS names. This option is available only on Windows 2000 and newer computers that run the DHCP Client service.

You should know and be comfortable with the `ipconfig` commands related to DNS for the exam.

Using the DNS Log File

You can configure the DNS server to create a log file that records the following information:

- Queries
- Notification messages from other servers
- Dynamic updates
- Content of the question section for DNS query messages
- Content of the answer section for DNS query messages
- Number of queries this server sends
- Number of queries this server has received
- Number of DNS requests received over a UDP port
- Number of DNS requests received over a TCP port
- Number of full packets sent by the server
- Number of packets written through by the server and back to the zone

The DNS log appears in *systemroot*\System32\dns\Dns.log. Because the log is in RTF format, you must use WordPad or Word to view it.

Once the log file reaches the maximum size, Windows Server 2008 writes over the beginning of the file. You can change the maximum size of the log. If you make the size value higher, data persists for a longer time but the log file consumes more disk space. If you make the value smaller, the log file uses less disk space but the data persists for a shorter time.

Summary

DNS was designed to be a robust, scalable, high-performance system for resolving friendly names to TCP/IP host addresses. We started by presenting an overview of the basics of DNS and how DNS names are generated. We then looked at the many new features available in the Microsoft Windows Server 2008 version of DNS and focused on how to install, configure, and manage the necessary services. Microsoft's DNS is based on a widely accepted set of industry standards. Because of this, Microsoft's DNS can work with both Windows and non-Windows based networks.

Exam Essentials

Understand the purpose of DNS.   DNS is a standard set of protocols that defines a mechanism for querying and updating address information in the database, a mechanism for replicating the information in the database among servers, and a schema of the database.

Understand the different parts of the DNS database.   The SOA record defines the general parameters for the DNS zone, including who the authoritative server is. NS records list the name servers for a domain; they allow other name servers to look up names in your domain. A host record (also called an address record or an A record) statically associates a host's name with its IP addresses. Pointer records (PTRs) map an IP address to a hostname, making it possible to do reverse lookups. Alias records allow you to use more than one name to point to a single host. The MX record tells you which servers can accept mail bound for a domain. SRV records tie together the location of a service (like a domain controller) with information about how to contact the service.

Know how DNS resolves names.   With iterative queries, a client asks the DNS server for an answer, and the client, or resolver, returns the best kind of answer it has. In a recursive query, the client sends a query to one name server, asking it to respond either with the requested answer or with an error. The error states either that the server can't come up with the right answer or that the domain name doesn't exist. With inverse queries, instead of supplying a name and then asking for an IP address, the client first provides the IP address and then asks for the name.

Understand the differences among DNS servers, clients, and resolvers.   Any computer providing domain name services is a DNS server. A DNS client is any machine issuing queries to a DNS server. A resolver handles the process of mapping a symbolic name to an actual network address.

Know how to install and configure DNS.   DNS can be installed before, during, or after installing the Active Directory service. When you install the DNS server, the DNS snap-in is installed, too. Configuring a DNS server ranges from very easy to very difficult, depending on what you're trying to make it do. In the simplest configuration, for a caching-only server, you don't have to do anything except make sure the server's root hints are set correctly. You can also configure a root server, a normal forward lookup server, and a reverse lookup server.

Know how to create new forward and reverse lookup zones.   You can use the New Zone wizard to create a new forward or reverse lookup zone. The process is basically the same for both types, but the specific steps and wizard pages differ somewhat. The wizard walks you through the steps, such as specifying a name for the zone (in the case of forward lookup zones) or the network ID portion of the network that the zone covers (in the case of reverse lookup zones).

Know how to configure zones for dynamic updates.   The DNS service allows dynamic updates to be enabled or disabled on a per-zone basis at each server. This is easily done in the DNS snap-in.

Know how to delegate zones for DNS.   DNS provides the ability to divide the namespace into one or more zones; these can then be stored, distributed, and replicated to other DNS servers. When delegating zones within your namespace, be aware that for each new zone you create, you need delegation records in other zones that point to the authoritative DNS servers for the new zone.

Understand the tools that are available for monitoring and troubleshooting DNS.   You can use the DNS snap-in to do some basic server testing and monitoring. More importantly, you use the snap-in to monitor and set logging options. Windows Server 2008 automatically logs DNS events in the event log under a distinct DNS server heading. Nslookup offers the ability to perform query testing of DNS servers and to obtain detailed responses at the command prompt. You can use the command-line tool ipconfig to view your DNS client settings, to view and reset cached information used locally for resolving DNS name queries, and to register the resource records for a dynamic update client. Finally, you can configure the DNS server to create a log file that records queries, notification messages, dynamic updates, and various other DNS information.

Review Questions

1. You are the network administrator for a large sales organization with four distinct regional offices situated in different areas of the United States. Your Windows Server 2008 computers are all in place, and you have almost finished migrating all the workstations to XP Professional and Vista. Your next step is to implement a single Active Directory tree, but you want to put your DNS infrastructure in place before you start building your tree. Because DNS is a critical component for the proper functioning of Active Directory, you want to make sure that each region will have service for local resources as well as good performance. What should you do to realize these requirements?

   A. Install a single DNS server at your location and create a separate domain name for each region for resolution of local resources.

   B. Install a DNS server at each regional location and create a single domain name for all the regions for resolution of local resources.

   C. Install a single DNS server at your location and create a single domain name for all the regions for resolution of local resources.

   D. Install a DNS server at each regional location and create a separate domain name for each region for resolution of local resources.

2. The following diagram outlines DNS name resolution through recursion. Move each item into the correct position so that the flow of DNS traffic is correct.

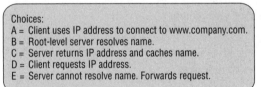

Choices:
A = Client uses IP address to connect to www.company.com.
B = Root-level server resolves name.
C = Server returns IP address and caches name.
D = Client requests IP address.
E = Server cannot resolve name. Forwards request.

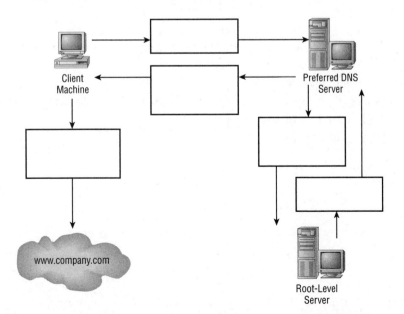

3. After upgrading your Windows NT network to Windows Server 2008, you decide to install Active Directory. Your network consists of 3 Windows Server 2008 computers, 65 XP Professional workstations, and 3 Unix workstations. One of the Unix stations is running a large laser printer and another is running a fax server. You've been using a DNS server on one of the Unix boxes for Internet browsing only, but now you'll need DNS for Active Directory. You deploy the Windows Server 2008 DNS service, replacing the DNS on the Unix box and configuring it for dynamic updates. After you deploy Active Directory, everything appears to work fine—the users can connect to resources on the network through hostnames. However, it becomes apparent that the fax server and the laser printer are no longer accessible via their hostnames. What is the most likely cause of this problem?

    A. You need to disable dynamic updates on the DNS server.

    B. You need to install WINS to resolve the hostnames on the Unix machines.

    C. You need to manually add A resource records for the Unix machines.

    D. You need to integrate the primary DNS zone into Active Directory.

4. You have been brought into an organization that has a variety of computer systems. Management is trying to tie these systems together and to minimize the administrative efforts required to keep the network-provided services running. The systems consist of 4 Windows NT servers, 7 Windows Server 2008 computers, 300 Vista and XP Professional workstations, 100 Windows NT workstations, 30 Unix clients, and 3 Unix servers. Management wants to continue the migration toward the new versions of Windows and also to expand the number of Unix servers as the need arises. Presently, they are using WINS on the Windows NT servers and a DNS service on one of the Unix servers that points to an ISP and provides all hostname resolution. What would be your recommendation for providing name resolution service for this organization?

    A. Install the Windows Server 2008 DNS service on the Windows Server 2008 computer.

    B. Install the WINS service on the Unix server.

    C. Upgrade the DNS on the Unix server to the Windows Server 2008 DNS.

    D. Use the standard DNS service that is already on the Unix server.

5. Jerry wants to configure a Windows Server 2008 DNS server so that it can answer queries for hosts on his intranet but not on the Internet. He can accomplish this by doing which of the following? (Choose two.)

    A. Installing the DNS server inside his company's firewall

    B. Configuring his server as a root server and leaving out root hints for the top-level domains

    C. Leaving forwarding turned off

    D. Disabling recursive lookups

6. Your company has been extraordinarily successful with its e-commerce site. In fact, because your customers have come to expect such a high level of reliability, you want to build several servers that mirror each other; just in case one of them fails, you will still be able to provide excellent service for your customers. The name of the web server is www.example.com, which you are duplicating on machines on different subnets, and you have made all the necessary host records in the DNS. After a while, you notice that only one machine is responding to client requests. You are not the original administrator for the company, so you suspect some of the default settings were changed before you arrived. What must you do so that your customers can utilize all the mirrored web servers?

   A. Enable DNS sharing.

   B. Enable IIS sharing.

   C. Enable round robin.

   D. Enable request redirector.

   E. Configure the proper priorities metric for this hostname.

7. You are the network administrator for a Windows Server 2008 network. You have multiple remote locations connected to your main office by slow satellite links. You want to install DNS into these offices so that clients can locate authoritative DNS servers in the main location. What type of DNS servers should be installed in the remote locations?

   A. Primary DNS zones

   B. Secondary DNS zones

   C. Active Directory Integrated zones

   D. Stub zones

8. The organization you work for has five Windows Server 2008 servers all running as domain controllers. Your DNS servers are all currently running as primary DNS zones. You need to set up a DNS strategy that allows all DNS servers to hold the same database and your company requires that you use secure DNS dynamic updates for all clients. What type of DNS strategy do you need to implement?

   A. Upgrade 1 server as a primary master and the rest as stub zones.

   B. Upgrade 1 server as a primary master and the rest as secondary servers.

   C. Upgrade all servers to Active Directory Integrated servers.

   D. Keep all servers primary servers and set up replication.

9. The company you work for has six locations around the country. You are part of the administrative team based in the central office, and you have finished upgrading the workstations and servers to Vista and Server 2008. Your team is now in the process of deploying DNS in order to support your manager's planned implementation of a single Active Directory tree so that you can support the network from your central location. Because you must support name resolution for six offices, you want to provide an efficient and responsive service for the users. Which of the following is the best approach to support your plans for a single Active Directory tree and provide efficiency and responsiveness for the users in this situation?

   A. Create a single second-level name and maintain all the DNS servers at your central office to ease administration.

   B. Create a single second-level name and deploy a DNS server at each location in the network.

   C. Create a second-level name for each city and maintain all the DNS servers at your central office to ease administration.

   D. Create a second-level name for each city and deploy a DNS server at each location in the network.

10. You want to quickly verify that your DNS service is running and listening to queries. What would you click or look at in the dialog box in order to do this?

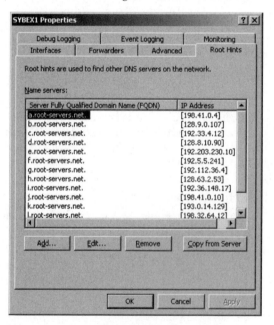

   A. The Name Servers area of the Root Hints tab

   B. The Add button

   C. The Monitoring tab

   D. The Interfaces tab

11. Acme Bowling Pin Company, with offices in 4 states, has been acquired by Roadrunner Enter-prises, which has offices in 14 states and is a highly diversified organization. Although the var-ious companies are managed independently, the parent company is very interested in minimizing costs by taking advantage of any shared corporate resources; it also wants to have overall cen-tral control. This means that you, the network administrator for Acme Bowling Pin Company, will manage your own DNS namespace but will still be under the umbrella of the parent organization. Which of the following will best accomplish these goals?

   A. Have each location, including yours, register its own namespace and manage its DNS system independently.

   B. Register a single domain name for Roadrunner Enterprises and use delegated subdomains on a single DNS server at corporate headquarters to provide name resolution across the enterprise.

   C. Register a single domain name for Roadrunner Enterprises and use delegated subdomains on DNS servers installed at each location to provide name resolution across the enterprise.

   D. Have each location, including yours, register its own namespace and add it on a single DNS server at corporate headquarters to provide name resolution across the enterprise.

12. A DNS client sends a recursive query to its local DNS server, asking for the IP address of www.bigbrother.gov. The DNS server finds no local zones corresponding to the requested domain name, so it sends a request to a root name server. What does the root name server reply with?

   A. The IP address of the name server for the bigbrother.gov domain

   B. The DNS name of the .gov top-level domain

   C. The IP address of www.bigbrother.gov

   D. The IP address of the name server for the .gov top-level domain

13. You have a private network that contains several DNS zones and servers, including a couple of root name servers. You never need to change any of your DNS data. You find that the load on one of your name servers is inordinately high. What can you do to reduce this load?

   A. Increase the TTL on the affected name server.

   B. Decrease the TTL on the affected name server.

   C. Add a service record to the affected name server.

   D. Edit the directory command in the DNS boot file.

14. You are charged with upgrading your Windows NT network to Windows Server 2008. You plan on installing Active Directory and upgrading all your client machines to Vista. Your company does not allow Internet access because the company president still views it, as well as email, as a time-wasting toy that distracts the employees. Despite what you feel is a short-sighted view by management, you begin to design the upgrade process. You realize that DNS is an important component of Windows Server 2008, even though you won't be using it to locate resources on the Internet. What DNS records must you include in the configuration of the Windows Server 2008 DNS service in this environment? (Choose all that apply.)

   A. Host record

   B. Pointer record

   C. Alias record

   D. Name server records

   E. Start of authority record

   F. Mail exchanger record

   G. Service record

15. A spammer is attempting to send junk mail through an unsuspecting mail server. The spammer uses a fake DNS name from which they think the mail server will accept mail, but the mail is rejected anyway. How does the mail server know to reject the spammer's mail?

   A. The spammer's DNS name is not in the cache file of the primary DNS server that serves the mail server's domain, so it gets rejected.

   B. A fake DNS name is automatically detected if the IP address isn't recognized by the mail server.

   C. The mail server employs a reverse lookup zone to verify that DNS names are not fake.

   D. The spammer does not have an MX record in the database of the DNS server that serves the mail server's domain.

16. Your web server's hostname within the LAN is `chaos.stellacon.com`. However, you need to add a DNS entry so that it can be found with the name `www.stellacon.com`. What type of record should you add to the DNS zone for `stellacon.com` in order for this to be configured properly?

   A. An Alias/CNAME record

   B. An A record

   C. An SRV record

   D. A PTR record

17. You have two master servers operating in your environment, a primary master and a secondary master. These DNS servers are authoritative for the zone `example.com`. When the secondary master transfers the domain, what part of the DNS zone does it use to determine if the zone data has changed?

A. The TTL, or time to live

B. The NS record

C. The serial number

D. The database record tombstone

18. This type of DNS query results in the server sending back its best answer from the cache or local data.

A. Recursive

B. Iterative

C. Forward

D. NS

19. You're troubleshooting an error whereby a client computer seems to have old DNS data. You've used ipconfig to see what DNS servers the client is using and you've used ping to verify connectivity to those servers. What command should you use in order to clear the DNS cache on the client so that it will start building a new cache of DNS lookups?

A. `ipconfig /cleardns`

B. `nslookup /flushdns`

C. `dns /register`

D. `ipconfig /flushdns`

20. Your organization has two DNS servers located at the home office location. However, clients in remote offices are reporting sporadic DNS lookup failures. The network team has informed you that some of the WAN links to the remote offices are nearing saturation. To relieve some of the burden, you decide to implement secondary DNS servers in the remote offices. However, the DNS servers will not be official name servers for the domain, and therefore you don't need to set up NS records for each server. You configure half of the new DNS servers to attempt zone transfer from the primary master and the other half from the secondary master server. After deploying the servers, you notice that none of the servers are able to complete a zone transfer. What is likely the cause of this?

A. The primary master server's firewall is not configured for zone transfer data.

B. The primary and secondary master servers are not configured to allow zone transfers from the new DNS servers.

C. The new DNS servers cannot perform zone transfers from secondary servers.

D. The primary server is configured to allow recursive queries only.

Answers to Review Questions

1. B. A DNS server installed at each regional location will provide name and service resolution even if the WAN links go down. The local location will also have better performance because the requests will not have to travel through the WAN links. A single domain name for all the locations is needed because your requirement is to have one Active Directory tree with a contiguous name space.

2. The client machine places its request with its preferred DNS server. If the DNS server doesn't have an entry in its DNS database, it forwards the request to a root-level server. The root-level server resolves the name and sends it back to the preferred DNS server. The DNS server caches the name so that any future requests don't need to be forwarded, and then it sends the IP address to the client. The client then uses the IP address to reach the intended target.

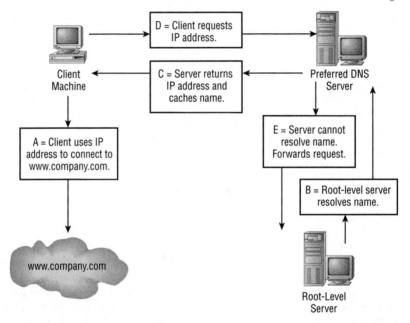

3. C. Windows 2000 and newer computers will register themselves in the DNS through dynamic updates. However, the Unix machines will not register themselves in the DNS. These machines will have to be added manually into the DNS so that the other clients can locate them. If you disabled the Dynamic DNS updates, you would then have to add all the workstations on the network to the DNS manually.

4. A. Installing the Windows DNS service on the Windows Server 2008 computer will provide dynamic updates. This will allow the newer Windows machines to publish themselves and to locate the Active Directory services through the SRV records that this version of DNS supports. The Windows Server 2008 DNS will also provide standard DNS services to the Unix and Windows NT machines. In addition, it can point to the DNS server that your ISP is supplying for searches beyond the local network.

No WINS service is available for Unix. It may remain on the Windows NT server until the upgrade is complete and the NetBIOS name resolution is no longer necessary.

5. B, C. Configuring his server as a root server and leaving forwarding off means that the server will either answer a query (for addresses it knows) or return a failure (for addresses it doesn't know).

6. C. The round robin option allows you to list a hostname with multiple IP addresses and then, as each request comes into the DNS server, rotate that list, presenting each of the IP addresses in turn. This will balance out the load across all the servers you have mirrored and configured in the DNS.

7. D. Stub zones are very useful for slow WAN connections. These zones store only three types of resource records: NS records, glue host (A) records, and SOA records. These three records are used to locate authoritative DNS servers.

8. C. Upgrading all the DNS servers to Active Directory Integrated zones will allow all DNS servers to share the same Active Directory DNS database. Active Directory Integrated zones also allow secure dynamic updates.

9. B. Installing a DNS server at each city as well as the central office allows the workstations in each city to obtain their name resolution from local servers, thereby providing good response time. If all the DNS servers were in the central office, name resolution would have to cross the routers, introducing latency and the potential for no service if the link ever went down. The namespace in a single Active Directory tree must be contiguous. If you create a second-level domain for each city, you need to create multiple Active Directory trees.

10. C. From the Monitoring tab, you can perform simple recursive queries to see if DNS servers are running and listening to queries. You can either run the tests immediately or set a schedule on which the tests will run.

11. C. DNS has the capability to create subdomains of a central corporate domain, and a subdomain can be delegated to a DNS server in each location for independent management. The entire company could use a single DNS server at corporate headquarters with the multiple domains, but then each namespace would not be managed locally at each location.

12. D. The root name server has authority for the root domain and will reply with the IP address of a name server for the .gov top-level domain. With the IP address of the top-level domain, the system can now query it for the bigbrother address.

13. A. If the TTL is too small, the load on the DNS server increases.

14. A, D, E, G. Even though it's best practice to have all the records associated with DNS as a part of each installation, name resolution will still function properly with just the fundamental records. The host record, or A record, is the basic record that contains the mapping between the logical name and the IP address. This is the heart of DNS. The name server records identify the DNS servers that are available for this network. The start of authority record, or SOA record, contains the basic configuration of the DNS service. The service record, while not essential to a traditional DNS, is critical to Active Directory because it's used to identify the domain controllers for login and other query information. The pointer record is used for reverse lookups; although it's very useful, it's not required for standard functionality. The alias record is needed only if you plan to have different names associated with the same physical address. The mail exchanger record is necessary only if you are using DNS to locate mail servers.

15. C. Most mail servers can be configured to reject incoming mail from servers whose IP addresses cannot be resolved with a reverse lookup.

16. A. Though it's possible to set up another A record pointing www.stellacon.com to the IP address of the server, such a record would not be configured properly. A CNAME record, sometimes called an Alias record, should be configured to point www at chaos.stellacon.com. Options C and D would not solve the problem.

17. C. The serial number is used by secondary servers to determine whether the zone data has changed. By default, this value is automatically updated with Windows Server 2008 DNS server. The zone's TTL is used to determine when to query for an update of the zone file from the master server unless a Notify message has been sent by the master server in the interim.

18. B. An iterative query results in the server sending back its best answer from data residing in its cache or local zones. A recursive query is one in which the server goes out and attempts to find the answer by querying other DNS servers.

19. D. The command ipconfig /flushdns clears the local DNS cache.

20. B. Since you didn't set up the new secondary servers with their own NS records, they aren't listed on the Name Servers tab of the zone's Properties dialog box. Therefore, by default these servers cannot transfer zone data. By going into the Zone Transfers tab, you can configure the servers to receive updates. Option A is incorrect because the main secondary master server can indeed receive zone transfers. Option C is incorrect because DNS servers can perform zone transfers from other secondary servers. Option D has nothing to do with zone transfers and cannot be true since the main secondary master can perform zone transfers.

Chapter

3

Active Directory Planning and Installation

In the previous chapters, you've seen some factors you need to take into account when planning for Active Directory, such as your company's physical and logical structure and the need for centralized or decentralized administration. The time you spend understanding these concepts is very important because the success of your Active Directory implementation depends on them.

Now that you are familiar with Domain Name System (DNS), you need to verify that the computer you upgrade to a domain controller (DC) meets the basic filesystem and network connectivity requirements so that Active Directory runs smoothly and efficiently in your organization.

Next, you'll explore the concept of domain functional levels, which essentially determine what sorts of domain controllers you can use in your environment. For instance, in the Windows Server 2000 Native domain functional level, you can include Server 2008, Server 2003, and 2000 Server domain controllers, but the functionality of the domain is severely limited.

Once you understand how to properly plan for your domain environment, you will learn how to install Active Directory, which you accomplish by promoting a Windows Server 2008 computer to a domain controller. We will also discuss a new feature in Windows Server 2008 called a read-only domain controller (RODC).

After you become familiar with the initial Active Directory installation, you will learn how to install and configure Application Directory partitions. These partitions provide replicable data repositories using the Active Directory paradigm, but they don't actually store any security principals, such as users or groups. As the name implies, you use Application Directory partitions primarily to store data generated by applications that need to be replicated throughout your network environments independently of the rest of Active Directory.

The final section of this chapter deals with integrating DNS with Active Directory. You learned about DNS in Chapter 2, but here we will review how DNS implements with Active Directory.

Verifying the Filesystem

When planning your Active Directory deployment, the filesystem the operating system uses is an important concern for many reasons. First, the filesystem can provide the ultimate level of security for all of the information stored on the server itself. Second, it is responsible for managing and tracking all of this data. Furthermore, certain features are available only on certain filesystems. These features include encryption support, remote file access, remote storage, disk redundancy, and disk quotas.

The Windows Server 2008 platform supports two filesystems:

- *File Allocation Table* 32 (FAT32) filesystem
- Windows *New Technology File System (NTFS)*

The fundamental difference between FAT32 and NTFS partitions is that NTFS allows for filesystem-level security. Support for FAT32 is mainly included in Windows Server 2008 for backward compatibility and machines that need to *dual-boot*. For example, if you want to configure a single computer to boot into Windows 98 and Windows Server 2003, you need to have at least one FAT or FAT32 partition.

Windows Server 2008 uses Version 5 of NTFS. There are many other benefits to using NTFS, including support for the following:

Disk quotas   In order to restrict the amount of disk space used by users on the network, systems administrators can establish disk quotas. By default, Windows Server 2008 supports disk quota restrictions at the volume level. That is, you can restrict the amount of storage space a specific user uses on a single disk volume. Third-party solutions that allow more granular quota settings are also available.

Filesystem encryption   One of the fundamental problems with network operating systems (NOSs) is that systems administrators are often given full permission to view all files and data stored on hard disks, which can be a security and privacy concern. In some cases, this is necessary. For example, in order to perform backup, recovery, and disk management functions, at least one user must have all permissions. Windows Server 2008 and NTFS address these issues by allowing for filesystem encryption. Encryption essentially scrambles all of the data stored within files before they are written to the disk. When an authorized user requests the files, they are transparently decrypted and provided. By using encryption, you can prevent the data from being used in the case where it is stolen or intercepted by an unauthorized user, even a system administrator.

Dynamic volumes   Protecting against disk failures is an important concern for production servers. Although earlier versions of Windows NT supported various levels of Redundant Array of Independent Disks (RAID) technology, software-based solutions had some shortcomings. Perhaps the most significant was that administrators needed to perform server reboots to change RAID configurations. Also, you could not make some configuration changes without completely reinstalling the operating system. With Windows Server 2008's support for dynamic volumes, systems administrators can change RAID and other disk configuration settings without needing to reboot or reinstall the server. The end result is greater data protection, increased scalability, and increased uptime.

Mounted drives   By using mounted drives, systems administrators can map a local disk drive to an NTFS directory name. This helps them organize disk space on servers and increase manageability. By using mounted drives, you can mount the C:\Users directory to an actual physical disk. If that disk becomes full, you can copy all of the files to another, larger drive without changing the directory pathname or reconfiguring applications.

Remote storage   Systems administrators often notice that as soon as they add more space, they must plan the next upgrade. One way to recover disk space is to move infrequently used files to tape. However, backing up and restoring these files can be quite difficult and time consuming. Systems administrators can use the remote storage features supported by NTFS to automatically off-load seldom-used data to tape or other devices, but the files remain available to users. If a user requests an archived file, Windows Server 2008 can automatically restore the file from a remote storage device and make it available. Using remote storage like this frees up systems administrators' time and allows them to focus on tasks other than micromanaging disk space.

Self-Healing NTFS   In previous versions of the Windows Server operating system, if you had to fix a corrupted NTFS volume, you used a tool called Chkdsk.exe. The disadvantage of this tool is that the Windows Server's availability was disrupted. If this server was your domain controller, that could stop domain logon authentication.

To help protect the Windows Server 2008 NTFS filesystem, Microsoft now uses a feature called self-healing NTFS. Self-healing NTFS attempts to fix corrupted NTFS filesystems without taking them offline. Self-healing NTFS allows an NTFS filesystem to be corrected without running the Chkdsk.exe utility. New features added to the NTFS kernel code allow disk inconsistencies to be corrected without system downtime.

Setting Up the NTFS Partition

Although the features mentioned in the previous section probably compel most systems administrators to use NTFS, more reasons make using it mandatory. The most important reason is that the Active Directory data store must reside on an NTFS partition. Therefore, before you begin installing Active Directory, make sure you have at least one NTFS partition available. Also, be sure you have a reasonable amount of disk space available (at least 4GB). Because the size of the Active Directory data store will grow as you add objects to it, also be sure you have adequate space for the future.

Exercise 3.1 shows you how to use the administrative tools to view and modify disk configuration.

WARNING   Before you make any disk configuration changes, be sure you completely understand their potential effects; then, perform the test in a lab environment and make sure you have good, verifiable backups handy. Changing partition sizes and adding and removing partitions can result in a total loss of all information on one or more partitions.

If you want to convert an existing partition from FAT or FAT32 to NTFS, you need to use the CONVERT command-line utility. For example, the following command converts the C: partition from FAT to NTFS:

```
CONVERT c: /fs:ntfs
```

EXERCISE 3.1

Viewing Disk Configuration

1. Click Start ➤Administrative Tools ➤ Computer Management.

2. Under the Storage branch, click Disk Management.

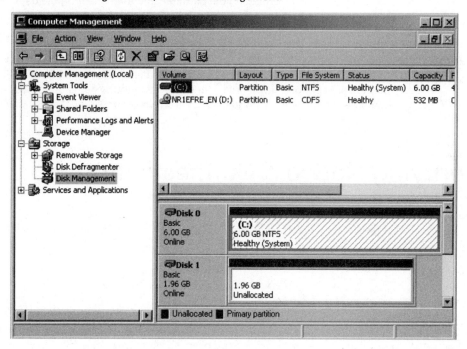

The Disk Management program shows you the logical and physical disks that are currently configured on your system. Note that information about the size of each partition is also displayed (in the Capacity column).

3. Use the View menu to choose various depictions of the physical and logical drives in your system.

4. To see the available options for modifying partition settings, right-click any of the disks or partitions. This step is optional.

    If the partition you are trying to convert contains any system files or the Windows Server 2008 virtual memory page file, a message informs you that the conversion will take place during the next machine reboot. After the partition is converted to NTFS, the computer automatically reboots again, and you will be able to continue using the system.

Windows Server 2008 allows you to convert existing FAT or FAT32 partitions to NTFS. However, this is a one-way process. You cannot convert an NTFS partition to any other filesystem without losing data. If you need to make such a conversion, the recommended process involves backing up all existing data, deleting and reformatting the partition, and then restoring the data.

Only the Windows NT, 2000, XP, Vista, 2003, and 2008 operating systems (all based on the original NT architecture) can read and write to and from NTFS partitions. Therefore, if you are using other operating systems on the same computer, be sure you fully understand the effects of converting the filesystem.

Verifying Network Connectivity

Although a Windows Server 2008 computer can be used by itself without connecting to a network, you will not harness much of the potential of the operating system without network connectivity. Because the fundamental purpose of a network operating system is to provide resources to users, you must verify network connectivity.

Basic Connectivity Tests

Before you begin to install Active Directory, you should perform several checks of your current configuration to ensure that the server is configured properly on the network. You should test the following:

Network adapter   At least one network adapter should be installed and properly configured on your server. A quick way to verify that a network adapter is properly installed is to use the Computer Management administrative tool. Under Device Manager, Network Adapters branch, you should have at least one network adapter listed. If you do not, use the Add Hardware icon in the Control Panel to configure hardware.

TCP/IP   Make sure TCP/IP is installed, configured, and enabled on any necessary network adapters. The server should also be given a valid IP address and subnet mask. Optionally, you may need to configure a default gateway, DNS servers, WINS servers, and other network settings. If you are using DHCP, be sure that the assigned information is correct. It is always a good idea to use a static IP address for servers because IP address changes can cause network connectivity problems if they are not handled properly.

You must understand TCP/IP to use Windows Server 2008 and Active Directory. See *MCTS: Windows Server 2008 Network Infrastructure Study Guide (70-642), First Edition* (Sybex, 2008) to learn more about TCP/IP.

Internet access   If the server should have access to the Internet, verify that it is able to connect to external web servers and other machines outside the large area network (LAN). If the server is unable to connect, you might have a problem with the TCP/IP configuration.

LAN access   The server should be able to view other servers and workstations on the network. You can quickly verify this type of connectivity by clicking Start ➤ Network. If other machines are not visible, ensure that the network and TCP/IP configuration are correct for your environment.

Client access   Network client computers should be able to connect to your server and view any shared resources. A simple way to test connectivity is to create a share and test whether other machines are able to see files and folders within it. If clients cannot access the machine, ensure that both the client and server are configured properly.

Wide area network (WAN) access   If you're working in a distributed environment, you should ensure that you have access to any remote sites or users that will need to connect to this machine. Usually, this is a simple test that can be performed by a network administrator.

Tools and Techniques for Testing Network Configuration

In some cases, verifying network access can be quite simple. You might have some internal and external network resources with which to test. In other cases, it might be more complicated. You can use several tools and techniques to verify that your network configuration is correct:

Using the ipconfig utility   By typing `ipconfig/all` at the command prompt, you can view information about the TCP/IP settings of a computer. Figure 3.1 shows the types of information you'll receive.

Using the `ping` command   The `ping` command was designed to test connectivity to other computers. You can use the command by simply typing `ping` and then an IP address or hostname at the command line. The following are some steps for testing connectivity using the `ping` command.

Ping other computers on the same subnet.   You should start by pinging a known active IP address on the network to check for a response. If you receive one, then you have connectivity to the network.

Next, check to see if you can ping another machine using its hostname. If this works, then local name resolution works properly.

Ping computers on different subnets. In order to ensure that routing is set up properly, you should attempt to ping computers that are local on other subnets (if any exist) on your network. If this test fails, try pinging the default gateway. Any errors may indicate a problem in the network configuration or a problem with a router.

Some firewalls, routers, or servers on your network or on the Internet might prevent you from receiving a successful response from a ping command. This is usually for security reasons (malicious users might attempt to disrupt network traffic using excessive pings as well as redirects and smurf attacks). If you do not receive a response, do not assume that the service is not available. Instead, try to verify connectivity in other ways. For example, you can use the TRACERT command to demonstrate connectivity beyond your subnet, even if other routers ignore Internet Control Message Protocol (ICMP) responses. Since the display of a second router implies connectivity, the path to an ultimate destination shows success even if it does not display the actual names and addresses.

FIGURE 3.1 Viewing TCP/IP information with the ipconfig utility

```
Command Prompt                                                          _ □ ×
C:\Documents and Settings\Administrator>ipconfig /all

Windows IP Configuration

    Host Name . . . . . . . . . . . . : sybex1
    Primary Dns Suffix  . . . . . . . : sybex1.com
    Node Type . . . . . . . . . . . . : Unknown
    IP Routing Enabled. . . . . . . . : Yes
    WINS Proxy Enabled. . . . . . . . : Yes
    DNS Suffix Search List. . . . . . : sybex1.com

Ethernet adapter Local Area Connection:

    Connection-specific DNS Suffix  . :
    Description . . . . . . . . . . . : ATI AT-2500TX PCI Fast Ethernet Adapter
    Physical Address. . . . . . . . . : 00-A0-D2-1B-C4-E2
    DHCP Enabled. . . . . . . . . . . : No
    IP Address. . . . . . . . . . . . : 192.168.0.2
    Subnet Mask . . . . . . . . . . . : 255.255.255.0
    Default Gateway . . . . . . . . . : 66.127.67.25
                                        192.168.0.1
    DNS Servers . . . . . . . . . . . : 206.13.28.12
                                        206.13.31.12

C:\Documents and Settings\Administrator>^@
```

Browsing the network To ensure that you have access to other computers on the network, be sure that they can be viewed by clicking Start ➢ Network. This verifies that your name resolution parameters are set up correctly and that other computers are accessible. Also, try connecting to resources (such as file shares or printers) on other machines.

Browsing the Internet You can quickly verify whether your server has access to the Internet by visiting a known website, such as www.microsoft.com. Success ensures that you have access outside of your network. If you do not have access to the Web, you might need to verify your proxy server settings (if applicable) and your DNS server settings.

By performing these simple tests, you can ensure that you have a properly configured network connection and that other network resources are available.

Understanding Domain and Forest Functionality

Windows Server 2008 Active Directory uses a concept called *domain and forest functionality*. The functional level that you choose during the Active Directory installation determines which features your domain can use.

Windows Server 2003 and 2008 include additional forest functionality compared to Windows 2000. Forest functionality applies to all of the domains in a forest.

About the Domain Functional Level

Windows Server 2008 will support the following domain functional levels:

- Windows 2000 Native
- Windows 2003
- Windows Server 2008

Which function level you use depends on the domain controllers you have installed on your network. This is an important fact to remember. You can use Windows NT 4, Windows 2000 Server, and Windows 2003 member servers in the Windows Server 2008 function level, as long as all domain controllers are running Windows Server 2008.

When you install the first domain controller in a new Windows Server 2008 forest, the domain functional level is set by default to Windows 2000 Native. Windows 2000 Native is the default setting because once a domain function level is upgraded, it cannot be downgraded.

Table 3.1 shows features available in Windows 2000 Native, Windows 2003, and Windows Server 2008 domain functional levels.

TABLE 3.1   Comparing Domain Functional Levels

Domain Functional Feature	Windows 2000 Native	Windows Server 2003	Windows Server 2008
Fine-grained password policies.	Disabled	Disabled	Enabled
Read-only domain controller (RODC).	Disabled	Enabled	Enabled
Last interactive logon information.	Disabled	Disabled	Enabled

TABLE 3.1   Comparing Domain Functional Levels *(continued)*

Domain Functional Feature	Windows 2000 Native	Windows Server 2003	Windows Server 2008
Advanced Encryption Services (AES 128 and 256) support for the Kerberos protocol.	Disabled	Disabled	Enabled
Distributed File System replication support for Sysvol.	Disabled	Disabled	Enabled
Ability to Redirect the Users and Computers containers.	Disabled	Enabled	Enabled
Ability to rename domain controllers.	Disabled	Enabled	Enabled
Logon Time stamp updates.	Disabled	Enabled	Enabled
Kerberos KDC key version numbers.	Disabled	Enabled	Enabled
InetOrgPerson objects can have passwords.	Disabled	Enabled	Enabled
Converts NT groups to domain local and global groups.	Enabled	Enabled	Enabled
SID history.	Enabled	Enabled	Enabled
Group nesting.	Enabled	Enabled	Enabled
Universal groups.	Enabled	Enabled	Enabled

About Forest Functionality

Windows Server 2008 includes new forest functionality features. Forest functionality applies to all of the domains in a forest. All domains have to be upgraded to Windows Server 2008 before the forest can be upgraded to Windows Server 2008.

There are three levels of forest functionality:

- Windows 2000—the default; supports Windows 2000, 2003, and 2008 domain controllers
- Windows Server 2003
- Windows Server 2008

Windows Server 2003 and 2008 have the same forest features. Some of the features are described in the following list:

Global Catalog replication enhancements   When an administrator adds a new attribute to the Global Catalog, only those changes are replicated to other global catalogs in the forest. This can significantly reduce the amount of network traffic generated by replication.

Defunct schema classes and attributes   You can never permanently remove classes and attributes from the Active Directory schema, but you can mark them as defunct so that they cannot be used. With Windows Server 2003 and 2008 forest functionality, you can redefine the defunct schema attribute so that it occupies a new role in the schema.

Forest trusts   Previously, system administrators had no easy way of granting permission on resources in different forests. Windows Server 2003 and 2008 resolve some of these difficulties by allowing trust relationships between separate Active Directory forests. Forest trusts act much like domain trusts, except that they extend to every domain in two forests. Note that all forest trusts are intransitive.

Linked value replication   Windows Server 2003 and 2008 use a concept called linked value replication. With linked value replication, only the user record that has been changed is replicated (not the entire group). This can significantly reduce network traffic associated with replication.

Renaming domains   Although the Active Directory domain structure was originally designed to be flexible, there were several limitations. Due to mergers, acquisitions, corporate reorganizations, and other business changes, you may need to rename domains. In Windows Server 2003 and 2008, you can change the DNS and NetBIOS names for any domain, as well as reposition a domain within a forest. Note that this operation is not as simple as just issuing a rename command. Instead, there's a specific process you must follow to make sure that the operation is successful. Fortunately, when you properly follow the procedure, Microsoft supports domain renaming.

Other features   Windows Server 2003 and 2008 support the following features:

- Improved replication algorithms and dynamic auxiliary classes are designed to increase performance, scalability, and reliability.
- Active Directory Federation Services (AD FS, also known as Trustbridge) handles federated identity management. Federated identity management is a standards-based information technology process that enables distributed identification, authentication, and authorization across organizational and platform boundaries. The AD FS solution

in Windows Server 2003 (Release 2) and 2008 helps administrators address these challenges by enabling organizations to securely share a user's identity information.

- Active Directory Application Mode (ADAM) was developed by Microsoft as part of
  Windows Server 2008 Active Directory for organizations that require flexible support
  for directory-enabled applications. ADAM, which uses the Lightweight Directory
  Access Protocol (LDAP), is a directory service that adds flexibility and helps organizations avoid increased infrastructure costs.

Many of the concepts related to domain and forest functional features are
covered in greater detail later in this book.

Planning the Domain Structure

Once you have verified the technical configuration of your server for Active Directory, it's time
to verify the Active Directory configuration for your organization. Since the content of this
chapter focuses on installing the first domain in your environment, you really only need to
know the following information prior to beginning setup:

- The DNS name of the domain
- The computer name or the NetBIOS name of the server (which will be used by previous
  versions of Windows to access server resources)
- Which domain function level the domain will operate in
- Whether or not other DNS servers are available on the network
- What type of and how many DNS servers are available on the network

However, if you will be installing additional domain controllers in your environment or
will be attaching to an existing Active Directory structure, you should also have the following
information:

- If this domain controller will join an existing domain, you should know the name of that
  domain. You will also either require a password for a member of the Enterprise Administrators group for that domain or have someone with those permissions create a domain
  account before promotion.
- You should know whether the new domain will join an existing tree and, if so, the name
  of the tree it will join.
- You should know the name of a forest to which this domain will connect (if applicable).

Installing Active Directory

Installing Active Directory is an easy and straightforward process as long as you planned adequately and made the necessary decisions beforehand. In this section, you'll look at the actual steps required to install the first domain controller in a given environment.

With early versions of the Windows NT operating system, you had to determine during installation the role of your server as it related to the domain controller or member server. Choices included making the machine a primary domain controller (PDC), a backup domain controller (BDC), or a member server. This was an extremely important decision because, even though you could promote a BDC to a PDC, you had to completely reinstall the operating system to make any changes to the server's role between a domain controller and a member server.

Instead of forcing you to choose during setup whether or not the machine will participate as a domain controller, Windows Server 2008 allows you to promote servers after you install Active Directory. Therefore, at the end of the setup process, all Windows Server 2008 computers are configured as either member servers (if they are joined to a domain) or stand-alone servers (if they are part of a workgroup). The process of converting a member server to a domain controller is known as *promotion*. Through the use of a simple and intuitive wizard, systems administrators can quickly configure servers to be domain controllers after installation.

Later in this section, you'll follow the steps you need to take to install Active Directory by promoting the first domain controller in the domain. These steps are performed using the Active Directory Installation Wizard *(DCPROMO)*. This tool is designed to be used after a server has been installed in the environment. As part of the promotion process, the server creates or receives information related to Active Directory configuration.

The first step in installing Active Directory is promoting a Windows Server 2008 computer to a domain controller. The first domain controller in an environment serves as the starting point for the forest, trees, domains, and the Operations Master roles.

Exercise 3.2 shows the steps you need to follow to promote an existing Windows Server 2008 to a domain controller. In order to complete the steps in this exercise, you must have already installed and configured a Windows Server 2003 or 2008 computer. You also need a DNS server that supports SRV records. If you do not have a DNS server available, the Active Directory Installation Wizard automatically configures one for you.

EXERCISE 3.2

Promoting a Domain Controller

1. Start the Active Directory Installation Wizard by clicking Start ➢ Run and typing **dcpromo**.

2. When the Welcome screen appears, check the box that says "Use Advanced Mode Installation" and then click Next

EXERCISE 3.2 *(continued)*

3. The "Choose a Deployment Configuration" box appears. Choose the second option, "Create a new domain in a new forest". Then click Next.

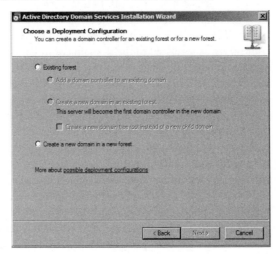

4. A warning box may appear stating that the local administrator account will become the domain administrator account. If this box appears, click Yes.

5. The Name the Forest Root Domain box appears, asking you to enter the full DNS name of your domain. Enter your domain's DNS name and click Next. (Use mycompany.com if you do not have a domain name.)

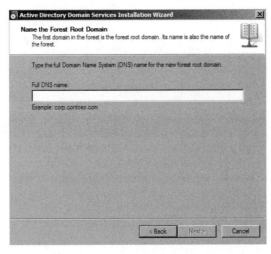

6. After the DNS name gets verified, a NetBIOS name box appears with your default NetBIOS name (for example, mycompany). Leave the default and click Next.

A NetBIOS name can be up to 15 characters. To make it easier to remember and type the name, you should limit yourself to the English alphabet characters and numbers.

7. The "Set Forest Functional Level" box appears. Use the pull down menu and choose Windows Server 2003 or Windows Server 2008 and then click Next.

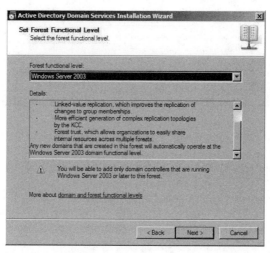

8. When the Additional Domain Controller Options page appears, make sure DNS Server is checked (if you need to install DNS). Also notice the option labeled "Read-Only Domain Controller (RODC)." This is where you will create your RODC (RODC installation and configuration are covered in later chapters of this book). Since this is the first domain controller in your new domain, the RODC option is grayed out. Click Next.

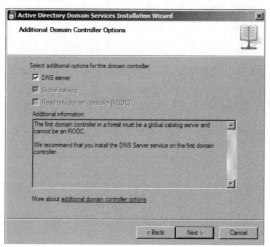

9. A Static IP Assignment box may appear. If it does, choose the Yes option and configure a static IP address for your computer. If this box does not appear, go on to the next step.

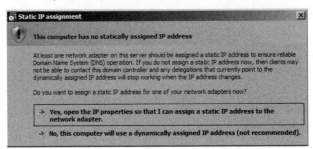

10. In the Location for Database, Log Files, and Sysvol page, specify the filesystem locations for the Active Directory database and log files. Microsoft recommends that these files reside on separate physical devices in order to improve performance and to provide for recoverability. The default filesystem location is in a directory called NTDS located within the system root. However, you can choose any folder located on a FAT32 or NTFS partition (Sysvol requires NTFS). After you've specified the filesystem locations (you can leave the defaults if you like), click Next.

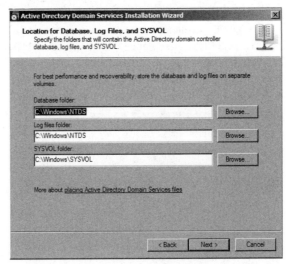

11. On the Directory Services Restore Mode Administrator Password page, provide a password to be used to restore Active Directory in the event of its loss or corruption. Note that this password does not have to correspond with passwords set for any other account. For this exercise, use the following password:

P@ssw0rd

After confirming the password, click Next.

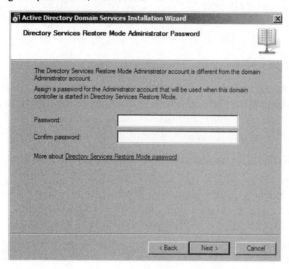

12. Based on the installation options you've selected, the wizard presents a summary of your choices. It is a good idea to copy and paste this information into a text file to refer to later. Verify the options, and then click Next to begin the Active Directory installation process.

A box with a book that is being written to will appear as Active Directory is installing.

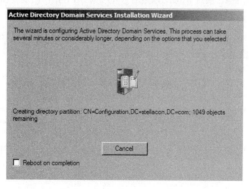

13. Once Active Directory has been installed, you are prompted to reboot the system. After the reboot, you can access the administrative tools that are related to the configuration and management of Active Directory.

Verifying Active Directory Installation

Once you have installed and configured Active Directory, you'll want to verify that you have done so properly. In the following sections, you'll look at methods for doing this.

Using Event Viewer

The first (and perhaps most informative) way to verify the operations of Active Directory is to query information stored in the Windows Server 2008 event log. You can do this using the Windows Server 2008 Event Viewer. Exercise 3.3 walks you through this procedure. Entries seen with the Event Viewer include errors, warnings, and informational messages.

 In order to complete the steps in this exercise, you must have configured the local machine as a domain controller.

EXERCISE 3.3

Viewing the Active Directory Event Log

1. Open the Event Viewer snap-in from the Administrative Tools program group.

2. In the left pane, under Applications and Services Logs, select Directory Service.

3. In the right pane, you can sort information by clicking column headings. For example, you can click the Source column to sort by the service or process that reported the event.

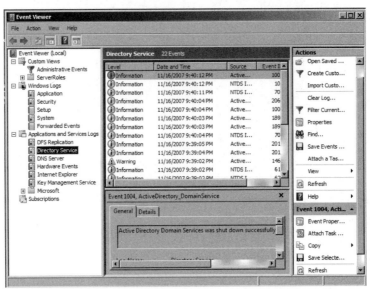

EXERCISE 3.3 *(continued)*

4. Double-click an event in the list to see the details for that item. Note that you can click the Copy button to copy the event information to the Clipboard. You can then paste the data into a document for later reference. Also, you can move between items using the up and down arrows. Click OK when you are done viewing an event.

5. Filter an event list by right-clicking the Directory Service item in the left pane, and selecting the Filter tab. Note that filtering does not remove entries from the event logs—it only restricts their display.

6. To verify Active Directory installation, look for events related to the proper startup of Active Directory, such as Event ID 1000 (Active Directory Startup Complete) and 1394 (Attempts To Update The Active Directory Database Are Succeeding). Also, be sure to examine any Error or Warning messages because these could indicate problems with DNS or other necessary services.

7. When you're done viewing information in the Event Viewer, close the application.

 Real World Scenario

Gaining Insight through Event Viewer

Despite its simple user interface and somewhat limited GUI functionality, the Event Viewer tool can be your best ally in isolating and troubleshooting problems with Windows Server 2008. The Event Viewer allows you to view information that is stored in various log files that are maintained by the operating system. This list of logs includes the following:

Application   Stores messages generated by programs running on your system. For example, SQL Server 2005 might report the completion of a database backup job within the Application log.

Security   Contains security-related information, as defined by your auditing settings. For example, you could see when users have logged onto the system or when particularly sensitive files have been accessed.

System   Contains operating system–related information and messages. Common messages might include a service startup failure or information about when the operating system was last rebooted.

Directory service   Stores messages and events related to how Active Directory functions. For example, details related to replication might be found here.

DNS server   Contains details about the operations of the DNS service. This log is useful for troubleshooting replication or name resolution problems.

Other log files   Contain various features of Windows Server 2008 and the applications that may run on this operating system that can create additional types of logs. These files allow you to view more information about other applications or services through the familiar Event Viewer tool.

Additionally, developers can easily send custom information from their programs to the Application log. Having all of this information in one place really makes it easy to analyze operating system and application messages. Also, many third-party tools and utilities are available for analyzing log files.

Although the Event Viewer GUI does a reasonably good job of letting you find the information you need, you might want to extract information to analyze other systems or applications. One especially useful feature of the Event Viewer is its ability to save the log file in various formats. You can access this feature by clicking Action ➢ Save As. You'll be given the option of saving in various formats, including tab- and comma-delimited text files. You can then open these files in other applications (such as Microsoft Excel) for additional data analysis.

Overall, in the real world, the Event Viewer can be an excellent resource for monitoring and troubleshooting your important servers and workstations!

In addition to providing information about the status of events related to Active Directory, the Event Viewer shows you useful information about other system services and applications. You should routinely use the tool.

Using Active Directory Administrative Tools

After a server has been promoted to a domain controller, you will see various tools added to the Administrative Tools program group (see Figure 3.2).

These include the following:

Active Directory Domains and Trusts   Use this tool to view and change information related to the various domains in an Active Directory environment. This MMC snap-in also allows you to set up shortcut trusts.

Active Directory Sites and Services   Use this tool to create and manage Active Directory sites and services to map to an organization's physical network infrastructure. Sites and services are covered in detail in Chapter 4, "Configuring Sites and Replication."

Active Directory Users and Computers   User and computer management is fundamental for an Active Directory environment. The Active Directory Users and Computers tool allows you to set machine- and user-specific settings across the domain. This tool is discussed throughout many chapters in this book.

FIGURE 3.2   Some of the many Windows Server 2008 administrative tools

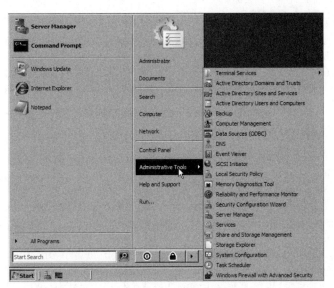

A good way to make sure that Active Directory is accessible and functioning properly is to run the Active Directory Users And Computers tool. When you open the tool, you should see a configuration similar to that shown in Figure 3.3. Specifically, you should make sure that the name of the domain you created appears in the list. You should also click the Domain Controllers folder and ensure that the name of your local server appears in the right pane. If your configuration passes these two checks, Active Directory is present and configured.

FIGURE 3.3   Viewing Active Directory information using the Active Directory Users and Computers tool

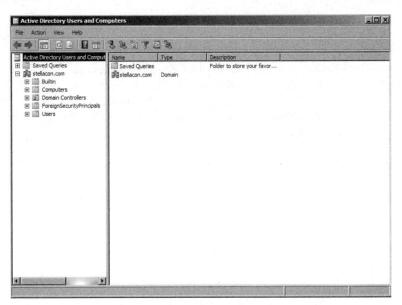

Testing from Clients

The best test of any solution is to simply verify that it works the way you had intended in your environment. When it comes to using Active Directory, a good test is to ensure that clients can view and access the various resources presented by Windows Server 2008 domain controllers. In the following sections, you'll look at several ways to verify that Active Directory is functioning properly.

Verifying Client Connectivity

Perhaps the most relevant way to test Active Directory is by testing client operations. Using computers running previous versions of Windows (such as Windows NT 4 or Windows 95/98), you should be able to see your server on the network. Earlier versions of Windows-based clients should recognize the NetBIOS name of the domain controller. Windows 2000 and newer computers should also be able to see resources in the domain, and users should be able to browse for resources using the My Network Places icon.

If you are unable to see the recently promoted server on the network, there is likely a network configuration error. If only one or a few clients are unable to see the machine, the problem is probably related to client-side configuration. To fix this, make sure the client computers have the appropriate TCP/IP configuration (including DNS server settings) and that they can see other computers on the network.

If the new domain controller is unavailable from any of the other client computers, you should verify the proper startup of Active Directory using the methods mentioned earlier in this chapter. If Active Directory has been started, ensure that the DNS settings are correct. Finally, test network connectivity between the server and the clients by accessing the My Network Places icon.

Joining a Domain

If Active Directory has been properly configured, clients and other servers should be able to join the domain. Exercise 3.4 outlines the steps you need to take to join a Windows XP Professional computer to the domain.

In order to complete this exercise, you must have already installed and properly configured at least one Active Directory domain controller and a DNS server that supports SRV records in your environment. In addition to the domain controller, you need at least one other computer, not configured as a domain controller, running one of the following operating systems: Windows 2000, Windows XP Professional (Windows XP Home Edition cannot join a domain), Vista, Windows Server 2003, or Windows Server 2008.

Once clients are able to successfully join the domain, they should be able to view Active Directory resources using the My Network Places icon. This test validates the proper functioning of Active Directory and ensures that you have connectivity with client computers.

EXERCISE 3.4

Joining a Computer to an Active Directory Domain

1. On the Desktop of the computer that is to be joined to the new domain, right-click the My Computer icon and click Properties (or select System from the Control Panel).

2. Select the Network Identification tab. You will see the current name of the local computer as well as information on the workgroup or domain to which it belongs.

3. If you want to change the name of the computer, click Change. This is useful if your domain has a specific naming convention for client computers. Otherwise, continue to the next step.

4. In the Member Of section, choose the Domain option. Type the name of the Active Directory domain that this computer should join. Click OK.

5. When prompted for the username and password of an account that has permission to join computers to the domain, enter the information for an administrator of the domain. Click OK to commit the changes. If joining the domain was successful, you will see a dialog box welcoming you to the new domain.

6. You will be notified that you must reboot the computer before the changes take place. Select Yes when prompted to reboot.

Creating and Configuring Application Data Partitions

Organizations store many different kinds of information in various places. For the IT departments that support this information, it can be difficult to ensure that the right information is available when and where it is needed. Windows Server 2008 uses a feature called *application data partitions*, which allows systems administrators and application developers to store custom information within Active Directory. The idea behind application data partitions is that, since you already have a directory service that can replicate all kinds of information, you might as well use it to keep track of your own information.

Developing distributed applications that can, for example, synchronize information across an enterprise is not a trivial task. You have to come up with a way to transfer data between remote sites (some of which are located across the world), and you have to ensure that the data is properly replicated. By storing application information in Active Directory, you can take advantage of its storage mechanism and replication topology. Application-related information stored on domain controllers benefits from having fault-tolerance features and availability.

Take a look at the following simple example to understand how this can work. Suppose your organization has developed a customer Sales Tracking and Inventory application. The company needs to make the information that is stored by this application available to all of its branch offices and users located throughout the world. However, the goal is to do this with the least amount of IT administrative effort. Assuming that Active Directory has already been deployed throughout the organization, developers can build support into the application for storing data within Active Directory. They can then rely on Active Directory to store and synchronize the information between various sites. When users request updated data from the application, the application can obtain this information from the nearest domain controller that hosts a replica of the Sales Tracking and Inventory data.

Other types of applications can also benefit greatly from the use of application data partitions. Now that you have a good idea of what application data partitions are, let's take a look at how you can create and manage them using Windows Server 2008 and Active Directory.

Creating Application Data Partitions

By default, after you create an Active Directory environment, you will not have any customer application data partitions. Therefore, the first step in making this functionality available is to create a new application data partition. You can use several tools to do this:

Third-party applications or application-specific tools   Generally, if you are planning to install an application that can store information in the Active Directory database, you'll receive some method of administering and configuring that data along with the application. For example, the setup process for the application might assist you in the steps you need to take to set up a new application data partition and to create the necessary structures for storing data.

 The creation and management of application data partitions is an advanced Active Directory–related function. Be sure that you have a solid understanding of the Active Directory schema, Active Directory replication, LDAP, and your applications' needs before you attempt to create new application data partitions in a live environment.

Active Directory Services Interface (ADSI)   ADSI is a set of programmable objects that can be accessed through languages such as Visual Basic Scripting Edition (VBScript), Visual C#, Visual Basic .NET, and many other language technologies that support the Component Object Modeling (COM) standard. Through the use of ADSI, developers can create, access, and update data stored in Active Directory and in any application data partitions.

The LDP tool   You can view and modify the contents of the Active Directory schema using LDAP-based queries. The LDP tool allows you to view information about application data partitions. In order to use this utility, you must first install the Windows Server 2008 Support Tools. The installer for this collection of utilities is located within the Windows Server 2008 installation media in the \Support\Tools folder. You'll need to run the SupTools.msi file in order to install the tools. Once the installation is complete, you can access the utility by clicking Start ➢ Run and typing **ldp.exe**. Figure 3.4 shows an example of connecting to a domain controller and browsing Active Directory information. For further details on using LDP, click the Support Tools Help icon (located within the Windows Support Tools program folder in the Start Menu). Additional details about working with the LDP tool are also available in the `LDP.doc` file, which is located within the folder into which you installed the Support Tools.

FIGURE 3.4   Using the LDP tool to view Active Directory schema information. Note: This tool isn't released for Server 2008 and the current screenshot is from 2003.

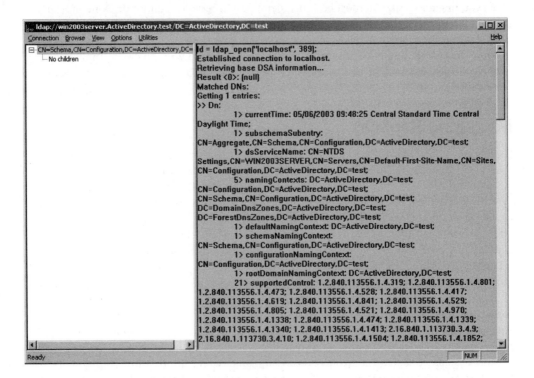

ntdsutil   The ntdsutil utility is the main method by which systems administrators create and manage application data partitions on their Windows Server 2008 domain controllers. This utility's specific commands are covered later in this chapter.

 Creating and managing application data partitions can be fairly complex; such a project's success depends on the quality of the architecture design. This is a good example of where IT staff and application developers must cooperate to ensure that data is stored effectively and that it is replicated efficiently.

You can create an application data partition in one of three different locations within an Active Directory forest:

- As a new tree in an Active Directory forest

- As a child of an Active Directory domain partition

  For example, you can create an Accounting application data partition within the Finance.MyCompany.com domain.

- As a child of another application data partition

  This method allows you to create a hierarchy of application data partitions.

As you might expect, you must be a member of the Enterprise Admins or Domain Admins group in order to be able to create application data partitions. Alternatively, you can be delegated the appropriate permissions to create new partitions.

Now that you have a good idea of the basic ways in which you can create application data partitions, let's look at how replicas (copies of application data partition information) are handled.

Managing Replicas

A replica is a copy of any data stored within Active Directory. Unlike the basic information that is stored in Active Directory, application partitions cannot contain security principals. Also, not all domain controllers automatically contain copies of the data stored in an application data partition. System administrators can define which domain controllers host copies of the application data. This is a very important feature, since, if replicas are used effectively, administrators can find a good balance between replication traffic and data consistency. For example, suppose that 3 of your organization's 30 locations require up-to-date accounting-related information. You might choose to only replicate the data to domain controllers located in the places that require the data. Limiting replication of this data reduces network traffic.

Replication is the process by which replicas are kept up to date. Application data can be stored and updated on designated servers, the same way basic Active Directory information (such as users and groups) is synchronized between domain controllers. Application data partition replicas are managed using the Knowledge Consistency Checker (KCC), which ensures that the designated domain controllers receive updated replica information. Additionally, the KCC uses all of Active Directory sites and connection objects (covered in Chapter 4) that you create to determine the best method to handle replication.

Removing Replicas

When you perform *demotion* on a domain controller, that server can no longer host an application data partition. If a domain controller contains a replica of application data partition information, you must remove the replica from the domain controller before you demote it. If a domain controller is the machine that hosts a replica of the application data partition, then the entire application data partition is removed and will be permanently lost. Generally, you want to do this only after you're absolutely sure that your organization no longer needs access to the data stored in the application data partition.

Using ntdsutil to Manage Application Data Partitions

The primary method by which systems administrators create and manage application data partitions is through the ntdsutil command-line tool. You can launch this tool by simply entering **ntdsutil** at a command prompt. The ntdsutil command is both interactive and context-sensitive. That is, once you launch the utility, you'll see an ntdsutil command prompt. At this prompt, you can enter various commands that set your context within the application. For example, if you enter the domain management command, you'll be able to use domain-related commands. Several operations also require you to connect to a domain, a domain controller, or an Active Directory object before you perform a command.

 For complete details on using ntdsutil, see the Windows Server 2008 Help and Support Center.

Table 3.2 provides a list of the domain management commands supported by the ntdsutil tool. You can access this information by typing the following sequence of commands at a command prompt.

```
ntdsutil
domain management
help
```

TABLE 3.2   ntdsutil Domain Management Commands

ntdsutil Domain Management Command	Purpose
Help or ?	Displays information about the commands that are available within the Domain Management menu of the ntdsutil command.
Connection or Connections	Allows you to connect to a specific domain controller. This will set the context for further operations that are performed on specific domain controllers.
Create NC *PartitionDistinguishedName DNSName*	Creates a new application directory partition.
Delete NC *PartitionDistinguishedName*	Removes an application data partition.
List NC Information *PartitionDistinguishedName*	Shows information about the specified application data partition.

TABLE 3.2   ntdsutil Domain Management Commands *(continued)*

ntdsutil Domain Management Command	Purpose
List NC Replicas *PartitionDistinguishedName*	Returns information about all replicas for the specific application data partition.
Precreate *PartitionDistinguishedName ServerDNSName*	Precreates cross-reference application data partition objects. This allows the specified DNS server to host a copy of the application data partition.
Remove NC Replica *PartitionDistinguishedName DCDNSName*	Removes a replica from the specified domain controller.
Select Operation Target	Selects the naming context that will be used for other operations.
Set NC Reference Domain *PartitionDistinguisedName DomainDistinguishedName*	Specifies the reference domain for an application data partition.
Set NC Replicate NotificationDelay *PartitionDistinguishedName FirstDCNotificationDelay OtherDCNotificationDelay*	Defines settings for how often replication will occur for the specified application data partition.

The ntdsutil commands are all case-insensitive. Mixed-case was used in the table to make them easier to read. NC in commands stands for *naming context*, referring to the fact that this is a partition of the Active Directory schema.

 Instead of focusing on details of specific commands and syntax related to ntdsutil, be sure that you really understand application directory partitions and how they and their replicas can be used.

Figure 3.5 provides an example of working with ntdsutil. The following commands were entered to set the context for further operations:

```
ntdsutil
domain management
connections
connect to server localhost
connect to domain ADTest
quit
list
```

FIGURE 3.5   Viewing naming contexts on the local domain controller

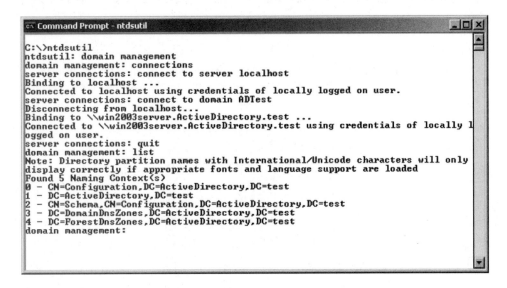

Configuring DNS Integration with Active Directory

There are many benefits to integrating Active Directory and DNS services.

- You can configure and manage replication along with other Active Directory components.

- You can automate much of the maintenance of DNS resource records through the use of dynamic updates.

- You will be able to set specific security options on the various properties of the DNS service.

Exercise 3.5 shows the steps that you can take to ensure that these integration features are enabled. You'll look at the various DNS functions that are specific to interoperability with Active Directory.

Before you begin this exercise, make sure that the local machine is configured as an Active Directory domain controller and that DNS services have been properly configured. If you instructed the Active Directory Installation Wizard to automatically configure DNS, many of the settings mentioned in this section may already be enabled. However, you should verify the configuration and be familiar with how the options can be set manually.

EXERCISE 3.5

Configuring DNS Integration with Active Directory

1. Open the DNS snap-in from the Administrative Tools program group.

2. Right-click the icon for the local DNS Server, and select Properties. Click the Security tab. Notice that you can now specify which users and groups have access to modify the configuration of the DNS server. Make any necessary changes, and click OK.

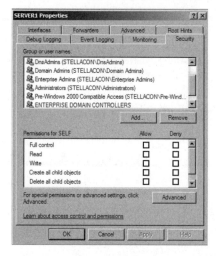

3. Expand the local server branch and the Forward Lookup Zones folder.

4. Right-click the name of the Active Directory domain you created, and select Properties.

5. On the General tab, verify that the type is Active Directory-Integrated and that the Data Is Stored In Active Directory message is displayed. If this option is not currently selected, you can change it by clicking the Change button next to Type.

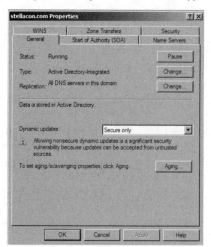

6. Verify that the Dynamic Updates option is set to Secure Only. This ensures that all updates to the DNS resource records database are made through authenticated Active Directory accounts and processes.

   The other options are Yes (to allow both secure and nonsecure dynamic updates) and No (to disallow dynamic updates).

7. Finally, notice that you can define the security permissions at the zone level by clicking the Security tab. Make any necessary changes, and click OK.

Summary

In this chapter, we covered the basics of implementing an Active Directory forest and domain structure, creating and configuring application data partitions, and setting the functional level of your domain and forest.

You are now familiar with how you can implement Active Directory. We carefully examined all the necessary steps and conditions you need to follow to install Active Directory on your network. First, you need to prepare for the Domain Name System (DNS) since Active Directory cannot be installed without the support of a DNS server. You also need to verify that the computer you upgrade to a domain controller (DC) meets some basic filesystem and network connectivity requirements so that Active Directory can run smoothly and efficiently in your organization. These are some of the most common things you will have to do when you deploy Active Directory.

We also covered the concept of domain functional levels, which essentially determine the kinds of domain controllers you can use in your environment. For instance, in the Windows 2000 functional level, you can include Server 2008, 2003 Server, and 2000 Server domain controllers, but the functionality of the domain is severely limited.

In this chapter, you also learned to install Active Directory, which you accomplish by promoting a Windows Server 2008 computer to a domain controller using DCPROMO. You also learned how to verify the installation by testing Active Directory from a client computer.

This chapter was limited in scope to examining the issues related to installing and configuring the first domain in an Active Directory environment. In later chapters, you'll see how to create and manage more complex configurations.

Exam Essentials

Know the prerequisites for promoting a server to a domain controller.   You should understand the tasks that you must complete before you attempt to upgrade a server to a domain controller. Also, you should have a good idea of the information you need in order to complete the domain controller promotion process.

Understand the steps of the Active Directory Installation Wizard (DCPROMO).   When you run the Active Directory Installation Wizard, you'll be presented with many different choices. You should understand the effects of the various options provided in each step of the wizard.

Be familiar with the tools that you will use to administer Active Directory.   Three main administrative tools are installed when you promote a Windows Server 2008 to a domain controller. Be sure you know which tools to use for which types of tasks.

Understand the purpose of application data partitions.   The idea behind application data partitions is that, since you already have a directory service that can replicate all kinds of security information, you can also use it to keep track of application data. The main benefit of storing application information in Active Directory is that you can take advantage of its storage mechanism and replication topology. Application-related information stored on domain controllers benefits from having fault-tolerance features and availability.

Review Questions

1. You are the system administrator of a large organization that has recently implemented Windows Server 2008. You have a few remote sites that do not have very tight security. You have decided to implement read-only domain controllers (RODC). What forest and function levels does the network need for you to do the install? (Choose all that apply.)

    A. Windows 2000 Mixed

    B. Windows 2000 Native

    C. Windows 2003

    D. Windows 2008

2. What is the maximum number of domains that a Windows 2008 Server computer, configured as a domain controller, may participate in at one time?

    A. 0

    B. 1

    C. 2

    D. Any number of domains

3. In order to support Windows Server 2000, 2003, and 2008 domain controllers in an Active Directory domain, which of the following modes must you use?

    A. Windows 2000 Native mode

    B. Windows Server 2003 mode

    C. Low-security mode

    D. Windows Server 2008 mode

4. The process of converting a Windows Server 2008 computer to a domain controller is known as

    A. Advertising

    B. Reinstallation

    C. Promotion

    D. Conversion

5. DNS server services can be configured using which of the following tools?

    A. The DNS administrative tool

    B. Computer Management

    C. Network Properties

    D. Active Directory Users and Computers

6.   You are the systems administrator for the XYZ Products, Inc. Windows Server 2008–based network. You are upgrading a Windows Server 2008 computer to an Active Directory domain controller and need to decide the initial domain name. Your business has the following requirements:

- The domain name must be accessible from the Internet.

- The domain name must reflect your company's proper name.

Which of the following domain names meet these requirements? (Choose two.)

A. XYZProducts.com

B. XYZProducts.domain

C. Server1.XYZProducts.org

D. XYZProductsServer2008

7.   Recently, you have received several alerts that Server1 is running low on disk space. Server1 primarily stores users' home directories. This problem has occurred several times in the past, and you want to restrict the amount of space that users can use on one of the volumes on the server. Which NTFS feature can you implement to limit the amount of disk space occupied by users?

A. Quotas

B. Encryption

C. Dynamic disks

D. Remote storage

E. Shared Folder Policy Objects

8.   A system administrator is trying to determine which filesystem to use for a server that will become a Windows Server 2008 file server and domain controller. His company's requirements include the following:

- The filesystem must allow for file-level security from within Windows 2008 Server.

- The filesystem must make efficient use of space on large partitions.

- The domain controller Sysvol must be stored on the partition.

Which of the following filesystems meets these requirements?

A. FAT

B. FAT32

C. HPFS

D. NTFS

9. For security reasons, you have decided that you must convert the system partition on your Windows Server 2008 from the FAT32 filesystem to NTFS. Which of the following steps must you take in order to convert the filesystem? (Choose two.)

   A. Run the command CONVERT /FS:NTFS from the command prompt.

   B. Rerun Windows Server 2008 Setup and choose to convert the partition to NTFS during the reinstallation.

   C. Boot Windows Server 2008 Setup from the installation CD-ROM and choose Rebuild File System.

   D. Reboot the computer.

10. You are attempting to join various machines on your network to an Active Directory domain. Which of the following scenarios describe machines that can be added to the domain? Choose all that apply.

   A. The machine is running Windows XP Professional.

   B. The machine is a member of another domain.

   C. The machine is running Windows Server 2008.

   D. The machine is a member of a workgroup.

11. Which of the following operations is *not* supported by the Active Directory Installation Wizard?

   A. Promoting a server to a domain controller

   B. Demoting a domain controller to a server

   C. Moving servers between domains

   D. Starting the DNS Installation Wizard

12. Windows Server 2008 requires the use of which of the following protocols or services in order to support Active Directory? (Choose two.)

   A. DHCP

   B. TCP/IP

   C. NetBEUI

   D. IPX/SPX

   E. DNS

13. You are promoting a Windows Server 2008 computer to an Active Directory domain controller for test purposes. This server will act alone on the network and does not need to be accessible from other machines. Which of the following domain names is a valid choice for the initial Active Directory domain? (Choose all that apply.)

   A. mycompany.com

   B. test.mycompany.com

   C. mycompany.org

   D. mycompany.net

14. You are promoting a Windows Server 2008 computer to an Active Directory domain controller for test purposes. The new domain controller will be added to an existing domain. While you are using Active Directory Installation Wizard, you receive an error message that prevents the server from being promoted. Which of the following might be the cause of the problem? (Choose all that apply.)

A. The system does not contain an NTFS partition on which the Sysvol directory can be created.

B. You do not have a Windows Server 2008 DNS server on the network.

C. The TCP/IP configuration on the new server is incorrect.

D. The domain has reached its maximum number of domain controllers.

15. You are installing the first domain controller in your Active Directory environment. What command do you run in order to begin the Active Directory Installation Wizard?

A. DCPromote.exe

B. DomainPromote.exe

C. DCPromo.exe

D. Promote.exe

16. You are the network administrator for a large company that creates widgets. You are asked by management to implement a new Windows Server 2008 system. You need to implement federated identity management. Which of the following will help you do this?

A. Active Directory Federation Services

B. Active Directory DNS Services

C. Active Directory IIS Services

D. Active Directory IAS Services

17. You are the systems administrator responsible for your company's infrastructure. You think you have an issue with name resolution and you need to verify that you are using the correct hostname. You want to test DNS on the local system and need to see if the hostname "server-1" resolves to the IP address 10.1.1.1. Which of the following actions provides a solution to the problem?

A. Add a DNS server to your local subnet.

B. Add the mapping for the hostname "server-1" to the IP address 10.1.1.1 in the local system's HOSTS file.

C. Add an A record to your local WINS server.

D. Add an MX record to your local DNS server.

18. As the lead administrator for 123 Inc., you are asked to solve a complex problem. Nobody on your staff can figure out why `server1.yourcompany.com` and `server1.yourcompany.com` can't communicate properly across the WAN. Choose the most likely cause of the problem.

    A. A firewall blocking the traffic.

    B. A router access list is assigned to the WAN port and it is blocking traffic.

    C. No route exists between the workstations.

    D. You need to create a unique FQDN.

19. You are the network administrator for your company, which consists of 3 new Windows Server 2008 servers and 40 workstations running Windows XP Professional. You design a new name for your domain while deploying Active Directory. You consider DNS and how your clients will use it. Because you don't own your DNS name publicly, only privately, what is your next step if you want to ensure that you are the owner of that domain for the future?

    A. Make a lease offer and hold the domain.

    B. Make a list of similar domain names to use.

    C. Register the name with a registration authority.

    D. Use a reverse lookup zone to configure this functionality.

20. You are the systems administrator for 123 Inc. You are in charge of your company's DNS infrastructure, and you want to ensure that naming remains accurate in a distributed network environment. Choose the proper way to ensure that DNS will stay accurate across the enterprise.

    A. You must designate one DNS server as the primary master database for a specific set of addresses.

    B. You need to implement round robin ordering.

    C. You need to implement a secondary transfer zone server to ensure accuracy.

    D. You must open Port 52 on all firewalls and access control lists enterprise-wide.

Answers to Review Questions

1. C, D. The forest and function levels have to be Windows 2003 or above to install a RODC.

2. B. A domain controller can contain Active Directory information for only one domain. If you want to use a multidomain environment, you must use multiple domain controllers configured in either a tree or forest setting.

3. A. In order to support Windows Server 2000, 2003, and 2008 domain controllers, you must use Windows 2000 Native mode. Note that in this configuration, several Windows 2000 Server Active Directory features will not be available.

4. C. Promotion is the process of making a Windows Server 2008 computer a new domain controller. This is the only way to install Active Directory.

5. A. The DNS administrative tool is designed to configure settings for the DNS server service. You can also manually edit DNS zone files using a standard text file editor.

6. A, C. Both of these domain names are based on the standard DNS top-level domain names and can therefore be made accessible over the Internet. Although you could use other top-level domain names (such as those provided in choices B and D), these names would not be automatically resolvable over the Internet.

7. A. Quotas allow systems administrators to place restrictions on the amount of disk space used on NTFS volumes. Quotas are native to NTFS and cannot be implemented on FAT32 drives. Options B, C, and D are available on NTFS partitions, but they cannot be used to restrict disk space. Option E is not an option related to disk storage management.

8. D. NTFS has file-level security and makes efficient usage of disk space. Since this machine is to be configured as a domain controller, the configuration requires at least one NTFS partition in order to store the Sysvol information.

9. A, D. In order to convert the system partition to NTFS, you must first use the CONVERT command-line utility and then reboot the server. During the next boot, the filesystem will be converted.

10. A, B, C, D. All of the above configurations can be joined to a domain. Note that if a machine is a member of another domain, it must first be removed from that domain before it can be joined to another. Join it to a workgroup to remove it from the old domain and then join it to the new domain.

11. C. The only way to move a domain controller between domains is to demote it from its current domain and then promote it into another domain. You cannot move a domain controller automatically using any of the built-in tools included with Windows Server 2008.

12. B, E. The use of LDAP and TCP/IP is required to support Active Directory. TCP/IP is the network protocol favored by Microsoft, who determined that all Active Directory communication would occur on TCP/IP. DNS is required because Active Directory is inherently dependent upon the domain model. DHCP is used for automatic address assignment, and is not required. Similarly, NetBEUI and IPX/SPX are not available network protocols in Windows Server 2008.

13. A, B, C, D. All of the domain names listed may be used. Although it is recommended, a registered Internet domain name is not required for installing Active Directory.

14. A, C. The Sysvol directory must be created on an NTFS partition. If such a partition is not available, you will not be able to promote the server to a domain controller. An error in the network configuration might prevent the server from connecting to another domain controller in the environment.

15. C. You use DCPromo.exe to begin the process of promoting or demoting a server to/from a domain controller.

16. A. You'll need to use Active Directory Federation Services (AD FS) in order to implement federated identity management. Federated identity management is a standards-based technology and information technology process that will enable distributed identification, authentication, and authorization across organizational and platform boundaries. The AD FS solution in Windows Server 2008 helps administrators address these challenges by enabling organizations to securely share a user's identity information.

17. B. The HOSTS file is a text file–based database of mappings between hostnames and IP addresses. It works like a file based version of DNS. Resolves a hostname to an IP address.

18. D. Each fully qualified domain name (FQDN), such as server1.yourcompany.com, must be unique. No two machines on the same network may have the same FQDN. This requirement ensures that each machine can be uniquely identified. The WAN link only connects what is still considered one network.

19. C. Ensure that you reserve your DNS names with a registration authority. You can also reserve your private names so that they cannot be used on the public Internet. Failure to reserve your internal name may prevent internal clients from accessing this namespace on the public Internet in the future; this is simply because the client would not be able to tell the difference between the internally selected name and the publicly assigned name via the registrar. You can set up zones for both the external and internal namespaces.

20. A. In order to ensure that naming remains accurate in a distributed network environment, one DNS server must be designated as the primary master database for a specific set of addresses. It is on this server that updates to hostname–to–IP address mappings can be updated. Whenever a DNS server is unable to resolve a specific DNS name, it simply queries other servers that can provide the information.

Chapter

4

Installing and Managing Trees and Forests

MICROSOFT EXAM OBJECTIVES COVERED IN THIS CHAPTER:

✓ **Configuring the Active Directory Infrastructure**

- Configure a forest or a domain. May include but is not limited to: remove a domain; perform an unattended installation; Active Directory Migration Tool (ADMT) v3 (pruning and grafting); raise forest and domain functional levels; interoperability with previous versions of Active Directory; alternate user principal name (UPN) suffix; forestprep; domainprep

- Configure trusts. May include but is not limited to: forest trust; selective authentication vs. forest-wide authentication; transitive trust; external trust; shortcut trust; SID filtering

- Configure the global catalog. May include but is not limited to: Universal Group Membership Caching (UGMC); partial attribute set; promote to global catalog

- Configure operations masters. May include but is not limited to: seize and transfer; backup operations master; operations master placement; Schema Master; extending the schema; time service

So far, you have seen the steps you need to take to install the Domain Name System (DNS) and to implement the first Active Directory domain. Although we briefly introduced you to multi-domain Active Directory structures earlier, we only focused on a single domain and the objects within it.

Many businesses find that using a single domain provides an adequate solution to meet their business needs. By working with *trees* and *forests*, however, organizations can use multiple domains to better organize their environments.

This chapter begins by covering some reasons why you should create more than one Active Directory domain. Then it moves on to look at the exact processes involved in creating a domain tree and in joining multiple trees together into a domain forest. In addition, you learn how to demote a domain controller and manage multiple domains after you've created trees and forests.

Reasons for Creating Multiple Domains

Before you look at the steps you must take to create multiple domains, become familiar with the reasons why an organization might want to create them.

In general, you should always try to reflect your organization's structure within a single domain. By using organizational units (OUs) and other objects, you can usually create an accurate and efficient structure within one domain. Creating and managing a single domain is usually much simpler than managing a more complex environment consisting of multiple domains.

That said, you should familiarize yourself with some real benefits and reasons for creating multiple domains as well as some drawbacks of using them.

Reasons for Using Multiple Domains

You might need to implement multiple domains for several reasons. These reasons include the following considerations:

Scalability Although Microsoft has designed Active Directory to accommodate millions of objects, this may not be practical for your current environment. Supporting thousands of users within a single domain requires more disk space, greater CPU (central processing unit) usage, and additional network burdens on your *domain controllers* (computers containing Active Directory security information). To determine the size of Active Directory domain your network can support, you need to plan, design, test, and analyze within your own environment.

Reducing replication traffic   All the domain controllers in a domain must keep an up-to-date copy of the entire Active Directory database. For small- to medium-sized domains, this is not generally a problem. Windows Server 2008 and Active Directory manage all the details of transferring the database behind the scenes. Other business and technical limitations might, however, affect Active Directory's ability to perform adequate replication. For example, if you have two sites that are connected by a very slow network link (or a sporadic link, or no link at all), replication is not practical. In this case, you would probably want to create separate domains to isolate replication traffic. Sporadic coverage across the wide area network (WAN) link would come from circuit switching technologies such as Integrated Services Digital Network (ISDN) technologies. If you didn't have a link at all, then you would have a service provider outage or some other type of disruption. Separate domains mean separate replication traffic, but the amount of administrative overhead is increased significantly.

Because it's common to have WAN links in your business environment, you will always need to consider how your users authenticate to a domain controller (DC). DCs at a remote site are commonly seen to authenticate users locally to their local area network (LAN). The most common design involves putting a DC at each remote site to keep authentication traffic from traversing the WAN. If it is the other way around, the authentication traffic may cause users problems if WAN utilization is high or if the link is broken and no other way to the central site is available. The design you are apt to see most often is one in which each server replicates its database of information to each other server so that the network and its systems converge.

However, is important to realize that the presence of slow WAN links alone is *not* a good reason to break an organization into multiple domains. The most common solution is to set up site links with the Site and Services Microsoft Management Console (MMC). When you use this MMC, you can manage replication traffic and fine-tune independently of the domain architecture. We'll cover these topics in detail in Chapter 5, "Configuring Sites and Replication."

The following are the reasons why you would want to use a multidomain architecture, such as when two companies merge through an acquisition.

Meeting business needs   Several business needs might justify the creation of multiple domains. Business needs can be broken down even further into organizational and political needs.

One of the organizational reasons for using multiple domains is to avoid potential problems associated with the Domain Administrator account. At least one user needs to have permissions at this level. If your organization is unable or unwilling to trust a single person to have this level of control over all business units, then multiple domains may be the best answer. Since each domain maintains its own security database, you can keep permissions and resources isolated. Through the use of trusts, however, you can still share resources.

A political need for separate domains might arise if you had two companies that merged with two separate but equal management staffs and two sets of officers. In such a situation, you might need to have Active Directory split into two separate databases to keep the security of the two groups separate. Some such organizations may need to keep the internal groups separate by law. A multidomain architecture provides exactly this type of pristinely separate environment.

Many levels of hierarchy   Larger organizations tend to have very complex internal and external business structures that dictate the need for many different levels of organization. For example, two companies might merge and need to keep two sets of officers who are managed under two different logical groupings. As you will see in Chapter 7, "Administering Active Directory," you can use OUs to help group different branches of the company so that you can assign permissions, or delegations, or whatever else you can think of without affecting anyone else. Managing data becomes much easier when you're using OUs, and if you design them correctly, OUs will help you control your network right from one console. You may only need one level of management—your company may be small enough to warrant the use of the default OU structure you see when Active Directory is first installed. If, however, you find that you need many levels of OUs to manage resources (or if large numbers of objects exist within each OU), it might make sense to create additional domains. Each domain would contain its own OU hierarchy and serve as the root of a new set of objects.

Decentralized administration   Two main models of administration are commonly used: a centralized administration model and a decentralized administration model. In the centralized administration model, a single IT organization is responsible for managing all of the users, computers, and security permissions for the entire organization. In the decentralized administration model, each department or business unit might have its own IT department. In both cases, the needs of the administration model can play a significant role in whether you decide to use multiple domains.

Consider, for example, a multinational company that has a separate IT department for offices in each country. Each IT department is responsible for supporting only the users and computers within its own region. Since the administration model is largely decentralized, creating a separate domain for each of these major business units might make sense from a security and maintenance standpoint.

Multiple DNS or domain names   Another reason you may need to use a multidomain architecture is if you want or plan to use multiple DNS names within your organization. If you use multiple DNS names or domain names, you must create multiple Active Directory domains. Each AD domain can have only one fully qualified domain name (FQDN). An FQDN is the full name of a system that consists of a local host, a second-level domain name, and a top-level domain (TLD). For example, www.wiley.com is an FQDN, .com is the TLD, www is the host, and wiley is the second-level domain name.

Legality   One final reason you may need to use a multidomain architecture is legality within your organization. Some corporations have to follow state or federal regulations and laws. For this reason, they may have to have multiple domains.

Drawbacks of Multiple Domains

Although there are many reasons why it makes sense to have multiple domains, there are also reasons why you should not break an organizational structure into multiple domains, many of which are related to maintenance and administration. Here are some of the drawbacks to using multiple domains:

Administrative inconsistency   One of the fundamental responsibilities of most systems administrators is implementing and managing security. When you are implementing Group Policy and security settings in multiple domains, you want to be careful to ensure that the settings are consistent. In Windows Server 2008, security policies can be different between and within the same domains. If this is what the organization intended, then it is not a problem. If, however, an organization wishes to make the same settings apply to all users, then each domain requires similar security settings.

Increased management challenges   Managing servers, users, and computers can become a considerable challenge when you are also managing multiple domains, because many more administrative units are required. In general, you need to manage all user, group, and computer settings separately for the objects within each domain. The hierarchical structure provided by OUs, on the other hand, provides a much simpler and easier way to manage permissions.

Decreased flexibility   Creating a domain involves the *promotion* of a DC to the new domain. Although the process is quite simple, it is much more difficult to rearrange the domain topology within an Active Directory environment than it is to simply reorganize OUs. When planning domains, you should ensure that the domain structure will not change often, if at all.

Now that you have examined the pros and cons related to creating multiple domains, it is time to see how to create trees and forests.

Creating Domain Trees and Forests

So far this chapter has covered some important reasons for using multiple domains in a single network environment; now it's time to look at how to create multidomain structures like domain trees and domain forests.

Regardless of the number of domains you have in your environment, you always have a tree and a forest. This might surprise those of you who generally think of domain trees and forests as belonging only to Active Directory environments that consist of multiple domains. However, recall that when you install the first domain in an Active Directory environment, that domain automatically creates a new forest and a new tree.

In the following sections, you will learn how to plan trees and forests as well as see how to promote domain controllers to establish a tree and forest environment.

Planning Trees and Forests

You have already seen several reasons why you might want to have multiple domains within a single company. What you haven't yet seen is how multiple domains can be related to each other and how their relationships can translate into domain forests and trees.

A fundamental commonality between the various domains that exist in trees and forests is that they all share the same Active Directory Global Catalog (GC) This means that if you modify the Active Directory schema, these changes must be propagated to all of the domain controllers in all of the domains. This is an important point because adding and modifying the structure of information in the GC can have widespread effects on replication and network traffic. Also, you need to ensure that any system you use in the GC role can handle it—you might need to size up the system's hardware requirements. This is especially true if there are multiple domains.

Every domain within an Active Directory configuration has its own unique name. For example, even though you might have a sales domain in two different trees, the complete names for each domain will be different (such as `sales.stellacon1.com` and `sales.stellacon2.com`).

In the following sections, you'll look at how you can organize multiple Active Directory domains based on business requirements.

Using a Single Tree

The concept of domain trees was created to preserve the relationship between multiple domains that share a common contiguous namespace. For example, you might have the following DNS domains (based on Internet names):

- `mycompany.com`
- `sales.mycompany.com`
- `engineering.mycompany.com`
- `europe.sales.mycompany.com`

Note that all of these domains fit within a single contiguous namespace. That is, they are all direct or indirect children of the `mycompany.com` domain. In this case, `mycompany.com` is called the root domain. All of the direct children (such as `sales.mycompany.com` and `engineering.mycompany.com`) are called child domains. Finally, parent domains are the domains that are directly above one domain. For example, `sales.mycompany.com` is the parent domain of `europe.sales.mycompany.com`. Figure 4.1 provides an example of a domain tree.

In order to establish a domain tree, you must create the root domain for the tree first. Then you can add child domains off this root. These child domains can then serve as parents for further subdomains. Each domain must have at least one domain controller, and domain controllers can participate in only one domain at a time. However, you can move a domain controller from one domain to another. To do this, you must first demote a domain controller to a member server and then promote it to a domain controller in another domain.

 You will learn how to demote a domain controller later in this chapter in the section titled "Demoting a Domain Controller."

FIGURE 4.1 A domain tree

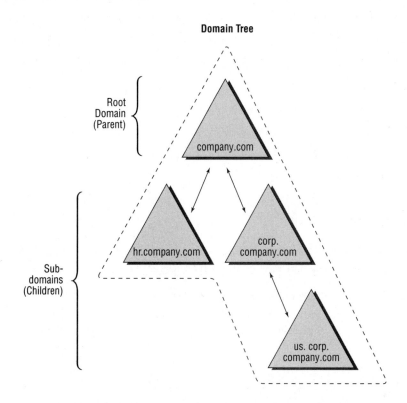

Domains are designed to be security boundaries. The domains within a tree are, by default, automatically bound together using a two-way transitive trust relationship, which allows resources to be shared among domains through the use of the appropriate user and group assignments. Because trust relationships are transitive, all of the domains within the tree trust each other. Note, however, that a trust by itself does not automatically grant any security permissions to users or objects between domains. Trusts are designed only to *allow* resources to be shared; you must still go through the process of sharing and managing them. Administrators must explicitly assign security settings to resources before users can access resources between domains.

Using a single tree makes sense when your organization maintains only a single contiguous namespace. Regardless of the number of domains that exist within this environment and how different their security settings are, they are related by a common name. Although domain trees make sense for many organizations, in some cases, the network namespace may be considerably more complicated. You'll look at how forests address these situations next.

Using a Forest

Active Directory forests are designed to accommodate multiple noncontiguous namespaces. That is, they can combine domain trees together into logical units. An example might be the following tree and domain structure:

- Tree: Organization1.com
  - Sales.Organization1.com
  - Marketing.Organization1.com
  - Engineering.Organization1.com
  - NorthAmerica.Engineering.Organization1.com
- Tree: Organization2.com
  - Sales.Organization2.com
  - Engineering.Organization2.com

Figure 4.2 provides an example of how multiple trees can fit into a single forest. Such a situation might occur in the acquisition and merger of companies or if a company is logically divided into two or more completely separate and autonomous business units.

FIGURE 4.2   A single forest consisting of multiple trees

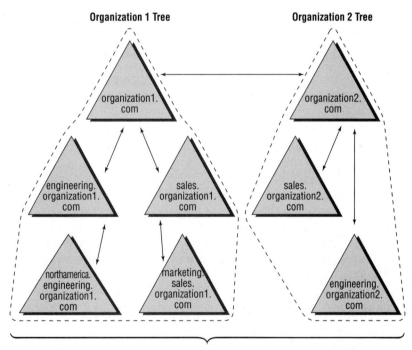

All of the trees within a forest are related through a single forest root domain. This is the first domain that was created in the Active Directory environment. The root domain in each tree creates a transitive trust with the forest root domain. The result is a configuration in which all of the trees within a domain and all of the domains within each tree trust each other. Again, as with domain trees, the presence of a trust relationship does not automatically signify that users have permissions to access resources across domains. It only allows objects and resources to be shared. Authorized network administrators must set up specific permissions.

All of the domains within a single Active Directory forest have the following features in common:

Schema   The schema is the Active Directory structure that defines how the information within the data store is structured. For the information stored on various domain controllers to remain compatible, all of the domain controllers within the entire Active Directory environment must share the same schema. For example, if you add a field for an employee's benefits plan number, all domain controllers throughout the environment need to recognize this information before you can share information among them.

Global Catalog (GC)   One of the problems associated with working in large network environments is that sharing information across multiple domains can be costly in terms of network and server resources. Fortunately, Active Directory uses the GC, which serves as a repository for information about a subset of all objects within *all* Active Directory domains in a forest. Systems administrators can determine what types of information should be added to the defaults in the GC. Generally, they decide to store commonly used information, such as a list of all of the printers, users, groups, and computers. In addition, they can configure specific domain controllers to carry a copy of the GC. Now, if you have a question about, for example, where to find all the color printers in the company, all you need to do is to contact the nearest GC server.

Configuration information   Some roles and functions must be managed for the entire forest. When you are dealing with multiple domains, this means that you must configure certain domain controllers to perform functions for the entire Active Directory environment. We will discuss some specifics of this later in this chapter.

The main purpose of allowing multiple domains to exist together is to allow them to share information and other resources. Now that you've seen the basics of domain trees and forests, take a look at how domains are actually created.

The Promotion Process

A domain tree is created when a new domain is added as the child of an existing domain. This relationship is established during the promotion of a Windows Server 2008 computer to a domain controller. Although the underlying relationships can be quite complicated in larger organizations, the *Active Directory Installation Wizard (DCPROMO)* makes it easy to create forests and trees.

Using the Active Directory Installation Wizard, you can quickly and easily create new domains by promoting a Windows Server 2008 stand-alone server or a member server to a domain controller. When you install a new domain controller, you can choose to make it part of an existing domain, or you can choose to make it the first domain controller in a new domain. In the following sections and exercises, you'll become familiar with the exact steps you need to take to create a domain tree and a domain forest when you promote a server to a domain controller.

Creating a Domain Tree

In the previous chapter (Chapter 3), you saw how to promote the first domain controller in the first domain in a forest, also known as the root. If you don't promote any other domain controllers, then that domain controller simply controls that one domain and only one tree is created. To create a new domain tree, you need to promote a Windows Server 2008 computer to a domain controller. In the Active Directory Installation Wizard, you select the option that makes this domain controller the first machine in a new domain that is a child of an existing domain. As a result, you will have a domain tree that contains two domains—a parent and a child.

Before you can create a new child domain, you need the following information:

- The name of the parent domain (for the exercises, you'll use the one you created in the previous chapter)

- The name of the child domain (the one you are planning to install)

- The filesystem locations for the Active Directory database, logs, and shared system volume

- DNS configuration information

- The NetBIOS name for the new server

- A domain administrator username and password

Exercise 4.1 walks you through the process of creating a new child domain using the Active Directory Installation Wizard. This exercise assumes that you have already created the parent domain and that you are using a server in the domain that is not a domain controller.

EXERCISE 4.1

Creating a New Subdomain

1. Log on to the computer as a member of the Administrators group and open the Active Directory Installation Wizard by clicking Start ➢ Run, and typing **dcpromo**. After the message about installing the binaries appears, Click Next to begin the wizard.

2. The Choose A Deployment Configuration screen appears. Click Existing Forest and then click Create A New Domain In An Existing Forest. Click Next.

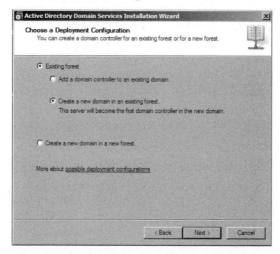

3. A warning box may appear stating that the local administrator account becomes the domain administrator account for the new domain. If it appears, Click Yes to continue.

4. On the Network Credentials page, specify the full name of the domain that you installed in the previous chapter. Then click the Set button. In the new Windows Security dialog box that appears, enter the username and password for the domain administrator of the domain you wish to join.

EXERCISE 4.1 *(continued)*

5. Click the OK button on the Alternate Credentials screen. The domain administrator account that you used in the previous chapter should now be listed. A warning may appear stating that the current user credentials cannot be selected because they are local to this computer. The warning appears because our local account is the same as our domain administrator's account. This warning will not affect the exercise. Click Next.

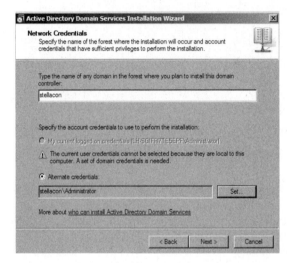

6. If the information you entered was correct, you will see the Name The New Domain page. Here, you will be able to confirm the name of the parent domain and then enter the domain name for the child domain. Enter the new child domain name (in the following example, we used **NH** for the state of New Hampshire). Click Next to continue.

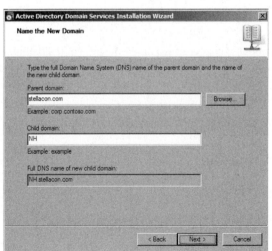

7. If the Select A Site screen appears, choose any site and click Next. (You may not have any sites created on your other domain. This server will then be added to the DefaultFirstSite.)

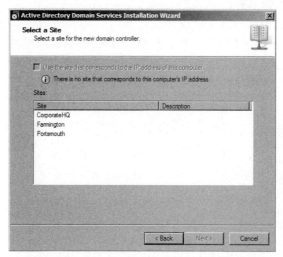

8. On the Additional Domain Controller Options page, uncheck any options and click Next.

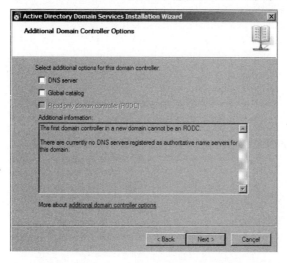

9. A warning box appears stating that you have chosen not to install DNS; just click Yes.

10. On the Location for Database, Log Files, and SYSVOL page, you'll need to specify the database and log locations. These settings specify where the Active Directory database resides on the local machine. As mentioned previously, it is good practice to place the log files on a separate physical hard disk because this increases performance. Enter the path for a local directory (you can also leave the defaults for these exercises), and click Next.

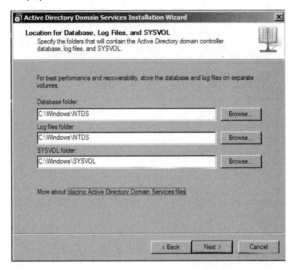

11. In order to be able to recover this server in the event of a loss of Active Directory information, you will need to provide a password on the Directory Services Restore Mode Administrator Password page. This password will allow you to use the built-in recovery features of Windows Server 2008 in the event that the Active Directory database is lost or corrupted. Enter **P@ssw0rd**, confirm it, and then click Next.

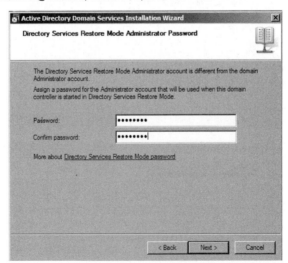

EXERCISE 4.1 *(continued)*

12. On the Summary page, you will be given a brief listing of all the choices you made in the previous steps. It's a good idea to copy this information and paste it into a text document for future reference. Click Next to continue.

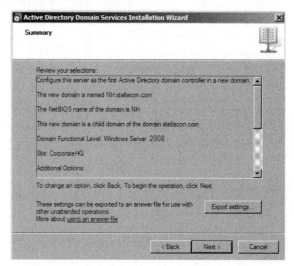

13. On the Completing the Active Directory Domain Services Installation Wizard, click Finish.

Joining a New Domain Tree to a Forest

A forest is one or more trees that do not share a contiguous namespace. For example, you could join the `organization1.com` and `organization2.com` domains together to create a single Active Directory environment.

Any two trees can be joined together to create a forest, as long as the second tree is installed after the first and the trees have noncontiguous namespaces. (If the namespaces were contiguous, you would actually need to create a new domain for an existing tree.) The process of creating a new tree to form or add to a forest is as simple as promoting a server to a domain controller for a new domain that does *not* share a namespace with an existing Active Directory domain.

The command-line tool adprep.exe is used to prepare a Microsoft Windows 2003 forest or a Windows 2003 domain for the installation of Windows Server 2008 domain controllers.

Before you promote a Windows Server 2008 domain controller into a Windows 2003 forest, an administrator should successfully run adprep /forestprep on the schema operations master and run adprep /domainprep on the infrastructure master in the Windows 2003 forest. The forestprep and domainprep processes prepare the Windows 2000 or 2003 network to accept the installation of the Windows Server 2008 servers.

In Exercise 4.2, you will use the Active Directory Installation Wizard to create a new domain tree to add to a forest. In order to add a new domain to an existing forest, you must already have at least one other domain, which is the root domain. Keep in mind that the entire forest structure is destroyed if the original root domain is ever entirely removed. Therefore, you should have at least two domain controllers in the Active Directory root domain; the second serves as a backup in case you have a problem with the first, and it can also serve as a backup solution for disaster recovery and fault tolerance purposes. Such a setup provides additional protection for the entire forest in case one of the domain controllers fails. In order to complete this exercise, you must have already installed another domain controller that serves as the root domain for a forest, and you must use a server in the domain that is not a domain controller.

EXERCISE 4.2

Creating a New Domain Tree in the Forest

1. Open the Active Directory Installation Wizard by clicking Start ➤ Run, and typing **dcpromo**. Click the Use Advanced Mode Installation box. Click Next.

2. On the Choose a Deployment Configuration page, select Existing Forest and then click Create A New Domain In An Existing Forest. Check the box "Create a new domain tree root instead of a new child domain." Click Next.

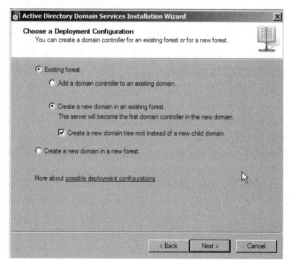

3. A warning box might appear stating that the local administrator account becomes the domain administrator account for the new domain. If it appears, Click Yes to continue.

4. On the Network Credentials page, specify the full name of the domain that you installed in the previous chapter. Click the Set button and enter the username and password for the domain administrator of a domain in the forest you wish to join. Click Next.

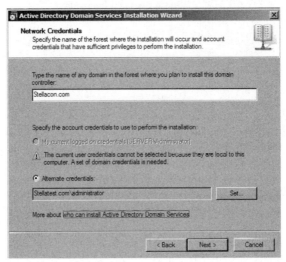

5. On the Name the New Domain Tree Root page, you need to specify the full name of the new domain you wish to create. Note that this domain may not share a contiguous namespace with any other existing domain. Once you have entered the appropriate information, click Next.

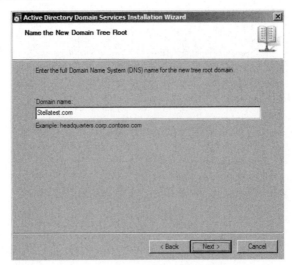

6. On the Domain NetBIOS Name page, you are prompted for the NetBIOS name of the domain controller. This is the name previous versions of Windows use to identify this machine. Choose a name that is up to 15 characters in length and includes only alpha-numeric characters. Click Next to continue.

7. If the Select A Site screen appears, choose any site and click Next. (You may not have any sites created on your forest. This server will then be added to the DefaultFirstSite.)

8. On the Additional Domain Controller Options page, make sure DNS Server is checked and click Next.

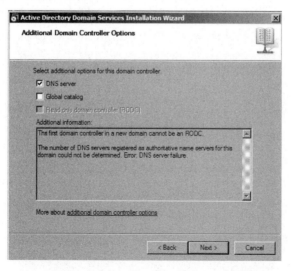

9. If a delegation for DNS message appears, click Yes.

10. The Source Domain Controller screen appears. Click the button labeled This Specific Domain Controller and highlight the domain controller that you created in Chapter 3. Click Next.

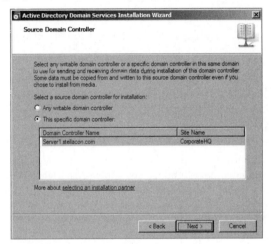

11. On the Location For Database, Log Files, And SYSVOL page, specify the database and log locations. These settings specify where the Active Directory database resides on the local machine. Click Next.

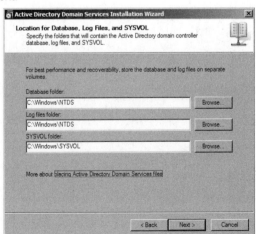

12. In order to be able to recover this server in the event of a loss of Active Directory information, you need to provide a Directory Services Restore Mode Administrator password. This password allows you to use the built-in recovery features of Windows Server 2008 if the Active Directory database is lost or corrupted. Enter **P@ssw0rd**, confirm it, and then click Next.

13. On the Summary page, you are given a brief listing of all of the choices you made in the previous steps. Click Next to continue.

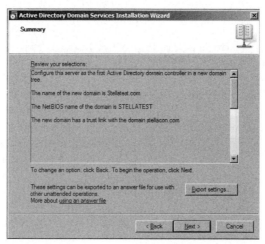

14. The Active Directory Installation Wizard automatically begins performing the steps required to create a new domain tree based on the information you provided. Note that you can press Cancel if you want to abort this process. When the setup is complete, you are prompted to reboot the system. Go ahead and do so, and once the process is finished, you will have a new domain tree.

Adding Additional Domain Controllers

In addition to the operations you've already performed, you can use the Active Directory Installation Wizard to create additional domain controllers for any of your domains. There are two main reasons to create additional domain controllers:

Fault tolerance and reliability   You should always consider the theory of disaster recovery (DR) and have a plan, sometimes referred to as a Disaster Recovery Plan (DRP). If you're part of one of those organizations that rely upon their network directory services infrastructures, you need Active Directory to provide security and resources for all users. For this reason, downtime and data loss are very costly. Through the use of multiple domain controllers, you can ensure that if one of the servers goes down, another one is available to perform the necessary tasks, such as user authentication and resource browsing. Additionally, data loss (perhaps from hard disk drive failure) will not result in the loss or unavailability of network security information since you can easily recover Active Directory information from the remaining, still functional domain controller.

Performance   The burden of processing login requests and serving as a repository for security permissions and other information can be quite extensive, especially in larger businesses. By using multiple domain controllers, you can distribute this load across multiple systems. Additionally, by strategically placing domain controllers, you can greatly increase response times for common network operations, such as authentication and browsing for resources.

As a rule of thumb, you should always plan and design your infrastructure to have at least two domain controllers per domain. For many organizations, this provides a good balance between the cost of servers and the level of reliability and performance. For larger or more distributed organizations, however, additional domain controllers greatly improve performance.

Demoting a Domain Controller

In addition to being able to promote member servers to domain controllers, the Active Directory Installation Wizard can do the exact opposite—demote domain controllers.

You might choose to demote a domain controller for a couple of reasons. First, if you have determined that the role of a server should change (for example, from a domain controller to a member or stand-alone server you might make into a web server), you can easily demote it to make this happen. Another common reason to demote a domain controller is if you wish to move the machine from one domain to another. You cannot do this in a single step: You need to first demote the existing domain controller to remove it from the current domain, then promote it into a new domain. The end result is that the server is now a domain controller for a different domain.

 Real World Scenario

Planning for Domain Controller Placement

You're the Senior Systems Administrator for a medium-sized Active Directory environment. Currently, the environment consists of only one Active Directory domain. Your company's network is spread out through 40 different sites within North America. Recently, you've received complaints from users and other system administrators about the performance of Active Directory–related operations. For example, users report that it takes several minutes to log on to their machines in the morning between the hours of 9 and 10am when activity is at its highest. Simultaneously, systems administrators complain that updating user information within the OUs for which they are responsible can take longer than expected.

One network administrator, who has a strong Windows NT 4 domain background but little knowledge of Active Directory design, suggests that you create multiple domains to solve some of the performance problems. However, you know that this would significantly change the environment and could make administration more difficult. Furthermore, the company's business goals involve keeping all company resources as unified as possible.

Fortunately, Active Directory's distributed domain controller architecture allows you to optimize performance for this type of situation without making dramatic changes to your environment. You decide that the quickest and easiest solution is to deploy additional domain controllers throughout the organization. The domain controllers are generally placed within areas of the network that are connected by slow or unreliable links. For example, a small branch office in Des Moines, Iowa receives its own domain controller. The process is quite simple: you install a new Windows Server 2008 computer and then run the Active Directory Installation Wizard (DCPROMO) to make the new machine a domain controller for an existing domain. Once the initial directory services data is copied to the new server, it is ready to service requests and updates of your domain information.

Note that there are potential drawbacks to this solution; for instance, you have to manage additional domain controllers and the network traffic generated from communications between the domain controllers. It's important that you monitor your network links to ensure that you've reached a good balance between replication traffic and overall Active Directory performance. In later chapters, you'll see how you can configure Active Directory sites to better map Active Directory operations to your physical network structure.

To demote a domain controller, you simply access the Active Directory Installation Wizard. The wizard automatically notices that the local server is a domain controller, and it asks you to verify each step you take, as with most things you do in Windows. You are prompted to decide whether you really want to remove this machine from the current domain (see Figure 4.3). Note that if the local server is a Global Catalog (GC) server, you will be warned that at least one copy of the GC must remain available so that you can perform logon authentication.

FIGURE 4.3   Demoting a domain controller using the Active Directory Domain Services Installation Wizard

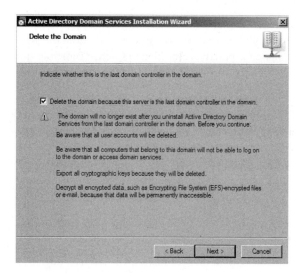

Real World Scenario

Removing the Last Domain Controller in a Domain

In order for a domain to continue to exist, at least one domain controller must remain in that domain. As noted in the dialog box in Figure 4.3, you must take some very important considerations into account if you are removing the last domain controller from the domain. Because all of the security accounts and information will be lost, you should ensure that the following requirements are met before you remove a domain's last domain controller:

Computers no longer log on to this domain.   Ensure that computers that were once members of this domain have changed domains. If computers are still attempting to log on, they will not be able to use any of the security features, including any security permissions or logon accounts. Users will, however, still be able to log on to the computer using cached authenticated information.

No user accounts are needed.   All of the user accounts that reside within the domain (and all of the resources and permissions associated with them) will be lost when the domain is destroyed. Therefore, if you have already set up usernames and passwords, you need to transfer these accounts to another domain; otherwise, you will lose all of this information.

All encrypted data is decrypted.   You need the security information (including User, Computer, and Group objects) stored within the Active Directory domain database to access any encrypted information. Once the domain no longer exists, the security information stored within it will no longer be available, and any encrypted information stored in the filesystem will become permanently inaccessible. So, you need to decrypt any encrypted data before you begin the demotion process so that you can make sure you can access this information afterward. For example, if you have encrypted files or folders that reside on NTFS volumes, you should decrypt them before you continue with the demotion process.

All cryptographic keys are backed up.   If you are using cryptographic keys to authenticate and secure data, you should export the key information before you demote the last domain controller in a domain. Because this information is stored in the Active Directory database, any resources locked with these keys become inaccessible once the database is lost as a result of the demotion process.

By now, you've probably noticed a running theme—a lot of information disappears when you demote the last domain controller in a domain. The Active Directory Installation Wizard makes performing potentially disastrous decisions very easy. Be sure that you understand these effects before you demote the last domain controller for a given domain.

By default, at the end of the demotion process, the server is joined as a member server to the domain for which it was previously a domain controller. If you demote the last domain controller in the domain, the server becomes a standalone.

WARNING   Removing a domain from your environment is not an operation that you should take lightly. Before you plan to remove a domain, make a list of all the resources that depend on the domain and the reasons why the domain was originally created. If you are sure your organization no longer requires the domain, then you can safely continue. If you are not sure, think again, because the process cannot be reversed and you could lose critical information!

Managing Multiple Domains

You can easily manage most of the operations that must occur *between* domains by using the Active Directory Domains And Trusts administrative tool. If, on the other hand, you want to configure settings *within* a domain, you should use the Active Directory Users And Computers tool. In the following sections, you'll look at ways to perform two common domain management functions with the tools just mentioned: managing *single master operations* and managing trusts. We'll also look at ways to manage UPN suffixes to simplify user accounts, and we'll examine GC servers in more detail.

Managing Single Master Operations

For the most part, Active Directory functions in what is known as multimaster replication. That is, every domain controller within the environment contains a copy of the Active Directory database that is both readable and writable. This works well for most types of information. For example, if you want to modify the password of a user, you can easily do this on *any* of the domain controllers within a domain. The change is then automatically propagated to the other domain controllers.

However, some functions are not managed in a multimaster fashion. These operations are known as *operations masters*. You must perform single-master operations on specially designated domain controllers within the Active Directory forest. There are five main single-master functions: two that apply to an entire Active Directory forest and three that apply to each domain.

Forest Operations Masters

You use the Active Directory Domains And Trusts tool to configure forest-wide roles. The following single-master operations apply to the entire forest:

Schema Master   Earlier, you learned that all of the domain controllers within a single Active Directory environment share the same schema. This ensures information consistency. Developers and systems administrators can, however, modify the Active Directory schema by adding custom information. A trivial example might involve adding a field to employee information that specifies a user's favorite color.

When you need to make these types of changes, you must perform them on the domain controller that serves as the *Schema Master* for the environment. The Schema Master is then responsible for propagating all of the changes to all of the other domain controllers within the forest.

Domain Naming Master   The purpose of the *Domain Naming Master* is to keep track of all the domains within an Active Directory forest. You access this domain controller whenever you need to add new domains to a tree or forest.

Domain Operations Masters

You use the Active Directory Users And Computers snap-in to administer roles within a domain. Within each domain, at least one domain controller must fulfill each of the following roles:

Relative ID (RID) Master   Every object within Active Directory must be assigned a unique identifier so that it is distinguishable from other objects. For example, if you have two OUs named IT that reside in different domains, you must have some way to easily distinguish between them. Furthermore, if you delete one of the IT OUs and then later re-create it, the system must be able to determine that it is not the same object as the other IT OU. The unique identifier for each object is made up of a domain identifier and a relative identifier (RID). RIDs are always unique within an Active Directory domain and are used for managing security information and authenticating users. The *RID Master* is responsible for creating these values within a domain whenever new Active Directory objects are created.

PDC Emulator Master   Within a domain, the *PDC Emulator Master* is responsible for maintaining backward compatibility with Windows NT domain controllers. When running in mixed-mode domains, the PDC Emulator is able to process authentication requests and serve as a primary domain controller (PDC) with Windows NT backup domain controllers (BDCs).

When running in Windows 2000 Native, Windows 2003, or Windows 2008 domain functional level (which does not support the use of pre–Windows 2000 domain controllers), the PDC Emulator Master serves as the default domain controller to process authentication requests if another domain controller is unable to do so. The PDC Emulator also receives preferential treatment whenever domain security changes are made.

Infrastructure Master   Whenever a user is added to or removed from a group, all of the other domain controllers should be made aware of this change. The role of the domain controller that acts as an *Infrastructure Master* is to ensure that group membership information stays synchronized within an Active Directory domain.

Another service that a server can control for the network is the Windows Time service. The Windows Time service uses a suite of algorithms in the Network Time Protocol (NTP). This helps to ensure that the time on all computers throughout a network are as accurate as possible. All client computers within a Windows Server 2008 domain are synchronized with the time of an authoritative computer.

Assigning Single-Master Roles

Now that you are familiar with the different types of single-master operations, take a look at Exercise 4.3. This exercise shows you how to assign these roles to servers within the Active Directory environment. In this exercise, you will assign single-master operations roles to various domain controllers within the environment. In order to complete the steps in this exercise, you need one Active Directory domain controller.

EXERCISE 4.3

Assigning Single-Master Operations

1. Open the Active Directory Domains And Trusts administrative tool by clicking Start ➢ Administrative Tools ➢ Active Directory Domains And Trusts.

2. Right-click Active Directory Domains And Trusts, and choose Operations Master.

3. In the Operations Master dialog box, note that you can change the operations master by clicking the Change button. If you want to move this assignment to another computer, you first need to connect to that computer and then make the change. Click Close to continue without making any changes.

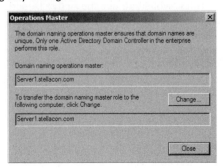

EXERCISE 4.3 *(continued)*

4. Close the Active Directory Domains And Trusts administrative tool.

5. Open the Active Directory Users And Computers administrative tool.

6. Right-click the name of a domain and select Operations Masters. This brings up the RID tab of the Operations Master dialog box.

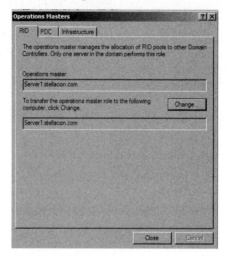

Notice that you can change the computer that is assigned to the role. In order to change the role, you first need to connect to the appropriate domain controller. Notice that the PDC and Infrastructure roles have similar tabs. Click Close to continue without making any changes.

7. When you are finished, close the Active Directory Users And Computers tool.

Remember that you manage single-master operations with three different tools. You use the Active Directory Domains And Trusts tool to configure forest-wide roles, while you use the Active Directory Users And Computers snap-in to administer roles within a domain. Although this might not seem intuitive at first, it can help you remember which roles apply to domains and which apply to the whole forest. The third tool, the Schema Master role, is a bit different than these other two. To change the Schema Master role, you must install the Active Directory Schema MMS snap-in and change it there.

Managing Trusts

Trust relationships make it easier to share security information and network resources between domains. As was already mentioned, standard transitive two-way trusts are automatically created between the domains in a tree and between each of the trees in a forest. Figure 4.4 shows an example of the default trust relationships in an Active Directory forest.

FIGURE 4.4   Default trusts in an Active Directory forest

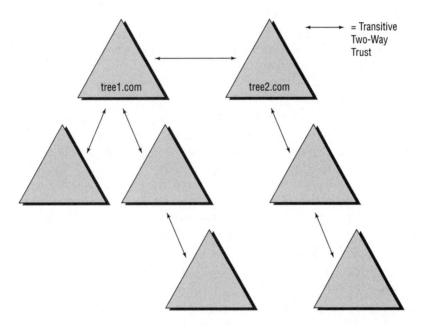

When configuring trusts, here are two main characteristics you need to consider:

Transitive trusts   By default, Active Directory trusts are *transitive trusts*. The simplest way to understand transitive relationships is through an example like the following: If Domain A trusts Domain B and Domain B trusts Domain C, then Domain A implicitly trusts Domain C. If you need to apply a tighter level of security, trusts can be configured as intransitive.

One-way vs. two-way   Trusts can be configured as one-way or two-way relationships. The default operation is to create *two-way trusts* or *bidirectional trusts*. This makes it easier to manage trust relationships by reducing the trusts you must create. In some cases, however, you might decide against two-way trusts. In one-way relationships, the trusting domain allows resources to be shared with the trusted domain, but not the other way around.

When domains are added together to form trees and forests, an automatic transitive two-way trust is created between them. Although the default trust relationships work well for most organizations, there are some reasons why you might want to manage trusts manually:

- You may want to remove trusts between domains if you are absolutely sure that you do not want resources to be shared between domains.

- Because of security concerns, you may need to keep resources isolated.

In addition to the default trust types, you can also configure the following types of special trusts:

External trusts   You use *external trusts* to provide access to resources on a Windows NT 4 domain or forest that cannot use a forest trust. Windows NT 4 domains cannot benefit from the other trust types that are used in Windows Server 2008, so in some cases, external trusts could be your only option. External trusts are always nontransitive, but they can be established in a one-way or two-way configuration.

> **Default SID filtering on external trusts**   When you set up an external trust, remember that it is possible for hackers to compromise a domain controller in a trusted domain. If this trust is compromised, a hacker can use the security identifier (SID) history attribute to associate SIDs with new user accounts, granting themselves unauthorized rights (this is called an elevation-of-privileges attack). To help prevent this type of attack, Windows Server 2008 automatically enables SID filter quarantining on all external trusts. SID filtering allows the domain controllers in the trusting domain (the domain with the resources) to remove all SID history attributes that are not members of the trusted domain.

Realm trusts   *Realm trusts* are similar to external trusts. You use them to connect to a non-Windows domain that uses Kerberos authentication. Realm trusts can be transitive or nontransitive, one-way or two-way.

Cross-forest trusts   *Cross-forest trusts* are used to share resources between forests. They have been used since Windows Server 2000 domains and cannot be intransitive, but you can establish them in a one-way or a two-way configuration. Authentication requests in either forest can reach the other forest in a two-way cross-forest trust.

> **Selective authentication vs. forest-wide authentication**   Forest-wide authentication on a forest trust means that users of the trusted forest can access all the resources of the trusting forest. Selective authentication means that users cannot authenticate to a domain controller or resource server in the trusting forest unless they are explicitly allowed to do so. Exercise 4.4 will show you the steps to change forest-wide authentication to selective authentication.

Shortcut trusts   In some cases, you may actually want to create direct trusts between two domains that implicitly trust each other. Such a trust is sometimes referred to as a *shortcut trust* and can improve the speed at which resources are accessed across many different domains.

Perhaps the most important aspect to remember regarding trusts is that creating them only *allows* you to share resources between domains. The trust does not grant any permissions between domains by itself. Once a trust has been established, however, systems administrators can easily assign the necessary permissions.

Exercise 4.4 walks you through the steps you need to take to manage trusts. In this exercise, you will see how to assign trust relationships between domains. In order to complete the steps in this exercise, you must have domain administrator access permissions.

EXERCISE 4.4

Managing Trust Relationships

1. Open the Active Directory Domains And Trusts administrative tool by clicking Start ➢ Administrative Tools ➢ Active Directory Domains And Trusts.

2. Right-click the name of a domain and select Properties.

3. Select the Trusts tab. You will see a list of the trusts that are currently configured. To modify the trust properties for an existing trust, highlight that trust and click Properties.

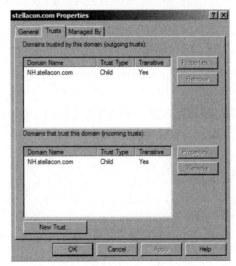

4.   The Properties window for the trust displays information about the trust's direction, transitivity, and type, along with the names of the domains involved in the relationship. Click Cancel to exit without making any changes.

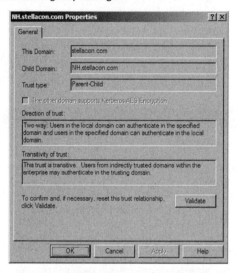

5.   To create a new trust relationship, click the New Trust button on the Trusts tab. The New Trust Wizard appears. Click Next to proceed with the wizard.

6.   On the Trust Name page, you are prompted for the name of the domain with which the trust should be created. Enter the name of the domain and click Next.

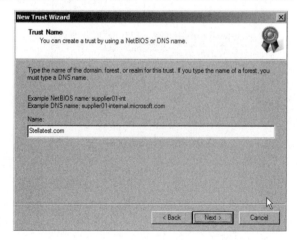

7. On the Trust Type page, you would normally choose the Trust With A Windows Domain option if you know that the other domain uses a Windows domain controller. In order to continue with this exercise (without requiring access to another domain), it is important to choose the Realm Trust option. This selection allows you to walk through the process of creating a trust relationship without needing an untrusted domain in the Active Directory environment. Click Next when you are done.

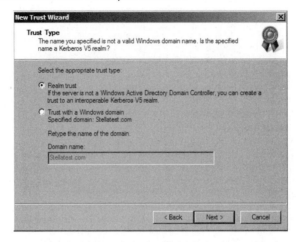

8. On the Transitivity Of Trust page, you choose whether the trust is transitive or intransitive. Choose the Nontransitive option and click Next to continue.

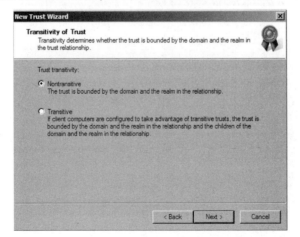

9. On the Direction Of Trust page, you select the direction of the trust. If you want both domains to trust each other, you select the two-way option. Otherwise you select either One-Way: Incoming or One-Way: Outgoing, depending on where the affected users are located. For the sake of this exercise, choose One-Way: Incoming and then click Next.

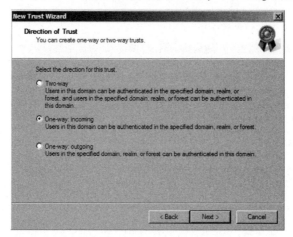

10. On the Trust Password page, you need to specify a password that should be used to administer the trust. Type **P@ssw0rd** and confirm it. Note that if there is an existing trust relationship between the domains, the passwords must match. Click Next to continue.

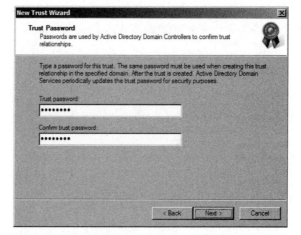

11. Now you see the Trust Selections Complete page that recaps the selections you have made. Because this is an exercise, you don't actually want to establish this trust. Click Cancel to cancel the wizard without saving the changes.

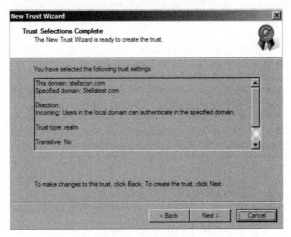

12. Exit the trust properties for the domain by clicking Cancel.

To Enable Selective Authentication

1. In the console tree, right-click the name of a domain and select Properties.

2. Select the Trusts tab. Under either Domains Trusted By This Domain (Outgoing Trusts) or Domains That Trust This Domain (Incoming Trusts), click the forest trust that you want to administer, and then click Properties.

3. On the Authentication tab, click Selective Authentication, and then click OK.

Managing UPN Suffixes

User principal name (UPN) suffixes are the part of a user's name that appears after the @ symbol. So, for instance, the UPN suffix of wpanek@stellacon.com would be stellacon.com. By default, the UPN suffix is determined by the name of the domain in which the user is created. In this example, the user wpanek was created in the domain stellacon.com, so the two pieces of the UPN logically fit together. However, you might find it useful to provide an alternative UPN suffix to consolidate the UPNs forest-wide.

For instance, if you manage a forest that consists of stellacon.com and stellacon2.com, you might want all of your users to adopt the more generally applicable stellacon.com UPN suffix. By adding additional UPN suffixes to the forest, you can easily choose the appropriate suffix when it comes time to create new users. Exercise 4.5 shows you how to add additional suffixes to a forest.

EXERCISE 4.5

Adding a UPN Suffix

1. Open the Active Directory Domains And Trusts administrative tool by clicking Start ➢ Administrative Tools ➢ Active Directory Domains And Trusts.

2. Right-click Active Directory Domains And Trusts in the left side of the window and select Properties.

3. On the UPN Suffixes tab of the Active Directory Domains And Trusts Properties dialog box, enter an alternate UPN suffix in the Alternate UPN Suffixes field. Click the Add button to add the suffix to the list.

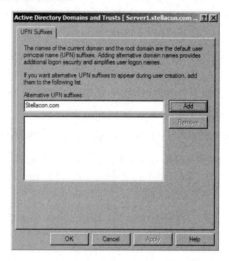

4. To remove a UPN suffix, select its name in the list and click the Remove button.

Managing Global Catalog Servers

One of the best features of a distributed directory service like Active Directory is that you can store different pieces of information in different places within an organization. For example, a domain in Japan might store a list of users who operate within a company's Asian operations business unit, while one in New York would contain a list of users who operate within its North American operations business unit. This architecture allows systems administrators to place the most frequently accessed information on domain controllers in different domains, thereby reducing disk space requirements and replication traffic.

However, you may encounter a problem when you deal with information that is segmented into multiple domains. The issue involves querying information stored within Active Directory. What would happen, for example, if a user wanted a list of all of the printers available in all domains within the Active Directory forest? In this case, the search would normally require information from at least one domain controller in each of the domains within the environment. Some of these domain controllers may be located across slow WAN links or may have unreliable connections. The end result would include an extremely long wait while retrieving the results of the query, that is, if any results came up without timing out.

Fortunately, Active Directory has a mechanism that speeds up such searches. You can configure any number of domain controllers to host a copy of the GC. The GC contains all of the schema information and a subset of the attributes for all domains within the Active Directory environment. Although a default set of information is normally included with the GC, systems administrators can choose to add additional information to this data store if it is needed. To help reduce replication traffic and to keep the GC's database small, only a limited subset of each object's attributes are replicated. This is called the partial attribute set (PAS). You can change the PAS by modifying the schema and marking attributes for replication to the GC.

Servers that contain a copy of the GC are known as GC servers. Now, whenever a user executes a query that requires information from multiple domains, they need only contact the nearest GC server for this information. Similarly, when users must authenticate across domains, they do not have to wait for a response from a domain controller that may be located across the world. The end result is that the overall performance of Active Directory queries increases.

Exercise 4.6 walks you through the steps you need to take to configure a domain controller as a GC server. Generally, GC servers are only useful in environments that use multiple Active Directory domains.

EXERCISE 4.6

Managing GC Servers

1. Open the Active Directory Sites And Services administrative tool by clicking Start ➢ Administrative Tools ➢ Active Directory Sites And Services.

2. Find the name of the local domain controller within the list of objects (typically under Default First Site Name ➢ Servers), and expand this object. Right-click NTDS Settings and select Properties.

3. In the NTDS Settings Properties dialog box, type **Primary GC Server for Domain** in the Description field. Note that there is a checkbox that determines whether this computer contains a copy of the Global Catalog. If the box is checked, then this domain controller contains a subset of information from all other domains within the Active Directory environment. Select the Global Catalog checkbox, and then click OK to continue.

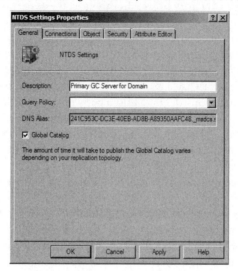

4. When you are finished, close the Active Directory Sites And Services administrative tool.

Managing Universal Group Membership Caching

Many networks run into problems due to available network bandwidth and server hardware limitations. For this reason, it may not be wise to install a GC in smaller branch offices. Windows Server 2008 can help these smaller sites by deploying domain controllers that use universal group membership caching.

Once enabled, universal group membership caching stores information locally once a user attempts to log on for the first time. With the use of a GC, the domain controller retains the universal group membership for that logged on user.

The next time that user attempts to log on, the authenticating domain controller running Windows Server 2008 will obtain the universal group membership information from its local cache without the need to contact a GC. The universal group membership information is retained, by default, on the domain controller for 8 hours.

Some of the advantages of using universal group membership caching are as follows:

Faster logon times   Since the domain controller does not need to contact a global catalog, logon authentication is faster.

Reduced network bandwidth   The domain controller does not have to handle object replication for all the objects located in the forest.

Ability to use existing hardware.   There is no need to upgrade hardware to support a GC.

Exercise 4.7 shows you the steps that you need to take to configure universal group membership caching.

EXERCISE 4.7

Managing Universal Group Membership Caching

1. Open the Active Directory Sites And Services administrative tool by clicking Start ➢ Administrative Tools ➢ Active Directory Sites And Services.

2. Click Sites, then Click DefaultFirstSite. In the right pane, right-click NTDS Settings and choose Properties.

3. In the NTDS Site Settings Properties dialog box, check the box labeled Enable Universal Group Membership Caching and then click OK to continue.

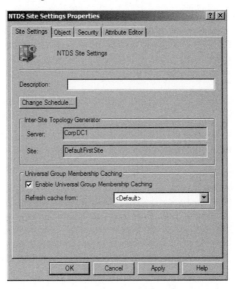

4. When you are finished, close the Active Directory Sites And Services administrative tool.

Summary

In this chapter, we covered the basics of linking multiple domains in trees and forests. You now know why you would want to plan for them and what the benefits and drawbacks are of using only one domain, or of having a multidomain environment. For example, you might decide to have multiple domains if you have an acquisitions and mergers situation where you need to keep multiple administrators. In addition, by using multiple domains, organizations can retain separate security databases; however, in such cases, they are also able to share resources between domains.

You also learned how to use multiple domains to provide two major benefits for the network directory services—security and availability. These benefits are made possible through Active Directory and the administrative tools that can be used to access it.

In addition, we covered how system administrators can simplify operations while still ensuring that only authorized users have access to their data, how multiple domains can interact to form Active Directory trees and forests, and how you can use the Active Directory Installation Wizard to create new Active Directory trees and forests.

Exam Essentials

Understand the reasons for using multiple domains.   There are seven primary reasons for using multiple domains: they provide additional scalability, they reduce replication traffic, they help with political and organizational issues, they provide many levels of hierarchy, they allow for decentralized administration, legality, and they allow for multiple DNS or domain names.

Understand the drawbacks of using multiple domains.   With multiple domains, maintaining administrative consistency is more difficult. The number of administrative units multiplies as well, which makes it difficult to keep track of network resources. Finally, it is much more difficult to rearrange the domain topology within an Active Directory environment than it is to simply reorganize OUs.

Know how to create a domain tree.   To create a new domain tree, you need to promote a Windows Server 2008 computer to a domain controller, select the option that makes this domain controller the first machine in a new domain, and make that domain the first domain of a new tree. The result is a new domain tree.

Know how to join a domain tree to a forest.   Creating a new tree to form or add to a forest is as simple as promoting a server to a domain controller for a new domain that does *not* share a namespace with an existing Active Directory domain. In order to add a domain to an existing forest, you must already have at least one other domain. This domain serves as the root domain for the entire forest.

Understand how to manage single-master operations. Single-master operations must be performed on specially designated machines within the Active Directory forest. There are five main single-master functions: two that apply to an entire Active Directory forest (Schema Master and Domain Naming Master) and three that apply to each domain (RID Master, PDC Emulator Master, and Infrastructure Master).

Understand how to manage trusts. When configuring trusts, you'll need to consider two main characteristics: transitivity and direction. The simplest way to understand transitive relationships is through an example like the following: If Domain A trusts Domain B and Domain B trusts Domain C, then Domain A implicitly trusts Domain C. Trusts can be configured as intransitive so that this type of behavior does not occur. In one-way relationships, the trusting domain allows resources to be shared with the trusted domain. In two-way relationships, both domains trust each other equally. Special trusts include external trusts, realm trusts, cross-forest trusts, and shortcut trusts.

Understand how to manage UPN suffixes. By default, the name of the domain in which the user is created determines the UPN suffix. By adding additional UPN suffixes to the forest, you can easily choose more manageable suffixes when it comes time to create new users.

Understand how to manage Global Catalog (GC) servers. You can configure any number of domain controllers to host a copy of the GC. The GC contains all of the schema information and a subset of the attributes for all domains within the Active Directory environment. Servers that contain a copy of the GC are known as GC servers. Whenever a user executes a query that requires information from multiple domains, they need only contact the nearest GC server for this information. Similarly, when users must authenticate across domains, they will not have to wait for a response from a domain controller that may be located across the world. The end result is increased overall performance of Active Directory queries.

Understanding Universal Group Membership Caching. You can enable a domain controller as a universal group membership caching server. The universal group membership caching machine will then send a request for the logon authentication of a user to the GC server. The GC will then send the information back to the universal group membership caching server to be cached locally for 8 hours (by default). The user can then authenticate without the need to contact the GC again.

Review Questions

1. You are a systems administrator for an environment that consists of two Active Directory domains. Initially, the domains were configured without any trust relationships. However, the business now needs to share resources between domains. You decide to create a trust relationship between Domain A and Domain B. Before you take any other actions, which of the following statements is true? Choose all that apply.

    A. All users in Domain A can access all resources in Domain B.

    B. All users in Domain B can access all resources in Domain A.

    C. Resources cannot be shared between the domains.

    D. Users in Domain A do not have permission to access resources in Domain B.

    E. Users in Domain B do not have permission to access resources in Domain A.

2. Jane is a systems administrator for a large Active Directory environment that plans to deploy four Active Directory domains. She is responsible for determining the hardware budget she needs to deploy the four domains. She has the following requirements:

    - The budget should minimize the number of servers to be deployed initially.

    - Each domain must implement enough fault tolerance to survive the complete failure of one domain controller.

    - If one domain controller fails, users in all domains should still have access to Active Directory information.

    In order to meet these requirements, what is the minimum number of domain controllers Jane can deploy initially?

    A. 0

    B. 1

    C. 2

    D. 4

    E. 8

3. Juan is a network administrator for three Active Directory domains that support offices based primarily in South America. His organization has recently decided to open several offices in North America and Asia, and many of the employees will be relocated to staff these offices. As part of the change, several offices in South America will either be closed or reduced in size.

Currently, the environment consists of many Windows Server 2008 computers in different configurations. In order to conserve hardware resources, Juan plans to reassign some of the servers located in South America to support operations in North America and Asia, which will include the creation of new domains. Which of the following server configurations can be directly promoted to become a domain controller for a new domain? Choose all that apply.

A. Member server

B. Stand-alone server

C. Domain controller

D. Secondary domain controller

4. Monica is the systems administrator for a mixed-domain environment that consists of Active Directory domain controllers and Windows NT 4 domain controllers. The server roles are as follows:

Server1: Schema Master

Server2: RID Master

Server3: Windows NT 4 BDC

Server4: Infrastructure Master

Server5: PDC Emulator Master

When the business finishes migrating the entire environment to Windows Server 2008, which of the following machines will no longer be required?

A. Server1

B. Server2

C. Server3

D. Server4

E. Server5

5. Implicit trusts created between domains are known as which of the following?

A. Two-way trusts

B. Transitive trusts

C. One-way trusts

D. Intransitive trusts

6. You are a developer for a small organization that has deployed a single Active Directory domain. Your organization has begun using the Active Directory schema in order to store important information related to each of the company's 350 employees. Most of the fields of information you plan to support are already included with the basic Active Directory schema. However, one field—a "security clearance level" value—is not supported. You want to take advantage of the extensibility of Active Directory by adding this field to the properties of a User object. On which of the following servers can the change be made?

A. Any domain controller

B. Any member server

C. The Schema Master

D. The Global Catalog

7. What are several Active Directory domains that share a contiguous namespace called?

A. A forest

B. A domain hierarchy

C. A tree

D. A DNS zone

8. A junior systems administrator who was responsible for administering an Active Directory domain accidentally demoted the last domain controller of your ADTest.com domain. He noticed that after the demotion process was complete, that none of the machines on the network could perform any Active Directory–related operations. He calls you to ask for advice about re-creating the domain. Your solution must meet the following requirements:

- No Active Directory security information can be lost.

- All objects must be restored.

- The process must not require the use of Active Directory or server backups because they were not being performed for the ADTest.com domain.

After the last domain controller in a domain has been demoted, how can the domain be re-created to meet these requirements?

A. By creating a new domain controller with the same name as the demoted one.

B. By creating a new domain with the same name.

C. By adding a new member server to the old domain.

D. None of the above solutions meets the requirements.

9. Which of the following item(s) does not depend on the DNS namespace? (Choose all that apply.)

   A. Organizational units (OUs)

   B. Domains

   C. Domain trees

   D. Domain forests

   E. DNS zones

   F. Active Directory sites

10. Which of the following types of computers contain a copy of the Global Catalog (GC)?

   A. All Windows NT domain controllers

   B. All Active Directory domain controllers

   C. Specified Active Directory domain controllers

   D. Active Directory workstations

11. Which of the following pieces of information should you have before you use the Active Directory Installation Wizard to install a new subdomain? Choose all that apply.

   A. The name of the child domain

   B. The name of the parent domain

   C. DNS configuration information

   D. NetBIOS name for the server

12. Which type of trust is automatically created between the domains in a domain tree?

   A. Transitive

   B. Two-way

   C. Transitive two-way

   D. Intransitive two-way

13. The Active Directory Installation Wizard can be accessed by typing which of the following commands?

   A. domaininstall

   B. domainupgrade

   C. dconfig

   D. dcinstall

   E. dcpromo

14. A systems administrator wants to remove a domain controller from a domain. Which of the following is the easiest way to perform the task?

   A. Use the Active Directory Installation Wizard to demote the domain controller.

   B. Use the `dcpromo /remove` command.

   C. Reinstall the server over the existing installation and make the machine a member of a workgroup.

   D. Reinstall the server over the existing installation and make the machine a member of a domain.

15. Which of the following is *true* regarding the sharing of resources between forests?

   A. All resources are automatically shared between forests.

   B. A trust relationship must exist before resources can be shared between forests.

   C. Resources cannot be shared between forests.

   D. A transitive trust relationship must exist before resources can be shared between forests.

16. You are a network administrator for your organization. Your company needs to implement a new remote location. Even though the company has a very slow WAN connection between sites, the new location must adhere to the following specs:

   ▪ Fast logon times

   ▪ Reduced network bandwidth

   ▪ Ability to use existing hardware

   What can you implement to achieve the above requirements?

   A. Global Catalog

   B. Universal group membership caching

   C. DNS Active Directory Integrated zone

   D. DNS Secondary zone

17. You are the network administrator for your company's infrastructure. You need to merge a company into your current domain and forest. The new company's domain is going to be created as a new domain that is added to your company's root name. From the following selections, what is the best way to accomplish this task?

   A. Join the new domain to a new forest.

   B. Join the new domain to a current one.

   C. Create a new FQDN and use a secondary zone.

   D. Allow for a canonical name record to translate to the new domain.

18. As the systems engineer installing the new Active Directory domain, you need to consider where you will have your five main single-master functions. Of the five main single master functions, two apply to an entire Active Directory forest. What are the three that apply to just the domain? Choose all that apply.

   A. Domain Naming Master

   B. RID Master

   C. PDC Emulator Master

   D. Infrastructure Master

19. When deploying Active Directory, you decide to create a new domain tree. What do you need to do to create this?

   A. Demote a Windows Server 2008 computer to a member server and select the option that makes this a tree master for the new domain.

   B. Use a Windows Server 2008 computer as a domain naming master and select the Tree Master option. This will force the selection.

   C. Use a system as a member server, promote it to a domain controller, and then select Use As Tree Master when prompted.

   D. Promote a Windows Server 2008 computer to a domain controller and select the option that makes this domain controller the first machine in a new domain that is a child of an existing one.

20. You are the network administrator for your company and are responsible for the current Active Directory layout. You are purchasing a new company soon and need to connect the two seamlessly. You need to make sure there is no more administrative overhead than absolutely necessary. You currently have two forests and two domains. You need to reduce administrative costs and the overhead and streamline Active Directory deployment. What is the best solution to this problem?

   A. Use multiple domains. Ensure that you are using the Active Directory Connector and make sure you set up QoS (quality of service) on the Active Directory Connector.

   B. Install a new domain controller and use it to offload processes.

   C. Do not use multiple domains. They increase overhead and shouldn't be used unless absolutely necessary. Redesign your network to fall under one domain and one forest, then plan and cutover accordingly.

   D. Make sure that you use a third-party load balancer to speed up Active Directory convergence.

Answers to Review Questions

1. D, E. A trust relationship only allows for the *possibility* of sharing resources between domains; it does not explicitly provide any permissions. In order to allow users to access resources in another domain, you must configure the appropriate permissions.

2. E. Every domain must have at least one domain controller; therefore, Jane needs at least four domain controllers in order to create the domains. Furthermore, to meet the requirements for fault tolerance and the ability to continue operations during the failure of a domain controller, each of the four domains must also have a second domain controller. Therefore, Jane must deploy a minimum of eight servers configured as Active Directory domain controllers.

3. A, B. Both member servers and stand-alone servers can be promoted to domain controllers for new Active Directory domains. In order to "move" an existing domain controller to a new domain, Juan must first demote the domain controller. He can then promote it to a domain controller for a new domain. Secondary domain controllers do not exist in Active Directory.

4. C. The Windows NT backup domain controller (BDC) will no longer be necessary once the environment moves to a Windows Server 2008 platform (although it may be upgraded to a Windows Server 2008 domain controller). The PDC Emulator Master is used primarily for compatibility with Windows NT domains; however, it will still be required for certain domain-wide functions in a Windows Server 2008 environment.

5. B. Trusts between domains that have not been explicitly defined are known as transitive trusts. Transitive trusts can be either one-way or two-way.

6. C. The Schema Master is the only server within Active Directory on which changes to the schema can be made.

7. C. A domain tree is made up of one or more domains that share the same contiguous namespace.

8. D. Once the last domain controller in an environment has been removed, there is no way to re-create the same domain. If adequate backups had been performed, you may have been able to recover information by rebuilding the server.

9. A, F. OUs do not participate in the DNS namespace—they are used primarily for naming objects within an Active Directory domain. The naming for Active Directory objects, such as sites, does not depend on DNS names either.

10. C. Systems administrators can define which domain controllers in the environment contain a copy of the GC. Although the GC does contain information about all domains in the environment, it does not have to reside on all domain controllers.

11. A, B, C, D. Before beginning the promotion of a domain controller, you should have all of the information listed. You must specify all of these pieces of information in the Active Directory Installation Wizard.

12. C. A transitive two-way trust is automatically created between the domains in a domain tree.

13. E. The dcpromo command can be used to launch the Active Directory Installation Wizard. None of the other commands are valid in Windows Server 2008.

14. A. The Active Directory Installation Wizard allows administrators to remove a domain controller from a domain quickly and easily without requiring them to reinstall the operating system.

15. B. When you create trust relationships, resources can be shared between domains that are in two different forests. To simplify access to resources (at the expense of security), a systems administrator could enable the Guest account in the domains so that resources would be automatically shared for members of the Everyone group.

16. B. Universal group membership caching stores information locally once a user attempts to log on for the first time. With the use of a Global Catalog, the domain controller retains the universal group membership for that logged on user. The next time that user attempts to log on, the authenticating domain controller running Windows Server 2008 will obtain the universal group membership information from its local cache without the need to contact a Global Catalog.

17. B. Creating a new tree to form or add to a forest is as simple as promoting a server to a domain controller for a new domain that does not share a namespace with an existing Active Directory domain. In order to add a new domain to an existing forest, you must already have at least one other domain. This domain serves as the root domain for the entire forest.

18. B, C, D. Single-master operations must be performed on specially designated machines within the Active Directory forest. The five main single-master functions are the following: two that apply to an entire Active Directory forest (Schema Master and Domain Naming Master) and three that apply to each domain (RID Master, PDC Emulator Master, and Infrastructure Master).

19. D. To create a new domain tree, you need to promote a Windows Server 2008 computer to a domain controller and select the option that makes this domain controller the first machine in a new domain. The result is a new domain tree.

20. C. With multiple domains, maintaining administrative consistency is more difficult. The number of administrative units multiplies as well, which makes it difficult to keep track of network resources.

Chapter

5

Configuring Sites and Replication

MICROSOFT EXAM OBJECTIVES COVERED IN THIS CHAPTER:

✓ **Configuring the Active Directory Infrastructure**

- ▪ Configure sites. May include but is not limited to: create Active Directory subnets; configure site links; configure site link costing; configure sites infrastructure

- ▪ Configure Active Directory replication. May include but is not limited to: Distributed File System; one-way replication; Bridgehead server; replication scheduling; configure replication protocols; force intersite replication

Microsoft has designed Active Directory to be an enterprise-wide solution for managing network resources. In previous chapters, you saw how to create Active Directory objects based on an organization's logical design. Domain structure and organizational unit (OU) structure, for example, should be designed based primarily on an organization's business needs.

Now it's time to learn how Active Directory can map to an organization's *physical* requirements. Specifically, you must consider network connectivity between sites and the flow of information between domain controllers (DC) under less-than-ideal conditions. These constraints determine how domain controllers can work together to ensure that the objects within Active Directory remain synchronized, no matter how large and geographically dispersed the network is.

Fortunately, through the use of the Active Directory Sites And Services administrative tool, you can quickly and easily create the various components of an Active Directory replication topology. Using this tool, you can create objects called sites, place servers in sites, and create connections between sites. Once you have configured Active Directory replication to fit your current network environment, you can sit back and allow Active Directory to make sure that information remains consistent across domain controllers.

This chapter covers the features of Active Directory that allow systems administrators to modify the behavior of replication based on their physical network design. Through the use of sites, systems and network administrators will be able to leverage their network infrastructure to best support Windows Server 2008 and Active Directory.

Overview of Network Planning

Before discussing sites and replication, you need to understand some basic physical and network concepts.

The Three Types of Network

When designing networks, systems and network administrators use the following terms to define the types of connectivity between locations and servers:

Local area networks (LANs)   A *local area network (LAN)* is usually characterized as a high-bandwidth network. Generally, an organization owns all of its LAN network hardware and software. Ethernet is by far the most common networking standard. Ethernet speeds are generally at least 10Mbps and can scale to multiple gigabits per second. Currently, the standard for Ethernet is the 10 Gigabit Ethernet, which runs at 10 times the speed of Gigabit Ethernet (1Gbps). Several LAN technologies, including routing and switching, are available to segment LANs and to reduce contention for network resources.

Wide area networks (WANs)   The purpose of a *wide area network (WAN)* is similar to that of a LAN—to connect network devices together. Unlike LANs, however, WANs are usually leased from third-party telecommunications carriers and Internet service providers (ISPs). Although extremely high-speed WAN connections are available, they are generally costly for organizations to implement through a distributed environment. Therefore, WAN connections are characterized by lower-speed connections and, sometimes, nonpersistent connections.

The Internet   If you have not heard of the Internet, you must have been locked away in a server room (without network access) for a long time. The Internet is a worldwide public network infrastructure based on the *Internet Protocol (IP)*. Access to the Internet is available through organizations known as ISPs. Because it is a public network, there is no single "owner" of the Internet. Instead, large network and telecommunications providers constantly upgrade the infrastructure of this network to meet growing demands.

Organizations now use the Internet regularly. For example, it's rare nowadays to see advertisements that don't direct you to one website or another. Through the use of technologies such as Virtual Private Networks (VPNs), organizations can use encryption and authentication technology to enable secure communications across the Internet.

Exploring Network Constraints

In an ideal situation, a high-speed network would connect all computers and networking devices. In such a situation, you would be able to ensure that any user of your network, regardless of location, would be able to quickly and easily access resources. When you are working in the real world, however, you have many other constraints to keep in mind, including network bandwidth and network cost.

Network Bandwidth

Network bandwidth generally refers to the amount of data that can pass through a specific connection in a given amount of time. For example, in a WAN situation, a T1 may have 1.544Mbps (megabits per second), or a standard analog modem may have a bandwidth of 56 or 57.6Kbps (kilobits per second) or less. However, your LAN's Ethernet connection may have a bandwidth of 100Mbps. Different types of networks work at different speeds; therefore, it's imperative that you always consider network bandwidth when you're thinking of how to deploy domain controllers in your environment.

Network Cost

Cost is perhaps the single biggest factor in determining a network design. If cost were not a constraint, organizations would clearly choose to use high-bandwidth connections for all of their sites. Realistically, trade-offs in performance must be made for the sake of affordability. Some of the factors that can affect the cost of networking include the distance between networks and the types of technology available at locations throughout the world. In remote or less-developed locations, you may not even be able to get access through an ISP or Telecom beyond a satellite connection or dial-up, and what is available can be quite costly. Network designers must keep these factors in mind, and often they must settle for less-than-ideal connectivity.

Before we considered the monetary value of doing business, let's consider another definition of cost. When designing and configuring networks, you can require certain devices to automatically make data transport decisions based on an assigned network cost. These devices are commonly known as routers, and they use routing protocols to make routing decisions. One of the elements a router uses to configure a routing protocol is its ability to adjust the cost of a route. For example, a router might have multiple ways to connect to a remote site, and it may have multiple interfaces connected to it, each with different paths out of the network to which it is connected locally. When two or more routes are available, you can set up a routing protocol that states that the route with the lower cost is automatically used first.

Another cost is personnel. Do you have the personnel to do the job or do you need to hire a consultant? Remember that even if you use individuals already on staff, they will be spending time on these projects. When your IT team is working on a project, that is a cost because they cannot also be working on day-to-day tasks.

All of these factors play an important role when you make your Active Directory implementation decisions.

Overview of Active Directory Replication and Sites

We now need to cover two topics that are not only covered heavily on the Microsoft exams, but are also two areas that all IT administrators should understand. Understanding Active Directory replication and sites can help you fine-tune a network to run at peak performance.

Replicating Active Directory

Regardless of the issues related to network design and technological constraints, network users have many different requirements and needs that must be addressed. First and foremost, network resources such as files, printers, and shared directories must be made available. Similarly, the resources stored within Active Directory—and, especially, its security information—are required for many operations that occur within domains.

With these issues in mind, take a look at how you can configure Active Directory to reach connectivity goals using replication.

Active Directory was designed as a scalable, distributed database that contains information about an organization's network resources. In previous chapters, we looked at how you can create and manage domains and how you can use domain controllers to store Active Directory databases.

Even in the simplest of network environments, you generally need more than one domain controller. The major reasons for this include fault tolerance (if one domain controller fails, others can still provide services as needed) and performance (the workload can be balanced between multiple domain controllers). Windows Server 2008 domain controllers have been designed to contain read-write copies of the Active Directory database as well as read-only copies of the Active Directory database. However, the domain controllers must also remain current when objects are created or modified on other domain controllers.

To keep information consistent between domain controllers, you use *Active Directory replication*. Replication is the process by which changes to the Active Directory database are transferred between domain controllers. The end result is that all of the domain controllers within an Active Directory domain contain up-to-date information and achieved convergence. Keep in mind that domain controllers may be located very near to each other (for example, within the same server rack) or they may be located across the world from each other. Although the goals of replication are quite simple, the real-world constraints of network connections between servers cause many limitations that you must accommodate. If you had a domain controller on your local LAN, you may find that between your server connections you have Gigabit Ethernet, which runs at 1000Mbps, whereas you may have a domain controller on the other side or a WAN where the network link runs at a fraction of a T1, 56Kbps. Replication traffic must traverse each link to ensure convergence no matter what the speed or what bandwidth is available.

Throughout this chapter, you will look at the technical details of Active Directory replication and how you can use the concept of sites and site links to map the logical structure of Active Directory to a physical network topology to help it work efficiently, no matter what type of link you are working with.

Understanding Active Directory Site Concepts

One of the most important aspects of designing and implementing Active Directory is understanding how Active Directory allows you to separate the logical components of the directory service from the physical components.

The logical components—Active Directory domains, OUs, users, groups, and computers—map to the organizational and business requirements of a company.

The physical components, on the other hand, are designed based on technical issues involved in keeping the network synchronized (that is, making sure all parts of the network have the same up-to-date information). Active Directory uses the concept of sites to map to an organization's physical network. Stated simply, a *site* is a collection of well-connected subnets. The technical implications of sites are described later in this chapter.

It is important to understand that no specified relationship exists between Active Directory domains and Active Directory sites. An Active Directory site can contain many domains. Alternatively, a single Active Directory domain can span multiple sites. Figure 5.1 illustrates this very important characteristic of domains and sites.

FIGURE 5.1 Potential relationships between domains and sites

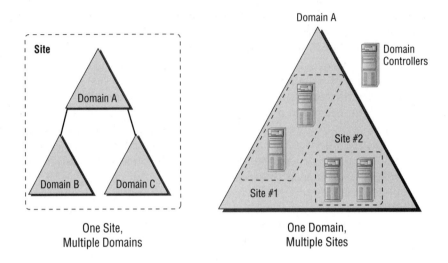

One Site,
Multiple Domains

One Domain,
Multiple Sites

There are two main reasons to use Active Directory sites: service requests and replication.

Service Requests

Clients often require the network services of a domain controller. One of the most common reasons for this is that they need the domain controller to perform network authentication. If your Active Directory network is set up with sites, clients can easily connect to the domain controller that is located closest to them. By doing this, they avoid many of the inefficiencies associated with connecting to distant domain controllers or to those that are located on the other side of a slow network connection. For example, by connecting to a local domain controller, you can avoid the problems associated with a saturated network link, which might cause two domain controllers to be out of synch with each other.

Other network services that clients might access include the Licensing service (for tracking licenses associated with Microsoft and other compatible products) and the services used by messaging applications (such as Exchange Server). All of these functions depend on the availability of network services.

Replication

As we mentioned earlier, the purpose of Active Directory replication is to ensure that the information stored on all domain controllers within a domain remains synchronized. In environments with many domains and domain controllers, usually multiple communication paths connect them, which makes the synchronization process more complicated. A simple method of transferring updates and other changes to Active Directory involves all of the servers communicating directly with each other as soon as a change occurs; they can all update with the change and reach convergence again. This is not ideal, however, since it places high requirements on network bandwidth and is inefficient for many network environments that use slower and more costly WAN links, especially if all environments update at the same time. Such simultaneous updating could cause the network connection at the core of your network to become saturated and decrease performance of the entire WAN.

Using sites, Active Directory can automatically determine the best methods for performing replication operations. Sites take into account an organization's network infrastructure, and Active Directory uses these sites to determine the most efficient method for synchronizing information between domain controllers. Systems administrators can make their physical network design map to Active Directory objects. Based on the creation and configuration of these objects, the Active Directory service can then manage replication traffic in an efficient way.

Whenever a change is made to the Active Directory database on a domain controller, the change is given an update sequence number. The domain controller can then propagate these changes to other domain controllers based on replication settings. In the event that the same setting (such as a user's last name) has been changed on two different domain controllers (before replication can take place), these sequence numbers are used to resolve the conflict.

Windows Server 2008 uses a feature called *linked value replication* that is only active when the domain is in Windows Server 2003 or 2008 domain functional level. In Windows 2000, if a change was made to a member of a group, the entire group was replicated. With linked value replication, only the group member is replicated. This greatly enhances replication efficiency and cuts down on network traffic utilization. Linked value replication is automatically enabled in Windows Server 2003 or 2008 domain functional level domains.

Planning Your Sites

Much of the challenge of designing Active Directory is related to mapping a company's business processes to the structure of a hierarchical data store. So far, you've seen many of these requirements. But what about the existing network infrastructure? Clearly, when you plan for and design the structure of Active Directory, you must take into account your LAN and WAN characteristics. Let's see some of the ways you can use Active Directory sites to manage replication traffic.

Synchronizing Active Directory is extremely important. In order to keep security permissions and objects within the directory consistent throughout the organization, you must use replication. Active Directory data store supports *multimaster replication*; that is, data can be modified at any domain controller within the domain because replication ensures that information remains consistent throughout the organization.

Ideally, every site within an organization has reliable, high-speed connections with the other sites. A much more realistic scenario, however, is one in which bandwidth is limited and connections are sometimes either sporadically available or completely unavailable.

Using sites, network and systems administrators can define which domain controllers are located on which areas of the network. These settings can be based on the bandwidth available between the areas of the network. Additionally, these administrators can define *subnets*—logically partitioned areas of the network—between areas of the network. Subnets are designed by subdividing IP addresses into usable blocks for assignment, and they are also objects found within the Sites and Services Microsoft Management Console (MMC) in the Administrative

Tools folder. The Windows Server 2008 Active Directory services use this information to decide how and when to replicate data between domain controllers.

Directly replicating information between all domain controllers might be a viable solution for some companies. For others, however, this might result in a lot of traffic traveling over slow or undersized network links. One way to efficiently synchronize data between sites that have slow connections is to use a *bridgehead server*. Bridgehead servers are designed to accept traffic between two remote sites and to then forward this information to the appropriate servers. Figure 5.2 provides an example of how a bridgehead server can reduce network bandwidth requirements and improve performance. Reduced network bandwidth requirements and improved performance can also be achieved by configuring replication to occur according to a predefined schedule if bandwidth usage statistics are available.

FIGURE 5.2   Using a bridgehead server

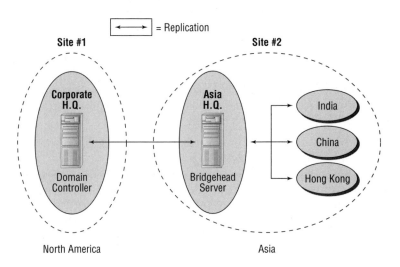

Bridgehead servers do not fit a normal hub-and-spoke WAN topology. Such a topology usually involves a core site (for example, company headquarters) with remote sites as links one off from the core. However, you can use a bridgehead server design to fit a distributed star, where you have a hub-and-spoke topology design, with additional spokes coming out of the first set of spokes. Doing so would make some of your spoke sites into smaller core sites; it is at these sites that you would place your bridgehead servers. In Figure 5.2, you can see that your Asia headquarters site is also where you can connect up to India, China, and Hong Kong—thus making Asia headquarters the ideal site for the bridgehead server.

In addition to managing replication traffic, sites also offer the advantage of allowing clients to access the nearest domain controller. This prevents problems with user authentication across slow network connections and it can help find the shortest and fastest path to resources such as files and printers. Therefore, Microsoft recommends that you place at least one domain controller at each site that contains a slow link. Preferably, this domain controller also contains a copy of the Global Catalog so that logon attempts and resource search queries do not occur across slow links. The drawback, however, is that deploying more copies of the Global Catalog to servers increases replication traffic.

Through proper planning and deployment of sites, organizations can best use the capabilities of the network infrastructure while keeping Active Directory synchronized.

Implementing Sites and Subnets

Now that you have an idea of the goals of replication, look at the following quick overview of the various Active Directory objects that are related to physical network topology.

The basic objects that are used for managing replication include the following:

Subnets A subnet is a partition of a network. As we started to discuss earlier, subnets are logical IP blocks usually connected to other IP blocks through the use of routers and other network devices. All of the computers that are located on a given subnet are generally well connected with each other.

 It is extremely important to understand the concepts of TCP/IP and the routing of network information when you are designing the topology for Active Directory replication. Although TCP/IP is not tested heavily in this exam, you should still generally understand it so that you know how to deploy sites properly. See *MCTS: Windows Server 2008 Network Infrastructure Study Guide (70-642)*, by William Panek, Tylor Wentworth, and James Chellis (Wiley, 2008) for more information on this topic.

Sites An Active Directory site is a logical object that can contain servers and other objects related to Active Directory replication. Specifically, a site is a grouping of related subnets. Sites are created to match the physical network structure of an organization. Sites are primarily used for slow WAN links. If your network is well connected (using fiber optics, Category 5 Ethernet, etc.), then sites are not needed.

Site links A *site link* is created to define the types of connections that are available between the components of a site. Site links can reflect a relative cost for a network connection and can reflect the bandwidth that is available for communications.

All of these components work together to determine how information is used to replicate data between domain controllers. Figure 5.3 provides an example of the physical components of Active Directory.

FIGURE 5.3   Active Directory replication objects

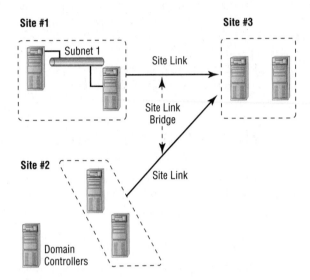

Many issues are related to configuring and managing sites; all are covered in this chapter. Overall, using sites allows you to control the behavior of Active Directory replication between domain controllers. With this background and goal in mind, let's look at how you can implement sites to control Active Directory replication so that it is efficient and in synch.

If you do not have replication set up properly, you will experience problems with your domain controllers after awhile. An example of a common replication problem is Event Log event ID 1311, which states that the Windows NT Directory Services (NTDS) Knowledge Consistency Checker (KCC) has found (and reported) a problem with Active Directory replication. This error message states that the replication configuration information in Active Directory does not accurately reflect the physical topology of the network. This error is commonly found on ailing networks that have replication problems for one reason or another.

Creating Sites

The primary method for creating and managing Active Directory replication components is to utilize the Active Directory Sites And Services tool or the MMC found within the Administrative Tools folder. Using this administrative component, you can graphically create and manage sites in much the same way you create and manage OUs.

Exercise 5.1 walks you through the process of creating Active Directory sites. In order for you to complete this exercise, the local machine must be a domain controller. Also, this exercise assumes that you have not yet changed the default domain site configuration.

Do not perform any testing on a production system or network—make sure you test site configuration in a lab setting only.

EXERCISE 5.1

Creating Sites

1. Open the Active Directory Sites And Services tool from the Administrative Tools program group.

2. Expand the Sites folder.

3. Right-click the Default-First-Site-Name item, and choose Rename. Rename the site to **CorporateHQ**.

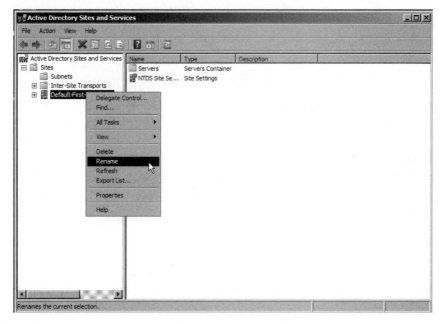

4. Create a new site by right-clicking the Sites object and selecting New Site.

EXERCISE 5.1 *(continued)*

5. On the New Object–Site dialog box, type **Farmington** for the site name. Click the DEFAULTIPSITELINK item, an information screen pops up, then click OK to create the site. Note that you cannot include spaces or other special characters in the name of a site.

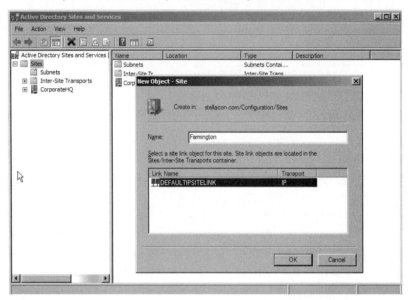

6. Notice the Farmington site is now listed under the Sites object.

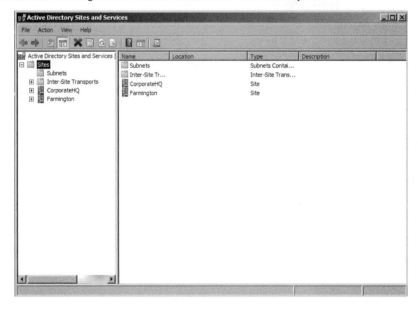

7. Create another new site and name it **Portsmouth**. Again, choose the DEFAULTIP-
    SITELINK item. Notice the new site is listed in the Sites object.

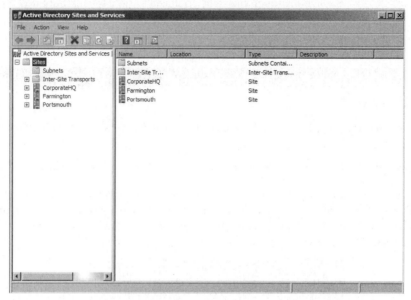

8. When you are finished, close the Active Directory Sites And Services tool.

Creating Subnets

Once you have created the sites that map to your network topology, it's time to define the subnets that define the site boundaries.

Subnets are based on TCP/IPv4 or TCP/IPv6 address information. For example, the IPv4
address may be 10.10.0.0, and the subnet mask may be 255.255.0.0. This information specifies that all of the TCP/IP addresses that begin with the first two octets are part of the same
TCP/IP subnet. All of the following TCP/IP addresses would be within this subnet:

- 10.10.1.5

- 10.10.100.17

- 10.10.110.120

The Active Directory Sites And Services tool expresses these subnets in a somewhat different notation. It uses the provided subnet address and appends a slash followed by the number
of bits in the subnet mask. In the example in the previous paragraph, the subnet would be
defined as 10.1.0.0/16.

Remember that sites typically represent distinct physical locations and almost always have their own subnets. The only way for a domain controller (DC) in one site to reach a DC in another site is to add subnet information about the remote site. Generally, information regarding the definition of subnets for a specific network environment will be available from a network designer. Exercise 5.2 walks you through the steps you need to take to create subnets and assign subnets to sites. In order to complete the steps in this exercise, you must have first completed Exercise 5.1.

EXERCISE 5.2

Creating Subnets

1. Open the Active Directory Sites And Services tool from the Administrative Tools program group.

2. Expand the Sites folder. Right-click the Subnets folder, and select New Subnet.

3. In the New Object–Subnet dialog box, you are prompted for information about the IPv4 or IPv6 details for the new subnet. For the prefix, type **10.1.1.0/24** (we are staying with the more commonly used IPv4). This actually calculates out to 10.10.0.0/16 with the mask of 255.255.255.0. Click the Farmington site, and then click OK to create the subnet.

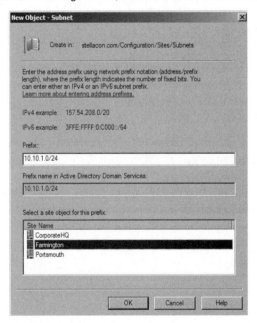

4.   In the Active Directory Sites And Services tool, right-click the newly created 10.1.1.0/24 subnet object, and select Properties.

5.   On the subnet's Properties dialog box, type **Farmington 100Mbit LAN** for the description. Click OK to continue.

6.   Create a new subnet using the following information:

Address: **160.25.0.0/16**

Site: **Portsmouth**

Description: **Portsmouth 100Mbit LAN**

7.   Finally, create another subnet using the following information:

Address: **176.33.0.0/16**

Site: **CorporateHQ**

Description: **Corporate 100Mbit switched LAN**

EXERCISE 5.2 *(continued)*

The Active Directory Sites And Services tool should now look like this:

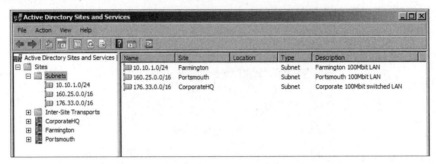

8. When finished, close the Active Directory Sites And Services tool.

So far, you have created the basic components that govern Active Directory sites: sites and subnets. You also linked these two components together by defining which subnets belong in which sites. These two steps—creating sites and subnets—form the basis of mapping the physical network infrastructure of an organization to Active Directory. Now, look at the various settings that you can make for sites.

Configuring Sites

Once you have created Active Directory sites and defined which subnets they contain, it's time to make some additional configuration settings for the site structure. Specifically, you'll need to assign servers to specific sites and configure the site licensing options. By placing servers in sites, you tell Active Directory replication services how to replicate information for various types of servers. Later in this chapter, you'll look at the details of working with replication within and between sites.

In Exercise 5.3, you will add servers to sites and configure CorpDC1 options. In order to complete the steps in this exercise, you must have first completed Exercises 5.1 and 5.2.

EXERCISE 5.3

Configuring Sites

1. Open the Active Directory Sites And Services tool from the Administrative Tools program group.

2. Expand the Sites folder, and click and expand the Farmington site.

3. Right-click the Servers container in the Farmington site, and select New ➢ Server. Type **FarmingtonDC1** for the name of the server, and then click OK.

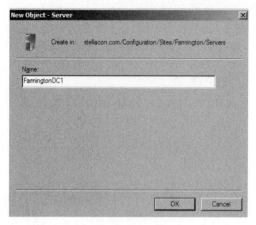

4. Create a new Server object within the CorporateHQ site, and name it **CorpDC1**. Note that this object also includes the name of the local domain controller.

5. Create two new Server objects within the Portsmouth site, and name them **PortsmouthDC1** and **PortsmouthDC2**. The Active Directory Sites And Service tool should now look like this:

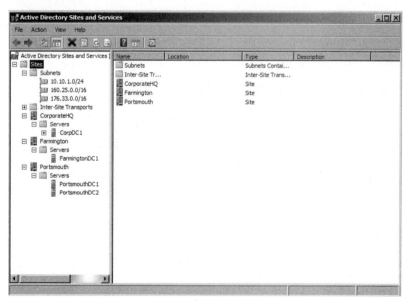

6. Right-click the CorpDC1 server object and select Properties. In the General tab of the CorpDC1 Properties box, select STMP in the Transports Available For Inter-site Data Transfer box, and click Add to make this server a preferred IP bridgehead server. Click OK to accept the settings.

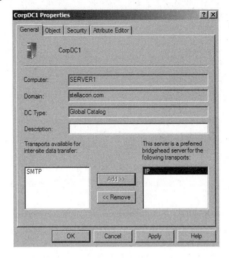

7. When you are finished, close the Active Directory Sites And Services tool.

With the configuration of the basic settings for sites out of the way, it's time to focus on the real details of the site topology—creating site links and site link bridges.

Configuring Replication

Sites are generally used to define groups of computers that are located within a single geographic location. In most organizations, machines that are located in close physical proximity (for example, within a single building or branch office) are well connected. A typical example is a LAN in a branch office of a company. All of the computers may be connected together using Ethernet, and routing and switching technology may be in place to reduce network congestion.

Often, however, domain controllers are located across various states, countries, and even continents. In such a situation, network connectivity is usually much slower, less reliable, and more costly than that for the equivalent LAN. Therefore, Active Directory replication must accommodate accordingly. When managing replication traffic within Active Directory sites, you need to be aware of two types of synchronization:

Intrasite *Intrasite replication* refers to the synchronization of Active Directory information between domain controllers that are located in the same site. In accordance with the concept of sites, these machines are usually well connected by a high-speed LAN.

Intersite   *Intersite replication* occurs between domain controllers in different sites. Usually, this means that there is a WAN or other type of low-speed network connection between the various machines. Intersite replication is optimized for minimizing the amount of network traffic that occurs between sites.

In the following sections, you'll look at ways to configure both intrasite and intersite replication. Additionally, you'll see features of Active Directory replication architecture that you can use to accommodate the needs of almost any environment.

Intrasite Replication

Intrasite replication is generally a simple process. One domain controller contacts the others in the same site when changes to its copy of Active Directory are made. It compares the update sequence numbers in its own copy of Active Directory with that of the other domain controllers, then the most current information is chosen by the DC in question, and all domain controllers within the site use this information to make the necessary updates to their database.

Because you can assume that the domain controllers within an Active Directory site are well connected, you can pay less attention to exactly when and how replication takes place. Communications between domain controllers occur using the *Remote Procedure Call (RPC) protocol*. This protocol is optimized for transmitting and synchronizing information on fast and reliable network connections. The RPC protocol provides for fast replication at the expense of network bandwidth, which is usually readily available because most LANs today are running on Fast Ethernet (100Mbps) at a minimum.

Intersite Replication

Intersite replication is optimized for low-bandwidth situations and network connections that have less reliability. Intersite replication offers several features that are tailored toward these types of connections. To begin with, two different protocols may be used to transfer information between sites:

RPC over IP   When connectivity is fairly reliable, IP is a good choice. IP-based communications require you to have a live connection between two or more domain controllers in different sites and let you transfer Active Directory information. RPC over IP was originally designed for slower WANs in which packet loss and corruption may occur often. As such, it is a good choice for low-quality connections involved in intersite replication.

Simple Mail Transfer Protocol (SMTP)   *Simple Mail Transfer Protocol (SMTP)* is perhaps best known as the protocol that is used to send and receive email messages on the Internet. SMTP was designed to use a store-and-forward mechanism through which a server receives a copy of a message, records it to disk, and then attempts to forward it to another email server. If the destination server is unavailable, it holds the message and attempts to resend it at periodic intervals.

This type of communication is extremely useful for situations in which network connections are unreliable or not always available. If, for instance, a branch office in Peru is connected to the corporate office by a dial-up connection that is available only during certain hours, SMTP would be a good choice for communication with that branch.

SMTP is an inherently insecure network protocol. Therefore, if you would like to ensure that you transfer replication traffic securely and you use SMTP for Active Directory replication, you must take advantage of Windows Server 2008's Certificate Services functionality.

Other intersite replication characteristics are designed to address low-bandwidth situations and less reliable network connections. These features give you a high degree of flexibility in controlling replication configuration. They include the following:

- Compression of Active Directory information. This compression is helpful because changes between domain controllers in remote sites may include a large amount of information and also because network bandwidth tends to be less available and more costly.

- Site links and site link bridges help determine intersite replication topology.

- Replication can occur based on a schedule defined by systems administrators.

You can configure intersite replication by using the Active Directory Sites And Services tool. Select the name of the site for which you want to configure settings. Then, right-click the NTDS Site Settings object in the right windowpane, and select Properties. By clicking the Change Schedule button in the NTDS Site Settings Properties dialog box, you'll be able to configure how often replication between sites will occur (see Figure 5.4).

FIGURE 5.4   Configuring intersite replication schedules

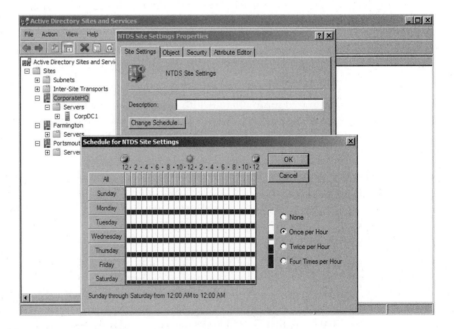

   You will see how to set the replication schedule in Exercise 5.4.

In the following sections, you will see how to configure site links and site link bridges, as well as how to manage connection objects and bridgehead servers.

Creating Site Links and Site Link Bridges

The overall topology of intersite replication is based on the use of site links and site link bridges. *Site links* are logical connections that define a path between two Active Directory sites. Site links can include several descriptive elements that define their network characteristics. *Site link bridges* are used to connect site links together so that the relationship can be transitive. Figure 5.5 provides an example of site links and site link bridges.

Both of these types of logical connection are used by Active Directory services to determine how information should be synchronized between domain controllers in remote sites. This information is used by the KCC, which forms a replication topology based on the site topology created. The KCC service is responsible for determining the best way to replicate information within and between sites.

FIGURE 5.5 An example of site links and site link bridges

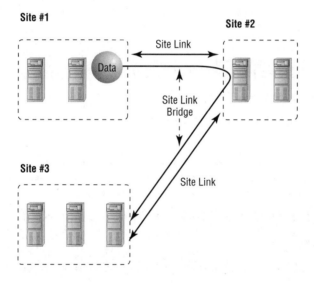

When creating site links for your environment, you'll need to consider the following factors:

Transporting information   You can choose to use either RPC over IP or SMTP for transferring information over a site link. You will need to determine which is best based on your network infrastructure and the reliability of connections between sites.

Assigning a cost value   You can create multiple site links between sites and assign site links a cost value based on the type of connection. The systems administrator determines the cost value, and the relative costs of site links are then used (by the system) to determine the optimal path for replication. The lower the cost, the more likely the link is to be used for replication.

For example, a company may primarily use a T1 link between branch offices, but it may also use a slower and circuit-switched dial-up ISDN connection for redundancy (in case the T1 fails). In this example, a systems administrator may assign a cost of 25 to the T1 line and a cost of 100 to the ISDN line. This ensures that the more reliable and higher-bandwidth T1 connection is used whenever it's available but that the ISDN line is also available.

Determining a replication schedule   Once you've determined how and through which connections replication will take place, it's time to determine when information should be replicated. Replication requires network resources and occupies bandwidth. Therefore, you need to balance the need for consistent directory information with the need to conserve bandwidth. For example, if you determine that it's reasonable to have a lag time of 6 hours between when an update is made at one site and when it is replicated to all others, you might schedule replication to occur once in the morning, once during the lunch hour, and more frequently after normal work hours.

Based on these factors, you should be able to devise a strategy that allows you to configure site links.

Exercise 5.4 walks you through the process of creating site links and site link bridges. In order to complete the steps in this exercise, you must have first completed Exercises 5.1, 5.2, and 5.3.

EXERCISE 5.4

Creating Site Links and Site Link Bridges

1. Open the Active Directory Sites And Services tool from the Administrative Tools program group.

2. Expand the Sites, Inter-site Transports, and IP objects. Right-click the DEFAULTIP-SITELINK item in the right pane, and select Rename. Rename the object **CorporateWAN**. The Active Directory Sites And Services tool should now look like this:

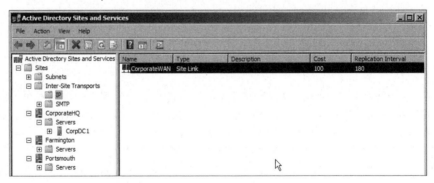

3. Right-click the CorporateWAN link, and select Properties. In the General tab of the CorporateWAN Properties dialog box, type **T1 Connecting Corporate and Portsmouth Offices** for
the description. Remove the Farmington site from the link by highlighting Farmington in
the Sites In This Site Link box and clicking Remove. For the Cost value, type **50**, and specify
that replication should occur every 60 minutes. To create the site link, click OK.

4. Right-click the IP folder, and select New Site Link. On the New Object - Site Link dialog
box, name the link **CorporateDialup**. Add the Farmington and CorporateHQ sites to the
site link and then click OK.

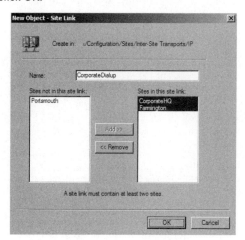

5. Right-click the CorporateDialup link, and select Properties. In the General tab of the CorporateDialup Properties dialog box, type **ISDN Dialup between Corporate and Farmington** for the description. Set the Cost value to 100, and specify that replication should occur every 120 minutes. To specify that replication should occur only during certain times of the day, click the Change Schedule button.

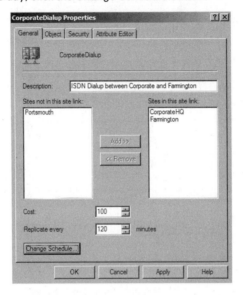

6. On the Schedule For CorporateDialup dialog box, highlight the area between 8:00am and 6:00pm for the days Monday through Friday, and click the Replication Not Available option. This will ensure that replication traffic is minimized during normal work hours.

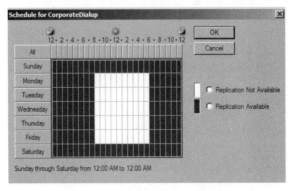

Click OK to accept the new schedule and then OK again to create the site link.

7. Right-click the IP object, and select New Site Link Bridge. On the New Object - Site Link Bridge dialog box, name the site link bridge **CorporateBridge**. Note that the Corporate-Dialup and CorporateWAN site links are already added to the site link bridge. Because there must be at least two site links in each bridge, you will not be able to remove these links. Click OK to create the site link bridge.

8. When finished, close the Active Directory Sites And Services tool. It should look like this now:

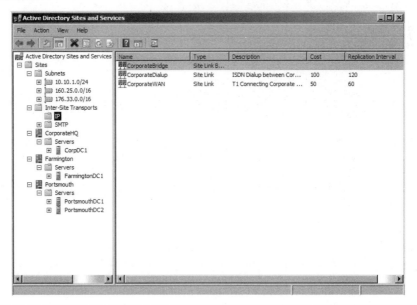

Creating Connection Objects

Generally, it is a good practice to allow Active Directory's replication mechanisms to automatically schedule and manage replication functions. In some cases, however, you may want to have additional control over replication. Perhaps you want to replicate certain changes on demand (for example, when you create new accounts). Or you may want to specify a custom schedule for certain servers.

Connection objects provide you with a way to set up these different types of replication schedules. You can create connection objects with the Active Directory Sites And Services tool by expanding a server object, right-clicking the NTDS Settings object, and selecting New Active Directory Domain Services Connection (see Figure 5.6).

FIGURE 5.6 Creating a new Active Directory Domain Services connection

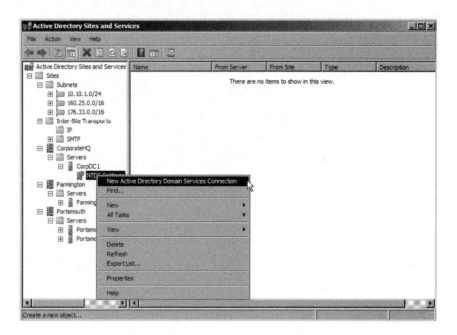

Within the properties of the connection object, which you can see in the right pane of the Active Directory Sites And Services tool, you can specify the type of transport to use for replication (RPC over IP or SMTP), the schedule for replication, and the domain controllers that participate in the replication. Additionally, you can right-click the connection object and select Replicate Now.

WARNING Ensure that if you kick off a manual replication, you don't do it during business hours if you think you do not have the bandwidth available to accomplish it. If you do it during business hours, you will most likely create a network slow-down if you do not plan properly. It's safer to plan a test during non-business hours or during times of very little activity on the network.

Moving Server Objects between Sites

Using the Active Directory Sites And Services tool, you can easily move servers between sites. To do this, simply right-click the name of a domain controller and select Move. You can then select the site to which you want to move the domain controller object.

Figure 5.7 shows the Move Server dialog box. After the server is moved, all replication topology settings are updated automatically. If you want to choose custom replication settings, you need to manually create connection objects (as described earlier).

FIGURE 5.7   Choosing a new site for a specific server

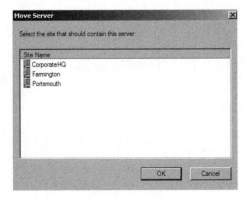

In Exercise 5.5, you move a server object between sites. In order to complete the steps in this exercise, you must have first completed the previous exercises in this chapter.

EXERCISE 5.5

Moving Server Objects between Sites

1. Open the Active Directory Sites And Services administrative tool.

2. Right-click the server named PortsmouthDC1, and select Move.

3. In the Move Server dialog box, select the Farmington site, and then click OK. This moves this server to the Farmington site.

4. To move the server back, right-click PortsmouthDC1 (now located in the Farmington site) and then click Move. Select Portsmouth for the destination site.

5. When finished, close the Active Directory Sites And Services administrative tool.

Creating Bridgehead Servers

By default, all of the servers in one site communicate with all of the servers in another site. You can, however, further control replication between sites by using *bridgehead servers*. As we mentioned earlier in the chapter, using bridgehead servers helps minimize replication traffic, especially in larger distributed star network topologies, and it allows you to dedicate machines that are better connected to receive replicated data. Figure 5.8 provides an example of how bridgehead servers work.

FIGURE 5.8 A replication scenario using bridgehead servers

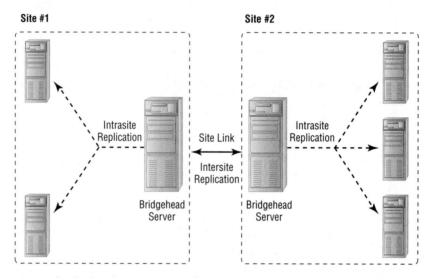

You can use a bridgehead server to specify which domain controllers are preferred for transferring replication information between sites. Different bridgehead servers can be selected for RPC over IP and SMTP replication, thus allowing you to balance the load. To create a bridgehead server for a site, simply right-click a domain controller and select Properties, which brings up the bridgehead server's Properties dialog box (See Figure 5.9). To make the server a bridgehead server, just select one or both replication types (called transports) from the left side of the dialog box and click the Add button to add them to the right side of the dialog box.

FIGURE 5.9 Specifying a bridgehead server

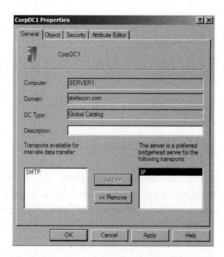

Configuring Server Topology

When you are using environments that require multiple sites, you must carefully consider where you place your servers. In doing so, you can greatly improve performance and the end user's experience by reducing the time they must spend performing common operations such as authentication or searching Active Directory for resources.

There are two main issues to consider when you are designing a distributed Active Directory environment. The first is how you should place domain controllers within the network environment. The second is how to manage the use of Global Catalog (GC) servers. Finding the right balance between servers, server resources, and performance can be considered an art form for network and systems administrators. In the following sections, you'll look at some of the important considerations you must take into account when you design a replication server topology.

Placing Domain Controllers

Microsoft highly recommends that you have at least two domain controllers in each domain of your Active Directory environment. As mentioned earlier in this chapter, using additional domain controllers provides the following benefits:

- Increased network performance:
  - The servers can balance the burden of serving client requests.
  - Clients can connect to the server closest to them instead of performing authentication and security operations across a slow WAN link.
- Fault tolerance (In case one domain controller fails, the other still contains a valid and usable copy of the Active Directory database).
- In Windows Server 2008, RODCs help increase security when users connect to a domain controller in a unsecured remote location.

As we just mentioned, having too few domain controllers can be a problem. However, you can also have *too many*. Keep in mind that the more domain controllers you choose to implement, the greater the replication traffic among them. Because each domain controller must propagate any changes to all of the others, compounding services can result in increased network traffic.

Placing Global Catalog Servers

A *Global Catalog (GC)* server is a domain controller that contains a copy of all the objects contained in the forest-wide domain controllers that compose the Active Directory database. Making a domain controller a GC server is very simple, and you can change this setting quite easily. That brings us to the harder part—determining which domain controllers should also be GC servers.

Where you place domain controllers and GC servers, and how many you deploy, are very important network planning decisions.

Generally, you want to make GC servers available in every site that has a slow link. This means that the most logical places to put GC servers are in every site and close to the WAN link for the best possible connectivity

However, having too many GC servers a bad thing. The main issue is associated with replication traffic—you must keep each GC server within your environment synchronized with the other servers. In a very dynamic environment, using additional GC servers causes a considerable increase in additional network traffic.

Therefore, you will want to find a good balance between replication burdens and GC query performance in your own environment.

To create a GC server, simply expand the Server object in the Active Directory Sites And Services tool, right-click NTDS settings, and select Properties to bring up the NTDS Settings Properties dialog box (see Figure 5.10). To configure a server as a GC server, simply place a check mark in the Global Catalog box.

FIGURE 5.10   Enabling the Global Catalog on an Active Directory domain controller

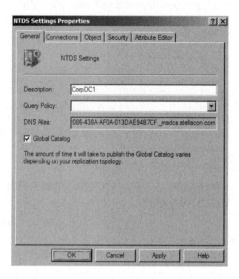

Monitoring and Troubleshooting Active Directory Replication

For the most part, domain controllers handle the replication processes automatically. However, systems administrators still need to monitor the performance of Active Directory replication, since failed network links and incorrect configurations can sometimes prevent the synchronization of information between domain controllers.

You can monitor the behavior of Active Directory replication and troubleshoot the process if problems occur.

Real World Scenario

Accommodating a Changing Environment

You're a systems administrator for a medium-sized business that consists of many offices located throughout the world. Some of these offices are well connected because they use high-speed, reliable links, while others are not so fortunate. Overall, things are going well until your CEO announces that the organization will be merging with another large company and that the business will be restructured. The restructuring will involve opening new offices, closing old ones, and transferring employees to different locations. Additionally, changes in the IT budget will affect the types of links that exist between offices. Your job as the systems administrator is to ensure that the network environment and, specifically, Active Directory, keep pace with the changes and ultimately outperform them.

An important skill for any technical professional is the ability to quickly and efficiently adapt to a changing organization. When a business grows, restructures, or forms relationships with other businesses, often many IT-related changes must also occur. You may have to create new network links, for example. Fortunately, Active Directory was designed with these kinds of challenges in mind. For example, you can use the Active Directory Sites And Services administrative tool to reflect physical network changes in Active Directory topology. If a site that previously had 64Kbps of bandwidth is upgraded to a T1 connection, you can change those characteristics for the site link objects. Conversely, if a site that was previously well con- nected is reduced to a slow, unreliable link, you can reconfigure the sites, change the site link transport mechanisms (perhaps from IP to SMTP to accommodate a nonpersistent link), and create connection objects (which would allow you to schedule replication traffic to occur during the least busy hours). Or suppose that many of your operations move overseas to a European division. This might call for designating specific domain controllers as preferred bridgehead servers to reduce the amount of replication traffic over costly and slow overseas links.

Sweeping organizational changes inevitably require you to move servers between sites. For example, an office may close and its domain controllers may move to another region of the world. Again, you can accommodate this change by using Active Directory administrative tools. You may change your OU structure to reflect new logical and business-oriented changes, and you can move server objects between sites to reflect physical network changes.

Rarely can the job of mapping a physical infrastructure to Active Directory be "complete." In most environments, it's safe to assume that you will always need to make changes based on business needs. Overall, however, you should feel comfortable that the physical components of Active Directory are at your side to help you accommodate these changes.

About System Monitor

The Windows Server 2008 System Monitor administrative tool was designed so that you can monitor many performance statistics associated with using Active Directory. Included within the various performance statistics that you may monitor are counters related to Active Directory replication.

Troubleshooting Replication

A common symptom of replication problems is that information is not updated on some or all domain controllers. For example, a systems administrator creates a User account on one domain controller, but the changes are not propagated to other domain controllers. In most environments, this is a potentially serious problem because it affects network security and can prevent authorized users from accessing the resources they require.

You can take several steps to troubleshoot Active Directory replication; each of these is discussed in the following sections.

Verifying Network Connectivity

In order for replication to work properly in distributed environments, you must have network connectivity. Although ideally all domain controllers would be connected by high-speed LAN links, this is rarely the case for larger organizations. In the real world, dial-up connections and slow connections are common. If you have verified that your replication topology is set up properly, you should confirm that your servers are able to communicate. Problems such as a failed dial-up connection attempt can prevent important Active Directory information from being replicated.

Verifying Router and Firewall Configurations

Firewalls are used to restrict the types of traffic that can be transferred between networks. They are mainly used to increase security by preventing unauthorized users from transferring information. In some cases, company firewalls may block the types of network access that must be available in order for Active Directory replication to occur. For example, if a specific router or firewall prevents data from being transferred using SMTP, replication that uses this protocol will fail.

Examining the Event Logs

Whenever an error in the replication configuration occurs, the computer writes events to the Directory Service and File Replication Service event logs. By using the Event Viewer administrative tool, you can quickly and easily view the details associated with any problems in replication. For example, if one domain controller is not able to communicate with another to transfer changes, a log entry is created. Figure 5.11 shows an example of the types of events you will see in the Directory Service log, and Figure 5.12 shows a specific example of a configuration error.

FIGURE 5.11   Viewing entries in the Directory Service event log

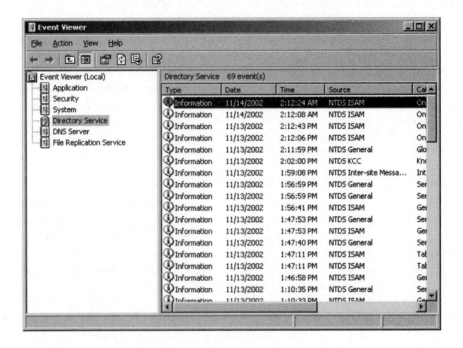

FIGURE 5.12   Viewing an entry in the event log

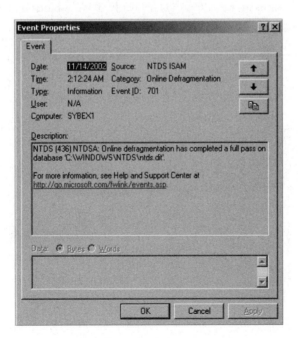

Verifying That Information Is Synchronized

It's often easy to forget to perform manual checks regarding the replication of Active Directory information. One of the reasons for this is that Active Directory domain controllers have their own read/write copies of the Active Directory database. Therefore, if connectivity does not exist, you will not encounter failures while creating new objects.

It is important to periodically verify that objects have been synchronized between domain controllers. This process might be as simple as logging on to a different domain controller and looking at the objects within a specific OU. This manual check, although it might be tedious, can prevent inconsistencies in the information stored on domain controllers, which, over time, can become an administration and security nightmare.

Verifying Authentication Scenarios

A common replication configuration issue occurs when clients are forced to authenticate across slow network connections. The primary symptom of the problem is that users complain about the amount of time it takes them to log on to Active Directory (especially during times of high volume of authentications, such as at the beginning of the workday).

Usually, you can alleviate this problem by using additional domain controllers or reconfiguring the site topology. A good way to test this is to consider the possible scenarios for the various clients that you support. Often, walking through a configuration, such as, "A client in Domain1 is trying to authenticate using a domain controller in Domain2, which is located across a slow WAN connection," can be helpful in pinpointing potential problem areas.

Verifying the Replication Topology

The Active Directory Sites And Services tool allows you to verify that a replication topology is logically consistent. You can quickly and easily perform this task by right-clicking the NTDS Settings within a Server object and choosing All Tasks ➢ Check Replication Topology (see Figure 5.13). If any errors are present, a dialog box alerts you to the problem.

FIGURE 5.13   Verifying Active Directory topology using the Active Directory Sites And Services tool

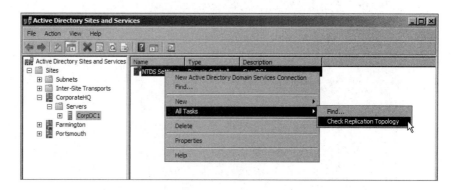

Summary

In this chapter we discussed the purpose of Active Directory replication. As you learned, replication is used to keep domain controllers synchronized and is important in Active Directory environments of all sizes. Replication is the process by which changes to the Active Directory database are transferred between domain controllers.

This chapter also covered the concepts of sites, site boundaries, and subnets. In addition to learning how to configure them, you learned that subnets define physical portions of your network environment and that sites are defined as collections of well-connected IP subnets. Site boundaries are defined by the subnet or subnets that you include in your site configuration.

We also covered the basics of replication and the differences between intrasite and intersite replication. We also covered the purpose and use of bridgehead servers in depth. Although replication is a behind-the-scenes type of task, the optimal configuration of sites in distributed network environments results in better use of bandwidth and faster response by network resources. For these reasons, you should be sure that you thoroughly understand the concepts related to managing replication for Active Directory.

We covered the placement of domain controllers and Global Catalog servers in the network and how when placed properly, they can increase the performance of Active Directory operations.

We also learned how to monitor and troubleshoot replication. The Windows Server 2008 System Monitor administrative tool was designed so that you can monitor many performance statistics associated with using Active Directory.

Exam Essentials

Understand the purpose of Active Directory replication.   Replication is used to keep domain controllers synchronized and is important in Active Directory environments of all sizes. Replication is the process by which changes to the Active Directory database are transferred between domain controllers.

Understand the concept of sites, site boundaries, and subnets.   Subnets define physical portions of your network environment. Sites are defined as collections of well-connected IP subnets. Site boundaries are defined by the subnet or subnets that you include in your site configuration.

Understand the differences between intrasite and intersite replication.   Intrasite replication is designed to synchronize Active Directory information to machines that are located in the same site. Intersite replication is used to synchronize information for domain controllers that are located in different sites.

Understand the purpose of bridgehead servers.   Bridgehead servers are designed to accept traffic between two remote sites and to then forward this information to the appropriate servers. One way to efficiently synchronize data between sites that are connected with slow connections is to use a bridgehead server.

Implement site links, site link bridges, and connection objects.   You can use all three of these object types to finely control the behavior of Active Directory replication and to manage replication traffic. Site links are created to define the types of connections that are available between the components of a site. Site links can reflect a relative cost for a network connection and can reflect the bandwidth that is available for communications. You can use site link bridges to connect site links together so that the relationship can be transitive. Connection objects provide you with a way to set up special types of replication schedules such as immediate replication on demand or specifying a custom schedule for certain servers.

Configure replication schedules and site link costs.   You can create multiple site links between sites and you can assign site links a cost value based on the type of connection. The systems administrator determines the cost value, and the relative costs of site links are then used to determine the optimal path for replication. The lower the cost, the more likely the link is to be used for replication. Once you've determined how and through which connections replication will take place, it's time to determine *when* information should be replicated. Replication requires network resources and occupies bandwidth. Therefore, you need to balance the need for consistent directory information with the need to conserve bandwidth.

Determine where to place domain controllers and Global Catalog servers based on a set of requirements.   Where you place domain controllers and Global Catalog servers can positively affect the performance of Active Directory operations. However, to optimize performance, you need to know where the best places are to put these servers in a network environment that consists of multiple sites.

Monitor and troubleshoot replication.   The Windows Server 2008 System Monitor administrative tool is designed so that you can monitor many performance statistics associated with using Active Directory. In addition to this monitoring, you should always verify basic network connectivity and router and firewall connections, as well as examine the event logs.

Review Questions

1. Daniel is responsible for managing Active Directory replication traffic for a medium-sized organization that has deployed a single Active Directory domain. Currently, the environment is configured with two sites and the default settings for replication. Each site consists of 15 domain controllers. Recently, network administrators have complained that Active Directory traffic is using a large amount of available network bandwidth between the two sites. Daniel has been asked to meet the following requirements:

    ▪ Reduce the amount of network traffic between domain controllers in the two sites.

    ▪ Minimize the amount of change to the current site topology.

    ▪ Require no changes to the existing physical network infrastructure.

    Daniel decides that it would be most efficient to configure specific domain controllers in each site that will receive the majority of replication traffic from the other site. Which of the following solutions meets the requirements?

    A. Create additional sites that are designed only for replication traffic and move the existing domain controllers to these sites.

    B. Create multiple site links between the two sites.

    C. Create a site link bridge between the two sites.

    D. Configure one server at each site to act as a preferred bridgehead server.

2. Which of the following does not need to be manually created when you are setting up a replication scenario involving three domains and three sites?

    A. Sites

    B. Site links

    C. Connection objects

    D. Subnets

3. Which of the following services of Active Directory is responsible for maintaining the replication topology?

    A. File Replication Service

    B. Knowledge Consistency Checker

    C. Windows Internet Name Service

    D. Domain Name System

4. Will, a systems administrator for an Active Directory environment that consists of three sites, wants to configure site links to be transitive. Which of the following Active Directory objects is responsible for representing a transitive relationship between sites?

    A. Additional sites

    B. Additional site links

    C. Bridgehead servers

    D. Site link bridges

5. You have configured your Active Directory environment with multiple sites and have placed the appropriate resources in each of the sites. You are now trying to choose a protocol for the transfer of replication information between two sites. The connection between the two sites has the following characteristics:

    ▪ The link is generally unavailable during certain parts of the day due to an unreliable network provider.

    ▪ The replication transmission must be attempted whether the link is available or not. If the link was unavailable during a scheduled replication, the information should automatically be received after the link becomes available again.

    ▪ Replication traffic must be able to travel over a standard Internet connection.

    Which of the following protocols meets these requirements?

    A. IP

    B. SMTP

    C. RPC

    D. DHCP

6. A network administrator has decided that it will be necessary to implement multiple sites in order to efficiently manage your company's large Active Directory environment. Based on her recommendations, you make the following decisions:

    ▪ You will create four sites to make the best configuration.

    ▪ You will connect the sites with site links and site link bridges.

    ▪ Two small offices must only receive replication traffic during non-business hours.

    ▪ The organization will own a single DNS name: supercompany.com.

    ▪ You want to keep administration as simple as possible, and you want to use the smallest possible number of domains.

    Based on this information, you must plan the Active Directory domain architecture. What is the minimum number of domains that you must create to support this configuration?

    A. 0

    B. 1

    C. 4

    D. 8

7. Andrew is troubleshooting a problem with Active Directory. One systems administrator has told him that she made an update to a User object and that another system administrator reported that he had not seen the changes appear on another domain controller. It has been over a week since the change was made. Andrew further verifies the problem by making a change to another Active Directory object. Within a few hours, the change appears on a few domain controllers, but not on all of them.

   Which of the following are possible causes for this problem? Choose all that apply.

   A. Network connectivity is unavailable.

   B. Connection objects are not properly configured.

   C. Sites are not properly configured.

   D. Site links are not properly configured.

   E. A WAN connection has failed.

   F. Andrew has configured one of the domain controllers for manual replication updates.

8. A systems administrator suspects that there is an error in the replication configuration. How can he look for specific error messages related to replication?

   A. By using the Active Directory Sites And Services administrative tool

   B. By using the Computer Management tool

   C. By going to Event Viewer ➢ System log

   D. By going to Event Viewer ➢ Directory Service log

9. Christina is responsible for managing Active Directory replication traffic for a medium-sized organization. Currently, the environment is configured with a single site and the default settings for replication. The site contains over 50 domain controllers and the system administrators are often making changes to the Active Directory database. Recently, network administrators have complained that Active Directory traffic is consuming a large amount of network bandwidth between portions of the network that are connected by slow links. Ordinarily, the amount of replication traffic is reasonable, but recently users have complained about slow network performance during certain hours of the day.

   Christina has been asked to alleviate the problem while meeting the following requirements:

   ▪ Be able to control exactly when replication occurs.

   ▪ Be able to base Active Directory replication on the physical network infrastructure.

   ▪ Perform the changes without creating or removing any domain controllers.

   Which two of the following steps can Christina take to meet these requirements?

   A. Create and define Connection objects that specify the hours during which replication will occur.

   B. Create multiple site links.

   C. Create a site link bridge.

   D. Create new Active Directory sites that reflect the physical network topology.

   E. Configure one server at each of the new sites to act as a bridgehead server.

10. James, a systems administrator, suspects that Active Directory replication traffic is consuming a large amount of network bandwidth. James is attempting to determine the amount of network traffic that is generated through replication. He wants to do the following:

- Determine replication data transfer statistics.
- Collect information about multiple Active Directory domain controllers at the same time.
- Measure other performance statistics, such as server CPU utilization.

Which of the following administrative tools is most useful for meeting these requirements?

A. Active Directory Users And Computers

B. Active Directory Domains And Trusts

C. Active Directory Sites And Services

D. Event Viewer

E. Performance

11. You are the administrator of a large, distributed network environment. Recently, your IT department has decided to add various routers to the environment to limit the amount of traffic going to and from various areas of the network. You need to reconfigure Active Directory replication to reflect the physical network changes. Which of the following Active Directory objects should you modify to define the network boundaries for Active Directory sites?

A. Site links

B. Site link bridges

C. Bridgehead servers

D. Subnets

12. You have recently created a new Active Directory domain by promoting several Windows Server 2008 computers to domain controllers. You then use the Active Directory Sites And Services tool to configure sites for the environment. You soon find that changes that are made on one domain controller may not appear in the Active Directory database on another domain controller. By checking the Directory Services log using the Event Viewer application, you find that one of the domain controllers at a specific site is not receiving Active Directory updates. Which of the following are possible reasons for this? (Choose all that apply.)

A. Network connectivity has not been established for this server.

B. A firewall is preventing replication information from being transmitted.

C. There are not enough domain controllers in the environment.

D. There are too many domain controllers in the environment.

E. You chose to disable Active Directory replication during the promotion of the machine to a domain controller.

13. You administer a network that consists of one domain spanning three physical locations: San Jose, Chicago, and Austin. All three locations contain domain controllers. You have a T1 line between San Jose and Chicago, with an ISDN for backup. The ISDN line must have the default site link cost assigned to it. You want Austin to always use San Jose for its replication communication even though a link exists between Austin and Chicago for other purposes.

In the following diagram, select and place the correct relative costs that should be assigned to the various site links. Each cost can only be used once.

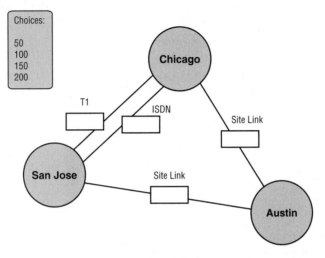

14. You need to create a new site named San Diego. Take a look at the following screen. What would you do next in order to create the new site?

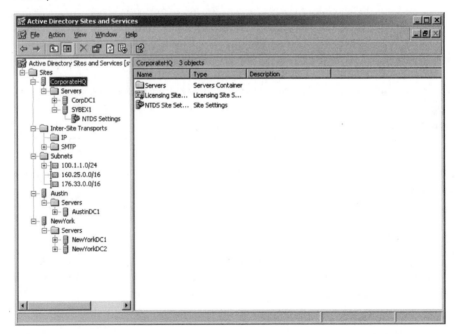

A. Right-click CorporateHQ.

B. Right-click Sites.

C. Double-click CorporateHQ.

D. Double-click Sites.

15. You administer a network with locations at two different sites. Both a T1 line and a dial-up line used for redundancy connect the sites. You want to ensure that replication normally occurs on the T1 line and that the dial-up line is only there as backup in case the T1 goes down. What should you do to meet these requirements? Choose all that apply.

A. Lower the cost of the T1 line.

B. Lower the cost of the dial-up line.

C. Raise the cost of the T1 line.

D. Raise the cost of the dial-up line.

16. You are the administrator for a network with locations at three different sites. You would like to specify the placement of the Global Catalog (GC) server. You have a central site located in New York, and two remote sites located in New Jersey and Connecticut. There are 100 users located in New York and 20 at each of the smaller locations. You have two full T1s connecting New Jersey and Connecticut to New York. What state would it make sense to put your GC in if you are only going to use one Global Catalog?

A. Connecticut

B. New Jersey

C. New York

D. All of the above

17. As the network administrator for RJS LLC, you are interested in specifying a bridgehead server at a location due to a recent merger. Your company just bought ABC Inc., and a large Active Directory domain comes from this acquisition. You need to bring up a new domain controller but you need to specify the intrasite replication. How do you specify this server as a bridgehead server?

A. In the Active Directory Sites And Services administrative tool, right-click a domain controller and select Properties. Select one or both replication transports from the left and click Add.

B. In the system Registry, change the `enum_bridgehead` value in `HKEY_LOCAL_MACHINE` to 1. Reboot the server.

C. In the Active Directory Sites and Services tool, right-click a domain controller and select Properties. Choose Add from the bridgehead server tab.

D. In the Control Panel, click the Active Directory Management applet, and in the Sites tab, select the Make This Server A Bridgehead Server option.

18. You are the administrator for your company's Active Directory infrastructure. The company has three domain controllers, each of which has Knowledge Consistency Checker (KCC) errors consistently popping up in the directory services Event Viewer log. What does this indicate?

A. Replication problems

B. DNS problems

C. Name resolution problems

D. Problems associated with Global Catalog placement

19. You need to keep track of licensing with the licensing server. Where can you configure the licensing server so that as the system administrator you can ensure you are compliant?

   A. Configure licensing in the Control Panel under the Licensing Applet.

   B. Configure licensing in the Registry under the HKEY_CIASSES_ROOT key.

   C. Configure licensing in the Computer Management MMC.

   D. Configure licensing in the Active Directory Sites And Services tool.

20. You are the network administrator responsible for deploying sites and subnets within your organization. You want to make sure you have set up your subnet objects correctly. From the following list, choose which subnet object cannot be used.

   A. 10.1.1.0

   B. 192.168.256.0

   C. 11.1.1.0

   D. 172.16.1.0

Answers to Review Questions

1. D. Preferred bridgehead servers receive replication information for a site and transmit this information to other domain controllers within the site. By doing this, Daniel can ensure that all replication traffic between the two sites is routed through the bridgehead servers and that replication traffic will flow properly between the domain controllers.

2. C. By default, Connection objects are automatically created by the Active Directory replication engine. You can choose to override the default behavior of Active Directory replication topology by manually creating Connection objects, but this step is not required.

3. B. The Knowledge Consistency Checker (KCC) is responsible for establishing the replication topology and ensuring that all domain controllers are kept up to date.

4. D. Site link bridges are designed to allow site links to be transitive. That is, they allow site links to use other site links to transfer replication information between sites. By default, all site links are bridged. However, you can turn off transitivity if you want to override this behavior.

5. B. The Simple Mail Transfer Protocol (SMTP) was designed for environments in which persistent connections may not always be available. SMTP uses the store-and-forward method to ensure that information is not lost if a connection cannot be made.

6. B. Because no relationship exists between domain structure and site structure, you only need one domain. Generally, if you have only one domain, you may need many domain controllers—at least one in each site.

7. A, B, C, D, E, F. Misconfiguration of any of these components of Active Directory may cause a replication failure.

8. D. The Directory Service event log contains error messages and information related to replication. These details can be useful when you are troubleshooting replication problems.

9. A, D. By creating new sites, Christina can help define settings for Active Directory replication based on the environment's network connections. She can use Connection objects to further define the details of how and when replication traffic will be transmitted between the domain controllers.

10. E. Through the use of the Performance administrative tool, systems administrators can measure and record performance values related to Active Directory replication. James can also use this tool to monitor multiple servers at the same time and view other performance-related statistics.

11. D. Subnets define the specific network segments that are well connected.

12. A, B. Because replication is occurring between most of the domain controllers, it is likely that a network problem is preventing this domain controller from communicating with the rest. A lack of network connectivity or the presence of a firewall can also prevent replication from occurring properly. The number of domain controllers in an environment will not prevent the replication of information, nor can replication be disabled during the promotion process.

13. The ISDN line is required to have the default cost of 100. That means that the T1 line's cost must be lower than 100 for this connection to be used by preference, and the only choice is 50. That leaves costs of 150 and 200 for the Austin links. Because Austin will never get replication information from Chicago, that link's cost should be 200. That only leaves 150 for the cost of the link between Austin and San Jose.

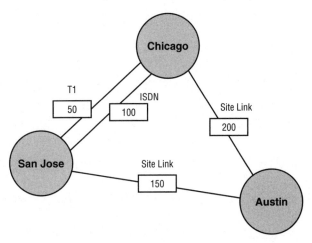

14. B. You can create new sites using the New Site action from the Sites contextual menu.

15. A, D. Lower costs are preferred over higher costs. However, if the lower cost connection fails for whatever reason, the higher cost link will be used.

16. C. Because you will only be using one GC server, it makes sense to position it centrally to the rest of the servers (New Jersey and Connecticut) on your network.

17. A. To make a bridgehead server, you simply need to right-click the domain controller you want to change to bridgehead server, select Properties, and add the transports.

18. A. Because of the nature of KCC errors, it's important to understand that they directly relate to replication problems, site linkage issues, and so on. KCC errors are indicative of replication problems.

19. D. As a systems administrator, you may want to use the Licensing Service to keep tabs on your compliance. You can do this in the Active Directory Sites And Services administration tool.

20. B. 192.168.256.0 is an invalid IP address and cannot be used as a subnet object.

Chapter

6

Configuring Active Directory Server Roles

MICROSOFT EXAM OBJECTIVES COVERED IN THIS CHAPTER:

✓ **Configuring Additional Active Directory Server Roles**

- Configure Active Directory Lightweight Directory Service (AD LDS). May include but is not limited to: migration to AD LDS; configure data within AD LDS; configure an authentication server; server core; Windows Server 2008 Hyper-V

- Configure Active Directory Rights Management Service (AD RMS). May include but is not limited to: certificate request and installation; self-enrollments; delegation; Active Directory Metadirectory Services (AD MDS); Windows Server virtualization

- Configure the read-only domain controller (RODC). May include but is not limited to: unidirectional replication; Administrator role separation; read-only DNS; BitLocker; credential caching; password replication; syskey; Windows Server virtualization

- Configure Active Directory Federation Services (AD FS). May include but is not limited to: install AD FS server role; exchange certificate with AD FS agents; configure trust policies; configure user and group claim mapping; Windows Server virtualization

✓ **Creating and Maintaining Active Directory Objects**

- Configure account policies. May include but is not limited to: domain password policy; account lockout policy; fine-grain password policies

✓ **Configuring Active Directory Certificate Services**

- Install Active Directory Certificate Services. May include but is not limited to: standalone vs. enterprise; CA hierarchies—root vs. subordinate; certificate requests; certificate practice statement

- Configure CA server settings. May include but is not limited to: key archival; certificate database backup and restore; assigning administration roles

- Manage certificate templates. May include but is not limited to: certificate template types; securing template permissions; managing different certificate template versions; key recovery agent

- Manage enrollments. May include but is not limited to: network device enrollment service (NDES); autoenrollment; Web enrollment; smart card enrollment; creating enrollment agents

- Manage certificate revocations. May include but is not limited to: configure Online Responders; Certificate Revocation List (CRL); CRL Distribution Point (CDP); Authority Information Access (AIA)

So far, you have learned how to install the main components of Active Directory. At this point, you should be able to install Domain Name System (DNS) and Active Directory. You should also understand what domains, sites, and trees can do for your organization.

In this chapter, we are going to take your domain a step further. First, we are going to talk about the Server Manager application, which allows you to install the many different server roles. Then we are going to dive into the five main Active Directory server roles and talk about what they can do to make your network run more securely and efficiently.

As you most likely noticed, this chapter covers many exam objectives. We cannot stress enough how important it is for you to know and understand these five Active Directory server roles before you attempt the MCTS 70-640 exam.

Understanding Server Manager

In Chapter 1, "Overview of Active Directory," we briefly mentioned some of the administration tools available in Windows Server 2003, including the Manage Your Server, Configure Your Server, and Add/Remove Windows components.

Windows Server 2008 combines many of these tools in a new Microsoft Management Console (MMC) snap-in called *Server Manager*. With Server Manager, an administrator can view the server configuration and installed roles. Server Manager also includes links for adding and removing features and roles (see Figure 6.1).

Server Manager is your one-stop shopping MMC snap-in. By that, I mean that you can take care of all your server management needs in one easy interface. In this chapter, we are going to discuss the following roles that you can install and manage using Server Manager.

- Active Directory Certificate Services
- Active Directory Domain Services
- Active Directory Federation Services
- Active Directory Lightweight Directory Services
- Active Directory Rights Management Services

FIGURE 6.1 Server Manager showing Windows Server 2008 server roles

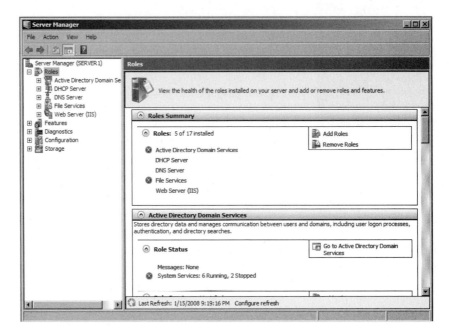

Configuring Active Directory Certificate Services

Using Active Directory Certificate Services (AD CS), administrators configure public key certificate services. AD CS security allows a private key to be combined with objects (such as users and computers), devices (such as routers), or services. The public-key infrastructure greatly increases data security.

In Windows Server 2008, AD CS provides services for creating and managing public key certificates used in software security systems that employ public key technologies. Organizations can use AD CS to enhance security by binding the identity of a user, device, or service to a corresponding private key. AD CS also includes features that allow you to manage certificate enrollment and revocation in a variety of environments.

Think of a digital certificate as a carrying case for a public key. A certificate contains the public key and a set of attributes, like the key holder's name and email address. These attributes specify something about the holder: their identity, what they're allowed to do with the certificate, and so on. The attributes and the public key are bound together because the certificate is digitally signed by the entity that issued it. Anyone who wants to verify the certificate's contents can verify the issuer's signature.

Certificates are one part of what security experts call a *public-key infrastructure (PKI)*. A PKI has several different components that you can mix and match to achieve the desired results.

Applications supported by AD CS include Secure/Multipurpose Internet Mail Extensions (S/MIME), secure wireless networks, Virtual Private Networks (VPN), IP security (IPsec), Encrypting File System (EFS), smart card logon, Secure Socket Layer/Transport Layer Security (SSL/TLS), and digital signatures.

The following are some of the AD CS components:

Cert Publishers group   Certificates are used to increase security by allowing for strong authentication methods. User accounts are placed within the Cert Publishers group if they need to be able to publish security certificates. Generally, these accounts are used by Active Directory security services.

PKI-savvy applications   These applications allow you and your users to do useful things with certificates, like encrypt email or network connections. Ideally, the user shouldn't have to know (or even necessarily be aware) of what the application is doing—everything should work seamlessly and automatically. The best-known examples of PKI-savvy applications are web browsers like Internet Explorer and Firefox and email applications like Outlook and Outlook Express.

Certificate templates   Certificate templates act like rubber stamps: By specifying a particular template as the model you want to use for a newly issued certificate, you're actually telling the CA which optional attributes to add to the certificate, as well as implicitly telling it how to fill in some of the mandatory attributes. Templates greatly simplify the process of issuing certificates because they keep you from having to memorize the names of all the attributes you might potentially want to put in a certificate. In Windows Server 2008, multiple templates are available and you also have the ability to secure templates using template permissions.

Online Responder service   Some applications—including S/MIME, SSL, EFS, and smart cards—need to validate the status of certificates. The Online Responder service authoritatively responds to such requests.

Certification practice statement   A Certification practice statement (CPS) is a statement that is issued by a certificate creator. It represents the creator's practices for issuing and validating certificates. The CPS represents the technical, procedural, and personnel policies and practices of the issuing certification authority (CA) organization.

Enrollment agents   Enrollment agents are administrators who have the ability to enroll users into the certificate services program. Enrollment agents can issue and manage certificate requests.

Network device enrollment service (NDES)   Network devices such as routers do not have accounts in the Active Directory Domain. The NDES allows such network devices to obtain certificates.

Web enrollment   With web enrollment, users can easily request certificates and retrieve certificate revocation lists (CRLs) through a web browser.

Installing Active Directory Certificate Services

When you are installing AD CS, the installation wizard will walk you through the installation process, and you will need to answer some configuration questions. If at any time during installation you do not know how to configure an option, you can click on the help link for explanations. Here are some of the AD CS options that you can configure during the installation:

Certificate authorities (CAs)   Certificate authorities issue, revoke, and publish certificates for their clients; big CAs like Thawte and VeriSign may do this for millions of users. You can also set up your own CA for each department or workgroup in your organization if you want.

Each CA is responsible for choosing what attributes it will include in a certificate and what mechanism it will use to verify those attributes before it issues the certificate.

There are three types of CA:

- Enterprise Root CAs (automatically integrated with Active Directory) are the most trusted CAs of the hierarchy. They hold the certificates that you issue to the users within your organization.

- Stand-Alone Root CAs hold the CAs that you issue to Internet users.

- Subordinate CAs are below the Enterprise and Stand Alone Root CAs in the hierarchy. The Enterprise or Stand Alone Root CAs give certificates to the Subordinate CAs, which in turn issue certificates to objects and services.

Cryptographic service provider (CSP)   The CSP is the mechanism that is responsible for authentication, encoding, and encryption services that Windows-based applications access through the Microsoft Cryptography application programming interface (CryptoAPI). Every CSP offers a unique implementation of the CryptoAPI. Some CSPs offer a strong cryptographic algorithm, while others use hardware components, such as smart cards.

Hash algorithm   An algorithm that produces a hash value of some piece of data, such as a message or session key, is called a *hash algorithm*. If you use a well-designed hash algorithm, the hash value changes when the data changes. Due to this characteristic, hash values are useful when you are trying to detect whether any modifications have been made to data (such as a message). Also, a well-designed hash algorithm makes it almost impossible for two independent inputs that have the same hash value.

Exercise 6.1 will show you the steps you need to follow to install the AD CS server. You need to complete the exercises in Chapter 3, "Active Directory Planning and Installation," before you attempt Exercise 6.1.

EXERCISE 6.1

Installing Active Directory Certificate Services

1. Open the Server Manager MMC by selecting Start ➢ Administrative Tools ➢ Server Manager.

2. Under Roles Summary, click the link labeled Add Role.

3. On the Select Server Roles screen, check the box next to Active Directory Certificate Services and click Next to continue.

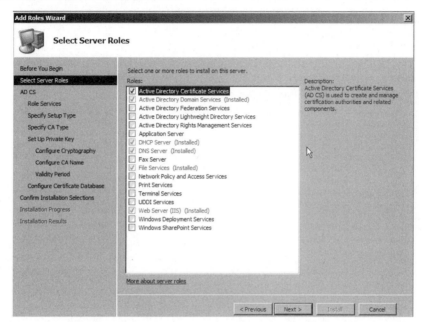

4. At the Active Directory Certificate Services (AD CS) screen, read the explanation of AD CS, then click Next.

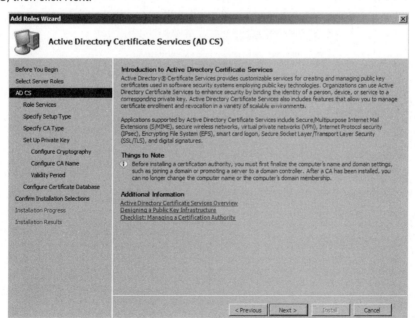

5. At the Select Role Services screen, make sure the Certificate Authority and Certificate Authority Web Enrollment boxes are both checked.

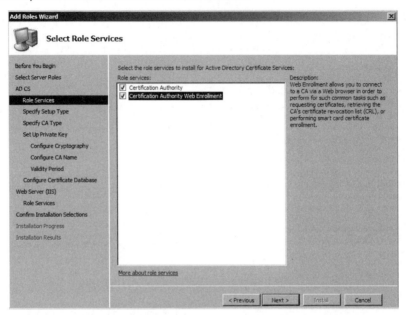

6. When you check the Certificate Authority Web Enrollment box, the Add Roles Wizard may appear, stating that you need to install supporting services. If you see this wizard, click the Add Required Role Services button. Otherwise go on to step 7.

7. Once both check boxes are checked on the Select Role Services screen, click Next.

8. At the Specify Setup Type screen, choose Enterprise (Recommended) and click Next.

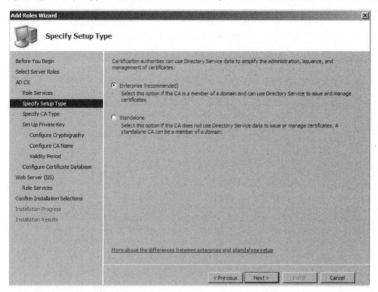

9. The Specify CA Type screen appears. This is where you decide what type of CA you will use. If you have only one CA or this is the first CA, choose Root CA (Recommended). If you are going to receive your certificates from a higher CA (either your own root or a third-party company) choose Subordinate CA. Click Next.

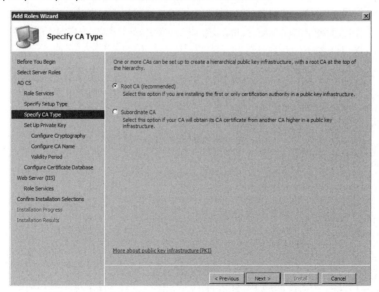

EXERCISE 6.1 *(continued)*

10. At the Set Up Private Key screen, choose Create A New Private Key, then click Next.

This option allows you to create a new key for our certificate server. You would choose Use Existing Private Key if you were reinstalling or using previously issued keys.

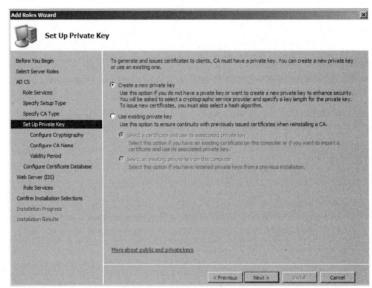

11. When the Configure Cryptography For CA screen appears, you must select a CSP. Choose RSA#Microsoft Software Key Storage Provider. Make sure that the Key Character Length is 2048 and choose sha1 for the hash algorithm. Click Next.

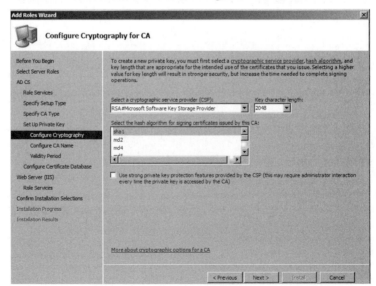

12. At the Configure CA Name screen, accept the defaults and click Next. The common name is the general name that is used to help identify the CA and the common name is also added to all issued certificates.

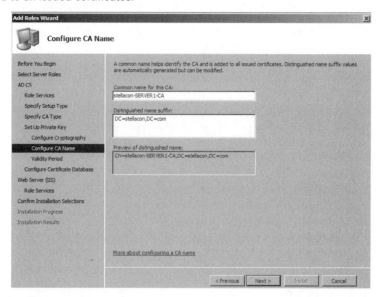

13. At the Set The Certificate Validity Period screen, change the default to 1 Years and click Next.

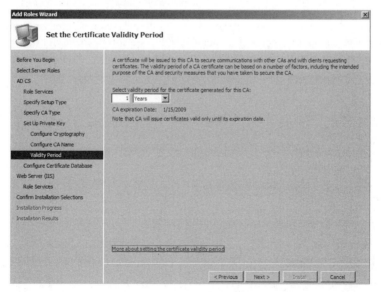

14. The Configure Certificate Database screen will prompt you to enter the storage location for your database files. Accept the defaults and click Next.

15. The Web Server IIS screen appears. This is an informational screen. Click Next.

16. At the Select Role Services screen, click Next. These are all the services you need to install IIS so it works with the certificate server.

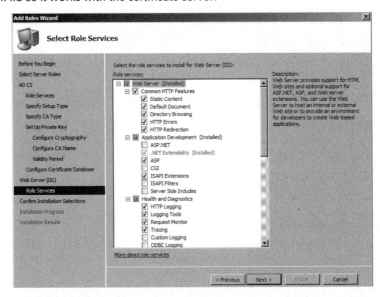

17. At the Confirm Installation Selections screen, you will see a warning message stating that the name of this server must remain unchanged for the certificate server to continue to run properly. Click Install.

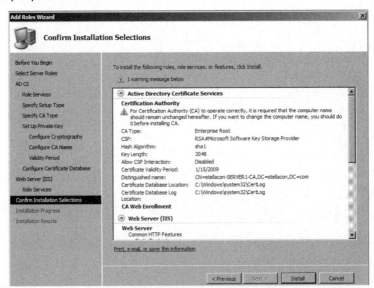

18. At the Installation Results screen, you will see the status of the installation. You should see an Installation Succeeded message. Click Close and exit the Server Manager.

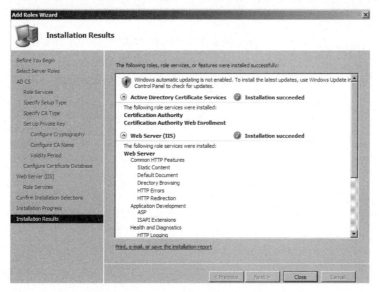

Enrolling User and Computer Certificates

Now that we have installed the AD CS, it's time for our users and computers to receive certificates. Users can receive their certificates three ways:

- Through Group Policy objects (GPOs)

  You can use group policies to automatically enroll user and computer certificates, making the entire certificate process transparent to your end users. See Chapter 8, "Configuring Group Policy Objects."

- Through web enrollment

  You can request a certificate by using `http://servername/certsrv` (see Exercise 6.3).

- Through certificate autoenrollment

  To set up certificate autoenrollment, you configure the local security policy (see Figure 6.2 and Exercise 6.2).

FIGURE 6.2   Configuring autoenrollment through the Local Security Policy application

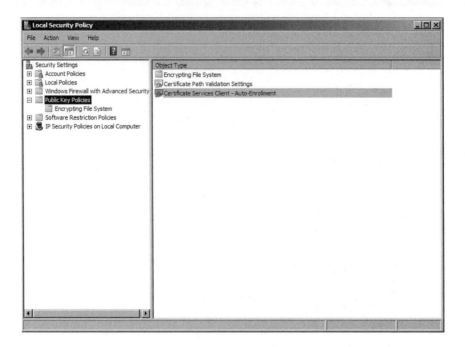

Real World Scenario

User Enrollment through autoenrollment

As an IT administrator, security is always a major concern on any network. When deciding to implement certificates, you must decide how you want to issue the certificates. It is always a good practice to auto enroll your end users. The fewer steps that an end user has to do, the better the chance that it will get done. We are not saying this in a bad way. Your end users are not as concerned with the network security as you are as an administrator. End users start doing their day-to-day tasks and before you know it, they forgot to implement the certificate. Try to make it a practice of auto enrolling your end users to make sure that the certificate gets issued and the network is secure.

Exercise 6.2 shows the steps you need to take to configure autoenrollment.

EXERCISE 6.2

Configuring Certificate Autoenrollment

1. Open the Local Security Policy MMC by selecting Start ➢ Administrative Tools ➢ Local Security Policy.

2. In the left pane, click Public Key Policies. In the right pane, right-click Certificate Services Client - Auto-Enrollment and choose Properties.

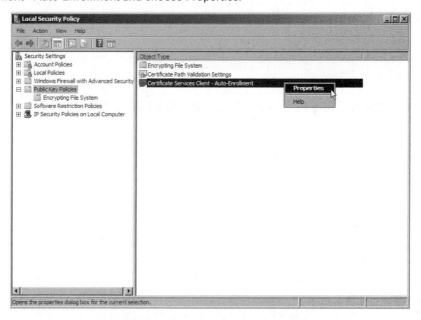

3. In the Configuration Model drop-down list, choose Enabled and click OK.

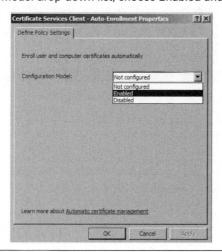

Exercise 6.3 will show you how to get a certificate using a web browser.

EXERCISE 6.3

Request a Certificate Using Your Web Browser

1. Open Internet Explorer by selecting Start ➢ Internet Explorer.

2. Enter **http://server1/certserv** in the Address bar. Note: server1 should be replaced with whtever the loca server name is.

3. Click the Request A Certificate link.

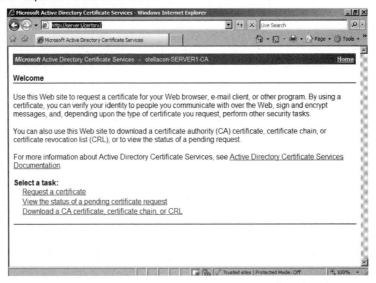

4. On the Request A Certificate page, click the Advanced Certificate Request link.

5. On the Advanced Certificate Request page, choose Create And Submit A Request To This CA.

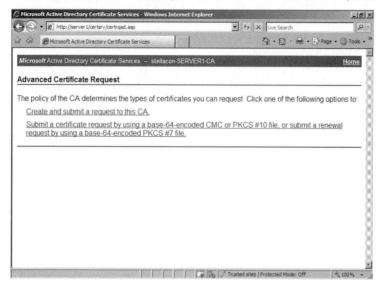

6. If you have a pop-up blocker enabled, you might receive a message about the information bar. Click Close and then right-click the information bar on the top of the website. If a second Information box appears telling you to add the website to the secure site list, click OK.

7. On the Advanced Certificate Request page, accept the defaults and click the Submit button. (If the Submit button is grayed out, your Internet security settings are too high. Reduce them and try again.)

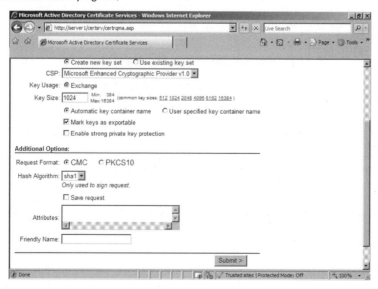

8. An information box will appear asking if you want this website to request a certificate. Click Yes.

9. A box will appear telling you that the certificate was issued to you. To accept this certificate, click Install This Certificate.

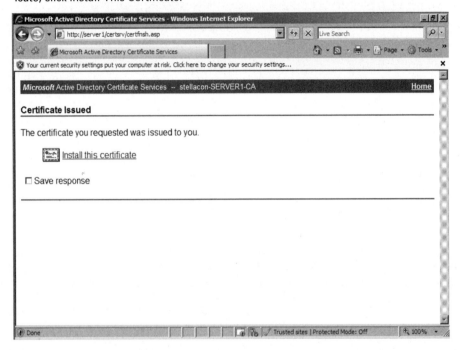

10. At the Web Access Confirmation screen, click Yes. (This confirmation is letting you know that a certificate is being added to your system.)

11. The Certificate Installed screen appears when installation is complete. Close the web browser.

Revoking Certificates

Occasionally, you will need to remove a certificate from a user or computer. This is known as *certificate revocation*. For example, if a user gets terminated from your organization, as an administrator, you have the ability to revoke this user's certificate so that they cannot access any data or confidential information after they leave the company.

The following are some of the certificate revocation components:

Certificate revocation list (CRL)   When certificates get revoked, they are listed in the *certificate revocation list (CRL)*. When configured properly by an administrator, this list is used by all the certificate servers. The CRL helps validate certificates and helps prevent revoked certificates from being used.

CRL distribution point (CDP)   You need to publish your CRL to a shared location called a *CRL distribution point (CDP)*. This gives your CRL a central location that all the certificate servers can share and use.

> Remember to change the URL distribution point for the authority information access (AIA) for any new root CA. You need to make this location accessible to all users in your organization's network. The offline root CA's default AIA points are not accessible to users on the network. If you do not change the location of the AIA, certificate chain verification fails.

Online Responder   The Online Responder is the server component of a certificate validation method called Online Certificate Status Protocol (OCSP). When certificates get revoked, your certificate server needs to make sure that these certificates don't get used again. You can perform this validation in many ways. The most common validation methods are CRLs, delta CRLs, and OCSP responses. Previous versions of Windows Server only supported CRLs. Windows Vista and the Windows Server 2008 operating system support both CRL and OCSP as methods for determining certificate status. The OCSP support applies to both the client component and the server component (called the Online Responder).

Exercise 6.4 walks you through the process of revoking a certificate using the Certificate Authority MMC snap-in (this MMC is installed automatically after the installation of your certificate server). You must have completed Exercise 6.1 and 6.3 in order to complete this exercise.

EXERCISE 6.4

Revoking a Certificate

1. Open the Certificate Authority MMC by selecting Start ➢ Administrative Tools ➢ Certificate Authority.

2. On the left pane, expand the server name. Click the Issued Certificates folder. Right-click the certificate (right pane), and in the menu, choose All Tasks ➢ Revoke Certificate.

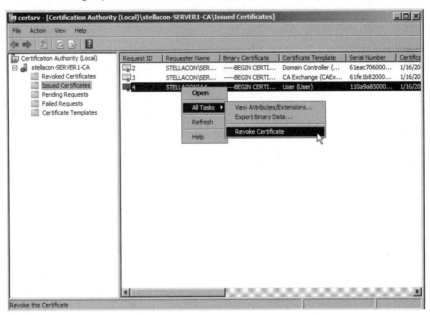

3. In the Certificate Revocation dialog box, you can choose the reason for the revocation and the effective date. Choose Unspecified and enter today's date. Click Yes. Close the Certificate Authority.

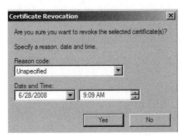

Configuring Additional CA Server Settings

You need to complete some important tasks while you are working on a certificate server. At this point, you have learned how to install an Enterprise Root CA, configure automatic certificate requests, set up web enrollment, and revoke a certificate. We will finish this section by covering some of the following tasks:

Key archival   Key archival allows a key to be stored for later recoverability if necessary. In a Windows Server 2008 CA, key archival is automatic. The private key portion of a public-private key pair is archived and can be recovered when needed.

Note that when a private key is recovered, the data or messages that it was associated with are not recovered. Key recovery only allows an individual to recover lost or damaged keys and allows an administrator to assume the role of an account for data access or recovery.

Key recovery agent   The *key recovery agent* is a role (a set of rights) that you can give an individual so that they have the permission to recover a lost or damaged key.

Assigning administrative roles   Using the Certificate Authority MMC, you can assign users or administrators rights to help manage the certificate server.

To assign an individual a role, right-click the name of the server in the Certificate Authority MMC and choose Properties. Click the Security tab. Add the individual and choose their roles.

> Rights and permissions are discussed in detail in Chapter 7, "Administering Active Directory."

Database backup and restore   One task that all administrators need to perform is backing up and restoring the certificates and keys. To back up and restore certificates, you use the Certificate Authority MMC. Exercise 6.5 will walk you through backing up your Certificate Authority server.

EXERCISE 6.5

Backing Up the Certificate Authority Server

1.   Open the Certificate Authority MMC by selecting Start ➤ Administrative Tools ➤ Certificate Authority.

EXERCISE 6.5 *(continued)*

2. In the left pane, right-click the name of the server, then choose All Tasks ➢ Back Up CA.

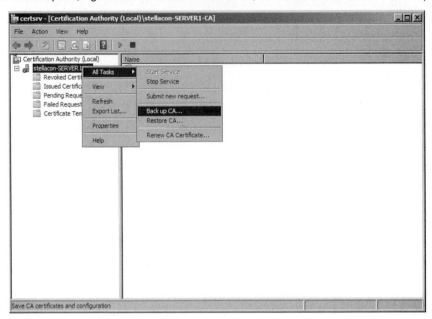

3. When the Certificate Authority Backup Wizard appears, click Next.

4. At the Items To Back Up screen, click the Private Key And CA Certificate check box. Next to the Back Up To This Location field, click the Browse button. Choose a location for your backup and click OK. Click Next.

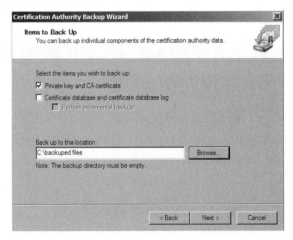

5. At the Select A Password screen, enter and confirm a password. For this exercise use **P@ssw0rd**. Click Next.

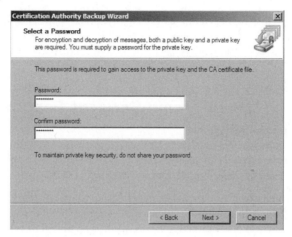

6. At the Completing The Certificate Authority Backup Wizard screen, click Finish.

7. Close the Certificate Authority MMC.

Understanding Active Directory Domain Services

With Active Directory Domain Services (AD DS), you manage objects (users, computers, printers, etc.) on a network. Active Directory is the database that stores all of your domain objects. In a Windows Server 2000, 2003, or 2008 network, you can not have a domain without Active Directory.

Introducing the New Domain Services Features in Windows Server 2008

Many new AD DS features have been added in Windows Server 2008. These features improve the security and efficiency of deploying and administering AD DS.

User interface improvements   Domain services are easier to install using the updated Installation Wizard for AD DS. Administrators can set up domain controllers anywhere in the organization. An improved AD DS user interface offers additional installation options for domain controllers. One of these is the ability to set up read-only domain controllers (RODCs).

Read-only domain controllers   Windows Server 2008 supports a new type of domain controller, the *read-only domain controller (RODC)*. You can safely install an RODC in a location that has limited security, such as a small offsite office. Offsite users no longer have to be authenticated across a slow WAN connection.

Auditing   Previous versions of Microsoft Windows Server supported auditing of successful or unsuccessful changes to Active Directory objects; however, the nature of the change was not included in the Security Log. In Microsoft Windows Server 2008, you can view the new and old values of the object and its attributes.

Fine-grained password policies   In Microsoft Windows Server 2000 and 2003, domain-based password policies and account lockout policies applied to all users in the domain. There was no inexpensive way to implement multiple such policies for individuals or groups. In Windows Server 2008, fine-grained password policies support multiple password and account lockout policies in the same domain.

Restartable Active Directory Domain Services   With Microsoft Windows Server 2008, administrators can stop or restart AD DS while other services not dependent on Active Directory (DNS, DHCP, etc.) continue to operate. For example, administrators can do an offline defragmentation of the Active Directory database or apply security updates without needing to restart the machine.

Database mounting tool   In previous versions of Active Directory, if an object got deleted, an administrator had to load multiple online backups until they found the object to restore. Windows Server 2008 Active Directory includes a database mounting tool (`Dsamain.exe`) that makes it quicker and easier to find and restore specific data. The tool supports online and Volume Shadow Copy Service (snapshot) backups.

Security Features Available for Domain Services

Two important security features are available for domain services in Windows Server 2008—RODCs and BitLocker Drive Encryption.

Read-Only Domain Controllers

As stated earlier, RODCs allow you to have a non-editable copy of Active Directory in an area that may be a security risk. RODCs hold an entire copy of Active Directory and the replication traffic is unidirectional. *Unidirectional replication* means that other domain controllers can talk to an RODC but an RODC cannot talk to other domain controllers.

One advantage to having an RODC is that you can give a normal user the administrator role for the RODC, and that user can do any type of maintenance on it. The user does not need to be a domain administrator; they are allowed to have the maintenance role for just the one RODC. This concept is known as administrator role separation.

You can also load DNS on an RODC. This makes a read-only copy of the DNS database. The downside to a read-only DNS server is that it does not allow dynamic updates (see Chapter 2, "Domain Name System (DNS)"). The benefit is that you do not have to worry about hackers or unauthorized domain users changing the DNS database.

RODCs do not store account credentials. They allow for authentication through credential caching, but not all accounts have to be cached. You can decide which accounts to cache on an RODC by using a *password replication policy*. This policy allows an administrator to determine which user groups will be allowed to use the RODC credential caching.

To install an RODC, use the `dcpromo.exe` application (discussed in Chapter 3, "Planning and Installing Active Directory," and Chapter 4, "Installing and Managing Trees and Forests"). In the Active Directory Domain Services Installation Wizard, on the Additional Domain Controller Options page, you check the box labeled Read-Only Domain Controller (RODC) (see Figure 6.3).

FIGURE 6.3   Installing an RODC

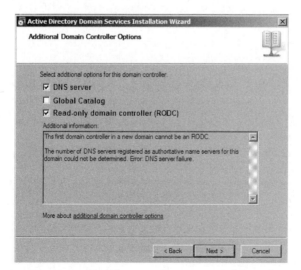

BitLocker Drive Encryption

Another way to add security in a non-secure location is through the use of BitLocker Drive Encryption. The BitLocker data-protection feature, new to Windows Server 2008, allows an IT administrator to encrypt both the operating system volume and additional data volumes within same server. However, BitLocker is not installed by default. To install the BitLocker security, use Server Manager (see Figure 6.4).

FIGURE 6.4   Using the Add Features Wizard of Server Manager to install BitLocker

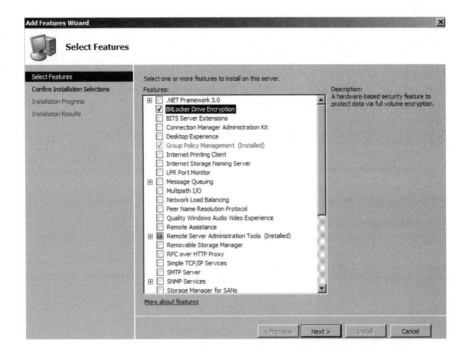

Active Directory Federation Services

Active Directory Federation Services (AD FS) provides Internet-based clients a secure identity access solution that works on both Windows and non-Windows operating systems.

Normally when a user from one network tries to access an application in another network, they must have a secondary username and password.

AD FS allows organizations to set up trust relationships between networks and supports single sign-on (SSO), which allows users to access applications on other networks without needing secondary passwords. Security is improved and administrators spend less time resetting passwords when users don't have to remember multiple passwords.

AD FS requires an AD FS server on both ends of the connection. For example, if company A is going to set up trust relationship with company B, the AD FS server needs to be configured at both company A and company B.

Installing AD FS

Exercise 6.6 shows you the steps you need to perform to install the AD FS through the Server Manager MMC.

EXERCISE 6.6

Installing the AD FS

1. Open the Server Manager MMC by selecting Start ➢ Administrative Tools ➢ Server Manager.

2. In the left pane, click Roles. In the Roles Summary section of right pane , click Add Roles.

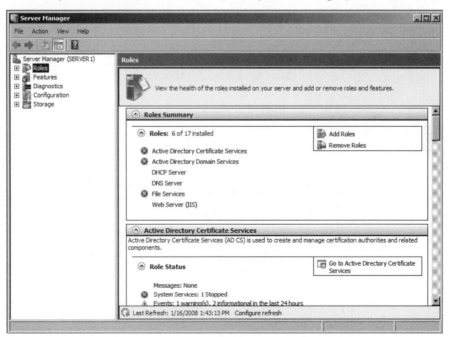

3. On the Select Server Roles screen, click the Active Directory Federation Services check box and click Next.

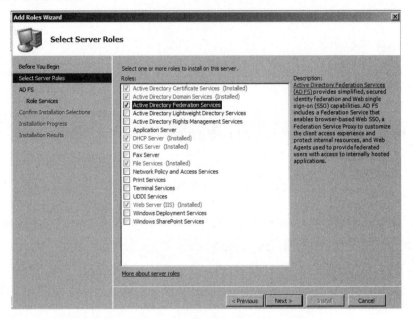

4. On the Introduction To AD FS screen, click Next.

5. On the Select Role Services screen, choose the AD FS Web Agent check box. A dialog box appears asking you to confirm the additional services that need to be installed. Click Add Required Role Services. When the Select Role Services screen reappears, Click Next.

EXERCISE 6.6 *(continued)*

6. On the Specify Federation Server screen, type the name of your server and domain and click Validate.

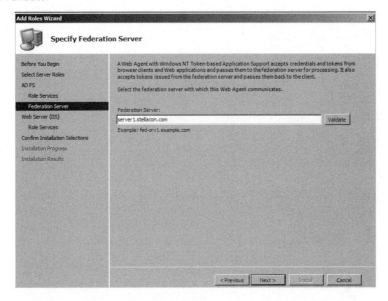

You will see an error message explaining that the other Federation server that you are trying to connect to is unavailable. That is OK for this exercise. Click Next.

7. At the Introduction To IIS screen, click Next.

8. On the Select Role Services screen, you see the additional services needed to install IIS. All the required boxes are already checked. Click Next.

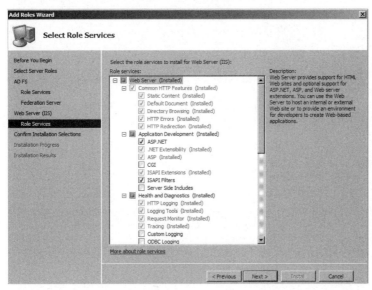

9. The Confirm Installation Selections screen shows you all the services and roles that you are about to install. Click Install.

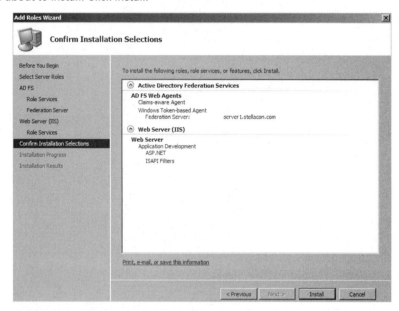

10. After the installation is finished, click Close.

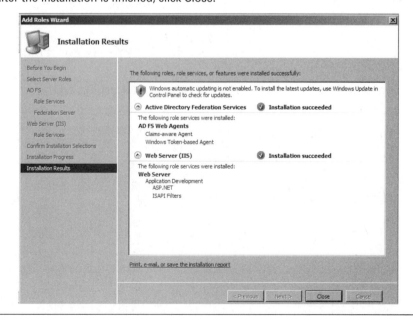

Configuring AD FS

Now that the AD FS is installed and running, you need to learn how to configure some of the important options. In the AD FS, you can configure trust policies, AD FS agents, and user and group mapping.

AD FS Web Agents   Administrators have the ability to configure a Windows NT token-based Web Agent. To support this new feature, Windows Server 2008 AD FS includes a user interface for the AD FS Web Agent role service. The Web Agent account is a service account that calls upon other services.

Trust policies   The AD FS trust policy is a file that outlines the set of rules that a Federation Service uses to recognize partners, certificates, account stores, claims, and the other numerous properties that are associated with the Federation Service.

User and group claim mapping   In basic terms, claims mean that each partnered location agrees and appropriately maps the AD FS trust policy for sharing between federation partner locations. A claim contains user information and helps users connect to a partner's resources. Three types of claims are supported by AD FS:

Identity claim   This claim type helps identify the user. The identity claim is included within a security token. A security token can contain up to three identity claims.

Group claim   This claim type indicates membership in a group or role.

Custom claim   This claim type provides any additional information that needs to be sent. An example might be DepartmentID. This is a custom field and then in turn would be a custom claim. A custom claim can provide any attribute that is located in Active Directory.

Active Directory Lightweight Directory Services

Active Directory Lightweight Directory Services (AD LDS) is a *Lightweight Directory Access Protocol (LDAP)* directory service. LDAP is an application protocol used for querying and modifying directory services. This type of service allows directory-enabled applications to store and retrieve data without needing the dependencies AD DS requires.

You can understand LDAP by thinking of directory services as something similar to an address book—a set of names (your objects) that you organize in a logical and hierarchical manner (for example, alphabetically). Each name in the address book has an address and phone number (the attributes of your objects) associated with it. LDAP allows you to query or modify this address book.

Installing AD LDS

In Exercise 6.7 we will install AD LDS by using the Server Manager MMC.

EXERCISE 6.7

Installing the AD LDS

1. Open the Server Manager MMC by selecting Start ➢ Administrative Tools ➢ Server Manager.

2. In the left pane, click Roles. In the Roles Summary section of the right pane, click Add Roles.

3. On the Select Server Roles screen, click the Active Directory Lightweight Directory Services check box and click Next.

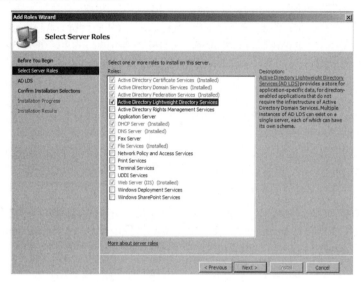

4. On the Introduction To AD LDS screen, click Next.

5. The Confirm Installation Selections screen shows you all the services and roles that you are about to install. Click Install.

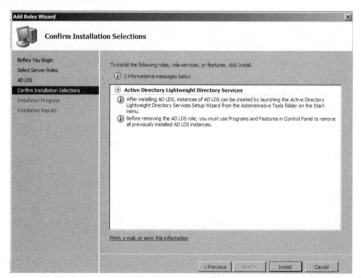

6. A progress screen will appear for a few minutes.

7. After the installation is finished, click Close.

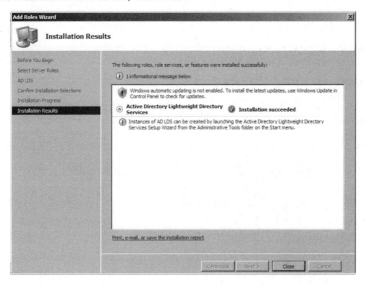

Configuring AD LDS

Now that we have installed AD LDS, we have to configure it. We have the ability to configure the following:

Configuring an authentication store   Let's say that you have a web or data server and you want a way to save authorization information for it. It is in this type of situation that configuring an AD LDS authentication store can help you out. AD LDS works well as an authentication store because it can host user account objects even though they are not Windows security principals. You can authenticate Non-Windows security principles by using LDAP simple binds.

Configuring the data within AD LDS   Remember, earlier we said that AD LDS is like an address book and you can edit who is in that address book by configuring the data within AD LDS. To configure the data within AD LDS, you can use the ADSI edit snap-in tool.

Migrating to AD LDS   What if your company was using an X.500-style directory service that was integrated into your company's legacy applications and you want to move to AD DS? You can use AD LDS to service the legacy applications while you use Active Directory for the shared security infrastructure.

Windows Server 2008 Hyper-V   Windows Server 2008 has a role-based utility called Hyper-V. Hyper-V is a hypervisor-based virtualization feature. (A hypervisor is a virtual machine monitor.) It includes all the necessary features to support machine virtualization. By using machine virtualization, a company can reduce costs, improve server utilization, and create a more dynamic IT infrastructure.

To configure AD LDS, you need to set up a service instance (or instance for short), which is a single running copy of AD LDS. You can have multiple instances as part of a configuration set. The reason for having multiple instances is load balancing and fault tolerance. This way if one instance becomes unavailable or overloaded, the other instances will pick up the slack.

In Exercise 6.8, we will use the Active Directory Lightweight Directory Services Wizard to set up our first AD LDS instance.

EXERCISE 6.8

Configuring an AD LDS Instance

1. Open the Server Manager MMC by selecting Start ➢ Administrative Tools ➢ Active Directory Lightweight Directory Services.

2. The Active Directory Lightweight Directory Services Wizard appears. Click Next.

3. At the Setup Options screen, choose the button labeled A Unique Instance. This option is for a new default instance. (If you choose the button labeled A Replica Of An Existing Instance, you are getting a copy of an instance from another machine.) Click Next.

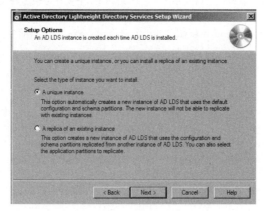

4. In the Instance Name screen, type the instance name you want to use and click Next.

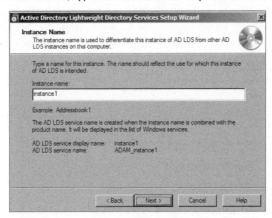

5. The Ports screen shows the first available ports on the machine. Whatever ports you choose, make sure that any internal firewalls know these port numbers. After you choose ports (or leave the defaults), click Next.

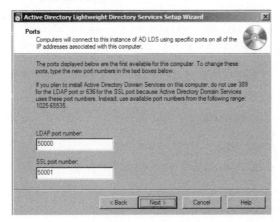

6. On the Application Directory Partition screen, you need to decide whether you want to create a directory partition (see Chapter 3). If your application (such as Exchange) installs its own partition, choose No, Do Not Create An Application Directory Partition. For this exercise, choose No, Do Not Create An Application Directory Partition and then click Next.

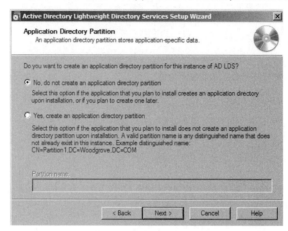

7. In the File Locations screen, you decide where you want to place your database files on your hard drive. For this exercise, leave the defaults and click Next.

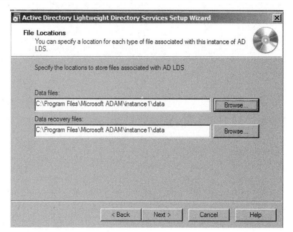

8. On the Service Account Selection screen, you need to choose which service account the AD LDS will use. This account has to have administrative rights. Choose Network Service Account and click Next.

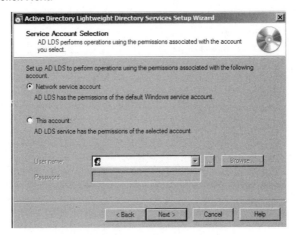

9. At the AD LDS Administrators screen, you choose which account will have the right to administer AD LDS. Choose Currently Logged On User and click Next.

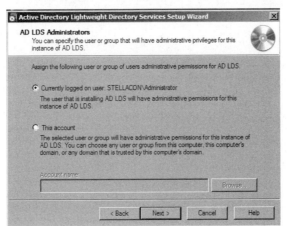

EXERCISE 6.8 *(continued)*

10. On the Importing LDIF Files screen, you can choose which LDIF (Lightweight Directory Interchange Format) services that you want to install. For the exercise, we will not install any services. Click Next.

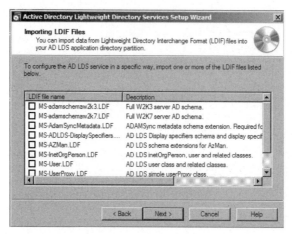

11. In the Ready To Install screen, look over all your choices before continuing. Click Next.

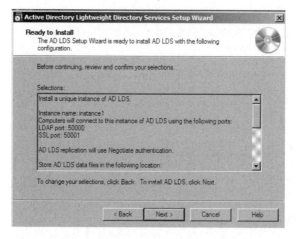

12. After the instance installation is complete, click Finish.

Now that you have created an initial instance, you can create more by choosing Active Directory Lightweight Directory Services Wizard and following the steps in Exercise 6.8 again. Now we are going to discuss the Active Directory Rights Management Services.

Active Directory Rights Management Services

Active Directory Rights Management Services (AD RMS), included with Microsoft Windows Server 2008, allows administrators or users to determine what access (open, read, modify, etc.) they give to other users in an organization. Access restrictions can improve security for email messages, internal websites, and documents.

 To secure documents, Microsoft Office 2003 Professional (Word, Excel, PowerPoint, and Outlook) or Microsoft Office 2007 Enterprise, Professional Plus, or Ultimate is required.

You can apply AD RMS usage policy templates directly to confidential information.

You can install AD RMS easily using Server Manager, and you can administer it through the MMC snap-in. These three new administrative roles allow for delegation of AD RMS responsibilities:

- AD RMS Enterprise Administrators
- AD RMS Template Administrators
- AD RMS Auditors

AD RMS is integrated with AD FS, which means that two organizations can share information without needing AD RMS installed in both organizations. Some other advantages of using AD RMS include the following:

Self enrollment AD RMS server enrollment allows for the creation and signing of a server licensor certificate (SLC). This SLC gives the AD RMS server the right to issue certificates and licenses whenever they are needed.

Active Directory Metadirectory Service (AD MDS) Microsoft uses an identity management product called Active Directory Metadirectory Service (AD MDS). AD MDS gives systems the tools they need to get identity data from directories and then expose that data through a directory service interface such as LDAP.

 AD RMS requires an AD RMS–enabled client. Windows Vista includes the AD RMS client by default. If you are not using Windows Vista or Windows Server 2008, you can download the AD RMS client for previous versions of Windows from Microsoft's Download Center.

Now that you have a basic understanding of what AD RMS does, let's take the next step and install AD RMS. In Exercise 6.9, we will install AD RMS by using the Server Manager MMC.

EXERCISE 6.9

Installing the AD RMS

1. Open the Server Manager MMC by selecting Start ➢ Administrative Tools ➢ Server Manager.

2. In the left pane, click Roles. In the Roles Summary section of the right pane, click Add Roles.

3. At the Select Server Roles screen, click the Active Directory Rights Management Services check box. A dialog box will appear stating that additional services need to be installed. Click the Add Required Role Services button. Then click Next.

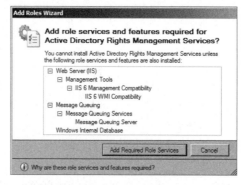

4. On the Introduction To AD RMS screen, click Next.

5. On the Select Role Services screen, make sure both check boxes (Active Directory Rights Management Server and Identity Federation Support) are checked. Identity Federation Support allows AD RMS to work with AD FS. Click Next.

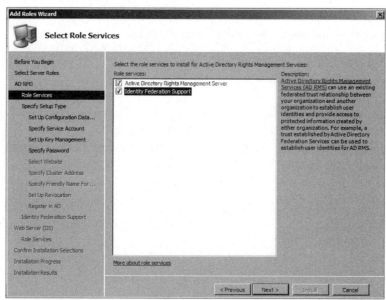

6. On the Specify Setup Type screen, choose Use This Server To Create A New AD RMS Cluster. (The other choice will not be available because we are installing the first AD RMS server and must start the cluster.) Click Next.

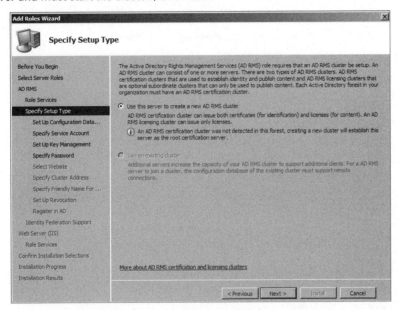

7. AD RMS uses a database to store configuration and policy information. At the Set Up Configuration Database screen, choose Use The Database Engine Built Into Windows. (The other option you have is to use a third-party database engine.) Click Next.

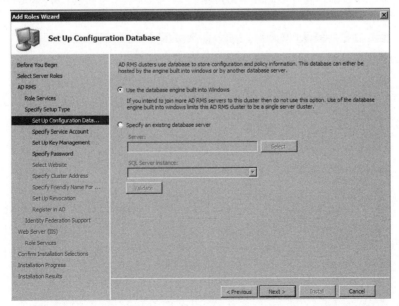

EXERCISE 6.9 *(continued)*

8.   On the Specify Service Account screen, you need to choose which service account the AD RMS will use. Chose Network Service Account and click Next. (An AD RMS account will be created to run the services.)

9.   At the Set Up Key Management screen, you decide which type of encryption you will use. Choose Use AD RMS Encryption Mechanism and click Next.

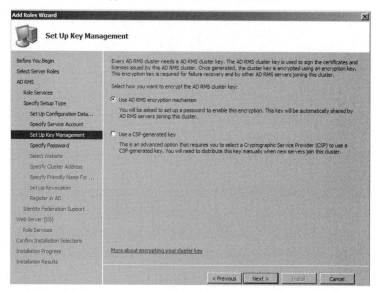

10. Next you will be asked to enter a password for AD RMS encryption. The AD RMS cluster key password is used to encrypt the AD RMS cluster key that is stored in the AD RMS database. Type **P@ssw0rd**, confirm it, and the click Next.

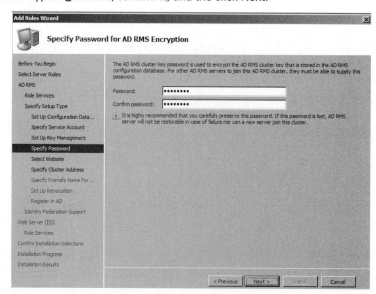

11. On the Select Website screen, leave the default and click Next. AD RMS needs to be hosted in IIS. This will set up a default website for AD RMS.

12. In the Specify Cluster Address screen, you choose whether to use a secure or a non-secure website. Choose Use A Secure (https://) Cluster Address and click the Validate button. After the address is verified, click Next.

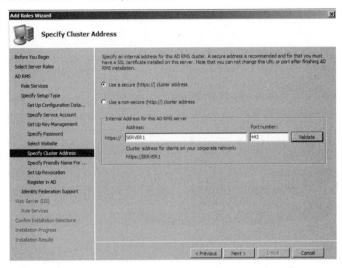

13. A dialog box appears asking you to put in a friendly name (a name you can use to access the server without knowing the entire UNC path). Leave the default and click Next.

14. In the Set Up Revocation screen, you can enable a revocation key, a third-party key that you can use to revoke licenses. For this exercise we are not going to use any third-party keys. Click Next.

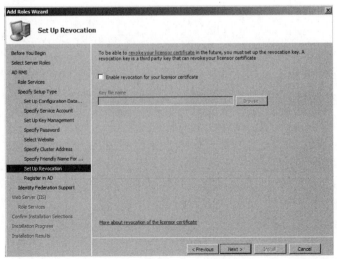

15. Next, you have the option to register AD RMS now or later. If you register the server now, AD RMS will take effect immediately. If you register the server later, AD RMS will not work until you register. We will not register during this exercise. Choose Register Later and click Next.

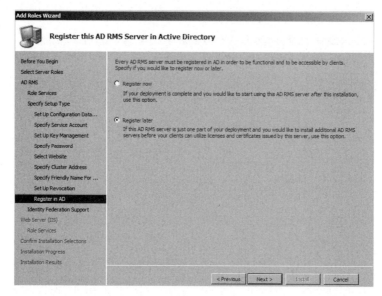

16. At the Configure Identity Federation Support screen, you specify the name of the web server that Identity Federation will use. Enter the friendly name from step 13 and click the Validate button. The Next button will become available after the server is validated. Click Next.

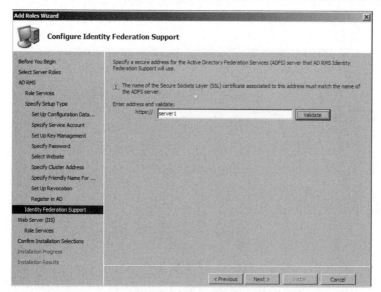

EXERCISE 6.9 *(continued)*

17. At the Introduction To IIS screen, click Next.

18. At the Select Roles Services screen, click Next. This will install all the necessary components for IIS.

19. At the Confirm Installation Selections screen, verify all your settings and click Install.

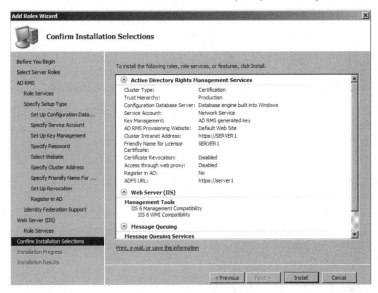

20. The install progress screen will appear. After the install is complete, click Close.

21. Close the Server Manager MMC.

Summary

In this chapter, we talked about the certificate authority (CA). We explained why you need to use certificates and how to configure them. We discussed how a computer or user gets a certificate through a GPO, autoenrollment, or web enrollment. We then reviewed the steps and reasons for revoking a certificate.

We went on to discuss the Active Directory Domain Service (AD DS) and the advantages of using a read-only domain controller (RODC). After that, we talked about the Active Directory Federation Services (AD FS), which provides Internet-based clients with a secure identity access solution that works on both Windows and non-Windows operating systems.

We continued with Active Directory Lightweight Directory Services (AD LDS), a Lightweight Directory Access Protocol (LDAP) directory service. We discussed how this type of service allows directory-enabled applications to store and retrieve data without needing the dependencies AD DS requires.

Finally, we talked about Active Directory Rights Management Services (AD RMS). We explained that the AD RMS is included with Microsoft Windows Server 2008 and described how it allows administrators or users to determine what access to give other users in an organization.

Exam Essentials

Understand the concepts behind certificate authority.   Certificate Authority servers manage certificates. Make sure you understand why companies use certificate servers and how they work.

Understand certificate enrollment.   You need to understand the many different ways to issue certificates to users and computers. You also need to understand the differences between installing certificates using GPOs, autoenrollment, and web enrollment.

Be familiar with the uses of read-only domain controllers.   Windows Server 2008 has a new type of domain controller called a read-only domain controller (RODC). This gives an organization the ability to install a domain controller in an area or location (on or offsite) that has limited security.

Know when to implement fine-grained password policies.   Understand that in Windows Server 2008 you have the ability to have multiple password and account lockout policies. In Microsoft Windows Server 2000 and 2003, when an organization implemented a domain-based password policy, it applied to all users in that domain. Fine-grained password policies allow an organization to have different password and account lockout policies for different sets of users in the same domain.

Understand Active Directory Federation Service.   Active Directory Federation Service (AD FS) gives users the ability to do a single sign-on (SSO) and access applications on other networks without needing a secondary password. Organizations can set up trust relationships with other trusted organizations so a user's digital identity and access rights can be accepted without a secondary password.

Know how to install Active Directory Rights Management Service.   Active Directory Rights Management Services (AD RMS), included with Microsoft Windows Server 2008, allows administrators or users to determine what access (open, read, modify, etc.) they give to other users in an organization. This access can be used to secure email messages, internal websites, and documents.

Understand how to configure Active Directory Lightweight Directory Services.   You need to know that Active Directory Lightweight Directory Services (AD LDS) is a Lightweight Directory Access Protocol (LDAP) directory service. This type of service allows directory-enabled applications to store and retrieve data without needing the dependencies AD DS requires.

Review Questions

1. Will, the administrator for your organization, has decided to implement certificates for all of your internal users. What type of root certificate authority (CA) would he implement?

    A. Enterprise

    B. Subordinate

    C. Stand Alone

    D. Web CA

2. You are the network administrator for your company. You have decided to implement the Active Directory Federation Services (AD FS). What application do you use to install the Active Directory Domain Services (AD DS)?

    A. Server Manager

    B. System Manager

    C. `Dcpromo.exe`

    D. Add/Remove Programs

3. You are hired as a contractor for a new organization that has no network currently in place. You decide to implement an Active Directory domain and the Active Directory Domain Services (AD DS). Which of the follow are requirements to install Active Directory?

    A. DNS

    B. DHCP

    C. WINS

    D. RIS

4. You have decided to implement certificate authority (CA) servers and you want all of your users to receive their certificates automatically without any user intervention. What two ways can you accomplish this goal?

    A. Autoenrollment

    B. GPO enrollment

    C. Internet enrollment

    D. Web enrollment

5. Which of the following provides Internet-based clients a secure identity access solution that works on both Windows and non-Windows operating systems?

    A. Active Directory Federation Services (AD FS)

    B. Active Directory Rights Management Service (AD RMS)

    C. Active Directory Lightweight Directory Service (AD LDS)

    D. Active Directory Domain Services (AD DS)

6. You have decided to place DNS on a read-only domain controller (RODC). What type of DNS zone do you now have?

    A. Primary with Active Directory integration

    B. Read-only DNS

    C. Secondary DNS

    D. Stub DNS

7. Which of the following allow administrators to configure services for issuing and managing public key certificates, which help organizations implement network security?

    A. Active Directory Federation Services (AD FS)

    B. Active Directory Rights Management Service (AD RMS)

    C. Active Directory Certificate Services (AD CS)

    D. Active Directory Domain Services (AD DS)

8. What role gives administrators the ability to enroll users into the certificate services program and allows for the issue and management of certificate requests?

    A. Enrollment agents

    B. Certificate agents

    C. Enrollment Admins

    D. Certificate Admins

9. You have decided to implement a certificate authority on your network. You have hired a third-party company to create and issue you the certificates you need to hand out to your Internet users. What type of certificate authority do you need to set up?

    A. Enterprise CA

    B. Enterprise Subordinate CA

    C. Stand-Alone CA

    D. Stand Alone Subordinate CA

10. Alexandria, the network administrator, has just hired a new junior administrator named Paige. Paige needs to be able to recover keys from the certificate authority server. What role does Alexandria need to give Paige so that she can recover keys?

    A. Certificate recovery agent

    B. Certificate admin agent

    C. Key recovery agent

    D. Certificate key admin

11. What file outlines the set of rules that a Federation Service uses to recognize partners, certificates, account stores, claims, and the numerous properties that are associated with the Federation Service?

A. Trust policy

B. AD FS rule set

C. Outline set

D. Outline policy

12. Which of the following is a Lightweight Directory Access Protocol (LDAP) directory service that allows directory-enabled applications to store and retrieve data without needing the dependencies AD DS requires?

A. Active Directory Federation Services (AD FS)

B. Active Directory Rights Management Service (AD RMS)

C. Active Directory Certificate Services (AD CS)

D. Active Directory Lightweight Directory Services (AD LDS)

13. You are the administrator of a network. Your company has decided to use server virtualization to help save money and add fault tolerance to your servers. What role-based utility is included with Windows Server 2008 making this possible?

A. Virtualization-H

B. Hyper-V

C. Hyper-Virtualization

D. Virtualization Manager

14. You are the administrator for a company. Your manager has explained to you that due to security requirements, you need to secure documents and emails using Microsoft Office 2007 Enterprise. What service do you need to install to help secure documents and emails?

A. Active Directory Federation Services (AD FS)

B. Active Directory Rights Management Service (AD RMS)

C. Active Directory Certificate Services (AD CS)

D. Active Directory Lightweight Directory Services (AD LDS)

15. Your company has one main location and five remote sites. One of the remote sites is having a problem with Active Directory and DNS being hacked into. What two of the following can you use to help solve this problem?

A. Read-only domain controller

B. Read-only stub server

C. Read-only DNS server

D. Read-only DHCP server

16. Your company has one main location and one remote site. The remote site is 300 miles from the main location and it has no IT staff on site. What type of domain controller can you install so that a normal user can have the rights to manage it?

A. Primary domain controller (PDC)

B. Read-only domain controller (RODC)

C. Backup domain controller (BDC)

D. Normal domain controller (DC)

17. You have decided to implement a certificate authority on your network. You have hired a third-party company to create and issue you the certificates you need to hand out to your internal users. What type of certificate authority do you need to set up?

A. Enterprise CA

B. Enterprise Subordinate CA

C. Stand Alone CA

D. Stand Alone Subordinate CA

18. You are the administrator of a mid-size organization. Your company has decided to install a certificate authority (CA). After you install the CA, you publish the certificate revocation list (CRL) to a central location for all CAs to use. What is this central location called?

A. CRL central point

B. CRL distribution location

C. CRL distribution point

D. CRL central location

19. You are an administrator of a mid-size organization. Your company currently uses Windows Server 2008 domain controllers. Your company wants to use multiple account lockout policies depending on what department people are in. What does Windows Server 2008 offer so that you can do this?

A. Multiple password policy

B. DSA password policy

C. OU password policy

D. Fine-grained password policy

20. You are the administrator for your organization. You have decided to implement certificate authority servers. You have routers located on your network. What component allows systems to receive a certificate even though they do not have an Active Directory account?

A. Hardware Device Enrollment Service

B. Network Device Enrollment Service

C. Router Enrollment Service

D. Network Hardware Enrollment Service

Answers to Review Questions

1. A. Enterprise Root CAs and Stand Alone Root CAs are the two types of CAs. Enterprise Root CAs (automatically integrated with Active Directory) are the top-most trusted CAs of the hierarchy. They hold the certificates that you issue to the users within your organization. The Stand Alone Root CAs hold the CAs that you issue to Internet users.

2. A. Server Manager is a new Windows Server 2008 feature. Server Manager allows an administrator to install and configure server roles and features and to view information about server configuration.

3. A. DNS is a requirement of Active Directory. You can install DNS before or during the installation of Active Directory. DHCP, WINS, and RIS are all optional (but not required) services that can run on a network.

4. A, B. GPO enrollment automatically issues a certificate to a user through the use of a Group Policy object (GPO). Web enrollment allows users to request certificates and retrieve certificate revocation lists (CRLs) through the use of a web browser. Autoenrollment automatically issues a certificate to a user after either the user or an administrator makes a setting on the user's computer.

5. A. Active Directory Federation Services (AD FS) provides Internet-based clients a secure identity access solution that works on both Windows and non-Windows operating systems. AD FS also gives users the ability to do a single sign-on (SSO) and access applications on other networks without needing a secondary password.

6. B. When you decide to load DNS on a RODC, that copy of DNS is a read-only copy. The downside to a read-only DNS server is that it will not allow dynamic updates. The benefit is that it can be placed in an non-secure location.

7. C. AD CS allows administrators to configure services for issuing and managing public key certificates. Companies can benefit from AD CS security by combining a private key with an object (such as users and computers), device (such as routers), or service.

8. A. Enrollment agents are administrators who have the ability to enroll users into the certificate services program. Enrollment agents can issue and manage certificate requests.

9. D. CAs that are below the Enterprise and Stand Alone Root CAs in the hierarchy are referred to as Subordinate CAs. The Enterprise or Stand Alone Root CAs give certificates to the Subordinate CAs, which in turn issue certificates to objects and services. The third-party company is the Stand Alone CA and your company would be the Stand Alone Subordinate CA. Standalone servers are for issuing certificates to Internet users.

10. C. The key recovery agent is a role (a set of rights) that you can give an individual so that they have the permission to recover a lost or damaged key.

11. A. The trust policy is the file that outlines the set of rules that a Federation Service uses to recognize partners, certificates, account stores, claims, and the numerous properties that are associated with the Federation Service.

12. D. AD LDS is a LDAP directory service. This type of service allows directory-enabled applications to store and retrieve data without needing the dependencies AD DS requires.

13. B. Windows Server 2008 has a role-based utility called Hyper-V. Hyper-V is a hypervisor-based virtualization feature. It includes all the necessary features to support machine virtualization. Using machine virtualization allows a company to reduce costs, to improve server utilization and to create a more-dynamic IT infrastructure.

14. B. AD RMS allows administrators or users to determine what access (open, read, modify, etc.) they give to other users. This access can be used to secure email messages, internal websites, and documents.

15. A, C. Read-only domain controllers allow you to have a non-editable copy of Active Directory in an area that may be a security risk. You can also place a read-only copy of DNS on that server. The other two options do not exist.

16. B. You can give a normal user the administrator role for only a RODC. The user can do any type of maintenance on the RODC without needing to be a domain administrator.

17. B. CAs that are below the Enterprise and Stand Alone Root CAs in the hierarchy are referred to as Subordinate CAs. The Enterprise or Stand Alone Root CAs give certificates to the Subordinate CAs, which in turn issue certificates to objects and services. The third-party company is the Enterprise CA and your company would be the Enterprise Subordinate CA. Enterprise certificate servers issue certificates to internal users.

18. C. When you have a CA, you need to publish your CRL to a shared location. This location is called a CRL distribution point. This gives your CRL a central location for all the certificate servers to share and use.

19. D. New to Windows Server 2008, fine-grained password policies allow an organization to have different password and account lockout policies for different sets of users in the same domain.

20. B. The Network Device Enrollment Service allows network devices (such as routers) to obtain certificates even though they do not have an account in the Active Directory domain.

Chapter

7

Administering
Active Directory

MICROSOFT EXAM OBJECTIVES COVERED IN THIS CHAPTER:

✓ **Creating and Maintaining Active Directory Objects**

- Automate creation of Active Directory accounts. May include but is not limited to: bulk import; Active Directory Migration Tool (ADMT) v3, configure the UPN; create computer, user, and group accounts (scripts, import, migration); template accounts; contacts; distribution lists

- Maintain Active Directory accounts. May include but is not limited to: configure group membership; account resets; delegation; AGDLP/AGGUDLP; deny domain local group; local vs. domain; Protected Admin; disabling accounts vs. deleting accounts; deprovisioning; contacts; creating organizational units (OUs); delegation of control

- Create and apply Group Policy objects (GPOs). May include but is not limited to: enforce, OU hierarchy, block inheritance, and enabling user objects; group policy processing priority; WMI; group policy filtering; group policy loopback (also in Chapter 8)

In the previous chapters, you learned how to install Domain Name System (DNS) and Active Directory, configure server roles, and work with sites, but you still haven't been introduced to the lower-level objects that exist in Active Directory.

In this chapter, you will look at the structure of the various components within a domain. You'll see how an organization's business structure can be mirrored within Active Directory through the use of organizational units (OUs) for ease of use and to create a seamless look and feel. Because the concepts related to OUs are quite simple, some systems administrators may underestimate their importance and not plan to use them accordingly. Make no mistake—one of the fundamental components of a successful Active Directory installation is the proper design and deployment of OUs.

You'll also see the actual steps you need to take to create common Active Directory objects and then learn how to configure and manage these objects. Finally, you'll look at ways to publish resources and methods for creating user accounts automatically.

An Overview of OUs

An *organizational unit (OU)* is a logical group of Active Directory objects, just as its name implies. OUs serve as containers within which other Active Directory objects can be created, but they do not form part of the DNS namespace. They are used solely to create organization within a domain.

OUs can contain the following types of Active Directory objects:

- Users
- Groups
- Computers
- Shared Folder objects
- Contacts
- Printers
- InetOrgPerson objects
- MSMQ Queue Aliases
- Other OUs

Perhaps the most useful feature of OUs is that they can contain other OU objects. As a result, systems administrators can hierarchically group resources and other objects according to business practices. The OU structure is extremely flexible and, as you will see later in this chapter, can easily be rearranged to reflect business reorganizations.

Another advantage to OUs is that each can have its own set of policies. Administrators can create individual and unique Group Policy objects (GPOs) for each OU. GPOs are rules or policies that can apply to all the objects within the OU. (GPOs are discussed in detail in Chapter 8, "Group Policy Objects.")

Each type of object has its own purpose within the organization of Active Directory domains. Later in this chapter, you'll look at the specifics of User, Computer, Group, and Shared Folder objects. For now, let's focus on the purpose and benefits of using OUs.

The Purpose of OUs

OUs are mainly used to organize the objects within Active Directory. Before you dive into the details of OUs, however, you must understand how OUs, users, and groups interact. Most importantly, you should understand that OUs are simply containers that you can use to logically group various objects. They are not, however, groups in the classical sense. That is, they are not used for assigning security permissions. Another way of stating this is that the user accounts, computer accounts, and group accounts that are contained in OUs are considered security principals while the OUs themselves are not.

OUs do not take the place of standard user and group permissions (covered in Chapter 9). A good general practice is to assign users to groups and then place the groups within OUs. This enhances the benefits of setting security permissions and of using the OU hierarchy for making settings. Figure 7.1 illustrates this concept.

FIGURE 7.1   Relationships of users, groups, and OUs

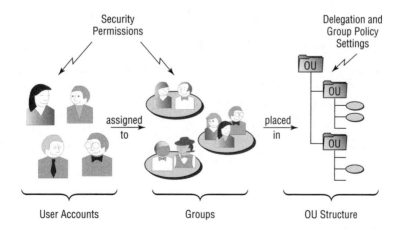

An OU contains objects only from within the domain in which it resides. As you'll see in the section titled "Delegating Administrative Control," later in this chapter, the OU is the finest level of granularity used for group policies and other administrative settings.

Benefits of OUs

There are many benefits of using OUs throughout your network environment:

- OUs are the smallest unit to which you can assign directory permissions.
- You can easily change the OU structure, and it is more flexible than the domain structure.
- The OU structure can support many different levels of hierarchy.
- Child objects can inherit OU settings.
- You can set Group Policy settings on OUs.
- You can easily delegate the administration of OUs and the objects within them to the appropriate users and groups.

Now that you have a good idea of why you should use OUs, take a look at some general practices you can use to plan the OU structure.

Planning the OU Structure

One of the key benefits of Active Directory is the way in which it can bring organization to complex network environments. Before you can begin to implement OUs in various configurations, you must plan a structure that is compatible with business and technical needs. In this section, you'll learn about several factors you should consider when planning for the structure of OUs.

Logical Grouping of Resources

The fundamental purpose of using OUs is to hierarchically group resources that exist within Active Directory. Fortunately, hierarchical groups are quite intuitive and widely used in most businesses. For example, a typical manufacturing business might divide its various operations into different departments like these:

- Sales
- Marketing
- Engineering
- Research and Development
- Support
- Information Technology (IT)

Each of these departments usually has its own goals and missions. In order to make the business competitive, individuals within each of the departments are assigned to various roles. Some types of roles might include the following:

- Managers
- Clerical staff
- Technical staff
- Planners

Each of these roles usually entails specific job responsibilities. For example, managers should provide direction to general staff members. Note that the very nature of these roles suggests that employees may fill many different positions. That is, one employee might be a manager in one department and a member of the technical staff in another. In the modern workplace, such situations are quite common.

All of this information helps you plan how to use OUs. First, the structure of OUs within a given network environment should map well to the business's needs, including the political and logical structure of the organization, as well as its technical needs. Figure 7.2 shows how a business organization might be mapped to the OU structure within an Active Directory domain.

FIGURE 7.2   Mapping a business organization to an OU structure

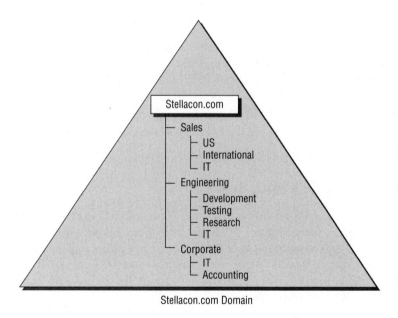

Stellacon.com Domain

When naming OUs for your organization, you should keep several considerations and limitations in mind:

Keep the names and descriptions simple.   The purpose of OUs is to make administering and using resources simple. Therefore, it's always a good idea to keep the names of your objects simple and descriptive. Sometimes, finding a balance between these two goals can be a challenge. For example, although a printer name like "The LaserJet located near Bob's cube" might seem descriptive, it is certainly difficult to type. Also, imagine the naming changes that you might have to make if Bob moves (or leaves the company)!

Pay attention to limitations.   The maximum length for the name of an OU is 64 characters. In most cases, this should adequately describe the OU. Remember, the name of an OU does not have to uniquely describe the object because the OU is generally referenced only as part of the overall hierarchy. For example, you can choose to create an OU named "IT" within two different parent OUs. Even though the OUs have the same name, users and administrators are able to distinguish between them based on their complete pathname.

Pay attention to the hierarchical consistency.   The fundamental basis of an OU structure is its position in a hierarchy. From a design standpoint, this means that you cannot have two OUs with the same name at the same level. However, you can have OUs with the same name at different levels. For example, you could create an OU named "Corporate" within the North America OU and another one within the South America OU. This is because the fully qualified name includes information about the hierarchy. When an administrator tries to access resources in a Corporate OU, they must specify which Corporate OU they mean.

If, for example, you create a North America OU, the Canada OU should logically fit under it. If you decide that you want to separate the North America and Canada OUs into completely different containers, then you might want to use other, more appropriate names. For example, you could change North America to U.S. Users and administrators depend on the hierarchy of OUs within the domain, so make sure that it remains logically consistent.

Based on these considerations, you should have a good idea of how to best organize the OU structure for your domain.

Understanding OU Inheritance

When you rearrange OUs within the structure of Active Directory, you can change several settings. When they are moving and reorganizing OUs, systems administrators must pay careful attention to automatic and unforeseen changes in security permissions and other configuration options. By default, OUs inherit the permissions of their new parent container when they are moved.

By using the built-in tools provided with Windows Server 2008 and Active Directory, you can move or copy OUs only within the same domain.

You cannot use the Active Directory Users And Computers tool to move OUs between domains. To do this, use the Active Directory Migration Tool (ADMT) v3.1. This is one of the many Active Directory support tools.

For more information on this, check out Microsoft's website at http://go.microsoft.com/fwlink/?LinkID=82740.

Delegating Administrative Control

We already mentioned that OUs are the smallest component within a domain to which administrative permissions and group policies can be assigned by administrators. Now, you'll take a look at specifically how administrative control is set on OUs.

Delegation occurs when a higher security authority assigns permissions to a lesser security authority. As a real-world example, assume that you are the director of IT for a large organization. Instead of doing all of the work yourself, you would probably assign roles and responsibilities to other individuals. For example, if you worked within a multidomain environment, you might make one systems administrator responsible for all operations within the Sales domain and another responsible for the Engineering domain. Similarly, you could assign the permissions for managing all printers and print queues objects within your organization to one individual user while allowing another individual user to manage all security permissions for users and groups.

In this way, you can distribute the various roles and responsibilities of the IT staff throughout the organization. Businesses generally have a division of labor that handles all of the tasks involved in keeping the company's networks humming. Network operating systems (NOSs), however, often make it difficult to assign just the right permissions, or in other words, do not support very granular permission assignments. Sometimes, fine granularity is necessary to ensure that only the right permissions are assigned. A good general rule of thumb is to provide users and administrators the minimum permissions they require to do their jobs. This way you can ensure that accidental, malicious, and otherwise unwanted changes do not occur.

You can use auditing to log events to the Security Log in the Event Viewer. This is a way to ensure that if accidental, malicious, and otherwise unwanted changes do occur, they are logged and traceable.

In the world of Active Directory, you use the process of delegation to define responsibilities for OU administrators. As a system administrator, you will be occasionally tasked with having to delegate responsibility to others—you can't do it all, although sometimes some administrators believe that they can. We understand the old IT logic of doing all the tasks yourself for job security, but this can actually make you look worse and not better.

You can delegate control only at the OU level and not at the object level within the OU.

If you do find yourself in a role to delegate, remember that Windows Server 2008 was designed to offer you the ability to do so. In its simplest definition, delegation allows a higher administrative authority to grant specific administrative rights for containers and subtrees to individuals and groups. What this essentially does is eliminate the need for domain administrators with sweeping authority over large segments of the user population. You can break up this control over branches within your tree, within each OU you create.

> To understand delegation and rights, you should first understand the concept
> of access control entries (ACEs). ACEs grant specific administrative rights on
> objects in a container to a user or group. The containers' access control list
> (ACL) is used to store ACEs.

When you are considering implementing delegation, keep these two main concerns in mind:

Parent-child relationships   The OU hierarchy you create will be very important when you consider the maintainability of security permissions. OUs can exist in a parent-child relationship, which means that permissions and group policies set on OUs higher up in the hierarchy (parents) can interact with objects in lower-level OUs (children). When it comes to delegating permissions, this is extremely important. You can allow child containers to automatically inherit the permissions set on parent containers. For example, if the North America division of your organization contains 12 other OUs, you could delegate permissions to all of them at once (saving time, and reducing the likelihood of human error) by placing security permissions on the North America division. This feature can greatly ease administration, especially in larger organizations, but it is also a reminder of the importance of properly planning the OU structure within a domain.

Inheritance settings   Now that you've seen how you can use parent-child relationships for administration, you should consider *inheritance*, the process in which child objects take on the permissions of a parent container. When you set permissions on a parent container, all of the child objects are configured to inherit the same permissions. You can override this behavior, however, if business rules do not lend themselves well to inheritance.

Applying Group Policies

One of the strengths of the Windows operating system is that it offers users a great deal of power and flexibility. From installing new software to adding device drivers, users can make many changes to their workstation configurations. However, this level of flexibility is also a potential problem. For instance, inexperienced users might inadvertently change settings, causing problems that can require many hours to fix.

In many cases (and especially in business environments), users only require a subset of the complete functionality the operating system provides. In the past, however, the difficulty associated with implementing and managing security and policy settings has led to lax security policies. Some of the reasons for this are technical—it can be very tedious and difficult to implement and manage security restrictions. Other problems have been political—users and management might feel that they should have full permissions on their local machines, despite the potential problems this might cause.

That's where the idea of group policies comes in. Simply defined, *group policies* are collections of permissions that you can apply to objects within Active Directory. Specifically, Group Policy settings are assigned at the site, domain, and OU levels, and they can apply to user accounts, computer accounts, and groups. Examples of settings that a systems administrator can make using group policies include the following:

- Restricting users from installing new programs
- Disallowing the use of Control Panel
- Limiting choices for display and Desktop settings

 Chapter 8 covers the technical issues related to group policies.

Creating OUs

Now that you have looked at several different ways in which OUs can be used to bring organization to the objects within Active Directory, it's time to look at how you can create and manage them.

Through the use of the Active Directory Users And Computers administrative tool, also called the MMC (Microsoft Management Console), you can quickly and easily add, move, and change OUs. This graphical tool makes it easy to visualize and create the various levels of hierarchy an organization requires.

Figure 7.3 shows a geographically based OU structure that a multinational company might use. Note that the organization is based in North America and it has a corporate office located there. In general, the other offices are much smaller than the corporate office located in North America.

FIGURE 7.3   A geographically based OU structure

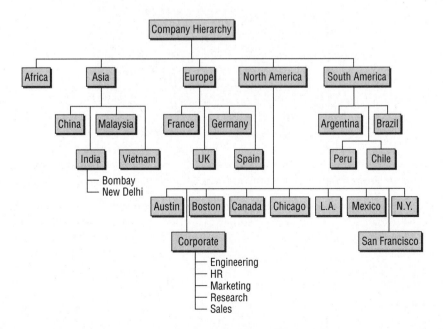

It's important to note that this OU structure could have been designed in several different ways. For example, we could have chosen to group all of the offices located in the United States within an OU named "U.S." However, due to the large size of these offices, we chose to place these objects at the same level as the Canada and Mexico OUs. This prevents an unnecessarily deep OU hierarchy while still logically grouping the offices.

Exercise 7.1 walks you through the process of creating several OUs for a multinational business. You'll be using this OU structure in later exercises within this chapter.

 In order to perform the exercises included in this chapter, you must have administrative access to a Windows Server 2008 domain controller.

EXERCISE 7.1

Creating an OU Structure

1. Open the Active Directory Users And Computers administrative tool.

2. Right-click the name of the local domain, and choose New ≻ Organizational Unit. You will see the dialog box shown in the following graphic. Notice that this box shows you the current context within which the OU will be created. In this case, you're creating a top-level OU, so the full path is simply the name of the domain.

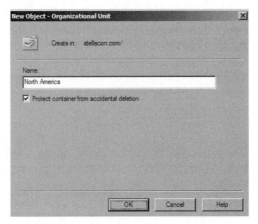

3. Type **North America** for the name of the first OU. Uncheck the box that states Protect Container From Accidental Deletion and click OK to create this object.

4. Create the following top-level OUs by right-clicking the name of the domain and choosing New ≻ Organizational Unit. Also make sure to uncheck Protect Container From Accidental Deletion for all OUs in these labs, because you'll be deleting some of these OUs in later exercises.

   Africa

   Asia

Europe

South America

Note that the order in which you create the OUs is not important. In this exercise, you are simply using a method that emphasizes the hierarchical relationship.

5. Create the following second-level OUs within the North America OU by right-clicking the North America OU and selecting New ➢ Organizational Unit:

   Austin

   Boston

   Canada

   Chicago

   Corporate

   Los Angeles

   Mexico

   New York

   San Francisco

6. Create the following OUs under the Asia OU:

   China

   India

   Malaysia

   Vietnam

7. Create the following OUs under the Europe OU:

   France

   Germany

   Spain

   UK

8. Create the following OUs under the South America OU:

   Argentina

   Brazil

   Chile

   Peru

EXERCISE 7.1 *(continued)*

9. Create the following third-level OUs Under the India OU by right-clicking India within the Asia OU, and selecting New ➢ Organizational Unit:

    Bombay

    New Delhi

10. Within the North America Corporate OU, create the following OUs:

    Engineering

    HR

    Marketing

    Research

    Sales

11. When you have completed the creation of the OUs, you should have a structure that looks similar to the one in the following graphic.

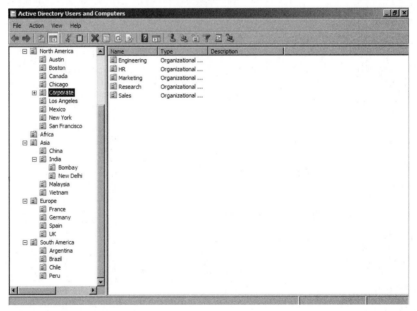

Managing OUs

Managing network environments would still be challenging even if things rarely changed. However, in the real world, business units, departments, and employee roles change frequently. As business and technical needs change, so should the structure of Active Directory.

Fortunately, changing the structure of OUs within a domain is a relatively simple process. In the following sections, you'll look at ways to delegate control of OUs and make other changes.

Moving, Deleting, and Renaming OUs

The process of moving, deleting, and renaming OUs is a simple one. Exercise 7.2 shows how you can easily change and reorganize OUs to reflect changes in the business organization. The specific scenario covered in this exercise includes the following changes:

- The Research and Engineering departments have been combined to form a department known as Research and Development (RD).
- The Sales department has been moved from the Corporate office to the New York office.
- The Marketing department has been moved from the Corporate office to the Chicago office.

This exercise assumes that you have already completed the steps in Exercise 7.1.

EXERCISE 7.2

Modifying OU Structure

1. Open the Active Directory Users And Computers administrative tool.

2. Right-click the Engineering OU (located within North America ➤ Corporate) and click Delete. When you are prompted for confirmation, click Yes. Note that if this OU contained objects, they all have been automatically deleted as well.

3. Right-click the Research OU and select Rename. Type **RD** to change the name of the OU and press Enter.

4. Right-click the Sales OU and select Move. In the Move dialog box, expand the North America branch and click the New York OU. Click OK to move the OU.

5. You will use an alternate method to move the Marketing OU. Drag the Marketing OU and drop it onto the Chicago OU.

6. When you have finished, you should see an OU structure similar to the one shown in the following graphic. Close the Active Directory Users And Computers administrative tool.

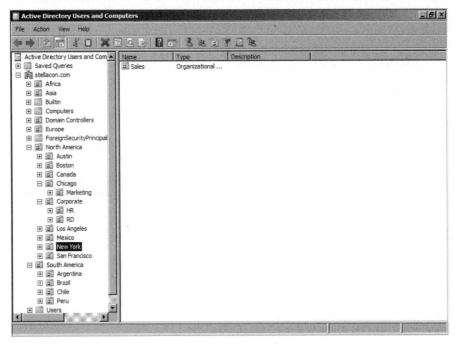

Administering Properties of OUs

Although OUs are primarily created for organizational purposes within the Active Directory environment, they have several settings that you can modify. To modify the properties of an OU using the Active Directory Users And Computers administrative tool, right-click the name of any OU and select Properties; when you do, the OU Properties dialog box appears. In the example shown in Figure 7.4, you see the options on the General tab.

In any organization, it helps to know who is responsible for managing an OU. You can set this information on the Managed By tab (see Figure 7.5). The information specified on this tab is very convenient because it is automatically pulled from the contact information on a user record. You should consider always having a contact for each OU within your organization so that users and other systems administrators know whom to contact if they need to make any changes.

FIGURE 7.4   The General tab of the OU's Properties dialog box

FIGURE 7.5   The Managed By tab of the OU's Properties dialog box

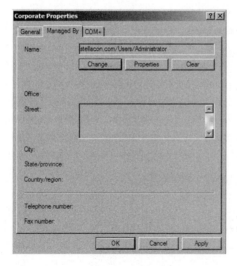

Delegating Control of OUs

In simple environments, one or a few systems administrators may be responsible for managing all of the settings within Active Directory. For example, a single systems administrator could manage all users within all OUs in the environment. In larger organizations, however, roles and responsibilities may be divided among many different individuals. A typical situation is one in which a systems administrator is responsible for objects within only a few OUs in an Active Directory domain. Or, one systems administrator might manage User and Group objects while another is responsible for managing file and print services.

Fortunately, using the Active Directory Users And Computers tool, you can quickly and easily ensure that specific users receive only the permissions they need. In Exercise 7.3, you will use the *Delegation of Control Wizard* to assign permissions to individuals. In order to successfully complete these steps, you must first have created the objects in the previous exercises of this chapter.

EXERCISE 7.3

Using the Delegation of Control Wizard

1. Open the Active Directory Users And Computers administrative tool.

2. Right-click the Corporate OU within the North America OU and select Delegate Control. This starts the Delegation of Control Wizard. Click Next to begin configuring security settings.

3. In the Users Or Groups page, click the Add button. In the Enter The Object Names To Select field, enter **Account Operators** and press Enter. Click Next to continue.

4. In the Tasks To Delegate page, select Delegate The Following Common Tasks and place a check mark next to the following items:

   Create, Delete, And Manage User Accounts

   Reset User Passwords And Force Password Change At Next Logon

   Read All User Information

   Create, Delete, And Manage Groups

   Modify The Membership Of A Group

   Click Next to continue.

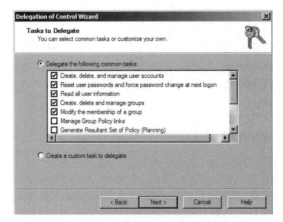

5. The Completing The Delegation of Control Wizard page then provides a summary of the operations you have selected. To implement the changes, click Finish.

Although the common tasks available through the wizard are sufficient for many delegation operations, you may have cases in which you want more control. For example, you might want to give a particular systems administrator permissions to modify only Computer objects. Exercise 7.4 uses the Delegation of Control Wizard to assign more granular permissions. In order to successfully complete these steps, you must first have completed the previous exercises in this chapter.

EXERCISE 7.4

Delegating Custom Tasks

1. Open the Active Directory Users And Computers administrative tool.

2. Right-click the Corporate OU within the North America OU and select Delegate Control. This starts the Delegation of Control Wizard. Click Next to begin making security settings.

3. In the Users Or Groups page, click the Add button. In the Enter The Object Names To Select field, enter **Server Operators** and press Enter. Click Next to continue.

4. In the Tasks To Delegate page, select the Create A Custom Task To Delegate radio button, and click Next to continue.

5. In the Active Directory Object Type page, choose Only The Following Objects In The Folder, and place a check mark next to the following items (you will have to scroll down to see them all):

User Objects

Computer Objects

Contact Objects

Group Objects

Organizational Unit Objects

Printer Objects

Click Next to continue.

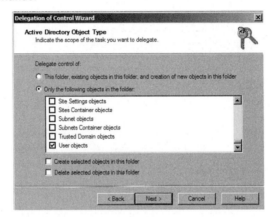

6. In the Permissions page, place a check mark next to the General option and make sure the other options are not checked. Note that if the various objects within your Active Directory schema had property-specific settings, you would see those options here. Place a check mark next to the following items:

Create All Child Objects

Read All Properties

Write All Properties

This gives the members of the Server Operators group the ability to create new objects within the Corporate OU and the permissions to read and write all properties for these objects. Click Next to continue.

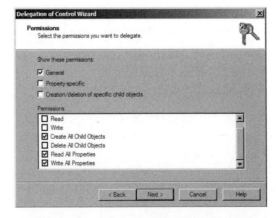

EXERCISE 7.4 *(continued)*

7. Click Next to continue.

8. The Completing The Delegation of Control Wizard page provides a summary of the operations you have selected. To implement the changes, click Finish.

 **Real World Scenario**

Delegation: Who's Responsible for What?

You're the IT director for a large, multinational organization. You've been with the company for quite a while—since the environment had only a handful of offices and a few network and systems administrators. But times have changed. Systems administrators must now coordinate the efforts of hundreds of IT staffers in 14 countries.

When the environment ran under a Windows NT 4 domain environment, the network was set up with many domains. For security, performance, and distribution of administration reasons, the computing resources in each major office were placed in their own domain. You have recently decided to move to Active Directory and to consolidate the numerous Windows NT domains into a single Active Directory domain. However, securely administering a distributed environment is still an important concern. So, the challenge involves determining how to coordinate the efforts of different systems administrators.

Fortunately, through the proper use of OUs and delegation, you are given a lot of flexibility in determining how to handle the administration. You can structure the administration in several ways. First, if you choose to create OUs based on geographic business structure, you could delegate control of these OUs based on the job functions of various systems administrators. For example, you could use one user account to administer the Europe OU. Within the Europe OU, this systems administrator could delegate control of offices represented by the Paris and London OUs. Within these OUs, you could further break down the administrative responsibilities for printer queue operators and security administrators.

Alternatively, the OU structure may create a functional representation of the business. For example, the Engineering OU might contain other OUs that are based on office locations such as New York and Paris. A systems administrator of the Engineering domain could delegate permissions based on geography or job functions to the lower OUs. Regardless of whether you build a departmental, functional, or geographical OU model, keep in mind that each model excludes other models. This is one of the most important decisions you need to make. When you are making this decision or modifying previous decisions, your overriding concern is how it will affect the management and administration of the network. The good news is that because Active Directory has so many features, the model you choose can be based on specific business requirements rather than imposed by architectural constraints.

Troubleshooting OUs

In general, you should find using OUs to be straightforward and relatively painless. With adequate planning, you'll be able to implement an intuitive and useful structure for OU objects.

The most common problems with OU configuration are related to the OU structure. When troubleshooting OUs, pay careful attention to the following factors:

Inheritance By default, Group Policy and other settings are transferred automatically from parent OUs to child OUs and objects. Even if a specific OU is not given a set of permissions, objects within that OU might still get them from parent objects.

Delegation of administration If you allow the wrong user accounts or groups to perform specific tasks on OUs, you might be violating your company's security policy. Be sure to verify the delegations you have made at each OU level.

Organizational issues Sometimes, business practices do not easily map to the structure of Active Directory. A few misplaced OUs, user accounts, computer accounts, or groups can make administration difficult or inaccurate. In many cases, it might be beneficial to rearrange the OU structure to accommodate any changes in the business organization. In others, it might make more sense to change business processes.

If you regularly consider each of these issues when troubleshooting problems with OUs, you will be much less likely to make errors in the Active Directory configuration.

Creating and Managing Active Directory Objects

Now that you are familiar with the task of creating OUs, you should find creating and managing other Active Directory objects quite simple. The following sections look at the details.

Overview of Active Directory Objects

When you install and configure a domain controller, Active Directory sets up some organization for you, and you can create and manage several types of objects. This section describes these features.

Active Directory Organization

By default, after you install and configure a domain controller, you will see the following organizational sections within the Active Directory Users And Computers tool (they look like folders):

Built-In The Built-In container includes all of the standard groups that are installed by default when you promote a domain controller. You can use these groups to administer the servers in your environment. Examples include the Administrators group, Backup Operators, and Print Operators.

Computers   By default, the Computers container contains a list of the workstations in your domain. From here, you can manage all of the computers in your domain.

Domain Controllers   The Domain Controllers container includes a list of all of the domain controllers for the domain.

Foreign security principals   *Foreign security principals* are any objects to which security can be assigned and that are not part of the current domain. *Security principals* are Active Directory objects to which permissions can be applied, and they can be used to manage permissions in Active Directory.

Users   The Users container includes all of the security accounts that are part of the domain. When you first install the domain controller, there will be several groups in this container. For example, the Domain Admins group and the Administrator account are created in this container.

Active Directory Objects

You can create and manage several different types of Active Directory objects. The following are specific object types:

Computer   Computer objects represent workstations that are part of the Active Directory domain. All computers within a domain share the same security database, including user and group information. Computer objects are useful for managing security permissions and enforcing Group Policy restrictions.

Contact   *Contact objects* are usually used in OUs to specify the main administrative contact. Contacts are not security principals like users. They are used to specify information about individuals within the organization.

Group   *Group objects* are logical collections of users primarily for assigning security permissions to resources. When managing users, you should place them into groups and then assign permissions to the group. This allows for flexible management without the need to set permissions for individual users.

Organizational Unit   An OU object is created to build a hierarchy within the Active Directory domain. It is the smallest unit that can be used to create administrative groupings, and it can be used to assign group policies. Generally, the OU structure within a domain reflects a company's business organization.

Printer   *Printer objects* map to printers.

Shared Folder   *Shared Folder objects* map to server shares. They are used to organize the various file resources that may be available on file/print servers. Often, Shared Folder objects are used to give logical names to specific file collections. For example, systems administrators might create separate shared folders for common applications, user data, and shared public files.

User   A *User object* is the fundamental security principal on which Active Directory is based. User accounts contain information about individuals, as well as password and other permission information.

InetOrgPerson   The *InetOrgPerson object* is an Active Directory object that defines attributes of users in Lightweight Directory Access Protocol (LDAP) and X.500 directories.

MSMQ Queue Alias   An *MSMQ Queue Alias object* is an Active Directory object for the MSMQ-Custom-Recipient class type. The MSMQ (Microsoft Message Queuing) Queue Alias object associates an Active Directory path and a user-defined alias with a public, private, or direct single-element format name. This allows a queue alias to be used to reference a queue that might not be listed in Active Directory Domain Services (AD DS).

Creating Objects Using the Active Directory Users And Computers Tool

Exercise 7.5 walks you through the steps you need to take to create various objects within an Active Directory domain. In this exercise, you create some basic Active Directory objects. In order to complete this exercise, you must have access to at least one Active Directory domain controller and you should have also completed the previous exercises in this chapter.

EXERCISE 7.5

Creating Active Directory Objects

1. Open the Active Directory Users And Computers tool.

2. Expand the current domain to list the objects currently contained within it. For this exercise you will use the second- and third-level OUs contained within the North America top-level OU, as shown in the following graphic.

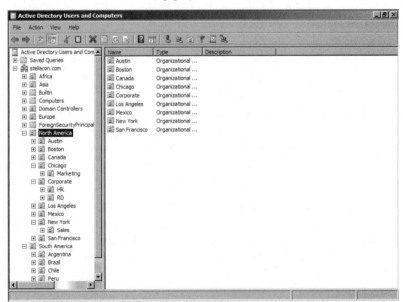

3. Right-click the Corporate OU, and select New ➢ User. Fill in the following information:

   First Name: **Maria**

   Initial: **D**

   Last Name: **President**

   Full Name: (leave as default)

   User Logon Name: **mdpresident** (leave default domain)

Click Next to continue.

4. Enter in "**P@ssw0rd**" for the password for this user, and then confirm it. Note that you can also make changes to password settings here. Click Next.

5. You will see a summary of the user information. Click Finish to create the new user.

6. Click on the RD container and create another user in that container with the following information:

    First Name: **John**

    Initials: **Q**

    Last Name: **Admin**

    Full Name: (leave as default)

    User Logon Name: **jqadmin** (leave default domain)

    Click Next to continue.

7. Assign the password "**P@ssw0rd**". Click Next, and then click Finish to create the user.

8. Right-click the RD OU, and select New ➢ Contact. Use the following information to fill in the properties of the Contact object:

    First Name: **Jane**

    Initials: **R**

    Last Name: **Admin**

    Display Name: **jradmin**

    Click OK to create the new Contact object.

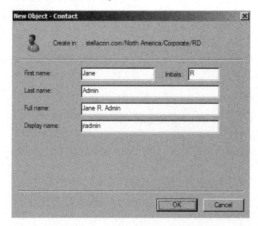

9. Right-click the RD OU, and select New ➤ Shared Folder. Enter **Software** for the name and
`\\server1\applications` for the network path (also known as the Universal Naming Convention [UNC] path). Note that you can create the object even though this resource (the
physical server) does not exist. Click OK to create the Shared Folder object.

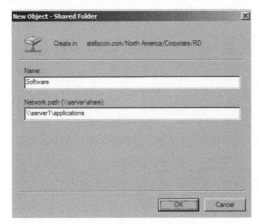

10. Right-click the HR OU, and select New ➤ Group. Type **All Users** for the group name. Do
not change the value in the Group Name (Pre–Windows 2000) field. For the Group Scope,
select Global, and for the Group Type, select Security. To create the group, click OK.

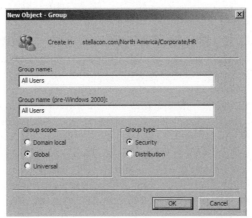

11. Right-click the Sales OU and select New ➤ Computer. Type **Workstation1** for the name of the computer. Notice that the pre–Windows 2000 name is automatically populated and that, by default, the members of the Domain Admins group are the only ones that can add this computer to the domain. Place a check mark in the Assign This Computer Account As A Pre–Windows 2000 Computer box, and then click OK to create the Computer object.

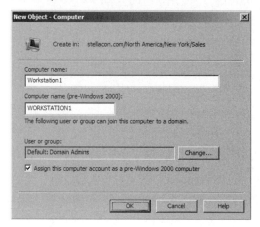

12. Close the Active Directory Users And Computers tool.

Importing Objects from a File

In Exercise 7.5 we created an account using the Active Directory Users And Computers tools. But what if we needed to bulk import accounts? There are two main applications for doing bulk imports of accounts: the `ldifde.exe` utility and the `csvde.exe` utility. Both utilities import accounts from files.

The `ldifde` utility imports from line-delimited files. This utility allows an administrator to export and import data, thus allowing batch operations like Add, Modify, and Delete to be performed in Active Directory. Windows Server 2008 includes `ldifde.exe` to help support batch operations.

`csvde.exe` performs the same export functions as `ldifde.exe`, but `csvde.exe` uses a comma-separated file format. The `csvde.exe` utility does not allow administrators to modify or delete objects. It only supports adding objects to Active Directory.

Active Directory Migration Tool (ADMT) v3

Another tool you can use to help import and migrate users is the Active Directory Migration Tool (ADMT) v3. The ADMT v3 allows an administrator to migrate users, groups, and computers from a Microsoft Windows NT 4.0 domain to a Windows Server 2008 Active Directory domain.

Administrators can also use the ADMT v3 to migrate users, groups, and computers between Active Directory domains in different forests (interforest migration) and between Active Directory domains in the same forest (intraforest migration).

ADMT v3 also helps administrators perform security translations from a Windows NT 4.0 domain to a Windows Server 2008 Active Directory domain. ADMT v3 will also allow the security translations between Active Directory domains in different forests.

Managing Object Properties

Once you've created the necessary Active Directory objects, you'll probably need to make changes to their default properties. In addition to the settings you made when you were creating Active Directory objects, you can configure several more properties. In addition, you can access object properties by right-clicking any object and selecting Properties from the pop-up menu.

Each object type contains a unique set of properties.

User Object Properties

The following list describes some of the properties of a user object.

- General: General account information about this user
- Address: Physical location information about this user
- Account: User logon name and other account restrictions, such as workstation restrictions and logon hours
- Profile: Information about the user's roaming profile settings
- Telephones: Telephone contact information for the user
- Organization: The user's title, department, and company information
- Member Of: Group membership information for the user
- Dial-In: Remote Access Service (RAS) permissions for the user
- Environment: Logon and other network settings for the user
- Sessions: Session limits, including maximum session time and idle session settings
- Remote Control: Remote control options for this user's session
- Terminal Services Profile: Information about the user's profile for use with Terminal Services
- COM+: Specifies a COM+ partition set for the user

Computer Object Properties

Computer objects have different properties than user objects. Computer objects refer to the systems that clients are operating to be part of a domain. The following list describes some computer object properties.

- General: Information about the name of the computer, the role of the computer, and its description

   You can enable an option to allow the Local System Account of this machine to request services from other servers. This is useful if the machine is a trusted and secure computer.
- Operating System: The name, version, and service pack information for the operating system running on the computer

- Member Of: Active Directory groups that this Computer object is a member of
- Location: A description of the computer's physical location
- Managed By: Information about the User or Contact object that is responsible for managing this computer
- Dial-in: Sets dial-in options for the computer

Setting Properties for Active Directory Objects

Now that you have seen the various properties that can be set for the Active Directory objects, let's go through an exercise on how to configure some of these properties.

Exercise 7.6 walks you through how to set various properties for Active Directory objects. In order to complete the steps in this exercise, you must have first completed Exercise 7.5.

 Although it may seem somewhat tedious, it's always a good idea to enter as much information as you know about Active Directory objects when you create them. Although the name Printer1 may be meaningful to you, users will appreciate the additional information when they are searching for objects.

EXERCISE 7.6

Managing Object Properties

1. Open the Active Directory Users And Computers tool.

2. Expand the name of the domain, and select the RD container. Right-click the John Q. Admin user account, and select Properties.

3. Here, you will see the various Properties tabs for the User account. Make some configuration changes based on your personal preferences. Click OK to continue.

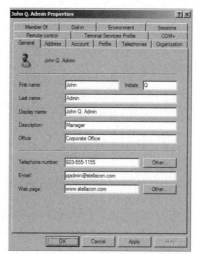

EXERCISE 7.6 *(continued)*

4. Select the HR OU. Right-click the All Users group, and click Properties. In the All Users Properties dialog box, you will be able to modify the membership of the group.

Click the Members tab, and then click Add. Add the Maria D. President and John Q. Admin User accounts to the Group. Click OK to save the settings and then OK to accept the group modifications.

5. Select the Sales OU. Right-click the Workstation1 Computer object. Notice that you can choose to disable the account or reset it (to allow another computer to join the domain under that same name). From the right-click menu, choose Properties. You'll see the properties for the Computer object.

Examine the various options and make changes based on your personal preference. After you have examined the available options, click OK to continue.

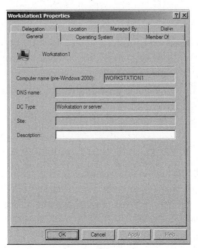

EXERCISE 7.6 *(continued)*

6. Select the Corporate OU. Right-click the Maria D. President User account, and choose Reset Password. You will be prompted to enter a new password and then you'll be asked to confirm it. Note that you can also force the user to change this password upon the next logon and you can also unlock the user's account from here. For this exercise, do not enter a new password; just choose Cancel.

7. Close the Active Directory Users And Computers tool.

By now, you have probably noticed that Active Directory objects have a lot of common options. For example, Group and Computer objects both have a Managed By tab.

Windows Server 2008 allows you to manage many user objects at once. For instance, you can select several user objects by holding down the Shift or Ctrl key while selecting. You can then right-click any one of the selected objects and select Properties to display the properties that are available for multiple users. Notice that not every user property is available, because some properties are unique to each user. You can configure the description field for multiple object selections that include both users and non-users, such as computers and groups.

A very important thing to think about when it comes to accounts is the difference between disabling an account and deleting an account. When you delete an account, the Security ID (SID) gets deleted. Even if you later create an account with the same username, it will have a different SID number and therefore, it will be a different account.

It is sometime better to disable an account and place it into a non-active OU called Disabled. This way if you ever need to re-access the account, you can do so.

Another object management task is the process of deprovisioning. Deprovisioning is managing Active Directory objects in the connector space (discussed in Chapter 6, "Configuring Server Roles"). To learn more about deprovisioning, visit Microsoft's website.

As was mentioned earlier, it's always a good idea to enter in as much information as possible about an object. This allows systems administrators and users alike to get the most out of Active Directory and its properties.

Understanding Groups

Now that you know how to create user accounts, it's time to learn how to create group accounts. As instructors, we are always amazed when students (who work in the IT field) have no idea why they should use groups. This is something every organization should be using.

To illustrate their usefulness, let's say we have a Sales department user by the name of wpanek. Our organization has 100 resources shared on the network for users to access.

Because wpanek is part of the Sales department, he has access to 50 of the resources. The other 50 are used by the Marketing department. If the organization is not using groups, and wpanek moves from Sales to Marketing, how many changes do we have to make? The answer is 100. We have to move him out of the 50 resources he currently can use and place his account in the 50 new resources that he now needs.

Now, let's say that we use groups. The Sales group has access to 50 resources and the Marketing group has access to the other 50. If wpanek moves from Sales to Marketing, we only need to make two changes. We just have to take wpanek out of the Sales group and place him in the Marketing group; after this is done wpanek can access everything he needs to do his job.

Group Properties

Now that you understand why you should use groups, let's go over setting up groups and their properties. When you are creating groups, it helps to understand some of the options that you need to use.

Group Type   You can choose from two group types—Security groups and Distribution groups.

- Security groups can have rights and permissions placed on them. For example, if you wanted to give a certain group of users access to a particular printer, but you wanted to control what the were allowed to do with this printer, you'd create a Security group and then apply certain rights and permissions to this group.

- Security groups can also receive emails. If someone sent an email to the group, all users within that group would receive it.

- Distribution groups are used for email *only*. You cannot place permissions and rights for objects on this group type.

Group Scope   When it comes to group scopes, your choices depend on what domain function level (discussed in Chapter 3, "Active Directory Planning and Installation") you are working with. If you are in Native mode (Windows 2000 Native, 2003, or 2008) you will have three choices:

Domain local groups   Domain local groups are groups that remain in the domain in which they were created. You use these groups to grant permissions within a single domain. For example, if you create a domain local group named HPLaser, you cannot use that group in any other domain and it has to reside in the domain in which you created it.

You can create domain local groups in domain Mixed or Native modes.

Global group   Global groups can contain other groups and accounts from the domain in which the group is created. In addition, you can give them permissions in any domain in the forest.

Global groups can be created in domain Mixed or Native modes.

Universal groups   Universal groups can include other groups and accounts from any domain in the domain tree or forest. You can give universal groups permissions in any domain in the domain tree or forest.

You can create universal groups *only* if you are in a domain Native mode.

Creating Group Strategies

When you are creating a group strategy, think of this acronym that Microsoft likes to use during the exam: AGDLP (or AGLP). This acronym stands for a series of actions you should perform. It always applies in Mixed mode and you can also apply it in Native mode. Here is how it expands:

A = Accounts (Create your user accounts.)

G = Global groups (Put user accounts into global groups.)

DL = Domain local groups (Put global groups into domain local groups.)

P = Permissions (Assign permissions like Deny or Apply on the domain local group.)

Another acronym that stands for a strategy you can use is AUDLP (or AULP). This is always used in native mode. Here is how it expands:

A = Accounts (Create your user accounts.)

U = Universal groups (Put the user accounts into universal groups.)

DL = Domain local groups (Put universal groups into domain local groups.)

P = Permissions (Place permissions on the local group.)

Creating a Group

To create a new group, open the Active Directory Users And Computers snap-in. Click the OU where the group is going to reside. Right-click and choose New and then Group. After you create the group, just click the Members tab and choose Add. Add the users that you want to reside in that group, and that's all there is to it.

Filtering and Advanced Active Directory Features

The Active Directory Users And Computers tool has a couple of other features that come in quite handy when you are managing many objects. You can access the Filter Options dialog box by clicking the View menu in the MMC and choosing Filter Options. You'll see a dialog box similar to the one shown in Figure 7.6. Here, you can choose to filter objects by their specific types within the display. For example, if you are an administrator who works primarily with user accounts and groups, you can select those specific items by placing check marks in the list. In addition, you can create more complex filters by choosing Create Custom. Doing so provides you with an interface that looks similar to that of the Find command.

Another option in the Active Directory Users And Computers tool is to view Advanced options. You can enable the Advanced options by choosing Advanced Features in the View menu. This adds two top-level folders to the list under the name of the domain.

The System folder (shown in Figure 7.7) provides additional features that you can configure to work with Active Directory. You can configure settings for the Distributed File System (DFS), IP Security (IPSec) policies, the File Replication Service (FRS), and more. In addition to the System folder, you'll see the LostAndFound folder. This folder contains any files that may not have been replicated properly between domain controllers. You should check this folder periodically for any files so that you can decide whether you need to move them or copy them to other locations.

FIGURE 7.6   The Filter Options dialog box

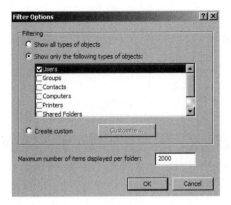

FIGURE 7.7   Advanced Features in the System folder of the Active Directory Users And Computers tool

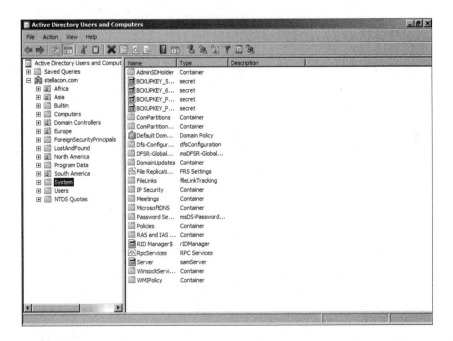

As you can see, managing Active Directory objects is generally a simple task. The Active Directory Users And Computers tool allows you to configure several objects. Let's move on to look at one more common administration function—moving objects.

Moving, Renaming, and Deleting Active Directory Objects

One of the extremely useful features of the Active Directory Users And Computers tool is its ability to easily move users and resources.

Exercise 7.7 walks you through the process of moving Active Directory objects. In this exercise, you will make several changes to the organization of Active Directory objects. In order to complete this exercise, you must have first completed Exercise 7.5.

EXERCISE 7.7

Moving Active Directory Objects

1. Open the Active Directory Users And Computers tool, and expand the name of the domain.

2. Select the Sales OU (Under the New York OU), right-click Workstation1, and select Move. A dialog box appears. Select the RD OU, and click OK to move the Computer object to that container.

3. Click the RD OU, and verify that Workstation1 was moved.

4. Close the Active Directory Users And Computers tool.

In addition to moving objects within Active Directory, you can also easily rename them by right-clicking an object and selecting Rename. Note that this option does not apply to all objects. For example, in order to prevent security breaches, Computer objects cannot be renamed.

You can remove objects from Active Directory by right-clicking them and choosing Delete.

Deleting an Active Directory object is an irreversible action. When an object is destroyed, any security permissions or other settings made for that object are removed as well. Because each object within Active Directory contains its own security identifier (SID), simply re-creating an object with the same name does not place any permissions on it. Before you delete an Active Directory object, be sure that you will never need it again.

Windows Server 2008 has a check box, "Protect container from accidental deletion," for all OUs. If this check box is checked, to delete or move an OU, you must go into the Active Directory Users And Computers Advanced options. Once you are in Advanced options, you can uncheck the box to move or delete the OU.

Resetting an Existing Computer Account

Every computer on the domain establishes a discrete channel of communication with the domain controller at logon time. The domain controller stores a randomly selected password (different from the user password) for authentication across the channel. The password is updated every 30 days.

Sometimes the computer's password and the domain controller's password don't match, and communication between the two machines fails. Without the ability to reset the computer account, you wouldn't be able to connect the machine to the domain. Fortunately, you can use the Active Directory Users And Computers tool to reestablish the connection.

Exercise 7.8 shows you how to reset an existing computer account. You should have completed the previous exercises in this chapter before you begin this exercise.

EXERCISE 7.8

Resetting an Existing Computer Account

1. Open the Active Directory Users And Computers tool and expand the name of the domain.

2. Click the RD OU, and then right-click the Workstation1 computer account.

3. Select Reset Account from the context menu. Click Yes to confirm your selection. Click OK at the success prompt.

4. When you reset the account, you break the connection between the computer and the domain, so after performing this exercise, reconnect the computer if you want it to continue working on the network.

Publishing Active Directory Objects

One of the main goals of Active Directory is to make resources easy to find. Two of the most commonly used resources in a networked environment are server file shares and printers. These are so common, in fact, that most organizations have dedicated file and print servers. When it comes to managing these types of resources, Active Directory makes it easy to determine which files and printers are available to users.

With that said, take a look at how Active Directory manages to publish shared folders and printers.

Making Active Directory Objects Available to Users

An important aspect of managing Active Directory objects is that a systems administrator can control which objects users can see. The act of making an Active Directory object available is known as *publishing*. The two main publishable objects are Printer objects and Shared Folder objects.

The general process for creating server shares and shared printers has remained unchanged from previous versions of Windows: You create the various objects (a printer or a file system folder) and then enable them for sharing.

To make these resources available via Active Directory, however, there's an additional step: You must publish the resources. Once an object has been published in Active Directory, clients will be able to use it.

You can also publish Windows NT 4 resources through Active Directory by creating Active Directory objects as you did in Exercise 7.5. When you publish objects in Active Directory, you should know the server name and share name of the resource. When system administrators use Active Directory objects, they can change the resource to which the object points without having to reconfigure or even notify clients. For example, if you move a share from one server to another, all you need to do is update the Shared Folder object's properties to point to the new location. Active Directory clients still refer to the resource with the same path and name as they used before.

Without Active Directory, Windows NT 4 shares and printers are accessible only by using NetBIOS-based shares. If you're planning to disable the NetBIOS protocol in your environment, you must be sure that these resources have been published or they will not be accessible.

Publishing Printers

Printers can be published easily within Active Directory. This makes them available to users in your domain.

Exercise 7.9 walks you through the steps you need to take to share and publish a Printer object by having you create and share a printer. In order to complete the printer installation, you need access to the Windows Server 2008 installation media (via the hard disk, a network share, or the CD-ROM drive).

EXERCISE 7.9

Creating and Publishing a Printer

1. Click Start ➢ Control Panel ➢ Printers ➢ Add Printer. This starts the Add Printer Wizard.

2. In the Choose A Local Or Network Printer page, select Add A Local Printer. This should automatically take you to the next page. If it does not, Click Next.

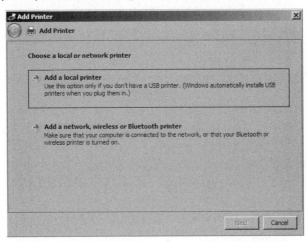

3. In the Choose A Printer Port page, select Use An Existing Port. From the drop-down list beside that option, make sure LPT1: (Printer Port) is selected. Click Next.

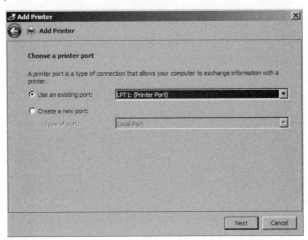

4. On the Install The Printer Driver page, select Generic for the manufacturer, and for the printer, highlight Generic / Text Only. Click Next.

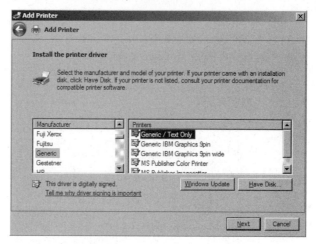

5. On the Type A Printer Name page, type **Text Printer**. Uncheck the Set As The Default Printer box and then click Next.

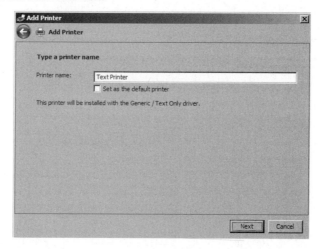

6. The Installing Printer screen appears. After the system is finished, the Printer Sharing page appears. Make sure the box labeled "Share this printer so that others on your network can find and use it" is selected and accept the default share name of Text Printer.

7. In the Location section, type **Building 203,** and in the Comment section, add the following comment: **This is a text-only Printer.** Click Next.

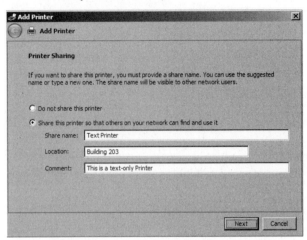

8. On the You've Successfully Added Text Printer page, click Finish.

9. Next, you need to verify that the printer will be listed in Active Directory. Click Start ➢ Control Panel ➢ Printers, then right-click the Text Printer icon and select Properties.

EXERCISE 7.9 *(continued)*

10. Next, select the Sharing tab, and ensure that the List In The Directory box is checked. Note that you can also add additional printer drivers for other operating systems using this tab. Click OK to accept the settings.

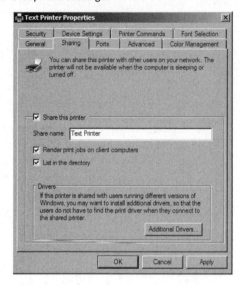

Note that when you create and share a printer this way, an Active Directory Printer object is not displayed within the Active Directory Users And Computers tool. The printer is actually associated with the Computer object to which it is connected. Printer objects in Active Directory are manually created for sharing printers from Windows NT 4 and earlier shared printer resources.

Publishing Shared Folders

Now that you've created and published a printer, you'll see how the same thing can be done to shared folders.

Exercise 7.10 walks through the steps required to create a folder, share it, and then publish it in Active Directory. This exercise assumes that you are using the C: partition; however, you may want to change this based on your server configuration. This exercise assumes that you have completed Exercise 7.5.

EXERCISE 7.10

Creating and Publishing a Shared Folder

1. Create a new folder in the root directory of your C: partition, and name it **Test Share**.

2. Right-click the Test Share. Choose Share.

3. In the File Sharing dialog box, enter the names of users you want to share this folder with. In the upper box, enter **Everyone,** then click Add. Note that Everyone appears in the lower box. Click in the Permission Level column next to Everyone and choose Contributor from the pop-up menu. Then click Share.

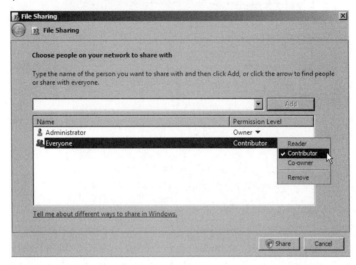

4. You see a message that your folder has been shared. Click Done.

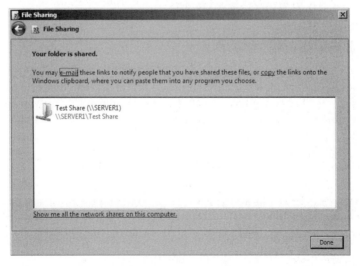

5. Open the Active Directory Users And Computers tool. Expand the current domain, and right-click the RD OU. Select New ➢ Shared Folder.

6. In the New Object - Shared Folder dialog box, type **Shared Folder Test** for the name of the folder. Then type the UNC path to the share (for example, **\\server1\Test Share**). Click OK to create the share.

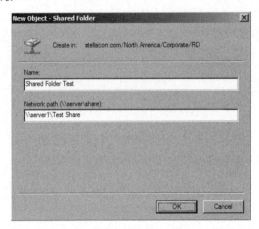

Once you have created and published the Shared Folder object, clients can use the My Network Places icon to find this object. The Shared Folder object will be organized based on the OU in which you created the Shared Folder object. When you use publication, you can see how this makes it easy to manage shared folders.

Querying Active Directory

So far you've created several Active Directory resources. One of the main benefits of having all of your resource information in Active Directory is that you can easily find what you're looking for using the Find dialog box. Recall that we recommended that you should always enter as much information as possible when creating Active Directory objects. This is where that extra effort begins to pay off.

Exercise 7.11 walks you through the steps to find specific objects in Active Directory. In order to complete this exercise, you must have first completed Exercise 7.5.

EXERCISE 7.11

Finding Objects in Active Directory

1. Open the Active Directory Users And Computers tool.

2. Right-click the name of the domain and select Find.

Publishing Active Directory Objects

EXERCISE 7.11 *(continued)*

3. In the Find Users, Contacts, And Groups dialog box, select Users, Contacts, And Groups from the Find drop-down list. For the In setting, choose Entire Directory. This searches the entire Active Directory environment for the criteria you enter.

   Note that if this is a production domain and there are many objects, searching the whole directory may be a time-consuming and network-intensive operation.

4. In the Name field, type **admin** and then click Find Now to obtain the results of the search.

5. Now that you have found several results, you can narrow down the list. Click the Advanced tab of the Find Users, Contacts, And Groups dialog box.

In the Field drop-down list, select User ➢ Last Name. For Condition, select Starts With, and for Value, type **admin**. Click Add to add this condition to the search criteria. Click Find Now. Now only the Users that have the last name Admin are shown.

6. When you have finished searching, close the Find Users, Contacts, And Groups dialog box and exit the Active Directory Users And Computers tool.

Using the many options available in the Find dialog box, you can usually narrow down the objects you're searching for quickly and efficiently. Users and systems administrators alike find this tool useful in environments of any size.

Summary

In this chapter, we covered the fundamentals of administering Active Directory. The most important part of administering Active Directory is learning about how to work with OUs. As a result, you should be aware of the purpose of OUs—they help you to organize and manage the directory. For instance, think of administrative control. If you wanted to delegate rights to another administrator (such as a sales manager), you could delegate that authority to that user within the SALES OU. As the systems administrator, you retain the rights to the castle.

We also looked at how to design an OU structure from an example. In our example, we looked at how to design proper OU layout. Once we finished designing, we looked at how to create, organize, and reorganize OUs if need be.

In addition, we took a look at groups and group strategies. We discussed the different types of groups—domain local, global, and universal groups. We talked about when each group is available and when to use each group.

Lastly, we covered how to use the Active Directory Users And Computers tool to manage Active Directory objects. If you're responsible for day-to-day systems administration, there's a good chance that you are already familiar with this tool, but if not, you should be now. Using this tool, you learned how to work with Active Directory objects such as Users, Computers, and Groups. You also learned how to import users by doing a bulk import and the two different file types that work for bulk imports. Bulk imports allow you to import multiple users without the need of adding one user at a time.

Exam Essentials

Understand the purpose of OUs.   OUs are used to create a hierarchical, logical organization for objects within an Active Directory domain.

Know the types of objects that can reside within OUs.   OUs can contain Active Directory User, Computer, Shared Folder, and other objects.

Understand how to use the Delegation of Control Wizard.   The Delegation of Control Wizard is used to assign specific permissions at the level of OUs.

Understand the concept of inheritance.   By default, child OUs inherit permissions and Group Policy assignments set for parent OUs. However, these settings can be overridden for more granular control of security.

Know groups and group strategies   We can use three groups in Native mode: domain local, global, and universal. Understand that universal groups cannot be created in Mixed mode. Understand the group strategies and when they apply.

Understand how Active Directory objects work.   Active Directory objects represent some piece of information about components within a domain. The objects themselves have attributes that describe details about them.

Understand how Active Directory objects can be organized.   By using the Active Directory Users And Computers tool, you can create, move, rename, and delete various objects.

Understand how to import bulk users.   You can import multiple accounts by doing a bulk import. Bulk imports use files to import the data into Active Directory. Know the two utilities (`ldifde.exe` and `csvde.exe`) you need to use to perform the bulk imports and how to use them.

Learn how resources can be published.   A design goal for Active Directory was to make network resources easier for users to find. With that in mind, you should understand how using published printers and shared folders can simplify network resource management.

Review Questions

1. Gabriel is responsible for administering a small Active Directory domain. Recently, the Engineering department within his organization has been divided into two departments. He wants to reflect this organizational change within Active Directory and plans to rename various groups and resources. Which of the following operations can he perform using the Active Directory Users And Computers tool? (Choose all that apply.)

   A. Renaming an organizational unit

   B. Querying for resources

   C. Renaming a group

   D. Creating a computer account

2. You are a domain administrator for a large domain. Recently, you have been asked to make changes to some of the permissions related to OUs within the domain. In order to further restrict security for the Texas OU, you remove some permissions at that level. Later, a junior systems administrator mentions that she is no longer able to make changes to objects within the Austin OU (which is located within the Texas OU). Assuming no other changes have been made to Active Directory permissions, which of the following characteristics of OUs might have caused the change in permissions?

   A. Inheritance

   B. Group Policy

   C. Delegation

   D. Object properties

3. Isabel, a systems administrator, has created a new Active Directory domain in an environment that already contains two trees. During the promotion of the domain controller, she chose to create a new Active Directory forest. Isabel is a member of the Enterprise Administrators group and has full permissions over all domains. During the organization's migration to Active Directory, many updates have been made to the information stored within the domains. Recently, users and other system administrators have complained about not being able to find specific Active Directory objects in one or more domains (although the objects exist in others).

   In order to investigate the problem, Isabel wants to check for any objects that have not been properly replicated among domain controllers. If possible, she would like to restore these objects to their proper place within the relevant Active Directory domains.

Which two of the following actions should she perform to be able to view the relevant information?

A. Change Active Directory permissions to allow object information to be viewed in all domains.

B. Select the Advanced Features item in the View menu.

C. Promote a member server in each domain to a domain controller.

D. Rebuild all domain controllers from the latest backups.

E. Examine the contents of the LostAndFound folder using the Active Directory Users And Computers tool.

4. You are a consultant hired to evaluate an organization's Active Directory domain. The domain contains over 200,000 objects and hundreds of OUs. You begin examining the objects within the domain, but you find that the loading of the contents of specific OUs takes a very long time. Furthermore, the list of objects can be very large. You want to do the following:

- Use the built-in Active Directory administrative tools, and avoid the use of third-party tools or utilities.

- Limit the list of objects within an OU to only the type of objects that you're examining (for example, only Computer objects).

- Prevent any changes to the Active Directory domain or any of the objects within it.

Which one of the following actions meets the above requirements?

A. Use the Filter option in the Active Directory Users And Computers tool to restrict the display of objects.

B. Use the Delegation of Control Wizard to give yourself permissions over only a certain type of object.

C. Implement a new naming convention for objects within an OU and then sort the results using this new naming convention.

D. Use the Active Directory Domains And Trusts tool to view information from only selected domain controllers.

E. Edit the domain Group Policy settings to allow yourself to view only the objects of interest.

5. Your organization is currently planning a migration from a Windows NT 4 environment that consists of several domains to an Active Directory environment. Your staff consists of 25 system administrators who are responsible for managing one or more domains. The organization is finalizing a merger with another company.

John, a technical planner, has recently provided you with a preliminary plan to migrate your environment to several Active Directory domains. He has cited security and administration as major justifications for this plan. Jane, a consultant, has recommended that the Windows NT 4 domains be consolidated into a single Active Directory domain. Which of the following statements provide a valid justification to support Jane's proposal? (Choose all that apply.)

A. In general, OU structure is more flexible than domain structure.

B. In general, domain structure is more flexible than OU structure.

C. It is possible to create a distributed system administration structure for OUs by using delegation.

D. The use of OUs within a single domain can greatly increase the security of the overall environment.

6. Miguel is a junior-level systems administrator and he has basic knowledge about working with Active Directory. As his supervisor, you have asked Miguel to make several security-related changes to OUs within the company's Active Directory domain. You instruct Miguel to use the basic functionality provided in the Delegation of Control Wizard. Which of the following operations are represented as common tasks within the Delegation of Control Wizard? (Choose all that apply.)

A. Reset passwords on user accounts.

B. Manage Group Policy links.

C. Modify the membership of a group.

D. Create, delete, and manage groups.

7. You are the primary systems administrator for a large Active Directory domain. Recently, you have hired another systems administrator to offload some of your responsibilities. This systems administrator will be responsible for handling help desk calls and for basic user account management. You want to allow the new employee to have permissions to reset passwords for all users within a specific OU. However, for security, reasons, it's important that the user not be able to make permissions changes for objects within other OUs in the domain. Which of the following is the best way to do this?

A. Create a special administration account within the OU and grant it full permissions for all objects within Active Directory.

B. Move the user's login account into the OU that he or she is to administer.

C. Move the user's login account to an OU that contains the OU (that is, the parent OU of the one that he or she is to administer).

D. Use the Delegation of Control Wizard to assign the necessary permissions on the OU that he or she is to administer.

8. You have been hired as a consultant to assist in the design of an organization's Active Directory environment. Specifically, you are instructed to focus on the OU structure (others will be planning for technical issues). You begin by preparing a list of information that you need to create the OU structure for a single domain. Which of the following pieces of information is not vital to your OU design?

    A. Physical network topology

    B. Business organizational requirements

    C. System administration requirements

    D. Security requirements

9. You want to allow the Super Users group to create and edit new objects within the Corporate OU. Using the Delegation of Control Wizard, you choose the Super Users group and arrive at the following screen. Where would you click in order to add the ability to create and edit new objects in the Corporate OU?

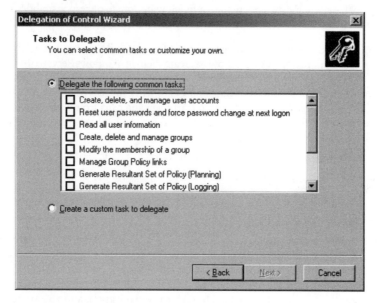

    A. Create, Delete, And Manage User Accounts

    B. Create, Delete And Manage Groups

    C. Manage Group Policy Links

    D. Create A Custom Task To Delegate

10. A systems administrator is using the Active Directory Users And Computers tool to view the objects within an OU. He has previously created many users, groups, and computers within this OU, but now only the users are showing. What is a possible explanation for this?

    A. Groups and computers are not normally shown in the Active Directory Users And Computers tool.

    B. Another systems administrator may have locked the groups, preventing others from accessing them.

    C. Filtering options have been set that specify that only User objects should be shown.

    D. The Group and Computer accounts have never been used and are, therefore, not shown.

11. The company you work for has a multilevel administrative team that is segmented by departments and locations. There are four major locations and you are in the Northeast group. You have been assigned to the administrative group that is responsible for creating and maintaining network shares for files and printers in your region. The last place you worked was a large Windows NT 4 network, where you had a much wider range of responsibilities. You are excited about the chance to learn more about Windows Server 2008.

    For your first task, you have been given a list of file and printer shares that need to be created for the users in your region. You ask how to create them in Windows Server 2008, and you are told that the process of creating a share is the same as with Windows NT. You create the shares and use NET USE to test them. Everything appears to work fine, so you send out a message that the shares are available. The next day, you start receiving calls from users who say that they cannot see any of resources that you created. What is the most likely reason for the calls from the users?

    A. You forgot to enable NetBIOS for the shares.

    B. You need to force replication for the shares to appear in the directory.

    C. You need to publish the shares in the directory.

    D. The shares will appear within the normal replication period.

12. Wilford Products has over 1,000 users in 5 locations across the country. The network consists of 4 servers and around 250 workstations in each location. One of the 4 servers in each location is a domain controller. As the new network administrator, you are now responsible for all aspects of the OUs within the directory. After meeting with the HR department, you have been informed that the vice president of sales has left the organization, and you are to remove his access to all resources on the network. You return to your office and remove his account from the directory. After you remove the account, you are immediately notified that you have been misinformed and the vice president of sales is not leaving the company. You quickly re-add him within the window of replication between the other domain controllers. What else must you do to reinstate his account and all his associated permissions?

    A. Nothing. Since you re-created the account before the replication window opened, the account will remain in the directory.

    B. Open the Tombstone folder and remove the object that is pending in order to remove the account before the replication window opens.

    C. After replication occurs, you need to manually synchronize his account in the domain controllers.

    D. You must re-establish every permission and setting manually.

13. You want to publish a printer to Active Directory. In the following screen, where would you click in order to accomplish this task?

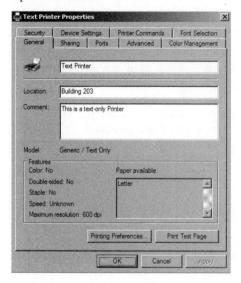

A. The Sharing tab

B. The Advanced tab

C. The Device Settings tab

D. The Printing Preferences button

14. You have inherited the administrator position of a network that has already completed its migration from Windows NT to Windows Server 2008. The network consists of a single domain that serves two locations with five servers at each site. The replication topology has proven to be solid, and the monitoring tasks that were in place when you arrived show no errors. Each site has two domain controllers for redundancy, each of which has a DNS server to support name resolution. Your first tasks are to learn how the directory has been designed and how the structure of the OUs is providing management capabilities to the domain. As you begin to settle in, you add some new users to the domain, but some of them complain that they cannot do what you have told them they could do. As you investigate the problem, you determine that Group Policy is not being applied when the users with the problems log on to the network. What are the possible reasons for this problem? (Choose all that apply.)

A. The policy has been blocked for the OU of which the users are members.

B. The users are not members of the OU that is subject to the Group Policy object.

C. The users are members of a security group whose Apply Group Policy ACE is set to Deny.

D. Policies must be applied to the specific OU that contains the users before they take effect.

15. A systems administrator creates a local Printer object, but it doesn't show up in Active Directory when a user executes a search for all printers. Which of the following are possible reasons for this? (Choose all that apply.)

    A. The printer was not shared.

    B. The List In Directory option is unchecked.

    C. The client does not have permissions to view the printer.

    D. The printer is malfunctioning.

16. As the network administrator for your company, you find that you need a plan for how to structure your OUs. You also need to accommodate the delegation of a few OUs to other administrators. Your current layout is as follows: you have a Sales department, a Marketing department, and an HR department. You need to plan and create OUs. You want to delegate control of each OU to each department supervisor. Which of the following solutions will help satisfy your plan?

    A. Build an OU called ADMIN, and then create three OUs below it called SALES, MARKET, and HR. Delegate control of each OU to each respective department head.

    B. Build an OU called SITEA, and then create two OUs below it called SALES and MARKET. Create a third OU under MARKET called HR. Delegate control of each OU to each respective department head.

    C. Build an OU called ADMIN, and then create three OUs below it called SALES, MARKET, and HR. Create Administrator accounts for each OU and then allow each to control their respective OUs.

    D. Build an OU called SITEA, and then create four OUs below it called SALES, ADMIN, MARKET, and HR. Delegate control of each OU to each respective department head and make sure that ADMIN keeps Executive Administrative privileges.

17. You are the Lead Administrator and Designer for your company. You have just installed the first of many Windows Server 2008 systems. You are building your infrastructure and now need to design the OU layout and implement it. You have to design an OU structure that includes the following departments: IT, HR, SALES, MARKETING, ENGINEERING, and CORPORATE. You also need to make sure that the supervisor within each department is able to manage each OU you create. You will need to delegate permissions. What is the best way to design your OU structure?

    A. Create an OU at the top level and call it DELEGATION. Create second-level OUs under DELEGATION and assign administrative rights to each. Create a policy that will allow each supervisor the right to manage the DELEGATION OU.

    B. Create an OU at the top level. Call it ADMIN1. Create IT, HR, SALES, MARKETING, ENGINEERING, and CORPORATE under ADMIN1. Set up delegation to the proper users for each OU.

    C. Design a top-level OU and create it with administrative rights. Name it US. Make an OU called COMP1 under US and then create SALES and MARKETING under it. Create a second OU called UK and create all the rest of the needed OUs under it. Rights will be assigned by default.

D. Create an OU at the top level. Call it TOP1. Create a Regional OU called US. Create IT1, HR1, SALES1, MARKETING1, ENGINEERING1, and CORPORATE1 under US1. Set up delegation to the proper users for each OU.

18. You are the network administrator responsible for administering and creating new OUs for your organization. You just changed an internal company name and need to make that change in Active Directory. Which of the following is the easiest way to make this change?

A. Rename the OU to SALESFORCE1.

B. Delete the OU and re-create it.

C. Using the Active Directory Sites And Services tool, use the Name option to make the change.

D. Create a new OU, name it SALESFORCE1, and delete the old OU.

19. As the lead systems administrator for your company, you are asked to delegate permissions to a user within the SALES OU. What tool is used to achieve this functionality? (Choose only one).

A. In Active Directory Sites And Services, right-click the OU where you want to delegate permissions and choose Delegate Control.

B. In Active Directory Trusts And Domains, right-click the OU where you want to delegate permissions and choose Delegate Control.

C. In Active Directory Users And Computers, right-click the OU where you want to delegate permissions and choose Delegate Control.

D. In Active Directory Domains And Forests, right-click the OU where you want to delegate permissions and choose Delegate Control.

20. You are asked to deploy Windows Server 2008 in your organization. You need to consider creating a management structure that will allow you to apply policies. What logical Active Directory object will allow you this functionality?

A. Containers

B. Forests

C. Domains

D. Organizational units (OUs)

Answers to Review Questions

1. A, B, C, D. The Active Directory Users And Computers tool was designed to simplify the administration of Active Directory objects. All of the above operations can be carried out using this tool.

2. A. Inheritance is the process by which permissions placed on parent OUs affect child OUs. In this example, the permissions change for the higher-level OU (Texas) automatically caused a change in permissions for the lower-level OU (Austin).

3. B, E. Enabling the Advanced Features item in the View menu will allow Isabel to see the LostAndFound and System folders. The LostAndFound folder contains information about objects that could not be replicated among domain controllers.

4. A. Through the use of filtering, you can choose which types of objects you want to see using the Active Directory Users And Computers tool. Several of the other choices may work, but they require changes to Active Directory settings or objects.

5. A, C. You can easily move and rename OUs without having to promote domain controllers and make network changes. This makes OU structure much more flexible and a good choice since the company may soon undergo a merger. Because security administration is important, delegation can be used to control administrative permissions at the OU level.

6. A, B, C, D. All of the options listed are common tasks presented in the Delegation of Control Wizard.

7. D. The Delegation of Control Wizard is designed to allow administrators to set up permissions on specific Active Directory objects.

8. A. OUs are created to reflect a company's logical organization. Because your focus is on the OU structure, you should be primarily concerned with business requirements. Other Active Directory features can be used to accommodate the network topology and technical issues (such as performance and scalability).

9. D. When you choose to delegate custom tasks, you have many more options for what you can delegate control of and what permissions you can apply. To do this, you must first select the Create A Custom Task To Delegate radio button, and then select the custom tasks. In this case, you would delegate control of Organizational Unit objects and set the permissions to Create All Child Objects, Read All Properties, and Write All Properties.

10. C. The filtering options would cause other objects to be hidden (although they still exist). Another explanation (but not one of the choices) is that a higher-level systems administrator modified the administrator's permissions using the Delegation of Control Wizard.

11. C. You need to publish shares in the directory before they are available to the users of the directory. If NetBIOS is still enabled on the network, the shares will be visible to the NetBIOS tools and clients, but you do not have to enable NetBIOS on shares. Although replication must occur before the shares are available in the directory, it is unlikely that the replication will not have occurred by the next day. If this is the case, then you have other problems with the directory as well.

12. D. When you delete an object in the directory, such as a user, it is gone and cannot be brought back. You could use a tape backup to bring an object back, but this would be a major undertaking for something like that and you would lose any other changes that occurred since the last backup. The best way to deal with an employee's leaving the organization is to disable the account and wait for a specified period before permanently removing it. In many cases, the person who replaces the former employee will need the same resources, so you can then simply rename the account, change the password, and re-enable the account for the new user.

13. A. The Sharing tab contains a check box that you can use to list the printer in Active Directory.

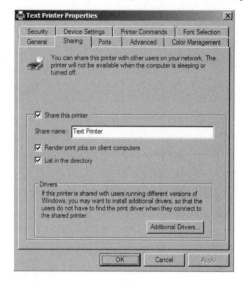

14. A, B, C. If you or a previous administrator has blocked a policy from flowing to an OU, then it will not apply to users in the OU. If the users are not in an OU that is subject to the policy, then the users will not receive that policy. If the users are members of a security group with an ACE set to Deny The Apply Group Policy, then it will block the policy. In general, policies flow down the directory tree if they are not blocked, so you do not have to apply the policy to each individual OU.

15. A, B, C. The first three reasons listed are explanations for why a printer may not show up within Active Directory. The printer will appear as an object in Active Directory even if it is malfunctioning.

16. A. The easiest way to achieve a desired result that is both easy to manage and secure is to build an OU called ADMIN, and then create three OUs below it called SALES, MARKET, and HR. Delegate control of each OU to each respective department head. If you do this, then you can retain control over the ADMIN OU and still be able to maintain control over your systems.

17. B. To lay out the OU design properly, you should consider the easiest possible way to get it done. In this example, that would be to create an administrative top-level OU and then branch off from there. This way, you can maintain control while still being able to delegate as you see fit. Also, your OU structure should be as simple as possible. You can make OUs by country code and so on—that is actually recommended—but you should also prepare for the future plans of the organization so that you do not have to do double the work.

18. A. The easiest way to achieve the desired result is to simply rename the OU.

19. C. If you need to delegate control, you can use Active Directory Users And Computers, right-click the OU where you want to delegate permissions, and choose Delegate Control.

20. D. OUs are extremely important to Active Directory's logical design. OUs allow you to delegate permissions, apply security, and so on.

Chapter

8

Configuring Group Policy Objects

MICROSOFT EXAM OBJECTIVES COVERED IN THIS CHAPTER:

✓ **Creating and Maintaining Active Directory Objects**

- Create and apply Group Policy objects (GPOs). May include but is not limited to: enforce OU hierarchy, block inheritance, and enabling user objects; group policy processing priority; WMI; RSoP; group policy filtering; group policy loopback

- Configure GPO templates. May include but is not limited to: user rights; ADMX Central Store; administrative templates; security templates; restricted groups; security options; starter GPOs; shell access policies

- Configure software deployment GPOs. May include but is not limited to: publishing to users; assigning software to users; assigning to computers; software removal

For many years in this industry, it was a time consuming process to make changes to computer or user environments. If you wanted to install a service pack or a piece of software, unless you had a third-party utility, you had to use sneakernet (that is, you had to walk from one computer to another with a disk containing the software).

Installing any type of software was one of the biggest challenges faced by systems administrators. It was difficult enough to deploy and manage workstations throughout the environment. When you added in the fact that users were generally able to make system configuration changes, it quickly became a management nightmare!

For example, imagine that a user noticed that they did not have enough disk space to copy a large file. Instead of seeking help from the IT help desk, they may have decided to do a little cleanup of their own. Unfortunately, this cleanup operation may have involved deleting critical system files! Or, consider the case of users who changed system settings "just to see what they do." Relatively minor changes, such as modifying TCP/IP bindings or Desktop settings, could cause hours of support headaches. Now, multiply these (or other common) problems by hundreds (or even thousands) of end users. Clearly, systems administrators needed to have a way to limit the options available to users of client operating systems.

So how do you prevent problems like these from occurring in a Windows Server 2008 environment? Fortunately, there's a solution that comes with the base operating system that's readily available and easy to implement. One of the most important system administration features in Windows Server 2008 and Active Directory is Group Policy. By using Group Policy objects (GPOs), administrators can quickly and easily define restrictions on common actions and then apply them at the site, domain, or organizational unit (OU) level. In this chapter, you will see how group policies work and then look at how you can implement them within an Active Directory environment.

Introducing Group Policy

One of the strengths of Windows-based operating systems is their flexibility. End users and systems administrators can configure many different options to suit the network environment and their personal tastes. However, this flexibility comes at a price—generally, many of these options should not be changed by end users on a network. For example, TCP/IP configuration and security policies should remain consistent for all client computers. In fact, end users really don't need to be able to change these types of settings in the first place because many of them do not understand what these setting are used for.

In previous versions of Windows (NT 4 and earlier), system administrators could use system policies (`config.pol` or `ntconfig.pol` files) to restrict some functionality at the Desktop level. They could make settings for users or computers, for instance; however, these settings focused primarily on preventing the user from performing such actions as changing their Desktop settings. The system administrators managed these changes by modifying Registry keys, which made creating and distributing policy settings difficult. Furthermore, the types of configuration options available in the default templates were not always sufficient, and systems administrators often had to dive through cryptic and poorly documented Registry settings to make necessary changes.

Windows Server 2008's *group policies* are designed to allow system administrators the ability to customize end user settings and to place restrictions on the types of actions that users can perform. Group policies can be easily created by systems administrators and then later applied to one or more users or computers within the environment. Although they ultimately do affect Registry settings, it is much easier to configure and apply settings through the use of Group Policy than it is to manually make changes to the Registry. To make management easy, Microsoft has set Windows Server 2008 up so that Group Policy settings are all managed from within the Microsoft Management Console (MMC) in the Group Policy Management Console (GPMC).

Group policies have several different potential uses. We'll cover the use of group policies for software deployment, and we will also focus on the technical background of group policies and how they apply to general configuration management.

Let's begin by looking at how group policies function.

Understanding Group Policy Settings

Group Policy settings are based on Group Policy *administrative templates*. These templates provide a list of user-friendly configuration options and specify the system settings to which they apply. For example, an option for a user or computer that reads, "Require a Specific Desktop Wallpaper Setting," would map to a key in the Registry that maintains this value. When the option is set, the appropriate change is made in the Registry of the affected user(s) and computer(s).

By default, Windows Server 2008 comes with several administrative template files that you can use to manage common settings. Additionally, systems administrators and application developers can create their own administrative template files to set options for specific functionality.

Most Group Policy items have three different settings options:

Enabled   Specifies that a setting for this GPO has been configured. Some settings require values or options to be set.

Disabled   Specifies that this option is disabled for client computers. Note that disabling an option *is* a setting. That is, it specifies that the systems administrator wants to disallow certain functionality.

Not Configured   Specifies that these settings have been neither enabled nor disabled. Not Configured is the default option for most settings. It simply states that this Group Policy will not specify an option and that other policy settings may take precedence.

The specific options available (and their effects) will depend on the setting. Often, you will need additional information. For example, when setting the Account Lockout policy, you must specify how many bad login attempts may be made before the account is locked out. With this in mind, let's look at the types of user and computer settings that can be managed.

Group Policy settings can apply to two types of Active Directory objects: Users and Computers. Because both Users and Computers can be placed into groups and organized within OUs, this type of configuration simplifies the management of hundreds, or even thousands, of computers.

The main options you can configure within User and Computer Group Policies are as follows:

Software Settings   Software Settings options apply to specific applications and software that might be installed on the computer. Systems administrators can use these settings to make new applications available to end users and to control the default configuration for these applications.

Windows Settings   Windows Settings options allow systems administrators to customize the behavior of the Windows operating system. The specific options that are available here are divided into two types: users and computers. User-specific settings let you configure Internet Explorer (including the default home page and other settings). Computer settings include security options, such as Account Policy and Event Log options.

Administrative Templates   Administrative Templates are used to further configure user and computer settings. In addition to the default options available, systems administrators can create their own administrative templates with custom options.

Figure 8.1 shows some of the options that you can configure with Group Policy.

ADMX Central Store   Another consideration in GPO settings is whether to set up an ADMX Central Store. GPO administrative template files are saved as .admx files. To get the most benefit out of using administrative templates, you should create an ADMX Central Store.

You create the Central Store in the SYSVOL folder on a domain controller. The Central Store is a repository for all of your administrative templates and it is checked by the Group Policy tools. The Group Policy tools then use any .admx files that they finds in the Central Store. These files then replicate to all domain controllers in the domain.

Security Template   Security Templates are used to configure security settings through a GPO. Some of the security settings that can be configured are settings for account policies, local policies, event log, restricted group, system services, and Registry. Security Templates are described in detail in Chapter 9, "Planning Security for Active Directory."

Later in this chapter, we'll look into the various options available in more detail.

Group Policy settings do not take effect immediately. You must run the gpupdate command at the command prompt or wait for the regular update cycle (90 minutes by default) in order for the policy changes to take effect.

FIGURE 8.1 Group Policy configuration options

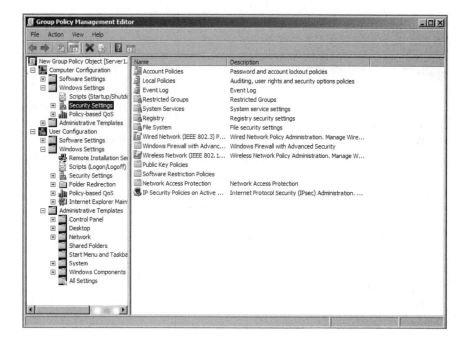

Group Policy Objects

So far, we have been talking about what group policies are designed to do. Now, it's time to drill down to determine exactly how you can set up and configure them.

To make them easier to manage, group policies may be placed in items called *Group Policy objects (GPOs)*. GPOs act as containers for the settings made within Group Policy files; this simplifies the management of settings. For example, as a systems administrator, you might have different policies for users and computers in different departments. Based on these requirements, you could create a GPO for members of the Sales department and another for members of the Engineering department. Then you could apply the GPOs to the OU for each department. Another important concept you need to understand is that Group Policy settings are hierarchical—that is, system administrators can apply Group Policy settings at three different levels:

Sites   At the highest level, system administrators can configure GPOs to apply to entire sites within an Active Directory environment. These settings apply to all of the domains and servers that are part of a site. Group Policy settings managed at the site level may apply to more than one domain. Therefore, they are useful when you want to make settings that apply to all of the domains within an Active Directory tree or forest.

> For more information on sites, see Chapter 5, "Configuring Sites and Replication."

Domains   Domains are the second level to which system administrators can assign GPOs. GPO settings placed at the domain level will apply to all of the User and Computer objects within the domain. Usually, systems administrators make master settings at the domain level.

Organizational units   The most granular level of settings for GPOs is at the OU level. By configuring Group Policy options for OUs, systems administrators can take advantage of the hierarchical structure of Active Directory. If the OU structure is planned well, you will find it easy to make logical GPO assignments for various business units at the OU level.

Based on the business need and the organization of the Active Directory environment, systems administrators might decide to set up Group Policy settings at any of these three levels. Because the settings are cumulative by default, a User object might receive policy settings from the site level, from the domain level, and from the OUs in which it is contained.

> You can also apply Group Policy settings to the local computer (in which case Active Directory is not used at all), but this limits the manageability of the Group Policy settings.

Group Policy Inheritance

In most cases, Group Policy settings are cumulative. For example, a GPO at the domain level might specify that all users within the domain must change their passwords every 60 days, and a GPO at the OU level might specify the default Desktop background for all users and computers within that OU. In this case, both settings apply, and users within the OU are forced to change their password every 60 days and have the default Desktop setting.

So what happens if there's a conflict in the settings? For example, suppose we create a scenario where a GPO at the site level specifies that users are to change passwords every 60 days, and one at the OU level specifies that they must change passwords every 90 days. Since Password policies for GPOs, though available, are not applied at the OU or site level, only Password policies at the domain level are applied. Although hypothetical, this raises an important point about *inheritance*. By default, the settings at the most specific level (in this case, the OU that contains the User object) override those at more general levels.

Although the default behavior is for settings to be cumulative and inherited, systems administrators can modify this behavior. Systems administrators can set two main options at the various levels to which GPOs might apply:

Block Policy Inheritance The Block Policy Inheritance option specifies that Group Policy settings for an object are not inherited from its parents. You might use this, for example, when a child OU requires completely different settings from a parent OU. Note, however, that you should manage blocking policy inheritance carefully because this option allows other systems administrators to override the settings made at higher levels.

Force Policy Inheritance The Enforced (sometimes referred as the NO Override) option can be placed on a parent object and ensures that all lower-level objects inherit these settings. In some cases, systems administrators want to ensure that Group Policy inheritance is not blocked at other levels. For example, suppose it is corporate policy that all Network accounts are locked out after five incorrect password attempts. In this case, you would not want lower-level systems administrators to override the option with other settings.

Systems administrators generally use this option when they want to globally enforce a specific setting. For example, if a password expiration policy should apply to all users and computers within a domain, a GPO with the Force Policy Inheritance option enabled could be created at the domain level.

We must consider one final case: if a conflict exists between the computer and user settings, the user settings take effect. If, for instance, a system administrator applies a default Desktop setting for the Computer policy, and a different default Desktop setting for the User policy, the one they specify in the User policy takes effect. This is because the user settings are more specific, and they allow systems administrators to make changes for individual users, regardless of the computer they're using.

Planning a Group Policy Strategy

Through the use of Group Policy settings, systems administrators can control many different aspects of their network environment. As you'll see throughout this chapter, system administrators can use GPOs to configure user settings and computer configurations. Windows Server 2008 includes many different administrative tools for performing these tasks. However, it's important to keep in mind that, as with many aspects of using Active Directory, a successful Group Policy strategy involves planning.

Because there are hundreds of possible GPO settings and many different ways in which you can implement them, start by determining the business and technical needs of your organization. For instance, first group your users based on their work functions. You might find, for example, that users in remote branch offices require particular network configuration options. In that case, you might implement Group Policy settings best at the site level. Or, you might find that certain departments have varying requirements for disk quota settings. In this case, it would probably make the most sense to apply GPOs to the appropriate department OUs within the domain.

The overall goal should be to reduce complexity (for example, by reducing the overall number of GPOs and GPO links), while still meeting the needs of your users. By taking into account the various needs of your users and the parts of your organization, you can often determine a logical and efficient method of creating and applying GPOs. Although it's rare that you'll come across a right or wrong method of implementing Group Policy settings, you will usually encounter some that are either better or worse than others.

By implementing a logical and consistent set of policies, you'll also be well prepared to trouble-shoot any problems that might come up, or to adapt to your organization's changing requirements. Later in this chapter, you'll see some specific methods for determining effective Group Policy settings before you apply them.

Implementing Group Policy

Now that we've covered the basic layout and structure of group policies and how they work, let's look at how you can implement them in an Active Directory environment. In this section, you'll start by creating GPOs. Then, you'll apply these GPOs to specific Active Directory objects and take a look at how to use administrative templates.

Creating GPOs

In previous versions of Windows Server (2000 and 2003) you could create GPOs from many different locations. For example, you could use Active Directory Users And Computers to create GPOs on your OUs along with other GPO tools. In Windows Server 2008, things are simpler. You can create GPOs for OUs in only one location: the Group Policy Management Console (GPMC). You have your choice of two applications for setting up policies on your Windows Server 2008 computers.

Local Computer Policy tool   This administrative tool allows you to quickly access the Group Policy settings that are available for the local computer. These options apply to the local machine and to users that access it. You must be a member of the local administrators group to access and make changes to these settings.

Group Policy Management Console (GPMC)   You must use the GPMC to manage Group Policy deployment. The GPMC provides a single solution for managing all Group Policy–related tasks and is also best suited to handle enterprise-level tasks such as forest-related work.

The GPMC allow administrators to manage the Group Policy and GPOs whether their enterprise solution spans multiple domains and sites within one or more forests, or whether it is local to one site all from one easy-to-use console. The GPMC adds flexibility, manageability, and functionality. Using this console, you can also perform other functions such as backup and restore, importing, and copying.

Exercise 8.1 walks you through the process of installing the Group Policy Management MMC snap-in for editing Group Policy settings and creating a GPO.

 WARNING You should be careful when making Group Policy settings because certain options might prevent the proper use of systems on your network. Always test Group Policy settings on a small group of users before you deploy GPOs throughout your organization. You'll probably find that some settings need to be changed in order for them to be effective.

EXERCISE 8.1

Creating a Group Policy Object Using the GPMC

1. Click Start ➤ Run, type **mmc**, and press Enter.

2. On the File menu, click Add/Remove Snap-In.

3. Click the Add button. In the Add Or Remove Snap-Ins dialog box, select Group Policy Management from the list, and click Add. If Group Policy Management is not on the list, go to step 4. If the choice is there, go to step 7.

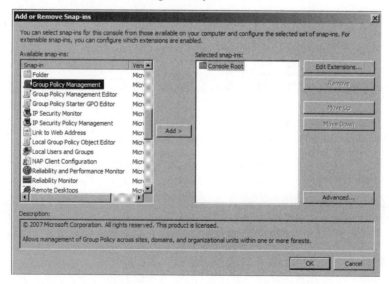

4.   (Only complete this step if Group Policy Management is missing from the list in the Add Or Remove Snap-Ins dialog box in step 3.) Click Start ➤ Administrative Tools ➤ Server Manager. In Server Manager, click Features. On the right side, click Add Features.

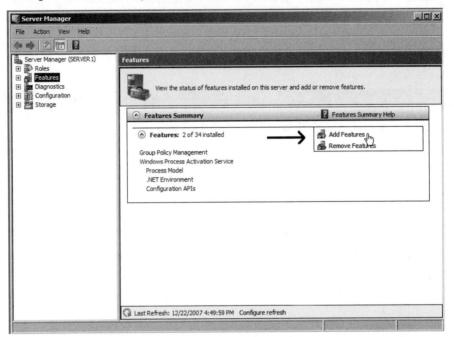

5.   Under the first section, check the box labeled Group Policy Management and then click Install. After it is installed, restart this exercise from step 1.

6.   Click Start ➤ Administrative Tools ➤ Group Policy Management. The Group Policy Management tool opens.

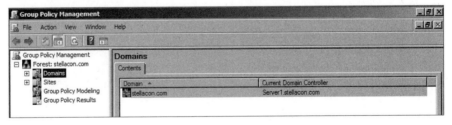

7. Expand the Forest, Domains, *your domain name,* and North America containers. Right-click the Corporate OU and then choose the menu item Create A GPO In This Domain, And Link It Here.

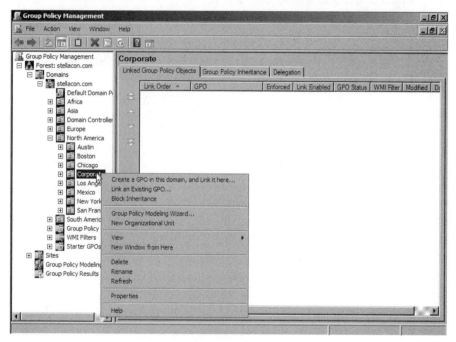

8. When the New GPO dialog box appears, type **Warning Box** in the Name field. Click OK.

EXERCISE 8.1 *(continued)*

9. The New GPO will be listed on the right side of the Group Policy Management window. Right-click the GPO and choose Edit.

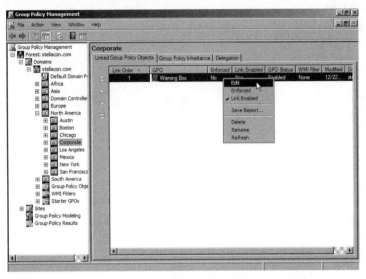

10. In the Group Policy Management Editor, expand the following: Computer Configuration, Windows Settings, Security Settings, Local Policies, and Security Options. On the right side, scroll down and double-click Interactive Logon: Message Text For Users Attempting To Log On.

11. Click the box labeled Define This Policy Setting In The Template. In the text box, type **Unauthorized use of this machine is prohibited** and then click OK. Close the GPO and return to the GPMC main screen.

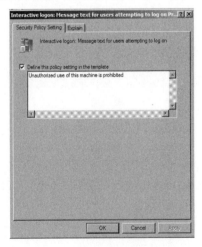

EXERCISE 8.1 *(continued)*

12. Under the domain name (in the GPMC) right-click Group Policy Objects and choose New.

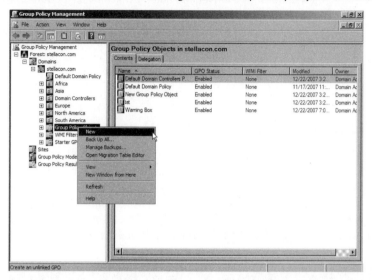

13. When the New GPO dialog box appears, type **Unlinked Test GPO** in the Name field. Click OK.

14. On the right side, the new GPO will appear. Right-click the Unlinked Test GPO and choose Edit.

15. Under the User Configuration section, click ➢ Administrative Templates ➢ Desktop. On the right side, double-click Hide And Disable All Items On The Desktop and then click Enabled. Click OK and then close the GPMC.

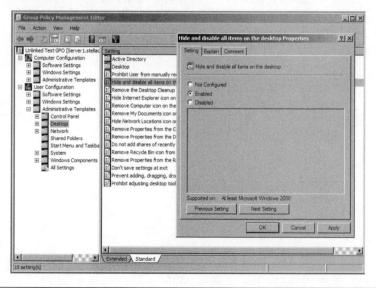

Note that Group Policy changes may not take effect until the next user logs in (some settings may even require that the machine be rebooted). That is, users who are currently working on the system will not see the effects of the changes until they log off and log in again. GPOs are reapplied every 90 minutes with a 30-minute offset. In other words, users who are logged on will have their policies reapplied every 60–120 minutes. Not all settings are reapplied (for example, software settings and Password policies).

Linking Existing GPOs to Active Directory

Creating a GPO is the first step in assigning group policies. The second step is to link the GPO to a specific Active Directory object. As mentioned earlier in this chapter, GPOs can be linked to sites, domains, and OUs.

Exercise 8.2 walks you through the steps you must take to assign an existing GPO to an OU within the local domain. In this exercise, you will link the Test Domain Policy GPO to an OU. In order to complete the steps in this exercise, you must have first completed Exercise 8.1.

EXERCISE 8.2

Linking Existing GPOs to Active Directory

1. Open the Group Policy Management Console (GPMC).

2. Expand the Forest and Domain containers and right-click on the Africa OU.

3. Choose Link An Existing GPO.

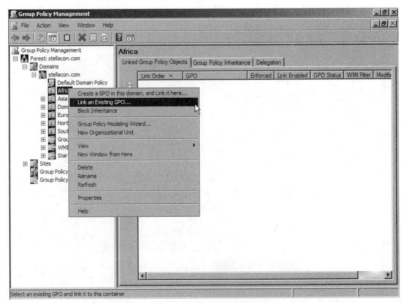

EXERCISE 8.2 *(continued)*

4. The Select GPO dialog box appears. Click Unlinked Test GPO and click OK.

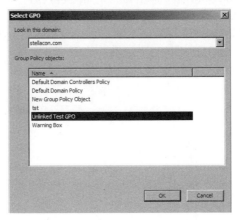

5. Close the Group Policy Management Console.

Note that the GPMC tool offers a lot of flexibility in assigning GPOs. You can create new GPOs, add multiple GPOs, edit them directly, change priority settings, remove links, and delete GPOs all from within this interface. In general, creating new GPOs using the GPMC tool is the quickest and easiest way to create the settings you need.

To test the Group Policy settings, you can simply create a User account within the Africa OU that you created in Exercise 8.2. Then, using another computer that is a member of the same domain, you can log on as the newly created user.

Managing Group Policy

Now that you have implemented GPOs and applied them to sites, domains, and OUs within Active Directory, it's time to look at some ways to manage them. In the following sections, you'll look at how multiple GPOs can interact with one another and ways you can provide security for GPO management. These features are a very important part of working with Active Directory, and if you properly plan Group Policy, you can greatly reduce the time the help desk spends troubleshooting common problems.

Managing GPOs

One of the benefits of GPOs is that they're modular and can apply to many different objects and levels within Active Directory. This can also be one of the drawbacks of GPOs if they're not managed properly. A common administrative function related to using GPOs is finding all of the Active Directory links for each of these objects. You can do this when you are viewing the Linked Group Policy Objects tab of the Site, Domain, or OU in the GPMC (shown in Figure 8.2).

FIGURE 8.2   Viewing GPO links to an Active Directory OU

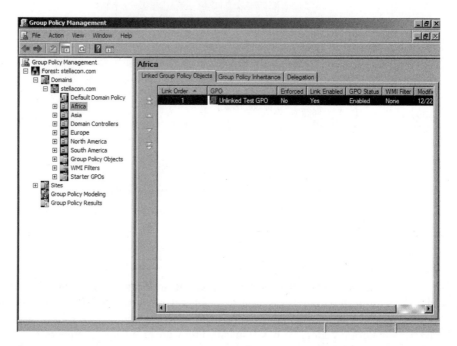

In addition to the common action of delegating permissions on OUs, you can set permissions regarding the modification of GPOs. The best way to accomplish this is to add users to the Group Policy Creator/Owners built-in security group. The members of this group are able to modify security policy. You saw how to add users to groups back in Chapter 7, "Administering Active Directory."

Security Filtering of a Group Policy

Another method of securing access to GPOs is to set permissions on the GPOs themselves. You can do this by opening the GPMC, selecting the GPO, and clicking the Advanced button in the Delegation tab. The Unlinked Test GPO Security Settings dialog box appears (see Figure 8.3).

The permissions options include the following:

- Full Control
- Read
- Write
- Create All Child Objects
- Delete All Child Objects
- Apply Group Policy

You might have to scroll the Permissions window to see the Apply Group Policy item.

FIGURE 8.3   A GPO's Security dialog box

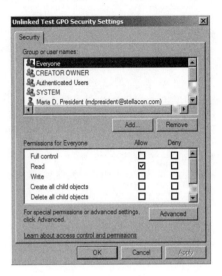

Of these, the Apply Group Policy setting is particularly important because you use it to filter the scope of the GPO. *Filtering* is the process by which selected security groups are included or excluded from the effects of the GPOs. To specify that the settings should apply to a GPO, you should select the Allow checkbox for both the Apply Group Policy setting and the Read setting. These settings will be applied only if the security group is also contained within a site, domain, or OU to which the GPO is linked. In order to disable GPO access for a group, choose Deny for both of these settings. Finally, if you do not want to specify either Allow or Deny, leave both boxes blank. This is effectively the same as having no setting.

In Exercise 8.3, you will filter Group Policy using security groups. In order to complete the steps in this exercise, you must have first completed Exercises 8.1 and 8.2.

EXERCISE 8.3

Filtering Group Policy Using Security Groups

1.   Open the Active Directory Users And Computers administrative tool.

2.   Create a new OU called **Group Policy Test**.

3.   Create two new Global Security groups within the Group Policy Test OU and name them **PolicyEnabled** and **PolicyDisabled**.

4.   Exit Active Directory Users And Computers and open the GPMC.

5.   Right-click the Group Policy Test OU, and select Link An Existing GPO.

6.   Choose Unlinked Test GPO and click OK.

7. Expand Group Policy Test OU so that you can see the GPO (Unlinked Test GPO) underneath the OU.

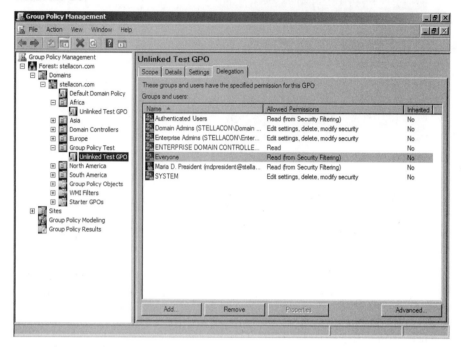

8. Click the Delegation tab and then click the Advanced button in the lower right corner of the window.

9. Click the Add button and type **PolicyEnabled** in the Enter The Object Names To Select field. Click the Check Names button. Then click OK.

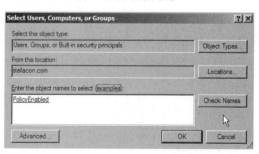

10. Add a group named **PolicyDisabled** in the same way.

11. Highlight the PolicyEnabled group, and select Allow for the Read and Apply Group Policy permissions. This ensures that users in the PolicyEnabled group will be affected by this policy.

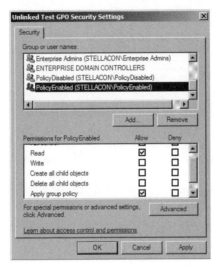

12. Highlight the PolicyDisabled group, and select Deny for the Read and Apply Group Policy permissions. This ensures that users in the PolicyDisabled group will not be affected by this policy.

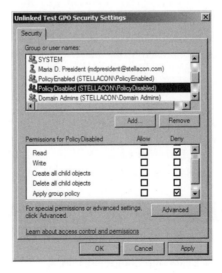

13. Click OK. You will see a message stating that you are choosing to use the Deny permission and that the Deny permission takes precedence over the Allow entries. Click the Yes button to continue.

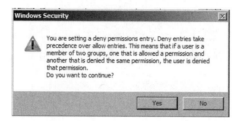

14. When you are finished, close the GPMC tool.

By using these settings, you can ensure that only the appropriate individuals will be able to modify GPO settings.

Delegating Administrative Control of GPOs

So far, you have learned about how you can use Group Policy to manage user and computer settings. What you haven't done is determine who can modify GPOs. It's very important to establish the appropriate security on GPOs themselves for two main reasons.

1. If the security settings aren't set properly, users and systems administrators can easily override them. This defeats the purpose of having the GPOs in the first place.

2. Having many different systems administrators creating and modifying GPOs can become extremely difficult to manage. When problems arise, the hierarchical nature of GPO inheritance can make it difficult to pinpoint the problem.

Fortunately, through the use of delegation, determining security permissions for GPOs is a simple task. You saw the usefulness of delegation in Chapter 7.

Exercise 8.4 walks you through the steps you must take to grant the appropriate permissions to a User account. Specifically, the process involves delegating the ability to manage Group Policy links on an Active Directory object (such as an OU). In order to complete this exercise, you must have first completed Exercises 8.1 and 8.2.

Delegating Administrative Control of Group Policy

1.   Open the Active Directory Users And Computers tool.

EXERCISE 8.4 *(continued)*

2. Expand the local domain, and create a user named **Policy Admin** within the Group Policy Test OU.

3. Exit Active Directory Users And Computers and open the GPMC.

4. Click the Group Policy Test OU and select the Delegation tab.

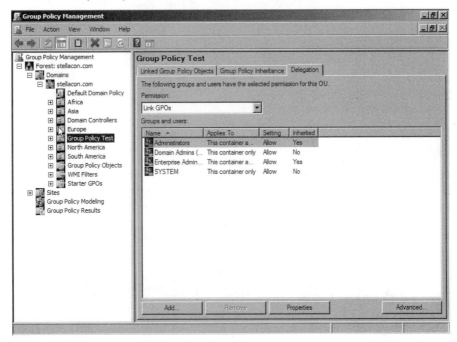

5. Click the Add button. In the field labeled Enter The Object Name To Select, type **Policy Admin** and click the Check Names button.

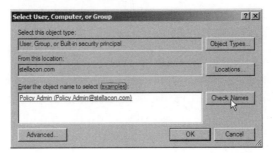

6. The Add Group or User dialog box appears. In the Permissions drop-down list, make sure the item labeled This Container And All Child Containers is chosen. Click OK.

7. At this point you should be looking at the Group Policy Test Delegation window. Click the Advanced button in the lower right corner.

8. Highlight the Policy Admin account and check the Allow Full Control box. This user now has full control of these OUs and all child OUs and GPOs for these OUs. Click OK.

    If you want to just give this user individual rights, then in the Properties window (step 8), click the Advanced button and then the Effective Permissions tab. This is where you can also choose a user and give them just the rights you need them to have.

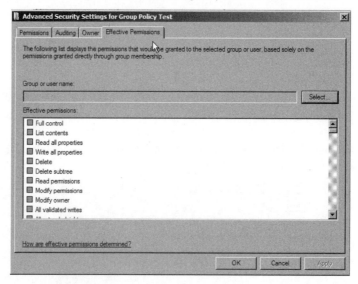

9. When you are finished, close the GPMC tool.

⊕ Real World Scenario

Understanding Delegation

Although we have talked about delegation throughout the text, it's important to discuss it again in the context of OUs, Group Policy, and Active Directory.

Once configured, Active Directory administrative delegation allows an administrator to delegate tasks (usually admin-related) to specific user accounts or groups. What this means is that if you don't manage it all, the user accounts (or groups) you choose will be able to manage their portions of the tree.

It's very important to be aware of the benefits of Active Directory Delegation (AD Delegation). AD Delegation will help you manage the assigning of administrative control over objects in Active Directory, such as users, groups, computers, printers, domains, and sites. AD Delegation is used to create more administrators, which essentially saves time.

For example, let's say you have a company whose IT department is small and located in the central location. The central location connects up three other smaller remote sites. These sites do not each warrant a full-time IT person, but the manager on staff (for example) can become an administrator for this portion of the tree. If the user accounts for the staff at the remote site are managed by that manager, this reduces the burden on the system administrator of trivial administrative work, such as unlocking user accounts or changing passwords, and thus it reduces costs.

Controlling Inheritance and Filtering Group Policy

Controlling inheritance is an important function when you are managing GPOs. Earlier in this chapter, you learned that, by default, GPO settings flow from higher-level Active Directory objects to lower-level ones. For example, the effective set of Group Policy settings for a user might be based on GPOs assigned at the site level, the domain level, and in the OU hierarchy. In general, this is probably the behavior you would want.

In some cases, however, you might want to block Group Policy inheritance. You can accomplish this easily by selecting the object to which a GPO has been linked. Right-click the object and choose Block Inheritance (see Figure 8.4). By enabling this option, you are effectively specifying that this object starts with a clean slate—that is, no other Group Policy settings will apply to the contents of this Active Directory site, domain, or OU.

FIGURE 8.4   Blocking GPO inheritance

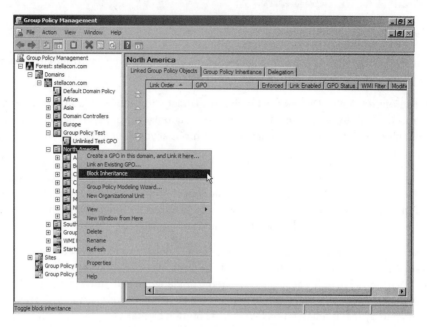

Systems administrators can also force inheritance. By setting the Enforced option, they can prevent other systems administrators from making changes to default policies. You can set the Enforced option by right-clicking the GPO and choosing the Enforced item (see Figure 8.5).

FIGURE 8.5   Setting the Enforced GPO option

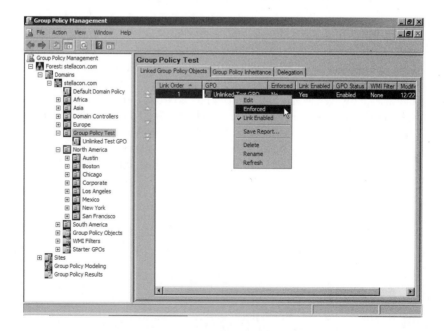

Assigning Script Policies

Systems administrators might want to make several changes and settings that would apply while the computer is starting up or the user is logging on. Perhaps the most common operation that logon scripts perform is mapping network drives. Although users can manually map network drives, providing this functionality within login scripts ensures that mappings stay consistent and that users need only remember the drive letters for their resources.

Script policies are specific options that are part of Group Policy settings for users and computers. These settings direct the operating system to the specific files that should be processed during the startup/shutdown or logon/logoff processes. You can create the scripts by using the *Windows Script Host (WSH)* or by using standard batch file commands. WSH allows developers and systems administrators to quickly and easily create scripts using the familiar Visual Basic Scripting Edition (VBScript) or JScript (Microsoft's implementation of JavaScript). Additionally, WSH can be expanded to accommodate other common scripting languages.

To set script policy options, you simply edit the Group Policy settings. As shown in Figure 8.6, there are two main areas for setting script policy settings:

FIGURE 8.6   Viewing Startup/Shutdown script policy settings

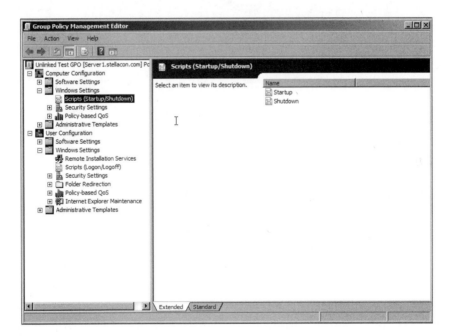

Startup/Shutdown Scripts   These settings are located within the Computer Configuration ➢ Windows Settings ➢ Scripts (Startup/Shutdown) object.

Logon/Logoff Scripts   These settings are located within the User Configuration ➢ Windows Settings ➢ Scripts (Logon/Logoff) object.

To assign scripts, simply double-click the setting, at which time its Properties dialog box appears. For instance, if you double-click the Startup setting, the Startup Properties dialog box appears, as shown in Figure 8.7. To add a script filename, click the Add button. When you do, you will be asked to provide the name of the script file (such as `MapNetworkDrives.vbs` or `ResetEnvironment.bat`).

FIGURE 8.7   Setting scripting options

Note that you can change the order in which the scripts are run by using the Up and Down buttons. The Show Files button opens the directory folder in which you should store the Logon script files. In order to ensure that the files are replicated to all domain controllers, you should be sure that you place the files within the SYSVOL share.

Managing Network Configuration

Group policies are also useful in network configuration. Although administrators can handle network settings at the protocol level using many different methods—such as Dynamic Host Configuration Protocol (DHCP)—Group Policy allows them to set which functions and operations are available to users and computers.

Figure 8.8 shows some of the features that are available for managing Group Policy settings. The paths to these settings are as follows:

Computer network options   These settings are located within the Computer Configuration, Administrative Templates, Network, Network Connections folder.

User network options   These settings are located within the User Configuration, Administrative Templates, Network folder.

Some examples of the types of settings available include the following:

- The ability to allow or disallow the modification of network settings.

    In many environments, the improper changing of network configurations and protocol settings is a common cause of help desk calls.

- The ability to allow or disallow the creation of Remote Access Service (RAS) connections.

  This option is very useful, especially in larger networked environments, because the use of modems and other WAN devices can pose a security threat to the network.

- The ability to set offline files and folders options.

  This is especially useful for keeping files synchronized for traveling users and is commonly configured for laptops.

Each setting includes detailed instructions in the description area of the GPO Editor window. By using these configuration options, systems administrators can maintain consistency for users and computers and can avoid many of the most common troubleshooting calls.

FIGURE 8.8   Viewing Group Policy User network configuration options

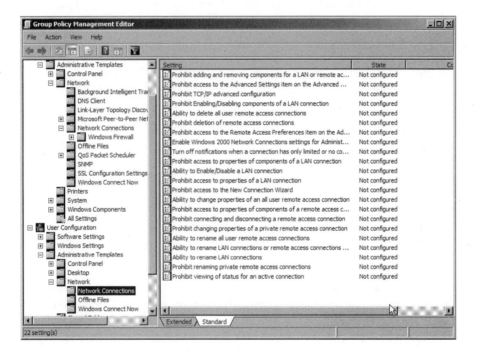

Automatically Enrolling User and Computer Certificates in Group Policy

You can also use Group Policy to automatically enroll user and computer certificates, making the entire certificate process transparent to your end users. Before you go on, you should understand what certificates are and why they are an important part of network security.

Think of a digital certificate as a carrying case for a public key. A certificate contains the public key and a set of attributes, including the key holder's name and email address. These attributes specify something about the holder: their identity, what they're allowed to do with the certificate, and so on. The attributes and the public key are bound together because the certificate is digitally signed by the entity that issued it. Anyone who wants to verify the certificate's contents can verify the issuer's signature.

Certificates are one part of what security experts call a public-key infrastructure (PKI). A PKI has several different components that you can mix and match to achieve the desired results. Microsoft's PKI implementation offers the following functions:

Certificate authorities (CAs)   Issue certificates, revoke certificates they've issued, and publish certificates for their clients. Big CAs like Thawte and VeriSign may do this for millions of users; you can also set up your own CA for each department or workgroup in your organization if you want. Each CA is responsible for choosing what attributes it will include in a certificate and what mechanism it will use to verify those attributes before it issues the certificate.

Certificate publishers   Make certificates publicly available, inside or outside an organization. This allows widespread availability of the critical material needed to support the entire PKI.

PKI-savvy applications   Allow you and your users to do useful things with certificates, like encrypt email or network connections. Ideally, the user shouldn't have to know (or even necessarily be aware of) what the application is doing—everything should work seamlessly and automatically. The best-known examples of PKI-savvy applications are web browsers like Internet Explorer and Netscape Navigator and email applications like Outlook and Outlook Express.

Certificate templates   Act like rubber stamps: By specifying a particular template as the model you want to use for a newly issued certificate, you're actually telling the CA which optional attributes to add to the certificate, as well as implicitly telling it how to fill some of the mandatory attributes. Templates greatly simplify the process of issuing certificates because they keep you from having to memorize the names of all the attributes you might potentially want to put in a certificate.

Learn More about PKI

The exam doesn't go deeply into PKI, but we recommended that you do some extra research on your own because it is a very important technology and shouldn't be overlooked. When discussing certificates, it's important to also mention PKI and its definition. PKI is actually a simple concept with a lot of moving parts. When broken down to its bare essentials, PKI is nothing more than a server and workstations utilizing a software service to add security to your infrastructure. When you use PKI, you are adding a layer of protection.

Installing and configuring a CA goes beyond the scope of this book. For more information, see the *MCTS: Windows Server 2008 Network Infrastructure Study Guide (70-642)*, by William Panek, Tylor Wentworth, and James Chellis (Sybex, 2008).

The auto-enrollment Settings policy determines whether or not users and/or computers are automatically enrolled for the appropriate certificates when necessary. By default, this policy is enabled if a Certificate Server is installed, but you can make changes to the settings as shown in Exercise 8.5.

In Exercise 8.5, you will learn how to configure automatic certificate enrollment in Group Policy. You must have completed the other exercises in this chapter in order to proceed.

EXERCISE 8.5

Configuring Automatic Certificate Enrollment in Group Policy

1. Open the Group Policy Management Console tool.

2. Right-click the North America OU you created in the previous exercises in this book.

3. Choose Create A GPO In This Domain And Link It Here and name it **Test CA**. Click OK.

4. Right-click the Test CA GPO and choose Edit.

5. Open Computer Configuration, Windows Settings, Security Settings, Public Key Policies.

6. Double-click Certificate Services Client - Auto-Enrollment in the right pane.

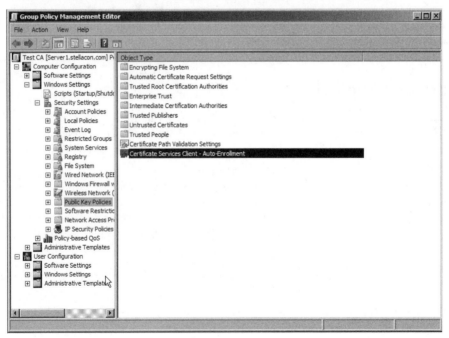

7. The Certificate Services Client - Auto-Enrollment Properties dialog box will appear.

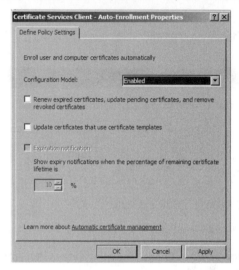

8. For now, you won't change anything. Just become familiar with the settings in this dialog box. Click OK to close it.

Redirecting Folders

Another set of Group Policy settings that you will learn about are the *folder redirection* settings. Group Policy provides a means of redirecting the My Documents, Desktop, and Start menu folders, as well as cached application data, to network locations. Folder redirection is particularly useful for the following reasons:

- When using roaming user profiles, a user's My Documents folder is copied to the local machine each time he logs on. This requires high bandwidth consumption and time if the My Documents folder is large. If you redirect the My Documents folder, it stays in the redirected location, and the user opens and saves files directly to that location.

- Documents are always available no matter where the user logs on.

- Data in the shared location can be backed up during the normal backup cycle without user intervention.

- Data can be redirected to a more robust server-side-administered disk that is less prone to physical and user errors.

When you decide to redirect folders, you have two options: basic and advanced.

- Basic redirection redirects everyone's folders to the same location (but each user gets their own folder within that location).

- Advanced redirection redirects folders to different locations based on group membership. For instance, you could configure the Engineers group to redirect their folders to //Engineering1/My_Documents/ and the Marketing group to //Marketing1/My_Documents/. Again, each individual user still gets their own folder within the redirected location.

To configure folder redirection, follow the steps in Exercise 8.6. You must have completed the other exercises in this chapter in order to proceed.

EXERCISE 8.6

Configuring Folder Redirection in Group Policy

1. Open the GPMC tool.

2. Open the North America OU and then edit the Test CA GPO.

3. Open User Configuration, Windows Settings, Folder Redirection, Documents.

4. Right-click Documents and select Properties.

5. On the Target tab of the Documents Properties dialog box, choose the Basic - Redirect Everyone's Folder To The Same Location selection from the Setting drop-down list.

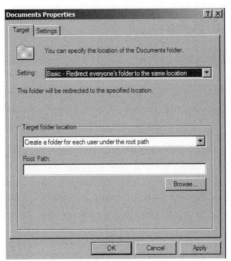

EXERCISE 8.6 *(continued)*

6. Leave the default option for the Target Folder Location drop-down list and specify a net-work path in the Root Path field.

7. Click the Settings tab. All of the default settings are self-explanatory and should typically be left with the default setting. Click OK when you are done.

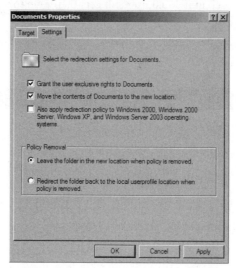

 Real World Scenario

Folder Redirection Facts

Try not to mix up the concepts of *folder redirection* and *offline folders*, especially in a world with ever-increasing numbers of mobile users. Folder redirection and offline folders are different features.

Windows Server 2008 folder redirection works as follows: the system uses a pointer that moves the folders you want to a location you specify. Users do not see any of this—it is trans-parent to them. One problem with folder redirection is that it does not work for mobile users (users who will be offline and who will not have access to files that they may need).

Offline folders, however, are copies of folders that were local to you. Files are now available locally to you on the system you have with you. They are also located back on the server where they are stored. Next time you log in, the folders are synchronized so that both folders contain the latest data. This is a perfect feature for mobile users, whereas folder redirection provides no benefit for the mobile user.

Deploying Software through a GPO

It's difficult enough to manage applications on a stand-alone computer. It seems that the process of installing, configuring, and uninstalling applications is never finished. Add in the hassle of computer reboots and reinstalling corrupted applications, and the reduction in productivity can be very real.

Software administrators who manage software in network environments have even more concerns.

- First and foremost, they must determine which applications specific users require.

- Then, IT departments must purchase the appropriate licenses for the software and acquire any necessary media.

- Next, the system administrators need to actually install the applications on users' machines. This process generally involves help desk staff visiting computers, or it requires end users to install the software themselves. Both processes entail several potential problems, including installation inconsistency and lost productivity from downtime experienced when applications were installed.

- Finally, they still need to manage software updates and remove unused software.

One of the key design goals for Active Directory was to reduce some of the headaches involved in managing software and configurations in a networked environment. To that end, Windows Server 2008 offers several features that can make the task of deploying software easier and less error prone. Before you dive into the technical details, though, you need to examine the issues related to software deployment.

The Software Management Life Cycle

Although it may seem that the use of a new application requires only the installation of the necessary software, the overall process of managing applications involves many more steps. When managing software applications, there are three main phases to the life cycle of applications:

Phase 1: Deploying software   The first step in using applications is to install them on the appropriate client computers. Generally, some applications are deployed during the initial configuration of a PC, and others are deployed when they are requested. In the latter case, this often used to mean that systems administrators and help desk staff would have to visit client computers and manually walk through the installation process. With Windows Server 2008 and GPOs, the entire process can be automated.

It is very important to understand that just because you can easily deploy software does not necessarily mean that you have the right to do so. Before you install software on client computers, you must make sure that you have the appropriate licenses for the software. Furthermore, it's very important to take the time to track application installations. As many systems administrators have discovered, it's much more difficult to inventory software installations after they've been performed. Another issue you may encounter is that you lack available resources (for instance, your system does not meet the minimum hardware requirements) and face problems such as limited hard disk space or memory that may not be able to handle the applications you want to load and use. You may also find that your user account does not have the permission to install software. It's important to consider not only how you will install software, but whether you can.

Phase 2: Maintaining software   Once an application is installed and in use on client computers, you need to ensure that the software is maintained. You must keep programs up to date by applying changes due to bug fixes, enhancements, and other types of updates. This is normally done with service packs, hot fixes, and updates. As with the initial software deployment, software maintenance can be tedious. Some programs require older versions to be uninstalled before updates are added. Others allow for automatically upgrading over existing installations. Managing and deploying software updates can consume a significant amount of the IT staff's time.

Using Windows Update

Make sure you learn about Windows Update, a service that allows you to connect to Microsoft's website and download what your system may need to bring it up to compliance. This tool is very helpful if you are running a stand-alone system, but if you want to deploy software across your enterprise, the best way to accomplish this is to first test the updates you are downloading and make sure you can use them and that they are not buggy. Then you can use a tool such as the Windows Server Update Service (WSUS), formally called the Software Update Services (SUS).

You can check for updates at Microsoft's website (http://update.microsoft.com). Microsoft likes to ask many types of questions about WSUS on its certification exams. WSUS is described in detail in other Sybex certification series books.

Phase 3: Removing software   At the end of the life cycle for many software products is the actual removal of unused programs. Removing software is necessary when applications become outdated or when users no longer require their functionality. One of the traditional problems with uninstalling applications is that many of the installed files may not be removed. Furthermore, the removal of shared components can sometimes cause other programs to stop functioning properly. Also, users often forget to uninstall applications that they no longer need, and these programs continue to occupy disk space and consume valuable system resources.

Each of these three phases of the software maintenance life cycle is managed by the Microsoft Windows Installer (MSI). Now that you have an overview of the process, let's move on to look at the actual steps involved in deploying software using Group Policy.

 The Microsoft Windows Installer (sometimes referred to as Microsoft Installer or Windows Installer) is an application installation and configuration service. An instruction file (the Microsoft Installer package) contains information about what needs to be done to install a product. It's common to confuse the two.

The Windows Installer

If you've installed newer application programs (such as Microsoft Office 2007), you probably noticed the updated setup and installation routines. Applications that comply with the updated standard use the *Windows Installer* specification and MSI software packages for deployment. Each package contains information about various setup options and the files required for installation. Although the benefits may not seem dramatic on the surface, there's a lot of new functionality under the hood.

The Windows Installer was created to solve many of the problems associated with traditional application development. It has several components, including the Installer service (which runs on Windows 2000, XP, Vista, Server 2003, and Server 2008 computers), the Installer program (`msiexec.exe`) that is responsible for executing the instructions in a *Windows Installer package*, and the specifications third-party developers use to create their own packages. Within each installation package file is a relational structure (similar to the structure of tables in databases) that records information about the programs contained within the package.

In order to appreciate the true value of the Windows Installer, you'll need to look at some of the problems with traditional software deployment mechanisms, and then at how the Windows Installer addresses many of these.

Application Installation Issues

Before the Windows Installer, applications were installed using a setup program that managed the various operations required for a program to operate. These operations included copying files, changing Registry settings, and managing any other operating system changes that might be required (such as starting or stopping services). However, this method included several problems:

- The setup process was not robust, and aborting the operation often left many unnecessary files in the filesystem.

- The process included uninstalling an application (this also often left many unnecessary files in the filesystem) and remnants in the Windows Registry and operating system folders. Over time, these remnants would result in reduced overall system performance and wasted disk space.

- There was no standard method for applying upgrades to applications, and installing a new version often required users to uninstall the old application, reboot, and then install the new program.

- Conflicts between different versions of dynamic link libraries (DLLs)—shared program code used across different applications—could cause the installation or removal of one application to break the functionality of another.

Benefits of the Windows Installer

Because of the many problems associated with traditional software installation, Microsoft created the Windows Installer. This system provides for better manageability of the software installation process and allows systems administrators more control over the deployment process. Specifically, benefits of the Windows Installer include the following:

Improved software removal   The process of removing software is an important one since remnants left behind during the uninstall process can eventually clutter up the Registry and filesystem. During the installation process, the Windows Installer keeps track of all of the changes made by a setup package. When it comes time to remove an application, all of these changes can then be rolled back.

More robust installation routines   If a typical setup program is aborted during the software installation process, the results are unpredictable. If the actual installation hasn't yet begun, then the installer generally removes any temporary files that may have been created. If, however, the file copy routine starts before the system encounters an error, it is likely that the files will not be automatically removed from the operating system. In contrast, the Windows Installer allows you to roll back any changes when the application setup process is aborted.

Ability to use elevated privileges   Installing applications usually requires the user to have Administrator permissions on the local computer because filesystem and Registry changes are required. When installing software for network users, systems administrators thus have two options. First, they can log off of the computer before installing the software and then log back on as a user who has Administrator permissions on the local computer. This method is tedious and time-consuming. The second option is to temporarily give users Administrator permissions on their own machines. This method could cause security problems and requires the attention of a systems administrator.

Through the use of the Installer service, the Windows Installer is able to use temporarily elevated privileges to install applications. This allows users, regardless of their security settings, to execute the installation of authorized applications. The end result is that this saves time and preserves security.

Support for repairing corrupted applications   Regardless of how well a network environment is managed, critical files are sometimes lost or corrupted. Such problems can prevent applications from running properly and can cause crashes. Windows Installer packages provide you with the ability to verify the installation of an application and, if necessary, replace any missing or corrupted files. This support saves time and lessens the end-user headaches associated with removing and reinstalling an entire application to replace just a few files.

Prevention of file conflicts   Generally, different versions of the same files should be compatible with each other. In the real world, however, this isn't always the case. A classic problem in the Windows world is the case of one program replacing DLLs that are used by several other programs. Windows Installer accurately tracks which files are used by certain programs and ensures that any shared files are not improperly deleted or overwritten.

Automated installations   A typical application setup process requires end users or systems administrators to respond to several prompts. For example, a user may be able to choose the program group in which icons will be created and the filesystem location to which the program will be installed. Additionally, they may be required to choose which options are installed. Although this type of flexibility is useful, it can be tedious when you are rolling out multiple applications. By using features of the Windows Installer, however, users are able to specify setup options before the process begins. This allows systems administrators to ensure consistency in installations and it saves users' time.

Advertising and on-demand installations   One of the most powerful features of the Windows Installer is its ability to perform on-demand software installations. Prior to Windows Installer, application installation options were quite basic—either a program was installed or it was not. When setting up a computer, systems administrators would be required to guess which applications the user might need and install all of them.

The Windows Installer supports a function known as advertising. Advertising makes applications appear to be available via the Start menu. However, the programs themselves may not actually be installed on the system. When a user attempts to access an advertised application, the Windows Installer automatically downloads the necessary files from a server and installs the program. The end result is that applications are installed only when they are needed, and the process requires no intervention from the end user. We'll cover the details of this process later in this chapter.

To anyone who has managed many software applications in a network environment, all of these features of the Windows Installer are likely welcome ones. They also make life easier for end users and application developers who can focus on the "real work" their jobs demand.

Windows Installer File Types

When performing software deployment with the Windows Installer in Windows Server 2008, you may encounter several different file types:

Microsoft Windows Installer (MSI) packages   In order to take full advantage of Windows Installer functionality, applications must include Microsoft Windows Installer packages. These packages are normally created by third-party application vendors and software developers, and they include the information required to install and configure the application and any supporting files.

Microsoft Transformation (MST) files   Microsoft Transformation (MST) files are useful when you are customizing the details of how applications are installed. When a systems administrator chooses to assign or publish an application, they may want to specify additional options for the package. If, for instance, a systems administrator wants to allow users to install only the

Microsoft Word and Microsoft PowerPoint components of Office XP, they could specify these options within a transformation file. Then, when users install the application, they will be provided with only the options related to these components.

Microsoft patches (MSP)   In order to maintain software, *patches* are often required. Patches may make Registry and/or filesystem changes. Patch files are used for minor system changes and are subject to certain limitations. Specifically, a patch file cannot remove any installed program components and cannot delete or modify any shortcuts created by the user.

Initialization files   In order to provide support for publishing non–Windows Installer applications, *initialization files* can be used. These files provide links to a standard executable file that is used to install an application. An example might be \\server1\software\program1\setup.exe. These files can then be published and advertised, and users can access the *Add or Remove Programs* icon to install them over the network.

Application assignment scripts (AAS)   *Application assignment scripts* store information regarding assigning programs and any settings that the systems administrator makes. These files are created when Group Policy is used to create software package assignments for users and computers.

Each of these types of files provides functionality that allows the system administrator to customize software deployment. Windows Installer packages have special properties that you can view by right-clicking the file in Windows Explorer and choosing Properties (see Figure 8.9).

FIGURE 8.9   Viewing the properties of an MSI package file

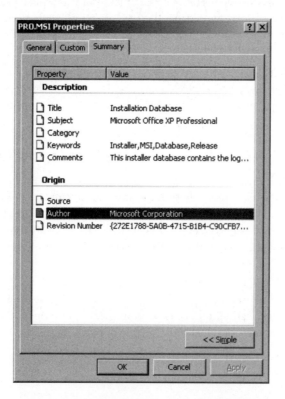

Deploying Applications

The functionality provided by Windows Installer offers many advantages to end users who install their own software. That, however, is just the beginning in a networked environment. As you'll see later in this chapter, the various features of Windows Installer and compatible packages allow systems administrators to centrally determine applications that users will be able to install.

There are two main methods of making programs available to end users using Active Directory: *assigning* and *publishing*. Both publishing and assigning applications greatly ease the process of deploying and managing applications in a network environment.

In the following sections, you'll look at how the processes of assigning and publishing applications can make life easier for IT staff and users alike. The various settings for assigned and published applications are managed through the use of GPOs.

Assigning Applications

Software applications can be assigned to users and computers. Assigning a software package makes the program available for automatic installation. The applications advertise their availability to the affected users or computers by placing icons within the Programs folder of the Start menu.

When applications are assigned to a user, programs will be advertised to the user, regardless of which computer they are using. That is, icons for the advertised program will appear within the Start menu, regardless of whether the program is installed on that computer. If the user clicks an icon for a program that has not yet been installed on the local computer, the application will automatically be accessed from a server and will be installed.

When an application is assigned to a computer, the program is made available to any users of the computer. For example, all users who log on to a computer that has been assigned Microsoft Office XP will have access to the components of the application. If the user did not previously install Microsoft Office, they will be prompted for any required setup information when the program first runs.

Generally, applications that are required by the vast majority of users should be assigned to computers. This reduces the amount of network bandwidth required to install applications on demand and improves the end user experience by preventing the delay involved when installing an application the first time it is accessed. Any applications that may be used by only a few users (or those with specific job tasks) should be assigned to users.

Publishing Applications

When applications are published, they are advertised, but no icons are automatically created. Instead, the applications are made available for installation using the Add Or Remove Programs icon in the Control Panel.

NOTE   Vista does not have the Add Or Remove Programs feature. In Vista, use the Programs icon in Control Panel to install the software.

Implementing Software Deployment

So far, you have become familiar with the issues related to software deployment and management from a theoretical level. Now it's time to drill down into the actual steps required to deploy software using the features of Active Directory and the GPMC. In the following sections, you will walk through the steps required to create an application distribution share point, to publish and assign applications, to update previously installed applications, to verify the installation of applications, and to update Windows operating systems.

Preparing for Software Deployment

Before you can install applications on client computers, you must make sure that the necessary files are available to end users. In many network environments, systems administrators create shares on file servers that include the installation files for many applications. Based on security permissions, either end users or systems administrators can then connect to these shares from a client computer and install the needed software. The efficient organization of these shares can save the help desk from having to carry around a library of CD-ROMs and can allow you to install applications easily on many computers at once.

 One of the problems in network environments is that users frequently install applications whether or not they really need them. They may stumble upon applications that are stored on common file servers and install them out of curiosity. These actions can often decrease productivity and may violate software licensing agreements. You can help avoid this by placing all of your application installation files in hidden shares (for example, "software$").

Exercise 8.7 walks you through the process of creating a software distribution share point. In this exercise, you will prepare for software deployment by creating a directory share and placing certain types of files in this directory. In order to complete the steps in this exercise, you must have access to the Microsoft Office 2007 installation files (via CD-ROM or through a network share) and have 2000MB of free disk space.

EXERCISE 8.7

Creating a Software Deployment Share

1. Using Windows Explorer, create a folder called **Software** that you can use with application sharing. Be sure that the volume on which you create this folder has at least 2000MB of available disk space.

2. Within the Software folder, create a folder called **Office 2007**.

3.   Copy all of the installation files for Microsoft Office 2007 from the CD-ROM or network share containing the files to the Office 2007 folder that you created in step 2.

4.   Right-click the Software folder (created in step 1), and select Share. In the Choose People On Your Network To Share With dialog box, type **Everyone**, and click the Add button. Next click the Share button. When you see a message that the sharing process is complete, click the Done button.

5.   Copy the Microsoft Office 2007 installation files (including the .MSI files) to the share.

Once you have created an application distribution share, it's time to actually publish and assign the applications. This topic is covered next.

Publishing and Assigning Applications

As we mentioned earlier in this section, system administrators can make software packages available to users by using publishing and assigning operations. Both of these operations allow systems administrators to leverage the power of Active Directory and, specifically, GPOs to determine which applications are available to users. Additionally, OUs can provide the organization that can help group users based on their job functions and software requirements.

The general process involves creating a GPO that includes software deployment settings for users and computers and then linking this GPO to Active Directory objects.

Exercise 8.8 walks you through the steps you need to take to publish and assign applications. In this exercise, you will create and assign applications to specific Active Directory objects using GPOs. In order to complete the steps in this exercise, you must have first completed Exercise 8.7.

Publishing and Assigning Applications Using Group Policy

1.   Open the Active Directory Users And Computers tool from the Administrative Tools program group.

2.   Expand the domain, and create a new top-level OU called **Software**.

3.   Within the Software OU, create a user named **Jane User** with a login name of **juser** (choose the defaults for all other options).

4.   Exit Active Directory Users And Computers and open the Group Policy Management Console (GPMC).

5. Right-click on the Software OU and choose Create A GPO In This Domain And Link It Here.

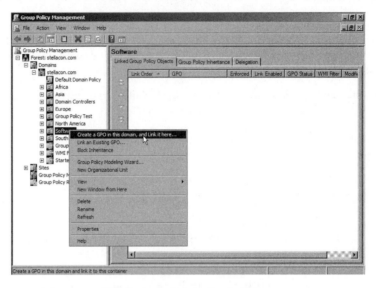

6. For the name of the new GPO, type **Software Deployment**.

7. To edit the Software Deployment GPO, right-click the Software Deployment GPO and choose Edit. Expand the Computer Configuration ➢ Software Settings object.

8. Right-click the Software Installation item, and select New ➢ Package.

9. Navigate to the Software share that you created in Exercise 8.7.

10. Within the Software share, double-click the Office 2007 folder and select the appropriate MSI file depending on the version of Office 2007 that you have. Office 2007 Professional is being used in this example, so you'll see that the OFFICEMUI.MSI file is chosen. Click Open.

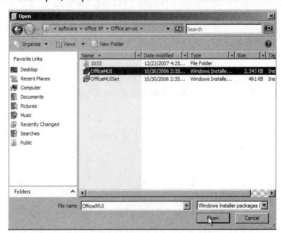

EXERCISE 8.8 *(continued)*

11. In the Deploy Software dialog box, choose Advanced. (Note that the Published option is unavailable because applications cannot be published to computers.) Click OK to return to the Deploy Software dialog box.

12. To examine the deployment options of this package, click the Deployment tab. Accept the default settings by clicking OK.

13. Within the Group Policy Object Editor, expand the User Configuration ➢ Software Settings object.

14. Right-click the Software Installation item, and select New ➢ Package.

15. Navigate to the Software share that you created in Exercise 8.7.

16. Within the Software share, double-click the Office 2007 folder, and select the appropriate MSI file. Click Open.

17. For the Software Deployment option, select Published in the Deploy Software dialog box and click OK.

18. Close the GPMC.

The overall process involved with deploying software using Active Directory is quite simple. However, you shouldn't let the intuitive graphical interface fool you—there's a lot of power under the hood of these software deployment features! Once you've properly assigned and published applications, it's time to see the effects of your work.

Applying Software Updates

The steps described in the previous section work only when you are installing a brand-new application. However, software companies often release updates that you need to install on top of existing applications. These updates usually consist of bug fixes or other changes that are required to keep the software up to date. You can apply software updates in Active Directory by using the Upgrades tab of the software package Properties dialog box found in the Group Policy Object Editor.

In Exercise 8.9, you will apply a software update to an existing application. You should add the upgrade package to the GPO in the same way that you added the original application in steps 8 through 12 of Exercise 8.8. You should also have completed Exercise 8.8 before attempting this exercise.

EXERCISE 8.9

Applying Software Updates

1. Open the Group Policy Management Console (GPMC) from the Administrative Tools program group.

2. Click the Software OU, right-click the Software Deployment GPO, and choose Edit.

3. Expand the Computer Configuration ➢ Software Settings ➢ Software Installation object.

4. Right-click the software package and select Properties from the context menu to bring up the Properties dialog box.

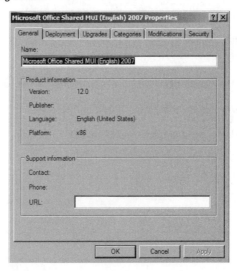

5. Select the Upgrades tab and click the Add button.

6. Click the Current Group Policy Object (GPO) radio button in the Choose a Package From section of the dialog box or click the Browse button to select the GPO to which you want to apply the upgrade. Consult your application's documentation to see if you should choose the Uninstall The Existing Package, Then Install The Upgrade Package radio button or the Package Can Upgrade Over The Existing Package radio button.

7. Click Cancel to close the Add Upgrade Package dialog box.

8. Click Cancel and exit the GPMC.

You should understand that not all upgrades make sense in all situations. For instance, if Stellacon 6 files are incompatible with the Stellacon 10 application, then your Stellacon 6 users might not want you to perform the upgrade without taking additional steps to ensure that they can continue to use their files. In addition, users might have some choice about which version they use when it doesn't affect the support of the network.

Regardless of the underlying reason for allowing this flexibility, you should be aware that there are two basic types of upgrades that are available for administrators to provide to the users:

Mandatory upgrade   Forces everyone who currently has an existing version of the program to upgrade according to the GPO. Users who have never installed the program for whatever reason will be able to install only the new upgraded version.

Nonmandatory upgrade   Allows users to choose whether they would like to upgrade. This upgrade type also allows users who do not have their application installed to choose which version they would like to use.

Verifying Software Installation

In order to ensure that the software installation settings you make in a GPO have taken place, you can log in to the domain from a Windows XP Professional or Vista computer that is within the OU to which the software settings apply. When you log in, you will notice two changes. First, the application is installed on the computer (if it was not installed already). In order to access the application, all a user needs to do is click one of the icons within the Program group of the Start menu. Note also that applications are available to any of the users who log on to this machine. Second, the settings apply to any computers that are contained within the OU and to any users who log on to these computers.

If you publish an application to users, the change may not be as evident, but it is equally useful. When you log on to a Windows XP Professional or Vista computer that is a member of the domain, and when you use a user account from the OU where you published the application, you will be able to automatically install any of the published applications. On a Windows XP Professional computer, you can do this by accessing the Add Or Remove Programs icon in the Control Panel. By clicking Add New Programs, you access a display of the applications available for installation. By clicking the Add button in the Add New Programs section of the Add Or Remove Programs dialog box, you will automatically begin the installation of the published application.

 Vista does not have the Add Or Remove Programs feature. In Vista, use the Programs icon in Control Panel to install the software.

Configuring Automatic Updates in Group Policy

So far you've seen the advantages of deploying application software in a Group Policy. Group policies also provide a way to install operating system updates across the network for Windows 2000, XP, Vista, Server 2003, and Server 2008 machines using Windows Update in conjunction with WSUS. WSUS is the newer version of SUS and is used on a Windows Server 2008 system to update systems. As you might remember from earlier, WSUS and SUS are patch management tools that help you deploy updates to your systems in a controlled manner.

Windows Update is available through the Microsoft website and is used to provide the most current files for the Windows operating systems. Examples of updates include security fixes, critical updates, updated help files, and updated drivers. You can access Windows Updates by clicking the Windows Updates icon in the system tray.

 Learn more about WSUS at http://technet.microsoft.com/en-us/wsus/ default.aspx.

WSUS is used to leverage the features of Windows Update within a corporate environment by downloading Windows updates to a corporate server, which in turn provides the updates to the internal corporate clients. This allows administrators to test and have full control over what updates are deployed within the corporate environment.

Within an enterprise network that is using Active Directory, you would typically see automatic updates configured through Group Policy. Group policies are used to manage configuration and security settings via Active Directory. Group Policy is also used to specify what server a client will use for automatic updates.

If the WSUS client is a part of an enterprise network that is using Active Directory, you would configure the client via a Group Policy.

Configuring Software Deployment Settings

In addition to the basic operations of assigning and publishing applications, you can use several other options to specify the details of how software is deployed. In the following sections, you will examine the various options that are available and their effects on the software installation process.

The Software Installation Properties Dialog Box

The most important software deployment settings are contained in the Software Installation Properties dialog box, which you can access by right-clicking the Software Installation item and selecting Properties from the pop-up menu. The following sections describe the features contained on the various tabs of the dialog box.

Managing Package Defaults

On the General tab of the Software Installation Properties dialog box, you'll be able to specify some defaults for any packages that you create within this GPO. Figure 8.10 shows the General options for managing software installation settings.

FIGURE 8.10 General tab of the Software Installation Properties dialog box

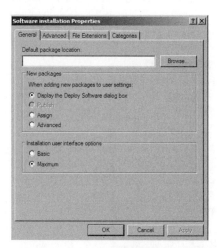

The various options available include the following:

Default Package Location   This setting specifies the default filesystem or network location for software installation packages. This is useful if you are already using a specific share on a file server for hosting the necessary installation files.

New Packages options   These settings specify the default type of package assignment that will be used when you add a new package to either the user or computer settings. If you'll be assigning or publishing multiple packages, you may find it useful to set a default here. Selecting the Advanced option enables Group Policy to display the package's Properties dialog box each time a new package is added.

Installation User Interface Options   When they are installing an application, systems administrators may or may not want end users to see all of the advanced installation options. If Basic is chosen, the user will only be able to configure the minimal settings (such as the installation location). If Maximum is chosen, all of the available installation options will be displayed. The specific installation options available will depend on the package itself.

The Advanced Tab

The Advanced tab (see Figure 8.11) includes several options for configuring advanced software installation properties. The only option you need to be concerned with is the following:

"Uninstall the applications when they fall out of the scope of management."   So far, you have seen how applications can be assigned and published to users or computers. But what happens when effective GPOs change? For example, suppose that User A is currently located within the Sales OU. A GPO that assigns the Microsoft Office XP suite of applications is linked to the Sales OU. Now, you decide to move User A to the Engineering OU, which has no software deployment settings. Should the application be uninstalled, or should it remain?

If the "Uninstall the applications when they fall out of the scope of management" option is checked, applications will be removed if they are not specifically assigned or published within GPOs. In our earlier example, this means that Office XP would be uninstalled for User A. If, however, this box is left unchecked, the application would remain installed.

FIGURE 8.11   The Advanced tab of the Software Installation Properties dialog box

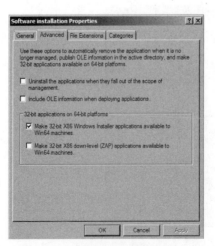

Managing File Extension Mappings

One of the potential problems associated with using many different file types is that it's difficult to keep track of which applications work with which files. For example, if you received a file with the extension .abc, you would have no idea which application you would need to view it. And Windows would not be of much help, either.

Fortunately, through software deployment settings, systems administrators can specify mappings for specific *file extensions*. For example, you could specify that whenever users attempt to access a file with the extension .vsd, the operating system should attempt to open the file using the Visio diagramming software. If Visio is not installed on the user's machine, the computer can automatically download and install it (assuming that the application has been properly advertised).

This method allows users to have applications automatically installed when they are needed. The following is an example of the sequence of events that might occur:

1. A user receives an email message that contains an Adobe Acrobat file attachment.

2. The computer realizes that Adobe Acrobat, the appropriate viewing application for this type of file, is not installed. However, it also realizes that a file extension mapping is available within the Active Directory software deployment settings.

3. The client computer automatically requests the Adobe Acrobat software package from the server and uses the Microsoft Windows Installer to automatically install the application.

4. The computer opens the attachment for the user.

Notice that all of these steps were carried out without any further interaction with the user.

You can manage file extension mappings by right-clicking the Software Installation item, selecting Properties, and then clicking the File Extensions tab.

Creating Application Categories

In many network environments, the list of supported applications can include hundreds of items. For users who are looking for only one specific program, searching through a list of all of these programs can be difficult and time-consuming.

Fortunately, methods for categorizing the applications are available on your network. You can easily manage the application categories for users and computers by right-clicking the Software Installation item, selecting Properties, and then clicking the Categories tab.

Figure 8.12 shows you how application categories can be created. It is a good idea to use category names that are meaningful to users because it will make it easier for them to find the programs they're looking for.

Once the software installation categories have been created, you can view them by opening the Add Or Remove Programs item in the Control Panel. When you click Add New Programs, you'll see that several options appear in the Category drop-down list. Now, when you select the properties for a package, you will be able to assign the application to one or more of the categories.

FIGURE 8.12 The Categories tab of the Software Installation Properties dialog box

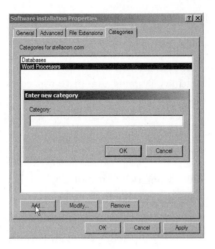

Removing Programs

As we discussed in the beginning of the chapter, an important phase in the software management life cycle is the removal of applications. Fortunately, using the GPMC and the Windows Installer packages, the process is simple. To remove an application, you can right-click the package within the Group Policy settings and select All Tasks ➢ Remove (see Figure 8.13).

FIGURE 8.13 Removing a software package

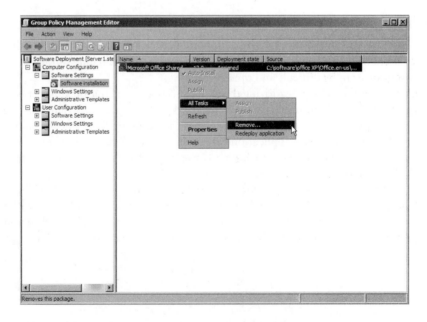

When choosing to remove a software package from a GPO, you have two options:

Immediately Uninstall The Software From Users And Computers Systems administrators can choose this option to ensure that an application is no longer available to users who are affected by the GPO. When this option is selected, the program will be automatically uninstalled from users and/or computers that have the package. This option might be useful, for example, if the license for a certain application has expired or if a program is no longer on the approved applications list.

Allow Users To Continue To Use The Software, But Prevent New Installations This option prevents users from making new installations of a package, but it does not remove the software if it has already been installed for users. This is a good option if the company has run out of additional licenses for the software, but the existing licenses are still valid.

Figure 8.14 shows these two removal options.

FIGURE 8.14   Software removal options

If you no longer require the ability to install or repair an application, you can delete it from your software distribution share point by deleting the appropriate Windows Installer package files. This will free up additional disk space for newer applications.

Microsoft Windows Installer Settings

Several options influence the behavior of the Windows Installer; you can set them within a GPO. You can access these options by navigating to User Configuration, Administrative Templates, Windows Components, Windows Installer. The options include the following:

Always Install With Elevated Privileges This policy allows users to install applications that require elevated privileges. For example, if a user does not have the permissions necessary to modify the Registry but the installation program must make Registry changes, this policy will allow the process to succeed.

Search Order This setting specifies the order in which the Windows Installer will search for installation files. The options include n (for network shares), m (for searching removal media), and u (for searching the Internet for installation files).

Disable Rollback When this option is enabled, the Windows Installer does not store the system state information that is required to roll back the installation of an application. Systems administrators may choose this option to reduce the amount of temporary disk space required during installation and to increase the performance of the installation operation. However, the drawback is that the system cannot roll back to its original state if the installation fails and the application needs to be removed.

Disable Media Source For Any Install   This option disallows the installation of software using removable media (such as CD-ROM, DVD-ROM, or floppy disks). It is useful for ensuring that users install only approved applications.

With these options, systems administrators can control how the Windows Installer operates for specific users who are affected by the GPO.

Troubleshooting Group Policies

Due to the wide variety of configurations that are possible when you are establishing GPOs, you should be aware of some common troubleshooting methods. These methods will help isolate problems in policy settings or GPO links.

One possible problem with GPO configuration is that logons and system startups may take a long time. This occurs especially in large environments when the Group Policy settings must be transmitted over the network and, in many cases, slow WAN links. In general, the number of GPOs should be limited because of the processing overhead and network requirements during logon. By default, GPOs are processed in a synchronous manner. This means that the processing of one GPO must be completed before another one is applied (as opposed to asynchronous processing, where they can all execute at the same time).

The most common issue associated with Group Policy is the unexpected setting of Group Policy options. In Windows Server 2000, administrators spent countless hours analyzing inheritance hierarchy and individual settings to determine why a particular user or computer was having policy problems. For instance, say a user named wpanek complains that the Run option is missing from his Start menu. The wpanek user account is stored in the New Hampshire OU, and you've applied group policies at the OU, domain, and site level. To determine the source of the problem, you would have to manually sift through each GPO to find the Start menu policy as well as figure out the applicable inheritance settings.

Windows Server 2008 has a handy feature called *Resultant Set of Policy (RSoP)* that displays the exact settings that actually apply to individual users, computers, OUs, domains, and sites after inheritance and filtering have taken effect. In the example just described, you could run RSoP on the wpanek account and view a single set of Group Policy settings that represent the settings that actually apply to the wpanek account. In addition, each setting's Properties dialog box displays the GPO that the setting is derived from, as well as the order of priority, the filter status, and other useful information, as you will see a bit later.

RSoP actually runs in two modes:

Logging mode   *Logging mode* displays the actual settings that apply to users and computers like in the example in the preceding paragraph.

Planning mode   *Planning mode* can be applied to users, computers, OUs, domains, and sites, and you use it before you actually apply any settings. Like its name implies, planning mode is used to plan GPOs.

Additionally, you can run the command-line utility `gpresult.exe` to quickly get a snapshot of the Group Policy settings that apply to a user and/or computer. Let's take a closer look at the two modes and the `gpresult.exe` command.

RSoP in Logging Mode

RSoP in logging mode can only query policy settings for users and computers. The easiest way to access RSoP in logging mode is through the Active Directory Users And Computers tool, although you can run it as a stand-alone MMC snap-in if you want to.

To analyze the policy settings for wpanek from the earlier example, you would right-click the user icon in Active Directory Users And Computers and select All Tasks ➢ Resultant Set of Policy (Logging). The Group Policy Results Wizard appears. The wizard walks you through the steps necessary to view the RSoP for wpanek.

The Computer Selection page, shown in Figure 8.15, requires you to select a computer for which to display settings. Remember that a GPO contains both user and computer settings, so you must choose a computer that the user has logged on to in order to continue with the wizard. If the user has never logged on to a computer, then you must run RSoP in planning mode, because there is no logged policy information for that user yet.

FIGURE 8.15   The Computer Selection page of the Resultant Set of Policy Wizard

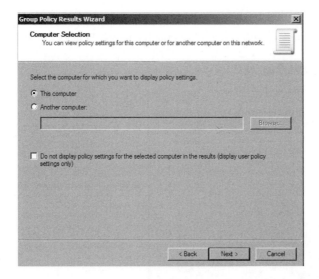

The User Selection page, shown in Figure 8.16, requires you to select a user account to analyze. Because we selected a user from the Active Directory Users And Computers tool, the username is filled in automatically. This page is most useful if you are running RSoP in MMC mode and don't have the luxury of selecting a user contextually.

FIGURE 8.16   The User Selection page of the Resultant Set of Policy Wizard

The Summary Of Selections page, shown in Figure 8.17, displays a summary of your choices and provides an option for gathering extended error information. If you need to make any changes before you begin to analyze the policy settings, you should click the Back button on the Summary screen. Otherwise, click Next.

FIGURE 8.17   The Summary of Selections page of the Group Policy Results Wizard

After the wizard is complete, you will see the window shown in Figure 8.18. This window looks very much like the Group Policy Object Editor window, but it only displays the policy settings that apply to the user and computer that you selected in the wizard. You can see these users and computers at the topmost level of the tree.

FIGURE 8.18   The User Selection page for user wpanek on computer SERVER1

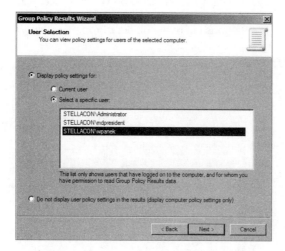

Any warnings or errors appear as a yellow triangle or red X over the applicable icon at the level where the warning or error occurred. To view more information about the warning or error, right-click the icon, select Properties, and select the Error Information tab. An error message is shown in Figure 8.19.

FIGURE 8.19   Details of error pertaining to user wpanek on computer SERVER1

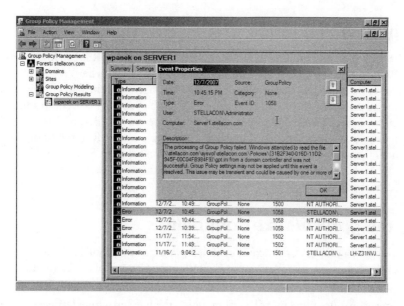

You cannot make changes to any of the individual settings because RSoP is a diagnostic tool and not an editor, but you can get more information about settings by clicking a setting and selecting Properties from the pop-up menu.

The Settings tab of the user's Properties window, shown in Figure 8.20, displays the actual setting that applies to the user in question based on GPO inheritance.

FIGURE 8.20   The Settings tab of the object's Properties window

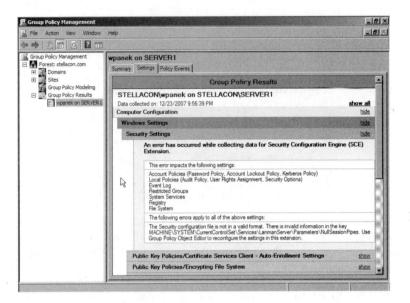

RSoP in Planning Mode

Running RSoP in planning mode isn't much different from running RSoP in logging mode, but the RSoP Wizard asks for a bit more information than you saw earlier.

In the earlier example, wpanek couldn't see the Run option in the Start menu because his user account is affected by the New Hampshire GPO in the San Jose OU. As an administrator, you could plan to move his user account to the North America OU. Before doing so, you could verify his new policy settings by running RSoP in planning mode. Run the RSoP on the user wpanek under the scenario that you've already moved him from the San Jose OU to the North America OU. At this point, you haven't actually moved the user, but you can see what his settings would be if you did.

Using the *gpresult.exe* Command

The command-line utility *gpresult.exe* is included as part of the RSoP tool. Running the command by itself without any switches returns the following Group Policy information about the local user and computer:

- The name of the domain controller from which the local machine retrieved the policy information
- The date and time in which the policies were applied
- Which policies were applied

- Which policies were filtered out
- Group membership

You can use the switches shown in Table 8.1 to get information for remote users and computers and to enable other options.

TABLE 8.1   gpresult Switches

Switch	Description
/S systemname	Generates RSoP information for a remote computer name
/USER username	Generates RSoP information for a remote username
/V	Specifies verbose mode, which displays more verbose information such as user rights information
/Z	Specifies an even greater level of verbose information
/SCOPE MACHINE	Displays maximum information about the computer policies applied to this system
/SCOPE USER	Displays maximum information about the user policies applied to this system
>textfile.txt	Writes the output to a text file

For example, to obtain information about user wpanek in a system called STELLACON, you would use the command gpresult /S STELLACON /USER wpanek.

Through the use of these techniques, you should be able to track down even the most elusive Group Policy problems. Remember, however, that good troubleshooting skills do not replace planning adequately and maintaining GPO settings!

Summary

In this chapter, we examined Active Directory's solution to a common headache for many systems administrators: policy settings. Specifically, we discussed topics that covered Group Policy.

We covered the fundamentals of Group Policy including its fundamental purpose. You can use Group Policy to enforce granular permissions for users in an Active Directory environment. Group policies can restrict and modify the actions they allow for users and computers within the Active Directory environment.

Also group policies can restrict and modify the actions that are allowed for users and computers within the Active Directory environment. Certain Group Policy settings may apply to users, computers, or both. Computer settings affect all users that access the machines to which the policy applies. User settings affect users, regardless of which machines they log on to.

You learned that you can link Group Policy objects (GPOs) to Active Directory sites, domains, or OUs. This link determines to which objects the policies apply. GPO links can interact through inheritance and filtering to result in an effective set of policies.

We covered inheritance and how GPOs filter down. We showed you how to use the Enforced option on a GPO issued from a parent and how to block a GPO from a child.

You also learned that you can use administrative templates to simplify the creation of GPOs. We covered the basic default templates that come with Windows Server 2008.

In addition, administrators can delegate control over GPOs in order to distribute administrative responsibilities. Delegation is an important concept because it allows for distributed administration.

You can also deploy software using GPOs. This feature can save time and increase productivity throughout the entire software management lifestyle by automating software installation and removal on client computers. The Windows Installer offers a more robust method for managing installation and removal, and applications that support it can take advantage of new Active Directory features. Make sure that you are comfortable using the Windows Installer.

You learned about publishing applications via Active Directory and the difference between publishing and assigning applications. We explained that you can assign some applications to users and computers so that they are always available. You can also publish them to users so that they may be installed by the user with a minimal effort when a user requires them.

You also learned how to prepare for software deployment. Before your users can take advantage of automated software installation, you must set up an installation share and provide the appropriate permissions.

The final portion of the chapter covered the Resultant Set of Policy (RSoP) tool, which you can use in logging mode or planning mode to determine exactly which set of policies apply to users, computers, OUs, domains, and sites.

Exam Essentials

Understand the purpose of Group Policy.   System administrators use Group Policy to enforce granular permissions for users in an Active Directory environment.

Understand user and computer settings.   Certain Group Policy settings may apply to users, computers, or both. Computer settings affect all users that access the machines to which the policy applies. User settings affect users, regardless of which machines they log on to.

Know the interactions between Group Policy objects and Active Directory.   GPOs can be linked to Active Directory objects. This link determines to which objects the policies apply.

Understand filtering and inheritance interactions between GPOs.   For ease of administration, GPOs can interact via inheritance and filtering. It is important to understand these interactions when you are implementing and troubleshooting Group Policy.

Know how Group Policy settings can affect script policies and network settings.   You can use special sets of GPOs to manage network configuration settings.

Understand how delegation of administration can be used in an Active Directory environment. Delegation is an important concept because it allows for distributed administration.

Know how to use the Resultant Set of Policy (RSoP) tool to troubleshoot and plan Group Policy. Windows Server 2008 includes the RSoP feature, which you can be run in logging mode or planning mode to determine exactly which set of policies apply to users, computers, OUs, domains, and sites.

Identify common problems with the software life cycle. IT professionals face many challenges with client applications, including development, deployment, maintenance, and troubleshooting.

Understand the benefits of the Windows Installer. Using the Windows Installer is an updated way to install applications on Windows-based machines. It offers a more robust method for making the system changes required by applications, and it allows for a cleaner uninstall. Windows Installer–based applications can also take advantage of new Active Directory features.

Understand the difference between publishing and assigning applications. Some applications can be assigned to users and computers so that they are always available. Applications can be published to users so that the user may install the application with a minimal amount of effort when it is required.

Know how to prepare for software deployment. Before your users can take advantage of automated software installation, you must set up an installation share and provide the appropriate permissions.

Know how to configure application settings using Active Directory and Group Policy. Using standard Windows Server 2008 administrative tools, you can create an application policy that meets the needs of your requirements. Features include automatic, on-demand installation of applications as well as many other features.

Create application categories to simplify the list of published applications. It's important to group applications by functionality or the users to whom they apply, especially in organizations that support a large number of programs.

Review Questions

1. A systems administrator is planning to implement Group Policy objects (GPOs) in a new Windows Server 2008 Active Directory environment. In order to meet the needs of the organization, he decides to implement a hierarchical system of Group Policy settings. At which of the following levels is he able to assign Group Policy settings? (Choose all that apply.)

   A. Sites

   B. Domains

   C. Organizational units (OUs)

   D. Local system

2. Ann is a systems administrator for a medium-sized Active Directory environment. She has determined that several new applications that will be deployed throughout the organization use Registry-based settings. She would like to do the following:

   - Control these Registry settings using Group Policy.
   - Create a standard set of options for these applications and allow other systems administrators to modify them using the standard Active Directory tools.

   Which of the following options can she use to meet these requirements? (Choose all that apply.)

   A. Implement the inheritance functionality of GPOs.

   B. Implement delegation of specific objects within Active Directory.

   C. Implement the No Override functionality of GPOs.

   D. Create administrative templates.

   E. Provide administrative templates to the systems administrators that are responsible for creating Group Policy for the applications.

3. Script policies can be set for which of the following events? (Choose all that apply.)

   A. Logon

   B. Logoff

   C. Startup

   D. Shutdown

4. John is developing a standards document for settings that are allowed by systems administrators in an Active Directory environment. He wants to maintain as much flexibility as possible in the area of Group Policy settings. In which of the following languages can script policies be written? (Choose all that apply.)

   A. Visual Basic Scripting Edition (VBScript)

   B. JScript

   C. Other Windows Script Host (WSH) languages

   D. Batch files

5. The process of assigning permissions to set Group Policy for objects within an OU is known as

    A. Promotion

    B. Inheritance

    C. Delegation

    D. Filtering

6. You are a systems administrator for a medium-sized Active Directory environment. Specifically, you are in charge of administering all objects that are located within the North America OU. The North America OU contains the Corporate OU. You want to do the following:

    ▪ Create a GPO that applies to all users within the North America OU except for those located within the Corporate OU.

    ▪ Be able to easily apply all Group Policy settings to users within the Corporate OU, should the need arise in the future.

    ▪ Accomplish this task with the least amount of administrative effort.

    Which two of the following options meets these requirements?

    A. Enable the Inheritance functionality of GPOs for all OUs within the North America OU.

    B. Implement delegation of all objects within the North America OU to one administrator and then remove permissions for the Corporate OU. Have this administrator link the GPO to the North America OU.

    C. Create a GPO link for the new policy at the level of the North America OU.

    D. Create special administrative templates for the Corporate OU.

    E. Enable the Block Inheritance option on the Corporate OU.

7. The process by which lower-level Active Directory objects inherit Group Policy settings from higher-level ones is known as

    A. Delegation

    B. Inheritance

    C. Cascading permissions

    D. Overriding

8. To disable GPO settings for a specific security group, which of the following permissions should you apply?

    A. Deny Write

    B. Allow Write

    C. Enable Apply Group Policy

    D. Disable Apply Group Policy

9. Trent is a systems administrator in a medium-sized Active Directory environment. He is responsible for creating and maintaining Group Policy settings. For a specific group of settings, he has the following requirements:

   - The settings in the Basic Users GPO should remain defined.
   - The settings in the Basic Users GPO should not apply to any users within the Active Directory environment.
   - The amount of administrative effort to apply the Basic Users settings to an OU in the future should be minimal.

   Which of the following options can Trent use to meet these requirements?

   A. Enable the No Override option at the domain level.

   B. Enable the Block Policy Inheritance option at the domain level.

   C. Remove the link to the Basic Users GPO from all Active Directory objects.

   D. Delete the Basic Users GPO.

   E. Rename the Basic Users GPO to break its link with any existing Active Directory objects.

10. Which of the following statements is true regarding the actions that occur when a software package is removed from a GPO that is linked to an OU?

   A. The application will be automatically uninstalled for all users with the OU.

   B. Current application installations will be unaffected by the change.

   C. The systems administrator may determine the effect.

   D. The current user may determine the effect.

11. GPOs assigned at which of the following level(s) will override GPO settings at the domain level?

   A. OU

   B. Site

   C. Domain

   D. Both OU and site

12. A systems administrator wants to ensure that only the GPOs set at the OU level affect the Group Policy settings for objects within the OU. Which option can they use to do this (assuming that all other GPO settings are the defaults)?

   A. The Enforced option

   B. The Block Policy Inheritance option

   C. The Disable option

   D. The Deny permission

13. In order to be accessible to other domain controllers, you should place logon/logoff and startup/shutdown scripts in which of the following shares?

   A. `Winnt`

   B. `System`

   C. `C$`

   D. `SYSVOL`

14. A systems administrator wants to ensure that a particular user will have access to Microsoft Office XP regardless of the computer to which they log on. Which of the following should they do?

   A. Assign the application to all computers within the environment and specify that only this user should have access to it.

   B. Assign the application to the user.

   C. Publish the application to all computers within the environment and specify that only this user should have access to it.

   D. Publish the application to the user.

15. Alicia is a systems administrator for a large organization. Recently, the company has moved most of its workstations and servers to the Windows Server 2008 platform and Alicia wants to take advantage of the new software deployment features of Active Directory. Specifically, she wants to do the following:

- Make applications available to users through the Add Or Remove Programs item in the Control Panel.
- Group applications based on functionality or the types of users who might require them.
- Avoid the automatic installation of applications for users and computers.

Which of the following steps should Alicia take to meet these requirements? (Choose all that apply.)

   A. Create application categories.

   B. Set up a software installation share and assign the appropriate security permissions.

   C. Assign applications to users.

   D. Assign applications to computers.

   E. Create new file extension mappings.

   F. Create application definitions using Active Directory and Group Policy administration tools.

16. You are the systems administrator for 123 Corp. You have been tasked with helping your mobile users find a way to access stored company files. You need to set up a solution that allows your mobile users the flexibility they need to use data stored on local servers within your organization's network. Which of the following is the best way to do this?

   A. Offline folders

   B. Folder redirection

   C. SYSVOL replication

   D. Folder replication

17. As the administrator responsible for your company's Active Directory deployment, you are asked to provide a solution for Group Policy management. You need to use a tool that allows you to manage Group Policy forest-wide. Which tool allows you to manage Group Policy across the enterprise, is downloadable from Microsoft, and adds features such as services for backing up Group Policy?

    A. Active Directory Sites And Services tool

    B. Active Directory Users And Computers tool

    C. Group Policy Management Console (GPMC)

    D. The Resultant Set of Policy (RSoP) tool

18. Emma wants to make a specific application available on the network. She finds that using Group Policy for software deployment will be the easiest way. She has the following requirements:

    ▪ All users of designated workstations should have access to Microsoft Office XP.

    ▪ If a user moves to other computers on which Microsoft Office XP is not installed, they should not have access to this program.

    Which of the following options should Emma choose to meet these requirements?

    A. Assign the application to computers.

    B. Assign the application to users.

    C. Publish the application to computers.

    D. Publish the application to users.

19. You are attempting to add a layer of security in your current domain of about 5 Windows Server 2008 systems and 40 Windows XP Professional workstations. You are asked about using certificates. What system is this technology part of?

    A. TKI—temporary-key infrastructure

    B. PKI—public-key infrastructure

    C. DCS—digital certificate system

    D. OTP—one-time passwords

20. You are the lead network administrator for your company. You have been tasked with the responsibility of creating GPOs and linking specific settings to targeted computers. You'll be using the GPOs to store the settings. You need to link specific settings to specific OUs and you may need to link them elsewhere. What are the other two levels in which you can link settings within Active Directory? (Choose all that apply.)

    A. Sites

    B. Groups

    C. Computers

    D. Domains

Answers to Review Questions

1. A, B, C, D. GPOs can be set at all of the levels listed. You cannot set GPOs on security principals such as users or groups.

2. D, E. Administrative templates are used to specify the options available for setting Group Policy. By creating new administrative templates, Ann can specify which options are available for the new applications. She can then distribute these templates to other systems administrators in the environment.

3. A, B, C, D. Script policies can be set for any of the events listed.

4. A, B, C, D. WSH can be used with any of these languages. Standard batch files can also be used.

5. C. The Delegation of Control Wizard can be used to allow other systems administrators permission to add GPO links to an Active Directory object.

6. C, E. The easiest way to accomplish this task is to create GPO links at the level of the parent OU (North America) and block inheritance at the level of the child OU (Corporate).

7. B. Inheritance is the process by which lower-level Active Directory objects inherit GPO settings from higher-level ones. You should always be aware of how inheritance will apply to your Active Directory hierarchy when you are configuring GPOs.

8. D. To disable the application of Group Policy on a security group, you should disable the Apply Group Policy option. This is particularly useful when you don't want GPO settings to apply to a specific group, even though that group may be in an OU that includes the GPO settings.

9. C. Systems administrators can disable a GPO without removing its link to Active Directory objects. This prevents the GPO from having any effects on Group Policy but leaves the GPO definition intact so that it can be enabled at a later date.

10. C. The systems administrator can specify whether the application will be uninstalled or if future installations will be prevented.

11. A. GPOs at the OU level take precedence over GPOs at the domain level. GPOs at the domain level, in turn, take precedence over GPOs at the site level.

12. B. The Block Policy Inheritance option prevents group policies of higher-level Active Directory objects from applying to lower-level objects as long as the Enforced option is not set.

13. D. By default, the contents of the SYSVOL share are made available to all domain controllers. Therefore, you should place scripts in these directories.

14. B. Assigning the application to the user ensures that the user will have access to Microsoft Office XP, regardless of the computer they use. The other options would mean that the user either wouldn't have access to the application at all, or would need to log on to a specific computer.

15. A, B, F. Alicia should first create an application share from which programs can be installed. Then, she can define which applications are available on the network. The purpose of application categories is to logically group applications in the Add Or Remove Programs item in the Control Panel. The other options can result in the automatic installation of applications for users and computers (something that she wants to avoid).

16. A. Folder redirection and offline folders are different features. The way that Windows Server 2008 folder redirection works is that the system uses a pointer that moves the folders you want to a location you specify. When data is needed, it's available, but once the user is mobile (not local), the data is no longer accessible. A way to fix this is to use the Offline Folders feature, which allows you to keep folders with information synchronized—thus you'd have a local copy on your local system that you'd take with you while you were on the move and you'd be able to synchronize it with a copy on the server when you returned. Copies of the data stay the same, which is a perfect feature for mobile users, whereas folder redirection provides no benefit for the mobile user.

17. C. The GPMC is a Microsoft-based downloadable tool that allows you full control and flexibility when you're deploying and managing Group Policy; it also provides add-on features and backup services.

18. A. Assigning the application to the computer will ensure that all users who access the workstation will have access to Microsoft Office XP. You cannot publish to computers, and assigning or publishing the application to users would mean that only those users could use the application and they would be able to access it from any machine on the network.

19. B. PKI stands for public-key infrastructure. Certificates are part of PKI, which is used to add a layer of security into your client/server infrastructure. The rest of the answers are incorrect distracters.

20. A, D. Group Policy settings are kept in GPOs. GPOs can be linked to sites, domains, and OUs.

Chapter

9

Planning Security for Active Directory

MICROSOFT EXAM OBJECTIVES COVERED IN THIS CHAPTER:

✓ **Creating and Maintaining Active Directory Objects**

- Maintain Active Directory accounts. May include but is not limited to: configure group membership; delegation; AGDLP/AGGUDLP; deny domain local group; local vs. domain; Protected Admin; disabling accounts vs. deleting accounts; deprovisioning; contacts; creating organizational units (OUs); delegation of control

- Configure GPO templates. May include but is not limited to: user rights; ADMX Central Store; administrative templates; security templates; restricted groups; security options; starter GPOs; shell access policies

- Configure audit policy by using GPOs. May include but is not limited to: audit logon events; audit account logon events; audit policy change; audit access privilege use; audit directory service access; audit object access

- Configure account policies. May include but is not limited to: domain password policy; account lockout policy; fine-grain password policies

✓ **Configuring Active Directory Certificate Services**

- Manage enrollments. May include but is not limited to: network device enrollment service (NDES); autoenrollment; Web enrollment; smart card enrollment; creating enrollment agents

So far in this book we have covered many important aspects of Active Directory. The most important aspect of any network, including Active Directory, is security. If your network is not secure, then hackers (internal or external) can make your life as an IT member a living nightmare.

All network operating systems (NOSs) offer some way to grant or deny access to resources, such as files and printers. Active Directory is no exception. You can define fundamental security objects through the use of the users, groups, and computers security principals. Then you can allow or disallow access to resources by granting specific permissions to each of these objects.

In this chapter, you'll learn how to implement security within Active Directory. By using Active Directory tools, you can quickly and easily configure the settings that you require in order to protect information.

Proper planning for security permissions is an important prerequisite of setting up Active Directory. Security is always one of the greatest concerns as an IT administrator.

If your security settings are too restrictive, users may not be able to perform their job functions. Worse yet, they may try to circumvent security measures. They may even complain to their management teams, and eventually you will receive these complaints. On the other end of the spectrum, if security permissions are too lax, users may be able to access and modify sensitive company resources.

You may continuously try to seek balance—to have enough security and, at the same time, be somewhat transparent to the end users, who simply want to do their jobs and not be bothered by what's between the lines.

You should have a security policy that states what is expected of every computer user in your company. Fine-tuning Active Directory to comply with your security policy and allowing end users to function without an issue should be your goal.

You should know how to use Active Directory to apply permissions to resources on the network. An administrator should pay particular attention to the evaluation of permissions when applied to different groups and the flow of permissions through the organizational units (OUs) via group policies. With all of this in mind, let's start looking at how you can manage security within Active Directory.

In order to complete the exercises in this chapter, you should understand the basics of working with Active Directory objects. If you are not familiar with creating and managing users, groups, computers, and OUs, you should review the information in Chapter 7, "Administering Active Directory," before you continue.

Active Directory Security Overview

One of the fundamental design goals for Active Directory is to define a single, centralized repository of users and information resources. Active Directory records information about all of the users, computers, and resources on your network. Each domain acts as a security boundary, and members of the domain (including workstations, servers, and domain controllers) share information about the objects within them.

The information stored within Active Directory determines which resources are accessible to which users. Through the use of *permissions* that are assigned to Active Directory objects, you can control all aspects of network security.

Throughout this chapter, you'll learn the details of security as it pertains to Active Directory. Note, however, that Active Directory security is only one aspect of overall network security. You should also be sure that you have implemented appropriate access control settings for the filesystem, network devices, and other resources. Let's start by looking at the various components of network security, which include working with security principals, and managing security and permissions, access control lists (ACLs), and access control entries (ACEs).

A fact that you should always keep in mind while you are setting up a network is that 80 percent of all hacks on a network are internal. This means that internal permissions and security (as well as external) need to be as strong as possible while still allowing users to do their jobs.

Understanding Security Principals

Security principals are Active Directory objects that are assigned *security identifiers (SIDs)*. A SID is a unique identifier that is used to manage any object to which permissions can be assigned. Security principals are assigned permissions to perform certain actions and access certain network resources.

The basic types of Active Directory objects that serve as security principals include the following:

User accounts   User accounts identify individual users on your network by including information such as the user's name and their password. User accounts are the fundamental unit of security administration.

Groups   There are two main types of groups: *security groups* and *distribution groups*. Both types can contain user accounts. Systems administrators use security groups to ease the management of security permissions. They use distribution groups, on the other hand, solely to send email. Distribution groups are not security principals. You'll see the details of groups in the next section.

Computer accounts   Computer accounts identify which client computers are members of particular domains. Because these computers participate in the Active Directory database, systems administrators can manage security settings that affect the computer. They use computer accounts to determine whether a computer can join a domain and for authentication purposes. As you'll see later in this chapter, systems administrators can also place restrictions on certain computer settings to increase security. These settings apply to the computer and, therefore, also apply to any user who is using it (regardless of the permissions granted to the user account).

Note that other objects—such as OUs—do not function as security principals. What this means is that you can apply certain settings (such as Group Policy) on all of the objects within an OU; however, you cannot specifically set permissions with respect to the OU itself. The purpose of OUs is to logically organize other Active Directory objects based on business needs, add a needed level of control for security, and create an easier way to delegate.

You can manage security by performing the following actions with security principals:

- You can assign them permissions to access various network resources.

- You can give them user rights.

- You can track their actions through auditing (covered later in this chapter).

The three types of security principals—user accounts, groups, and computer accounts—form the basis of the Active Directory security architecture. As a systems administrator, you will likely spend a portion of your time managing permissions for these objects.

 It is important to understand that, since a unique SID defines each security principal, deleting a security principal is an irreversible process. For example, if you delete a user account and then later re-create one with the same name, you need to reassign permissions and group membership settings for the new account. Once a user account is deleted, its SID is deleted.

Users and groups are two types of fundamental security principals employed for security administration. In the following sections, you'll learn how users and groups interact and about the different types of groups that you can create.

Types of Groups

When dealing with groups, you should make the distinction between local security principals and domain security principals:

- You use *local users and groups* to assign the permissions necessary to access the local machine. For example, you may assign the permissions you need to reboot a domain controller to a specific local group.

- *Domain users and groups*, on the other hand, are used throughout the domain. These objects are available on any of the computers within the Active Directory domain and between domains that have a trust relationship.

Here are the two main types of groups used in Active Directory:

Security groups Security groups are considered security principals. They can contain user accounts. To make administration simpler, systems administrators usually grant permissions to groups. This allows you to change permissions easily at the Active Directory level (instead of at the level of the resource on which the permissions are assigned).

You can also place Active Directory Contact objects within security groups, but security permissions will not apply to them.

Distribution groups Distribution groups are not considered security principals, because they do not have SIDs. As mentioned earlier, they are used only for the purpose of sending email messages. You can add users to distribution groups just as you would add them to security groups. You can also place distribution groups within OUs so they are easier to manage. You will find them useful, for example, if you need to send email messages to an entire department or business unit within Active Directory.

Understanding the differences between security and distribution groups is important in an Active Directory environment. For the most part, systems administrators use security groups for daily administration of permissions. On the other hand, systems administrators who are responsible for maintaining email distribution lists generally use distribution groups to logically group members of departments and business units. (A system administrator can also email all of the users within a security group, but to do so, they would have to specify the email addresses for the accounts.)

When you are working in Windows 2000 Native, Server 2003, or Server 2008 functional level domains, you can convert security groups to or from distribution groups. When group types are running in a Windows 2000 Mixed domain functional level, you cannot change them.

It is vital that you understand Group types when you are getting ready to take the Microsoft exams. Microsoft likes to include trick questions about putting permissions on Distribution groups. Remember, only Security groups can have permissions assigned to them.

Group Scope

In addition to being classified by type, each group is also given a specific scope. The scope of a group defines two characteristics. First, it determines the level of security that applies to a group. Second, it determines which users can be added to the group. Group scope is an important concept in network environments because it ultimately defines which resources users are able to access.

The three types of group scope are as follows:

Domain local   The scope of *domain local groups* extends as far as the local machine. When you're using the Active Directory Users And Computers tool, domain local accounts apply to the computer for which you are viewing information. Domain local groups are used to assign permissions to local resources, such as files and printers. They can contain global groups, universal groups, and user accounts.

Global   The scope of *global groups* is limited to a single domain. Global groups may contain any of the users that are a part of the Active Directory domain in which the global groups reside. Global groups are often used for managing domain security permissions based on job functions. For example, if you need to specify permissions for the Engineering Department, you could create one or more global groups (such as EngineeringManagers and Engineering-Developers). You could then assign security permissions to each group for any of the resources within the domain.

Universal   *Universal groups* can contain users from any domains within an Active Directory forest. Therefore, system administrators use them to manage security across domains. Universal groups are available only when you're running Active Directory in the Windows 2000 Native, Windows Server 2003, or Windows Server 2008 domain functional level. When you are managing multiple domains, it often helps to group global groups within universal groups. For instance, if you have an Engineering global group in the `research.stellacon.com` domain and an Engineering global group in the `asia.stellacon.com` domain, you can create a universal AllEngineers group that contains both of the global groups. Now, whenever you must assign security permissions to all engineers within the organization, you need only assign permissions to the AllEngineers universal group.

For domain controllers to process authentication between domains, information about the membership of universal groups is stored in the Global Catalog (GC). Keep this in mind if you ever plan to place users directly into universal groups and bypass global groups because all of the users will be enumerated in the GC, which will impact size and performance.

Fortunately, universal group credentials are cached on domain controllers that universal group members use to log on. This process is called universal group membership caching (discussed in Chapter 4: Installing and Managing Trees and Forests). The cached data is obtained by the domain controller whenever universal group members log on, and then it is retained on the domain controller for eight hours by default. This is especially useful for smaller locations, such as branch offices, that run less expensive domain controllers. Most domain controllers at these locations cannot store a copy of the entire GC, and frequent calls to the nearest GC would require an inordinate amount of network traffic.

When you create a new group using the Active Directory Users And Computers tool, you must specify the scope of the group. Figure 9.1 shows the New Object - Group dialog box and the available options for the group scope.

FIGURE 9.1   The New Object—Group dialog box

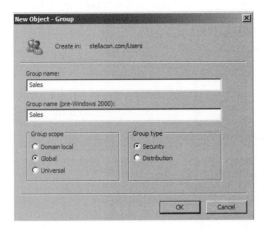

As you can see, the main properties for each of these group types are affected by whether Active Directory is running in Windows 2000 Mixed, Windows 2000 Native, Server 2003, or Server 2008 domain functional level (Figure 9.1 shows that you are in Native mode because all three options are available). Each of these scope levels is designed for a specific purpose and will ultimately affect the types of security permissions that you can assign to them.

The following are limitations on group functionality when you are running in Windows 2000 Mixed domain functional level:

- Universal security groups are not available.

- You are not allowed to change the scope of groups.

- Limitations to group nesting exist. Specifically, the only nesting allowed is global groups contained in domain local groups.

When you are running in Native mode domains, you can make the following group scope changes:

- You can change domain local groups to a universal group. You can make this change only if the domain local group does not contain any other domain local groups.

- You can change a global group to a universal group. You can only make this change if the global group is not a member of any other global groups.

Universal groups themselves cannot be converted into any other group scope type. However, changing group scope can be helpful when your security administration or business needs change. You can change group scope easily using the Active Directory Users And Computers tool. To do so, access the properties of the group. As shown in Figure 9.2, you can make a group scope change by clicking one of the options.

FIGURE 9.2   A group's Properties dialog box

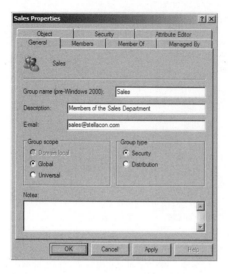

Built-In Domain Local Groups

Systems administrators use built-in domain local groups to perform administrative functions on the local server. Because these have preassigned permissions and privileges, they allow systems administrators to easily assign common management functions. Figure 9.3 shows the default built-in groups that are available on a Windows Server 2008 domain controller.

FIGURE 9.3   Default built-in local groups

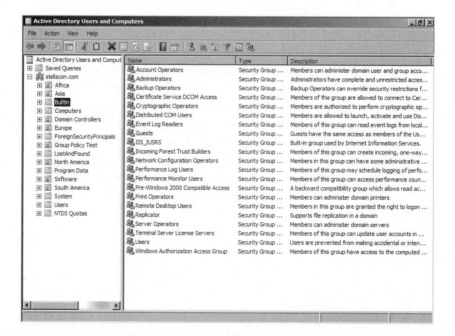

The list of built-in local groups includes some of the following:

Account Operators   These users can create and modify domain user and group accounts. Members of this group are generally responsible for the daily administration of Active Directory.

Administrators   Members of the Administrators group, by default, are given full permissions to perform any functions within the Active Directory domain and on the local computer. This means they can access all files and resources that reside on any server within the domain. As you can see, this is a very powerful account.

In general, you should restrict the number of users who are included in this group because most common administration functions do not require this level of access.

Backup Operators   One of the problems associated with backing up data in a secure network environment is that you need to provide a way to bypass standard file system security so you can copy files. Although you could place users in the Administrators group, doing so usually provides more permissions than necessary. Members of the Backup Operators group can bypass standard filesystem security for the purpose of backup and recovery only. They cannot, however, directly access or open files within the filesystem.

Generally, backup software applications and data use the permissions assigned to the Backup Operators group.

Certificate Service DCOM Access   Members of the Certificate Service DCOM Access group can connect to certificate authority servers in the Enterprise.

Cryptographic Operators   Members of the Cryptographic Operators group are authorized to perform cryptographic operations. Cryptography allows the use of codes to convert data, which then allows a specific recipient to read it using a key.

Guests   Typically, you use the Guests group to provide access to resources that generally do not require security. For example, if you have a network share that provides files that should be made available to all network users, you can assign permissions to allow members of the Guest group to access those files.

Print Operators   By default, members of the Print Operators group are given permissions to administer all of the printers within a domain. This includes common functions such as changing the priority of print jobs and deleting items from the print queue.

Replicator   The Replicator group allows files to be replicated among the computers in a domain. You can add accounts used for replication-related tasks to this group to provide those accounts with the permissions they need to keep files synchronized across multiple computers.

Server Operators   A common administrative task is managing server configuration. Members of the Server Operators group are granted the permissions they need to manage services, shares, and other system settings.

Users   The Users built-in domain local group is used to administer security for most network accounts. Usually, you don't give this group many permissions and use it to apply security settings for most employees within an organization.

The remaining built-in groups, such as Network Configuration Operators and Performance Monitor Users, are beyond the scope of this book and are not part of the 70-640 exam.

Windows Server 2008 also includes many different default groups you can find in the Users folder. As shown in Figure 9.4, these groups are of varying scopes, including domain local, global, and universal groups. You'll see the details of these groups in the next section.

FIGURE 9.4 Contents of the default Users folder

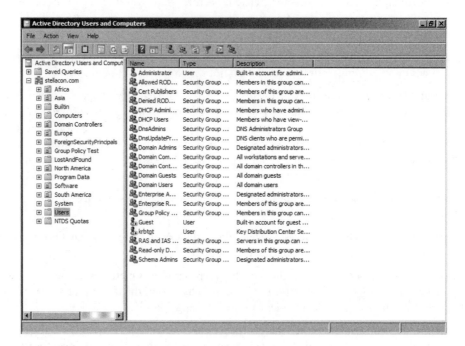

Three important user accounts are created during the promotion of a domain controller:

- The Administrator account is assigned the password a systems administrator provides during the promotion process, and it has full permissions to perform all actions within the domain.

- The Guest account is disabled by default. The purpose of the Guest account is to provide anonymous access to users who do not have an individual logon and password to use within the domain. Although the Guest account might be useful in some situations, it is generally recommended that this account be disabled to increase security.

- Only the operating system uses the krbtgt or Key Distribution Center Service account for Kerberos authentication while it is using DCPromo.exe. This account is disabled by default. Unlike other user accounts, the krbtgt account cannot be used to log on to the domain, and therefore it does not need to be enabled. Since only the operating system uses this account, you do not need to worry about hackers gaining access by using this account.

Predefined Global Groups

As we mentioned earlier in this chapter, you use global groups to manage permissions at the domain level. Members of each of these groups can perform specific tasks related to managing Active Directory.

The following predefined global groups are installed in the Users folder:

Cert Publishers   Certificates are used to increase security by allowing for strong authentication methods. User accounts are placed within the Cert Publishers group if they must publish security certificates. Generally, Active Directory security services use these accounts.

Domain Computers   All of the computers that are members of the domain are generally members of the Domain Computers group. This includes any workstations or servers that have joined the domain, but it does not include the domain controllers.

Domain Admins   Members of the Domain Admins group have full permissions to manage all of the Active Directory objects for this domain. This is a powerful account; therefore, you should restrict its membership to only those users who require full permissions.

Domain Controllers   All of the domain controllers for a given domain are generally included within this group.

Domain Guests   Generally, by default, members of the Domain Guests group are given minimal permissions with respect to resources. Systems administrators may place user accounts in this group if they require only basic access or temporary permissions within the domain.

Domain Users   The Domain Users group usually contains all of the user accounts for the given domain. This group is generally given basic permissions to resources that do not require higher levels of security. A common example is a public file share.

Enterprise Admins   Members of the Enterprise Admins group are given full permissions to perform actions within the entire domain forest. This includes functions such as managing trust relationships and adding new domains to trees and forests.

Group Policy Creator Owners   Members of the Group Policy Creator Owners group are able to create and modify Group Policy settings for objects within the domain. This allows them to enable security settings on OUs (and the objects that they contain).

Schema Admins   Members of the Schema Admins group are given permissions to modify the Active Directory schema. As a member of Schema Admins, you can create additional fields of information for user accounts. This is a very powerful function because any changes to the schema will be propagated to all of the domains and domain controllers within an Active Directory forest. Furthermore, you cannot undo changes to the schema (although you can disable some).

In addition to these groups, you can create new ones for specific services and applications that are installed on the server (you'll notice the list in Figure 9.4 includes more than just the ones in the preceding list). Specifically, services that run on domain controllers and servers will be created as security groups with domain local scope. For example, if a domain controller is running the DNS service, the DNSAdmins and DNSUpdateProxy groups become available. In addition, there are two read-only domain controller (RODC) local groups: the Allowed RODC Password Replication and the Denied RODC Password Replication. Similarly, if you install the DHCP service, it automatically creates the DHCPUsers and DHCPAdministrators groups. The purpose of these groups depends on the functionality of the applications being installed.

Foreign Security Principals

In environments that have more than one domain, you may need to grant permissions to users who reside in multiple domains. Generally, you manage this using Active Directory trees and forests. However, in some cases, you may want to provide resources to users who belong to domains that are not part of the forest.

Active Directory uses the concept of *foreign security principals* to allow permissions to be assigned to users who are not part of an Active Directory forest. This process is automatic and does not require the intervention of systems administrators. You can then add the foreign security principals to domain local groups, which, in turn, you can grant permissions for resources within the domain. You can view a list of foreign security principals by using the Active Directory Users And Computers tool. Figure 9.5 shows the contents of the ForeignSecurityPrincipals folder.

FIGURE 9.5   The ForeignSecurityPrincipals folder

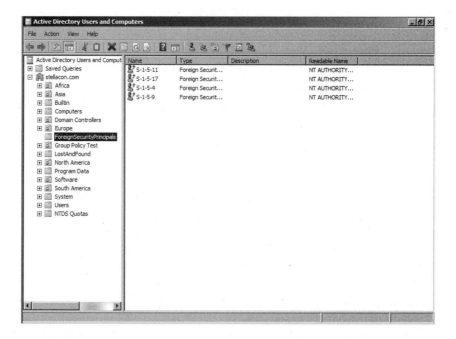

Managing Security and Permissions

Now that you understand the basic issues, terms, and Active Directory objects that pertain to security, it's time to look at how you can apply this information to secure your network resources. The general practice for managing security is to assign users to groups and then grant permissions and logon parameters to the groups so that they can access certain resources.

For management ease and to implement a hierarchical structure, you can place groups within OUs. You can also assign Group Policy settings to all of the objects contained within an OU. By using this method, you can combine the benefits of a hierarchical structure (through OUs) with the use of security principals. Figure 9.6 provides a diagram of this process.

FIGURE 9.6   An overview of security management

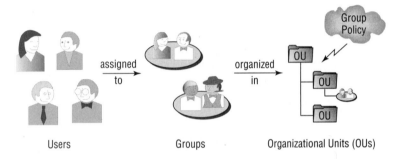

| Users | Groups | Organizational Units (OUs) |

The primary tool you use to manage security permissions for users, groups, and computers is the Active Directory Users And Computers tool. Using this tool, you can create and manage Active Directory objects and organize them based on your business needs. Common tasks for many systems administrators might include the following:

- Resetting a user's password (for example, in cases where they forget their password)

- Creating new user accounts (when, for instance, a new employee joins the company)

- Modifying group memberships based on changes in job requirements and functions

- Disabling user accounts (when, for example, users will be out of the office for long periods of time and will not require network resource access)

Once you've properly grouped your users, you need to set the actual permissions that affect the objects within Active Directory. The actual permissions available vary based on the type of object. Table 9.1 provides an example of some of the permissions that you can apply to various Active Directory objects and an explanation of what each permission does.

TABLE 9.1   Permissions of Active Directory Objects

Permission	Explanation
Control Access	Changes security permissions on the object
Create Child	Creates objects within an OU (such as other OUs)
Delete Child	Deletes child objects within an OU
Delete Tree	Deletes an OU and the objects within it
List Contents	Views objects within an OU
List Object	Views a list of the objects within an OU
Read	Views properties of an object (such as a username)
Write	Modifies properties of an object

Using ACLs and ACEs

Each object in Active Directory has an access control list (ACL). The ACL is a list of user accounts and groups that are allowed to access the resource. For each ACL, there is an access control entry (ACE) that defines what a user or a group can actually do with the resource. Deny permissions are always listed first. This means that if users have Deny permissions through user or group membership, they will not be allowed to access the object, even if they have explicit Allow permissions through other user or group permissions. Figure 9.7 shows an ACL for the Sales OU.

FIGURE 9.7   The ACL for an OU named Sales

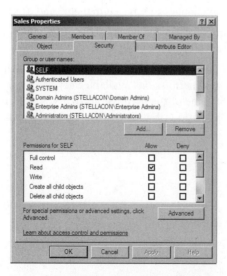

The Security tab is only enabled if you selected the Advanced Features option from the View menu in the Active Directory Users And Computers tool.

 Real World Scenario

Using Groups Effectively

You are a new systems administrator for a medium-sized organization, and your network spans a single campus-type environment. The previous administrator whom you replaced was the main person who migrated the network from Windows 2000 to Windows Server 2008. No one is really complaining about the network, and everyone seems happy with their new workstations. The environment is very collegial, with most employees on a first-name basis, and a great deal of your job is done in the hallway as you bump into people. As you familiarize yourself with the network, you soon realize that the previous administrator had a very ad hoc approach to administration. Many of the permissions to resources had been given to individual accounts as people asked for them. There doesn't seem to be any particular strategy in the design of the directory or the allocation of resources.

In one of your meetings with management, they tell you that the company has acquired another company, and if this acquisition goes well, several more acquisitions will follow. Management tells you about these sensitive plans because they do not want any hiccups in the information system as these new organizations are absorbed into the existing company.

You immediately realize that management practices of the past for this network have to vanish, and they need to be replaced with the best practices that have been developed for networks over the years. One of the fundamental practices you need to establish for this environment is the use of groups to apply permissions and give privileges to users through-out the network.

It is quite simple to give permissions individually, and in some cases, it seems like overkill to create a group, give permissions to the group, and then add a user to the group. But using group-based permissions really pays off in the long run, regardless of how small your net-work is today. One constant in the networking world is that networks grow. And when they grow, it is much easier to add users to a well-thought-out system of groups and consistently applied policies and permissions than it is to patch these elements together for each indi-vidual user.

Don't get caught up in the "easy" way of dealing with each request as it comes down the pike. Take the time to figure out how the system will benefit from a more structured approach. Visualize your network as already large with numerous accounts, even if it is still small; this way, when it grows, you will be well positioned to manage the network as smoothly as possible.

Implementing Active Directory Security

So far, you have looked at many different concepts that are related to security within Active Directory. You began by exploring security principals and how they form the basis for administering Active Directory security. Then, you considered the purpose and function of groups, how group scopes can affect how these groups work, and how to create a list of the predefined users and groups for new domains and domain controllers. Based on all of this information, it's time to see how you can implement Active Directory security.

In this section, you'll take a look at how you can create and manage users and groups. The most commonly used tool for working with these objects is the Active Directory Users And Computers tool. Using this tool, you can create new user and group objects within the relevant OUs of your domain, and you can modify group membership and group scope.

In addition to these basic operations, you can use some additional techniques to simplify the administration of users and groups. One method involves using user templates. Additionally, you'll want be able to specify who can make changes to user and group objects. That's the purpose of delegation. Both of these topics are covered later in this section.

Let's start with the basics. In Exercise 9.1, you learn how to create and manage users and groups.

 This exercise involves creating new OUs and user accounts within an Active Directory domain. Be sure that you are working in a test environment to avoid any problems that might occur due to the changes that you make.

EXERCISE 9.1

Creating and Managing Users and Groups

1. Open the Active Directory Users And Computers tool.

2. Create the following top-level OUs:

    Sales

    Marketing

    Engineering

    HR

3. Create the following User objects within the Sales container (use the defaults for all fields not listed):

    a. First Name: **John**

        Last Name: **Sales**

User Logon Name: **JSales**

   b. First Name: **Linda**

       Last Name: **Manager**

       User Logon Name: **LManager**

4. Create the following User objects within the Marketing container (use the defaults for all fields not listed):

   a. First Name: **Jane**

       Last Name: **Marketing**

       User Logon Name: **JMarketing**

   b. First Name: **Monica**

       Last Name: **Manager**

       User Logon Name: **MManager**

5. Create the following User object within the Engineering container (use the defaults for all fields not listed):

       First Name: **Bob**

       Last Name: **Engineer**

       User Logon Name: **BEngineer**

6. Right-click the HR container, and select New ➢ Group. Use the name **Managers** for the group, and specify Global for the group scope and Security for the group type. Click OK to create the group.

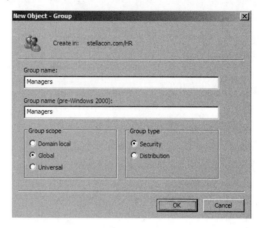

7. To assign users to the Managers group, right-click the Group object and select Properties. Change to the Members tab, and click Add. Enter Linda Manager and Monica Manager, and then click OK. You will see the group membership list. Click OK to finish adding the users to the group.

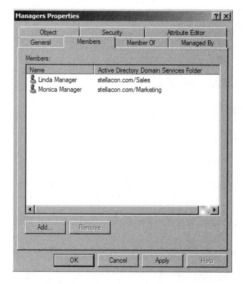

8. When you are finished creating users and groups, close the Active Directory Users And Computers tool.

Notice that you can add users to groups regardless of the OU in which they're contained. In Exercise 9.1, for example, you added two user accounts from different OUs into a group that was created in a third OU. This type of flexibility allows you to easily manage user and group accounts based on your business organization.

The Active Directory Users And Computers tool also allows you to perform common functions by simply right-clicking an object and selecting actions from the context menu. For example, you could right-click a user account and select Add Members To Group to quickly change group membership. You even have the ability in Active Directory Users And Computer to drag a user from one OU and drop them into another.

You may have noticed that creating multiple users can be a fairly laborious and a potentially error-prone process. As a result, you are probably ready to take a look at a better way to create multiple users—by using user templates, discussed in the next section.

Using User Templates

Sometimes you will need to add several users with the same security settings. Rather than creating each user from scratch and making configuration changes to each one manually, you can create one user template, configure it, and copy it as many times as necessary. Each copy retains the configuration, group membership, and permissions of the original, but you must specify a new username, password, and full name to make the new user unique.

In Exercise 9.2, you create a user template, make configuration changes, and create a new user based on the template. This exercise shows you that the new user you create will belong to the same group as the user template that you copied it from. You should have completed Exercise 9.1 before you begin this one.

EXERCISE 9.2

Creating and Using User Templates

1. Open the Active Directory Users And Computers tool.

2. Create the following User object within the Sales container (use the defaults for all fields not listed):

    First Name: **Sales User**

    Last Name: **Template**

    User Logon Name: **SalesUserTemplate**

3. Create a new global security group called **Sales Users**, and add SalesUserTemplate to the group membership.

4. Right-click the SalesUserTemplate user object and select Copy from the context menu.

5. Enter the username, first name, and last name for the new user.

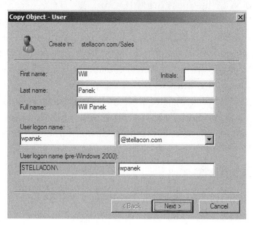

6. Click the Next button to move on to the password screen and enter the new user's password information. Close the Copy Object - User dialog box when you're done.

7. Right-click the user you created in step 5, select Properties, and click the Member Of tab.

8. Verify that the new user is a member of the Sales Users group.

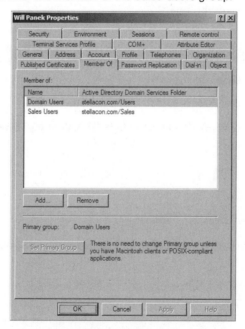

Delegating Control of Users and Groups

A common administrative function related to the use of Active Directory involves managing users and groups. You can use OUs to logically group objects so that you can easily manage them. Once you have placed the appropriate Active Directory objects within OUs, you are ready to delegate control of these objects.

Delegation is the process by which a higher-level security administrator assigns permissions to other users. For example, if Admin A is a member of the Domain Admins group, he is able to delegate control of any OU within the domain to Admin B. You can access the Delegation of Control Wizard through the Active Directory Users And Computers tool. You can use it to quickly and easily perform common delegation tasks. The wizard walks you through the steps of selecting for which object(s) you want to perform delegation, what permission you want to allow, and which users will have those permissions.

Exercise 9.3 walks through the steps required to delegate control of OUs. In order to complete the steps in this exercise, you must have already completed Exercise 9.1.

EXERCISE 9.3

Delegating Control of Active Directory Objects

1. Open the Active Directory Users And Computers tool.

2. Create a new user within the Engineering OU, using the following information (use the default settings for any fields not specified):

    First Name: **Robert**

    Last Name: **Admin**

    User Logon Name: **radmin**

3. Right-click the Sales OU, and select Delegate Control. This starts the Delegation of Control Wizard. Click Next.

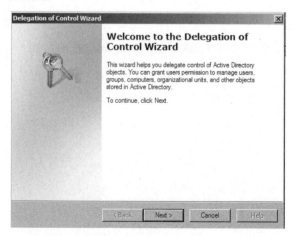

4.   To add users and groups to which you want to delegate control, click the Add button. In the Add dialog box, enter **Robert Admin** for the name of the user to add. Note that you can specify multiple users or groups using this option.

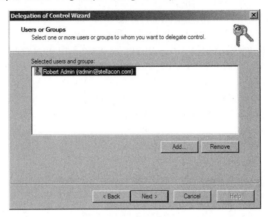

5.   Click OK to add the account to the delegation list, which is shown in the Users Or Groups page. Click Next to continue.

6.   On the Tasks To Delegate page, you must specify which actions you want to allow the selected user to perform within this OU. Select the Delegate The Following Common Tasks option, and place a check mark next to the following options:

Create, Delete, And Manage User Accounts

Reset User Passwords And Force Password Change At Next Logon

Read All User Information

Create, Delete And Manage Groups

Modify The Membership Of A Group

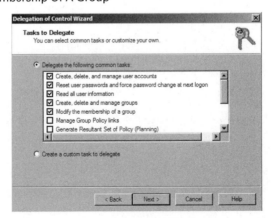

7. Click Next to continue. The wizard provides you with a summary of the selections that you have made on the Completing The Delegation Of Control Wizard page. To complete the process, click Finish to have the wizard commit the changes.

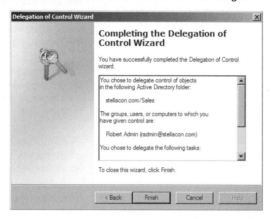

Now, when the user Robert Admin logs on (using `radmin` as his logon name), he will be able to perform common administrative functions for all of the objects contained within the Sales OU.

8. When you are finished, close the Active Directory Users And Computers tool.

Using Group Policy for Security

As discussed in Chapter 8, "Configuring Group Policy Objects," a very useful and powerful feature of Active Directory is a technology known as a Group Policy. Through the use of Group Policy settings, systems administrators can assign literally hundreds of different settings and options for users, groups, and OUs. Specifically, in relation to security, you can use many different options to control how important features such as password policies, user rights, and account lockout settings can be configured.

The general process for making these settings is to create a Group Policy object (GPO) with the settings that you want, and to then link it to an OU or other Active Directory object.

Table 9.2 lists many Group Policy settings that are relevant to creating a secure Active Directory environment. Note that this list is not complete—many other options are available through Windows Server 2008's administrative tools.

TABLE 9.2 Group Policy Settings Used for Security Purposes

Setting Section	Setting Name	Purpose
Account Policies ➢ Password Policy	Enforce PasswordHistory	Specifies how many passwords will be remembered. This option prevents users from reusing the same passwords, whenever they're changed.
Account Policies ➢ Password Policy	Minimum Password Length	Prevents users from using short, weak passwords by specifying the minimum number of characters that the password must include.
Account Policies ➢ Account Lockout Policy	Account Lockout Threshold	Specifies how many bad password attempts will be entered before the account gets locked out.
Account Policies ➢ Account Lockout Policy	Account LockoutDuration	Specifies how long an account will remain locked out after too many bad password attempts have been entered. By setting this option to a reasonable value (such as "30 minutes"), you can reduce administrative overhead while still maintaining fairly strong security.
Account Policies ➢ Account Lockout Policy	Reset Account Lockout Counter After	Specifies how long the Account Lockout Threshold counter will hold failed logon attempts before resetting to 0.
Local Policies ➢ Security Options	Accounts: RenameAdministrator Account	Often, when trying to gain unauthorized access to a computer, individuals attempt to guess the Administrator password. One method for increasing security is to rename this account so that no password allows entry using this logon.
Local Policies ➢ Security Options	Domain Controller: Allow Server Operators To Schedule Tasks	This option specifies whether members of the built-in Server Operators group are allowed to schedule tasks on the server.

TABLE 9.2   Group Policy Settings Used for Security Purposes

Setting Section	Setting Name	Purpose
Local Policies ➢ Security Options	Interactive Logon: Do Not Display Last User Name	Increases security by not displaying the name of the last user who logged into the system.
Local Policies ➢ Security Options	Shutdown: Allow System To Be Shut Down Without Having To Log On	Allows systems administrators to perform remote shutdown operations without logging on to the server.

You can use several different methods to configure Group Policy settings using the tools included with Windows Server 2008. Exercise 9.4 walks through the steps required to create a basic Group Policy for the purpose of enforcing security settings. In order to complete the steps of this exercise, you must have already completed Exercise 9.1.

EXERCISE 9.4

Applying Security Policies by Using Group Policy

1. Open the Group Policy Management Console tool.

2. Expand Domains and then click the domain name.

3. In the right pane, right-click the Default Domain Policy and choose Edit.

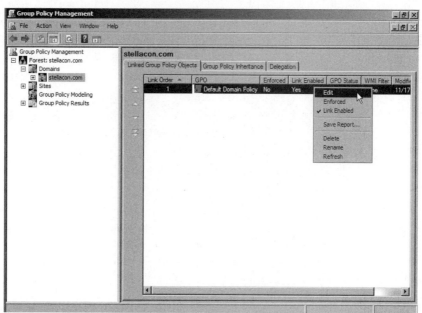

EXERCISE 9.4 *(continued)*

4. In the Group Policy Management Editor window, expand the Computer Configuration, Windows Settings, Security Settings, Account Policies, and Password Policy objects.

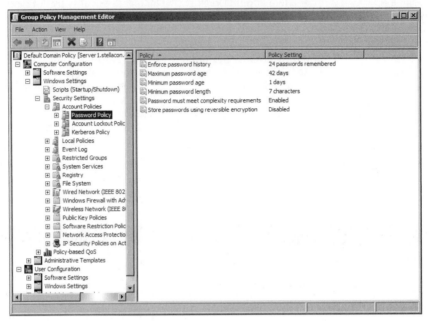

5. In the right pane, double-click the Minimum Password Length setting.

6. In the Security Policy Setting dialog box, make sure the box labeled Define This Policy Setting option is checked. Increase the Password Must Be At Least value to 8 characters.

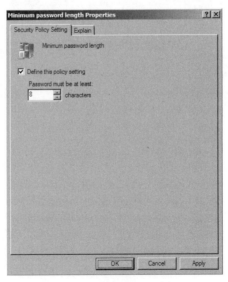

7. Click OK to return to the Group Policy Management Editor window.

8. Expand the User Configuration, Administrative Templates, and Control Panel objects. Double-click Prohibit Access To The Control Panel, select Enabled, and then click OK.

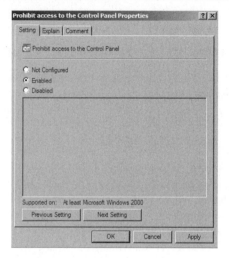

9. Close the Group Policy window.

Understanding Smart Card Authentication

In the previous section, we discussed password policies and account lockout policies that increase security for Windows Server 2008. However, the standard account logon process is still fairly insecure due to the fact that a malicious attacker only needs a single piece of information—a password—to log on to the network. This problem is compounded by the fact that users or administrators probably would not detect a stolen password until after it had been used by a hacker to break into the system. Smart cards, which are similar in appearance to credit cards, solve both of these problems.

Smart cards store user certificate information in a magnetic strip (barcode) or on a gold chip on a plastic card. As an alternative to the standard username and password logon process, users can insert a smart card into a special smart card reader attached to the computer and enter a unique PIN on the keyboard. This provides the system with a double-verification (two-factor authentication) secure logon (the smart card and the PIN) and reduces the likelihood that a user's authentication method will be stolen without detection.

To deploy a smart card solution in the enterprise you must have a certificate authority (CA) and a public-key infrastructure (PKI) on your intranet. In each domain, you must configure the security permissions of the Smart Card User, Smart Card Logon, and Enrollment Agent certificate templates to allow smart card users to enroll for certificates. You must also set up the CA to issue smart card certificates and Enrollment Agent certificates.

After you've configured your certificate server to meet the requirements for smart card authentication, you can set up a smart card enrollment station and begin issuing smart cards to users. Most organizations that use smart card authentication don't allow standard authentication at all, so Microsoft provides a Group Policy setting that requires the use of smart cards.

Preparing a Smart Card Certificate Enrollment Station

To begin issuing smart cards, you must prepare a smart card certificate enrollment station where you physically transfer the authentication information to smart cards. You need to install a smart card reader on the enrollment station, which in this case doubles as a smart card writer.

Smart card readers are available from a variety of manufacturers, so you should always make sure that any smart card reader your company purchases is listed on the Windows Server 2008 hardware compatibility list (HCL).

After you've properly installed the smart card reader, you need to install an Enrollment Agent certificate on the enrollment station, which you obtain from your CA.

Exercises 9.5 and 9.6 walk you through the process of configuring an enrollment station. Note that you must have access to a company CA configured to meet the requirements of smart card authentication in order to complete this exercise.

We understand that most people reading this book do not have a smart card reader just lying around. If you do not have a smart card reader, do as much of the exercise as possible. This will still give you a feel for the process. If you would like to practice on a smart card reader, you can pick up a reader and a card for very little money on an online auction site.

EXERCISE 9.5

Installing a Certificate for a Smart Card Enrollment Station

1. Log on as the user or administrator who will issue the smart card certificates.

2. Open a Microsoft Management Console (MMC) by selecting Start ➢ Run and entering **mmc** in the Run dialog box.

3. Add the Certificates snap-in by selecting File ➢ Add/Remove Snap-in. Select the Certificates snap-in and click the Add button. When the Certificate Snap-in dialog box appears, choose My User Account and click Finish.

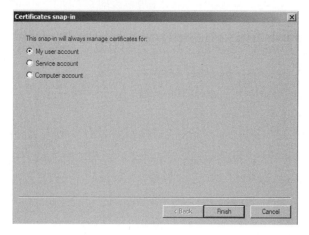

4. Click OK to return to the MMC and display the newly added snap-in.

5. Double-click the Certificates—Current User node in the MMC window.

6. Right-click Personal in the Logical Store Name pane and select All Tasks ➢ Request New Certificate.

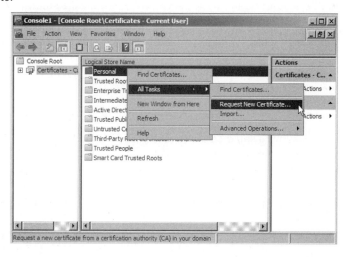

7. In the Certificate Request Wizard, select the Enrollment Agent certificate template. Enter a name and description for the template. When prompted, click Install Certificate.

Writing Certificate Information onto Smart Cards

After you've prepared the enrollment station to enroll smart cards certificates, you can actually begin writing certificate information to the physical cards. Follow the steps in Exercise 9.6 to enroll a smart card for user logon. Note that you must complete Exercise 9.5 before continuing. In addition, you must have a smart card reader and at least one blank smart card available.

EXERCISE 9.6

Setting Up a Smart Card for User Logon

1.   Log on to the computer as the user or administrator that you configured in the previous exercise.

2.   Open Internet Explorer by selecting Start ➤ All Programs ➤ Internet Explorer.

3.   In the Address field, enter the address of the CA that issues smart card certificates and press Enter.

4.   In the Internet Explorer (IE) window, click Request a Certificate, and then click Advanced Certificate Request.

5.   Click "Request a certificate for a smart card on behalf of another user using the smart card certificate enrollment station". If prompted, click Yes to accept the smart card signing certificate.

6.   Click Smart Card Logon on the Smart Card Certificate Enrollment Station web page.

7.   Under Certification Authority, select the CA you want to issue the smart card certificate.

8.   Under Cryptographic Service Provider, select the cryptographic service provider of the smart card's manufacturer.

9.   Under Administrator Signing Certificate, click the Enrollment Agent certificate from the previous exercise.

10.   Under User To Enroll, click Select User. Select the user to enroll and click Enroll.

11.   When prompted, insert the smart card into the smart card reader and click OK. When prompted, enter a new PIN for the smart card.

Configuring Group Policy Settings for Smart Cards

Now that you've seen how to configure a smart card enrollment station and set up smart cards for user logon, you should begin to think about Group Policy settings for enforcing smart card logon. One of the most common mistakes that administrators make when administering a smart card policy is to not require smart card logon at all. This means that users with smart cards can log on with either their smart cards or through the standard username and password procedure, which defeats the point of issuing smart cards in the first place! Exercise 9.7 shows you how to configure Group Policy to require smart card authentication.

EXERCISE 9.7

Configuring Group Policy to Require Smart Card Logon

1. Open the Active Directory Users And Computers tool.

2. Create a new top-level OU called **Smart Card Test**.

3. Close the Active Directory Users And Computers tool and open the Group Policy Management Console.

4. Right-click the Smart Card Test OU and select Create A GPO In This Domain And Link It Here.

5. In the New GPO dialog box, enter **Smart Card GPO Test** in the Name box and Click OK. Right-click the new GPO and then click the Edit button.

6. In the Group Policy Object Editor window, expand Computer Configuration ➢ Windows Settings ➢ Security Settings ➢ Local Policies ➢ Security Options.

7. Double-click the Interactive Logon: Require Smart Card policy.

8. Check the box labeled Define This Policy Setting and then select Enabled and click OK.

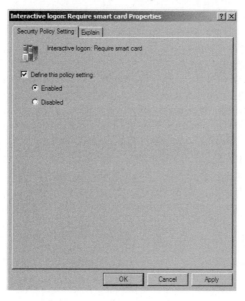

9. Close the Group Policy Management Console.

Understanding Security Configuration and Analysis Tools

The power and flexibility of Windows-based operating systems are both benefits and liabilities. On the plus side, the many configuration options available allow users and systems administrators to modify and customize settings. On the negative side, however, when systems administrators allow all users full functionality, problems can arise. For example, novice users might attempt to delete critical system files or incorrectly uninstall programs to free up disk space.

So how can you prevent these types of problems? One method is to control the types of actions that users can perform. Because you can configure most settings for the Windows Server 2008 interface in the Registry, you could edit the appropriate settings using the RegEdit command. However, this process can become quite tedious. Furthermore, manually modifying the Registry is a dangerous process and one that is bound to cause problems due to human error. In order to make creating and applying security settings easier, Microsoft has included the Security Configuration And Analysis utility with Windows Server 2008. They have also built this utility's functionality into a command-line utility called secedit.exe.

Using the Security Configuration And Analysis Utility

You can use the *Security Configuration And Analysis utility* together with security template files to create, modify, and apply security settings in the Registry . *Security templates* allow systems administrators to define security settings once and then store this information in a file that can be applied to other computers.

These template files offer a user-friendly way to configure common settings for Windows Server 2008 operating systems. For example, instead of searching through the Registry (which is largely undocumented) for specific keys, a systems administrator can choose from a list of common options. The template file provides a description of the settings, along with information about the Registry key(s) to which the modifications must be made. Templates can be stored and applied to users and computers. For example, we could create three configurations named Level 1, Level 2, and Level 3. We may use the Level 3 template for high-level managers and engineers, and the Level 1 and Level 2 templates for all other users who need only basic functionality.

The overall process for working with the Security Configuration And Analysis utility is as follows:

1. Open or create a security database file.

2. Import an existing template file.

3. Analyze the local computer.

4. Make any setting changes.

5. Save any template changes.

6. Export the new template (optional).

7. Apply the changes to the local computer (optional).

The Security Configuration And Analysis utility has no default icon. In order to access it, you must manually choose this snap-in from within the MMC.

Exercise 9.8 walks you through the steps you need to take to use the Security Configuration And Analysis utility. In this exercise, you will use this utility to create and modify security configurations.

EXERCISE 9.8

Using the Security Configuration And Analysis Utility

1. Click Start ➢ Run, type **mmc**, and press Enter. This opens a blank MMC.

2. In the File menu, select Add/Remove Snap-In. Select the Security Configuration And Analysis item, then click Add. You will see that the Security Configuration And Analysis snap-in has been added to the configuration. Click OK to continue.

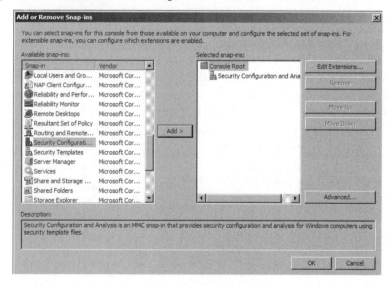

3. Within the MMC, right-click Security Configuration And Analysis, and select Open Database. This displays a standard file selection (Open) dialog box. Change to a local directory on your computer, and create a new security database file named `SecurityTest.sdb`. Note the location of this file because you'll need it in later steps. Click Open.

4. You'll be prompted to open a Security Template file. By default, these files are stored within the Security\Templates directory of your Windows system root. In the Import Template dialog box, select DC Security, and place a check mark in the Clear This Database Before Importing box. Click Open to load the Security Template file.

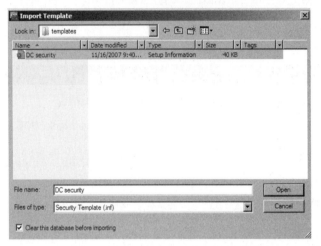

5. Within the Security Configuration And Analysis utility, you have access to several tasks. To analyze the security configuration of the local computer, right-click the Security Configuration And Analysis utility, and select Analyze Computer Now.

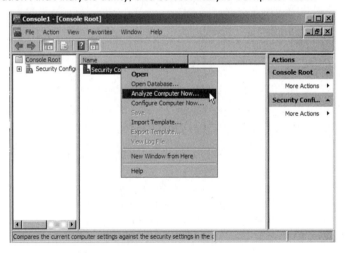

6. When prompted, enter the path to a local directory with the filename `securityTest.log`. Click OK to begin the analysis process. You will now see the Security Configuration And Analysis utility begin to analyze your computer.

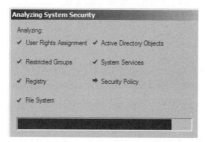

7. When the process has been completed, you can view the current security settings for the local computer. Navigate through the various items to view the current security configuration.

8. To make changes to this template, expand the Password Policy object under Account Policies. Double-click the Enforce Password History item. In the Enforce Password History Properties dialog box, place a check mark next to the Define This Policy In The Database, and enter **2** for Passwords Remembered.

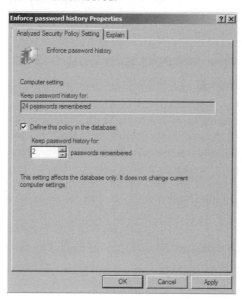

9. Click OK to make the setting change.

   Note that this change in setting was not enabled for the local computer—the change was implemented only within the security database file.

10. To save the changes to the Security Database file, right-click the Security And Configuration Analysis utility, and select Save.

11. To export the current settings to a Template file, right-click the Security And Configuration Analysis utility, and select Export Template. You are prompted for the location and filename to which these settings should be saved. Be sure to choose a meaningful name so that other systems administrators will understand the purpose of this template.

12. As of yet, the configuration change you made has not yet been applied to any machines. To apply the change to the local computer, right-click the Security And Configuration Analysis utility, and select Configure Computer Now. You are prompted to enter the path for a log file. Enter any path on the local computer, and specify **SecurityTest2.log** as the filename. Click OK. You should see the settings being applied to the local computer.

13. To quickly view the contents of the log file for the most recent operation, right-click the Security And Configuration Analysis utility, and select View Log.

14. When you are finished, exit the Security And Configuration Analysis utility by closing the MMC.

Understanding the *secedit.exe* Command

All of the functionality of the Security Configuration And Analysis utility has also been built into a command-line utility called secedit.exe. One advantage of using secedit.exe is that you can perform a batch analysis without having to use the graphical tools.

Just like the Security Configuration And Analysis utility, the command-line utility is database driven, meaning that you can use switches to access database and configuration files. The secedit.exe command performs the following high-level functions: analysis, configuration, export function, and validation. These are the same functions carried out by the Security Configuration And Analysis graphical utility (described in the previous section and exercise).

Table 9.3 lists the secedit.exe switches and their functions.

If any errors occur during the security configuration and analysis process, the results will be stored in the log file that is created. Be sure to examine this file for any errors that might be present in your configuration.

TABLE 9.3   *secedit.exe* Switches

Switch	Valid with Switch	Function
/analyze	Independent function	Analyzes system security.
/configure	Independent function	Configures system security by applying a stored template.
/refreshpolicy	Independent function	Reapplies security settings to the GPO.
/export	Independent function	Exports a template from the database to the template file.
/validate	Independent function	Validates the syntax of a security template.
[/DB *filename*]	/analyze, /configure, /export	Required with the /analyze and /configure commands. Optional with others. Specifies the path to the database file.
[/CFG *filename*]	/analyze, /configure, /export	Required if a new database file is specified. Specifies the path to a security template to import into the database.
[/log *logpath*]	/analyze, /configure, /export	Specifies the path to the log file generated during the operation.
[/verbose]	/analyze, /configure, /export	Specifies more detailed progress information.
[/quiet]	/analyze, /configure, /export	Suppresses screen output during the operation.
[/overwrite]	/configure	Optional only if [/CFG *filename*] is used. Completely overwrites the database rather than appending the database.
[/areas *area1 area2*]	/configure, /export	Specifies security areas to be applied to the system. Default is all areas. Options are SECURITYPOLICY, GROUP_MGMT, USER_RIGHTS, REGKEYS, FILESTORE, and SERVICES.

TABLE 9.3 *secedit.exe* Switches *(continued)*

Switch	Valid with Switch	Function
Machine_policy	/refreshpolicy	Refreshes security settings for the local computer.
User_policy	/refreshpolicy	Refreshes security settings for the current local user account.
/enforce	/refreshpolicy	Refreshes security settings even if no changes have been made to the GPO.
/MergedPolicy	/export	Merges local and domain policy in the export file.
Filename	/validate	Indicates the filename of the template to validate.

 Real World Scenario

Enforcing Consistent Security Policies

You are one of 50 systems administrators for a large, multinational organization. As is the case for most of these administrators, you're responsible for all operations related to a portion of an Active Directory domain. Specifically, your job is to manage all of the aspects of administration for objects contained within the Portsmouth OU. The Portsmouth office supports nearly 500 employees. Recently, security has become an important concern because the company is growing quickly and new employees are being added almost daily. In addition, the organization deals with customers' sensitive financial information, and the success of the business is based on this information remaining secure. You've been tasked with creating and implementing an Active Directory security policy for the Portsmouth OU.

At first you start looking into the Group Policy settings that might be appropriate for attaining the desired level of security. You create different levels of security based on users' job functions. Specific policy options include restricting when users can access network resources and which resources they can access. You also begin to implement settings that "harden" your production servers, especially those that contain sensitive data.

A few days after you begin your analysis, you join the weekly company-wide IT conference call and learn that you're not alone in this task. It seems that systems administrators throughout the company have been given similar tasks. The only difference is that they're all asked to implement policies only for the specific Active Directory objects for which they're responsible. That gets you thinking about pooling resources: That is, although it might make sense to attack this task for just the Portsmouth OU, wouldn't it be great if the entire organization could implement a consistent and uniform security policy? If every systems administrator decided to implement security policies in a different way, this would compromise consistency and ease of administration within the environment. And it's likely that many systems administrators will create useful security policies that the others overlooked. The idea of "think globally, act locally" may apply here.

The Security Configuration And Analysis utility that is included with Windows Server 2008 is designed to solve exactly this type of problem. You find that by using this tool, you can design a set of security configurations and then apply those policies to various computers within the environment. You decide to begin by creating security templates based on business needs. Because the environment has many different requirements (and some that are specific only to a few offices), your goal is to minimize the number of different security templates that you create while still meeting the needs of the entire organization. Perhaps the best way to proceed in this scenario is to pool resources: Many tech-heads are better than one! However, keep in mind that this will be more of a political task than a technical one, at least until the various administrators can come together. One of the results—and benefits—of Active Directory is that many of these decisions can be centralized so that the departmental administrators can spend their time helping users with specific issues rather than on duplicating effort. Regardless, creating the appropriate security policies is unlikely to be an easy task—you'll need to confer with systems administrators throughout the company and you'll need to talk to managers and business leaders as well. However, it will be worth the effort to ensure that the entire organization has implemented consistent security policies. Overall, a little extra work up front can save a lot of headaches in the long run.

Implementing an Audit Policy

One of the most important aspects of controlling security in networked environments is ensuring that only authorized users are able to access specific resources. Although systems administrators often spend much time managing security permissions, it is almost always possible for a security problem to occur.

Sometimes, the best way to find possible security breaches is to actually record the actions specific users take. Then, in the case of a security breach (the unauthorized shutdown of a server, for example), systems administrators can examine the log to find the cause of the problem.

The Windows Server 2008 operating system and Active Directory offer you the ability to audit a wide range of actions. In the following sections, you'll see how to implement auditing for Active Directory.

Overview of Auditing

The act of auditing relates to recording specific actions. From a security standpoint, auditing is used to detect any possible misuse of network resources. Although auditing does not necessarily prevent resources from being misused, it does help determine when security violations occurred (or were attempted). Furthermore, just the fact that others know that you have implemented auditing may prevent them from attempting to circumvent security.

You need to complete several steps in order to implement auditing using Windows Server 2008:

- Configure the size and storage settings for the audit logs.

- Enable categories of events to audit.

- Specify which objects and actions should be recorded in the audit log.

Note that there are trade-offs to implementing auditing. First and foremost, recording auditing information can consume system resources. This can decrease overall system performance and use up valuable disk space. Second, auditing many events can make the audit log impractical to view. If too much detail is provided, systems administrators are unlikely to scrutinize all of the recorded events. For these reasons, you should always be sure to find a balance between the level of auditing details provided and the performance-management implications of these settings.

Implementing Auditing

Auditing is not an all-or-none type of process. As is the case with security in general, systems administrators must choose specifically which objects and actions they want to audit.

The main categories for auditing include the following:

- Audit account logon events

- Audit account management

- Audit directory service access

- Audit logon events

- Audit object access

- Audit policy change

- Audit privilege use

- Audit process tracking

- Audit system events

In the above list of categories, there are four of these categories that are related to Active Directory. Let's discuss these four auditing categories in a bit more detail.

Audit account logon events   You enable this auditing event if you want to audit when a user authenticates with a domain controller and log onto the domain. This event is logged in the security log on the domain controller.

Audit account management   This auditing event is used when you want to watch what changes are being made to Active Directory accounts. For example, when another administrator creates or deletes a user account, it would be an audited event.

Audit directory service access   This auditing event occurs whenever a user or administrator accesses Active Directory objects. Let's say an administrator opens Active Directory and clicks on a user account, even if nothing is changed on that account, an event is audited.

Audit logon events   Account logon events are created for domain account activity. For example, you have a user that logons to a server so that they can access files; the act of logging onto the server creates this audit event.

In order to audit access to objects stored within Active Directory, you must enable the Audit Directory Service Access option. Then you must specify which objects and actions should be tracked.

Exercise 9.9 walks through the steps you must take to implement auditing of Active Directory objects on domain controllers. In order to complete the steps in this exercise, you must have already completed Exercise 9.1.

EXERCISE 9.9

Enabling Auditing of Active Directory Objects

1.   Open the Local Security Policy tool (located in the Administrative tools program group).

2.   Expand Local Policies and then expand Audit Policy.

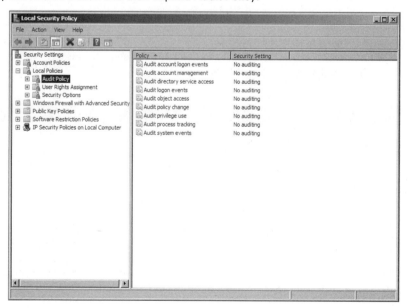

EXERCISE 9.9 *(continued)*

3. Double-click the setting for Audit Directory Service Access.

4. In the Audit Directory Service Access Properties dialog box, place check marks next to Success and Failure. Click OK to save the settings.

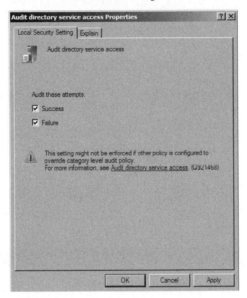

5. Close the Local Security Policy Tool.

Once you have enabled auditing of Active Directory objects, it's time to specify exactly which actions and objects should be audited. Exercise 9.10 walks through the steps required to enable auditing for a specific OU. In order to complete the steps in this exercise, you must have already completed Exercise 9.1 and Exercise 9.9.

EXERCISE 9.10

Enabling Auditing for a Specific OU

1. Open the Active Directory Users And Computers tool.

2. To enable auditing for a specific object, right-click the Engineering OU, and select Properties. Select the Group Policy tab on the Engineer Properties dialog box.

3. Highlight the Engineering Security Settings Group Policy object, if present, and select Properties.

4. Select the Security tab on the GPO Properties dialog box, and then click Advanced. Select the Auditing tab. You will see the current auditing settings for this GPO.

5. Click the Edit button. Notice that you can view and change auditing settings based on the objects and/or properties. To retain the current settings, click OK. (You may need to create a new GPO. For more information, see Chapter 8.)

6. To exit the configuration for the Engineering object, click OK three more times.

7. When you are finished with the auditing settings, close the Active Directory Users And Computers tool.

Viewing Auditing Information

One of the most important aspects of auditing is regularly monitoring the audit logs. If this step is ignored, as it often is in poorly managed environments, the act of auditing is useless. Fortunately, Windows Server 2008 includes the *Event Viewer* tool, which allows systems administrators to quickly and easily view audited events. Using the filtering capabilities of Event Viewer, they can find specific events of interest.

Exercise 9.11 walks through the steps you must take to generate some auditing events and to examine the data collected for these actions. In this exercise, you will perform some actions that will be audited, and then you will view the information recorded within the audit logs. In order to complete this exercise, you must have already completed the steps in Exercise 9.1 and Exercise 9.10.

Generating and Viewing Audit Logs

1. Open the Active Directory Users And Computers tool.

2. Within the Engineering OU, right-click the Bob Engineer User account, and select Properties.

3. On the Bob Properties dialog box, add the middle initial **A** for this User account, and specify **Software Developer** in the Description box. Click OK to save the changes.

4. Within the Engineering OU, right-click the Robert Admin User account, and select Properties.

5. On the Robert Properties dialog box add a description of **Engineering IT Admin**, and click OK.

6. Close the Active Directory Users And Computers tool.

7. Open the Event Viewer tool from the Administrative Tools program group. Select the Security item under Windows Logs. You will see a list of audited events categorized under Directory Service Access. Note that you can obtain more details about a specific item by double-clicking it.

8. When you are finished viewing the Security Log, close the Event Viewer tool.

Real World Scenario

Real World Security Hacks for Your Windows Server 2008 Accounts

Always secure your domain controllers. In production environments, you could wind up very vulnerable to attack by not securing your accounts, which is not what you want. Once you have installed Windows Server 2008, you need to begin the lockdown process. Now more than ever, you need to analyze and address security issues for any default installation of any operating system or platform. With such an emphasis placed on security these days, each install you do needs to be addressed, and it's no different with Windows Server 2008. After you complete a basic install, you should start a checklist of items that you want to lock down, remove, and audit, or at least know about to keep yourself and your systems safe from threat.

After you install the system, you need to address a few issues pertaining to the installation. First, remember that most of the time, the new system has much in common with the old one as well as many other systems out there. The first common issues for Windows-based systems are the Guest and Administrator accounts. Not only can a hacker try to expose a weakness in this commonality, but also malware-based attacks have been known to use the built-in Administrator account as a potential starting point from which to gain entry to or compromise your system. This is very common these days; many of the virus attacks on most corporate networks have depended on this weakness.

When you keep default accounts in your server, you may be asking for trouble. Any password attack known to IT professionals today is based on the hacker's knowing two things, the username and the password. If they have half the equation, as they do in the case of credentials (most of the time these are just a password tied to an account), then all they need is a good password cracking tool, a huge dictionary file, and some time.

Another option is to set those accounts up completely so that they function as an early alert system that lets you know someone is picking the lock on your door. If you get an account lockout (if you set it up and find it logged in your Event Viewer) on the default accounts, you can be pretty sure that you are under attack. You can't avoid this scenario when you leave default accounts in your design. Although you can't delete many of the default accounts, you will have the option of renaming them.

By default, the Guest account is not operational on either member servers or domain controllers. This is good news because it means that you don't really have to worry about it being exploited unless someone enables it. However, it is important that you check to make sure that it is not and does not become active.

The Administrator account, on the other hand, is a more powerful account that needs to be handled with care. This is because the server can be easily compromised if a hacker just compromises the administrative credentials of the system. Therefore, it is very important for you to know about this account and lock it down immediately after you finish installing the base NOS. To do so, you can rename the account with Group Policy or set it up as an account that is used only to log and audit attempts for use. If you decide to make a new Administrator account under a different name, make sure you don't give out the new name and, in addition, make sure you secure it. Normally, in smaller organizations, it's easier to just rename the account and then set it up as a trap, but doing so is up to you. Always try to create a backup Administrator account and use it instead, but if you do, you want to make sure you never lock yourself out of the system. To prevent this from happening, make sure you note what the new account will be called.

Summary

In this chapter, we talked about planning for and implementing security with Active Directory. You cannot overlook security; it's important to always consider how security may affect your deployment or lack of it—how it will ultimately affect your system if it is hacked.

We also looked at the differences between security and distribution groups. Distribution groups are used for only one thing: email distribution lists. These groups are used with email applications (such as Microsoft Exchange Server 2007) to send email to the members of the group you create. They will not allow you to assign permissions, and you cannot use them to filter Group Policy settings. In the Windows Server 2008 operating system, security groups are used to manage user account and computer account access to shared resources and to filter Group Policy settings.

We also explained other important items that pertain to security, such as what default groups are available after a base install of the operating system, and how to secure the most vulnerable accounts.

We then examined how permissions are managed. You can change permissions with Group Policy or simply by altering them right on the object. We also covered how delegation of control can be used to distribute administrative responsibilities. We wrapped up this chapter by discussed auditing—why it's important and how to get it done.

Thoroughly understanding each of these topics is important when you're implementing Active Directory in a business environment (and when you're preparing for the exam). In the next chapter, we focus on Active Directory reliability and how to optimize it.

Exam Essentials

Understand the purpose of security principals. Security principals are Active Directory objects that can be assigned permissions. Understanding how they work is vital to creating a secure Active Directory environment. Security principals include users, groups, and computers.

Understand group types and group scope. The two major types of groups are security and distribution groups, and they have different purposes. Groups can be local, global, or universal. Domain local groups are used to assign permissions to local resources, such as files and printers. The scope of global groups is limited to a single domain. Universal groups can contain users from any domains within an Active Directory forest.

Understand the purpose and permissions of built-in groups. The Active Directory environment includes several built-in local and global groups that are designed to simplify common systems administration tasks. For instance, members of the Administrators group are given full permissions to perform any functions within the Active Directory domain and on the local computer.

Understand how to use Group Policy to manage password and other security-related policies. Through the use of Group Policy settings, you can configure password and account-related options. You can also specify to which users, groups, and OUs many of the settings apply.

Understand how to configure smart card authentication. Smart card authentication requires a CA for issuing smart card certificates. To enroll a smart card certificate, you must first prepare a smart card enrollment station and then write certificate information to the smart cards using a smart card reader. Finally, to make smart cards useful, you should enable the Interactive Logon: Require Smart Card policy in the Group Policy Object Editor.

Understand how to use the Delegation of Control Wizard to allow distributed administration. Delegation is the process by which a higher-level security administrator assigns permissions to other users. The Delegation of Control Wizard walks you through the steps of selecting for which object(s) you want to perform delegation, what permission you want to allow, and which users will have those permissions.

Learn how the Security Configuration And Analysis utility can simplify the implementation of security policies. You can use the Security Configuration And Analysis utility together with security template files to create, modify, and apply security settings in the Registry. Security templates allow systems administrators to define security settings once and then store this information in a file that can be applied to other computers.

Understand the purpose and function of auditing. Auditing helps determine the cause of security violations and helps troubleshoot permissions-related problems.

Review Questions

1. You are the systems administrator for a medium-sized Active Directory domain. Currently, the environment supports many different domain controllers, some of which are running Windows NT 4 and others that are running Windows 2003 and Server 2008. When you are running domain controllers in this type of environment, which of the following types of groups can you not use?

   A. Universal security groups

   B. Global groups

   C. Domain local groups

   D. Computer groups

2. Isabel is a systems administrator for an Active Directory environment that is running in Native mode. Recently, several managers have reported suspicions about user activities and have asked her to increase security in the environment. Specifically, the requirements are as follows:

   - The accessing of certain sensitive files must be logged.
   - Modifications to certain sensitive files must be logged.
   - Systems administrators must be able to provide information about which users accessed sensitive files and when they were accessed.
   - All logon attempts for specific shared machines must be recorded.

   Which of the following steps should Isabel take to meet these requirements? (Choose all that apply.)

   A. Enable auditing with the Computer Management tool.

   B. Enable auditing with the Active Directory Users And Computers tool.

   C. Enable auditing with the Active Directory Domains And Trusts tool.

   D. Enable auditing with the Event Viewer tool.

   E. View the audit log using the Event Viewer tool.

   F. View auditing information using the Computer Management tool.

   G. Enable failure and success auditing settings for specific files stored on NTFS volumes.

   H. Enable failure and success auditing settings for logon events on specific computer accounts.

3. A systems administrator wants to allow another user the ability to change user account information for all users within a specific OU. Which of the following tools would allow them to do this most easily?

   A. Domain Security Policy

   B. Domain Controller Security Policy

   C. Computer Management

   D. Delegation of Control Wizard

4. Will, an IT manager, has full permissions over several OUs within a small Active Directory domain. Recently, Will has hired a junior systems administrator named Crystal to take over some of the responsibilities of administering the objects within these OUs. Will gives Crystal access to modify user accounts within two OUs. This process is known as what?

   A. Inheritance

   B. Transfer of control

   C. Delegation

   D. Transfer of ownership

5. Paige, a systems administrator, wants to prevent users from starting or stopping a specific service on domain controllers. Which of the following tools can she use to prevent this from occurring?

   A. Active Directory Users And Computers tool

   B. Domain Controller Security Policy

   C. Domain Security Policy

   D. Local System Policy

6. As the network administrator of Wanton Accounting Services, you are just getting settled into a comfortable routine. The network was converted from Windows NT and is now deployed as a Windows Server 2008 network with two sites and one domain. Most of the problems that you have encountered have been from users who needed education on how to search the directory and other nuances of the new system. Recently, you were brought into a meeting with top management and you were told that a few employees who recently left the company joined a competitor. Management wanted to know if any attempts were made to obtain information about the company's accounts. They also wanted to know if anyone internal to the company was trying to access the information improperly. When you informed them that you didn't know, the experience was not one that you would want to repeat. Because you are the network administrator, you do not have any control over the perimeter security of the network. What can you audit on the network to make sure that you can answer any future inquiries by management with confidence?

   A. Logon/logoff—success

   B. Logon/logoff—failure

   C. File access and object access—success and failure

   D. Write access for program files—success and failure

   E. User rights—success and failure

7. You are almost finished helping with the migration of a Windows NT network to a Windows Server 2008 network. The current domain functional level is Windows 2000 Mixed mode. There are three locations, and the engineers are creating a single domain for now. Many rumors are surfacing that a merger with one of your competitors is going to happen, and the designers are considering adding a new domain to bring those users into the network. One of your jobs is to help come up with the administrative plans for the designers to manage the users. To outline your task, you are going to build a best-practices approach to giving permissions to resources on your mixed network. Which of the following approaches best suits your situation?

A. Apply permissions to the domain local group and add the accounts to this group.

B. Apply permissions to the domain local groups, add users to global groups, and add the global groups to the domain local groups.

C. Apply permissions to global groups, add users to universal groups, and place these universal groups into global groups.

D. Apply permissions to domain local groups, add the users to global groups, add the global groups into universal groups, and add the universal groups into the domain local groups.

8. Which of the following folders in the Active Directory Users And Computers tool is used when users from outside the forest are granted access to resources within a domain?

A. Users

B. Computers

C. Domain Controllers

D. Foreign Security Principals

9. Alexis is a systems administrator for an Active Directory environment that contains four domains. Recently, several managers have reported suspicions about user activities and have asked him to increase security in the environment. Specifically, the requirements are as follows:

- Audit changes to User objects that are contained within a specific OU.

- Allow a special user account called Audit to view and modify all security-related information about objects in that OU.

Which of the following steps should Alexis take to meet these requirements? (Choose all that apply.)

A. Convert all volumes on which Active Directory information resides to NTFS.

B. Enable auditing with the Active Directory Users And Computers tool.

C. Create a new Active Directory domain and create restrictive permissions for the suspected users within this domain.

D. Reconfigure trust settings using the Active Directory Domains And Trusts tool.

E. Specify auditing options for the OU using the Active Directory Users And Computers tool.

F. Use the Delegation of Control Wizard to grant appropriate permissions to view and modify objects within the OU to the Audit user account.

10. You are installing a new software application on a Windows Server 2008 domain controller. After reading the manual and consulting with a security administrator, you find that you have the following requirements:

    ▪ The software must run under an account that has permissions to all files on the server on which it is installed.

    ▪ The software must be able to bypass filesystem security in order to work properly.

    ▪ The software must be able to read and write sensitive files stored on the local server.

    ▪ Users of the software must not be able to view sensitive data that is stored within the files on the server.

    You decide to create a new User account for the software and then assign the account to a built-in local group. To which of the following groups should you assign the account?

    A. Account Operators

    B. Backup Operators

    C. Guests

    D. Domain Admins

11. Members of which of the following groups have permissions to perform actions in multiple domains?

    A. Domain Admins

    B. Domain Users

    C. Administrators

    D. Enterprise Admins

12. The Association of Firefighters has offices throughout the United States. It has a Windows Server 2008 network that is running in Windows 2000 Mixed domain functional level. The Firefighters' association has confidential information from several companies that needs to be kept that way. You created a shared folder named Confidential and published it in the directory to contain this confidential information. The manager of the department that manages this information has requested that you disable Alexandria's access to the share. When checking the properties of the share, you notice that a domain local group called Secret and another domain local group called Temporary have permissions to the Confidential share. You notice that Alexandria is the only member of the Temporary group, so instead of modifying Alexandria's account directly with a Deny to the share, you simply delete the group. You immediately get a call from the manager that he has changed his mind and that Alexandria needs access to the resources. You re-create the Temporary group and add Alexandria back into the group. The next day you get a call from Alexandria telling you that she cannot access the resources. What is the best way for you to provide her access to the resource?

    A. Add Alexandria to the Secret group.

    B. Grant Alexandria direct access to the share.

    C. Grant access to the Confidential folder for the Temporary group.

    D. Add the Temporary group into the Secret group.

13. Alex, a systems administrator, has created a top-level OU called Engineering. Within the Engineering OU, he has created two OUs: Research and Development. Alex wants to place security permissions on only the Engineering OU, so he blocks the inheritance of properties for the OUs. However, when he does so, he finds that the permissions settings for the child OUs are now unacceptable. Which of the following actions should he take to change the permissions for the child OUs?

A. Open the ACL for each child OU and set permissions for each ACE.

B. Rename the parent OU.

C. Delete and re-create the child OUs.

D. Delete and re-create the parent OU.

14. You are the systems administrator for a small Active Directory domain. Recently, you hired an intern to assist you with managing user objects within the domain. You want to do the following:

- Provide the intern with permissions to access Active Directory using the Active Directory Users And Computers tool.

- Provide the intern with sufficient permissions to change the properties of user accounts and to create and delete user accounts.

- Provide the intern with the ability to create groups and computers.

- Prevent the intern from being able to make any other changes to the Active Directory environment.

To which of the following groups should you add the user?

A. Backup Operators

B. Account Operators

C. Enterprise Admins

D. Domain Admins

E. Guests

15. You want the Security Log to overwrite events that are more than nine days old. Take a look at the following screen. What would you do next in order to accomplish this task?

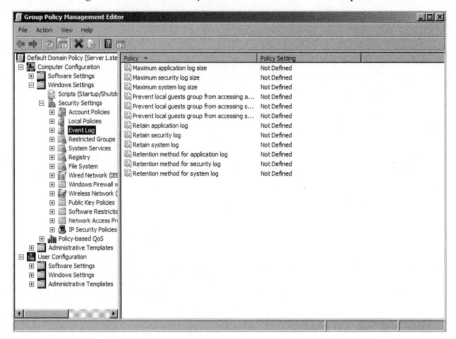

A. Double-click Maximum Security Log Size.

B. Double-click Retention Method For Security Log.

C. Double-click Retain Security Log.

D. Right-click Retention Method For Security Log.

16. As the network administrator for your company, you need to implement security on your Administrator account. Recently you have detected four attempts to access your server very late at night during business off hours. Which of the following is the best solution to this problem?

A. Delete the Administrator account.

B. Rename the Administrator account.

C. Activate the second Administrator account, the Guest account.

D. Active the second Administrator account, the Backup Operator account.

17. You are asked to implement security into your Active Directory deployment. You need to ensure that you have auditing set up properly. If you wanted to check and see if you had unauthorized access to your server, what would you consider checking?

A. Event Viewer logs ➤ application log

B. Event Viewer logs ➤ FRS log

C. Event Viewer logs ➤ system log

D. Event Viewer logs ➤ Security Log

18. You have just installed a Windows Server 2008 system into your current network. You are looking at the default accounts that are domain local. Which of the following accounts is not set up by default?

A. Remote Administrators

B. Administrators

C. Backup Operators

D. Print Operators

E. Guests

F. Users

19. The finance department has classified documents that are payroll related. The company wants you to audit the finance documents to make sure that no unauthorized users are accessing the documents. Which of the following needs to be enabled?

A. Process access

B. Policy change

C. Privilege use

D. Object tracking

20. After monitoring the Event Viewer logs on your Windows Server 2008 systems, you find that a driver fails to load during startup. If the event is recorded, what log would you examine to find the entry?

A. Event log

B. Application log

C. System log

D. Security log

Answers to Review Questions

1. A, D. Because you are supporting Windows NT 4, Server 2003, and Server 2008 domain controllers, you must run the environment in Windows 2000 Mixed domain functional level. Universal security groups are not available when you are running in Windows 2000 Mixed domain functional level. Computer groups is not an actual group type.

2. B, E, G, H. The Active Directory Users And Computers tool allows systems administrators to change auditing options and to choose which actions are audited. At the filesystem level, Isabel can specify exactly which actions are recorded in the audit log. She can then use Event Viewer to view the recorded information and provide it to the appropriate managers.

3. D. The Delegation of Control Wizard is designed to assist systems administrators in granting specific permissions to other users.

4. C. Delegation is the process of granting permissions to other users. Delegation is often used to distribute systems administration responsibilities. Inheritance is the transfer of permissions and other settings from parent OUs to child OUs. Transfer of control and transfer of ownership are not terms applicable to OUs.

5. B. The settings made in the Domain Controller Security Policy tool apply only to domain controllers.

6. C. By auditing for the success or failure of file access and object access you can learn who is accessing any files that you want to watch. You can then create a report and notify management of who has accessed the files and who has tried and failed to access those files. However, because outsiders may be collusion with someone inside the company, the success or failure of logon/logoff will not provide clear results in this situation. User rights refer to the process of changing the authority of a user to system privileges and are not related to this problem. Auditing access for program files is usually associated with determining whether a virus is attempting to embed itself into your program files.

7. B. Because this is still a Windows 2000 Mixed domain functional-level network, universal groups are not available, so the best practice is to add users to global groups and apply permissions to the domain local groups where the resources reside. Even in a Native mode network, you do not want to place users into a universal group because the contents of universal groups are included in the Global Catalog and therefore will unnecessarily add to its size. When the migration is complete, you can use the universal groups to include global groups from multiple domains and then you can placed them in domain local groups that have permissions applied to them.

8. D. When resources are made available to users who reside in domains outside the forest, Foreign Security Principal objects are automatically created. These new objects are stored within the ForeignSecurityPrincipals folder.

9. B, E, F. The first step is to enable auditing. With auditing enabled, Lance can specify which actions are recorded. To give permissions to the Audit user account, he can use the Delegation of Control Wizard.

10. B. Members of the Backup Operators group are able to bypass filesystem security in order to back up and restore files. The requirements provided are similar to those for many popular backup software applications.

11. D. Members of the Enterprise Admins group are given full permissions to manage all domains within an Active Directory forest.

12. C. Once you delete a security principal such as a local domain group, it is lost forever, and any new one, even with the same name, needs to have the permissions reapplied to become effective. You could add Alexandria to the Secret group, but you don't know what other resources she would get access to by becoming a member of this group. Giving Alexandria direct access to the share would work, but it is not the best practice. You should always use groups to apply resources in order to maintain manageability of the network. Because the network is in Windows 2000 Mixed domain functional level, you cannot nest groups other than by adding a global group into a domain local group.

13. A. When Alex blocked inheritance, the child OUs did not retain the permissions of the parent OU. Therefore, he must use the ACL for each child and set specific permissions for each ACE in the list.

14. B. The user should be added to the Account Operators group. Although membership in the Enterprise Admins or Domain Admins group provides the user with the requisite permissions, these choices exceed the required functionality.

15. C. The Retain Security Log setting allows you to specify how long the Security Log should be retained before it gets overwritten.

16. B. When installing and using Windows Server 2008, always make sure you keep tabs on the use of the Administrator account. Often, this account can be manipulated and used for wrongdoing. You should rename the Administrator account if you have a problem with it or want to protect it because most hackers can easily find out half the credentials they need to get into the heart of your system.

17. D. The Event Viewer is used to view logs. The Security Log records events such as valid and invalid logon attempts, as well as events related to resource use, such as the creating, opening, or deleting of files. For example, when logon auditing is enabled, an event is recorded in the Security Log each time a user attempts to log on to the computer. You must be logged on as Administrator or as a member of the Administrators group in order to turn on, use, and specify which events are recorded in the Security Log.

18. A. All domain local groups are correct except for Remote Administrators; this is not a default group created with the base OS install.

19. D. To audit documents (objects) you need to enable auditing on object access. You can audit successes or failures.

20. C. The Event Viewer is used to view logs. The system log contains events logged by Windows system components. For example, if a driver fails to load during startup, an event is recorded in the system log. Windows predetermines the events that are logged by system components.

Chapter

10

Active Directory Optimization and Reliability

MICROSOFT EXAM OBJECTIVES COVERED IN THIS CHAPTER:

✓ **Maintaining the Active Directory Environment**

- Configure backup and recovery. May include but is not limited to: using Windows Server Backup; back up files and system state data to media; back up and restore by using removable media; perform an authoritative or non-authoritative Active Directory restore; Directory Services Recovery Mode (DSRM) (reset admin password); back up and restore GPOs

- Perform offline maintenance. May include but is not limited to: offline defragmentation and compaction; Restartable Active Directory; Active Directory database storage allocation

- Monitor Active Directory. May include but is not limited to: Network Monitor; Task Manager; Event Viewer; ReplMon; RepAdmin; Windows System Resource Manager; Reliability and Performance Monitor; Server Performance Advisor

One of the most important tasks of an IT team is to keep the network up and running. Making sure that Active Directory is running at its peak performance is one way you can guarantee that your end users continue to use the network and its resources without problems or interruptions. Remember, everyone has clients; sales people have theirs as do we as system administrators. Our clients are the end users. It's our job to make sure our clients can do their jobs.

When you are working with Active Directory it is important that you make sure your system information is safely backed up. Backups become useful when you lose data because of system failures, file corruptions, or accidental modifications of information. As consultants, we can tell you from experience that backups are one of the most important tasks that an IT person performs daily. In this chapter, we cover the many different types of backup strategies.

Sometimes, performance optimization can feel like a luxury, especially if you can't get your domain controllers to the point where they are actually performing the services you intended for them, such as servicing printers or allowing users to share and work on files. The Windows Server 2008 operating system platform has been specifically designed to provide high availability services intended solely to keep your mission-critical applications and data accessible even in times of disaster. Occasionally, however, you might experience intermittent server crashes on one or more of the domain controllers or other computers in your environment.

The most common cause of such problems is a hardware configuration issue. Poorly written device drivers and unsupported hardware can cause problems with system stability. Similarly, a failed hardware component (such as system memory) can also cause problems. For instance, memory chips can be faulty, electrostatic discharge (ESD) can ruin them, and other hardware issues can occur. No matter what, a problem with your memory chip only spells disaster for your server. Usually, third-party hardware vendors provide utility disks with their computers that you can use to perform hardware diagnostics on machines to help find your problems. These utilities are a good first step when you are working on resolving intermittent server crashes. When you use these utility disks combined with the troubleshooting tips we provide in this and other chapters of this book, you should be able to pinpoint most Active Directory–related problems that might occur on your network.

In this chapter, we'll cover tools and methods for measuring performance and troubleshooting failures in Windows Server 2008. Before you dive into the technical details, however, you should thoroughly understand what we're trying to accomplish and how we'll meet this goal.

It would be almost impossible to cover everything that could go wrong with your Windows Server 2008 system and/or Active Directory. This book covers many of the most likely and/or common issues you might come across, but anything is likely. Make sure you focus on the methodology we use and the steps we show you to locate and isolate a problem, even if you are not 100 percent sure what the problem may be. In addition, use online resources to help you locate and troubleshoot the problem, but don't believe everything you read (something that is posted online can be wrong or misleading); test your changes in a lab environment and try to read multiple sources. Always use Microsoft Support (http://support.microsoft.com/) as one of your sources, because this site is most likely the right source of information (it's the product vendor, after all). You won't be able to find and fix everything, but knowing where to find critical information that will aid you definitely won't hurt you either. One of the tools that many of us use in the industry is Microsoft TechNet. The full version of TechNet (paid subscription) is a resource that will help you find and fix many real world issues.

Overview of Windows Server 2008 Performance Monitoring

The first step in any performance optimization strategy is to accurately and consistently measure performance. The insight that you'll gain from monitoring factors such as network and system utilization, will be extremely useful when you go to measure the effects of any changes.

The overall process of performance monitoring usually involves the following steps:

1. Establish a baseline of current performance.
2. Identify the bottleneck(s).
3. Plan for and implement changes.
4. Measure the effects of the changes.
5. Repeat the process, based on business needs.

Note that the performance optimization process is never really finished because you can always try to gain more performance from your system by modifying settings and applying other well-known tweaks. Before you get discouraged, realize that you'll reach some level of performance that you and your network and system users consider acceptable enough; at this point, you will find that it's not worth the additional effort it'll take to optimize performance further. Also note that as your network and system load increases (more users or users doing more), as will the need to reiterate this process. By continuing to monitor, measure, and optimize, you will keep ahead of the pack and keep your end users happy.

Now that you have an idea of the overall process, let's focus on how you should make changes. Some important ideas to keep in mind when monitoring performance include the following:

Plan changes carefully. Here's a rule of thumb we always try to follow: An hour of planning can save you a week of work. When you are working in an easy-to-use GUI-based operating system like the Windows Server 2008 platform, it's tempting to randomly remove a check mark here or there and then retest the performance. You should resist the urge to do this because some changes can cause large decreases in performance or can impact functionality. Before you make haphazard changes (especially on production servers), take the time to learn about, plan for, and test your changes. Plan for outages and testing accordingly.

Utilize a test environment. Test in a test lab that simulates a production environment. Do not make changes on production environments without first giving warning. Ideally, change production environments in off hours when fewer network and system users will be affected. Making haphazard changes in a production environment can cause serious problems. These problems will likely outweigh any benefits you could receive from making performance tweaks.

Make only one change at a time. The golden rule of scientific experiments is that you should always keep track of as many variables as possible. When the topic is server optimization, this roughly translates into making only one change at a time.

One of the problems with making multiple system changes is that, although you may have improved performance overall, it's hard to determine exactly *which* change created the positive effects. It's also possible, for example, that changing one parameter increased performance greatly while changing another decreased it slightly. Although the overall result was an increase in performance, the second, performance-reducing option should be identified so the same mistake is not made again. To reduce the chance of obtaining misleading results, always try to make only one change at a time.

But the main reason to make one change at a time is that if you do make a mistake or create an unexpected issue, you can easily back out of the change. If you make two or three changes at the same time and are not sure which one created the problem, you will have to undo all the changes and then make one alteration at a time to find the problem. If you make only one change at a time and follow that methodology every time, you won't find yourself in this situation.

It's important to remember that many changes (for example, Registry changes) take place immediately; they do not need to be explicitly applied. Once the change is made, it's live. Be careful to plan your changes wisely.

Ensure consistency in measurements. When you are monitoring performance, consistency is extremely important. You should strive toward having repeatable and accurate measurements. Controlling variables, such as system load at various times during the day, can help.

Assume, for instance, that you want to measure the number of transactions that you can simulate on the accounting database server within an hour. The results would be widely different if you ran the test during the month-end accounting close than if you ran the test on a Sunday morning. By running the same tests when the server is under a relatively static amount of load, you will be able to get more accurate measurements.

Maintain a performance history.   In the introduction to this chapter, we mentioned that the performance optimization cycle is a continuous improvement process. Because many changes may be made over time, it is important to keep track of the changes you have made and the results you have experienced. Documenting this knowledge will help solve similar problems if they arise. We understand that many IT professionals do not like to document, but documentation can make life much easier in the long run.

As you can see, you need to keep a lot of factors in mind when optimizing performance. Although this might seem like a lot to digest and remember, do not fear; as systems administrators, you will learn some of the rules you need to know to keep your system running optimally. Fortunately, the tools included with Windows Server 2008 can help you organize the process and take measurements. Now that you have a good overview of the process, let's move on to look at the tools you can use to set it in motion.

Using Windows Server 2008 Performance Tools

Because performance monitoring and optimization are vital functions in network environments of any size, Windows Server 2008 includes several performance-related tools.

The first and most useful tool is the Windows Server 2008 *Reliability and Performance Monitor*, which was designed to allow users and systems administrators to monitor performance statistics for various operating system parameters. Specifically, you can collect, store, and analyze information about CPU, memory, disk, and network resources using this tool, and these are only a handful of the things that you can monitor. By collecting and analyzing performance values, systems administrators can identify many potential problems. As you'll see later in this chapter, you can also use the Reliability and Performance Monitor to monitor the performance of Active Directory and its various components.

Here are the two ways in which you can use the Reliability and Performance Monitor:

Reliability and Performance Monitor ActiveX Control   The Windows Server 2008 Reliability and Performance Monitor is an ActiveX control that you can place within other applications. Examples of applications that can host the Reliability and Performance Monitor control include web browsers and client programs like Microsoft Office's Word XP or Excel XP. This functionality can make it very easy for applications developers and systems administrators to incorporate the Reliability and Performance Monitor into their own tools and applications.

Reliability and Performance MMC   For more common performance monitoring functions, you'll want to use the built-in Microsoft Management Console (MMC) version of the Reliability and Performance Monitor called the Performance Monitor.

To access the Reliability and Performance Monitor MMC, you open Computer Management in the Administrative Tools program group within your Start menu. This launches the Reliability and Performance MMC and loads and initializes Reliability and Performance Monitor with a handful of default counters.

You can choose from many different methods of monitoring performance when you are using Performance Monitor. A couple of examples are listed here:

- You can look at a snapshot of current activity for a few of the most important counters; this allows you to find areas of potential bottlenecks and monitor the load on your servers at a certain point in time.

- You can save information to a log file for historical reporting and later analysis. This type of information is useful, for example, if you want to compare the load on your servers from three months ago to the current load.

You'll get to take a closer look at this method and many others as you examine Performance Monitor in more detail.

In the following sections, you'll learn about the basics of working with the Windows Server 2008 Performance Monitor and other performance tools. Then, you'll apply these tools and techniques when you monitor the performance of Active Directory.

 Your Performance Monitor grows as your system grows, and whenever you add services to Windows Server 2008 (such as installing Exchange Server 2007 SP1), you also add to what you can monitor. You should make sure that, as you install services, you take a look at what it is you can monitor.

Deciding What to Monitor

The first step in monitoring performance is to decide *what* you want to monitor. In Windows Server 2008, the operating system and related services include hundreds of performance statistics that you can track easily. All of these performance statistics fall into three main categories that you can choose to measure:

Performance objects   A performance object within Performance Monitor is a collection of various performance statistics that you can monitor. Performance objects are based on various areas of system resources. For example, there are performance objects for the processor and memory, as well as for specific services such as web services. Later in this chapter, you'll see how you can use the Windows NT Directory Service (NTDS) performance object to monitor performance of Active Directory.

Counters   Counters are the actual parameters measured by Performance Monitor. They are specific items that are grouped within performance objects. For example, within the Processor performance object, there is a counter for % Processor Time. This counter displays one type of detailed information about the Processor performance object (specifically, the amount of total CPU time all of the processes on the system are using).

Instances   Some counters will have instances. An instance further identifies which performance parameter the counter is measuring. A simple example is a server with two CPUs. If you decide that you want to monitor processor usage (using the Processor performance object)—specifically, utilization (the %Total Utilization counter)—you must still specify *which* CPU(s) you want to measure. In this example, you would choose between monitoring either of the two CPUs or a total value for both (using the Total instance).

To specify which performance objects, counters, and instances you want to monitor, add them to Performance Monitor using the Add Counters dialog box. Figure 10.1 shows the various available options when you add new counters to monitor using Performance Monitor.

FIGURE 10.1   Adding a new Performance Monitor counter

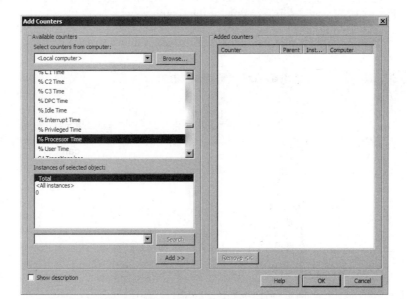

The items that you will be able to monitor will be based on your hardware and software configuration. For example, if you have not installed and configured the Internet Information Server (IIS) service, the options available within the Web Server performance object will not be available. Or, if you have multiple network adapters or CPUs in the server, you will have the option of viewing each instance separately or as part of the total value. You'll see which counters are generally most useful later in this chapter.

Viewing Performance Information

The Windows Server 2008 Performance Monitor was designed to show information in a clear and easy-to-understand format. Performance objects, counters, and instances may be displayed in each of three views. This flexibility allows systems administrators to quickly and easily define the information they want to see once and then choose how it will be displayed based on specific needs. Most likely you will only use one view, but it's helpful to know what other views are available depending on what it is you are trying to assess.

You can use the following main views to review statistics and information on performance:

Graph view The Graph view is the default display that is presented when you first access the Windows Server 2008 Performance Monitor. The chart displays values using the vertical axis and time using the horizontal axis. This view is useful if you want to display values over a period of time and or see the changes in these values over that time period. Each point that is plotted on the graph is based on an average value calculated during the sample interval for the measurement being made. For example, you may notice overall CPU utilization starting at a low value at the beginning of the chart and then becoming much higher during later measurements. This indicates that the server has become busier (specifically, with CPU-intensive processes). Figure 10.2 provides an example of the Graph view.

FIGURE 10.2 Viewing information in Performance Monitor Graph view

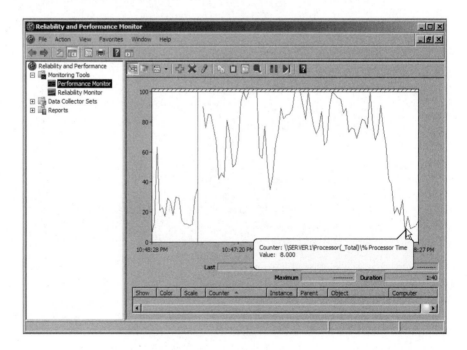

A quick way to get to the Performance Console and view Performance Monitor is to go to Start ➤ Run and enter **perfmon** in the Open box. The Performance Console opens directly to Performance Monitor.

Histogram view   The Histogram view shows performance statistics and information using a set of relative bar charts. This view is useful if you want to see a snapshot of the latest value for a given counter. For example, if we were interested in viewing a snapshot of current system performance statistics during each refresh interval, the length of each of the bars in the display would give us a visual representation of each value. It would also allow us to visually compare measurements relative to each other. You can set the histogram to display an average measurement as well as minimum and maximum thresholds. Figure 10.3 shows a typical Histogram view.

FIGURE 10.3   Viewing information in Performance Monitor Histogram view

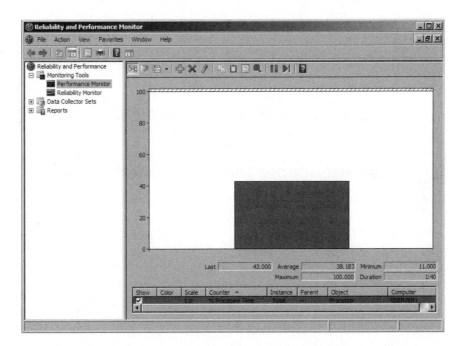

Report view   Like the Histogram view, the Report view shows performance statistics based on the latest measurement. You can see an average measurement as well as minimum and maximum thresholds. This view is most useful for determining exact values because it provides information in numeric terms, whereas the Chart and Histogram views provide information graphically. Figure 10.4 provides an example of the type of information you'll see in the Report view.

FIGURE 10.4   Viewing information in Performance Monitor Report view

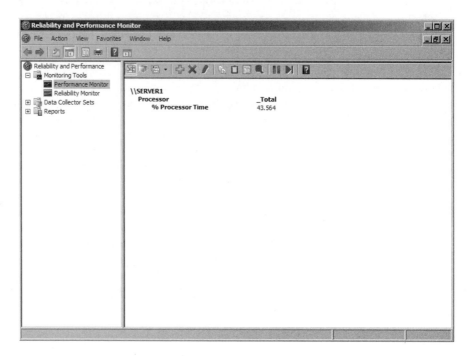

Managing Performance Monitor Properties

You can specify additional settings for viewing performance information within the properties of Performance Monitor. You can access these options by clicking the Properties button in the taskbar or by right-clicking Performance Monitor display and selecting Properties. You can change these additional settings using the following tabs:

General tab   On the General tab (shown in Figure 10.5), you can specify several options that relate to Performance Monitor view.

- You can enable or disable legends (which display information about the various counters), the value bar, and the toolbar.

- For the Report and Histogram views, you can choose which type of information is displayed. The options are Default, Current, Minimum, Maximum, and Average. What you see with each of these options depends on the type of data being collected. These options are not available for the Graph view, because the Graph view displays an average value over a period of time (the sample interval).

- You can also choose the graph elements. By default, the display will be set to update every second. If you want to update less often, you should increase the number of seconds between updates.

FIGURE 10.5   General tab of Performance Monitor Properties dialog box

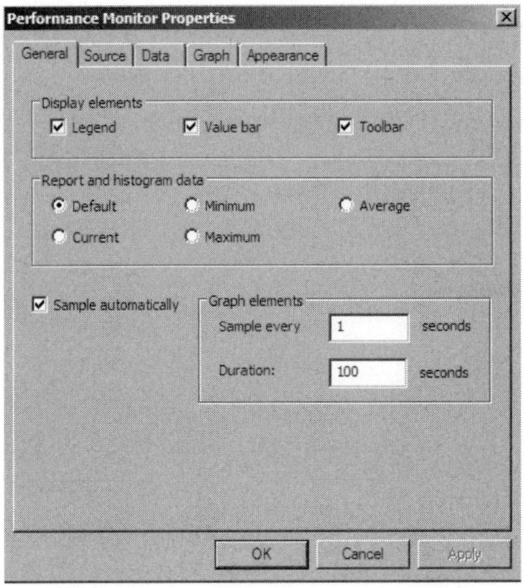

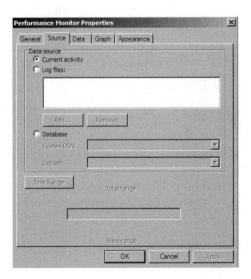

Source tab   On the Source tab (shown in Figure 10.6), you can specify the source for the performance information you would like to view. Options include current activity (the default setting) or data from a log file. If you choose to analyze information from a log file, you can also specify the time range for which you want to view statistics. We'll cover these selections in the next section.

FIGURE 10.6   Source tab of Performance Monitor Properties dialog box

Data tab   The Data tab (shown in Figure 10.7) displays a list of the counters that have been added to Performance Monitor display. These counters apply to the Chart, Histogram, and Report views. Using this interface, you can also add or remove any of the counters and change properties, such as the width, style, and color of the line, and the scale used for display.

FIGURE 10.7   The Data tab of Performance Monitor Properties dialog box

Graph tab   On the Graph tab (shown in Figure 10.8), you can specify certain options that will allow you to customize the display of Performance Monitor views. First you can specify what type of view you want to see (Line, Histogram Bar, or Report). Then you can add a title for the graph, specify a label for the vertical axis, choose to display grids, and specify the vertical scale range.

FIGURE 10.8   The Graph tab of Performance Monitor Properties dialog box

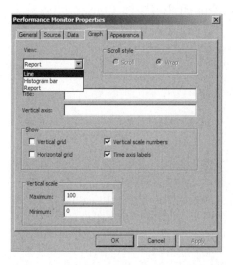

Appearance tab   Using the Appearance tab (see Figure 10.9), you can specify the colors for the areas of the display, such as the background and foreground. You can also specify the fonts that are used to display counter values in Performance Monitor views. You can change settings to find a suitable balance between readability and the amount of information shown on one screen. Finally, you can set up the properties for a border.

FIGURE 10.9   The Appearance tab of Performance Monitor Properties dialog box

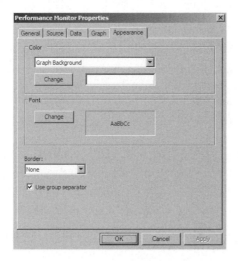

Now that you have an idea of the types of information Performance Monitor tracks and how this data is displayed, take a look at another feature that you will use to save and analyze performance data.

Saving and Analyzing Data with Performance Logs and Alerts

One of the most important aspects of monitoring performance is that it should be done over a given period of time (referred to as a baseline). So far, we have discussed how you can use Performance Monitor to view statistics in real time. We have, however, also alluded to using Performance Monitor to save data for later analysis. Now let's take a look at how this is done.

When viewing information in Performance Monitor, you have two main options with respect to the data on display:

View Current Activity   When you first open the Performance icon from the Administrative Tools folder, the default option is to view data obtained from current system information. This method of viewing measures and displays various real-time statistics on the system's performance.

View Log File Data   This option allows you to view information that was previously saved to a log file. Although the performance objects, counters, and instances may appear to be the same as those you saw using the View Current Activity option, the information itself was actually captured at a previous point in time and stored into a log file.

Log files for the View Log File Data option are created in the Performance Logs and Alerts section of the Windows Server 2008 Performance tool.

Three items allow you to customize how the data is collected in the log files:

Counter logs   *Counter logs* record performance statistics based on the various performance objects, counters, and instances available in Performance Monitor. The values are updated based on a time interval setting and are saved to a file for later analysis.

Circular logging   In circular logging, the data that is stored within a file is overwritten as new data is entered into the log. This is a useful method of logging if you only want to record information for a certain time frame (for example, the last four hours). Circular logging also conserves disk space by ensuring that the performance log file will not continue to grow over certain limits.

Linear logging   In linear logging, data is never deleted from the log files, and new information is added to the end of the log file. The result is a log file that continually grows. The benefit is that all historical information is retained.

Now that we have an idea of the types of functions that are supported by the Windows Server 2008 Performance tool, let's move on to look at how this information can be applied to the task at hand—monitoring and troubleshooting Active Directory.

 Real World Scenario

Real World Performance Monitoring

In our daily jobs as systems engineers and administrators, we come across systems that need of our help...and may even be asking for it. Of course you check your Event Viewer, Performance Monitor, and perform other tasks that help you troubleshoot. But what is really the most common problem that occurs? From our experience, we'd say that many times you suffer performance problems if you have your Windows Server 2008 operating system installed on a sub-par system. Either the server hardware isn't enterprise class, or the minimum hardware requirements weren't addressed. Most production servers suffer from slow response times, lagging, and so on, because money wasn't spent where it should have been—on the server's hardware requirements.

Take a look at www.microsoft.com/windowsserver2008/evaluation/overview.mspx to see the minimum Windows Server 2008 requirements. You have to make very sure that you follow these minimum requirements. That's not all though; as you will see by reading this chapter, most times the minimum requirements are just that—the bare minimum and not necessarily good enough, especially if you are running many services on your server or you have many network clients who will access the server.

Would you drive a truck over a glass bridge? No. Then why would you run an enterprise class server operating system hosting a mission-critical application such as Active Directory, email, and messaging on an antiquated desktop system? This seems illogical when you read it, but in practice, it's common to find budgets squeezed to the point where your secondary domain controller is running on a high-end desktop. Just make sure that you consider this when you deploy a new system. Once you deploy it, open up Performance Monitor and see if you are having issues just opening and running programs on the server itself.

It's also common to blame the network first, but it is usually not the problem at all. Be careful of false positives and keep your mind focused on finding the root of the problem. If you come across other problems, document them, but continue to focus on finding (and fixing) the real issue.

If your enterprise-level servers aren't running with Redundant Array of Independent Disks (RAID), then you will most likely need an upgrade on your system hardware. Most enterprise-level server systems come with RAID as the minimum fault tolerance you should have on any server of any size. RAID can help you in a pinch; when you lose a disk—and you will, based on the Mean Time Between Failure (MTBF)—you can quickly recover with minimal downtime and no loss of data.

Monitoring and Troubleshooting Active Directory Components

Active Directory utilizes many different types of server resources in order to function properly. For example, it uses memory to increase the speed of accessing data, CPU time to process information, and network resources to communicate with clients and Active Directory domain controllers. Additionally, it uses disk space for storing the Active Directory data store itself and the Global Catalog (GC).

The types and amount of system resources consumed by Active Directory are based on many factors. Some of the more obvious ones include the size of the Active Directory data store and how many users are supported in the environment. Other factors include the replication topology and the domain architecture. As you can see, all of the design issues you learned about in earlier chapters will play a role in the overall performance of domain controllers and Active Directory.

So how do all of these Active Directory requirements impact the server overall? Although the answer isn't always simple to determine, Performance Monitor is usually the right tool for the job. In the following sections, we'll look at how you can use Windows Server 2008's Performance tool to monitor and optimize the performance of Active Directory.

Monitoring Domain Controller Performance

When it comes to performance, domain controllers have the same basic resource requirements as the other machines in your environment. The major areas to monitor for computers include the following:

- Processor (CPU) time
- Memory
- Disk I/O (Input/Output)
- Disk space
- Network utilization

When you're deciding to monitor performance, you should carefully determine which statistics will be most useful. For example, if you're measuring the performance of a database server, CPU time and memory may be the most important. However, some applications may have high disk I/O and network requirements. Choosing what to monitor can be difficult because so many different options are available. Many times it just takes experience and trial and error using various performance objects to learn exactly how best to monitor things. This chapter at least starts you on your journey if performance monitoring is new to you, and it fills you in on how to monitor Active Directory if you are already a performance-monitoring guru.

Table 10.1 describes some common System Monitor counters and performance objects you might want to choose.

TABLE 10.1   Useful Counters for Monitoring Domain Controller Performance

Performance Object	Counter	Notes
Memory	Available MB	Displays the number of megabytes of physical memory (RAM) available for use by processes.
Memory	Pages/Sec	Indicates the number of pages of memory that must be read from or written to disk per second. A high number may indicate that more memory is needed.
Network Interface	Bytes Total/Sec	Measures the total number of bytes sent to or received by the specified network interface card.
Network Interface	Packets Received Errors	Specifies the number of received network packets that contained errors. A high number may indicate problems with the network connection.

TABLE 10.1   Useful Counters for Monitoring Domain Controller Performance   *(continued)*

Performance Object	Counter	Notes
Network Segment	% Net Utilization	Specifies the percentage of total network resources being consumed. A high value may indicate network congestion.*
Paging File	% Usage	Indicates the amount of the Windows virtual memory file (paging file) in use. If this is a large number, the machine may benefit from a RAM upgrade.
Physical Disk	Disk Reads/Sec Disk Writes/Sec	Indicates the amount of disk activity on the server.
Physical Disk	Avg. Disk Queue Length	Indicates the number of disk read or write requests that are waiting to access the disk. If this value is high, disk I/O could potentially be a bottleneck.
Processor	% Processor Time	Indicates the overall CPU load on the server. High values generally indicate processor-intensive tasks. In machines with multiple processors, you can monitor each processor individually, or you can view a total value.
Server	Bytes Total/Sec	Specifies the number of bytes sent by the Server service on the local machine. A high value usually indicates that the server is responsible for fulfilling many outbound data requests (such as a file/print server).
Server	Server Sessions	Indicates the number of users who may be accessing the server.
System	Processor Queue Length	Specifies the number of threads that are awaiting CPU time. A high number might indicate that a reduction in available CPU resources is creating a potential bottleneck.

TABLE 10.1   Useful Counters for Monitoring Domain Controller Performance   *(continued)*

Performance Object	Counter	Notes
System	Processes	Indicates the number of processes currently running on the system.
Web Service	Bytes Total/Sec	Indicates the number of bytes of data that have been transmitted to or from the local web service. This option is only available if IIS is installed and the web server is running.

*You must have the full version of Network Monitor installed on the local computer in order to view this counter.

Keep in mind that this is not by any means a complete list of the items of interest—it's just a good guideline for some of the more common items that you may want to include. The key to determining what to monitor is to first understand the demands imposed by applications or services and then make appropriate choices. When monitored and interpreted properly, these performance values can be extremely useful in providing insight into overall system performance.

Monitoring Active Directory Performance with Performance Monitor

As you may have already guessed, the Windows Server 2008 operating system automatically tracks many performance statistics that are related to Active Directory. You can easily access these same statistics by using Performance Monitor. The specific counters you'll want to monitor are part of the NTDS performance object and are based on several different functions of Active Directory, including some of those that follow:

- The Address Book (AB)
- The Directory Replication Agent (DRA)
- The Directory Service (DS)
- The Lightweight Directory Access Protocol (LDAP)
- The Security Accounts Manager (SAM)

You may find each of these performance objects useful when you are monitoring specific aspects of Active Directory. The specific counters you choose to monitor will depend on the aspects of Active Directory performance you're planning to examine. For example, if you want to measure performance statistics related to Active Directory replication (covered in Chapter 5, "Configuring Sites and Replication"), you will probably want to monitor the DRA counters. Similarly, if you're interested in performance loads generated by Windows NT computers, you will want to monitor the SAM.

Perhaps the best way to learn about the various types of performance objects, counters, and instances that are related to Active Directory is by actually measuring these values and saving them for analysis. Exercise 10.1 walks you through the steps of working with various features of the Windows Server 2008 Performance Monitor. In this exercise, you will use various features of the Windows Server 2008 Performance Monitor to analyze performance information on a Windows Server 2008 domain controller.

EXERCISE 10.1

Monitoring Domain Controller and Active Directory Performance with Windows Server 2008 Performance Monitor

1. Open the Reliability and Performance Monitor by selecting Start ➤ Run and entering **perfmon**.

2. In the left pane, right-click Performance Monitor and select New ➤ Data Collector Set. In the Name box of the Create New Data Collector Set dialog box, type **Domain Controller Performance** and click Next.

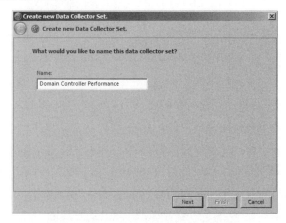

3. A dialog box showing the location of the saved data appears. This is the location on the hard disk where the data will be stored. Keep the defaults and click Next.

4. In the Create New Data Collector Set dialog box, make sure the Save And Close radio button is selected and click Finish.

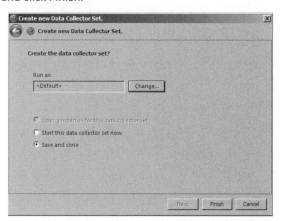

5. In the left pane of the Reliability and Performance Monitor, expand Data Collector Sets, User Defined and click the new collector set you just created (Domain Controller Performance). Right-click System Monitor Log in the right pane and choose Properties.

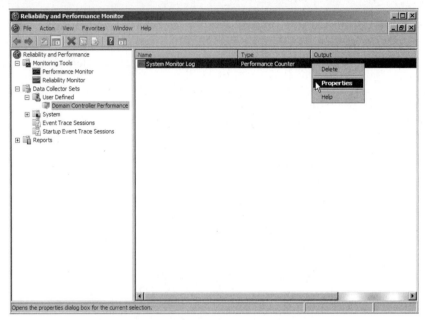

6. In the System Monitor Log Properties dialog box, click the Add button.

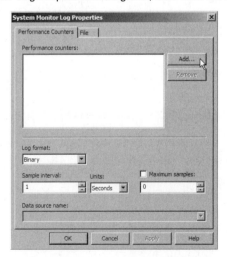

7. In the dialog box that appears, select <Local Computer> in the Select Counters From Computer drop-down list. Expand the Processor object from the Available Counters list. Select the % Processor Time counter and the _Total instance. Note that you can click the Show Description box to find more information about the various parameters that are available. Click the Add button to add the counter to the Added Counters list.

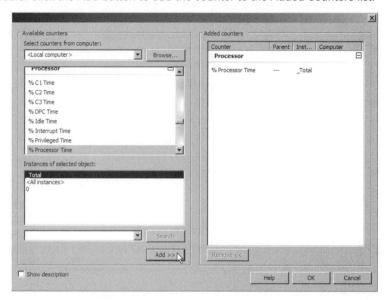

8. When you are finished adding these counters, click the OK button to return to the System Monitor Log Properties dialog box and view the counters that you selected.

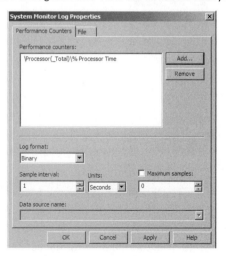

9. Click the File tab of the System Monitor Log Properties dialog box. Change the log file name to **Domain Controller log**. Click the Append check box. Click OK.

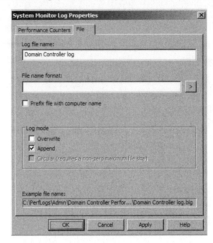

10. In the left pane of the Reliability and Performance Monitor, right-click the collector set Domain Controller Performance. Choose Start.

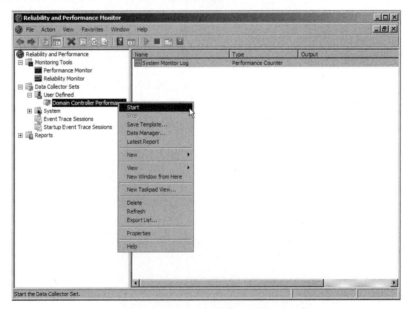

11. Let the system run for five minutes. During this time, open applications or windows on the server. After five minutes, in the left pane of the Reliability and Performance Monitor, right-click the collector set Domain Controller Performance. Choose Stop.

EXERCISE 10.1 *(continued)*

12. Right-click the collector set Domain Controller Performance. Choose Latest Report.

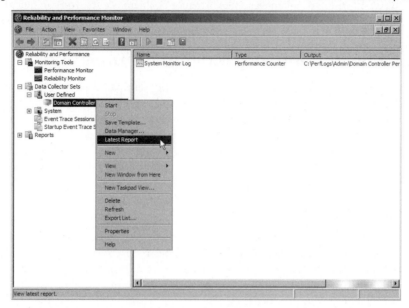

13. View the data that was captured.

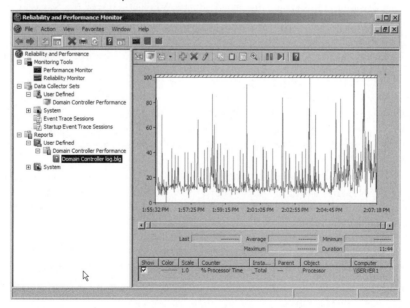

14. When you are done viewing the captured data, close the Reliability and Performance Monitor.

It is useful to have a set of performance monitor counters saved to files so that you can quickly and easily monitor the items of interest. For example, you may want to create a System Monitor log that includes statistics related to database services while another focuses on network utilization. In that way, whenever a performance problem occurs, you can quickly determine the cause of the problem (without having to create a System Monitor log from scratch).

Using Other Performance Monitoring Tools

Performance Monitor allows you to monitor various different parameters of the Windows Server 2008 operating system and associated services and applications. However, you can use three other tools to monitor performance in Windows Server 2008. They are *Network Monitor*, *Task Manager*, and *Event Viewer*. All three of these tools are useful for monitoring different areas of overall system performance and for examining details related to specific system events. In the following sections, we'll take a quick look at these tools and how you can best use them.

The Network Monitor

Although Performance Monitor is a great tool for viewing overall network performance statistics, it isn't equipped for packet-level analysis and doesn't give you much insight into what types of network traffic are traveling on the wire. That's where the Network Monitor tool comes in. There are two main components to the Network Monitor: the Network Monitor Agent and the Network Monitor tool itself.

The Network Monitor Agent is available with Windows 2000, XP, Server 2003, and Server 2008. The agent allows you to track network packets. When you install the Network Monitor Agent, you will also be able to access the Network Segment System Monitor counter.

On Windows Server 2008 computers, you'll see the Network Monitor icon appear in the Administrative Tools program group. You can use the Network Monitor tool to capture data as it travels on your network.

A limited version of Network Monitor is available for free with Windows Server 2008. The full version of Network Monitor is available at Microsoft's download server. For more information, see www.microsoft.com/downloads/.

Once you have captured the data of interest, you can save it to a capture file or further analyze it using the Network Monitor. Experienced network and systems administrators can use this information to determine how applications are communicating and the types of data that are being passed via the network.

For the exam, you don't need to understand the detailed information that Network Monitor displays, but you should be aware of the types of information that you can view and when you should use Network Monitor.

The Task Manager

Performance Monitor is designed to allow you to keep track of specific aspects of system performance over time. But what do you do if you want to get a quick snapshot of what the local system is doing? Creating a System Monitor chart, adding counters, and choosing a view is overkill. Fortunately, the Windows Server 2008 Task Manager has been designed to provide a quick overview of important system performance statistics without requiring any configuration. Better yet, it's always readily available.

You can easily access the Task Manager in several ways:

- Right-click the Windows taskbar, and then click Task Manager.

- Press Ctrl+Alt+Del, and then select Task Manager.

- Press Ctrl+Shift+Esc.

Each of these methods allows you to quickly access a snapshot of the current system performance.

Once you access the Task Manager, you will see the following six tabs:

Applications tab   The Applications tab (see Figure 10.10) shows you a list of the applications currently running on the local computer. This is a good place to check to determine which programs are running on the system. You can also use this tab to shut down any applications whose status is listed as [Not Responding] (meaning either that the application has crashed or that it is performing operations and is not responding to Windows Server 2008).

FIGURE 10.10   The Applications tab of the Task Manager

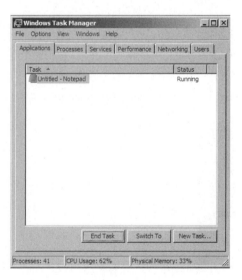

Processes tab   The Processes tab shows you all of the processes that are currently running on the local computer. By default, you'll be able to view how much CPU time and memory a particular process is using. By clicking any of the columns, you can quickly sort by the data values in that particular column. This is useful, for example, if you want to find out which processes are using the most memory on your server.

By accessing the performance objects in the View menu, you can add additional columns to the Processes tab. Figure 10.11 shows a list of the current processes running on a Windows Server 2008 computer.

FIGURE 10.11 Viewing process statistics and information using the Task Manager

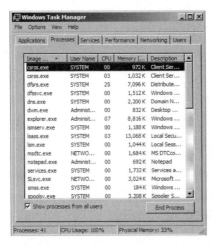

Services tab The Services tab (see Figure 10.12) shows you what services are currently running on the system. From this location, you can stop a service from running by right-clicking the service and choosing Stop. The Services button launches the Services MMC.

FIGURE 10.12 Viewing services information using the Task Manager

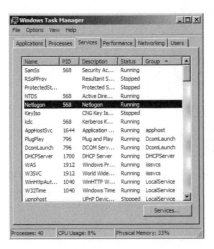

Performance tab   One of the problems with using Performance Monitor to get a quick snap-shot of system performance is that you have to add counters to a chart. Most systems administrators are too busy to take the time to do this when all they need is basic CPU and memory information. That's where the Performance tab of the Task Manager comes in. Using the Performance tab, you can view details about how memory is allocated on the computer and how much of the CPU is utilized (see Figure 10.13).

FIGURE 10.13   Viewing CPU and memory performance information using the Task Manager

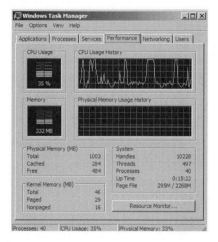

Networking tab   Like the Performance tab, the Networking tab (see Figure 10.14) displays a graph of the current network utilization. The active connections are displayed at the bottom of the tab along with their connection speed, percentage of utilization, and status. The graph in the top part of the tab displays the percentage of utilization in real time.

FIGURE 10.14   Viewing network information using the Task Manager

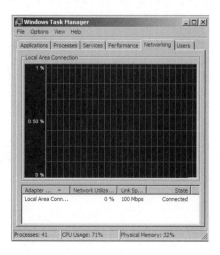

Users tab   The Users tab (see Figure 10.15) displays a list of the currently active user accounts. This is particularly helpful if you want to see who is online and quickly log off or disconnect users. You can also send a console message to any remote user in the list by clicking the Send Message button. (The button is grayed out in Figure 10.15 because you cannot send a message to yourself. If you select a different user, the button will be available.)

FIGURE 10.15   Viewing user information using the Task Manager

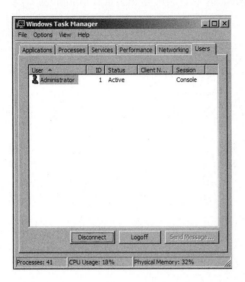

As you can see, the Task Manager is very useful for quickly providing important information about the system. Once you get used to using the Task Manager, you won't be able to get by without it!

Make sure you use Task Manager often and familiarize yourself with all that it can do; you can end processes that have become intermittent, kill applications that may hang the system, view NIC performance, and so on. In addition, you can access this tool quickly to get an idea of what could be causing you problems. All the performance monitoring tools (Task Manager, Event Viewer, Network Monitor, and Performance Monitor) are great at getting granular information on potential problems.

The Event Viewer

The Event Viewer is also useful for monitoring Active Directory information. Specifically, you can use the Directory Service log to view any information, warnings, or alerts related to the proper functioning of the directory services. You can access the Event Viewer by selecting Start ➤ Programs ➤ Administrative Tools ➤ Event Viewer. Clicking any of the items in the left pane displays the various events that have been logged for each item. The contents of Directory Service log are shown in Figure 10.16.

FIGURE 10.16   The Directory Service log in Event Viewer

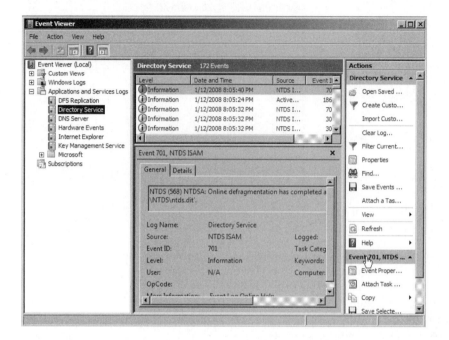

Each event is preceded by a blue "i" icon. That icon designates that these events are informational and do not indicate problems with the Directory Service. Rather, they record benign events such as Active Directory startup or a domain controller finding a Global Catalog server.

Problematic or potentially problematic events are indicated by a yellow Warning icon or a red Error icon, both of which are shown in Figure 10.17. Warnings usually indicate a problem that wouldn't prevent a service from running but might cause undesired effects with the service in question. For example, we were configuring a site with some fictional domain controllers and IP addresses. Our local domain controller's IP address wasn't associated with any of the sites, and the Event Viewer generated a Warning. In this case, the local domain controller could still function as a domain controller, but the site configuration could produce undesirable results.

FIGURE 10.17   Information, Errors, and Warnings in Event Viewer

Error events almost always indicate a failed service, application, or function. For instance, if the dynamic registration of a DNS client fails, the Event Viewer generates an Error. As you can see, errors are more severe than warnings, because in this case, the DNS client cannot participate in DNS at all.

Double-clicking any event opens the event's Properties dialog box, as shown in Figure 10.18. The Event Properties dialog box displays a detailed description of the event.

FIGURE 10.18   The Event Properties dialog box

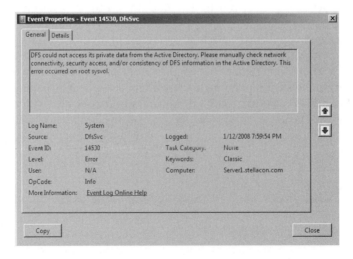

The Event Viewer can display thousands of different events, so it would be impossible to list them all here. Just be aware that information events are always benign, warnings indicate noncritical problems, and errors indicate show-stopping events.

Troubleshooting Active Directory Performance Monitoring

Monitoring performance is not always an easy process. As mentioned earlier, the act of performance monitoring can use up system resources. One of the problems that may then occur is that Performance Monitor cannot obtain performance statistics and information quickly enough. If this occurs, you'll receive an error message. In this case, the suggestion is to increase the sample interval. This will reduce the number of statistics Performance Monitor has to record and display, and it may prevent the loss of performance information.

Sometimes, when you're viewing performance information in the Chart or Histogram view, the data is either too small (the bar or line is too close to the baseline) or too large (the bar or line is above the maximum value). In either case, you'll want to adjust the scale for the counter so that you can accurately see information in the display. For example, if the scale for the number of logons is 1 when it displays values from 0 to 100 and you frequently have more than 100 users per server, you might want to change the scale to a value less than 1. If you choose $\frac{1}{10}$, you will be able to accurately see up to 1000 user logons in the Chart and Histogram views. You can adjust the scale by right-clicking Performance Monitor display, selecting Properties, and then accessing the Data tab.

Backup and Recovery of Active Directory

If you have deployed Active Directory in your network environment, your users now depend on it to function properly in order to do their jobs. From network authentications to file access to print and web services, Active Directory has now become a mission-critical component of your business. Therefore, the importance of backing up the Active Directory data store should be evident. As we discussed in earlier chapters, it is important to have multiple domain controllers available to provide backup in case of a problem. The same goes for Active Directory itself—it too should be backed up by being saved. This way, if a massive disaster occurs in which you need to restore your directory services, you will have that option available to you.

Backups are just good common sense, but here are several specific reasons to back up data:

Protect against hardware failures.   Computer hardware devices have finite lifetimes, and all hardware eventually fails. We discussed this when we mentioned MTBF earlier. MTBF is the average time a device will function before it actually fails. There is also a rating derived from benchmark testing of hard disk devices that tells you when you may be at risk for an unavoidable disaster. Some types of failures, such as corrupted hard disk drives, can result in significant data loss.

Protect against accidental deletion or modification of data. Although the threat of hardware failures is very real, in most environments, mistakes in modifying or deleting data are much more common. For example, suppose a systems administrator accidentally deletes all of the objects within a specific OU. Clearly, it's very important to be able to retrieve this information from a backup.

Keep historical information. Users and systems administrators sometimes modify files and then later find that they require access to an older version of the file. Or a file is accidentally deleted, and a user does not discover that fact until much later. By keeping multiple backups over time, you can recover information from prior backups when necessary.

Protect against malicious deletion or modification of data. Even in the most secure environments, it is conceivable that unauthorized users (or authorized ones with malicious intent!) could delete or modify information. In such cases, the loss of data might require valid backups from which to restore critical information.

Windows Server 2008 includes a Backup utility that is designed to back up operating system files and the Active Directory data store. It allows for basic backup functionality, such as scheduling backup jobs and selecting which files to back up. Figure 10.19 shows the main screen for the Windows Server 2008 Backup utility.

FIGURE 10.19 The main screen of the Windows Server 2008 Backup utility

In the following sections, we'll look at the details of using the Windows Server 2008 Backup utility and how you can restore Active Directory when problems do occur.

Overview of the Windows Server 2008 Backup Utility

Although the general purpose behind performing backup operations—protecting information—is straightforward, systems administrators must consider many options when determining the optimal backup and recovery scenario for their environment. Factors include what to back up, how often to back up, and when the backups should be performed.

In this section, you'll see how the Windows Server 2008 Backup utility makes it easy to implement a backup plan for many network environments.

Although the Windows Server 2008 Backup utility provides the basic functionality required to back up your files, you may want to investigate third-party products that provide additional functionality. These applications can provide options for specific types of backups (such as those for Exchange Server and SQL Server), as well as disaster recovery options, networking functionality, centralized management, and support for more advanced hardware.

Backup Types

One of the most important issues you will have to deal with when you are performing backups is keeping track of which files you have backed up and which files you need to back up. Whenever a backup of a file is made, the Archive bit for the file is set. You can view the attributes of system files by right-clicking them and selecting Properties. By clicking the Advanced button on the Properties dialog box, you will access the Advanced Attributes dialog box. Here you will see the option File Is Ready For Archiving. Figure 10.20 shows an example of the attributes for a file.

FIGURE 10.20   Viewing the Archive attributes for a file

Although it is possible to back up all of the files in the filesystem during each backup operation, it's sometimes more convenient to back up only selected files (such as those that have changed since the last backup operation). When performing backups, you can backup to

removable media (such as tape) or to a network location. It is not recommended to do a backup to a network location unless absolutely necessary. The reason for this is that if your company suffers from a disaster (fire, hurricane, etc..), your data can all still be lost—including the backup. If you backup to a removable media source, a copy of the backup can be taken off-site. This protects against a major disaster. Several types of backups can be performed:

 The Windows Server 2008 Backup Utility supports Normal (full) and Incremental backups. We also explain other backup methods in the event that you use a third-party backup utility.

Normal   *Normal backups* (also referred to as full backups) back up all of the selected files and then mark them as backed up. This option is usually used when a full system backup is made.

Copy   *Copy backups* back up all of the selected files, but do not mark them as backed up. This is useful when you want to make additional backups of files for moving files offsite or you want to make multiple copies of the same data for archival purposes.

Incremental   *Incremental backups* copy any selected files that are marked as ready for backup (typically because they have not been backed up, or they have been changed since the last backup) and then mark the files as backed up. When the next incremental backup is run, only the files that are not marked as having been backed up are stored. Incremental backups are used in conjunction with Normal (Full) backups. The most common backup process is to make a full backup and then to make subsequent incremental backups. The benefit to this method is that only files that have changed since the last full or incremental backup will be stored. This can reduce backup times and disk or tape storage space requirements.

When recovering information from this type of backup method, a systems administrator must first restore the full backup and then restore each of the incremental backups.

Differential   *Differential backups* are similar in purpose to incremental backups with one important exception: Differential backups copy all files that are marked for backup but do not mark the files as backed up. When restoring files in a situation that uses normal and differential backups, you only need to restore the normal backup and the latest differential backup.

Daily   *Daily backups* back up all files that have changed during a single day. This operation uses the file time/date stamps to determine which files should be backed up and does not mark the files as having been backed up.

Figure 10.21 shows the Windows Server 2008 Backup Utility Optimize Backup Performance dialog box and the three choices for backup types.

Note that systems administrators might choose to combine normal, daily, incremental, and differential backup types as part of the same backup plan. In general, however, it is sufficient to use only one or two of these methods (for example, normal backups with incremental backups). If you require a combination of multiple backup types, be sure that you fully understand which types of files are being backed up.

FIGURE 10.21   Options for optimizing backup performance

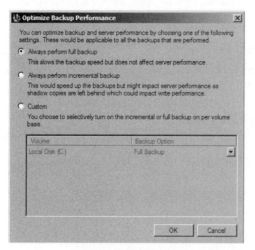

Backing Up System State Data

When you are planning to back up and restore Active Directory, be aware that the most important component is known as the *System State data*. System State data includes the components that the Windows Server 2008 operating system relies on for normal operations. The Windows Server 2008 Backup utility offers you the ability to back up the System State data to another type of media (such as a hard disk, network share, or tape device). Specifically, it will back up the following components for a Windows Server 2008 domain controller.

Active Directory   The Active Directory data store is at the heart of Active Directory. It contains all of the information necessary to create and manage network resources, such as users and computers. In most environments that use Active Directory, users and systems administrators rely on the proper functioning of these services in order to do their jobs.

Boot files   Boot files are the files required for booting the Windows Server 2008 operating system and can be used in the case of boot file corruption.

COM+ Class Registration database   The COM+ Class Registration database is a listing of all of the COM+ Class registrations stored on the computer. Applications that run on a Windows Server 2008 computer might require the registration of various share code components. As part of the System State backup process, Windows Server 2008 stores all of the information related to Component Object Model+ (COM+) components so that it can be quickly and easily restored.

Registry   The Windows Server 2008 Registry is a central repository of information related to the operating system configuration (such as desktop and network settings), user settings, and application settings. Therefore, the Registry is absolutely vital to the proper functioning of Windows Server 2008.

SYSVOL **Directory**   The SYSVOL directory includes data and files that are shared between the domain controllers within an Active Directory domain. This information is relied upon by many operating system services for proper functioning.

Scheduling Backups

In addition to specifying which files to back up, you can schedule backup jobs to occur at specific times. Planning *when* to perform backups is just as important as deciding what to back up. Performing backup operations can reduce overall system performance; therefore, you should plan to back up information during times of minimal activity on your servers. Figure 10.22 shows the Backup Schedule Wizard of the Window Server 2008 Backup utility.

FIGURE 10.22   Scheduling jobs using the Windows Server 2008 Backup utility

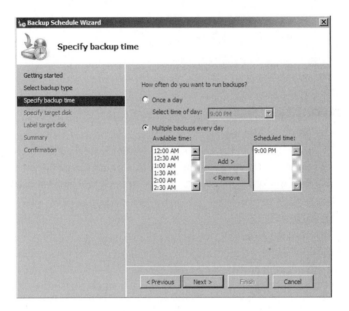

To add a backup operation to the schedule, you can simply click the Add button on the Specify Backup Time window.

Restoring System State Data

In some cases, the Active Directory data store or other System State data may become corrupt or unavailable. This could be due to many different reasons. A hard disk failure might, for example, result in the loss of data. Or the accidental deletion of an OU and all of its objects might require a restore operation to be performed.

The actual steps involved in restoring System State data are based on the details of what has caused the data loss and what effect this data loss has had on the system. In the best case, the System State data is corrupt or inaccurate, but the operating system can still boot. If this is the case, all that you must do is boot into a special *Directory Services Restore mode (DSRM)* and then restore the System State data from a backup. This process will replace the current System

State data with that from the backup. Therefore, any changes that have been made since the last backup will be completely lost and must be redone.

In a worst-case scenario, all of the information on a server has been lost or a hardware failure is preventing the machine from properly booting. If this is the case, here are several steps that you must take in order to recover System State data:

1. Fix any hardware problem that might prevent the computer from booting (for example, replace any failed hard disks).

2. Reinstall the Windows Server 2008 operating system. This should be performed like a regular installation on a new system.

3. Reinstall any device drivers that may be required by your backup device. If you backed up information to the filesystem, this will not apply.

4. Restore the System State data using the Windows Server 2008 Backup utility.

We'll cover the technical details of performing restores later in this section. For now, however, you should understand the importance of backing up information and, whenever possible, testing the validity of backups.

Backing up Group Policy Objects

Group Policy Objects (GPOs) are a major part of Active Directory. When you back up Active Directory, GPOs can also get backed up. You also have the ability to backup GPOs through the Group Policy Management Console (GPMC). This gives you the ability to back up and restore individual GPOs.

 Group Policy management Console is discussed in detail in Chapter 8, "Configuring Group Policy Objects."

To back up all GPOs, open the GPMC and right click on the Group Policy Objects container. You will see an option to Back Up All. After you choose this option, a wizard will start asking you for the backup location. Choose a location and click backup.

To back up an individual GPO, right click on the GPO (in the Group Policy Objects container) and choose Backup. Again, after you choose this option, a wizard will start asking you for the backup location. Choose a location and click Backup.

To restore a GPO, it's the same process as above except instead of choosing Backup, you will either choose Manage Backups (to restore all GPOs) or Restore (for an individual GPO).

Backing Up Active Directory

The Windows Server 2008 Backup utility makes it easy to back up the System data (including Active Directory) as part of a normal backup operation. We've already covered the ideas behind the different backup types and why and when they are used. Exercise 10.2 walks you through the process of backing up the domain controller. In order to complete this exercise, the local machine must be a domain controller, and you must have sufficient free space to back up the System State (usually at least 500MB).

Windows Server 2008 Backup utility is not installed by default. If you have already installed Windows Server 2008 Backup utility, skip to step 5.

EXERCISE 10.2

Backing Up Active Directory

1. To install the Windows Server 2008 Backup utility, click Start ≻ Administrative Tools ≻ Server Manager. In the left pane, click Features. In the right pane click Add Features.

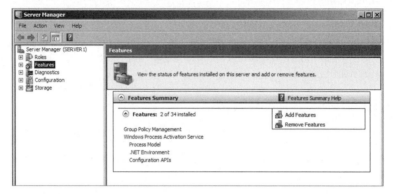

2. In the Select Features window, scroll down and check the Windows Server Backup check box. Click Next.

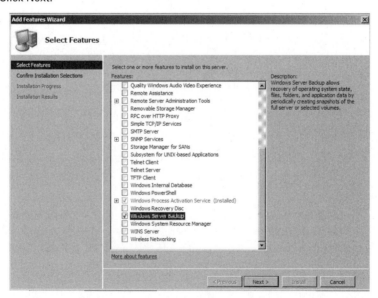

3. On the Confirm Installation Selections screen, click the Install button.

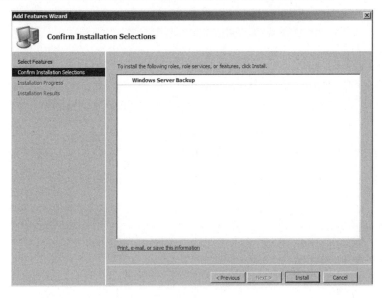

4. After the installation is complete, close Server Manager.

5. Open the Backup utility by clicking Start ➢ Administrative Tools ➢ Backup.

6. In the Windows Server Backup utility, click Action ➢ Backup Once. This is how you schedule a one-time backup. The Action menu also contains the Backup Schedule (set a daily backup time), Recover, and Configure Performance Settings commands.

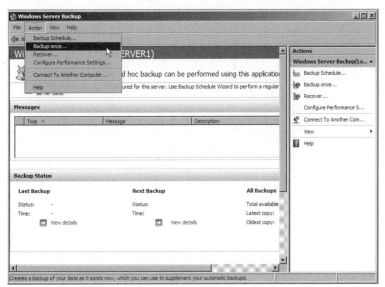

7. The Backup Once Wizard appears. Make sure the radio button labeled Different Options is checked and click Next.

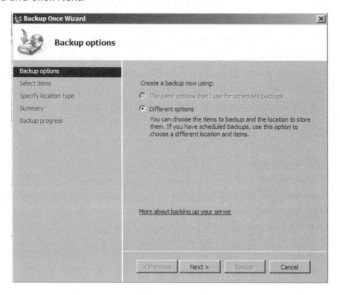

8. In the Select Items window, click the Custom radio button. Click Next.

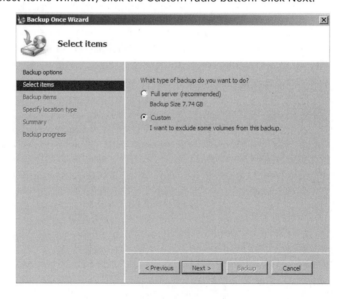

The Full Server—Recommended option does a complete backup of the system.

9. In the Backup Items window, make sure that the check box labeled "I want to be able to perform a system recovery using this backup" is checked. Once this box is checked, the local disk box will also be checked. Click Next.

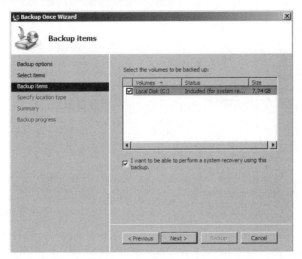

10. In the Specify Location Type screen, choose Local Drives. These options help you determine where your backup file is going to be stored. Click Next.

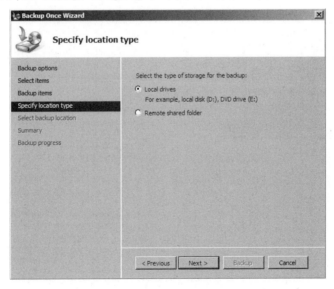

11. In the Select Backup Location screen, choose a local drive that has enough space for the backup. Click Next.

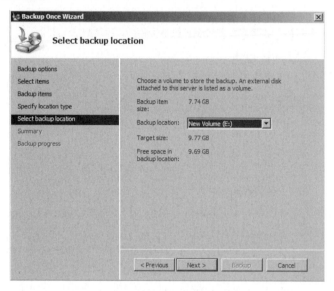

12. Verify all your choices in the Summary screen and choose the Backup button.

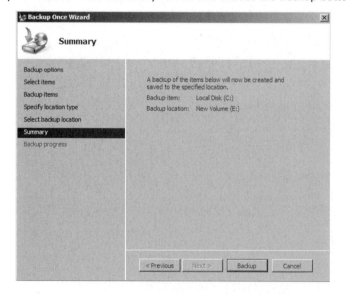

13. The Backup Progress screen will show you the status of your backup. Once the backup is complete, close the Windows Server 2008 Backup utility.

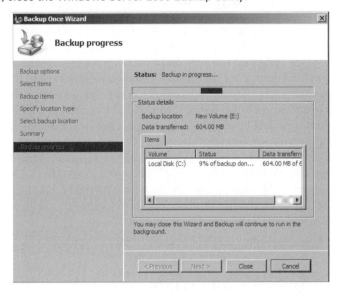

Restoring Active Directory

Active Directory has been designed with fault tolerance in mind. For example, it is highly recommended by Microsoft that each domain have at least two domain controllers. Each of these domain controllers contains a copy of the Active Directory data store. Should one of the domain controllers fail, the available one can take over the failed server's functionality. When the failed server is repaired, it can then be promoted to a domain controller in the existing environment. This process effectively restores the failed domain controller without incurring any downtime for end users because all of the Active Directory data is replicated to the repaired server in the next scheduled replication.

In some cases, you might need to restore Active Directory from a backup. For example, suppose a systems administrator accidentally deletes several hundred users from the domain and does not realize it until the change has been propagated to all of the other domain controllers. Manually re-creating the accounts is not an option because the objects' security identifiers will be different (and all permissions must be reset). Clearly, a method for restoring from backup is the best solution. You can elect to make the Active Directory restore authoritative or non-authoritative, as described in the following sections.

Overview of Authoritative Restore

Restoring Active Directory and other System State data is an important process should system files or the Active Directory data store become corrupt or otherwise unavailable. Fortunately, the Windows Server 2008 Backup utility allows you to easily restore data from a backup, should the need arise.

We mentioned earlier that in the case of the accidental deletion of information from Active Directory, you may need to restore the Active Directory from a recent backup. But what happens if there is more than one domain controller in the environment? Even if you did perform a restore, the information on this domain controller would be seen as outdated and it would be overwritten by the data from another domain controller. This data from the older domain controller is exactly the information you want to replace. The domain controller that was reloaded using a backup would have an older timestamp and the other domain controllers would re-delete the information from the backup.

Fortunately, Windows Server 2008 and Active Directory allow you to perform what is called an *authoritative restore*. The authoritative restore process specifies a domain controller as having the authoritative (or master) copy of the Active Directory data store. When other domain controllers communicate with this domain controller, their information will be overwritten with Active Directory data stored on the local machine.

Now that we have an idea of how an authoritative restore is supposed to work, let's move on to looking at the details of performing the process.

Performing an Authoritative Restore

When you are restoring Active Directory information on a Windows Server 2008 domain controller, make sure Active Directory services are not running. This is because the restore of System State data requires full access to system files and the Active Directory data store. If you attempt to restore System State data while the domain controller is active, you will see the error message shown in Figure 10.23.

FIGURE 10.23   Attempting to restore System State while a domain controller is active

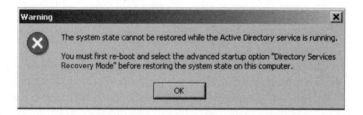

In general, restoring data and operating system files is a straightforward process. It is important to note that restoring a System State backup will replace the existing Registry, Sysvol, and Active Directory files, so any changes you made since the last backup will be lost.

Exercise 10.3 walks you through the process of performing an authoritative restore on the System State and Active Directory information. This process uses the ntdsutil utility—which we first saw back in Chapter 3, "Active Directory Planning and Installation"—to set the authoritative restore mode for a domain controller after the System State is restored but before the domain controller is rebooted. In order to complete this process, you must have first completed the steps in Exercise 10.2.

Any changes made to Active Directory after the backup performed in Exercise 10.2 will be lost after you complete Exercise 10.3.

EXERCISE 10.3

Restoring the System State and Active Directory

1. Reboot the local machine. When the machine starts to boot up, press the F8 key to enter the Windows Server 2008 advanced options.

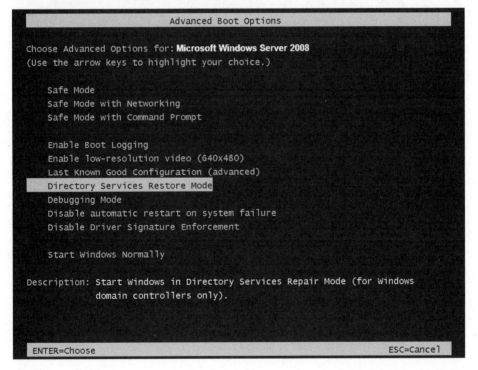

2. From the boot menu, choose Directory Services Restore Mode and press Enter. The operating system will begin to boot in safe mode.

3. Log on to the computer as a member of the *local* Administrators group. Note that you cannot log on using an Active Directory account since network services and Active Directory have not been started.

4. You may see a message warning you that the machine is running in safe mode and that certain services will not be available. For example, a minimal set of drivers has been loaded, and you will not have access to the network. Click OK to continue. You will notice the label Safe Mode in the corners of the screen.

5. When the operating system has finished booting, open the Backup utility by clicking Start ➢ Administrative Tools ➢ Backup.

6. The Backup utility will begin. Click Action and then choose Recover.

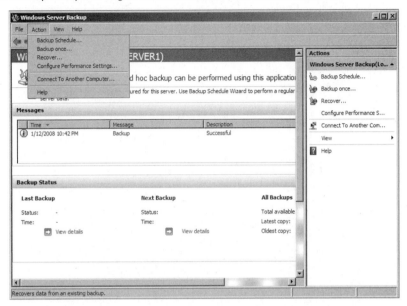

7. The Recovery Wizard appears. Make sure the button labeled This Server is selected and click Next.

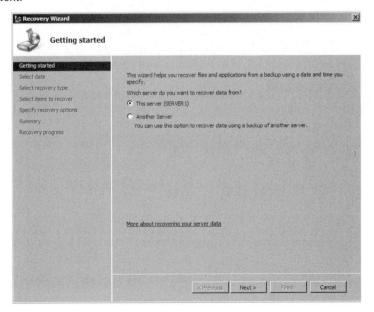

8. On the Select Date page, click the date of the backup that you created in the previous exercise. Click Next to continue.

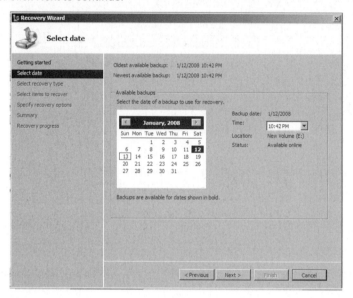

9. On the Select Recovery Type page, click the Files And Folders radio button. Click Next to continue.

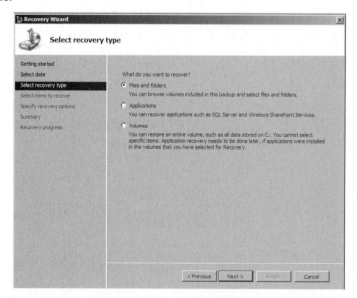

10. On the Select Items To Recover page, you will see the server you backed up in the last exercise. Click the Local Disk (C:) and then click Next.

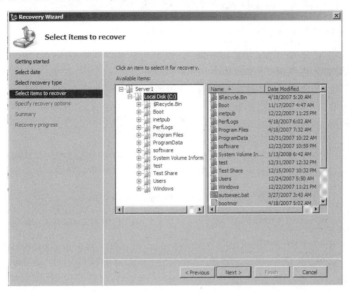

11. If a warning box appears, just click OK.

12. On the Specify Recovery Options page, choose Another Location and click the Browse button. Choose a location on your hard disk to restore the files. Do not overwrite your hard disk for this exercise! Click Next.

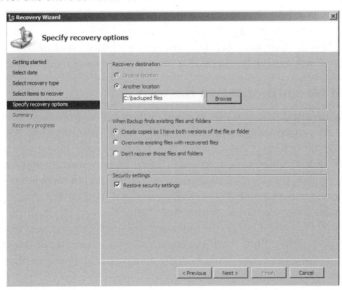

13. On the Summary Page, click Finished.

14. You will be asked whether you want to restart the computer. Select No.

15. Close the Backup Utility.

16. Now, you will need to place the domain controller in authoritative restore mode. To do this, click Start ➤ Run and type **cmd**. At the command prompt, enter **ntdsutil**. Note that you can enter the question mark symbol (**?**) to view help information for the various commands available with the ntdsutil utility.

17. At the ntdsutil prompt, type **authoritative restore** and press Enter.

18. At the authoritative restore prompt, type **restore database** and press Enter. You will be asked whether or not you want to perform an authoritative restore. Click Yes.

19. The ntdsutil utility will begin the authoritative restore process.

20. Type **quit** twice to exit ntdsutil. Then, close the command prompt by typing **exit**.

21. Finally, click Start ➤ Shut Down, and restart the computer. Following a reboot of the operating system, Active Directory and System State data will be current to the point of the last backup.

In addition to restoring the entire Active Directory database, you can also restore just specific subtrees within Active Directory using the `restore subtree` command in the ntdsutil utility. This allows you to restore specific information and is useful in the case of an accidental deletion of isolated material.

Following the authoritative restore process, Active Directory should be updated to the time of the last backup. Furthermore, all other domain controllers for this domain will have their Active Directory information overwritten by the results of the restore operation. The end result is an Active Directory environment that has been recovered from media.

Overview of Nonauthoritative Restore

Now that you understand why you would use an authoritative restore and how it is performed, it's an easy conceptual jump to understand what a nonauthoritative restore is. Remember that by making a restore authoritative, you are simply telling other domain controllers in the domain to recognize the restored machine as the newest copy of Active Directory for replication purposes. If you only have one domain controller, the authoritative restore process becomes moot; you can simply skip the steps required to make the restore authoritative and begin using the domain controller immediately after the normal restore is complete.

If you have more than one domain controller in the domain and you need to perform a nonauthoritative restore, simply allow the domain controller to receive Active Directory database information from other domain controllers in the domain using normal replication methods.

Offline Maintenance with *ntdsutil.exe*

As you have seen in the last section, there are times when you have to be offline to do maintenance. For example, you need to perform authoritative and nonauthoritative restores while the domain controller is offline. The main utility we use for offline maintenance is ntdsutil.

The primary method by which systems administrators can do offline maintenance is through the ntdsutil command-line tool. You can launch this tool by simply entering `ntdsutil` at a command prompt. The `ntdsutil` command is both interactive and context-sensitive. That is, once you launch the utility, you'll see an ntdsutil command prompt. At this prompt, you can enter various commands that set your context within the application. For example, if you enter **domain management**, you'll be able to enter in domain-related commands. Several operations also require you to connect to a domain, a domain controller, or an Active Directory object before you perform a command.

Table 10.2 provides a list of the domain management commands supported by the ntdsutil tool. You can access this functionality by typing the command at a command prompt.

TABLE 10.2   ntdsutil Offline Maintenance Commands

ntdsutil Domain Management Command	Purpose
Help or ?	Displays information about the commands that are available within the Domain Management menu of the `ntdsutil` utility.
compact to (At the file maintenance prompt)	Allows you to compact the active directory database.
metadata cleanup	Removes metadata's from decommissioned domain controllers.
Set DSRM Password	Resets directory service restore mode administrator account password.

Monitoring Replication

At times you may need to keep on eye on how your replication traffic is working on your domain controllers. We are going to examine two replication utilities that you can use to help determine problems on your domain.

RepAdmin Utility

The RepAdmin utility is included when you install Windows Server 2008. This command-line tool helps administrators diagnose replication problems between Windows domain controllers.

RepAdmin can allow administrators to view the replication topology of each domain controller as seen from the domain controller's perspective. Administrators can also use RepAdmin to manually create the replication topology. By manually creating the replication topology, administrators can force replication events between domain controllers and view the replication metadata vectors.

To access the RepAdmin utility, open a command prompt (Run ➢ CMD). At the command prompt, type **RepAdmin.exe** and all the available options will appear.

Replication Monitor

Replication Monitor has been used for years to monitor replication traffic. At the time that this book was written, a version of Replication Monitor for Windows Server 2008 had not yet been released. Instead, we will discuss Replication Monitor as it has been for many years. To see if a current version has been released, visit **www.microsoft.com**.

Replication Monitor is not installed on Windows Server 2008 computers by default; it is a support package installation. You can access the Replication Monitor by entering **replmon** in the Run dialog box.

The Replication Monitor window is initially empty; you must add one or more servers to the monitor window in order to derive any meaningful information from the tool. To add a server, right-click the Monitored Servers item in the left pane and select Add Monitored Server. The Add Monitored Server Wizard prompts you to enter or select a server from a list, which is a very straightforward process.

After you add a server to Replication Monitor, you can begin monitoring replication traffic. Figure 10.24 displays a single server in the left pane. You can see the different Active Directory partitions under the server name. You can use the Replication Monitor primarily for the following two purposes: checking for replication errors and initiating immediate domain controller synchronization.

FIGURE 10.24   The Replication Monitor

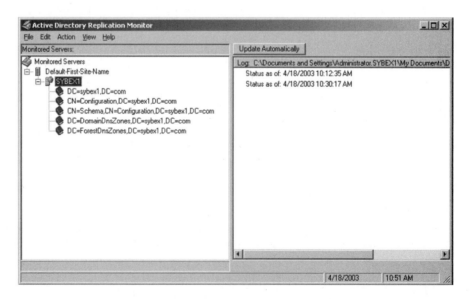

To check for replication errors, click the Action menu and select Domain ➤ Search Domain Controllers For Replication Errors. In the Search Domain Controllers For Replication Errors dialog box, click the Run Search button to search domain controllers in the domain for errors. Any errors are displayed in the main section of the dialog box.

To synchronize Active Directory immediately, right-click a server name and select Synchronize Each Directory Partition With All Servers from the pop-up menu. Alternately, you can synchronize partitions individually by right-clicking a partition name and selecting Synchronize This Directory Partition with All Servers from the pop-up menu.

Summary

Although the tasks related to performance optimization and ensuring reliability of Active Directory domain controllers are only a small part of the seemingly endless tasks performed by systems administrators, they are very important in the overall health of a network environment. In this chapter, we covered many aspects associated with optimizing Active Directory and making it reliable. We showed you how to use many tools that can help you monitor and manage your systems and we discussed the basics of troubleshooting Active Directory in times of problem or disaster.

It is imperative that you monitor performance on domain controllers in order to root out any issues that may affect your systems. If your systems are not running optimally, your end users may experience issues such as latency, or worse, you may experience corruption in your Active Directory database. Either way, it's important to know how to monitor the performance of domain controllers. In this chapter, we also looked at ways systems administrators can optimize the operations of domain controllers to ensure that end users receive adequate performance.

We also looked at how to use the various performance-related tools that are included with Windows Server 2008. Tools such as the Performance Monitor utility, Task Manager, Network Monitor, and Event Viewer can help you diagnose and troubleshoot system performance issues. As an administrator, you will often use these tools and they will definitely help you find typical problems related to memory, disk space, and any other hardware-related issues you may experience. Knowing how to use tools to troubleshoot and test your systems is not only imperative to passing the exam, but also to performing your duties at work. In order to have a smoothly running network environment, it is vital that you understand the issues related to the reliability and performance of Active Directory and domain controllers.

We also covered the details of performing backups, the most commonly used form of reliability you can implement. You learned how to back up and restore System State data using the Windows Server 2008 Backup utility. Through the use of wizards and prompts, this backup tool can simplify an otherwise tedious process. Knowing how to restore System State data and the Active Directory database can really put you a cut above the rest, especially in times of disaster. By using the authoritative restore functionality, you can revert all or part of an Active Directory environment back to an earlier state.

Exam Essentials

Understand the methodology behind troubleshooting performance. By following a set of steps that involves making measurements and finding bottlenecks, you can perform systematic troubleshooting of performance problems.

Be familiar with the features and capabilities of the Windows Server 2008 Performance Monitor tool for troubleshooting performance problems. Using the Performance administrative tool is a very powerful method for collecting data about all areas of system performance. Through the use of performance objects, counters, and instances, you can choose to collect and record only the data of interest and use this information for pinpointing performance problems.

Know the importance of common performance counters. Several important performance-related counters deal with general system performance. Know the importance of monitoring memory, CPU, and network usage on a busy server.

Understand the role of other troubleshooting tools. The Windows Task Manager, Network Monitor, and Event Viewer can all be used to diagnose and troubleshoot configuration- and performance-related issues.

Understand how to troubleshoot common sources of server reliability problems. Windows Server 2008 has been designed to be a stable, robust, and reliable operating system. Should you experience intermittent failures, you should know how to troubleshoot device drivers and buggy system-level software.

Understand the various backup types available with the Windows Server 2008 Backup utility. The Windows Server 2008 Backup utility can perform full and incremental backup operations. Some third-party backup utilities also support differential and daily backups. You can use each of these operations as part of an efficient backup strategy.

Know how to back up Active Directory. The data within the Active Directory database on a domain controller is part of the System State data. You can back up the System State to a file using the Windows Server 2008 Backup utility.

Know how to restore Active Directory. Restoring the Active Directory database is considerably different from other restore operations. In order to restore some or all of the Active Directory database, you must first boot the machine into Directory Services Restore mode.

Understand the importance of an authoritative restore process. You use an authoritative restore when you want to restore earlier information from an Active Directory backup and you want the older information to be propagated to other domain controllers in the environment.

Understand offline maintenance using ntdsutil. The ntdsutil command-line tool is a primary method by which systems administrators perform offline maintenance. Understand how to launch this tool by entering **ntdsutil** at a command prompt.

Be familiar with replication utilities. Know the two utilities for monitoring replication—repadmin.exe and replmon.exe. Know that the RepAdmin command-line tool helps administrators diagnose replication problems between Windows domain controllers.

Review Questions

1. Crystal is a systems administrator who is responsible for performing backups on several servers. Recently, she has been asked to take over operations of several new servers. Unfortunately, no information about the standard upkeep and maintenance of those servers is available. Crystal wants to begin by making configuration changes to these servers, but she wants to first ensure that she has a full backup of all data on each of these servers.

    Crystal decides to use the Windows Server 2008 Backup utility to perform the backups. She wants to choose a backup type that will back up all files on each of these servers, regardless of when they were last changed or if they have been previously backed up. Which of the following types of backup operations store all of the selected files, without regard to the Archive bit setting?

    A. Normal

    B. Incremental

    C. Copy

    D. Differential

2. What utility is a command-line tool that helps administrators diagnose replication problems between Windows domain controllers?

    A. RepAdmin

    B. RepWatch

    C. RepUtility

    D. RepAlert

3. A systems administrator boots the operating system using the Directory Services Restore mode. He attempts to log in using a Domain Administrator account, but is unable to do so. What is the most likely reason for this?

    A. The account has been disabled by another domain administrator.

    B. The permissions on the domain controller do not allow users to log on locally.

    C. The Active Directory service is unavailable, and he must use the local Administrator password.

    D. Another domain controller for the domain is not available to authenticate the login.

4. Which of the following types of backup operations should a systems administrator use to back up all of the files that have changed since the last full backup or incremental backup and to mark these files as having been backed up?

    A. Differential

    B. Copy

    C. Incremental

    D. Normal

5. Following an authoritative restore of the entire Active Directory database, what will happen to the copy of Active Directory on other domain controllers for the same domain?

   A. The copies of Active Directory on other domain controllers will be overwritten.

   B. The information on all domain controllers will be merged.

   C. The other domain controllers will be automatically demoted.

   D. The copies of Active Directory on the restored domain controller will be overwritten.

6. Which of the following ntdsutil commands is used to perform an authoritative restore of the entire Active Directory database?

   A. restore active directory

   B. restore database

   C. restore subtree

   D. restore all

7. You are responsible for managing several Windows Server 2008 domain controller computers in your environment. Recently, a hard disk on one of these machines failed, and the Active Directory database was lost. You want to perform the following tasks:

   - Determine which partitions on the server are still accessible.

   - Restore as much of the system configuration (including the Active Directory database) as is possible.

   Which of the following could you use to help meet these requirements?

   A. Event Viewer

   B. Performance Monitor

   C. A hard disk from another server that is not configured as a domain controller

   D. A valid System State backup from the server

8. You have been hired as a consultant to research a network-related problem at a small organization. The environment supports many custom-developed applications that are not well documented. A manager suspects that one or more computers on the network are generating excessive traffic and bogging down the network. You want to do the following:

   - Determine which computers are causing the problems.

   - Record and examine network packets that are coming to/from specific machines.

   - View data related only to specific types of network packet.

   What tool should you use to accomplish all of the requirements?

   A. Task Manager

   B. Performance Monitor

   C. Event Viewer

   D. Network Monitor

9. Which of the following is not backed up as part of the Windows Server 2008 System State on a domain controller?

A. Registry

B. COM+ Registration information

C. Boot files

D. Active Directory database information

E. User profiles

10. Which of the following System Monitor performance objects can you use to measure performance statistics related to Active Directory? (Choose all that apply.)

A. Directory Services

B. LDAP

C. Network

D. Replication

E. NTDS

11. You are the system administrator for your company. Your new users have not been replicating properly on your Windows Server 2008 server. Which utility can you use to check the replication of your domain controllers?

A. RepConsole

B. RepAdmin

C. RepView

D. RepMonitor

12. Robert is a systems administrator who is responsible for performing backups on several servers. Recently, he has been asked to take over operations of several new servers, including backup operations. He has the following requirements:

- The backup must finish as quickly as possible.
- The backup must use the absolute minimum amount of storage space.
- He must perform backup operations at least daily with a full backup at least weekly.

Robert decides to use the Windows Server 2008 Backup utility to perform the backups. He wants to choose a set of backup types that will meet all of these requirements. He decides to back up all files on each of these servers every week. Then, he decides to store only the files that have changed since the last backup operation (regardless of type) during the weekdays. Which of the following types of backup operations should he use to implement this solution? (Choose two.)

A. Normal

B. Daily

C. Copy

D. Differential

E. Incremental

13. A systems administrator suspects that a domain controller is not operating properly. Another systems administrator has been monitoring the performance of the server and has found that this is not a likely cause of the problems. Where can the first systems administrator look for more information regarding details about any specific problems or errors that may be occurring?

A. Task Manager

B. Network Monitor

C. Performance Monitor

D. Event Viewer

14. Which of the following System Monitor views displays performance information over a period of time?

A. Graph

B. Histogram

C. Report

D. Current Activity

15. You are using the Backup Wizard to back up Active Directory. You want to ensure that the entire Active Directory is backed up while maintaining a minimum backup file size. In the following screen, where would you click in order to accomplish this task?

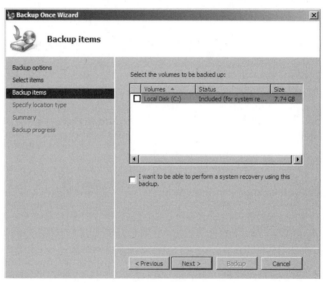

A. "I want to be able to perform a system recovery using this backup."

B. Local Disk (C:).

C. Nothing—This screen does not back up the System State data.

D. The Next button.

16. In your current capacity as network administrator, you are looking to diagnose a problem with your current network infrastructure. You have 20 Windows Server 2008 servers and 1000 Windows XP Professional workstations spread out across 6 subnets. You need to test the connections between each pair of servers and determine how each server connects to the network switches that are used to build the core of the network. All servers run fine except for one. Which of the following lists of tools would you use to troubleshoot this server?

A. Event Viewer, Performance Monitor, Network Monitor

B. Task Manager, Network Monitor, Server Monitor

C. Performance Monitor, System logs, Task Manager

D. Event Viewer, Network Sniffer, NTBACKUP

17. You are the systems engineer responsible for 123 Ltd.'s new division. You need to deploy five new Windows Server 2008 systems. What do you need to do in order to make sure that you understand the normal load put on the systems under normal operations?

A. Set up Task Manager.

B. Establish a baseline of current performance.

C. Deploy the Alerts in the Performance Console.

D. Use Network Monitor to see current and future load.

18. As the IT Manager for your company's technology division, you are asked to deploy a method of finding problems on your connection to the network. You have three Windows Server 2008 systems and each is set up as a domain controller. What tools are incorporated with each server that will help you find problems on the network, more specifically on the network medium?

A. Task Monitor

B. Performance Monitor

C. Network Monitor

D. Event Monitor

19. You are the systems administrator for your company and are responsible for the Active Directory infrastructure. After a disaster, you are asked to restore the Active Directory System State data information on a Windows Server 2008 domain controller. You try to run the restore and you get an error message. You are unable to perform the restore. From the list of possible choices, what may be causing this problem to occur?

A. Active Directory services are running.

B. DNS services are still running.

C. The Backup service is not running.

D. The TCP/IP service is not running.

20. You have been asked to deploy counters to monitor your CPU on a server that is performing poorly. What is the process of adding the % Processor Time counter and the _Total instance counters on a Windows Server 2008 system?

A. In the Add Counters dialog box, select Use Local Computer Counters. Choose the CPU performance object from the Performance Object list, and then click Select Counters From List. Select the % Processor Time counter and the _Total instance.

B. In the Add Counters dialog box, select Use Local Computer Counters. Choose the PROC performance object from the Performance Object list, and then click Select Counters From List. Select the % Processor Time counter and the _Total instance.

C. In the Add Counters dialog box, select Use Local Computer Counters. Choose the DISK performance object from the Performance Object list, and then click Select Counters From List. Select the % Processor Time counter and the _Total instance.

D. In the Add Counters dialog box, select Use Local Computer Counters. Choose the Processor performance object from the Performance Object list, and then click Select Counters From List. Select the % Processor Time counter and the _Total instance.

Answers to Review Questions

1. A. Normal and Copy backup operations do not use the Archive bit to determine which files to back up, and they will include all files that are selected for backup on the server. The other backup types will store only a subset of files based on their dates or whether or not they have been previously backed up. The Windows Server 2008 Backup utility supports Normal backups but does not support Copy backups. For this reason, Crystal should choose a Normal backup to ensure that she performs a valid backup of all files on the servers before she makes any configuration changes.

2. A. The RepAdmin command-line tool is included when you install Windows Server 2008. RepAdmin helps administrators diagnose replication problems between Windows domain controllers.

3. C. When booting in Directory Services Restore mode, Active Directory is not started, and network services are disabled. Therefore, the systems administrator must use a local account in order to log in.

4. C. Incremental backup operations copy files and mark them as having been backed up. Therefore, a system administrator uses them when they want to back up only the files that have changed since the last full or incremental backup. Differential backups, although they will also back up only files that were created or changed since the last full or incremental backup, will not mark the files as having been backed up.

5. A. In an authoritative restore of the entire Active Directory database, the restored copy will override information stored on other domain controllers.

6. B. The `restore database` command instructs the ntdsutil application to perform an authoritative restore of the entire Active Directory database.

7. D. You can recover System State data from a backup, which always includes the Active Directory database. In this case, the Event Viewer and System Monitor wouldn't help you recover the database, but they might help you determine why the hard drive crashed in the first place.

8. D. Through the use of the Network Monitor application, you can view all of the network packets that are being sent to or from the local server. Based on this information, you can determine the source of certain types of traffic, such as pings. The other types of monitoring can provide useful information, but they do not allow you to drill down into the specific details of a network packet, nor do they allow you to filter the data that has been collected based on details about the packet.

9. E. The System State backup includes information that can be used to rebuild a server's basic configuration. All of the information listed, except for user profile data, is backed up as part of a System State backup operation.

10. A, B, C, D, E. The various counters that are part of the NTDS performance object provide information about the performance of various aspects of Active Directory. By collecting information for each of these performance objects, you can determine what areas of system performance might be having problems.

11. B. RepAdmin is a command line utility used to view and configure Windows Server 2008 replication between domain controllers.

12. A, E. In order to meet the requirements, Robert should use the normal backup type to create a full backup every week and the incremental backup type to back up only the data that has been modified since the last full or incremental backup operation.

13. D. The Event Viewer is the best tool for viewing information, warnings, and alerts related to Windows Server 2008 functions.

14. A. Using the Graph view, you can view performance information over a period of time (as defined by the sample interval). The Histogram and Report views are designed to show the latest performance statistics and average values.

15. A. "I want to be able to perform a system recovery using this backup" is what you want to click. Once this check box is checked, the Local Disk (C:) will automatically become checked.

16. A. Event Viewer is used to show you informational- and warning-based events tracked by the system. The logs are useful for finding problems in your system. Performance Monitor is used to monitor performance objects, set counters, and establish a baseline of your system. Network Monitor is used to look at the traffic (to the packet level) on your network. All tools are used to help find problems in your system.

17. B. By establishing a baseline of the current performance of your systems, you get an idea of how they perform normally, and then you will know when they aren't performing as expected because the charts will be off. Make sure you document this procedure and consider setting up a linear rather than circular log.

18. C. Network Monitor is used to find network problems at the packet level. Make sure you are familiar with this tool for both the exam and in production environments where you can use it.

19. A. When you are restoring Active Directory System State data information on a Windows Server 2008 domain controller, make sure Active Directory services are not running. You need to do this because the restore of System State data requires full access to system files and the Active Directory data store. If you attempt to restore System State data while the domain controller is active, you will see an error message. All other listed services will not interfere with the restore.

20. D. In the Add Counters dialog box, you first need to select Use Local Computer Counters. Then you need to choose the Processor performance object from the Performance Object list, and then click Select Counters From List. Finally, select the % Processor Time counter and the _Total instance.

Appendix

A

About the Companion CD

IN THIS APPENDIX:

✓ What you'll find on the CD

✓ System requirements

✓ Using the CD

✓ Troubleshooting

What You'll Find on the CD

The following sections are arranged by category and provide a summary of the software and other goodies you'll find on the CD. If you need help with installing the items provided on the CD, refer to the installation instructions in the ìUsing the CDî section of this appendix.

Some programs on the CD might fall into one of these categories:

Shareware programs are fully functional, free, trial versions of copyrighted programs. If you like particular programs, register with their authors for a nominal fee and receive licenses, enhanced versions, and technical support.

Freeware programs are free, copyrighted games, applications, and utilities. You can copy them to as many computers as you like—for free—but they offer no technical support.

GNU software is governed by its own license, which is included inside the folder of the GNU software. There are no restrictions on distribution of GNU software. See the GNU license at the root of the CD for more details.

Trial, demo, or *evaluation* versions of software are usually limited either by time or functionality (such as not letting you save a project after you create it).

Sybex Test Engine

For Windows

The CD contains the Sybex Test Engine, which includes all of the Assessment Test and Chapter Review questions in electronic format, as well as two bonus exams located only on the CD.

PDF of the Book

For Windows

We have included an electronic version of the text in .pdf format. You can view the electronic version of the book with Adobe Reader.

Adobe Reader

For Windows

We've also included a copy of Adobe Reader, so you can view PDF files that accompany the book's content. For more information on Adobe Reader or to check for a newer version, visit Adobe's website at http://www.adobe.com/products/reader/.

Electronic Flashcards

For PC, Pocket PC and Palm

These handy electronic flashcards are just what they sound like. One side contains a question or fill in the blank, and the other side shows the answer.

System Requirements

Make sure that your computer meets the minimum system requirements shown in the following list. If your computer doesn't match up to most of these requirements, you may have problems using the software and files on the companion CD. For the latest and greatest information, please refer to the ReadMe file located at the root of the CD-ROM.

- A PC running Microsoft Windows 98, Windows 2000, Windows NT4 (with SP4 or later), Windows Me, Windows XP, or Windows Vista
- An Internet connection
- A CD-ROM drive

Using the CD

To install the items from the CD to your hard drive, follow these steps:

1. Insert the CD into your computer's CD-ROM drive. The license agreement appears.

 Windows users: The interface won't launch if you have Autorun disabled. In that case, click Start ➤ Run (for Windows Vista, Start ➤ All Programs ➤ Accessories ➤ Run). In the dialog box that appears, type D:**Start.exe**. (Replace D with the proper letter if your CD drive uses a different letter. If you don't know the letter, see how your CD drive is listed under My Computer.) Click OK.

2. Read through the license agreement, and then click the Accept button if you want to use the CD.

The CD interface appears. The interface allows you to access the content with just one or two clicks.

Troubleshooting

Wiley has attempted to provide programs that work on most computers with the minimum system requirements. Alas, your computer may differ, and some programs may not work properly for some reason.

The two likeliest problems are that you don't have enough memory (RAM) for the programs you want to use, or you have other programs running that are affecting installation or running of a program. If you get an error message such as "Not enough memory" or "Setup cannot continue," try one or more of the following suggestions and then try using the software again:

Turn off any antivirus software running on your computer. Installation programs sometimes mimic virus activity and may make your computer incorrectly believe that it's being infected by a virus.

Close all running programs. The more programs you have running, the less memory is available to other programs. Installation programs typically update files and programs; so if you keep other programs running, installation may not work properly.

Have your local computer store add more RAM to your computer. This is, admittedly, a drastic and somewhat expensive step. However, adding more memory can really help the speed of your computer and allow more programs to run at the same time.

Customer Care

If you have trouble with the book's companion CD-ROM, please call the Wiley Product Technical Support phone number at (800) 762-2974. Outside the United States, call +1(317) 572-3994. You can also contact Wiley Product Technical Support at http://sybex.custhelp.com. John Wiley & Sons will provide technical support only for installation and other general quality control items. For technical support on the applications themselves, consult the program's vendor or author.

To place additional orders or to request information about other Wiley products, please call (877) 762-2974.

Glossary

A

Active Directory Installation Wizard (DCPROMO) A command-line tool used to promote a Windows Server 2008, 2003, or 2000 Server computer to a domain controller. Using the Active Directory Installation Wizard, systems administrators can create trees and forests. See also *promotion*.

Active Directory Integrated DNS zone Primary zone with Active Directory Integration. The zone database is stored in Active Directory.

Active Directory replication A method by which Active Directory domain controllers synchronize information. See also *intersite replication* and *intrasite replication*.

Add or Remove Programs Pre-Vista and Windows Server 2008 Control Panel applet that allows software applications and components of the operating system to be installed and uninstalled.

administrative template Template that specifies additional options that can be set by an administrator using the Group Policy Editor tool. This template provides a list of user-friendly configuration options and specifies the system settings to which they apply. When an option is set, the appropriate change is made in the Registry. Windows Server 2008 comes with several administrative template files. You can also create your own administrative templates.

application assignment script Script file that specifies which applications are assigned to users of the Active Directory. These files are created by administrators when Group Policy is used to create software package assignments for users and computers.

application data partitions Applications that rely on Active Directory have the ability to use an application's data partitions to store application-specific data. Applications, services, or administrators can create application data partitions as container objects.

assigning One of two processes by which applications are made available to computers and/or users. See also *publishing*.

auditing The act of recording specific actions that are taken within a secure network operating system. Auditing is often used by administrators as a security measure to provide for accountability. Typical audited events include logon and logoff events, as well as accessing files and objects.

authoritative restore Specifies that the contents of a certain portion of the Active Directory on a domain controller should override any changes on other domain controllers, regardless of their sequence numbers. An authoritative restore is used to restore the contents of the Active Directory to a previous point in time.

B

background zone loading   An Active Directory feature that allows an Active Directory Integrated DNS zone to load in the background. This means that a DNS server can service client requests while the zone is still loading into memory.

bidirectional trust   See *two-way trust*.

bottleneck   Occurs when the flow of packets transmitted across network media slows down. Packets then accumulate and get backed up on the network.

bridgehead server   Used in Windows Server 2008 replication to coordinate the transfer of replicated information between Active Directory sites.

C

certificate revocation   The process of revoking a certificate from a user or computer. See also *certificate revocation list (CRL)*.

certificate revocation list (CRL)   This list shows all the certificates that have been revoked. This list is published to a location that all certificate authority servers can access. See also *CRL distribution point (CDP)*.

client   Host that connects to a server based machine.

Computer object   An Active Directory object that is a security principal and that identifies a computer that is part of a domain.

Connection object   An object that can be defined as part of the Active Directory's replication topology using the Active Directory Sites And Services tool. Connection objects are automatically created to manage Active Directory replication, and administrators can use them to manually control details about how and when replication operations occur.

connector   A software add-on that allows different types of applications or servers to communicate with each other. A connector acts as a translator for computer systems or applications. Many connectors are included with Active Directory.

Contact object   Active Directory object that defines the contact information for a single entity such as an individual or company. Usually used in organizational units (OUs) to specify the main administrative contact and other individuals within the organization. Contact objects are not security principals like User objects. They are primarily used for reference or automatic mailing lists.

Copy backup   A backup type that backs up selected folders and files but does not set the archive bit.

Counter logs   Files that contain information collected by the Windows Performance tool. Counter logs can be used to track and analyze performance-related statistics over time.

CRL distribution point (CDP)   A shared location containing the certificate revocation list. See also *certificate revocation list (CRL)*.

cross-forest trust   A Windows Server 2008 feature that lets you implement trusts between all domains in one forest and all domains in another forest.

D

Daily backup   A backup type that backs up all of the files that have been modified on the day that the daily backup is performed. The Archive attribute is not set on the files that have been backed up.

DCPROMO   See *Active Directory Installation Wizard (DCPROMO)*.

delegation   The process by which a user who has higher-level security permissions grants certain permissions over Active Directory objects to users who are lower-level security authorities. Delegation is often used to distribute administrative responsibilities in a network environment.

Delegation of Control Wizard   A Windows Server 2003 and 2008 tool used for delegating permissions over Active Directory objects. See also *delegation*.

demotion   The process of downgrading a Windows Server 2008 domain controller to a member server.

differential backup   A backup type that copies only the files that have been changed since the last normal (full) backup or incremental backup. A differential backup backs up only those files that have changed since the last full backup, but it does not set the archive bit.

Directory Services Restore mode (DSRM)   A special boot mode for Windows Server 2008 domain controllers. The Directory Services Restore mode is used to boot a domain controller without starting Active Directory services. This enables systems administrators to log on locally to restore or to troubleshoot any problems with the Active Directory.

distinguished name   The fully qualified name of an object within a hierarchical system. Distinguished names are used for all Active Directory objects and in the Domain Name System (DNS). No two objects in these systems should have the same distinguished name.

Distribution group   Collection of Active Directory users used primarily for email distribution. Distribution groups do not have security identifiers (SIDs).

DNS client   Any machine issuing queries to a DNS server. The client hostname may or may not be registered in a domain name system (DNS) database.

DNS name server   Any computer providing domain name resolution services.

DNS Notify   A mechanism that allows the process of initiating notifications to secondary servers when zone changes occur (RFC 1996).

DNS zone   A portion of the DNS namespace over which a specific DNS server has authority.

domain   In Microsoft networks, an arrangement of client and server computers referenced by a specific name that shares a single security permissions database. On the Internet, a domain is a named collection of hosts and subdomains, registered with a unique name by the InterNIC.

domain controller   A Windows Server 2008 computer that includes a copy of the Active Directory data store. Domain controllers contain the security information required to perform services related to the Active Directory.

Domain Local group   An Active Directory security or distribution group that can contain Universal groups, Global groups, or accounts from anywhere within an Active Directory forest.

Domain Name System (DNS)   The TCP/IP network service that translates textual Internet network addresses into numerical Internet network addresses.

Domain Naming Master   The Active Directory domain controller responsible for adding and removing domains within the Active Directory environment.

domain trees   A set of Active Directory domains that share a common namespace and are connected by a transitive two-way trust. Resources can be shared between the domains in an Active Directory tree.

dual-boot   A computer system that can have multiple operating systems loaded. Only one operating system can run at any given time, but dual-booting allows you to choose at startup which operating system you would like to start.

dynamic   In computer terms, a system or application that builds its own records.

Dynamic DNS standard (DDNS)   A standard that allows clients or DHCP to register with DNS automatically. This means that DNS can build its zone database on the fly.

Dynamic Host Configuration Protocol (DHCP)   A protocol that automatically assigns TCP/IP addresses to DHCP clients.

E

elevation-of-privileges attack   An attack against a domain controller in a trusted domain, accomplished through an external trust. The hacker uses the security identifier (SID) history attribute to associate SIDs with new user accounts, granting themselves unauthorized rights.

Event Viewer   A Windows Server 2008 utility that tracks information about the computer's hardware and software, as well as security events. This information is stored in three log files: the Application log, the Security log, and the System log.

external trust   A way to provide access to resources on a Windows NT 4 domain or forest that cannot use a forest trust.

F

File Allocation Table (FAT)   A filesystem, created by Microsoft, that was used for MS-DOS and Microsoft Windows up to and including Windows Me, and also by virtually all other existing personal computer operating systems, floppy disks, and solid-state memory cards. The FAT filesystem (sometimes known as FAT16) is a standard for mass-storage compatibility. Windows Server 2008 does not support FAT because it has fewer fault-tolerance features than the NTFS filesystem and can become corrupted through normal use over time.

file extension   The three-letter suffix that follows the name of a standard filesystem file. Using Group Policy and software management functionality, systems administration can specify which applications are associated with which file extensions.

filtering   The process by which permissions on security groups are used to identify which Active Directory objects are affected by Group Policy settings. Using filtering, systems administrators can maintain a fine level of control over Group Policy settings.

folder redirection   A Group Policy setting that automatically redirects special folders (such as My Documents) to an alternate network location. Mobile users find folder redirection useful because their documents are always available in the same location.

foreign security principal   Active Directory object used to give permissions to other security principals that do not exist within an Active Directory domain. Generally, foreign security principals are automatically created by the services of the Active Directory.

forest   A collection of Windows 2008 domains in a trust relationship that does not necessarily share a common namespace. All of the domains within a forest share a common schema and Global Catalog, and domains can share resources in a forest.

G

Global Catalog (GC)   A portion of the Active Directory that contains a subset of information about all of the objects within all domains of the Active Directory data store. The Global Catalog is used to improve performance of authentications and for sharing information between domains.

Global group   An Active Directory security group that contains accounts only from its own domain.

gpresult.exe   A command-line interface for RSoP. See also *Resultant Set of Policy (RSoP)*.

Group object   Logical collection of users that is used primarily for assigning security permissions to resources.

Group Policy   Settings that can affect the behavior of, and the functionality available to, users and computers. *Group policies* allow system administrators to customize end user settings and to place restrictions on the types of actions that users can perform. Group policies can be applied to one or more users or computers within the Active Directory environment. See also *Group Policy object (GPO)*.

Group Policy object (GPO)   A collection of settings (group policies) that control the behavior of users and computers. GPOs act as containers for the settings made within Group Policy files; this simplifies the management of settings. See also *Group Policy*.

H

hash algorithm   An algorithm that produces a hash value of some piece of data, such as a message or session key. If you use a well designed hash algorithm, when input data changes are made, the resulting hash value can alter. Hash values are useful in detecting modifications to data. A well-designed hash algorithm makes it almost impossible for two independent inputs that have the same hash value.

host record   A record that is used to statically associate a host's name to its IP addresses. Also called an A record for TCP/IP v4 and AAAA record for TCP/IP v6.

I

incremental backup   A backup type that backs up only the files that have changed since the last normal or incremental backup. It sets the archive attribute on the files that are backed up.

InetOrgPerson object   An Active Directory object that defines attributes of users in Lightweight Directory Access Protocol (LDAP) and X.500 directories.

Infrastructure Master   The Windows Server 2008 domain controller that is responsible for managing group memberships and transferring this information to other domain controllers within the Active Directory environment.

inheritance   The process by which settings and properties defined on a parent object implicitly apply to a child object.

initialization file   A file used to specify parameters that are used by an application or a utility. Setup programs often use initialization files to determine application installation information.

Internet Protocol (IP)   The Network layer protocol upon which the Internet is based. IP provides a simple connectionless packet exchange. Other protocols such as TCP use IP to perform their connection-oriented (or guaranteed delivery) services.

intersite replication   The transfer of information between domain controllers that reside in different Active Directory sites.

intrasite replication   The transfer of information between domain controllers that reside within the same Active Directory site.

K

key recovery agent   A user or administrator who has the right to revoke certificates from users or computers.

L

LDAP   See *Lightweight Directory Access Protocol (LDAP)*.

Lightweight Directory Access Protocol (LDAP)   A protocol used for querying and modifying information stored within directory services. The Active Directory can be queried and modified through the use of LDAP-compatible tools.

linked value replication   A Windows Server 2003 and 2008 feature that only replicates the part of the Active Directory that changed since the last replication cycle.

load balancing   A method of distributing network load among multiple network hosts.

local area network (LAN)   A network of well-connected computers that usually reside within a single geographic location (such as an office building). An organization typically owns all of the hardware that makes up its LAN.

Logging mode   An RSoP mode that pulls policy information from a log based on actual logon activity. Logging mode displays the actual settings that apply to users and computers. See also *Planning mode* and *Resultant Set of Policy (RSoP)*.

M

MSMQ Queue Alias object   Active Directory object for the MSMQ-Custom-Recipient class type. This object associates an Active Directory path and a user-defined alias with a public, private, or direct single-element format name, allowing a queue alias to be used to reference a queue that might not be listed in Active Directory Domain Services (AD DS).

N

name server   A server that can give an authoritative answer to name resolution queries about that domain.

name server (NS) record   This record lists the name servers for a domain and allows other name servers to look up names in your domain.

Network Monitor   A Windows Server 2008 utility that can be used to monitor and decode packets that are transferred to and from the local server.

New Technology File System (NTFS)   Filesystem used for Windows NT–based operating systems (Windows NT, Windows 2000, Windows XP, Windows Server 2003, Windows Server 2008, and Windows Vista). NTFS offers features such as local security on files and folders, data compression, disk quotas, and data encryption.

Non-Dynamic DNS (NDDNS)   A DNS database that needs to be built manually. Clients cannot automatically update the DNS server.

Normal backup   A backup type that backs up all selected folders and files and then marks each file that has been backed up as archived.

Nslookup   Command line utility for testing a DNS server.

O

objects   Units stored within Active Directory.

operations master   A special domain controller that is solely responsible for specific parts of the Active Directory, such as the schema, domain naming, or relative ID (RID).

organizational unit (OU)   Used to logically organize the Active Directory objects (such as similar accounts or machines) within a domain. An OU is the smallest component within a domain to which administrative permissions and group policies can be assigned. OUs serve as containers within which other Active Directory objects can be created, but they do not form part of the DNS namespace.

P

packet sniffer   A utility that allows an individual to watch or retrieve packets from a network cable.

partial attribute set (PAS)   A subset of an object's attributes that is stored in the Global Catalog (GC) to reduce replication traffic. The PAS can be changed by modifying the schema and marking attributes for replication to the GC.

password replication policy A policy that allows an administrator to determine which user groups will be allowed to use the read-only domain controller (RODC) credential caching.

patch A Windows Installer file that updates application code. Patches can be used to make sure that new features are installed after an application has already completed installation. A patch file does not remove any installed components.

PDC Emulator Master Within a domain, the PDC Emulator Master is responsible for maintaining backward compatibility with Windows NT domain controllers. When running in mixed-mode domains, the PDC Emulator is able to process authentication requests and serve as a primary domain controller (PDC) with Windows NT backup domain controllers (BDCs).

permissions Security constructs used to regulate access to resources by username or group affiliation. Administrators can assign permissions to allow any level of access (such as read-only, read/write, or delete) by controlling the ability of users to initiate object services. Security is implemented by the system checking the user's security identifier (SID) against each object's access control list (ACL).

Planning mode An RSoP mode that is used to plan Group Policy changes before putting them into effect. See also *Logging mode, Resultant Set of Policy (RSoP)*.

pointer (PTR) record Used to associate an IP address to its host's name. This record is necessary because IP addresses begin with the least-specific portion first (the network) and end with the most-specific portion (the host); whereas hostnames begin with the most specific portion at the beginning and the least specific at the end.

Primary Domain Controller (PDC) Emulator Master A special domain controller responsible for maintaining backward compatibility with Windows NT domain controllers.

primary zone This zone is responsible for maintaining all of the records for the DNS zone. It contains the primary copy of the DNS database and all record updates occur here. You create a new primary zone whenever you create a new DNS domain.

Printer object Active Directory object that identifies printers that are published within domains.

promotion The act of converting a Windows Server 2008, 2003, or 2000 Server computer to a domain controller. See also *Active Directory Installation Wizard (DCPROMO)*.

public-key infrastructure (PKI) A structure that binds public keys with respective user identities through the use of a certificate authority.

publishing One of two processes by which applications are made available to computers and/or users. Publishing makes applications available for use by users through Group Policy and Software Installation settings. End users can install published applications on demand or when they need them by using the Add Or Remove Programs item in the Control Panel. See also *assigning*.

R

read-only domain controller (RODC)   A domain controller containing a read-only full copy of an Active Directory database. The Active Directory database on a RODC cannot be altered. A RODC is used in an area or location that has limited security and is new in Windows Server 2008.

realm trust   A way to connect to a non-Windows domain that uses Kerberos authentication. Realm trusts can be transitive or nontransitive, one-way or two-way.

relative distinguished name (RDN)   Also referred to as the common name. This name specifies only part of the object's path relative to another object. For example, if a username is wpanek@stellacon.com, wpanek is the RDN.

Reliability and Performance Monitor   A Windows Server 2008 utility used to log and view performance-related data. The Reliability and Performance Monitor includes chart, histogram, and report views.

Remote Procedure Call (RPC) protocol   A protocol used to allow communications between system processes on remote computers. Active Directory uses the RPC protocol for intrasite replication. See also *intrasite replication.*

replication   The transfer of information between domain controllers. Replication allows a database to be distributed among many different servers in a network environment.

resolver   Any machine issuing queries to a DNS server is called a resolver, although technically a resolver is a software process that finds answers to queries for DNS data. Clients issue DNS requests through processes called resolvers.

resource record (RR)   An entry in a DNS database that specifies the availability of specific DNS services. For example, an MX record specifies the IP address of a mail server, and (A) host records specify the IP addresses of workstations on the network.

Resultant Set of Policy (RSoP)   A Windows Server 2008 tool that automatically calculates the actual policy for a user or group based on site, domain, and OU placement, as well as inheritance settings.

RID Master   The domain controller that is responsible for generating unique identifiers for each of the domains within an Active Directory environment.

root domain   By default, the root domain is the first domain created in an Active Directory forest.

S

scavenging The DNS process of cleaning up old resource records in the DNS database. Scavenging uses the resource record timestamp to determine if the record is stale.

schema The organizational structure of a database. The Active Directory schema defines the attributes, objects, and classes available in Active Directory.

Schema Master A Windows Server 2008 domain controller that is responsible for maintaining the master copy of the Active Directory schema. There is only one Schema Master per Active Directory forest.

script policy A setting within Group Policy objects that specifies login, logoff, startup, and shutdown script settings. You can create the scripts by using the Windows Script Host (WSH) or by using standard batch file commands.

secondary DNS zone Noneditable copy of the DNS database that is used for load balancing (also referred to as load sharing). A secondary zone gets its database from the primary zone and provides for fault tolerance and increased network performance, especially in organizations with WAN connections.

Security Configuration And Analysis utility A Windows Server 2008 utility used for creating security profiles and managing security settings across multiple machines.

security group Active Directory object that can contain users or other groups and that are used for the management and assignment of permissions. Users are placed into security groups, and then permissions are granted to these groups. Security groups are considered to be security principals. See also *security principal*.

security identifier (SID) A unique number given to Active Directory objects (such as users, computers, and groups) to identify those object within Active Directory.

security principal An Active Directory object that is used to assign and maintain security settings. The primary security principals are Users, Groups, and Computers.

security template File used by the Security Configuration And Analysis tool for defining and enforcing security settings across multiple computers.

Server Manager A Microsoft Management Console (MMC) snap-in that allows an administrator to install and administer server roles, view information about server configuration, and keep track of the status of installed roles.

service (SRV) record Ties the location of a service (like a domain controller) with information about how to contact the service.

Shared Folder object Active Directory object that specifies the name and location of specific shared resources that are available to users of the Active Directory. Often, Shared Folder objects are used to give logical names to specific file collections. For example, systems administrators might create separate shared folders for common applications, user data, and shared public files.

shortcut trust   A direct trust between two domains that implicitly trust each other.

Simple Mail Transfer Protocol (SMTP)   A TCP/IP-based protocol that is primarily used for the exchange of Internet email. Active Directory can also use SMTP to manage intersite replication between domain controllers. See also *intersite replication.*

single master operations   Specific functions that must be managed within an Active Directory environment but are only handled by specific domain controllers. Some single master operations are unique to each domain, and some are unique to the entire Active Directory forest.

single sign-on (SSO)   A way of accessing applications or servers without needing a secondary password. Active Directory Federation Services offers this feature.

site   A collection of well-connected TCP/IP subnets. Sites are used to define the topology of Active Directory replication.

site link   A link between two or more Active Directory sites. See also *site.*

site link bridge   A connection between two or more Active Directory site links. A site link bridge can be used to create a transitive relationship for replication between sites. See also *site* and *site link.*

smart card   A credit-card-sized card with embedded integrated circuits that can process information. A smart card can be used to implement two-factor authentication: The card stores user certificate information and is used with a PIN as an alternative to the standard user-name and password logon process.

subdomain   A lower level domain. Normally a child domain off of a parent domain.

subnet   A collection of TCP/IP addresses that define a particular network location. All of the computers within a subnet share the same group of TCP/IP addresses and have the same subnet mask.

System State data   Information used to manage the configuration of a Windows Server 2008 operating system. For Windows Server 2008 domain controllers, the System State data includes a copy of the Active Directory data store.

T

Task Manager   A Windows Server 2008 utility that can be used to quickly and easily obtain a snapshot of current system performance.

transitive trust   A trust relationship that allows for implicit trusts between domains. For example, if Domain A trusts Domain B and Domain B trusts Domain C, then Domain A implicitly trusts Domain C.

tree A set of Active Directory domains that share a common namespace and are connected by a transitive two-way trust. Resources can be shared between the domains in an Active Directory tree.

trust A relationship between domains that allows users who are contained within one domain to be granted access to resources in other domains.

two-way trust A relationship between domains in which two domains trust each other equally.

U

unidirectional replication One-way replication. Replication travels in one direction only.

Universal group An Active Directory security or distribution group that can contain members from, and be accessed from, any domain within an Active Directory forest. A domain must be running in native mode to use Universal groups.

User account See user object.

User object Active Directory object that is a security principal and that identifies individuals that can log on to a domain. User accounts contain information about individuals, as well as password and other permission information.

W

Web enrollment A method of receiving a certificate. Allows users to use a web browser to request a certificate from a certificate server.

wide area network (WAN) A distributed network, typically connected through slow, and sometimes unreliable, links. The various sites that make up a WAN are typically connected through leased lines.

Windows Installer A Windows service that provides for the automatic installation of applications through the use of compatible installation scripts.

Windows Installer package Special files that include the information necessary to install Windows-based applications.

Windows Internet Name Service (WINS) A service that resolves a NetBIOS name to a TCP/IP address. WINS is used primarily in older operating systems (95, 98, and NT).

Windows Script Host (WSH) A utility for running scripts on Windows-based computers. By default, WSH includes support for the VBScript and JScript languages. Through the use of third-party extensions, scripts can be written in other languages.

Index

Note to the reader: Throughout this index **boldfaced** page numbers indicate primary discussions of a topic. *Italicized* page numbers indicate illustrations.

P

Wiley Publishing, Inc. End-User License Agreement

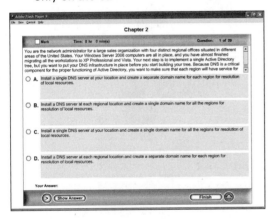
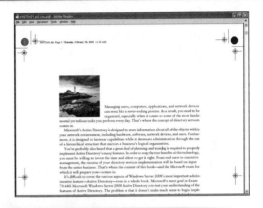

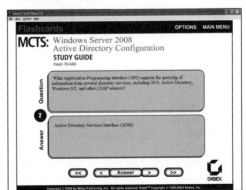